W9-AWU-215

The Official Guide

CorelDRAW™ 9

Foster D. Coburn, III
Pete McCormick

Osborne **McGraw-Hill**

Berkeley   New York   St. Louis   San Francisco
Auckland   Bogotá   Hamburg   London
Madrid   Mexico City   Milan   Montreal   New Delhi
Panama City   Paris   São Paulo
Singapore   Sydney   Tokyo   Toronto

Osborne/**McGraw-Hill**
2600 Tenth Street
Berkeley, California 94710
U.S.A.

For information on translations or book distributors outside the U.S.A., or to arrange bulk purchase discounts for sales promotions, premiums, or fund-raisers, please contact Osborne/**McGraw-Hill** at the above address.

CorelDRAW™ 9 The Official Guide

1234567890 DOC DOC 90198765432109

ISBN 0-07-211986-1

Publisher: Brandon A. Nordin
Associate Publisher and Editor-in-Chief: Scott Rogers
Acquisitions Editor: Megg Bonar
Project Editor: Jennifer Wenzel
Editorial Assistant: Stephane Thomas
Technical Editor: Debbie Cook
Copy Editor: Nancy Crumpton
Proofreader: Rhonda Holmes
Indexer: Irv Hershman
Computer Designers: Roberta Steele, Jani Beckwith
Illustrators: Brian Wells, Beth Young, Robert Hansen
Series Design: Roberta Steele

This book was composed with Corel VENTURA.

The Official Guide

CorelDRAW™ 9

This book is dedicated to the loyal readers of our previous books and to our Boot Camp attendees who keep coming back year after year.

We would also like to express a special dedication to two little three-year-olds—Julia and Natalie.

Contents At a Glance

Contents

Foreword

With the availability of CorelDRAW™ 9, graphics professionals the world over have at their fingertips a powerful suite of integrated tools for illustration, page layout, photo editing and painting. The new version of CorelDRAW builds on the exceptional creation tools and outstanding output capabilities of CorelDRAW 8 and now offers even better design tools and productivity features for better flexibility and free range of creative expression.

Experience the dynamic interactive tools, sophisticated effects and high-end output capabilities found in the new publish to HTML and PDF features, and the expanded support for a wider choice of color palettes now available in CorelDRAW 9. Maximize your graphical creativity with professional pre-press features—including the new Service Bureau Wizards—numerous import/export filters—including the new Digital Camera interface and a variety of valuable media asset-management tools. The combination of new features and tools and the solid assets already available in CorelDRAW will make it easier for you to create stunning designs and special effects on the way to creating your own digital masterpieces. At Corel, we are excited about CorelDRAW 9, and know you will benefit from the design time we have all invested.

In the same way that CorelDRAW 9 provides a powerful solution to enhance your creative productivity, so, too, does this book, *CorelDRAW 9: The Official Guide.* Foster Coburn and Pete McCormick are Corel-certified instructors who travel the country to teach CorelDRAW and provide hands-on training in an entertaining and informative manner. This book is their personal version of a CorelDRAW training seminar and will lead you to mastery of the software, complete with sample files from the book's exercises on the CD. Let the authors introduce you to the power of CorelDRAW as they explain the tools, features and techniques that make CorelDRAW such a great product.

Corel is excited about the new technologies now available with CorelDRAW 9, and we invite you to follow along in this CorelPRESS ™ guide. Let the experts show you the way! The authors and the team at Corel have spent many hours on this book and CorelDRAW 9 to make sure that your experience is a good one. CorelPRESS guides are designed to bring out the best in your Corel software, and have been designed with our readers in mind. Together with Osborne/McGraw-Hill, Corel is proud to bring you another fine effort in disseminating solid information about a great family of products. Congratulations to the team at Osborne who created this excellent book, and to the team at Corel who supported their efforts.

Michael C. J. Cowpland
President and CEO
Corel Corporation
June 1999

Introduction

Writing this chapter is always a joy. It means that we've finished everything else and it gives us the opportunity to thank all of the people who helped us to complete this book.

The hardest part about putting this book to bed is that we never feel that it is finished. There is always one more tip or technique that needs to be added. And as soon as this book hits the shelves, we know we'll find a great feature hidden beneath the surface. Not to mention the fact that there are always several ways to accomplish the same task. Each user will find a way that works best for him or her. So as we find these new gems, we'll add them to the book's companion Web site at http://www.unleash.com.

On the color pages you'll see some really incredible images from Corel's World Design Contest. We are frequently asked how they are created. Most of them are rather simple to create if one has the time and talent. This book will show you how to use the tools and effects—the time and talent is up to you. Even those of us who are "artistically challenged" can create some great work thanks to the power of CorelDRAW.

We are always eager to hear what you, the reader, think of our books. We want to know what you liked and what we've missed. This allows us to continue building on this book so that the next edition can be ever bigger and better. Visit our Web page, send us a letter, fire off an e-mail, or just give us a call. The more we hear from you, the more that we can give back in future editions and on our Web site.

The number of people who must be thanked is enormous. Some of them don't even realize how important their help has been. Sue McCormick has known exactly where to find Pete the past few months, and he can finally emerge from his cave for a little bit of relaxation and golf. And Foster can now resume his search for someone to coax him out of his cave. Our friends and families have been extremely patient as we made excuses for working nights and weekends. We can finally turn off the computers for a few hours and enjoy ourselves for a little while.

Jodi, our office manager, has been wonderful throughout this whole ordeal. We even made her read many of the chapters to find our typos. By the time you read this, she will have left to be a full-time mother and we wish her all the best. So thank you Jodi, enjoy the many years to come with your two wonderful kids!

Debbie Cook worked through each chapter to make sure that what we had written was correct. In doing so, she also provided lots of helpful tips. Thanks Debbie for the great work!

"Doctor" Dickson is responsible for getting a decent picture out of us. We aren't nearly as beautiful as the models he normally photographs but he did a wonderful job with the subjects he had. Doug Dickson has educated us tremendously on the printing and pre-press industry. We are probably his most irritating client and he still accepts our jobs and gets them off press looking fantastic.

The crew at Corel has been wonderful. Without their help, the book couldn't have been written. Tony Severenuk and Cory Cooperman not only had to get CorelDRAW 9 out the door, but also had to deal with our many questions. They did a great job with both projects. Chip Maxwell has got to be sick of hearing from us as well. Being in charge of authors, he gets to deal with us a lot. This book is really his project as well and he did a tremendous job. And we must single out Rus Miller, the engineer extraordinaire who handles the print engine. Not only does he write great code, but he is always willing to explain it to us mere mortals. Thanks to all those we mentioned and to the many others who we've accidentally missed. Keep up all the great work, eh?

To our fellow betazoids, thanks for all of your input. You'll undoubtedly find something in this book that you provided in one way or another. Reading through the beta newsgroups not only provided a much needed break from writing, but was also an inspiration as new features were deciphered. Get some rest, it's about time to start the beta cycle all over again!

Each year we marvel at the work of the artists who use CorelDRAW. Thanks to all of the artists whose work is featured within our color pages. It is your work that inspires all of us to use the product, and maybe one day we can join you on the winners platform.

Most of all, we must thank you, the reader, for purchasing this book. We sincerely hope that we've been able to enlighten and inspire you to push CorelDRAW to its limits and beyond.

PART I

The Basics

CHAPTER 1

Getting the Most Out of CorelDRAW 9

COREL.COM

CorelDRAW 9

This chapter is designed to give you an overview of what you will find in the rest of this book so that you can get most from CorelDRAW 9. As you work through this book, we expect that you will skip around to the chapters that are most appropriate to the task at hand. So we suggest that you read this chapter completely before you move forward. Here we will help you install the program, direct you to the new features, answer the most common questions, describe how you can use the CD-ROM included with the book, and direct you to additional ways to learn about CorelDRAW.

What's in the Box?

CorelDRAW 9 is really a suite of applications, beginning with the flagship illustration program CorelDRAW. Also included is Corel PHOTO-PAINT, the image-editing and pixel-based paint program. Besides the two main applications, there are various other graphic utilities and tools. Because of the complexities of the two main programs, this book covers CorelDRAW 9 only. Detailed information on Corel PHOTO-PAINT can be found in *Corel PHOTO-PAINT 9: The Official Guide,* also published by Osborne/McGraw-Hill. To incorporate information about the other applications into a single book would make the book unmanageable for the reader and would kill quite a few trees.

What Is CorelDRAW?

CorelDRAW is a vector-based drawing and illustration program. This means that when you draw an object on the CorelDRAW drawing page, the shape of the object displayed onscreen is defined by a mathematical formula. In fact, its accuracy can be measured to one tenth of a micron. Sounds complicated, doesn't it? Forget the technical definition. What it really is, is a program that lets you draw shapes to illustrate ideas in a graphical and text-based fashion. The capabilities and potential of the program are limited only by your imagination.

Before You Install

Corel provides a large quantity of useful information regarding the installation of CorelDRAW and issues you may face as you use the product. This information is contained in the readme.html file that is supplied on CD1. Before you install the product, it is a good idea to load this file in your Web browser and read it very carefully. You may also want to print a copy so that you will have it for reference. This file is updated with every maintenance release, so it can contain information that became available after this book was printed. Of special interest are instructions on installation and hardware compatibility. Pay particular attention to the section on video display problems and the section on fonts or installing multilingual fonts. The remainder of the readme file primarily contains portions of the Help files that are in the various other programs that come with CorelDRAW.

Installing CorelDRAW 9

Before you insert the installation CD, you may want to look at what's included on the three CD-ROMs that come with the application. The contents of each CD are listed here:

- *CD1*   Programs, fonts, symbols, and samples

- *CD2*   Clipart images (26,618), 3D models, templates, and electronic documentation

- *CD3*   Photos, tiles, image lists, spraylists, brush textures, frames, objects, sounds, videos, and Web clipart

You need to know what's on the CD if you want to be able to find a photograph or a certain piece of clipart.

Installing the Programs

Before you begin the installation process, be sure to close any open programs and any TSRs running in the background, especially virus checkers and crash utilities. These utilities will drastically slow the installation or not allow CorelDRAW to install at all.

Whether you're installing CorelDRAW for the first time or adding programs and files you didn't originally install, start by inserting CD1. The auto-run program will begin the installation process by displaying the initial screen of the Corel Setup Wizard.

If for some reason the auto-run program does not start the Setup Wizard, follow these steps:

1. Click the Windows Start button, and choose Settings from the Start menu. When the Settings flyout appears, choose Control Panel.

2. In the Control Panel dialog box, double-click the Add/Remove Programs icon. The Add/Remove Programs Properties dialog box will appear.

3. Click the Install button. The Install Program from Floppy Disk or CD-ROM Drive dialog box will appear.

4. Click the Next button to go to the Run Installation Program dialog box. If the CD is in the correct drive, the drive letter of your CD will appear along with the Setup.exe command in the Command Line for Installation box. If it doesn't appear, type the correct path to the CD plus the words **Setup32.exe** in the Command Line for Installation box.

After a short period of time, the Corel Setup Wizard will appear. If you wish to read the Release Notes, you can do so at this time. When you're ready to move on, click the Next button to view the License Agreement. Read it carefully, and click the Accept button to go to the next screen. The next screen asks you to enter your Full name and Company name. If you don't have a company name, just leave that line blank. Click Next to move on to the next screen. Now you need to enter the serial number listed on your Product Authenticity Card that was supplied in the CorelDRAW box. If you don't have such a card, you're either working with an illegal version of CorelDRAW, or you'll need to contact Corel Customer Service to get a serial number. You can reach Corel Customer Service by phone at 1-800-77-COREL or by e-mail at custserv2@corel.ca.

The fifth screen, shown in Figure 1-1, is the beginning of the installation process. The Setup Options screen offers three choices: Typical Setup, Compact Setup, and Custom Setup. Next to each option is the approximate space required to install on your hard drive. The actual space required is dependent upon the type of file allocation table (FAT) you have used to format your hard drive. The FAT system used by DOS and Windows 95 is inefficient on larger hard drives, and so you'll find that CorelDRAW will take more space. If you have installed FAT32, which came with Windows 95 OSR2 and Windows 98, then the sizes will be more accurate. Windows NT users with NTFS will also find the values to be fairly accurate. Obviously if you choose Custom Setup, the size listed is just the starting point.

If you don't want to get involved making choices during the setup procedure, you should choose the Typical Setup installation option. This option asks you only two questions during the installation process. It would be a good idea to read further to learn about each setup option before making your final choice.

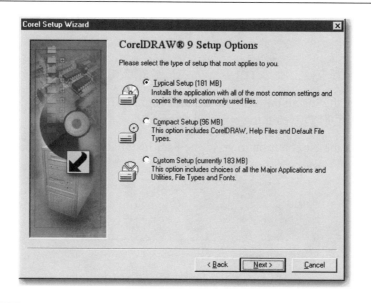

FIGURE 1-1   CorelDRAW 9 Setup Wizard Setup Options dialog box

Using the Typical Setup Option

If you choose the Typical Setup option, the first screen provides you with a list of languages supported by the Writing Tools. In the version distributed in the U.S., the default is English. Other localized versions will default to other languages. Select the languages you will need supported, and click Next.

Now you are asked to choose a destination folder (see Figure 1-2). The top parameter box lets you enter the drive letter and name of the folder where you want CorelDRAW 9 and all its other programs and utilities to reside. A drive letter and folder will appear by default. If the drive letter and folder are acceptable, you don't need to make any changes.

The second parameter box on the Destination Folder screen shows the amount of free space available in the drive on which you chose to install the programs and the amount of space the programs require. If you chose a drive other than drive C, this box will still show a small amount of space used on the C drive because some files must be installed as part of the operating system. When you click Next, you'll be asked the name of the folder to be used to store the shortcuts. This is what will appear on your Start menu.

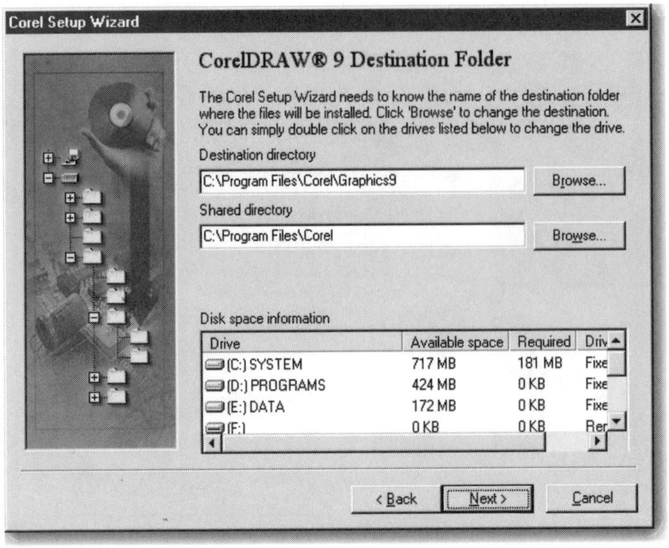

FIGURE 1-2   CorelDRAW 9 Setup Wizard Destination Folder dialog box

The last screen to appear is the Ready to Install screen, shown in Figure 1-3. It simply verifies the name of the registered owner and the Destination and Shared folders you designated earlier. If any information is incorrect, click the Back button to return to the previous screens and make corrections. You can review the components that will be installed by putting a check mark in the Show Selected Components box. Expanding the various folders will reveal all the components. You can't make any changes to the component list. It is merely there to show you what is being installed. If you see a component that you don't want or one that is missing, use the Custom Setup option. When everything is correct, click the Install button.

The programs, graphic utilities, productivity tools, and filters that will be installed automatically when you choose the Typical Setup option are listed next.

PROGRAMS   CorelDRAW 9 includes Program Files, Help Files, Tutors and Examples, Outlines & Fills, Scripts, and Presets.

Corel PHOTO-PAINT 9 includes Program Files, Help Files, Tutors and Examples, and Scripts and Script Effects.

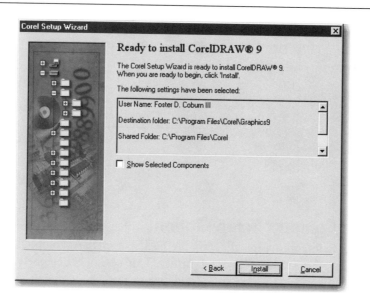

FIGURE 1-3   CorelDRAW 9 Setup Wizard Ready to Install dialog box

Graphics Utilities

Corel CAPTURE
Corel TRACE
All plug-in filters

Productivity Tools

Labels (North America only)
Duplexing Wizard

Filters

Bitmap filters   CPT, TIF, PCX, BMP, GIF, JPG, PCD, PSD, MAC, PP5,
TGA, SCT, FPX, PNG, RAW, DCS, WI, IMG, FPX, RIFF Painter 5
Vector filters   WPG, AI, DXF, CGM, CMX, CDR, CPX, CDX, EPS, EMF,
HPGL/PLT, PCT, Interpreted PostScript, WMF, PDF, PSF, DWG, 3DMF,

VSD, TTF
Animation filters   All
Text filters   WP8, DOC, RTF, TXT, XLS, WQ/WB, WK
Internet filters   All

Other

Sixty-six default fonts
Corel Uninstall
Readme files

Using the Compact Setup Option

The Compact Setup option installs only the basic CorelDRAW application along
with the readme files and the Uninstall utility. This option is designed for the
laptop user or the user with very little hard disk space. The application includes all
import and export filters previously listed. This installation requires approximately
96MB. No fonts will be installed if you use the Compact Setup.

As you proceed, you will see the same dialog boxes described earlier and shown in
Figures 1-2 and 1-3.

Using the Custom Setup Option

If you are comfortable choosing your components, you may want to use the Custom
Setup option. Because the Typical Setup leaves off several important utilities, it is a
good idea for all users to use the Custom Setup option. This option allows you to
decide what will be installed. For example, the Typical Setup option installs many
filters, but most users use only a few of these filters. Installing all of them serves no
purpose other than taking up valuable hard disk space. Additionally, you may want
to install only one or two of the applications that come with CorelDRAW 9 instead
of the entire suite.

If you choose the Custom Setup option on the Setup Options screen, the next
screen you see is the Components screen, shown in Figure 1-4. This is where you
decide which components of CorelDRAW you want to install. Click the plus icon (+)
next to each program to see the list of components within the program. Remove any
component you don't think you will need. For example, Figure 1-4 shows all the parts
of CorelDRAW itself. If you do not want to install any of the components, just
uncheck the box that corresponds to that component. You may decide you don't
want an entire program, in which case you should remove the check mark from the

box next to the name of the program. Make sure to go through the entire list carefully, and choose what you'll need. Don't worry, you can always run the install later, and add a component that you left off.

We highly recommend installing the Font Navigator program located in the Productivity Tools folder. This is a fantastic program for managing your fonts. You'll learn more about it in Chapter 32.

Be sure to click the + box next to each of the Filter categories to see the list of available file types. This is one area where you can save some hard disk space. Look through each category for file types you know you won't ever use. For example, if you know you will never handle a file created in Microsoft Word, you can remove the check mark next to that file type's name. If you are not familiar with a particular file type, it is best to install it, to be safe.

The next screen following the Components screen is the Writing Tools screen described a bit earlier. You're instructed to put a check beside each language you wish to install. The spell checker defaults to the language of the program. If you bought the English version, the spell checker defaults to English.

The Color Profile screen shown in Figure 1-5 follows the Writing Tools screen. Click on the + next to each option to expand the folder. Choose your monitor from the

| FIGURE 1-4 | CorelDRAW 9 Setup Wizard Components dialog box |

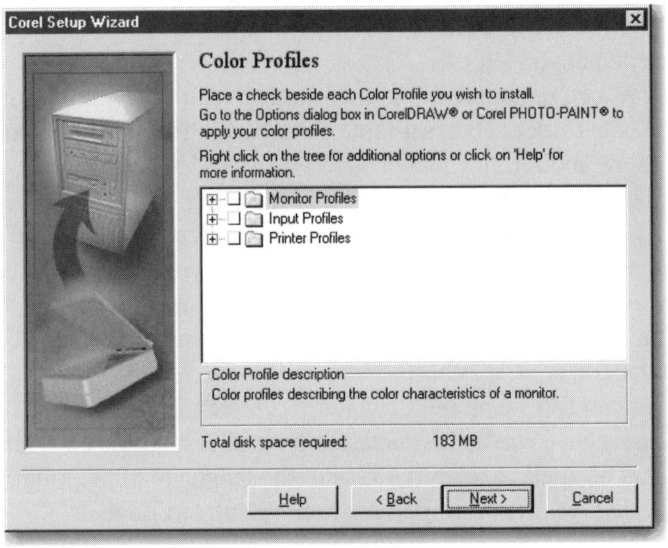

FIGURE 1-5 CorelDRAW 9 Setup Wizard Color Profiles dialog box

list. Do the same for Input Profiles and Printer Profiles. Remember to include printers that your service bureau might have as well as the printers in your office. If you do not see your devices on the list, it is best to contact the hardware vendors directly to get a profile. You'll learn more about the color profiles in Chapter 22.

Digital camera support is new in CorelDRAW 9. On the next screen you can choose which cameras you want directly supported by CorelDRAW and Corel PHOTO-PAINT from the list shown in Figure 1-6. For those of you with multiple cameras, make sure to select them all.

Next you will see the Fonts screen, shown in Figure 1-7. We recommend that you remove the check mark from the Default check box, ensuring that no fonts are installed in the installation process. We suggest not installing any fonts at this point because we feel the better way to install fonts is by using a font management system such as the Font Navigator utility supplied with CorelDRAW 9. Refer to Chapter 32 for a detailed explanation of how to install fonts. Selecting the default fonts will install 66 new fonts in your Windows Fonts folder. You can also select additional fonts from categories provided in this screen.

If you do install fonts during the installation process, do not install every available font in the list. If you did, you could easily overload your system. Additionally, if you install fonts using the Install program, only TrueType fonts will be installed.

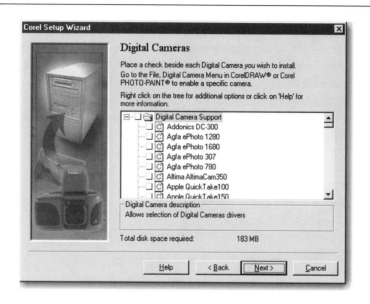

FIGURE 1-6   CorelDRAW 9 Setup Wizard Digital Cameras dialog box

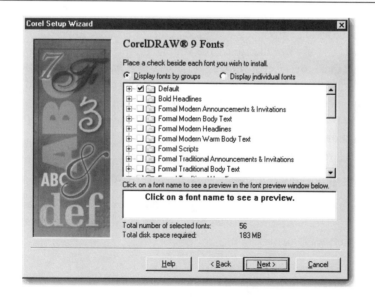

FIGURE 1-7   CorelDRAW 9 Setup Wizard Fonts dialog box

After you have made your font choices, the Destination Folder dialog box shown earlier in Figure 1-2 appears. From this point on, follow the instructions provided earlier to complete your installation. When everything is correct, click the Install button. From this point forward, the Installation Wizard takes over and completes the installation process.

If you installed every program and every available component, you would end up adding all the programs, graphics utilities, productivity tools, and filters installed in the Typical Setup plus the following:

Corel TEXTURE
Corel SCRIPT
Corel BARCODE Wizard
Bitstream Font Navigator 3.0
Corel Versions
Microsoft Visual Basic for Applications
Microsoft Internet Explorer 5.0

When the installation is complete, you will be told to reboot your system so all of the newly selected components can be installed correctly. You will have the option to reboot as soon as the installation process is complete or at a later time. Unless you have a specific reason for not rebooting, you should reboot as soon as the installation process is complete.

If you need to add components later, the Setup program will detect that CorelDRAW is already installed and give you the option of adding components. As you have seen, there are several choices to make when installing CorelDRAW on your system. If you feel you have minimal technical expertise, we recommend using the Custom Setup method; this will conserve hard disk space by not installing some things you may never use. If you later decide to use a particular program or add fonts, you can run the installation program again.

Other Programs

Several other utility programs are included on the CorelDRAW 9 CDs that are not installed by the Setup Wizard. We've listed them in the following sections with instructions on how to install them.

Adobe Acrobat Reader 4

With CorelDRAW 9's new and improved Publish to PDF feature, you'll want to install a copy of Acrobat Reader to view the PDF files you create. You'll find the setup program at x:\Acrobat Reader 4.0\ar40eng.exe where x represents the letter of your CD-ROM drive.

Canto Cumulus Desktop

Corel has licensed Canto Cumulus Desktop as a way to create catalogs of artwork. This replaces programs like Corel Mosaic and Corel Multimedia Manager that appeared in earlier versions of CorelDRAW. You'll find the Setup program at x:\Cumulus Desktop\Installer\setup.exe where x represents the letter of your CD-ROM drive.

Apple QuickTime 3.0

One of the new file formats supported in Corel PHOTO-PAINT 9 is the QuickTime VR format. If you want to view these files, you'll need to install Apple's QuickTime 3.0. You'll find the Setup program at x:\Apple\QuickTime30.exe where x represents the letter of your CD-ROM drive.

Microsoft Internet Explorer 5

As Microsoft Internet Explorer 4.01 or 5 is required to use the Digital Signatures portion of Visual Basic for Applications (VBA), you'll find a copy of Internet Explorer 5.0 on CD1. If you already installed VBA and Digital Signatures, then there is no reason to install the browser separately. But for those who just want to update their copy of Internet Explorer, you'll find the Setup program at x:\Config\Redist\ Digital Signatures\ie5setup.exe where x represents the letter of your CD-ROM drive.

Begin at the Beginning

If you're completely new to CorelDRAW, you may feel intimidated when you first open the application. If you're like most of us, your concern will grow when you try to draw your first object on the screen. The anxiety will become even greater when you try to color your object with something other than a color from the palette on the right side of the screen. After trying one tool and another, many first-time users feel that a degree in rocket science is required to use the program. Before you start looking for the receipt so you can return the box for a refund, remember one thing: We've all been where you are, and we got through it. What most of us didn't have was a book like this one to make the learning process easier.

What's on the Screen

When you first open CorelDRAW 9, the screen will look like the one shown in Figure 1-8. Before you can begin, you must select one of the options on the Welcome screen. Select New Graphic, and the default screen shown in Figure 1-9, displaying the drawing page, will appear. The remaining options are self-explanatory. If you have used the program before, you may wish to choose the What's New? option first.

The following is a brief description of the CorelDRAW screen. The entire area below the title bar, with the exception of the actual drawing page in the center of the screen, is called the *workspace*. Down the left side of the screen is the toolbox. The Color palette is displayed on the right side. Across the top of the screen are displayed the title bar, menu bar, standard toolbar, and Property Bar in descending order. The bottom of the screen displays a scrollbar and below that the Status Bar. In the center of the screen is the drawing page. The drop shadow around the page is called the *page border*. The white area surrounding the page is called the *desktop*. Each of these elements that make up the screen will be covered in the following chapters as they are introduced. This chapter will introduce the toolbox, the Hints window, and CorelTUTOR.

FIGURE 1-8   The Welcome screen that appears when you first start CorelDRAW 9

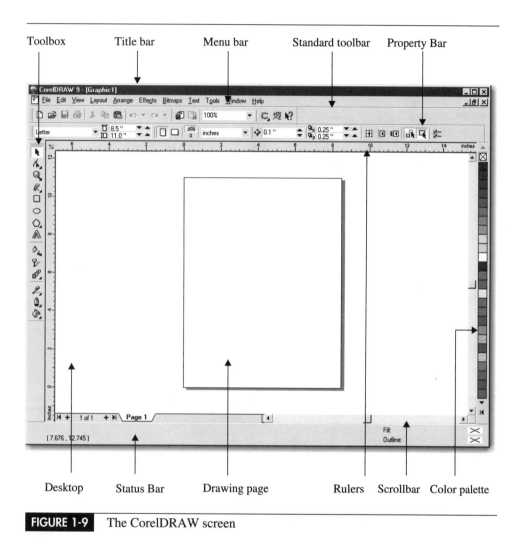

FIGURE 1-9   The CorelDRAW screen

The Toolbox

The toolbox, shown in Figure 1-10, contains the tools you'll need to create the shapes to illustrate your ideas. There are additional tools in the toolbox that allow you to modify the basic shapes and to change the fill and outline colors of those shapes. Some icons in the toolbox have small black triangles at the lower-right corner. If you click and hold on the triangle with the left mouse button, a flyout

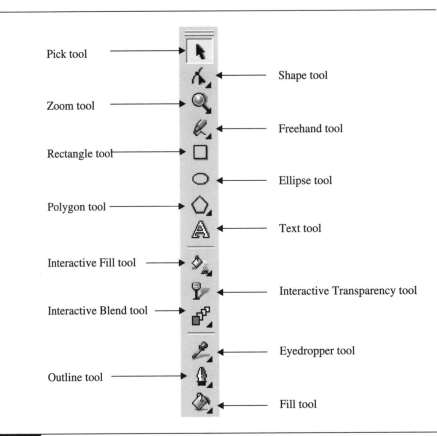

Pick tool

Shape tool

Zoom tool

Freehand tool

Rectangle tool

Ellipse tool

Polygon tool

Text tool

Interactive Fill tool

Interactive Transparency tool

Interactive Blend tool

Eyedropper tool

Outline tool

Fill tool

FIGURE 1-10   Toolbox for creating shapes in CorelDRAW 9

will appear, containing either additional shape creation tools or, in some cases, icons that provide access to dialog boxes. You can create a floating toolbar from a flyout by left-clicking and dragging the flyout out onto the drawing window. This technique is called *tearing off* a flyout. You'll find you frequently use certain tools whose flyouts contain additional tools. Creating a floating toolbar from these flyouts will provide quicker access to them.

The following table lists each tool in the toolbox, including any additional tools on their respective flyouts; it includes a description of each tool's basic function. Also noted is the chapter number where a complete description of each tool's functions can be found.

Tool	Flyout	Basic Function
Pick (Chapter 6)		Selects and transforms objects
Shape (Chapter 7)		Changes the shape of objects by node manipulation
	Knife	Cuts away portions of objects and welds lines
	Eraser	Erases portions of objects
	Free Transform	Transforms objects
Zoom (Chapter 11)		Views objects from close up or farther away
	Pan	Moves the page within the drawing window
Freehand (Chapter 4)		Draws shapes freehand as if you had a pencil in your hand
	Bézier	Draws shapes in a "connect the dots" style while also controlling the shape
	Artistic Media	Allows your cursor to function similar to a paintbrush with a wide variety of options
	Dimension	Draws measurement lines on or between objects, including callouts
	Connector Line	Draws connecting lines between objects
	Interactive Connector Line	Draws connecting lines between objects using only horizontal and vertical lines
Rectangle (Chapter 3)		Draws rectangles of all sizes
Ellipse (Chapter 3)		Draws ellipses of all sizes
Polygon (Chapter 3)		Draws polygons and stars with varying numbers of sides
	Spiral	Draws spirals with varying revolutions
	Graph Paper	Draws graph paper with varying numbers and sizes of cells
Text (Chapter 5)		Types Artistic or Paragraph text
Interactive Fill (Chapter 9)		Interactively fills objects
Interactive Transparency (Chapter 20)		Applies transparencies to objects interactively

Tool	Flyout	Basic Function
Interactive Effects (Chapters 17–19)	Interactive Blend	Blends objects interactively
	Interactive Contour	Contours objects interactively
	Interactive Distortion	Distorts objects interactively
	Interactive Envelope	Warps objects interactively
	Interactive Extrude	Adds 3D effects to objects interactively
	Interactive Drop Shadow	Adds a soft drop shadow to objects interactively
Eyedropper (Chapter 8)		Captures fill colors from objects
	Paintbucket	Applies sampled fill colors to objects

NOTE *The Fill and Outline tools at the bottom of the toolbox were not included in the preceding table because they are not technically considered tools. The Fill tool allows you to fill the inside of a shape with various colors, patterns, and textures using Dockers and dialog boxes. The Outline tool allows you to control the color, size, and style of the outline on shapes, also through the use of Dockers and dialog boxes. Both tools are described in detail in Chapters 8, 9, and 10.*

New Features in CorelDRAW 9

With each new version of CorelDRAW comes a long list of new features.

Onscreen Look and Feel

- Multiple palettes onscreen at once is described in Chapter 8.
- Sound feedback can be added in the Control Panel for various actions in CorelDRAW.
- Docker windows have been enhanced. Dockers are discussed in Chapter 2.
- Web links listed in the menu can be updated automatically.

Productivity and Performance

1

■ Workspaces now have a common appearance between the Mac and Windows versions of CorelDRAW. Workspaces are described in Chapter 34.

■ Publish to PDF allows you to easily create Acrobat files. You'll learn all the details in Chapter 27.

■ Microsoft Visual Basic for Applications gives you another powerful tool for automating your workflow.

■ IXLA Digital Camera Interface allows you to directly access your digital camera. This is described in Chapter 23.

■ Use multiple page sizes and orientations in the same document. We'll show you how in Chapter 25.

Interactive Tools

■ Interactive Connector Lines allow you to more easily create a dynamic connection between two objects. They are discussed in Chapter 4.

■ Mesh fills give you a way to create realistic looking fills by dropping colors onto a mesh grid. You'll learn all about it in Chapter 9.

■ Contours can now be created with the Interactive Contour tool, which is described in Chapter 19.

■ Interactive Drop Shadows now have a Perspective mode. Learn all the details in Chapter 19.

■ Placing Text on a Path has a number of new options. See how they all work in Chapter 21.

Convenience Features

■ Node reduction has been enhanced, allowing you to more easily smooth curves. Learn how to do this in Chapter 7.

■ Rectangles can now have a separate radius on each corner. See how this works in Chapter 3.

■ Sets of guidelines can now be saved as sets of presets, and many presets are included. Discover this time-saving procedure in Chapter 13.

■ An object's position and size is now reported live on the Property Bar as it is drawn. Learn more about this in Chapter 3.

■ As you draw lines, they can be automatically smoothed. You'll see how this works in Chapter 4.

Bitmap Effects

■ A wide variety of new bitmap effects have been added. Learn how to access these great new effects in Chapter 22.

■ Use the Scanning script enclosed in this book to scan at the correct resolution. We'll provide the details in Chapter 23.

Color and Printing

■ The Print dialog box now contains a mini-preview. Learn all about this dialog box in Chapter 26.

■ Imposition layouts are a breeze to create. You'll learn the technique in Chapter 26.

■ The Preflight dialog box helps you to discover printing problems before they happen. See how this works in Chapter 26.

■ The Palette Editor makes it much easier for you to create custom palettes and edit existing palettes. See how it works in Chapter 8.

■ By using the Eyedropper, you can easily capture the color from the fill or outline of one object and apply it to another. You'll learn how to do this in Chapter 8.

Supporting Applications

■ Bitstream Font Navigator provides a powerful tool for managing the thousand fonts included with CorelDRAW 9. Learn how to put it to use in Chapter 32.

■ Corel SCRIPT can automate your CorelDRAW tasks, starting with the most basic to extremely complex. You'll learn to write a simple script in Chapter 35.

Technical Support

Technical support is much like the Help topics discussed earlier but focuses on the more technical aspects of the program. Clicking Help | Technical Support will bring up the Corel Technical Support tabbed dialog box. The first tab shows the Contents page, displaying a list of technical topics from which you can choose to get help. When you choose one of these topics, you will be taken to a second dialog box, which offers additional topics related to your first choice.

The second tab is the Index tab. This tab provides an alphabetical list of topics that you can choose to find technical help on. It also provides a parameters box above the list box that lets you type in the key words you are looking for.

The third tab on the dialog box is the Find tab. It offers the same options as the Find page in the general Help dialog box. As stated previously, we do not recommend creating the Find database unless you are unable to find the help you need using the first two Help methods.

Chapter 2 will continue your introduction to CorelDRAW by discussing the menus, standard toolbar, Property Bar, and dialog boxes.

About CorelDRAW

When you click Help | About CorelDRAW, the About CorelDRAW 9 dialog box, shown in Figure 1-11, appears. At first glance, this dialog box may not seem to be very interesting. However, it is a very important dialog box that contains information that can be helpful when you're troubleshooting a problem or simply requesting tech support from Corel itself.

To begin, this dialog box shows the current version of the program you're using. This information can be extremely important to know when you're experiencing problems with the program. Oftentimes, Corel sends out revised versions of the program to fix problems that surface in early versions. Knowing which version you have will tell you if you are using the most current version. The lower portion of the dialog box lists the name of the person to whom the program is registered, along with the serial number and pin number. This information is required when you are asking for tech support.

Perhaps the most important information to be found in this dialog box appears when you click the button labeled System Info at the upper right. Clicking this

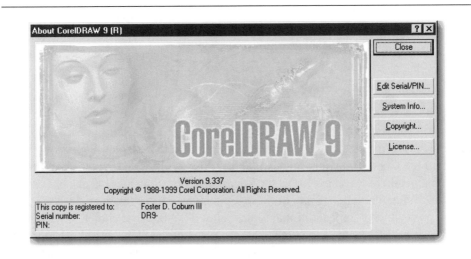

FIGURE 1-11   The About CorelDRAW 9 dialog box

button displays the System Info dialog box, shown in Figure 1-12. This dialog box, by default, shows you a list containing complete system information about your computer system. When you click the down arrow of the Choose a Category list box, you can display information about four more areas pertaining to your system and to the CorelDRAW program itself. These include:

■ Your computer's display data

■ A listing of the printers installed on your system

■ A complete list of all Corel .exe and .dll files

■ A complete list of all the system .dll files

This information can be vital in troubleshooting a problem. Bet you didn't know how important this dialog box really was!

Answers to Your Most Common Questions

With all the classes we've taught and support messages we've seen on the Internet, we've encountered some questions that come up all the time. So we thought we'd point you in the right direction, and help you get these problems solved first.

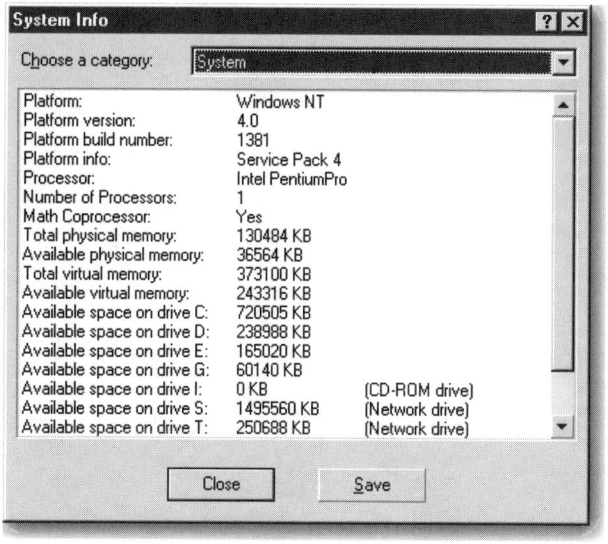

FIGURE 1-12 System Info dialog box

How Do I Set the Default Fill, Outline, and Fonts?

These options are all controlled by the styles that are associated with the current document. To access the style definitions, select Tools | Options, and navigate the tree on the left side of the dialog box until you find the Document | Styles dialog box shown in Figure 1-13.

In the list of styles, Default Graphic controls the fill and outline applied to objects you draw. Default Artistic Text controls all aspects of text you create with the Artistic Text tool, and Default Paragraph Text controls Paragraph Text that you create. Select the style you wish to modify. Click the Edit button at the right side of the dialog box for the options you wish to change, and you can change the defaults for the current document.

If you want to save these defaults so that they will apply to all new documents, click directly on the word *Document* in the list on the left side of the dialog box. Place a check in the Save options as defaults for new documents check box. Then place a check in only the Styles check box, and remove all other checks. When you click OK, you'll have saved the defaults for all new documents.

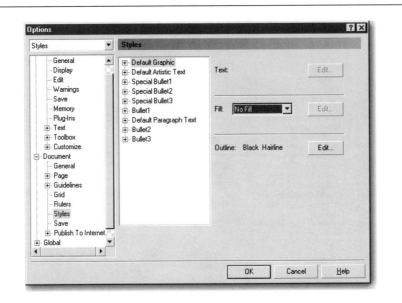

FIGURE 1-13   Tools Options Styles dialog box

How Can I Install All the Fonts Supplied with CorelDRAW?

The short answer is that you can't install them all without having serious problems with your computer. Technically you can install them on Windows NT, but it is not suggested. But that doesn't mean that you can't have all the fonts available for use with CorelDRAW at a moments notice. The key here is to use Bitstream Font Navigator to manage your fonts and to copy the fonts from the CorelDRAW CD appropriately. In Chapter 32, we provide detailed instructions on how to set up your fonts properly.

Why Do the Colors on My Screen Look Dull?

A few years ago the question we always heard was "How come the colors onscreen don't match the colors on my printer?" The simple answer is that the screen is an RGB device, and quality color printers are CMYK devices. Earlier versions of CorelDRAW had color management software, but few users used it. In CorelDRAW 8 and 9, the color management is turned on by default, and that is what causes the onscreen colors to look "dull." But you should find that the colors more closely match the output of your printer.

You can easily turn off the color management so that you get the bright, unprintable colors again. Select Tools | Color Management, and uncheck the Calibrate colors for display check box. In Chapter 8, you'll learn more about choosing the appropriate color model for the job you are creating, and how to best use color management.

How Do I Get Rid of the White Box Around Bitmaps?

There are ways to get rid of it in CorelDRAW, including using the Bitmap Color Mask and PowerClip, and by just node-editing the shape of the bitmap. But the best solution involves Corel PHOTO-PAINT. You'll need to mask the area that you wish to keep, convert it to a floating object, and then save the file in CPT format. When you import the CPT file into CorelDRAW, you will find that it is a group of objects. Ungroup the group, and delete the unwanted objects (the white box). For detailed instructions on this process, visit http://www.unleash.com/articles/whitebox.

My Machine Crashes Quite Often, How Can I Solve This?

If you are crashing often, the cause is most likely something that has gone wrong in your computer. Occasionally it will be a problem with CorelDRAW itself. The most common suspects for these crashes are the drivers that control the video card in your computer. To test this theory, reboot your computer in "Safe" mode (press F8 when you see "Starting Windows 9x", or choose VGA for NT users). Understand that this is only a test. You'll need to work for a while at this lower resolution with a minimum number of colors. Did the problem go away? If so, the video drivers probably need to be changed. Contact the manufacturer of your video card to get a different driver. It is also possible that the problem lies with drivers for other hardware such as network drivers, CD-ROM drivers, etc.

The full troubleshooting process is much more detailed, and we've provided a step-by-step worksheet on our Web site that you can work through. These documents are found at http://www.unleash.com/articles/crash.

Using the Enclosed CD-ROM

In Appendix A, you'll find detailed instructions about the contents of the CD-ROM as well as how to install the software it contains. You'll also find a file entitled readme.html in the root folder that will help you get the most from the CD-ROM. Just load readme.html in your favorite Web browser, and enjoy all the great stuff we've provided for you.

Learning More About CorelDRAW

With well over 900 pages, you'd think that we could cover everything there is to know about CorelDRAW 9. Unfortunately, we could fill many more pages if we had the time and energy. Since we can't cover it all, we thought we'd point you to several other sources of free information on getting the most from CorelDRAW 9.

What's This?

When you click What's This? (SHIFT-F1) on the Help menu, the cursor is replaced by a cursor with a question mark. You then use this cursor to click on various elements of the CorelDRAW screen. For example, if you click on the Rectangle tool in the toolbox, a Tool Tip pops up, telling you how the tool is used. If you click on the drawing page in the center of the screen, a message tells you that this is the area that can be printed by your printer. This tool is great for getting fast feedback about certain elements of the screen. It can also be accessed by clicking the What's This? button on the toolbar. You can also right-click almost anywhere and find What's This in the pop-up menu.

Using the Hints Window

The Hints window, shown in Figure 1-14, is accessed by clicking its name in the Help menu. Its primary purpose is to provide hints on how to use the tools in the toolbox. It is also context-sensitive, so when a tool is selected, a hint on how to use the tool is displayed. Figure 1-15 shows the Hints window when the Rectangle tool has been selected.

FIGURE 1-14   The initial Hints window

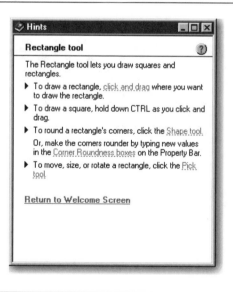

FIGURE 1-15   The Hints window when the Rectangle tool is selected

Practice drawing a rectangle with the Hints window displayed while following these steps:

1. Click the Rectangle tool, and follow the first instruction on the Hints window telling you how to draw a rectangle.

2. After you have drawn the rectangle, drag the crosshair portion of the cursor over the X in the middle of the rectangle (the cursor will change to a pair of crossed double-headed arrows). The Hints window will change to look like the one shown in Figure 1-16. In this configuration, additional hints are given on how to transform the rectangle you just created. Practice the first three instructions on the Hints window while in this configuration. If you followed the instructions correctly, you will have learned how to move, stretch, resize, rotate, and skew your rectangle.

If you want more information pertaining to the tool you are using or the object you have selected, click the question mark button at the upper right of the Hints window. This action will display the CorelDRAW Help screen with even more information about the tool or object.

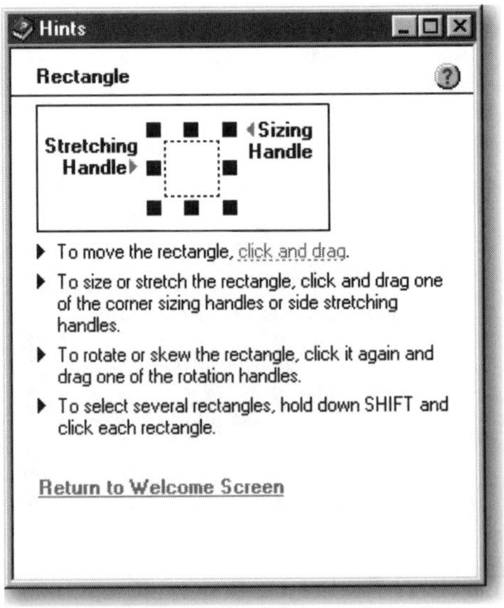

FIGURE 1-16   Hints window with details on modifying an object

As you can readily see, the Hints window can provide a wealth of information on how to use the various tools in CorelDRAW. If you take advantage of this storehouse of information, it will make your learning curve much shorter.

If you have clicked on one of the five buttons on the default Hints window to view the corresponding information, you can return to the default window by clicking the arrow to the left of the question mark button at the upper right of the window. If the window has changed configuration because a tool has been selected, you must close and reopen the Hints window to display the default Hints window again.

Using CorelTUTOR

CorelTUTOR, shown in Figure 1-17, is an online tutor that is activated by either choosing it from the Help menu, Help | CorelTUTOR (ALT-H-T), or by clicking the Apple button on the toolbar. The Tutor provides step-by-step instructions and, in many cases, interactive instruction on how to complete specific tasks. You can learn something as simple as creating a simple shape or more complex tasks that

FIGURE 1-17   CorelTUTOR provides several helpful tutorials

require several steps. It's an excellent learning tool for the new user and a good quick review source for the experienced user.

Corel on the Web

Corel on the Web is a new method of providing up-to-date help. It allows you to go to Corel's Web site while working in CorelDRAW. When you click the Help menu and then hold the cursor over the words "Corel on the Web," a flyout is revealed, offering several Help topics that can be found on Corel's Web site. When you click one of the topics, your default Web browser will be activated. If you're currently connected, it will take you directly to the specific page you clicked on. If you're not connected, you'll need to connect (on some systems, your dial-up networking dialog box will appear, asking if you want to connect). If you click Update Links at the bottom of the flyout, Corel's Web site will be contacted, and your menu will be updated with any changes to the list of links.

Companion Web Site

There is a lot of information that we haven't covered in this book, and some of it changes constantly. We keep that information on the companion Web site to this book. You can find it at http://www.unleash.com. There you will find lots of free tutorials for using CorelDRAW and Corel PHOTO-PAINT, helpful utilities, and a number of other training aids. To get the most out of the site, make sure to sign up for the Graphics Unleashed Newsletter, and we'll send you an occasional e-mail to let you know about the latest information added to the site.

CHAPTER 2

Menus, Standard Toolbar, Property Bar, and Dialog Boxes

COREL.COM

CorelDRAW 9

The CorelDRAW menus, standard toolbar, Property Bar, and dialog boxes are all discussed in this chapter because they share a commonality: each contains tools or commands that allow you to change or modify objects.

Menu Bar

The menu bar, shown as part of the default screen in Figure 2-1, is located at the top of the screen, just under the title bar. It is the only one of the various bars in CorelDRAW that you cannot move from its default position on the screen. The menu bar provides 11 default menus. In addition, you can add your own personalized menus to the menu bar (see Chapter 34).

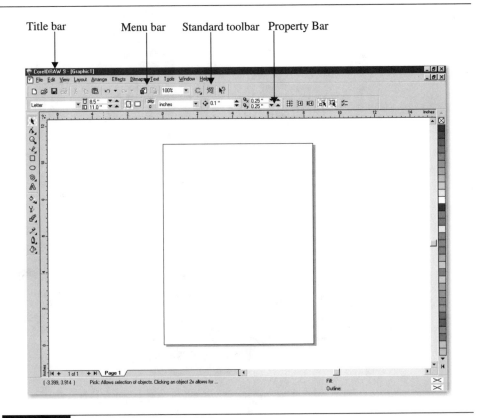

FIGURE 2-1   The default CorelDRAW screen

2

When you click a menu, a drop-down menu of commands appears. For example, if you click the View menu, the drop-down menu displays all of the available ways to view the document onscreen along with a few other commands that fall into the view category. To select a command when the drop-down menu is displayed, you can either use the mouse or simply press the underlined letter in the command name. For example, if you want to open the Color Management dialog box, you can click the Tools menu and press the letter C. You can select many menu items using only shortcut keys. For example if you want to display the Transformation Docker window discussed in Chapter 6, press ALT-A-T (A is for Arrange and T is for Transformation). If you are new to shortcut keys, here's how they work: for the shortcut just described, you press the ALT key, then press the A key, and then press the T key. As you become more familiar with the contents of each menu, you may find you can work more quickly using the shortcut keys.

TIP   *Two of the more important items in the Help menu are the CorelTUTOR program and the Hints window. CorelTUTOR is an interactive program that runs on top of the CorelDRAW window. You select the subject you want to learn about, and the CorelTUTOR program guides you through the process of creating the effect or locating the information you need.*

The Hints widow provides you with hints on how to use the tools in the toolbox. It is context sensitive, so when you select a tool, you receive a hint on how to use it.

Here's how you use the three buttons at the far right of the menu bar. If you click the leftmost button, the current graphic is minimized at the bottom of the CorelDRAW window. The middle button toggles between maximizing the screen so it fills the entire window and reducing the screen to half, or the last size the window was before you maximized. The rightmost button closes the current image file.

Windows Control Menu

The Windows control menu is located on the far left of the menu bar, next to the File menu, and is represented by the Corel balloon icon on a page. The Windows control menu contains the basic Windows commands Restore, Move, Size, Minimize, Maximize, Close, and Next. You can also access this menu by clicking the Corel balloon next to the word "CorelDRAW" on the title bar or by holding down the ALT key and pressing the SPACEBAR.

Menu Access Using a Right Mouse Click

In Windows 95 or 98 and Windows NT 4.0, users can right-click almost anything on the screen, and something will happen. CorelDRAW 9 uses this feature extensively. For example, you can right-click to open menus. The Document menu, shown next, displays if you right-click either the CorelDRAW desktop or the page with nothing selected. We have clicked on the Create Object command in this menu to display its child menu. This child menu contains commands that actually select the tool from the toolbox. For example, if you choose Spiral the cursor changes to the Spiral tool.

Full-Screen Preview	F9			
View	▶			
Create Object	▶	Rectangle	F6	
Import...	Ctrl+I	Ellipse	F7	
Insert New Object...		Curve		
Paste	Ctrl+V	Polygon	Y	
Undo Delete	Ctrl+Z	Spiral		
		Graph Paper		
What's This?		Dimension	▶	
Document Info...				
Properties...		Text	F8	

The Object menu, shown next, displays when you right-click a group of objects. This menu is context sensitive, so the items it contains vary depending on the objects selected when you right-click the mouse. The Object menu appears when two basic objects have been selected.

Convert To Curves	Ctrl+Q
Ungroup	Ctrl+U
Ungroup All	
Wrap Paragraph Text	
Undo Move	Ctrl+Z
Cut	Ctrl+X
Copy	Ctrl+C
Delete	Delete
Lock Object	
Order	▶
Styles	▶
Internet Links	▶
Overprint Fill	
Overprint Outline	
Drape Fills	
What's This?	
Properties...	

Toolbar Menu

One of the more useful menus is the toolbar menu, which is shown next. You open it either by right-clicking on the standard toolbar, the Property Bar, or the toolbox. This menu lets you choose which of the various toolbars to display onscreen.

```
Toolbars...
Customize...

✔ Standard
✔ Property Bar
✔ Toolbox
  Text
  Zoom
  Internet Objects
  Transform
  Visual Basic for Applications

✔ Status Bar
```

Standard Toolbar

The standard toolbar is located just underneath the menu bar (see below). This toolbar includes many shortcut buttons that perform various functions in CorelDRAW. In addition to the shortcut buttons is a Zoom levels list box.

Zoom levels list box

```
CorelDRAW 9 - [Graphic2]
File  Edit  View  Layout  Arrange  Effects  Bitmaps  Text  Tools  Window  Help
□ ☞ 🖫 🖨 ⅛ 🖹 🖺 ↻ ▼ ↺ 🗗 🖺 100% ▼ ⟳ 💥 ▶?
```

The Zoom levels list box lets you select from 12 different Zoom levels:

- To Selected

- To Fit

- To Page

- To Width

- To Height

- 10%

- 25%

- 50%

- 75%

- 100%

- 200%

- 400%

You can also type in custom zoom levels directly in the Zoom levels list box. Simply type in a zoom percentage, and press the ENTER key. For more information on creating custom zoom levels, see Chapter 11.

The standard toolbar is completely customizable, letting you add or remove the shortcut icons to suit your particular way of working in CorelDRAW. For information on customizing the toolbar, see Chapter 34.

When you hold the cursor over a shortcut icon, a Tool Tip appears with a short description of the tool's function. Additional information about the function of the tool appears in the status line at the bottom of the screen.

Table 2-1 lists the default shortcut icons, in the order in which they appear on the toolbar from left to right, and the functions they perform. When an icon is grayed out, it is unavailable in the current context.

Property Bar

The Property Bar is a context-sensitive command bar. The settings and options available on the bar change depending on the tool or object selected. The Property Bar, shown here, is located just below the standard toolbar.

Icon	Function
New	Opens a new graphic.
Open	Opens an existing graphic.
Save	Saves the current file you are working on. If the file has never been saved before, the Save As dialog box appears.
Print	Displays the Print dialog box.
Cut	Deletes the selected objects from the screen and puts them on the clipboard.
Copy	Places the selected objects on the clipboard without deleting them.
Paste	Places the contents of the clipboard on the CorelDRAW page.
Undo	Reverses the most recent operation.
Undo Multiple actions	Displays an undo list box allowing you to select the previous actions to undo in the sequence in which they were applied.
Redo	Reverses the most recent undo operation.
Redo Multiple actions	Displays a redo list box allowing you to select the previous actions to redo in the sequence in which they were applied.
Import	Opens the Import dialog box.
Export	Opens the Export dialog box.
Zoom levels list box	See the explanation earlier in this chapter.
Application Launcher	Opens a drop-down list that lets you open another CorelDRAW application or utility.
Corel Graphics Community	Takes you to a site on a Corel Web page that offers tips and tricks for getting the most out of CorelDRAW applications. Accessing this page requires that you be connected to the Internet.
What's This Help	Invokes context-sensitive help by adding a question mark to your cursor. You can use the cursor to click on various parts of the screen and dialog boxes to get help information about the particular item you click on.

TABLE 2-1   Default Toolbar Icons

The major benefit of the Property Bar is that it reduces the need to use the menu commands or access many of the dialog boxes. As you work in CorelDRAW, you will soon discover the real value of this incredible tool.

Because the Property Bar changes every time you change tools, this chapter doesn't discuss the dozens of possible configurations. The versatility of this toolbar will be apparent as you learn about the commands and effects in the chapters that follow.

Dialog Boxes

A *dialog box* is a window that appears when CorelDRAW needs additional information before it can perform an action or carry out a command. You can navigate through these dialog boxes either with the mouse or the keyboard. Most people find it easier to move around in dialog boxes using the mouse. You simply click a button or check box and then, where applicable, use the appropriate keystrokes to complete the task.

The second way to navigate through dialog boxes is to use the TAB key. When a dialog box is on the screen, pressing TAB cycles through the various radio buttons, check boxes, and so on. When a particular button or parameter box is highlighted, you can use various keys to toggle the item on or off or enter data. Table 2-2 lists the keystrokes to use for the various types of items.

Docker Windows

Docker windows have replaced many of the dialog boxes and roll-ups used in previous versions of CorelDRAW. The Color Palette Browser window is shown here:

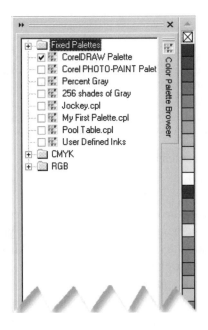

Item	Keystrokes
Buttons (OK, Cancel, etc.)	Press the ENTER key to activate.
Radio buttons (choice buttons)	Press the SPACEBAR to toggle on and off.
Check boxes	Press the SPACEBAR to toggle on and off.
Num boxes	Press the UP or DOWN ARROW keys to change numbers.
List boxes	Press the UP or DOWN ARROW keys to select a name.
Parameter boxes	Type in data.

TABLE 2-2   Keystrokes for Various Types of Dialog Box Items

By default, these Docker windows are docked on the right side of the desktop, next to the color palette. You can redock a window elsewhere on the desktop or "tear" it off into a Docker group on the desktop, as shown here:

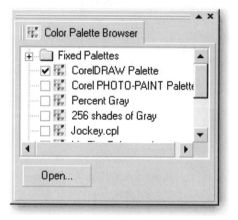

To tear off a Docker window, you must click the double parallel lines across the top of the window and drag the window out onto the desktop. You can also redock the dialog box after it has been torn off by dragging on the same parallel lines to the side of the desktop.

You can access all Docker windows by clicking Window I Dockers. These windows include

■ Object Manager

■ Object Data Manager

- View Manager (CTRL-F2)

- Link Manager

- Internet Bookmark manager

- HTML Object Conflict

- Bitmap Color Mask

- Lens (ALT-F3)

- Artistic Media

- Transformation

- Shaping

- Color

- Color Palette Browser

- Color Styles

- Graphic and Text Styles (CTRL-F5)

- Symbols and Special Characters (CTRL-F11)

- Scrapbook

- Script and Preset Manager

 NOTE *Some Docker windows from the previous list can also be accessed from the other menus that relate to their function.*

Grouping, Collapsing, and Closing Dockers

When you open more than one Docker on screen, the last Docker opened will be displayed together with the previous Docker. Two or more Docker windows form a group of Dockers. The names of each Docker appear on a tab at the side of the Docker group. Click the name of the Docker you want to use to replace the currently displayed Docker. This grouping of Dockers allows you to have ready access to multiple Dockers.

Collapsing the Docker is a way of keeping these multiple Dockers conveniently accessible without having to access them each time from the

<u>W</u>indows | <u>D</u>ockers menu. When Dockers are collapsed, they appear as tabs along the right side of the desktop next to the color palette. To collapse the Dockers, click on the double arrows at the upper left of the Docker window. Figure 2-2 shows the Script and Preset Manager, Artistic Media, and Color Docker windows alongside the color palette in the grouped state. Dockers can also be collapsed when in the "torn off" state by clicking the single arrow at the upper right of the Docker. When a Docker is collapsed in this manner, it remains "floating" onscreen in a toolbar mode.

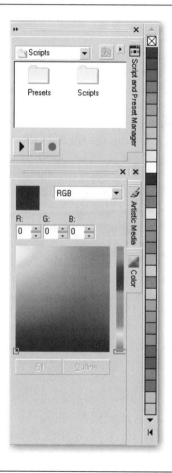

FIGURE 2-2   The Script and Preset Manager, Artistic Media, and Color Docker windows in a grouped state

To display a Docker again in its natural state after being collapsed, click on the same arrows or arrow you used to collapse the Docker.

To close an active Docker window, click on the X at the upper right of the window. To close a Docker group, click on the X with the drop shadow at the far right of the window.

It's also possible to drag a Docker window that has been "torn off" onto another Docker window located in its natural state at the side of the CorelDRAW window. When these torn off Dockers are dragged onto an existing Docker window, all the windows become a group.

Tabbed Dockers

CorelDRAW sometimes uses tabbed Dockers. They replace most of the tabbed dialog boxes used in previous versions. Tabbed Dockers are Docker windows that when selected appear onscreen in an undocked state. They appear in an undocked state when they are first displayed but can be docked like any other Docker window by dragging them to any edge of the desktop (usually the right side of the screen). They cannot be grouped with the other Dockers as described earlier. The reason they are not originally displayed like Docker windows is they take up a lot of screen space. In the undocked state, they are smaller. They also contain tabs (which normal Dockers don't), like the older tabbed dialog boxes. These tabs are like folders; select a tab and the Docker changes to display the settings available for that tab. Press CTRL-TAB to highlight the individual tabs in an open Docker, or simply click a tab with your mouse. Once you have selected a tab, you can use just the TAB key to move around in the active Docker. A good example of a tabbed Docker is the Object Properties Docker shown in Figure 2-3. As a point of reference, the display showing in the figure results when an object with a red fill is selected.

NOTE   *The two tabbed dialog boxes still remaining in CorelDRAW 9 are the Uniform Fill and Outline Color dialog boxes.*

This chapter has given you the knowledge that will help you as you learn how to locate and use the many commands and features contained in the CorelDRAW program. Being able to move within a dialog box or knowing where to look for a command or Docker window can make your life a lot easier when you're working in CorelDRAW.

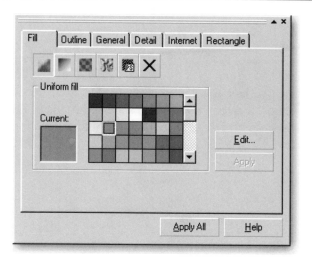

FIGURE 2-3   The Object Properties Docker group

The following chapters will teach you how to use the tools and effects so you can take advantage of the many features in the program.

CHAPTER 3

Rectangles, Ellipses, Polygons, Stars, Spirals, and Graph Paper

CorelDRAW 9

COREL.COM

Most CorelDRAW users want to create something as fast as possible. Often they will turn to the Freehand tool (see Chapter 4) and be disappointed with the results. This chapter starts with the tools for creating primitive shapes like rectangles, ellipses, and polygons. As you continue to use the program, you'll find these tools to be much more valuable than you originally thought. Although the primitive shapes may not be that interesting by themselves, you can use them to create many other shapes that are both interesting and useful.

Drawing Rectangles

The rectangle is the most basic of the primitive shapes provided in the toolbox. Plain and simple, it draws rectangles of all shapes and sizes.

Select the Rectangle tool by clicking its icon in the toolbox, by pressing the F6 function key, or by right-clicking the drawing window and choosing Create Object | Rectangle (F6) from the pop-up menu that appears.

Once the Rectangle tool is selected, your cursor will change into a small crosshair to indicate where the rectangle will be drawn. At the lower-right corner of the crosshair, a small rectangle reminds you which tool is currently selected, as shown here.

To draw a rectangle, simply click where you want to begin a rectangle, and drag your mouse (or pen) to the opposite corner. When you release the mouse button, the rectangle will be drawn on the screen. As you draw the rectangle, the Property Bar gives you feedback on the width, height, and center point of the rectangle in progress. Once you release the mouse button, the Status Bar indicates that a rectangle is selected, and the final dimensions are shown on the Property Bar. Here is an example of the Property Bar information.

Property Bar : Rectangle		
x: 4.076 "	↔ 3.95 "	
y: 3.928 "	↕ 3.018 "	

Just drawing rectangles won't garner you any praise as an artist, but you can modify the rectangle in several ways to make it a bit more useful. To do this, you'll need to use the modifier keys: CTRL and SHIFT.

If you hold down the CTRL key while drawing a rectangle, it will be constrained to a perfect square. A good way to remember this is that CTRL means constrain throughout CorelDRAW—for example, if you hold down the CTRL key while drawing an ellipse, it will be constrained to a perfect circle. Holding down the SHIFT key while drawing a rectangle allows you to draw from the center point outward rather than from corner to corner. This approach can be especially handy if you know where the center point should be located. You can also use the modifier keys together to draw squares from the center out. Note that you can change the default behavior of these modifier keys in DRAW 9, as described in Chapter 34. They also work differently by default on the Macintosh. For Mac users, SHIFT will constrain and COMMAND will draw from the center.

When you've finished drawing a rectangle, it will look something like this.

Notice that an *X* appears in the center of the object. Grabbing and dragging this *X* with your cursor allows you to quickly move the object without having to select the Pick tool first. You'll also note that each of the nodes at the corners of the rectangle is visible. For those of you new to CorelDRAW, they are the tiny unfilled squares that appear on each corner of the rectangle. For those of you familiar with other software, you may know nodes by another name. You'll learn how these nodes can be useful a little later in this chapter.

Rounding the Corners

There is not a special tool labeled the Rounded Rectangle tool, as in other programs. However, it's easy to draw rounded rectangles by first drawing a rectangle and then rounding the corners. This method actually gives you more control over the final shape.

In previous versions, the only way to round a rectangle's corners was by using the Shape tool. Each corner has one node. Click any of these nodes with the Shape tool, and drag away from the corner. All of the corners will become rounded as you drag. When you are done, simply release the mouse button. If the rectangle has been stretched since being originally drawn, the Status Bar will indicate that the corners are "distorted." This means that they won't be perfectly round but, rather, stretched in the same proportions as the rectangle. Using this old method allows you to create a corner radius of an exact amount.

There are visible nodes on the rectangle immediately after you draw it. If you move your cursor over one of the nodes while the Rectangle tool is still selected, the cursor changes to the Shape tool, shown here.

It will now behave just like the Shape tool. So without changing tools, you can round the corners of the rectangle interactively. This method is certainly faster than those in earlier versions.

New to CorelDRAW 9 is the ability to round each corner separately. You can do this interactively by pressing the Z key on your keyboard and then clicking on the node. After you've clicked on the node, click and drag the node with the Shape tool or the Shape tool behavior of other tools described earlier. If you would like to select more than one corner, hold down the SHIFT key along with the Z key, and click on the corners you wish to add.

When a rectangle is the active object, the Property Bar has four textboxes for setting the percentage of roundness as shown here. The percentage shown is related to the shortest side of the rectangle. You simply change the amount on the Property Bar until the roundness is what you want. Note that this is not the true radius of the corner. To the right of the textboxes is a lock icon. When the lock icon is depressed, all corners are changed when you change any of the values. But if it is not depressed, you can change the individual roundness values. When you type a number, remember to press ENTER so that the roundness takes effect. If you set the percentage to 100, the shortest side will be completely rounded.

NOTE   *There is no way in CorelDRAW 9's default feature set to enter a value for the radius of the corner. So we've included a script on the enclosed CD-ROM for you that will draw a rectangle of any size you desire and any corner radius you like. All measurements in this script are inches.*

Putting Rectangles to Use

Users don't always appreciate how often they'll use rectangles. So we've put together a drawing that uses only rectangles to create a small building. Figure 3-1 shows the original layouts of the building and the finished building. The file is provided on the enclosed CD-ROM as Building.cdr with each of the stages on a separate page.

Drawing Ellipses

The ellipse is the most useful of all the primitive shape tools. You can use it as a starting point for almost any free-form shape imaginable.

When drawing ellipses, you need to understand how their size is determined. You will draw a rectangular shape that is invisible, commonly referred to as the

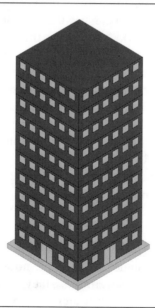

FIGURE 3-1   A simple building was drawn using nothing but rectangles. With a little stretching, skewing, and moving, we got the building shown here.

bounding box. The extreme points of the ellipse will be tangent to the midpoint of each side of the invisible bounding box. This sounds a little bit complicated, but after you draw a few ellipses, it will seem very natural.

Select the Ellipse tool by clicking its icon in the toolbox. Alternatively, you can use the F7 shortcut key or right-click the page with the Pick tool and choose Create Object | Ellipse (F7) from the pop-up menu. Note that your cursor will change to the one shown here.

Once you've selected the tool, click one corner of the imaginary rectangle, and drag to the opposite corner. As you do this, the Property Bar reports the width, height, and center point of the ellipse. Release the mouse button to complete the ellipse. The Status Bar will report that you have an ellipse selected. The final size and position of the center point is shown on the Property Bar. Remember that the size of the ellipse is updated dynamically on the Property Bar as you draw.

As with the Rectangle tool, you can use the modifier keys when drawing ellipses. Holding down the CTRL key constrains the new ellipse to a perfect circle. Holding down the SHIFT key causes the ellipse to be drawn from the center outward. Holding down both keys draws a circle from the center out. Remember to release the mouse button before releasing the modifier key.

As with rectangles, after you've drawn an ellipse, you can move it simply by clicking the *X* in the middle and dragging it to the desired location.

Ellipses may seem like a simple shape, but they can lead to much more advanced shapes. In Chapter 14 you'll see a series of ellipses transformed into a dolphin. Chapter 15 will show you how you can create all kinds of fantastic shapes from rectangles and ellipses through the use of Weld, Trim, and Intersection.

Creating Pie Wedges and Arcs

Just as there is no rounded rectangle tool, there are no special tools in CorelDRAW for creating arcs and pie wedges. Nevertheless, they are easy to create with some minor editing of an ellipse. You can draw arcs and pie wedges directly, by just clicking the appropriate button on the Property Bar shown a bit later.

Each ellipse has one node. The node is at the top of the ellipse if you draw the ellipse from top to bottom. If you draw the ellipse from the bottom to the top, the node is at the bottom. To create an arc, select this single node with the Shape tool, and drag your cursor around the outside perimeter of the ellipse. To create a pie wedge, drag the node around the inside perimeter of the ellipse. Remember that you can select the node without changing to the Shape tool. If you hold down the CTRL key while dragging the node, the arc or wedge will be constrained to an angle that is a multiple of the angle you set in the Options dialog box that is described in Chapter 34. This will normally be 15 degrees unless you've changed the default setting. This original way to create arcs and wedges gives you lots of visual feedback, but it is not always the quickest way to get the job done, especially if you are trying to create exact angles.

You'll find the beginning and ending angles, whether to create an arc or a wedge, and the direction right on the Property Bar when an ellipse, arc, or pie wedge is selected as shown here. Remember that after you type an angle in the textboxes, you'll need to press the ENTER key to make the changes take effect.

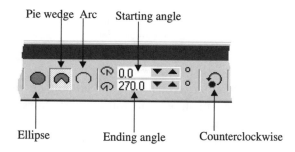

Here are examples of an ellipse, a pie wedge, and an arc.

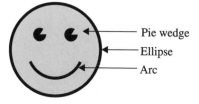

Drawing Polygons and Stars

The polygon is the most complex of the primitive shapes included in CorelDRAW. You can choose the number of points or sides it will have, whether it will have flat sides or points, and how those points will be constructed and shaped.

Let's start with the simple polygon. In the default configuration, it has five flat sides. Click the Polygon tool in the toolbox (it is on the Object flyout shown here), or right-click in the drawing window and choose Create Object | Polygon from the pop-up menu.

Spiral tool

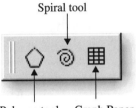

Polygon tool   Graph Paper tool

Your cursor will change to reflect that you are drawing a polygon, as shown here.

Now drag out an imaginary rectangle while holding down the left mouse button. You should have a plain old polygon with five sides, as shown here. If you want to constrain the aspect ratio (so the width and height are the same), just use the CTRL modifier key while drawing the polygon. And, yes, the SHIFT key allows you to draw from the center out, as with the other tools.

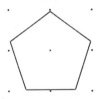

Now that you've seen the basic polygon, you will start changing the attributes. You can do this either before or after you draw the polygon with the exception of sharpness, which can only be changed after drawing the polygon. First you'll change the number of sides. You can change attributes right on the Property Bar, as shown here. Type the number **8** in the textbox just to the right of the star, and press ENTER. The polygon will change into an octagon (like a stop sign). If you're having trouble seeing this shape, just color it red, and it should look more familiar. For those who like to push the limits, you can create polygons with as many as 500 sides.

TIP   *Lowering the number of sides to three allows you to easily draw triangles.*

Number of points on polygon   Polygon/Star

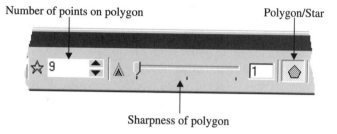

Sharpness of polygon

NOTE   *If you change these values while no object is selected, you automatically change the default values.*

If you'd rather create a star, simply click the Polygon/Star button on the Property Bar. If you have a polygon selected, the icon will be a polygon. Click once, and the icon will change into a star—as will the polygon you had selected. Notice that inside of the star are construction lines. If you want a star without these lines, you can use another method that will be described a little later in this chapter.

Just to the left of the Polygon/Star button is a slider that controls the sharpness of the points in stars. If you still have only five points in your star, you'll notice that this slider is dimmed. It becomes undimmed when the selected star has at least seven points. If the star has seven points, you can set the sharpness to either 1 or 2. As the number of points increases, the number of sharpness levels also increases as this number specifies the number of points in between the points that are joined. Basically, the higher the sharpness level, the more pointy your star will be. Here are two 12-pointed stars. The left star has a sharpness level of 1, and the right one has a sharpness level of 4.

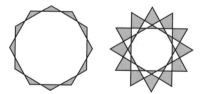

By now, you can see that the Polygon tool can create the shapes you always tried to create with a Spirograph as a child. However, the really interesting behavior of the Polygon tool becomes apparent when you edit the polygon with

the Shape tool. You'll learn the basics in this chapter, and in Chapter 7 you'll learn some really awesome techniques.

When you draw a polygon, it has a single node where each of the sides meet and another node in the middle of each side. Thus, the standard five-sided polygon has ten nodes. When you move one node, all the other "similar" nodes move by the same amount. Moving the node in the center of the polygon's side therefore affects the nodes in the middle of the other sides.

With the Polygon tool still selected, click one of the nodes. Move it toward the center of the polygon, and watch how the other nodes behave the same way. Now rotate the nodes counterclockwise inside of the polygon. Again the other nodes do the same. You'll see that the simple polygon has now become much more interesting (or at least more intricate) than the original. As you move the nodes, you might notice a light outline of the original polygon. This is the bounding box. Don't worry; it is just visual feedback and will not print. Holding down the CTRL key constrains the movement of the nodes so they can only be moved closer or farther from the center of the polygon. One of the side effects of this behavior in polygon editing is the time you will spend just playing with the many cool shapes that you can create—and the more points to the polygon, the more nodes you have to manipulate! If you finish by filling the modified polygon, it becomes even more interesting.

CAUTION   *Because it is quite easy to draw a polygon with many overlapping paths, you can run into problems with complexity when printing. Chapter 26 describes various ways to decrease the complexity of a drawing.*

Drawing Spirals

The Spiral tool is the middle of the three tools on the Object flyout. When you select the Spiral tool, your cursor changes into the one shown here.

Before drawing your spiral, make sure to change the settings on the Property Bar, shown next, to your desired settings. Spirals are elliptical in shape, so drawing them is similar to drawing an ellipse. Drag from one corner of the imaginary box to the opposite corner. As you draw, the Status Bar reports the width and height of the spiral. If you wish to constrain the width and height so they are the same, simply hold down the CTRL key as you draw the spiral. Of course, the SHIFT key allows you to draw from the center outward. Note that if you have a slow system, it may be nearly impossible for you to use these modifier keys because of the irregular redrawing of the screen.

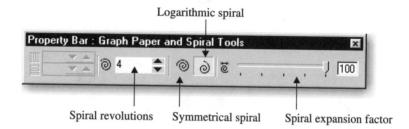

You can specify anything from a single rotation to 100 rotations. Changing the number of rotations only affects new spirals, not spirals that you've already drawn. Spirals are not a dynamic shape like rectangles, ellipses, and polygons. The tool is simply an automated way to create a complex line.

Next to the number of rotations on the Property Bar are two buttons for defining the type of spiral. The default is symmetrical. Each rotation of a symmetrical spiral is spaced evenly from the previous rotation. The button on the right allows you to create a logarithmic spiral. Each rotation of a logarithmic spiral is increasingly farther away from the previous rotation. The rate at which the rotation increases is based on the spiral expansion factor, which you control by using the slider just to the right of the Logarithmic spiral button.

No special editing properties are associated with spirals. However, you can do some interesting things with spirals and the Shape tool, as described in Chapter 7.

Creating Graph Paper

The Graph Paper tool actually creates a grid of a specified number of rows and columns. You can access the tool by selecting its icon from the Object flyout or by right-clicking your drawing and choosing Create Object Graph Paper from the pop-up menu. After you've selected the Graph Paper tool, your cursor will change into the one shown here.

Before drawing the grid, you need to set the number of rows and columns that you want. You can easily do this on the Property Bar, as shown here; the maximum number of rows or columns is 50. Then simply drag out a rectangle, just as you've done with the Rectangle tool. Within that rectangle will appear a grid containing the exact number of rows and columns you specified. Note that the Status Bar will say that you have a group of objects. That is because the Graph Paper tool is nothing more than an automated way to draw a group of rectangles.

Graph Paper columns

Graph Paper rows

Once you've drawn the grid, you cannot change the number of rows or columns without deleting the entire grid and starting over. If you want to work with the individual rectangles, you'll need to ungroup them, as described in Chapter 14. At that point, each cell in the grid will be a separate rectangle and will behave just like any other rectangle you draw.

CHAPTER 4

Drawing Lines of all Shapes and Sizes

CorelDRAW 9

In the previous chapter, you learned how to create various shapes. This chapter explains how to create your own freehand shapes from scratch. Many users gravitate to the Freehand tool as the obvious way to draw, but if you don't understand exactly how it works, it can be rather frustrating. You'll also find that your skills will be hampered if you choose to draw with a brick on a string or a billiard ball (a mouse or trackball). Using a graphic tablet will give you much greater control over the shapes you create, and it is by far the best way to take advantage of the Artistic Media tool.

Activate any of the tools on the Curve flyout, shown here, by pressing the F5 key. The tool selected on the flyout will be the last tool used. Pressing it will bring up the Artistic Media tool, but there are no other shortcuts to get to any of the individual tools.

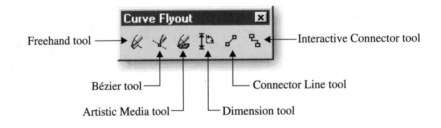

Freehand Tool

The Freehand tool works very much like a pencil. When you drag, a line will follow your cursor. If you've drunk too much coffee, the line will show the shakiness of your hand. It's extremely difficult to draw smooth lines without using a graphics tablet because of the inaccuracy of a mouse. And if you really want to drive yourself nuts, try to draw with the little red eraser tip or touchpad found on laptops! When you select the Freehand tool, your cursor will look like this:

As you draw, CorelDRAW adds nodes at various intervals along the line. The technical details of nodes are described fully in Chapter 7. But for now you should understand that usually, the fewer the nodes along the curve, the better. There are exceptions to this rule, but a curve with more nodes is less smooth because each node adds another point of inflection. How closely the line tracks your movement is also controlled by the Freehand Smoothing slider on the Property Bar, shown here, and by the Freehand tool settings, which are discussed in Chapter 34. The Freehand Smoothing slider, which defaults to 100, ranges from 0 to 100. To use it, click directly on the control, and drag your cursor to the left or right without releasing the left mouse button. You'll see a slider control appear under the Property Bar that indicates the actual movement of the slider.

 TIP _Hold down the SHIFT key while drawing a line, and you can backtrack to erase part of the line. Once you release the SHIFT key, you can resume drawing._

You create straight lines in a slightly different way. Instead of dragging, you click at the start of the line, move your cursor to the end of the line, and then click again. This generates a straight line between those two points. Many users want perfectly horizontal or vertical lines and mistakenly call them straight lines. You create such lines in the same manner, except that you hold down the CTRL key before and during the second click. This constrains the line to a multiple of the constrain angle set in the Options dialog box (which is discussed in Chapter 34).

You can also switch between drawing a curved line and a straight line. Begin drawing the line freehand and when you get to the place where the straight line should begin, just press the TAB key. The straight line will end when you either release the left mouse button or press the TAB key again. If you press the TAB key to end the straight line, you will still be drawing with a freehand line.

 NOTE _Depending on the smoothness setting for freehand lines, the straight lines may be converted to curved lines._

Auto-Tracing Bitmaps

If you have imported a bitmap into your drawing, it is quite easy to convert it into a vector drawing. First, select the bitmap with the Pick tool, and then activate the Freehand tool. The Status Bar will indicate that you are auto-tracing. Click the Freehand tool just outside of the shape you want auto-traced, and a vectorized version of it will soon appear. This functionality is described in Chapter 23. We'll discuss the process for manually tracing bitmaps a little bit later in this chapter.

Bézier Tool

The first time you use the Bézier tool, you might find it difficult to understand. This tool definitely takes a little practice to master, but the benefits are worth it. The Bézier tool gives you the most control over the shaping of a curve while drawing. Each time you click the mouse, it creates a node and connects the node with any previous node. But by clicking and dragging, you can shape the curve entering the node. This technique will make more sense after you've completed the section in Chapter 7 on shaping objects. You are actually moving the bézier control handle of the node when you click and drag; it is what controls the angle of the line entering and exiting the node. To change the last node to a cusp node, just press C. In fact, you can hold down the C key while drawing, and all the nodes will be cusps. When you are finished drawing the line, either press the SPACEBAR, or select another tool.

    TIP   *You can move any of the nodes created previously while the Bézier tool is still creating a line. Just move the cursor over the node until it changes into the Interactive Shape cursor, and edit away.*

One area where the Bézier tool really shines is in the manual tracing of bitmaps. Earlier we mentioned CorelDRAW's built-in auto-tracing features. By using the Bézier tool and adding nodes at each inflection point on a curve, you can quickly and accurately recreate scanned artwork. Although it may seem to take longer to do it manually, it is almost always quicker than auto-tracing and then cleaning up the mess of extra nodes that CorelDRAW created. Even if you don't shape the curves as you create the nodes, you can place them quickly and then use the Shape tool to modify them later.

A Simple Project

To help you get a better idea of how to use the Bézier tool, we're going to work through a simple project. Since this project involves drawing, your results will vary from the results we show. The most important thing is that you learn how the tool works.

1. Select the Bézier tool if it isn't already selected.

2. Click on the page to create the node labeled 1 in the image that follows.

3. Click a second time to create the node labeled 2. Before releasing the mouse button, drag as indicated by the arrow just above the node. The dotted line indicates the handles for the node.

4. Click and drag again to create the node labeled 3. Again follow the arrow when dragging.

5. Repeat the process to create the node labeled 4. Note that the arrow is at an angle so you'll need to drag in that direction.

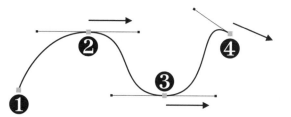

This was a simple project, and the result was just a squiggly line. Keep practicing these techniques to create some simple objects like an apple with a bite out of it or the outline of a car. With a little practice, you'll find that the Bézier tool is the best way to create freehand shapes and to trace scanned images.

Artistic Media Tool

Those of you who've had a few versions of CorelDRAW may have noticed that PowerLines have disappeared from the current version. The Artistic Media tool has taken their place. PowerLines never did seem to work because they created a large number of objects with an overwhelming number of nodes. You'll find that the Artistic Media tool can do almost everything that PowerLines could do and much more.

Presets

When you select the Artistic Media tool from the Curve flyout, the Property Bar initially changes to the one shown here:

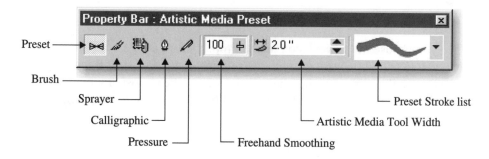

The first five buttons allow you to select which type of pen you would like to use. Choices include Preset, Brush, Sprayer, Calligraphic, and Pressure. Each of these pen types are discussed a later in this chapter. Note that as you select a pen type, the Property Bar will change to reflect settings for that pen type. The Property Bar shown previously is applicable only when Preset is selected.

Just to the right of the buttons is a parameter box that gives the maximum width of the line (or shape) being created. This value is used in different ways, depending on which type of pen you are using. The next parameter box contains the Nib Angle options. It is available only when you have the Calligraphic pen selected. In all other cases it is grayed out. On the far right is a drop-down list of the various available presets, which is available only when the Preset pen type is selected.

OK, that's enough talk. For now, just select one of the presets from the drop-down list at the far right of the Property Bar, and draw something on the page. You might perceive a slight delay between drawing the line and actually seeing the finished object. Can you see how the Preset Stroke that you chose was fit to the line you drew? The value in the Artistic Media Tool Width num box is used to determine the maximum width of the line. Feel free to change the width now, and watch how the line on the page will change. While you're at it, change to a different Preset Stroke, and the line width change again. Not happy with the line you drew? No problem, just switch to the Shape tool, and you can modify the actual stroke of the line. Details on editing with the Shape tool are provided in Chapter 7. A simple example of a line being edited is shown here:

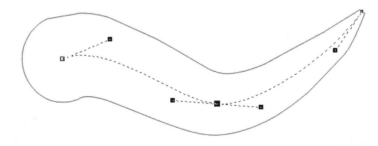

Brush

When you choose the second icon on the Property Bar, the Artistic Media tool will allow you to paint brushstrokes with the settings on the Property Bar shown here. These are similar to presets, but they allow you to take almost any image you can create in CorelDRAW and paint with it. Just by clicking on the Brush Stroke drop-down list, you can set a number of interesting brushes. Go ahead and paint with them for a little while to see how they work. The changes we described with the presets are equally applicable here.

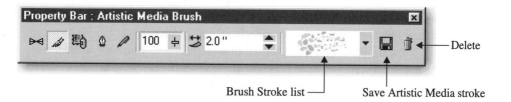

Brush Stroke list ———
Save Artistic Media stroke

The Brush Stroke that you choose will be fit to the stroke you draw with the width of the stroke determined by the Artistic Media Tool Width setting on the Property Bar. One of the neatest features is that you can create your own brushes. Create the shape or shapes that you want to use for your brush. Make sure that all objects that should be part of the shape are selected, and click the Save Artistic Media Stroke button. Give the stroke a name, and you should see a preview of your objects at the top of the drop-down list. That's all there is to it. And since the strokes are in CMX format, it is easy to edit the existing strokes to change their shapes or colors. If you choose to design your own brushes, you may want to consider keeping their complexity to a minimum to avoid any output problems and to keep them working fast.

Object Sprayer

Have you ever used the Image Sprayer in Corel PHOTO-PAINT? If so, you'll be familiar with the Object Sprayer. When you choose the Object Sprayer, the Property Bar changes to the one shown here:

Choice of spray order ——— Dabs/Spacing of Object(s) to be Sprayed

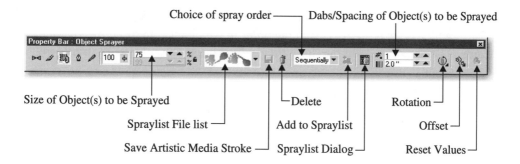

Size of Object(s) to be Sprayed

Spraylist File list ———
Save Artistic Media Stroke ———

Delete
Add to Spraylist
Spraylist Dialog ———

Rotation ———
Offset ———
Reset Values ———

To use the Object Sprayer, you'll first want to choose a Spraylist from the drop-down list on the Property Bar. Just to the left of the drop-down list is the size of the object being sprayed. You can adjust this size to fit your needs. By default, the width and height are the same, but you can click the lock icon just to its right and adjust the two values separately. The size is based on the first image in the list, and the other images are sized proportionally larger or smaller.

Since a Spraylist can contain a number of different shapes, you can choose how the shapes are used. This is different from the Brush, which may have contained many different shapes that were always used together. The Choice of spray order drop-down allows you to choose from Randomly, Sequentially, and By Direction. Let's say that the spraylist has ten objects that it can spray. Randomly has no particular sequence for choosing which of the ten objects will be sprayed. Sequentially uses the first object, then the second object, and so on. By Direction chooses the object sprayed by the direction of the line. So if you are moving horizontally, you spray one object. Start drawing at a 45-degree angle, and you spray another object. This is especially useful for a list containing arrows that point in various directions, or the like.

For each place along the stroke that an object is sprayed, you can actually have multiple objects. The number is controlled by the number of Dabs you specify. It is set to 1 by default. How often an object (or objects) is painted is controlled by the Spacing specified on the Property Bar. By default it is 1 inch.

Rotation provides settings that will rotate the objects relative either to the path drawn or to the page. Clicking the Rotation icon will bring down a mini dialog box for entering various settings. Similarly, you can specify an Offset value by clicking on the Offset icon and entering appropriate values in the mini dialog box. Here, you can also choose if the offset will always be on one side of the line, alternate from side to side, or change randomly. Experiment with these settings until you find something that gives you the exact results that you want. If all goes awry and you just want to start again, click the Reset button at the far right of the Property Bar.

At times, the spraylist will contain objects that you don't want to use. You can control which objects are used, and the order in which they are used by creating a Playlist. To do so, click on the Spraylist Dialog button on the Property Bar to get the dialog box shown next.

On the left side of the dialog box, all of the objects within the Spraylist are listed. The right side of the dialog contains the playlist that will be used as you paint with the Object Sprayer. In the middle of the dialog box there is a series of buttons that allow you to modify the list. The top three buttons allow you to select an object and move it up or down in the list. If two objects are selected, their order can be reversed by clicking the rightmost of the three buttons. The other buttons are clearly labeled and allow you to add objects from the spraylist to the Playlist or to delete objects from the Playlist. Alternatively, you can add all the objects, or clear them. Note that these changes are used only while the spraylist is selected, and no permanent changes are made to the spraylist.

Creating Your Own Spraylist

This is an interesting feature, but only a handful of lists are supplied with CorelDRAW. So to get the most out of it, you'll want to create your own spraylists. You'll need to follow the instructions carefully so that your list will work properly.

1. First, create all the objects on your drawing page.

2. Select the Artistic Media tool in the Object Sprayer mode.

3. Select New Spraylist from the Spraylist File List drop-down dialog box on the Property Bar drop-down dialog box. Note that it is the topmost option.

4. With the Artistic Media tool, click and/or SHIFT-click the objects on the page. If you select more than one object, they will be treated as a single object in the spraylist.

5. Click the Add to Spraylist button on the Property Bar.

6. Repeat as necessary until you've added all the objects you want to add to the spraylist.

7. Click the Save icon to save to a named list. It is possible that you'll need to change a number in one of the num boxes and then change it back to activate the Save icon.

Completing these steps will create the list, what if you want to delete objects from the list? With no objects selected on the page, bring up the Spraylist Dialog using the icon on the Property Bar. There is no way to *delete* the object from the spraylist, so you'll just have to *remove* it from the playlist. Select the object you want to remove, and click the Remove button. When you get back to the Property Bar, click the Save icon to make this change to the playlist permanent.

If you really want to delete the object, you'll have to open the CDR file that is the spraylist. Delete the object you don't want. Now it is gone, but the preview is wrong. So bring up the Spraylist dialog box, and move an object up in the playlist and then down again. When you get back to the Property Bar, click the Save icon, and the preview will be updated. This would be much easier if you could just select the object in the spraylist and press the Remove button, but that feature will have to come in a future release.

Calligraphic

Unlike the previous two Artistic Media tools, the Calligraphic tool just draws fillable shapes. You can control the Freehand Smoothing and Width of the line as with the Presets described earlier. The only unique option is the Calligraphic Angle found at the far right of the Property Bar. A simple way to see how this tool works is to draw an *S*. Note how the thickness of the line is determined by the direction of your brushstroke. With the default settings, the line should have little or no thickness for purely horizontal lines and full thickness for perfectly vertical lines. As the angle changes, the points of maximum and minimum thickness will change.

Pressure

Drawing pressure lines requires a graphics tablet. You can draw them with a mouse, but since there is no pressure, the line will have a minimum amount of width to start. If you use the Up and Down arrows on your keyboard, it will increase and decrease pressure as you draw with the mouse. The Artistic Media Tool Width will now be used as the width of the line when the maximum pressure is applied. If you apply less pressure, the line will be thinner.

Artistic Media Docker

So far we've concentrated on using the Artistic Media tool, but there is another way. With CorelDRAW, isn't there always another way? You can access the Docker by selecting <u>W</u>indow I <u>D</u>ockers I A<u>r</u>tistic Media. The Docker is shown here in an undocked state:

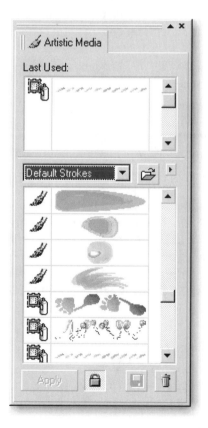

One benefit to using the Docker is that you can apply a preset, brush, or spraylist to a line you've already drawn. This allows you to tweak the original line until it is perfect before applying the Artistic Media. Select the line you want to paint, and then single-click on the stroke you wish to apply. If you want to change to another stroke, just click on the new stroke, and the change will happen automatically.

You can also create a new stroke by dragging an object onto the Docker. If it is a single object and you drop it on an existing spraylist, it will be added to the spraylist. If you drop it elsewhere, you'll be asked if you want a new brush or a spraylist. If you plan on creating a spraylist, it is best to drag the first object in to get it started, then drag in new objects one by one. When they can be added, you'll see a small + next to your cursor. If you select all the objects and drag them at once, they will all be considered a single object in the spraylist.

Graphics Tablets

To get the most out of the Artistic Media tool, you need a graphics tablet. You can create some of the effects without one, but you can't easily simulate the Pressure effect.

Tablets are something that we've been recommending for years. Sure, they cost more than a standard mouse, but they also deliver much more in terms of accuracy. Obviously, using a pen to draw is much more natural than a mouse which can sometimes feel like a bar of soap.

Tablets are also ergonomically better for you. They decrease your chances of getting Carpal Tunnel Syndrome, which is commonly attributed to using a mouse. The savings in health costs alone can make the tablet a worthwhile purchase.

Most tablet manufacturers offer tablets in three sizes of interest to graphic designers. The smallest tablet is usually in the neighborhood of 4"×5" and is also the cheapest at less than $150. Many users are attracted by the price, but you do get what you pay for. A bit larger are the 6"×8" and 9" x 12" tablets. The larger tablets give you much more room to work with, and you can commonly find them for under $300. Lastly, there are the 12"×12" tablets. If you are tracing artwork from a full 8.5"×11" page, these tablets can be useful, but most CorelDRAW users will find that the 6"×8" size is optimal.

All tablets have at least two buttons, just like a mouse. The "left mouse button" is typically the tip of the pen. Pressing down on the tip is the same as left-clicking with a mouse. Nowadays, the tips measure the amount of pressure you use when drawing. This information is used by almost all paint programs, including PHOTO-PAINT, and also by the Pressure Artistic Media Tool. The "right mouse button" is found on the barrel of the pen, which you press with your finger. Many pens have another button on the barrel that you can program for a double-click. This feature is especially handy since it can be difficult to tap the tip twice in the same place. The latest trend is to add an "eraser" to the other end of the pen. Turn the pen over, and this "tip" will act as an eraser in CorelDRAW. In Corel PHOTO-PAINT, you can program it to activate the tool of your choice.

So next time you have a little extra money for computer "toys," put a graphics tablet at the top of your list—you won't be disappointed.

Dimension Tool

When you select the Dimension tool from the Curve flyout, you can actually create several types of dimensions. The Property Bar has a series of icons for each of the dimension types, as shown here.

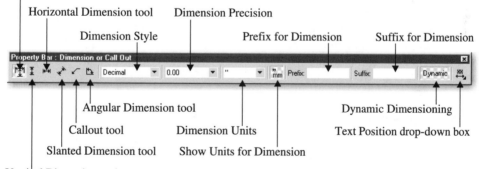

Most of the time, you'll want to link a dimension line with another object. By selecting View | Snap to Objects, you activate linking. By default, it is automatically selected when you choose the Dimension tool. If Snap to Objects has been previously activated, there is no need to select it again. With auto, vertical, horizontal, and slanted dimension lines, three clicks are required to complete a line. The first left mouse click is where the line begins measuring. Next, click where the line ends measuring. Finally, click where you would like the text of the measurement. Here is an example dimension line:

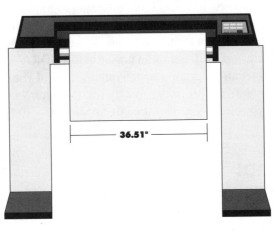

CAUTION   *If you use an inappropriate dimension line type, the amount may be zero. For example, if you use the vertical dimension line to measure the width of an object, it will display zero since there is no change in the vertical direction. The new Auto Dimension tool is a way to avoid this problem. It can draw either vertical, horizontal, or slanted lines, based on your mouse movement. You can also press the TAB key to toggle between the three states.*

Once a dimension line has been drawn, you can't modify it by selecting the line itself. You can, however, move the text closer or farther from the linked object, and the dimension line will adjust automatically. Also, if you resize the linked object, the dimension line will update to fit the object and change the measurement value. To change the font of the text, simply select it and change it just like any other text.

NOTE   *Dimension Text uses the properties of default Artistic text.*

4

When the dimension line is selected, you can make several changes to the way the measurement is represented. The Property Bar includes several drop-down lists and buttons.

The Dimension Style drop-down list lets you choose between Decimal, Fractional, US Engineering, and US Architecture. Decimal represents the amount as a whole number followed by a decimal point and up to ten significant digits. The number of significant digits is selected from the Precision drop-down list. Fractional represents the amount as a whole number followed by a fraction that can have a precision to 1/1024 of a unit that is specified in the Precision drop-down list. US Engineering shows the amount in feet and inches with a precision of up to ten decimal places on the inches. No matter which unit is selected, US Engineering is always measured in feet and inches. US Architecture is similar in that it shows feet and fractional inches, with a precision that can be as small as 1/1024 of an inch.

The Dimension Units drop-down list allows you to choose any of the units that are available in CorelDRAW. Several of the units are available in more than one form. For example, inches can be represented with the double-tick symbol, the abbreviation "in," or the word "inches." Remember that you cannot specify units if you've chosen US Engineering or US Architecture for the style.

When you don't want the units to be displayed, simply deselect the Show Units for Dimension button. When the Dynamic Dimensioning button is selected, the amount shown as part of the dimension line will change any time you resize the dimension line. If you want the amount to remain static, deselect the Dynamic Dimensioning button. You can place text before or after the dimension by typing text in the Prefix for Dimension and Suffix for Dimension boxes. Note that if you want space between the text and the amount, you must add it manually. Finally, you can control the position of the text relative to the dimension line through the options in the Text Position drop-down list.

 TIP *If you want to show a unit abbreviation other than one listed, turn off Show Units for Dimension, and type your own abbreviation in the Suffix for Dimension box.*

Angular Dimension

The main difference between angular dimensions and the other dimensions is that they require four distinct clicks rather than three. The first click is at the origin of the angle, the second click is at the starting point, the third click is at the ending point, and the last click is where the text should appear. The Units drop-down box will allow only degrees, radians, and gradians since the other units don't apply to measuring angles. Here is an example of an angular dimension:

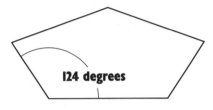

Callouts

Callouts are not dimension lines. It's unclear why they are located on the Dimension Property Bar, and not the Curve flyout, which just makes them hard to find. They do require three clicks just like dimension lines, though. The first click should be near the point that the callout will reference. This end quite often will have an arrow added. The second click, if it is a single one, creates an elbow in the line. Double-clicking for the second click will leave the line straight rather than with an elbow. The third click or the previous double-click produces a text cursor for the description of the callout. Callouts automatically link the line and the text so that they move together. You can format the text and line just as you would format any other lines and text. Here is an example of a callout:

TIP   *Callouts can be dynamically linked to an object if Snap to Objects is selected when they are drawn. If you move the object to which the callout is linked, the callout line will update as well.*

Connector Line Tool

The Connector Line tool is the fifth icon in the Curve flyout. You use it to draw a line between two objects that dynamically change when either or both of the objects is moved. When the tool is selected, Snap to Objects is activated automatically, without having to be selected. The line will snap to any of the nodes on a nearby object. If you click away from any objects, you will simply draw a straight line. Once you've connected two objects, you can specify whether the line is to be locked to the initial node you clicked, or whether it can float freely to the node closest to the connected object. To control this, simply select or deselect the Lock to Connector Node button on the Property Bar; it should be the only available button.

Connector lines are especially useful when drawing a flow chart or an organization chart that changes frequently. Simply moving one of the boxes will automatically move the lines. Connector lines can be drawn at any angle. Read on for an even better variation on this tool.

4

Interactive Connector Tool

At the far right of the Curve flyout is the Interactive Connector tool. It is similar to the Connector Line tool in that it draws lines that connect two objects. The lines dynamically update as well. The big difference is that the connection lines drawn by the Interactive Connector are limited to horizontal and vertical lines. To draw a Flow line (the result of using the Interactive Connector tool), click and drag from a node on one object to a node on another object. Flow lines give a cleaner look to a drawing when compared with lines drawn with the Connector Line tool. Examples of a flowchart created with each tool are shown here. Connector lines are on the left, and Flow lines are on the right.

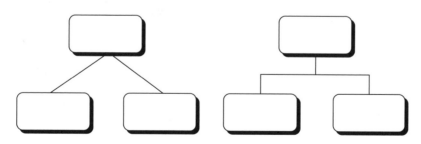

A Flow line will connect only to a node or to the midpoint of a line segment. If you wish to connect with the midpoint as in the previous example, you may have to hover your cursor for a while so that the point will appear under the cursor.

Each of the tools on the Curve flyout allows you to create some form of line. Some of these lines are freeform lines, some have a "thickness," and some are associated with a measurement. Most of the time you will be using either the Freehand tool or the Bézier tool to create a freeform shape. The other tools are used under special circumstances.

CHAPTER 5

Creating and Manipulating Text

CorelDRAW 9

If you are upgrading from an older version of CorelDRAW, you may notice that there is now just a single Text tool. We'll describe how this single tool can be used to create both Artistic and Paragraph Text. Symbols and Special Characters are accessed through the Windows | Docker menu. This chapter will describe each of the text types and how to work with each type, and we'll give you an example of how to create a page layout project in CorelDRAW. But before you decide to use CorelDRAW for all your page layout needs, please keep in mind that documents of more than a few pages really should be created in a package such as Corel VENTURA.

Artistic Text

Artistic Text is used when a short block of text will have a special effect applied. Quite often you will use it without applying special effects, but you must first have Artistic Text before even attempting most effects. You can have no more than 32,000 characters in a single block of Artistic Text. Older versions of CorelDRAW had a 250-character limit on text blocks that could receive an effect. That limit is gone, but remember that the longer the block, the more time consuming the effect will be to implement.

Creating Artistic Text

To create a block of Artistic Text, you first need to select the Text tool from the toolbox or right-click the drawing window and choose Create Object | Text from the pop-up menu. An even quicker way to select the Text tool is with the F8 shortcut key.

Once the Text tool is selected, click anywhere in the drawing window, and begin typing. By default, the text is 24-point Avant Garde Bk BT. As you type, the text will not automatically wrap to the next line. If you want a new paragraph or line, you must press the ENTER key.

You can change the default font for the current document by changing the font name and size on the Property Bar when no text object is selected. After you select the new attributes, you will be presented with the Text Attributes dialog box, shown next, asking whether the change applies to Artistic Text, Paragraph Text, or both.

Text Attributes   [?] [X]

Changing text properties when nothing is selected will modify the attributes used by the text tools when creating new objects.

Click on the boxes below to choose which tools will receive new default settings.

☑ <u>A</u>rtistic Text
☐ <u>P</u>aragraph Text

[OK]   [Cancel]

5

TIP   *You can also change the default font in the <u>T</u>ools | <u>O</u>ptions dialog box as described in Chapter 1.*

Artistic Text behaves like any other graphical object. It can be stretched, mirrored, rotated, extruded, contoured, and placed on a path. If you wish to directly edit the shapes of text characters, you need to convert the text to curves. You can also break apart and arrange blocks of Artistic Text. You can use <u>A</u>rrange | <u>B</u>reak Apart (CTRL-K) to make each line of text a separate object. If you apply this command to a single line of text, each word becomes a separate object. And if you apply Break Apart to a single word, the word becomes separate characters. This can be handy when converting text blocks to curves to ensure that they do not become too complex. If you wish to combine together separate lines of text, simply use the <u>A</u>rrange | <u>C</u>ombine (CTRL-L) command. This will place the text in a single block, with the first block selected being the top line in the block. And separate words can be combined into a line of text, but be sure to add a space at the beginning or end of the separate words or you will end up with one really long word!

CAUTION   *When converting text to curves, do not allow any object to exceed 500 nodes. Doing so can lead to serious printing problems.*

If you wish to edit the text, you can simply click with the Text tool anywhere within the text block, and a cursor will appear. If you'd rather edit the text in a dialog box, choose Text | Edit Text or use the CTRL-SHIFT-T shortcut key. Often it is easier to edit the text within the dialog box because it will automatically wrap the lines for editing purposes; for tiny text using the dialog box is a must, since the text will always be presented in a readable size in the correct font. An example of Artistic Text on screen is shown here.

ARTISTIC TEXT

Artistic Text Attributes

You can change the attributes of Artistic Text in two places: the Property Bar and the Format Text dialog box. Not all of the attributes are available on the Property Bar, so this chapter discusses the procedures for using the Format Text dialog box. In many instances, however, when an attribute is available, it is much quicker to use the Property Bar. You access the Format Text dialog box by choosing Text | Format Text (CTRL-T).

If you select the text with the Pick tool, all formatting changes will apply to the whole block of text. You can also select individual characters with either the Shape tool or the Text tool. Both tools allow you to change the attributes of only the selected characters.

The Format Text dialog box in CorelDRAW 9 is modeless, which means that you can continue working with text objects onscreen while the dialog box is active. You can then easily apply formatting changes to separate text objects or even separate characters within a text block. In addition to the OK button, there is now an Apply button to use in these instances.

 TIP   *For those of you who have complained that you can't boldface or underline a single word in a block of text, here's the solution: simply select that word with the Shape or Text tool, and activate Bold, Underline, or whatever effect you desire.*

Font

The first tab in the Format Text dialog box is the Font tab, as shown in Figure 5-1. The left side of the dialog box presents a drop-down list of all available fonts. PostScript Type 1 fonts are preceded by a T1 symbol, and TrueType fonts are preceded by a TT symbol. If the icons are dimmed, the font has been temporarily installed by Font Navigator (see Chapter 32). Just above the list of fonts is the name of the currently selected font. You can manually type in a name. With each letter that you type, you are moved down the list to the first font that matches. For instance, if you're looking for Zapf Dingbats, simply type **Z**, and you'll be moved to the first font that begins with the letter Z. You can continue to type the name until the correct font is chosen or use the mouse to click the desired font. The typing method just makes it easier to get to fonts farther down the list. Note that a preview of the chosen font is shown at the bottom of the dialog box.

Below the Font is the <u>S</u>ize spin box. Font sizes by default are shown in points. The up arrow increases the value by 1 point, and the down arrow decreases it by 1 point. The smallest point size possible is .001 point, and the largest is 3,000 points.

The next value is the font's weight. Up to four values are available in the St<u>y</u>le list, depending on the font chosen. Only weights that exist are shown, unlike in word processing programs, where the program will "fake" a bold or italic weight. The four possible weights are Normal, Italic, Bold, and Bold Italic. These names are based upon attributes set within the font rather than the font's actual name.

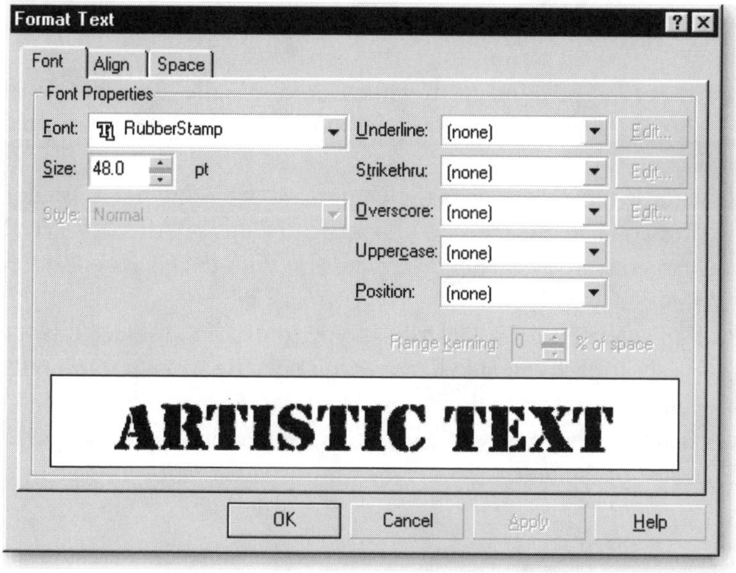

FIGURE 5-1   The Font tab of the Format Text dialog box for Artistic Text

CAUTION *The weight names are always reported as Normal, Normal-Italic, Bold, and Bold-Italic even though this nomenclature is not correct for many fonts. Although this may seem to be just an irritation, it can lead to problems when exporting files to other programs that work with the correct font names.*

On the right side of the dialog box are three drop-down lists labeled Underline, Strikethru, and Overscore. Each of them has an option for Single Thin, Single Thick, or Double Thin outline, and each type of outline can be applied to just words or to the whole text block (including spaces). When you choose any of the ruling lines, you can choose Edit to change the appearance of the lines in the Edit Underline dialog box shown here.

The Thickness and Baseline Shift values are originally a percentage of the font's point size, but they can also be specified in specific points using the Units drop-down list.

Below the three types of lines is the Uppercase drop-down list. By default, it is set to None. But you can change it to either Small Caps or All Caps. You'll also see how you can convert everything to uppercase with the Change Case command a bit later in this chapter.

The Position selection for a font allows you to make the selected text a superscript or subscript. In most instances, you will use these options only when you have selected characters within a text block rather than the text block as a whole. Note that there is no way to customize the percentage of these effects in relation to the rest of the text.

Alignment

When you select the Align tab in the Format Text dialog box, six types of alignment are available for Artistic Text, as shown in Figure 5-2. The default alignment is None. This selection does exactly what it says: nothing. Many people assume it is the same as left justification, but it is not. When None is selected, you can use the Shape tool to move individual characters past the left margin of the text block. Left alignment justifies everything to the left margin, leaving the right edge ragged. Center alignment centers all of the text. Initially, the centering will be relative to where the text cursor was first clicked in the drawing window. As you move the center-aligned text, however, it will be relative to the center of the text block. Right alignment justifies everything to the right margin, leaving the left edge ragged. Again, the initial alignment is relative to where the text cursor was first clicked in the drawing window.

Full justify justifies both the left and right edges of the text. If the last line is only one word, that word will remain just left justified. Unfortunately, this format looks really strange when two words are fully justified with a huge white area between them. Use this form of alignment with caution. Force justify takes full justification one step further: it forces everything to be justified to both left and right margins. So if only one word appears on a line, a lot of space is added between characters to justify the word to both the left and right margins. Again, use this option with caution.

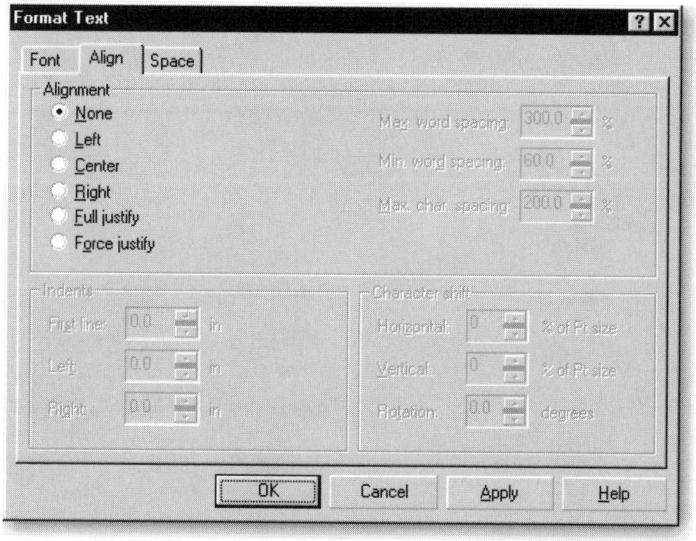

FIGURE 5-2 The Format Text dialog box with the Align tab selected

When you select individual characters within a text block using either the Shape or Text tool before or while accessing the Align tab of the Format Text dialog box, extra controls are available, as shown in Figure 5-3. These extra controls are described next.

You can control the character shift of the selected characters by moving them a certain percentage in either the Horizontal or the Vertical direction. By *character shift*, we are referring to the amount that a character is moved above or below the normal baseline for text. These characters can also be rotated individually.

Spacing

The Space tab of the Format Text dialog box, shown in Figure 5-4, is used to control text spacing and alignment. With Artistic Text, you have three spacing controls: Character, Word, and Line. Character spacing is measured as a percentage of the space taken up by the space character in the font used by the text. By default, it is set to zero so that no extra space is added between characters. By clicking the spin arrows, you can increase or decrease the value by 1 percentage

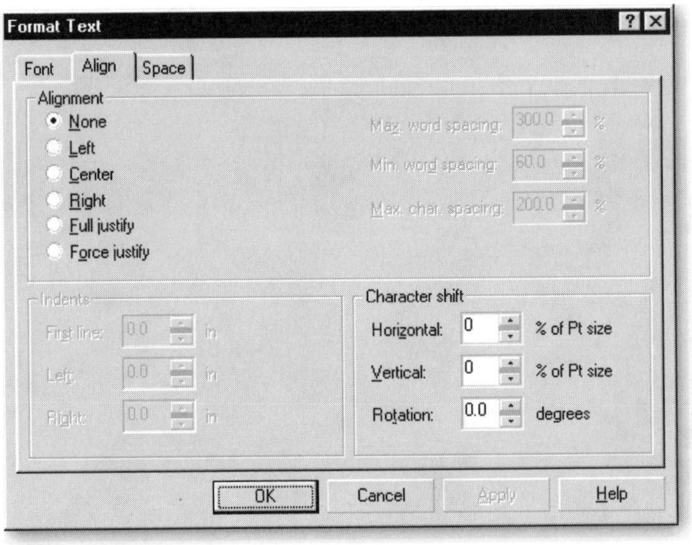

FIGURE 5-3   The Align tab of the Format Text dialog box for selected characters

point; you can also simply type a value. Word spacing is measured in the same way, but since you generally want a full space between words, this value defaults to 100 percent.

Line spacing by default is measured as a percentage of the character height. You can also measure line spacing in points or as a percentage of the point size. Plain and simple, the default selection is probably the worst way to measure line spacing. Line spacing (or leading) traditionally is measured in points by graphic artists. Typically, spacing is the font size plus two points. Thus, for 10-point text, the leading would be 12 points. For point sizes over about 24 points, the point size itself tends to work fine as the line spacing measure; in fact, you may even want the leading to be less than the point size. It is a good habit to start measuring text in points if you do not already do so. You can make that your default selection if you select Points in this dialog box when no text is selected and then save that as your default font, as previously described.

There are also several other ways to change the character spacing. If you have more than one character selected, CTRL-SHIFT-> will increase the space between letters (commonly called *kerning*), and CTRL-SHIFT-< will decrease the space.

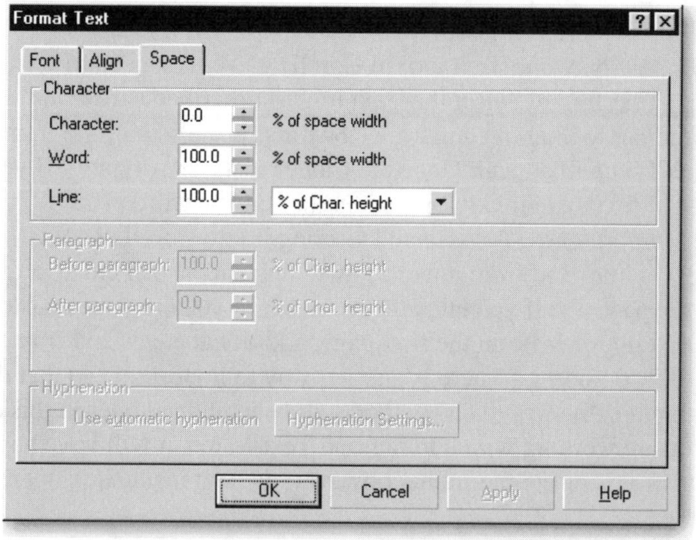

5

FIGURE 5-4   The Format Text dialog box with the Space tab displayed

Kerning the characters in this way is much more visual than using the dialog box. With the Shape tool selected, you can click the node to the left of the character and drag it anywhere you like. Holding the CTRL key constrains the movement along the baseline of the text. Finally, you can kern with the Pick tool. Press the Z key on the keyboard, which will allow you to again select the node to the left of the character. Once selected, drag the character wherever you like.

Paragraph Text

Paragraph Text is used for larger blocks of text that contain multiple paragraphs, multiple columns, or multiple frames. Because its purpose is to handle long blocks of text, only the enveloping, drop shadow and transparency effect can be applied to Paragraph Text. Each paragraph of text can have up to 32,000 characters. Each frame of Paragraph Text can contain up to 32,000 paragraphs, and up to 32,000 frames can be linked together. If you need that much text, you sure as heck shouldn't be using CorelDRAW for that particular project! For projects of that size, we highly recommend that you use Corel VENTURA.

Creating Paragraph Text

Since there is now only one Text tool in CorelDRAW, you need to actually draw the Paragraph Text frame. Select the Text tool as described earlier in this chapter. Use the text cursor to drag out a marquee box that is the size of the frame where the Paragraph Text will appear. Once the frame exists, start typing. If you have a large amount of text that already exists in your favorite word processor, you can use the File | Import (CTRL-I) command to bring it into CorelDRAW.

When text is imported from a word processing file, it will create a frame that is the same as the page size if you click the space bar or you drag out a custom frame. If all of the text does not fit on the first page, additional pages and frames will be added until all text appears. There is another way to import text so that the text does not automatically flow. This method will be explained later in this chapter.

When you are working with a Paragraph Text frame, it will have handles like other objects. If you resize the frame, however, the text inside it is not resized.

Instead, only the container into which the text flows is resized. An example of a Paragraph Text frame is shown here.

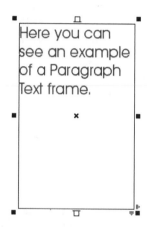

 TIP   *If you wish to resize the text at the same time as the frame, hold down the ALT key while resizing.*

Paragraph Text Attributes

Changing the attributes of Paragraph Text is much like changing Artistic Text except that many more options are available.

Font

The Font tab of the Format Text dialog box for Paragraph Text is exactly the same as that for Artistic Text, as shown in Figure 5-1.

Align

The Align tab of the Format Text dialog box is the same as for Artistic Text, with the addition of more controls, as shown in Figure 5-5. Max. word spacing, Min. word spacing, and Max. char. spacing allow more control when Full justify and Force justify are used. The problem we described earlier of Artistic Text creating large areas of white space can be eliminated by adjusting these settings. Since Artistic Text was not designed for large blocks of text, it doesn't include these controls. But Paragraph Text is geared more toward page layout tasks, and you therefore have much greater control over the text flow within the frame.

To change the indents, use the spin boxes labeled First line, Left, and Right. Note that the Left value indicates the left indentation of the paragraph as a whole. None of these values can be negative, but if the First line indent is less than the Left, you will actually be creating an outdent.

Spacing

All of the spacing options that are available to Artistic Text are also available for Paragraph Text. In addition, the Format Text dialog box includes many other options, as shown in Figure 5-6.

The Before paragraph and After paragraph settings specify the amount of extra leading, or line spacing, that will be added before or after a paragraph. By default, the setting for spacing before a paragraph is the same as the line spacing. If line

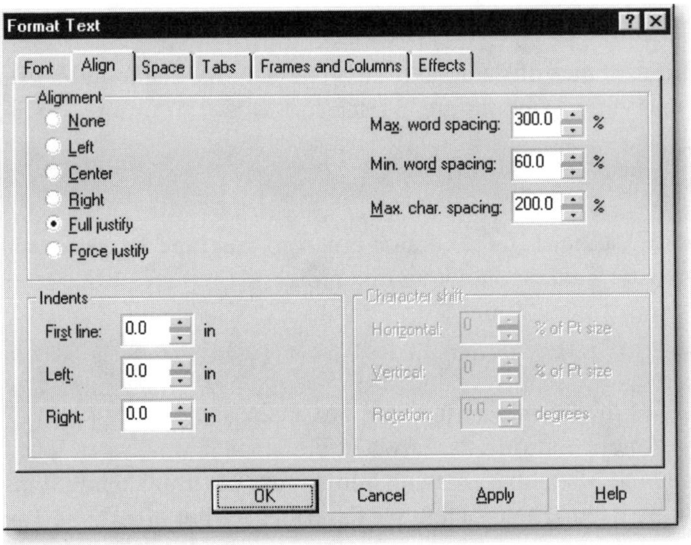

FIGURE 5-5   The Align tab of the Format Text dialog box for Paragraph Text

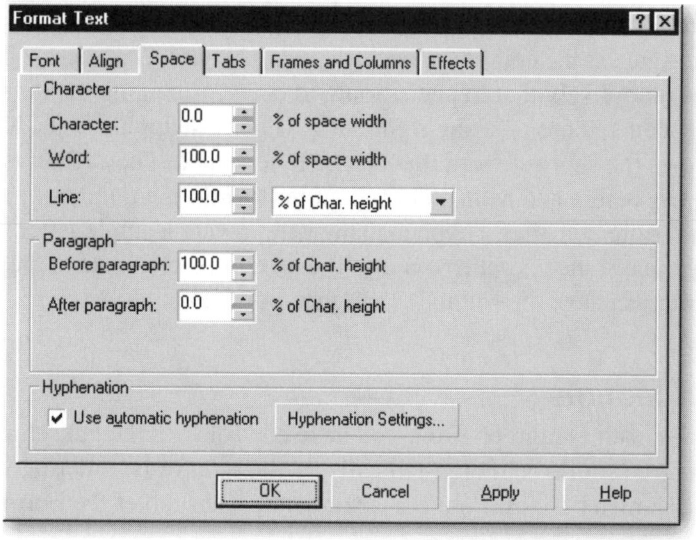

Font | **Align** | **Space** | **Tabs** | **Frames and Columns** | **Effects**

Character
- Character: 0.0 — % of space width
- Word: 100.0 — % of space width
- Line: 100.0 — % of Char. height ▼

Paragraph
- Before paragraph: 100.0 — % of Char. height
- After paragraph: 0.0 — % of Char. height

Hyphenation
- ✔ Use automatic hyphenation   Hyphenation Settings...

OK   Cancel   Apply   Help

5

FIGURE 5-6   The Space tab of the Format Text dialog box for Paragraph Text

---

spacing has been changed, however, this will not be true. If the setting for spacing before a paragraph is decreased, the end of one paragraph could overlap the beginning of the next one. Thus, this setting should be a value at least equal to the line spacing value. To add extra space, simply increase the Before paragraph value by the amount of extra space you desire.

After paragraph works in much the same way as Before paragraph. But instead of adding the space before a paragraph, it will add it to the bottom of a paragraph. Depending on the layout of your document, each of these values must be carefully adjusted to get just the right look.

By default, the Hyphenation controls are turned off. You can activate them by checking the Use automatic hyphenation check box. Clicking the Hyphenation Settings button displays the Hyphenation Settings dialog box, shown here.

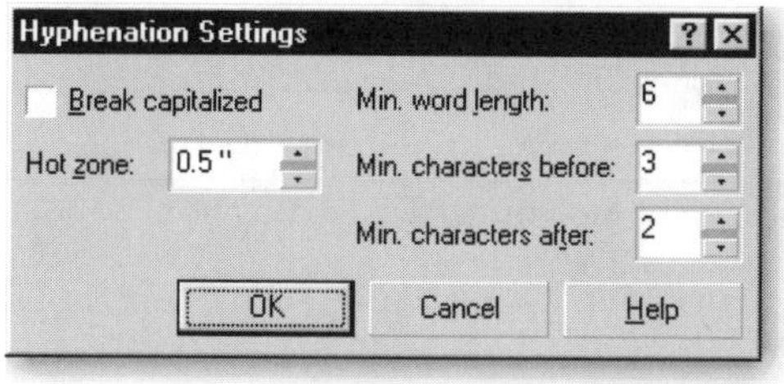

Hyphenation Settings

- ☐ Break capitalized   Min. word length: 6
- Hot zone: 0.5"   Min. characters before: 3
-    Min. characters after: 2

OK   Cancel   Help

By default, a break cannot occur between capital letters. To allow this type of break, you check the Break capitalized check box. The Hot zone value indicates the size of the area at the end of the line where hyphenation can occur. The smaller the zone, the more likely that hyphenation will occur. Changing the default to .3 inches will produce more pleasing right margins in most applications. Min. word length specifies the shortest word that can be hyphenated. The default is six letters. Min. characters before and Min. characters after specify the number of letters that must appear before and after a hyphen. This will prevent a single letter from being stranded on a line somewhere. If you don't want two letters to stand alone, for example, simply change the setting to a higher value.

Tabs and Indents

When working with Paragraph Text, you have control over the tab settings. These settings can be controlled either graphically on the ruler or by entering values in the various parameter boxes. Figure 5-7 shows the Tabs tab of the Format Text dialog box.

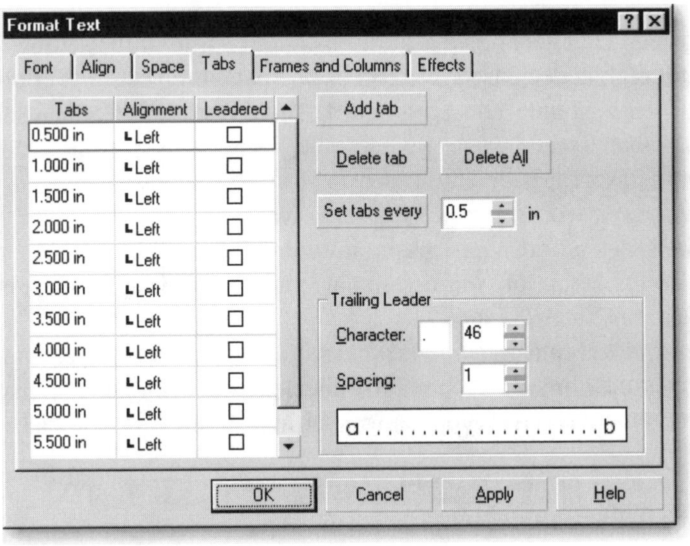

FIGURE 5-7   The Tabs tab of the Format Text dialog box

The left side of the dialog box presents a list of all the existing tabs. The first column in the table indicates the position of the tab. Double-clicking a value allows you to edit it either by typing a new value or using the spin controls. Clicking any of the values in the Alignment column displays a drop-down list from which you can choose Left, Right, Center, or Decimal alignment. Left, Right, and Center tabs align text exactly as you would expect. The Decimal option aligns the decimal point in a number at the tab position, which allows you to easily align a column of numbers. The numeric characters in a font are usually not proportionally spaced as are the alphabetic characters. This is so that the numbers will line up properly. You will occasionally come across a font that does have proportional spacing for numbers. If so, you may have to change fonts if you need to accurately align columns of numbers.

The Leadered column indicates whether a particular tab stop uses leaders. Leaders provide actual characters for a tab rather than just a blank space. The most common type of leader is a dot leader, which provides a series of dots or periods within the tab area.

You specify the leader character either by typing it directly in the Character box or by entering its ASCII value in the second Character box. Note that extended characters are not available as leaders. The default leader character is a space. You use the Spacing parameter box to indicate the spacing between leader characters. Spacing can vary from a very tight setting of 0 to an extremely loose setting of 10; the smaller the value, the closer together the characters in the leader line will be. As you adjust the value, a preview just below the Spacing box shows you exactly how the leader will look. Note that even though you can set leaders on more than one tab stop, all leader characters in a paragraph will be the same.

You can set up to 64 tabs for each paragraph—not that you would ever need that many. To set them so they are evenly spaced, use the Set tabs every button. Type the spacing value in the spin box, and click the button. Tabs will automatically be added at the interval you specified.

To simply add a single tab, click the Add tab button. If you wish to delete a single tab, you must first select the tab in the table and then click the Delete tab button. To eliminate all of the tab stops, click the Delete All button.

Frames and Columns

All Paragraph Text is in a frame. Inside of that frame, the text can flow into columns. This value is the first value you set on the Frames and Columns tab of the Format Text dialog box, shown in Figure 5-8. Each frame can contain up to eight columns.

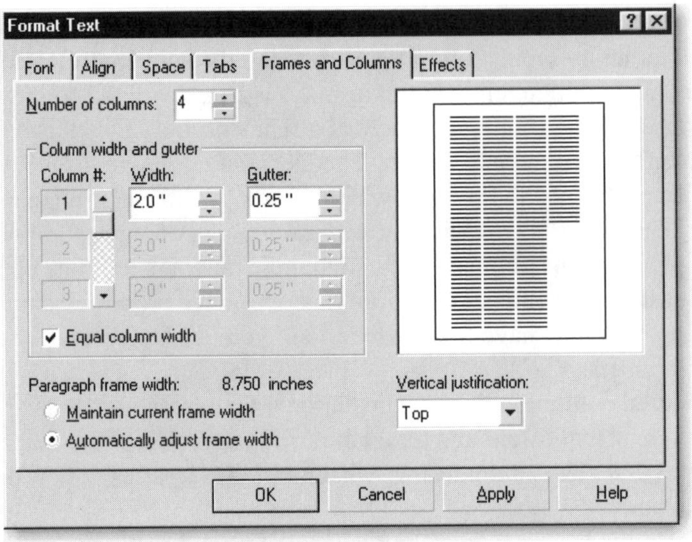

FIGURE 5-8   The Frames and Columns tab of the Format Text dialog box

The dialog box displays values only for up to three columns at a time, but a scrollbar appears next to the column numbers when more than three are selected. The Width column controls the width of a single column of text within a frame. The Gutter column controls the amount of white space between columns. If the Equal column width check box is checked, you can change these values only for the first column, and all other columns will use identical values. Otherwise, you can enter column widths for each individual column and gutter widths between every pair of columns. Note that there will always be one less gutter width than the number of columns.

At the bottom of the dialog box, the total value of the paragraph frame width is shown. This value is simply the column and gutter widths added together. If you select the Maintain current frame width radio button, the value of the paragraph frame must equal the current frame width. If it doesn't, the values will be adjusted accordingly. Selecting the Automatically adjust frame width radio button resizes the frame to match the values you've entered.

The Vertical justification value indicates how the text fits within the paragraph frame from top to bottom. You can align text at the top, center, or bottom, or you can choose the Full option, which will add leading between the lines of text so that it is evenly spaced to fill the whole frame. Full justification can be useful for fitting ad copy into an ad, for example.

As you are making the various changes, the preview window in the upper-right corner of the dialog box gives you an idea of how the frame will look. Remember that it is only a rough preview and is not entirely a WYSIWYG view.

Effects

The last tab in the Format Text dialog box is Effects. This is a rather deceiving name as it is used for creating bullets and drop caps. By default, None is selected in the Effect Type drop-down list, and the dialog box is completely dimmed. If you select Bullet or Drop cap, however, the tab will become usable.

SPECIFYING BULLET EFFECTS   Figure 5-9 shows the dialog box displayed when you choose Bullet. Note that the fonts you see could be different as this list shows the fonts installed on your system.

A bullet is a character that precedes a paragraph to give it a special emphasis. Normally, it is represented by a symbol character rather than an alphabetic character. The name comes from the filled circle that is the most common type of bullet used. Since it resembles a bullet hole, it is called a *bullet*.

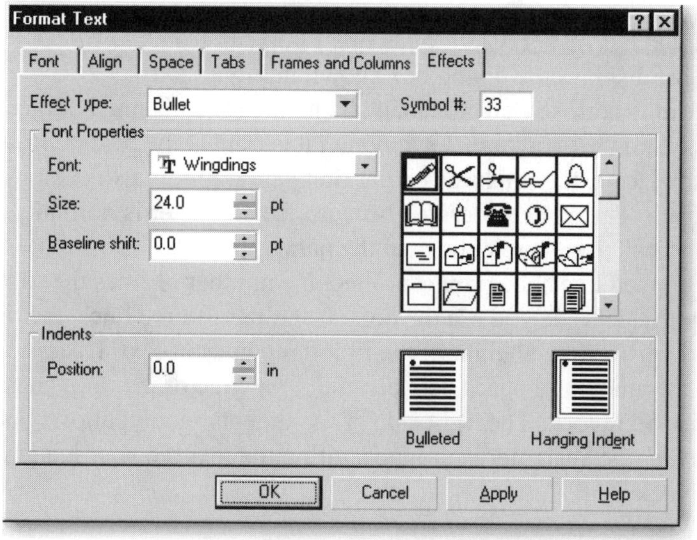

FIGURE 5-9   The Effects tab of the Format Text dialog box when Bullet is selected

When you choose a font, all of the characters in the font will be displayed in the grid. Click the character you desire, and it will become the bullet character for the paragraph. If you'd rather enter the character's number, you can use the Symbol # textbox. This number is simply the character's ASCII value. ASCII values for the most common fonts used for bullets are provided in the back of the Libraries Catalog that comes in your CorelDRAW box.

Just below the Font drop-down list, you can adjust the Size and Baseline shift. The size of the bullet defaults to the same size as the rest of the text in the paragraph. The baseline shift indicates how far above or below the baseline the bullet character is placed. Some bullet characters need to be shifted up or down so that they look right. Either enter a value for the shift, or use the spin buttons to change the current value. Negative values will shift the bullet below the baseline, while positive values will move it above the baseline.

The Position indicates how far the bullet character itself will be from the left margin. If the paragraph has a first-line indent larger than the bullet indent, white space will be between the bullet and the rest of the text; the text begins at the position that is specified by the first-line indent value.

You also have two placement options. Bulleted places the bullet within the paragraph so that the second line aligns with the bullet rather than the rest of the text. Hanging Indent leaves the bullet "hanging" in the margin so that the text in the paragraph is left aligned on all lines.

SPECIFYING DROP CAP EFFECTS   Selecting Drop cap from the Effect Type drop-down list displays the dialog box shown in Figure 5-10.

A drop cap is normally an alphabetical character that is much larger than the size of text within the paragraph. Commonly, it is used at the beginning of a section or chapter to place extra emphasis on the first paragraph. It also can provide a nice graphical touch. The name is derived because the character is normally a capital letter that "drops" over several lines of the paragraph.

In the Dropped lines box, you can select the number of lines the first character will be dropped. Thus, if you use the default setting of three lines, the first character will grow to the height of the first three lines of text. Distance from text determines the amount of space between the right edge of the drop character and the rest of the text block. The right side of the Indents section allows you to specify whether the character is dropped within the text block or hanging outside of the text block.

```
Format Text                                            ? X
  Font | Align | Space | Tabs | Frames and Columns | Effects |

  Effect Type:      Drop cap              ▼

       Dropped lines:  3   ▲▼



  ─Indents─────────────────────────────────────────────────
     Distance from text:  0.0   ▲▼  in    ┌───┐      ┌───┐
                                          │A ≡│      │A ≡│
                                          │ ≡ │      │  ≡│
                                          │ ≡ │      │  ≡│
                                          └───┘      └───┘
                                          Dropped   Hanging Indent

         ┌─────────┐   ┌────────┐   ┌────────┐   ┌────────┐
         │   OK    │   │ Cancel │   │ Apply  │   │  Help  │
         └─────────┘   └────────┘   └────────┘   └────────┘
```

FIGURE 5-10	The Effects tab of the Format Text dialog box when Drop cap is selected

Flowing Paragraph Text

Since Paragraph Text is usually a large block of text, quite often it will span more than one page or two areas on the same page. In this case, text will automatically flow from one frame to another. When the text extends beyond the bottom of a frame, the bottom-middle handle will have a downward-pointing arrow in it. Click the handle with the Pick tool, and your cursor will look like the cursor shown here.

Go to the place in your drawing where you want more text to appear. If you want a paragraph frame to be created automatically, just click. Automatically created frames will be drawn the same size as the page. You can also drag out a frame instead, to create a paragraph frame of the size you want. Text will flow into the new frame from the previous frame. If there is still more text, the bottom-middle handle will again have a downward-pointing arrow inside of it. You'll also notice that the top-middle handle of this new frame will have "greeked text" inside of it to indicate that it is linked to another frame above it. If you check the first frame, you'll notice that it now has the same symbol in the bottom-middle handle, indicating that there is text in a frame following it. When frames are linked, a small line will be drawn between them to indicate the link. This line is purely for informational purposes and is not printed. Here is an example of text flowing between two frames.

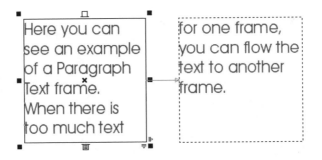

If you wish to break the link between two linked frames, use the Arrange | Separate command. To relink paragraphs, click again on the bottom window shade of the first text frame and then click on the frame where you want the text to continue. Note that your cursor will show a large arrow when you are over a text frame that can be linked.

Wrapping Text Around Graphics

Text can easily flow around a graphic object. Select the graphic object or group of objects that you wish the text to flow around. Bring up the Object Properties dialog box using the ALT-ENTER shortcut key. The General tab contains a Wrap paragraph text check box. When it is checked, you can specify the Text wrap offset. Click the Apply button, and adjust the offset until you are satisfied. At that point, click OK. We'll explore this further in the project at the end of this chapter.

TIP *If you wish to wrap the text around a bitmap or a group of objects, it is better to draw a simple shape and wrap around that shape. Trying to wrap around a bitmap will always give you a rectangle, and wrapping around groups of objects can take a long time with uncertain results.*

Other methods for wrapping Paragraph Text are discussed in Chapter 17.

Converting Between Artistic and Paragraph Text

5

In the past, if you created the "wrong" kind of text, you usually had to recreate it to convert it to the other kind of text. Now CorelDRAW provides the Text | Convert command. It will convert Artistic Text to Paragraph Text and vice versa. The conversion is not always perfect, but it sure does save a lot of work.

Note that if you have Paragraph Text selected and not all of the text is displayed in a single frame, the Convert command will be dimmed. Also, text that has been wrapped or is in columns will not look the same after conversion. It will be changed to flush left in a single column.

Changing Case

You can change the case of either form of text. Choose the Text | Change Case command. The Change Case dialog box shown here will be displayed.

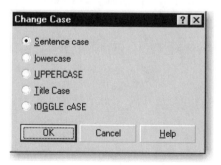

Five options are available. Sentence case will capitalize the first word of every sentence. The lowercase option will make all of the characters lowercase. UPPERCASE will capitalize all of the characters. Title Case will capitalize the first letter of each word. The tOGGLE cASE option will change the case of each character to the opposite of its current setting.

Symbols

Symbols are found in the Symbols Docker. Choose Window | Dockers | Symbols and Special Characters (CTRL-F11) to display the Docker-up onscreen, as shown here. Note that we've undocked it.

Many users get confused about the symbols and assume that they are clipart. They are, but they are stored as fonts and therefore must be installed as fonts in order to be used. At the top of the window is a drop-down list that shows each of the fonts that can be accessed as symbols. Normally, these are only fonts that notify themselves to Windows that they contain symbols. So, you won't see alphabetical fonts in the list without changing the default settings of CorelDRAW. To make this change, click the flyout arrow to the right of the font list, and turn on either TrueType fonts or Type1 fonts depending on the font you wish to use. You can also limit the part of these fonts shown to only the extended characters by choosing Show Special Characters only from the flyout menu.

Just below the drop-down list are the graphical characters of the selected symbol font. A scrollbar at the right side of the window lets you scroll through the characters until you find just the one you desire. If you know the ASCII value of the symbol you need, you can type it directly into the # parameters box below the character showing.

Once you've selected the symbol you want, simply drag it into the drawing window. It will become a graphic within your drawing at the size specified in the Size parameters box in the Docker window.

TIP *If your cursor is within a text block, you can drag the symbol and drop it onto the cursor to automatically insert it into the text. To take this one step further, copy any graphic to the clipboard, place your cursor within text, and then select Paste. This will insert the graphic into the text. Or right-click, and then drag and drop the graphic on the place within the text where you would like it to appear.*

By default, you'll only get a single symbol. But you can get several symbols tiled onto your page by choosing Tile Symbol/Special Character from the flyout menu. If you do choose to tile a symbol, you can control the Horizontal and Vertical grid size of each tile by selecting Tile Options from the flyout menu to get the dialog box shown here. Note that you must drag the symbol inside of the page borders for the tiling to work.

Page Layout Project

So that you can better understand how to flow large amounts of text and how to wrap text around a graphic, we've developed a little project for you. Some of the tasks required for this project have not been covered yet, so we've provided a template to get you started. The process of creating this template will be described in later chapters. But for now, open the file news.cdr from the book's CD. This template requires that you have loaded the Futura family of fonts. If you're unsure of how to load fonts, this topic is covered in Chapter 32.

You'll notice that we've already created guidelines to delineate the margins and columns for the page. We teach you how to do this in Chapter 13. A masthead and some notes are also included. But for now, we want to start by working with the frame that already exists in the leftmost column. With it selected, use the CTRL-SHIFT-T shortcut key to bring up the Edit Text dialog box.

Currently the frame contains some text that we don't need. Select it all, and press the DEL key. Now we're ready to bring in our own text. We could type it here, but it is much easier to create it in a word processor and import the results. Press the Import button on the right side of the dialog box. We want to use the news.doc file supplied on the CD. When it is imported, you'll see the text in the dialog box. Now click OK to return to the page.

Notice that the text completely fills the first column. We're going to create an additional column in a minute, and it would be helpful if Snap to Guidelines is enabled. Select View | Snap to Guidelines if it is not already enabled. Notice that the window shade at the bottom of the column has an arrow in it. This indicates that there is more text. Click on the arrow, and your cursor should change to the "page" cursor shown earlier in this chapter. Using this cursor, drag out a new frame of text in the second column. Text will flow to fill this column as well. Repeat this process to create the third and fourth columns.

At this point, all the text should be visible. We would like to change the text to a different font, which can be done by selecting all the text and formatting it by hand. But we're going to use a style. You'll learn more about styles in Chapter 29. For now, you're just going to use styles that we've created for you.

Place your cursor somewhere in the first line of text, and drag across to the last column so that you have at least some portion of each paragraph selected. From the drop-down list at the left of the Property Bar, select Default Paragraph Text. Now you should see that the text fills three columns and it automatically reflowed with this formatting change.

You will find headings throughout the text. Place your cursor within these paragraphs, and select the Level 2 Heading style from the leftmost drop-down on the Property Bar. The paragraphs will automatically be formatted, and the text will automatically reflow to reflect the changes.

We'd like to make one other change. Throughout the text are several URLs (Web addresses). We would like these URLs to appear in blue so that they are more prominent. Find the first URL in the text, highlight just the URL, and left-click blue in the color palette. The change should be apparent immediately. Repeat this process until all of the URLs are in blue.

The headline also needs to be changed. You'll note that it is set in Artistic Text as Paragraph Text cannot span more than one column. Swipe this text with your cursor, and replace it with the headline of your choice.

Next, we would like to have a character at the end of the article to indicate that it is indeed the end. Bring up the Symbols Docker by choosing Window | Symbols and Special Characters. Place your cursor at the very end of the text. Select the Wingdings font from the drop-down list at the top of the Symbols Docker. Now drag any of the symbols, and drop it on your cursor. This will insert the character into your text.

Our last step is to add a graphic and wrap the text around it. In the previous chapters, you've learned to create lots of different shapes. So create the shape of your choice, and fill it with red. Make sure that the shape covers some of the text, or it won't do us much good to wrap around it. A new way to wrap text is to click the Wrap Paragraph Text icon on the Property Bar (see the circle in the following illustration). If you click and hold the button, you'll receive the pop-up menu with a number of wrap options for the text. Choose the settings you like, and then feel free to move the shape around or resize it. You'll notice that the text will automatically reflow around the new shape.

Congratulations, you've now created a simple newsletter. An example of the finished piece is shown in Figure 5-11.

Getting the Most From www.unleash.com

Logos for the Design Challenged

Each month Gary Priester provides a new tutorial to expand your creativity. Many CorelDRAW users do not have a background in graphic design and Gary's tutorials will help you learn ways to improve your design skills. You'll learn about creating logos, putting them to use, outputting your creations and much more. Visit http://www.unleash.com/gary/lo go to see a complete index of articles.

Drawing Conclusions

Rick Altman always has an opinion. Sometimes you'll agree with him and sometimes you won't. In his monthly column, he shares his opinion with you on a variety of subjects. Visit http://www.unleash.com/rick to read the latest column.

Video Training

Some users want to learn by watching. If that is the case, we've got the most complete set of videotapes available on the CorelDRAW suite. Each tape is packed by two hours of training hosted by Foster Coburn. In the bottom corner of the tape, you'll see the section number for the topic being covered. This makes it much easier for you to fast forward to the lesson you want to learn or to rewind to watch a lesson again. You'll find detailed descriptions of these videos and many others at http://www.unleash.com/store.

Problem Solving

There are times when it seems that your computer just doesn't want to cooperate. The best example of this is when you get a message tel ling you that a program has crashed. Most users will blame the program that crashed when the problem lies elsewhere. We provide problem solving documents that give you a list of tasks you can perform to help prevent these crashes. If you follow the documents closely,

you will find that most of the crashing should go away. You'll find these documents at http://www.unleash.com/articles /crash

Everything You Wanted to Know About Fonts

People can never have enough fonts. The one you really need is always one that you don't have. And the process of installing fonts is baffling. So we've prepared a series of tutorials that will help you find more fonts, solve problems involved with too many fonts and how to install them easily. All of this information can be found at http://www.unleash.com/articles /fonts

Grandpa B's PHOTO-PAINT Tutorials

Mike Bresciani recently started using PHOTO-PAINT as a hobby. He discovers some really interesting techniques and love to pass those along to other new users. You'll find a complete list of his tutorials at http://www.unleash.com/mikeb

Building the Perfect Computer

We are frequently asked questions about which computer to buy to run CorelDRAW the best. A list of our favorite components is found at http://www.unleash.com/picks/d reampc.html

CorelDRAW Utilities and PHOTO-PAINT Plug-ins

There are a number of little utilities that will help you get the job done in CorelDRAW. We've included many of them on the CD in this book. But they do change from time to time and so we keep a list of the best ones and links to get them at

http ://www.unleash.com/picks /drawutils.html. PHOTO-PAINT comes with a number of really cool effects filters. But there are hundreds more of them available to use as plug-ins. Some of them are free, some will cost you a bit of money. We've

got a list of our favorites at http://www.unleash.com/picks/p lugin.html.

Boot Camps

Do you want to get the most out of CorelDRAW and Corel PHOTO-PAINT? If so, you're the perfect candidate for a three-day Boot Camp. Twice a month we offer a Boot Camp in picturesque Cave Creek, Arizona. The Boot Camps are hosted by Foster Coburn and Peter McCormick which means you'll get the information straight from the experts.

Boot Camps are designed for people who are already using the software and want to advance their skills. If you've never used CorelDRAW then you would be better served by taking a class at your local training center. All of the information is taught "hands off" so that you're not always waiting on the slowest student in the class. We also limit class size to 18 students so that you can get all of your questions answered.

In addition to serving you the information you need, we also serve you a continental breakfast and hot lunch each day. If that isn't enough good food, we throw in a barbecue dinner on Friday night! You certainly won't go away hungry.

To learn more about the Boot Camp; including dates, cost and travel information; visit http://www.unleash.com/trainin g/bootcamp.html ☺

Get a FREE CorelDRAW Newsletter!

This is a real newsletter and you can get it for **free**! Just visit http://www.unleash.com and sign the guest book. You'll receive the newsletters by e-mail approximately twice a month. Each issue is loaded with tips and tricks to help you get the most from CorelDRAW.

FIGURE 5-11   A sample of the finished newsletter

CHAPTER 6

Selecting and Transforming Objects

CorelDRAW 9

The Pick tool doesn't create anything, yet it is the most versatile tool in the CorelDRAW toolbox. It is used to select, position, resize, rotate, and skew objects. All of these functions can be accomplished in a variety of ways.

Selecting Objects

Before you can work with an object, you must select it. You select objects in CorelDRAW in four basic ways: using the mouse, marquee selection, tabbing, and the menus. If you've just drawn an object, it is automatically selected.

Selecting Objects with the Mouse

The simplest way to select an object is to click it using the left mouse button. Even if the object has no fill, you can click within the object to select it. This wasn't always the default for previous versions where you needed to click an object's outline rather than inside the object. Once selected, the object will have eight object handles surrounding its bounding box. (Note that the bounding box of an object may extend beyond the edges of the object.) Four of the handles are at the middle of each side and are the stretching handles, and four of them are at the extreme corners and are the sizing handles. The following illustration shows examples of the object handles on a selected object.

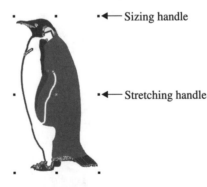

Sizing handle

Stretching handle

TIP   *If you do not want to select unfilled objects by clicking inside of them, select Tools | Options | Workspace | Toolbox | Pick Tool, and make sure the Treat all objects as filled check box is not checked. You can also toggle the settings on the Property Bar using the button shown next:*

When an object is selected, the Property Bar supplies valuable information about the object, such as the height, width, and center point. The Status Bar provides the number of nodes when the Shape tool is active.

To select more than one object, hold down the SHIFT key while clicking the object or objects that you wish to add to the selection. With each object added, the object handles change so that they surround all of the selected objects, and the Status Bar reports the number of objects that have been selected, as shown here.

134 Objects Selected on Layer 1

If you find that you have selected more objects than you want, simply click the object you wish to remove from the selection while holding down the SHIFT key. If you watch the Status Bar, you will see that you now have one less object selected than before.

Sometimes you want to select an object that is within a group. You can ungroup and then select the object you want, but a simpler way is to select the group and then the object while holding down the CTRL key. When you do this, the object handles will be round instead of square, and the selected object will be referred to as a *child object* on the Status Bar. Here is an example of a selected child object.

Child object
handle

TIP *Another way to select an object within a group is to select it in the Object Manager, which is described in Chapter 12.*

NOTE *Neither method allows you to select multiple objects within a group.*

Sometimes you have nested groups—that is, a group within a group. In those cases, a CTRL-click may result in the selection of another group. Continue to use CTRL-click until you get the object you want.

CTRL-click can also work with some effect groups. Unfortunately, it does not work with Blend or Contour groups. Those groups must first be separated before anything other than the whole group can be selected. You can select the control objects, but not the objects created by these effects.

Digger Tool

You can now easily select objects that are hidden behind other objects. Hold down the ALT key, and click the area where the hidden object is located. As you click, the X in the middle of the object and the object handles appear. This function is called the Digger tool. If the object is several levels deep, continue to hold down the ALT key and click until it is selected. You can also use this method to select multiple hidden objects. Hold down ALT-SHIFT while clicking, and the newly selected objects will be added to the previously selected objects. Finally, you can select hidden objects within a group by holding down ALT-CTRL while clicking. If all else fails, you might want to change into Wireframe view (described in Chapter 11) or use the Object Manager (described in Chapter 12).

Marquee Selection

Selecting objects by clicking them is great if you just have one or two objects. Often, however, you'll want to select a bunch of objects that are adjacent to one another. In this case, you'll want to *marquee select* the objects.

Creating a marquee selection is very similar to drawing a rectangle that encloses all of the objects you wish to select. However, instead of drawing the rectangle with the Rectangle tool, you draw it with the Pick tool. As you draw, a dotted blue box is displayed. Once all of the objects are within the dotted blue box, simply release the mouse button to select all of the objects.

When marquee selecting objects, quite often you may select an extra object or two. Remember that you can SHIFT-click an object to deselect it. Hold down the ALT key while marquee selecting to select any object within the marquee and any objects intersected by the marquee. Using the CTRL key constrains the marquee to a square.

You can also use marquee selection to deselect objects. Hold down the SHIFT key while marquee selecting, and any selected objects within the marquee will be deselected. This technique is handy when you need to deselect a small area of objects within a larger area of objects that you do want selected.

Tabbing Around

Yet another way to select objects is by using the TAB key on your keyboard. Pressing TAB selects the next object forward in the stacking order. (Chapter 12 provides more information on stacking order.) Tabbing is a great way to move through your drawing one object at a time to search for a problem object or a particular fill. SHIFT-TAB moves you through the stacking order backward.

TIP   *If you tab through a group of objects, only objects within the group will be selected if you've already selected a child object.*

Using the Menus

If you just want to select all of the objects, you can use the Edit | Select All | Objects (CTRL-A) command. Another shortcut is to double-click the Pick tool itself. Note that there are also menu commands for selecting all text, guidelines, or nodes.

TIP   *To deselect all objects, use the ESC key.*

Manipulating Objects

Rarely will you select objects just for the sake of selecting them. Usually you will want to make a change to the object. That change could be moving the object, changing its size, rotating it, or skewing it. As with most functions in CorelDRAW, there are a variety of ways to accomplish these tasks. The best method to use depends on the results you desire.

Positioning Objects

Simply put, if you want to position a selected object somewhere else in your drawing, push it there. Clicking a selected object or objects and then dragging them to the desired destination is all you need to do. Once you release the mouse button, the objects are dropped into place. As you move the objects, you'll notice that a blue outline appears to show you where the object is currently located. Some of you may see something other than a blue line showing the new position of the object. That is the simplest rendering. But if you click the TAB key while repositioning the object, it will toggle between three different modes, as shown in Figure 6-1. If you hesitate slightly on the object after selecting it but before moving it, the object will render as XOR when being moved.

We've already discussed the first method, which is the blue outline. The next method is a kind of transparent fill (actually an XOR), which allows you to partially see the objects behind the object you are moving and doesn't require that the screen be redrawn. Thus, it is fast. Finally, there is the opaque fill. This fill gives the highest quality rendering of the object, but you can't see what is behind it, and it does take a while to redraw. You will see a grid pattern on the object

Blue outline   XOR fill   Opaque fill

 FIGURE 6-1   The three ways that objects are displayed as they are being moved

being moved that represents other objects below it. Our recommendation is to use the transparent fill.

If you need to know the distance the objects are moving, the Status Bar tells you the distance of the move horizontally (in the *x* direction) and vertically (in the *y* direction), the distance of the move in a straight line, and the angle of the movement, as shown here:

DX:1.879 in DY:0.722 in Distance: 2.013 Angle: 21.014

During a move, you may notice that the objects begin to snap or stick at certain intervals. This happens because objects can snap to a grid, to guidelines, or to other objects, depending on the settings in the Layout menu. Chapter 13 contains more information on these options.

To make a duplicate of the objects being moved, simply press the + key on the numeric keypad, or click the right mouse button. You must be sure to do so before you release the left mouse button. You can also move an object by right-clicking and dragging it. When you release the right mouse button, you'll see a pop-up menu (as shown next). One of the options is to copy the object. Note that the other options may come in handy as well. Depending on where you drop the object, the menu choices you see may be different than those shown here.

 TIP   *New to CorelDRAW 9 is the capability to press the* SPACEBAR *to create a duplicate. Users of laptops will appreciate this capability because they typically don't have a numeric keypad and therefore a + key.*

Using the methods described so far, you may find it difficult to place objects in an exact location. If you want to place objects in an exact place in your drawing, you can use the Property Bar. Whenever an object is selected and the Pick tool is the active tool, the far-left side of the Property Bar shows the absolute *x* and *y* coordinates of the object's center (shown next).

x: 2.964 "
y: 5.667 "

If you change these numbers, the selected objects are moved automatically when you press the ENTER key. You can use the TAB key to move to the next textbox, or you can simply click it, but the changes are not reflected until you press the ENTER key.

TIP   *After typing the number, type the abbreviation of the number's measurement system, and you can use any available system regardless of the system used for the rulers. Note that the value you enter will automatically be converted into the ruler units after you press the ENTER key. You can also perform math in these num boxes.*

Relative Positioning

Many times you'll want to move an object an exact amount in a particular direction. In this case, you want the positioning to be relative to the current position. You can achieve this by moving the object with your mouse, but it can be difficult to move the exact amount you desire. Select Arrange | Transformation to bring up the Transform Docker. Click the leftmost icon to get the Docker shown here.

Transformation

Position:
H: 0.0   in
V: 0.0   in

✔ Relative Position

Apply To Duplicate

Apply

You can enter any amount you desire for relative movement. In the middle of the Docker is the Relative Position check box. When this check box is checked, all values you enter in the H (horizontal) and V (vertical) boxes will be a relative amount of movement from the current position relative to the 0, 0 position on the page. To execute the movement, simply click the Apply button at the bottom of the Docker or press the ENTER key. To leave a duplicate object behind, click the Apply to Duplicate button instead.

Absolute Positioning

The Transformation Position Docker also allows you to specify the absolute coordinates of any of nine locations on objects. These positions are the four corners of the selection box, the four midpoints of the sides of the selection box, and the center of the selection box.

When you are working in the absolute positioning mode, choosing a different check box in the coordinate grid will not move the object, but will change the coordinates shown to the current position of the chosen location in the grid. The idea here is that you will enter the exact H and V coordinates of where you want a particular part of the object to be located. If you are working with a rectangular object, this is quite easy to understand. However, if you choose the upper-left check box in the grid and the selected object is an ellipse, then you'll be positioning the upper-left corner of the selection box instead.

Consider an example in which several objects are selected whose selection box is exactly two inches square. The objects are currently near the center of your drawing page.

1. Select the upper-left check box in the grid.

2. Type **0** for H and **11** for V.

3. Click Apply.

Notice that your objects are in the upper-left corner of the page. Now try another example:

1. Select the lower-right check box in the grid.

2. Type **8.5** for H and **0** for V (assuming that your page size is 8.5 x 11). If necessary, modify these numbers so that they equal your page size.

3. Click Apply.

Now the objects will be in the lower-right corner of the page. You might want to experiment a little further with this dialog box before moving on as it can take a little while to get used to.

Nudging

There is yet another way to move objects—nudging them. Nudging is extremely useful when you just need to push the selected objects into place. To nudge objects, you simply press the arrow key on your keyboard that corresponds to the direction you want to move the selection. Each press of the arrow moves the objects by the amount specified in the Tools | Options | Workspace | Edit dialog box's Nudge section.

The default value is 0.1 inches, which you may find too large. Modify this number to your liking, and it will be used on all drawings using the current Workspace. Note that you can save multiple Workspaces, which can each have different nudge settings. This is explained in detail in Chapter 34. A quick way to change your nudge setting is on the Property Bar. Make sure that no objects are selected, and change the value in the text box shown here to the desired setting. Remember to press ENTER when you're done.

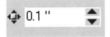

Another variation is the super nudge. This allows you to use the SHIFT key to multiply the amount of nudge. Again you can set the amount of multiplication with the Tools | Options | Workspace | Edit dialog box. Now hold down the SHIFT key as you press the arrow keys on your keyboard. Notice that the amount of movement has increased. If this isn't clear to you, increase the amount of multiplication. This is one of those features that won't look great in the ads, but sure will save you a lot of work!

Locking Objects

In early versions of CorelDRAW, you could place objects on a layer and then lock that layer, but there was no way to lock an individual object. Now an object can be locked so that it can't be moved, transformed, filled, or outlined. It can, however, be selected so that it can be unlocked.

To lock an object, select the object, and then choose Arrange | Lock Object. An alternative is to right-click the object and select Lock Object from the pop-up menu. After the object is locked, you'll notice that the square object handles are now small lock icons as shown here. If you attempt to do anything with a selected, but locked, object, CorelDRAW will behave as if you don't have any objects selected.

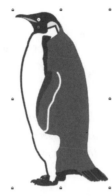

To unlock an object, you first need to select it. Then choose Arrange I Unlock Object, or right-click and choose Unlock Object from the pop-up menu. You can easily unlock all objects in a drawing by selecting Arrange I Unlock All Objects. Before selecting the command, you do not need to select any of the objects. After you select the command, all of the previously locked objects will be selected.

Resizing Objects

When you create objects in your drawing, very rarely will they be the exact size you need; you were more worried about making the object look correct than getting the exact size. There are several ways that you can resize an object in CorelDRAW.

When an object is selected, you simply need to grab one of the object handles around the perimeter of the selection box and drag it in the direction you want to increase or decrease the size of the object. If you grab a corner handle, the resized object will retain its original aspect ratio. If you instead grab a center handle, then the object will be stretched in only one direction and will thus become distorted.

You can also use the modifier keys to help control the resizing. Hold down the CTRL key while resizing to constrain the size to 100 percent increments of the original size. Remember that you'll have to resize at least 100 percent before anything will happen so it may take a fairly large mouse movement. Dragging across the object in either the horizontal or vertical direction creates a mirror image of the object. Combined with the CTRL key, it creates a perfect mirror, while without the CTRL key, it would be a distorted mirror. You can press the right mouse button or the + key before you release the left mouse button to make a duplicate of the object being resized. Pressing and holding the SHIFT key resizes the selection from the center outward. Pressing CTRL and SHIFT together resizes the object from the center outward in 100 percent increments.

 CAUTION *In trying to follow Windows standards, Corel provides the capability to use "standard" Windows conventions for the CTRL and SHIFT keys. By default, they work as described here, but you can change this behavior by using the dialog box that appears when you select the Tools | Options | Workspace | Toolbox command, and choose the Pick tool so that CTRL leaves a duplicate, SHIFT constrains, and ALT stretches from the center. Those of you using the Macintosh versions of CorelDRAW will note that the modifier keys follow the Macintosh conventions. Mac users should use Command to constrain and Option to stretch from the center.*

Exact Sizing

Sometimes you'll need to make an object an exact size. This is especially important for technical drawings but can also apply to making an ad fit in a specified area. The quickest way to resize the selected objects is to use the controls found on the Property Bar, shown here.

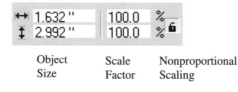

| Object Size | Scale Factor | Nonproportional Scaling |

 NOTE *The object size shown on the Property Bar does not take into account the thickness of the outline. So to be completely accurate, you'd need to add one half of the outline thickness to edge side of the object. This can be very important if you're designing an ad that cannot exceed an exact size. It might be handy to convert the outline to an object so that it can be sized to fit within the specified size.*

Type the size you desire in the textbox, and press the ENTER key. Remember that you can use the TAB key to move between the textboxes on the Property Bar. If you want to retain the aspect ratio, you can use the small lock icon on the Property Bar. When the lock icon is depressed, the aspect ratio is not constrained.

TIP   *After making changes with the Property Bar, you can use the CTRL-R shortcut key to repeat the changes. This is especially useful when you use Apply To Duplicate.*

Similar functionality is available in the Transformation Docker, which you can display by choosing Arrange | Transformation and selecting the fourth icon as shown here.

6

Type the desired size in the H and V textboxes, and then click Apply. If you want to apply the changes to a duplicate object, click Apply To Duplicate instead. To retain the aspect ratio of the object being resized, simply uncheck the Non-proportional check box. When you enter a number in one of the textboxes, the other will change automatically to a proportional value.

The control handle corresponding to the check box you select in the coordinate grid will remain anchored when you apply the resizing. This is similar to grabbing the handle opposite the point and dragging with the mouse.

Scaling Objects

When resizing objects you can also scale them as a percentage of their current size. As usual, you can do this in more than one way. The easiest way is to again use the Property Bar's scaling controls that were shown a bit earlier.

Instead of entering the exact measurement of the object, now you are entering a percentage by which the object will be scaled. Thus, if you typed 50 percent for each value, the object would be half of its original size, and if you typed 200 percent for each value, the object would double its size. Again, the lock icon next to the scaling boxes can be used to constrain the aspect ratio of the object. Note that when you type a value, you must press ENTER to make it take effect.

CAUTION *After you press ENTER, both scaling boxes return to 100 percent rather than reflecting the exact amount of cumulative scaling. While this isn't technically a bug, it can be very frustrating if you want to know how much an object was previously scaled.*

These same transformations can be performed in the Scale & Mirror Docker shown here.

Activate the Docker with the <u>A</u>rrange | <u>T</u>ransformation command, and click the third icon. Type a value in the H and V textboxes, and click Apply to implement the changes. Again, you can constrain the aspect ratio by unchecking the Non-proportional check box.

The coordinate grid allows you to select an anchor point for the scaling. Whichever check box you have checked will remain stationary, and the object will be scaled from that point.

Mirroring Objects

A true mirror requires that the size of the original object be retained. Often, however, you'll use this feature to create a shadow or reflection of the object that is a different size. In those cases, you can create the effect with the mouse. Simply grab one of the side handles (not a corner handle), and drag across the object in the direction you want the mirror to appear. When you are satisfied, release the mouse button. Click the right mouse button or press the + key to create a duplicate, just as with the other transformations. As you drag, the Status Bar tells you the exact scale, and the word "Mirrored" indicates that you are mirroring. You can mirror the object at the exact same size by holding down the CTRL key while dragging.

 TIP   *Mirroring is nothing more than using a negative scaling value.*

Entering a negative value into the scaling boxes also creates the mirroring effect. Thus, you can simply use the Property Bar and Scale & Mirror Docker that were previously discussed. If you want an exact mirror, both the Property Bar and the Scale & Mirror Docker provide buttons for this. The Property Bar buttons are shown here.

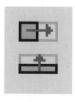

Rotating and Skewing Objects

To rotate or skew an object manually, you need to click the selected object a second time or double-click it as you select it. This changes the object handles to rotation handles on each corner and skew handles in the middle of each side. You'll also see a thumbtack representing the center of rotation. An example of an object selected in this way is shown here.

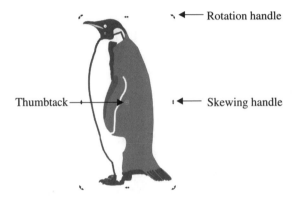

Drag any of the rotation handles, and the selected object will begin to rotate. As the object rotates, the Status Bar specifies the amount of rotation. When you release the left mouse button, the object will be dropped. You can constrain rotation to a particular angle by holding down the CTRL key while rotating the object. By default, it will be constrained to multiples of 15 degrees, but you can change the amount by choosing Tools | Options | Workspace | Edit and selecting Constrain angle. You can make a duplicate of the object by clicking the right mouse button or using the + key before releasing the left mouse button.

By default, an object rotates around its true center, but you can move the center of rotation to any place inside or outside of the object's selection box. Simply drag the thumbtack (the circle with the dot in the middle) to where you want the center of rotation to be. If you hold down the CTRL key while dragging, the thumbtack will snap to any of the places where a handle appears or to the true center of the object's bounding box.

Precision Rotation

You can also rotate objects by using the Property Bar. You simply type the exact value of rotation you desire and click ENTER. The Property Bar controls are shown here. CorelDRAW 9 will retain the rotation value so that you'll know exactly how much an object has been previously rotated.

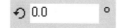

You can also use the Rotate Docker, accessed with the Arrange I Transformation command, and choose the second icon. The Docker allows you to type a numeric value for the center of rotation along with the rotation angle, as shown here.

6

As with the other transformation Dockers, you can work with the coordinate grid when measuring the position of the center of rotation. Clicking any of the nine check boxes will automatically move the center of rotation to that point on the selected object. If you check the Relative Center check box, the center of rotation will be measured relative to the true center of the object's bounding box.

Skewing

Skewing refers to distorting an object in either the vertical or horizontal direction. It makes an object look as if it is leaning. When using the mouse, simply grab one of the skew handles and drag it. Remember that you click twice on an object to display the rotation and skew handles. To skew vertically, you use one of the handles on a vertical side, and to skew horizontally, you use one of the handles on a horizontal side. As you skew, the Status Bar displays the angle of skew. This angle can be either positive or negative, depending on the direction and the handle you've chosen to use. The following table gives you an idea of which handle to drag in which direction to get a particular angle.

Direction	Left	Right
Top Handle	Positive	Negative
Bottom Handle	Negative	Positive
Direction	Up	Down
Left Side Handle	Negative	Positive
Right Side Handle	Positive	Negative

As when you rotate objects, you can hold down the CTRL key to constrain the skew to an angle that is a multiple of 15 degrees (unless the default has been changed). Unlike all of the other transformations, there are no skew controls on the Property Bar.

To access the Skew Docker, select Arrange | Transformation, and choose the rightmost icon. As shown here, you can type the horizontal and vertical skew angles.

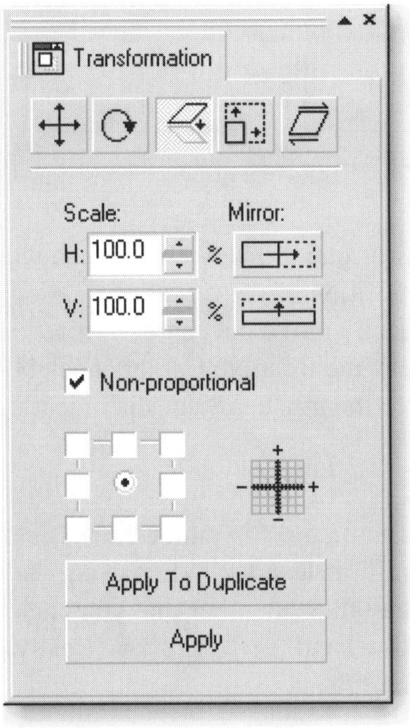

By default, the skew is relative to the center of the object, but by checking the Use Anchor Point check box, you can select any of the check boxes in the coordinate grid.

Manipulating Objects with Other Tools

When you learned how to create objects in Chapters 3, 4, and 5, you learned about the X that appears in the center of each object and the handles that surround it. So as you are creating objects, you can easily transform them without having to use the Pick tool.

Drag the X at the center of the object to move it to the desired location. This is slightly different than using the Pick tool because you can only click the X itself and not anywhere within the object. The handles work just the same as with the Pick tool. The corner handles size the object and retain the aspect ratio, while the side handles distort the shape.

If you quickly click the X, the handles change into rotation and skewing handles, and the X changes into a thumbtack. So you can easily rotate and skew the object by clicking and dragging on the appropriate handle.

You can even select multiple objects by holding down the SHIFT key and clicking on another object. So with all this new functionality, the Pick tool becomes less important, and you'll become more productive since you will switch tools less often.

Free Transformation Tools

As if there weren't already enough ways to transform objects, Corel added a series of free transformation tools that mimic the tools found in other illustration programs. At first glance, they seem to be just a duplication of the existing tools, but a longer look reveals that they provide a set of useful tools. When you select the Free Transform tool from the Shape Edit flyout, the Property Bar changes to the one shown here.

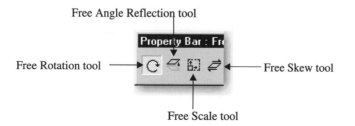

Free Angle Reflection tool

Free Rotation tool

Free Skew tool

Free Scale tool

Each of these tools requires you to click and drag. As you drag, you'll see a preview of the transformation (unless you've disabled this feature, as described earlier). The initial click sets the anchor point, and the transformation will be relative to that point. It may take you a while to get the hang of this if you are familiar with the other methods of transforming objects.

Free Rotation Tool

With the Free Rotation tool, the initial click sets the center of rotation for the object. As you drag, a line appears to indicate the angle of rotation relative to the original object along with a preview of the rotated object, as shown here. When you release the mouse button, the rotation is completed.

Free Angle Reflection Tool

The initial click of the Free Angle Reflection tool sets the point around which the object is reflected. So if this point is several inches from the objects, the result will be twice that amount in the direction in which you drag your cursor. Here you can see the original object, the plane around which the object is being reflected, and the dotted outline indicating the transformed object.

Free Scale Tool

You'll probably find the Free Scale tool the hardest to initially understand. The first click sets the position from which the object will scale. As you drag, the shape resizes itself based on the original point and the direction in which you drag. By default, the scaling is not proportional, and so the object will become rather distorted, as shown here. You can hold down the CTRL key to constrain the aspect ratio of the original object.

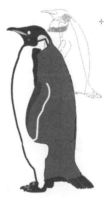

   TIP   *After the initial click, the farther your cursor is from the object, the more control you'll have over the transform.*

Free Skew Tool

When using the Free Skew tool, as when using the other free transformation tools, you begin by clicking to set the anchor point for the skew. As you drag, you are skewing in both the *x* and the *y* axis, so it is quite different from using the skew handles, which affect only one direction. Holding down the CTRL key while dragging constrains the skewing to only one direction. Here you can see the original object and the transformation.

The Transform Toolbar

You saw earlier how many of the transform commands are available on the Property Bar. But there are a few that are not available. A separate toolbar, the Transform toolbar shown here, contains the same tools as the Property Bar plus some additional tools.

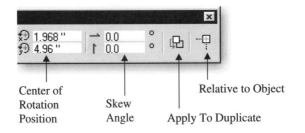

To access the Transform toolbar, select <u>W</u>indow I <u>T</u>oolbars, and place a check in the Transform check box. Or right-click the gray area within any existing toolbar, and select Transform from the pop-up menu that appears.

The Center of Rotation textboxes allow you to precisely place the center of rotation for an object, which you would do in place of moving the thumbtack. You can also enter the skew angles as exact values rather than using the skew handles to do your skewing interactively.

Probably the most important benefit of this toolbar is the Apply To Duplicate button. This means that any transformations you apply will be to a new object and the existing object will be retained. The last button, Relative to Object, controls whether the values shown on the toolbar are relative to the page or to the object. When the button is up, they are relative to the page, and that is how the Property Bar will always work. But with the button depressed, all measurements are relative to the object.

6

Undoing All Transformations

With all the various transformations you can apply, you may decide at times that the original object was the best. You always have the Edit | Undo (CTRL-Z) command to undo the last few transformations. But that won't always save you if you've done many other things to the drawing since transforming the object. CorelDRAW does remember what you've done, and it is quite easy to get rid of these transformations. Simply choose Arrange | Clear Transformations to return the object to its original shape even after the drawing has been saved, closed, and reopened. And if you now choose Edit | Undo, the object will return to its fully transformed state.

CHAPTER 7

Shaping Objects

COREL.COM

CorelDRAW 9

After you've created an object, you'll inevitably need to make changes to it. You'll want to mold the shape so it is just perfect. You may need to make only a minor change or two, but you'll soon discover that fully understanding how to shape objects is essential to using CorelDRAW. The Shape Edit flyout, shown here, includes four tools: the Shape, Knife, Eraser, and Free Transform tools. The most comprehensive of these is the Shape tool, commonly referred to as the Node Edit tool. Chapter 6 covers the Free Transform tool.

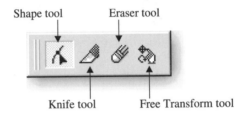

Shape tool   Eraser tool

Knife tool   Free Transform tool

The Shape Tool

There is no tool that you'll use more than the Shape tool. It can be used on curves, rectangles, ellipses, polygons, stars, text, bitmaps, envelopes, and more. With each type of shape, it works just a little bit differently.

Understanding Nodes

Nodes are the building blocks of vector artwork. A node is nothing more than a point in space that has a set of *x, y* coordinates. In the following sections we will examine why you need to use nodes and then show how to use them.

Vectors versus Bitmaps

To fully understand nodes, you need to understand how CorelDRAW creates objects. All of the shapes you create are vector objects, although many bitmaps are now used within CorelDRAW. That means that they are drawn using vector geometry (you know, that class you hated). Anything you create can be resized without a loss of quality, and large drawings take no more file space than small ones. Everything you draw is created using mathematical equations. When a graphic is resized, the equations are simply updated for the new size, and therefore, there is no loss of quality.

Now consider bitmaps, the domain of Corel PHOTO-PAINT. Everything you see on the screen is composed of thousands of tiny pixels (picture elements). Each of those dots can be one of 16.7 million colors if you use the RGB model. So to create a drawing with thousands of pixels in full color, you need a lot of memory and hard drive space. Consider a simple program icon that you might find on the desktop. It may look pretty bland, but every such icon is composed of 1,024 tiny dots. Just imagine how many dots are required for artwork that has to be printed! With bitmaps, resizing can leave either lots of information that is unused or a great lack of information, which leads to jaggies.

Thus, any time you create artwork as a vector image rather than a bitmap, you'll get higher quality and save lots of hard drive space. Some images, such as full-color photos, are nearly impossible to recreate as vector images and work much better as bitmaps. A good example of a vector image that looks like a photo is the Hedy Lamarr image that is featured on the CorelDRAW 9 box. It looks like a photograph, but it was done completely with vector shapes. To pull off this look, the artist took nearly 200 hours to create it.

A common graphic that can easily be represented in either format is a logo. To properly use a logo in bitmap format, you must have it available in many different sizes. However, in vector format, the logo can be resized at will without any loss of quality. If a logo was originally created in CorelDRAW, you already have it as a vector, but if the logo was scanned or is in a bitmap file, you'll need to convert it.

A Brief Introduction to Bézier Curves

You've already seen the Bézier tool in Chapter 4. Now we're going to talk about bézier curves, and you're probably wondering how they got such an interesting name. They were created by a French mathematician named Pierre Bézier. He discovered that any irregular curve can be defined by a fixed point (we'll call it x, y) and two control handles (we'll call them x1, y1 and x2, y2). Here is a diagram that shows how these points relate.

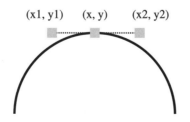

(x1, y1)   (x, y)   (x2, y2)

Now that you know the theory, we'll put it into plain language. The fixed point is known as a *node* in CorelDRAW. The two control handles are called *bézier control handles*. We'll explore how these two interact as we move forward in this chapter. There are a couple of rules that you should follow to get the best results. Certain types of nodes will only have one control handle because they are connecting a straight line to a curve. Your results will be improved if you have either two control handles or none at all. All you'll need to do is change the straight line to a curve to fix change the number of control handles. Also try to make it so that the bézier control handle is no more than 30 percent of the length of the line segment itself. You'll find that this gives you a better-looking curve.

Two Types of Lines

Although you can have a single point in space, no node can exist by itself. When another node is added, a segment is created between the two. This segment can be either a line or a curve. The first node will always be displayed larger than the second, and when it is selected, the Status Bar will indicate that it is the first node.

LINES   A line segment is a straight line between any two nodes. Just because a line is straight does not mean it is a line segment. At the end of a line segment is a node called a *line node*, and this node will not have a bézier control handle on the segment side of the node. Remember that if the overall path contains more than two nodes, some of the segments can be lines, and some can be curves, so the nodes are what separate the segments.

CURVES   A curve segment can be straight, but what differentiates it from a line segment is that it has bézier control points, so the curve can be shaped. Here is an example of a curved path with nodes and bézier control points.

Just as the node itself is a point in space, so is each bézier control point. You'll see a dotted line between the control point handle and the node itself. This line forms a tangent with the curve entering the node. Remember that since there are two control handles for each node, the "launch angle" of the curve entering the node can be quite different from the angle exiting the node.

Five Types of Nodes

There are five types of nodes: cusp, smooth, symmetrical, line cusp, and line smooth. The behavior of the two bézier control handles entering and exiting a node is controlled by the type of node. When you understand the behavior of each of these node types, you will be able to fully control the shape of the curve you are creating.

You can move the bézier control handles toward or away from the node, and you can rotate them about the node. Moving the handle closer to the node produces a tight curve, and moving it farther away makes the curve wider.

CUSP NODES   In situations where a curve must come to a point, use a cusp node. You can move the handles in and out to adjust the curve's shape. You can also rotate each handle independently around the node. Here are some examples of cusp nodes.

CAUTION   *You can rotate the handles so that the curve will cross itself, which may create the effect you desire. However, because it can cause problems when printing, this should be avoided if possible.*

SMOOTH NODES   Smooth nodes cannot be used where two line segments meet since they will require a cusp node. You can use a smooth node to connect a line segment to a curve segment, but the results can be rather strange. Most of the time when you want a smooth curve, you'll use a smooth node.

The two bézier control handles of a smooth node always remain in a straight line. This means that rotating the handle on one side of a node automatically rotates the handle on the opposite side of the node by the same amount. You can, however, move the handles in and out independently of one another. Just be careful as you move the handles so as not to accidentally rotate them. Here are some examples of smooth nodes.

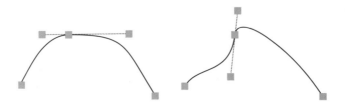

SYMMETRICAL NODES   Symmetrical nodes cannot be used with a line segment on either side of the node. They can be used only with curve segments since the bézier control handles on either side of the node must be on a straight line and must be equidistant from the node. Moving either control handle causes the opposite handle to mimic that movement. Symmetrical nodes are useful when you want perfectly symmetrical curves, but you probably won't use them very often. Here are some examples of symmetrical nodes.

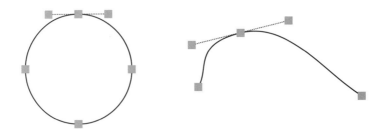

 TIP   *When a node is selected, pressing C will toggle the node between a Smooth and a Cusp. Pressing S will toggle between Smooth and Symmetrical.*

Selecting and Moving Nodes

Many of the same techniques used to select objects can be used when selecting nodes. First you need to select the Shape tool itself by clicking its icon in the toolbox or pressing the F10 shortcut key.

TIP *Remember that in CorelDRAW 9, each of the tools will behave like the Shape tool when the cursor is over a node.*

Selecting Nodes

You can select any individual node simply by clicking on it with the Shape tool. If you hold down the SHIFT key, you can select several nodes or deselect nodes if they are already selected. You can also marquee select nodes: drag an imaginary rectangle with the Shape tool, and all of the nodes within the rectangle will be selected. If you hold down the SHIFT key while marquee selecting, you will toggle the current selection status of each node within the marquee box. The CTRL key will constrain the marquee box to a square. If you use the ALT key, you can draw a freehand marquee around the nodes you wish to select.

For those of you who are real keyboard fans, the HOME key takes you to the first node of a curve, and the END key takes you to the last node. If the path is closed, the first and last nodes will be the same node. The TAB key moves you to the next node on the path, and SHIFT-TAB moves you to the previous node on the path. SHIFT-HOME toggles the selection status of the first node, and SHIFT-END toggles the selection status of the last node. Either CTRL-SHIFT-HOME or CTRL-SHIFT-END selects all of the nodes on the path. You can also select all nodes by double-clicking the Shape tool.

NOTE *When all nodes on a path have been selected, line segment nodes will be hollow, and curve nodes will be solid.*

Moving Nodes

Once you have selected a node, you can simply drag it to a new location. If multiple nodes have been selected, they will all move in unison. The movement of the nodes can be constrained to only horizontal or only vertical by holding down the CTRL key while moving the nodes.

Just as you can nudge and supernudge objects, you can do the same thing with nodes. This technique is especially useful when you are fine-tuning the shape of a curve. Use the arrow keys on the keyboard to nudge nodes in the direction of the arrow. Use the SHIFT key in conjunction with the arrow keys to supernudge a node.

 TIP   *You can also use nudge and supernudge in conjunction with a selected bézier control handle.*

 TIP   *If you are unable to grab a bézier control handle because it is on top of the node itself, simply hold down the SHIFT key while dragging it away from the node.*

Node Editing Tools

So far, we've covered a lot of the theory behind nodes. Now you'll see how you can begin modifying things. All of the node editing tools are found in two different places: the Node pop-up menu, and the Property Bar.

If you right-click a node with the Shape tool, or any other tool for that matter, CorelDRAW displays the pop-up menu shown here:

CorelDRAW 9 displays all of the same commands on the Property Bar when the Shape tool is selected. The Property Bar is shown here:

Convert Line to Curve

Convert Curve to Line ———

Break Curve ———

Join Two Nodes ———

Make Node a Cusp

Make Node Smooth

Make Node Symmetrical

Curve Smoothness

Elastic Mode

Property Bar : Edit curve, polygon & envelope [x]

Reverse Curve Direction ———

Extend Curve to Close ———

Extract Subpath ———

Auto-Close Curve

Align Nodes

Rotate and Skew Nodes

Stretch and Scale Nodes

Delete Node(s)

Add Node(s)

7

The various commands will be described according to their position on the Property Bar.

Adding and Deleting Nodes

When you are shaping curves, you'll often find that more nodes are needed to get the exact shape that you desire. To position a new node at an exact location, click the path where you wish the new node to appear. A round black dot will appear where you clicked. Click the + icon on the Property Bar or press the + key on the numeric keypad, and a node will appear where the circle was located.

TIP *Double-click with the Shape tool anywhere on the line where you'd like a node, and presto, it will appear!*

You can also select an existing node before clicking the + icon, which will create a new node that is located at the midpoint of the segment preceding the selected node. Note that after a node is added, both nodes will be selected. Clicking the + icon a second time will therefore add two more nodes at the midpoints of each of the preceding segments, and then four nodes will be selected. Thus, clicking the + icon several times quickly adds many nodes.

You can delete nodes in much the same manner. Highlight the node or nodes you wish to delete, and click the – icon on the Property Bar or simply press the DEL key.

 TIP *Double-click an existing node with the Shape tool, and it will be deleted.*

AUTO-REDUCING NODES AND CURVE SMOOTHNESS As you are creating artwork, sometimes you'll come across an overabundance of nodes. This can be caused by auto-tracing bitmaps, using the Artistic Media tool or Eraser tool, or just plain node craziness. You can spend a lot of time selecting the least important nodes and manually deleting them—or the Curve Smoothness slider can do this for you.

To fully understand the Curve Smoothness function, you need to understand another math term: *standard deviation*. The higher the curve smoothness, the fewer the nodes. This also means that the reduction in nodes will have a higher amount of standard deviation from the original line. For you nonmathematicians, the standard deviation is the largest distance the node can be from the path that will exist after the node is deleted. The larger the amount of curve smoothness, the more nodes will be deleted. However, deleting more nodes can compromise the integrity of the path. You will find that the default setting of zero works very well under all but the most extreme circumstances. You can easily change the Curve Smoothness by clicking on the node and then dragging the Curve Smoothness slider.

Breaking Apart and Joining Nodes

Select any node, and click the Break Curve icon. This will create two nodes on top of one another and will automatically split the path into two subpaths. Move either of the nodes out of the way, and you'll see that they are no longer connected. If the path had been closed (and therefore, able to be filled), it will now be open, and any fill will be gone unless you have changed the default so that open curves are filled. There is still only one path, however, even though there may appear to be two, as shown here in two different examples.

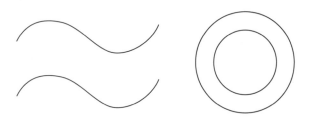

A good example of a single object with two subpaths is the letter *O*. The outside ellipse is one subpath, and the inside ellipse is a second subpath; when combined, they are a single object with two subpaths. Subpaths don't have to overlap one another; they can be anywhere in a drawing.

Sometimes when an object contains two or more subpaths, you will want to combine them into a single path. Select one of the end nodes from each subpath, and click the Join Two Nodes icon. The combined node will appear equidistant between the original locations of the separate nodes; therefore, it is a good idea to position the two nodes together in the area where you want the combined node to appear.

Stretching and Rotating Nodes

In Chapter 6, you saw how whole objects could be stretched and rotated, and this can also be done with selected nodes. The commands for stretching and rotating nodes are available only when two or more nodes are selected.

The best way to see how these commands work is to complete a simple project:

1. Draw a circle (remember to hold down the CTRL key).

2. Convert the circle to curves using the CTRL-Q shortcut keys.

3. Marquee select all four nodes, and click the + key on the numeric keypad twice to create a total of 16 nodes.

4. Select every other node by SHIFT-clicking them.

5. Click the Stretch and Scale Nodes icon on the Property Bar.

6. You'll now see handles around the selected nodes just as if they were a selected object. Hold down the SHIFT key, and stretch them about two-thirds of the way toward the center of the circle. You should now have a shape similar to the one shown here.

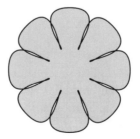

7. Click the Rotate and Skew Nodes icon on the Property Bar.

8. The familiar rotation handles should appear. Hold down the CTRL key, and rotate the nodes 90 degrees.

9. The final shape should look similar to the one shown here.

Note that the shape you just created has lines that overlap quite a bit, so it may be difficult to print on some printers.

All of the same concepts you learned when stretching and rotating objects also apply when working with nodes.

Reversing Curve Direction

New to CorelDRAW 9 is the option to reverse the direction of a curve. When you press the button on the Property Bar, you won't see any changes. And I'm sure that you may not understand the benefit of such a feature. Meanwhile, a large group of users are thrilled to see this. For those who are cutting vinyl signs, the direction of the curve dictates the direction of the knife cutting the vinyl. This can be important because if the knife is going the wrong direction, it can cause the vinyl to buckle. If you're creating graphics for printing or for the Web, this feature is not something that you'll need often. It can be useful if you plan on fitting text to a path, blending paths together, or adding Artistic Media. The direction of the curve can affect how these features will work.

Closing Open Paths

Suppose you draw this really cool shape and then realize that it isn't closed. Sure, you could grab the Freehand tool and close the shape, but just as easily you can select the end nodes of the open path and click the Extend Curve to Close button on the Property Bar. This will create a straight line between the two end nodes.

This button is available only when you have the two end nodes selected. Just selecting one of them will not make the button available.

Another way to accomplish the same feat is to click the Auto-Close Curve button on the Property Bar. It will be available when any nodes of an open path are selected.

Extracting Subpaths

When a curve consists of more than one subpath, there are several ways to make a subpath separate again. The traditional way is to use the Arrange | Break Apart (CTRL-K) command. A problem arises, however, if the curve has more than two subpaths. You may want to separate just one subpath from several others, but Break Apart separates them all.

You can now simply select a node from the subpath that you wish to extract and then click the Extract Subpath button on the Property Bar. This will extract only the selected subpath (or subpaths) and leave the others intact.

Aligning Nodes

When two or more nodes are selected, you have the option of aligning them with one another. Selecting the Align Nodes button on the Property Bar will produce the Node Align dialog box shown here.

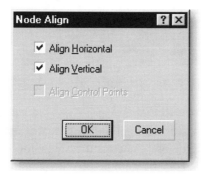

You can align the nodes in either the horizontal or the vertical direction. Deselect the option you don't want, and then click OK. You can also align the nodes in both the horizontal and vertical directions. This will place all selected nodes on top of one another, but the curve will look strange because the control points will not be aligned. Therefore, when aligning nodes in both directions, you'll probably want to align the control points as well so the curve remains smooth.

Working in Elastic Mode

Normally, when two or more nodes are moved together, they move the exact same distance. When Elastic Mode is activated, the nodes closest to the node being selected will move proportionally farther. The distance is measured not in a straight line, but along the path itself. A great example of this movement is the "explosion" of a spiral.

1. Draw a spiral with eight rotations, constraining it by holding down the CTRL key.

2. Select all of the nodes.

3. Select Elastic Mode from the Property Bar.

4. Click and drag the bottommost node of the spiral to an area above the spiral.

This should provide a twister, as shown here in a before and after view.

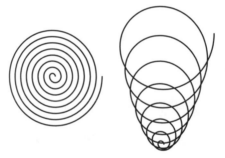

Advanced Ellipse Shaping

In earlier chapters, you saw various methods for creating shapes. One of the best ways is to start with an ellipse and then use the Shape tool to mold it into the shape you desire. Before you begin to manipulate the ellipse, make sure to convert it to curves (CTRL-Q). If you don't, you will instead be creating arcs and pie wedges, as described in Chapter 3.

Once you have an ellipse that has been converted to curves, just begin pushing and pulling on nodes, adjusting the bézier handles, and even adding more nodes until the shape begins to take form. Usually you'll need to add many more nodes to the standard ellipse since it only has four to begin with.

This method is desirable because it will often give you curves that are much smoother than what you would get if you drew them using the Freehand tool. In addition, you may find it easier to visualize shapes with this method.

Here is a scene that was created using this method. Some of the shapes are still somewhat elliptical, but others have changed dramatically from the originals. Take a little time to try this method; we think you'll find it quite useful.

In Chapter 14, you'll see how a dolphin was created by reshaping ellipses.

Advanced Polygon Shaping

In Chapter 3, you saw how to create some incredible designs by using the Shape tool with a polygon. At that time, you just used the polygon's existing nodes and moved them around a bit. However, you aren't limited to just the existing nodes, and the lines don't have to be straight.

Now that you understand how the Shape tool works, draw another polygon, and begin to adjust the nodes. If you want a line to curve, convert that segment to a curve segment, and adjust the bézier control handles. If you want more nodes, add however many you desire. Notice that all of these changes are reflected all the way around the polygon.

With this capability, you can create even more incredible shapes for your projects. Here is an example of a shape created by adding a couple of nodes to a polygon and just playing for a few minutes.

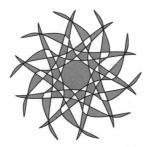

Shaping Bitmaps

When you used the Shape tool on bitmaps in early versions of CorelDRAW, you could crop the edges of the bitmap only in a straight line. There was a single node at each corner of the bitmap, and you could crop the bitmap to any shape—as long as it was rectangular.

Now the rules have changed. You can add nodes, change segments to curves, and basically create any shape you wish. Remember that you are only cropping the bitmap, so the extra information is still contained in your file; it is just hidden from view. This is similar to using the PowerClip effect described in Chapter 20, but it is just as easy to crop some bitmaps as it is to PowerClip them. If you right-click and choose Crop Bitmap from the pop-up menu, the extra data will be thrown out.

Here is an example of a bitmap before and after cropping.

Before cropping

After cropping

TIP   *The best way to alter the parts of a bitmap that are visible is to mask the bitmap in PHOTO-PAINT, save the file as a .cpt (PHOTO-PAINT's native format) file, and import it into CorelDRAW. Only the area of the bitmap within the mask will display. For more information on importing bitmaps, see Chapter 24.*

The Knife Tool

The Knife tool is the second tool on the Node Edit flyout. It is similar to the Break Curve button, except that you don't select a node prior to using the Knife tool. Anywhere you click on a path with the Knife tool will create a node and break the curve. If you are working with a closed path, you will need to make two separate cuts to break it into two objects: the first cut will turn the closed path into an open path; the second cut will break the path into two pieces. By default, each object will be closed automatically after the second cut.

You can change the defaults by selecting the Knife tool with no objects selected. The buttons on the Property Bar allow you to keep the chopped-up object as a single object, and you can choose not to close additional objects that are created by the Knife tool.

Freehand Knifing

Older versions just allowed you to click on the outline of an object and cut in a straight line to another cut on the outline. Now you can do much more by simply clicking and dragging. The following project will show you how to draw a cracked egg:

1. Draw an ellipse that looks something like an egg, and color it yellow.

2. Select the Knife tool, and place it over one side of the egg. The Knife cursor should rotate to indicate that it is ready to cut.

3. Drag the Knife across the object in somewhat of a zigzag pattern until you reach the other side of the object. Note that the cursor will again rotate when it reaches the opposite edge.

4. Before releasing the left mouse button, press the TAB key. You'll notice that half of the egg has been removed. Press TAB again, and the other half is removed instead. Press TAB yet again, and the whole egg will be retained, but it will be cracked in two. Keep pressing on TAB until the piece or pieces you wish to keep are displayed, and then release the left mouse button.

Here is the egg prior to cracking and then each of the three stages that can be achieved after cracking. Although this is just a simple tool, it sure can help you to create some cool stuff!

The Eraser Tool

A few years back, someone at one of our Boot Camps commented that it would be nice to have an Eraser tool in CorelDRAW. We looked at the person strangely and thought to ourselves that this is a vector program, not a bitmap program. If you want to erase something, just delete it. Then Corel went and added an Eraser tool, and we can see its usefulness. It just goes to show you that some of the best ideas don't always make sense at first.

When you select the Eraser tool from the Shape Edit flyout, the Property Bar will have two different settings that are relevant to the Eraser tool, as shown here.

The first setting controls the thickness of the eraser. Just as you can buy different sizes of erasers at your favorite art supply store, you can work with different sizes of erasers in CorelDRAW. Your cursor will change to reflect the size currently chosen so you'll know exactly how big of an area will be erased.

The other setting is controlled by the Auto-Reduce on Erase button. Because the Eraser tool can cause quite a few extra nodes to appear, you will probably want this button depressed. It is just an automated way of using the Curve Smoothness function (described earlier in this chapter) immediately after you finish erasing. Finally, you can choose to have a round or square eraser head.

To use the Eraser tool, you can first select the object you wish to erase. If nothing is selected, just select the object with the Eraser tool. If you have more than one object selected, you will receive an error message. When you have only a single object selected and the Eraser tool is active, simply start erasing the object. As you do so, the parts of the object you've erased will disappear, which can be somewhat misleading because the true erasing doesn't take place until after you release the mouse button. Then the area you've erased will be subtracted from the object.

At times, you may miss certain areas and leave pieces behind. Just continue to erase those areas until you are pleased with the result.

 NOTE *If you have a graphics tablet with an eraser, the Eraser tool is automatically invoked when you turn over your pen—or at least it should be. You may need to make some changes in the tablet's control panel so that it is context sensitive. You can also get pressure sensitivity using the erase on your pen!*

7

Here is an example of an object before and after parts of it were erased.

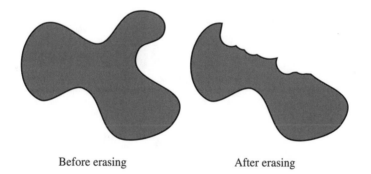

Before erasing   After erasing

As you are creating artwork, you'll find that the Shape tool is used more often than any other tool in the toolbox. If you are at all unclear about how nodes work, you might want to go over this chapter again until you fully understand this important concept.

CHAPTER 8

Colors, Models, Color Palettes, and Uniform Fills

CorelDRAW 9

B efore you can use any of the fill types in CorelDRAW, you have to decide whether to use colors selected from a color palette or a color model. For many CorelDRAW users, not knowing when to use a color from a palette or a model has led to disappointing results when a project was printed or displayed on the Internet. To help you make this important decision, the following paragraphs describe the difference between color models and color palettes.

Color Models

Color models contain colors that are either subtractive or additive. Both types of models are made up of colors derived from a mathematical formula. This formula provides a basis for measurement using a color standard.

When artists begin an oil painting, they prepare by squeezing colors onto a palette. When artists want a different color or hue of a color, they simply mix the colors on the palette. This mixing of colors allows artists to create millions of colors. Think of a color model in terms of mixing colors on an artist's palette. CorelDRAW's color models contain colors made up of mixtures of either process colors or RGB colors. CorelDRAW supplies seven color models plus a grayscale model and a Registration model. Each color model contains slightly different colors, giving you millions of colors to choose from.

Subtractive Models

Subtractive models use inks to create color. The more pigment in the ink, the darker the color, and the darker the ink, the less light is reflected off the paper.

Subtractive colors are used for printing to process-color printers using cyan, magenta, yellow, black (CMYK) transparent inks. Process colors can produce millions of colors by simply mixing them together.

Spot colors are subtractive colors as well, but they are made from opaque inks. These inks cannot be mixed with other spot colors, but tints of a specific ink color can be used. When printing spot colors, a separate plate is generated for each spot color used in the image.

When printing process colors, only four plates are required to print the entire color range. Some desktop printers can use only CMY colors. These printers simulate the color black by mixing together 100 percent of each of the CMY colors. Blacks created using this method generally are not as black as those created using the fourth plate containing the black ink.

Additive Models

Additive models use light to create color. Additive colors are made from red, green, blue (RGB) colors. Your computer monitor uses RGB to display colors. The greater a color's intensity, the darker the color. If you use the highest intensity setting, 255, for each of the three colors, you will produce the color white. Conversely, if you use the lowest intensity setting, 0, for each of the colors, you will produce the color black.

Colors can be displayed using the hue, saturation, brightness (HSB) color values of red, green, and blue. The human eye sees colors displayed in HSB more accurately than those using any other color model. Hue is the actual color, saturation is the purity of the color, and brightness is the amount of white in the color.

The additive color models available in CorelDRAW are RGB, HSB, HLS, Lab, and YIQ. These color models differ mainly in that they were developed by different companies, each using its own formula.

The model of choice in most cases is the Lab model. The Lab model uses the color ranges of both the CMYK and RGB color models. The Lab model is device independent and represents the way the human eye sees color, similar to the HSB color model. Because it is device independent, in theory it produces more predictable results than any of the other models. Device independence means that the colors are displayed without any bias toward a particular monitor. This being said, most users still don't take advantage of the LAB model even though it really does provide the best onscreen color representation.

Table 8-1 lists the eight models available, the type of colors used in each model, and the best use of each model.

Color Palettes

An electronic color palette is like the artist's palette except it contains many more separate colors than an artist could place on a palette. The electronic palette displays the many individual colors in color wells. Each of the many color palettes in CorelDRAW contains a different set of colors. Color palettes contain individual colors that either have been mixed from a color palette or have been specifically supplied by a particular provider. The best examples of colors supplied by a provider are the PANTONE spot and process colors.

Color Model	Colors Used in Model	Best Use
CMY	Cyan, magenta, yellow	Four-color printing
CMYK	Cyan, magenta, yellow, black	Four-color printing
RGB	Red, green, blue	Screen presentations, Web displays, and slides
HSB	Hue, saturation, brightness	Screen presentations, Web displays, and slides
HLS	Hue, lightness, saturation	Screen presentations, Web displays, and slides
Lab	Encompasses the range of both CMYK and RGB color models	Four-color printing
YIQ	Luminance and chromatic values (NTSC American video standard)	Television broadcast images
Grayscale	256 shades of gray	

TABLE 8-1   Color Models

There are four basic RGB color palettes, seven spot color palettes, and a basic CMYK color palette. The Lab color palette is in a category of its own because it combines elements of both RGB and CMYK colors.

The default palette docked on the right side of the drawing window is called the Custom palette, which contains the CMYK color palette. To view one of seven basic palettes other than the default palette, choose Window | Color Palettes. When the flyout menu appears, click one of the palette types. The benefit of being able to replace the default palette is that when you want to work exclusively with another palette, you can display them onscreen for easy access. We will discuss the other options at the bottom of the flyout later in this chapter.

Spot colors are most often used when you need a specific color or when your project contains only one or two colors. A spot color is a pre-mixed printer ink that prints the same each time it is used. Think of spot inks as similar to going to the hardware store to match paint swatches to a particular shade of blue in your wallpaper. The actual paint is then mixed based on a formula and theoretically will be exactly the same color every time it is mixed. Process colors are more like watercolors. They are transparent colors whose perceived color values will change depending upon the media used, the amount of paint applied, etc.

Spot colors are used in conjunction with a swatch book that contains all the colors in the particular palette. You begin by choosing the color you want from the swatch book. Each color has a corresponding name and number assigned to it. You simply choose the color you want and then choose its matching name or number from the palette in the Uniform Fill dialog box when the Fixed Palette tab is selected.

Some projects require the use of both process colors and spot colors. For example, a sales brochure may use process colors for the main brochure and a spot color for the client's logo. Keep in mind that a separate plate is used for each spot color, adding to the cost of the project.

 TIP Two newer process color palettes called PANTONE Hexachrome coated and PANTONE Hexachrome uncoated have been available since 1997. Hexachrome color uses six different process inks (cyan, magenta, yellow, black, orange, and green) to produce full-color images. Ask your service bureau and your printer whether you should use hexachrome colors. For you to use them, your service bureau must be able to produce a match print using the six process colors. Remember that using this palette will require two more color plates, which will add to the cost of the project. However, the increase in the quality of the final print may be worth it.

The Default CorelDRAW Palette

The default CorelDRAW palette docked on the right side of the drawing window contains 89 CMYK colors, 10 grays, and white—for a total of 100 choices. The default palette contains CMYK colors because most color printing is done using process colors. It's important to understand that you don't have to use the colors in this palette to print with CMYK process colors. In fact, you can select a color from any of the available color models and palettes and still print in CMYK colors. This is possible because the print engine in CorelDRAW treats all colors except spot colors as CMYK colors. You can even print spot colors as CMYK colors if you check the Convert Spot Colors to CMYK box on the Separations page in the Print dialog box.

 NOTE Although you can use RGB colors when creating your drawings, if your final output is to paper, don't count on the conversion to CMYK process. Use the CMYK color models and palettes to start with to ensure optimum results.

You may be wondering why there are so many "brand name" palettes to choose from if, when you print, everything is printed in process colors or spot colors. The answer is that many of the process color palettes and all the spot color palettes have color swatch books available that contain printed colors corresponding to every color in their respective palettes. Choosing your colors from the swatch book ensures that the colors will print the same in your projects.

This brings up the subject of screen color versus the color that is actually printed. Until recently, screen color rarely came close to the actual color printed on paper or film. CorelDRAW includes a Color Management system that allows you to choose a color profile based on your scanner and monitor as well as the desktop printer or separations output device. You will learn how to choose a color profile for your system later in the chapter. These color profiles go a long way toward matching the screen colors to the final printed color by using a built-in artificial intelligence system. You notice we say these color profiles "go a long way toward matching" colors; we don't say they "match them perfectly." If you wonder why the color management system can't perfectly match the colors on your screen to the printed colors, it's because your screen uses additive colors, and the printer uses subtractive colors. Additive colors are represented by the light from your monitor (RGB colors), and subtractive colors are made up of the inks the printer uses (CMYK colors). The only absolute way to match CMYK colors is to use the swatch books referred to earlier.

After learning that you can't really trust the screen color, you should be asking, "Then what's the purpose of the default CorelDRAW color palette?" The original purpose of this color palette was to provide a place to store custom colors. The CorelDRAW color palette in previous versions was called the Custom color palette and was the only palette that allowed you to add your own custom colors. Now because of all the other custom palettes available, it could be considered just another palette. You will learn how to create your own custom palettes using the new Palette Editor later in this chapter.

Determining Which Palette to Use

Before you decide which palette to use in a project, you need to know how the image will be used. Will it be printed with process colors or spot colors? Will it be used for screen presentations or slides? Will it be used on the Internet? CorelDRAW lists all the available palettes in the Color Palette Browser window, which you access by Choosing Window I Color Palette I Color Palette Browser.

When you select one of the palettes from the Docker window, it is placed next to any existing palettes already on screen. By default, the CorelDRAW palette, using CMYK colors, is displayed when you open CorelDRAW.

Table 8-2 lists the 18 basic palettes available, the type of colors included in each palette, and the best use of each palette. There are also an additional 49 custom theme palettes for both RGB and CMYK colors.

Color Matching System Colors and Spot Color Palettes

The term "color matching system" in Table 8-2 may be new to you. The common names for colors contained in color matching systems are *spot* and *process colors.* These spot colors contain the colors from universally accepted color matching systems such as PANTONE® Process Color System. Companies that produce these spot color inks offer swatch books that show the colors as they appear when printed. The benefit of using a spot color is that you can select a color from the swatch book and then choose the corresponding color in the color palette, and you know what the color will look like when it's printed. You will want to use a spot color when, for example, your client tells you that you must match the company colors exactly. You do not need to use spot and process colors for all your projects, but note that the color that you see on your monitor is not what is going to print on paper, regardless of whether you're using spot or process colors.

Also available on the third-party market is a swatch book for CMYK process colors. This author uses one produced by AGFA called Postscript Process Color Guide. You can reach them at 1-800-395-7007 or their Web site at agfahome.com.

 NOTE   *If you are producing files that are being sent to a service bureau or printer, you should buy one of the color matching system swatch books. Onscreen colors can provide a fairly accurate representation of what the colors will look like when printed. However, their accuracy depends on several variables, especially your video card and monitor. A swatch book provides an accurate representation of each color in the color matching system. Being able to compare the colors in the swatch book to the colors you see on your screen can save you time and money at printing time.*

Palette Type	Colors Used in Palette	Best Use
Uniform	RGB	Screen presentations, slides, and desktop inkjet printers
HKS	Spot color	Color matching system (spot colors)
Custom (the default CorelDRAW palette)	CMYK	Four-color printing
RGB	RGB	Screen presentations , slides, and desktop inkjet printers
FOCOLTONE colors	CMYK	Color matching system for four-color printing
CMYK	CMYK	Four-color printing
PANTONE MATCHING SYSTEM (Coated and Uncoated)	Spot color	Color matching system (spot colors)
PANTONE Corel 8	Spot color	Based on the Pantone spot color specifier used in CorelDRAW 8 colors. Old CDRs using this palette will be remapped to new Pantone CV or Pantone CU palettes included in CorelDRAW 9, when applicable. Otherwise mapped to User Inks palette so that spot colors will still separate to spot plates.
PANTONE HEXACHROME (Coated and Uncoated)	CMYKOG (O = Orange; G = Green)	Color matching system
PANTONE Metallic Colors	Spot color	Color matching system (spot colors)
PANTONE Pastel Colors (Coated and Uncoated)	Spot color	Color matching system (spot colors)
PANTONE Process Color System	CMYK	Color matching system for four-color printing
TRUMATCH Colors	CMYK	Process color specifier
Netscape Navigator	RGB	Screen presentations on the Internet using Netscape Navigator. Same as IE below but in different order
Microsoft Internet Explorer	RGB	Screen presentations on the Internet using Microsoft Internet Explorer. Same as Netscape above but in different order
Spectramaster colors	LAB	For automobile paint; viewed in RGB, prints to CMYK model.

TABLE 8-2   Color Palettes

Palette Type	Colors Used in Palette	Best Use
TOYO Color Finder system	Spot	Color matching system (spot colors)
DIC colors	Spot	Color matching system (spot color)
LAB colors	LAB	Four-color printing
Grayscale RGB and K	256 and 100 shades of gray	Black-and-white printing

TABLE 8-2   Color Palettes *(continued)*

Creating Your Own Swatch Book from the Custom Color Palette

If the only purpose for custom palettes was to store custom colors, they would not have much value, but if you could choose a color from a swatch book that related to the colors in your custom palettes, you could then have confidence in the colors being printed. There are no swatch books for CorelDRAW's default palette or for any custom palettes you create, but you can create your own.

Creating a swatch book for the default palette is not a gimmick dreamed up for inclusion in this book. It's an extremely important step in ensuring that the colors you choose from the Custom palette print correctly.

Creating a swatch book, which will actually be a single sheet of paper, involves drawing small rectangles on the page, one for each custom color, and filling each one with a color from the palette you will be using for your projects. If you frequently use more than one palette, you need to create separate swatch book files. Underneath the colored squares, you type the CMYK values that make up each color. You then print the file on the paper you will use for your projects.

You use this pseudo-swatch book to choose your colors instead of choosing the colors from the on screen palette. Make additional swatch books for every medium on which you will be printing. For example, if you will be printing on cups using the sublimation method, create a print using the colors you will be using and print it on a cup. The next time you will be printing on cups, pick the colors from those on the cup, and you will be assured that the colors will print correctly. If you are outputting to film, spend money to have a match print made of the Custom color palette.

NOTE   *We aren't suggesting that you pick colors from a custom printed swatch book for every color you will ever use in a project. What we recommend is that you use this method when the color used on certain objects, like a client's logo or headline text, must be exact to meet the client's requirements.*

If you don't create custom swatch books, you will have to rely on the colors displayed on your monitor. If you use a ICC color profile, you will have to trust the accuracy of the artificial intelligence of the color management system. Since most users will probably procrastinate and put off creating a custom color swatch file for printing on various media, we have created a .cdr file of all 100 colors in the CorelDRAW Custom palette that you get from the CD in back of this book. The path to the file is /Chap08/Colorcht.cdr. Print this palette with the corresponding CMYK values on the medium you will be printing to, and use it as your Custom palette swatch book. A sample of the color palette is printed in the color pages of this book.

Using Color Models and Palettes

Now that you understand the differences between color models and palettes and know about the different colors contained in them, its time to put this knowledge to use.

The average CorelDRAW user tends to pick colors from the default CorelDRAW palette displayed on the right side of the CorelDRAW window. With all the new palettes in CorelDRAW 9, it's time to be adventuresome. To change to another palette, you have two options. The first option is to Choose Window | Color Palettes, and choose one of the listed palettes from the child menu (see Figure 8-1). This option will display the most frequently used palettes. Instead of choosing one of the palettes listed, you can select the second option, which is to choose Color Palette Browser near the bottom of the child menu to display the Color Palette Browser Docker shown in Figure 8-2. This Docker lets you choose from all the palettes available in CorelDRAW 9.

When you choose a palette from this Docker, the new palette is immediately displayed. Figure 8-3 shows a close-up view of the Docker with the CMYK | Misc folder expanded to show the various theme palettes available in this category.

| FIGURE 8-1 | The Window menu and the Color Palettes child menu |

CorelDRAW version 9 now allows you to have multiple palettes open at the same time. Notice three different palettes are displayed in Figure 8-3: the default CorelDRAW palette, CMYK I Misc I Pastels, and CMYK I Misc I Sunset. The Open button at the bottom of the Docker window lets you access any custom palettes you may have stored in a folder other than the default palette folders.

This method of choosing new palettes should be the preferred method for most users.

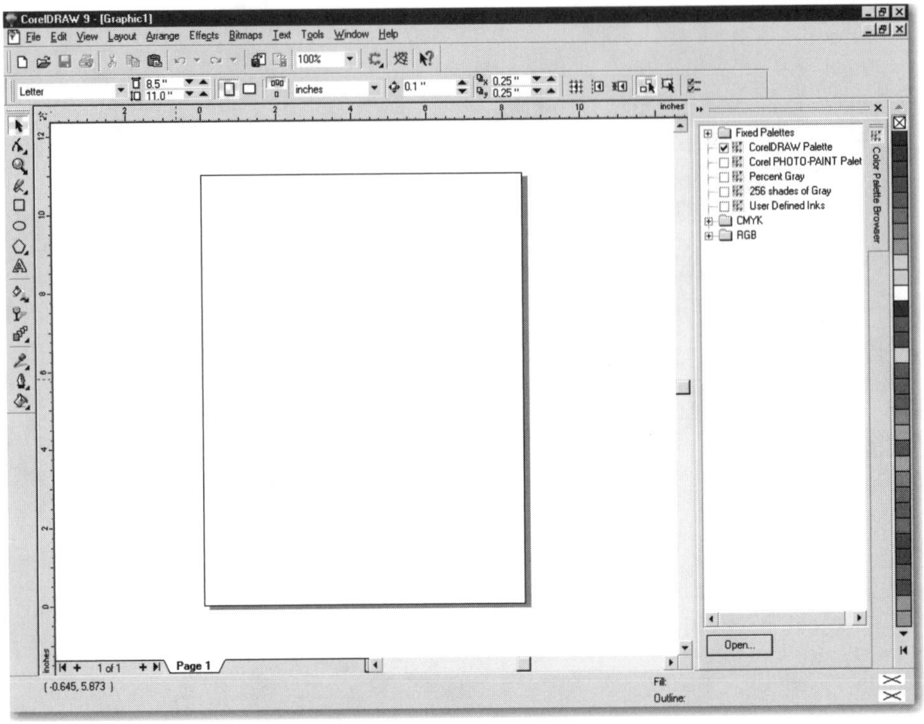

FIGURE 8-2   The CorelDRAW window with the Color Palette Browser
Docker displayed

Using the Pop-Up Tint Palettes

A pop-up tint palette lets you select tints from selected colors. To use the new
pop-up tint palette, follow the same steps you normally use to select a color, but
instead of clicking and immediately releasing the mouse button, click and hold
down the mouse button for a second or two. A palette of 49 tints of the color you
clicked will appear. When the palette appears, release the mouse button. Click one
of the 49 tints to use as your fill. This pop-up palette is HSL-based, with the hue of

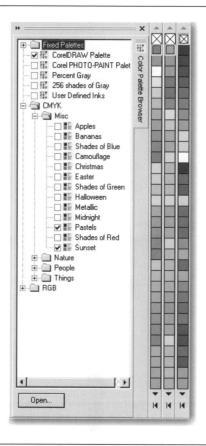

FIGURE 8-3   The Color Palette Docker showing the CMYK | Misc folder expanded and multiple palettes displayed

the color being used horizontally and a combination of saturation and lightness used vertically. The original color from the palette is the center color in the pop-up, unless the color is at the extreme end of the scale. For example, 100 percent black, grayscale, and spot colors will be a one-dimensional grid of density (represented by a bar rather than a box).

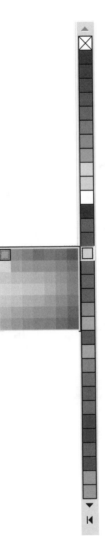

The pop-up tint palette shown next shows the PANTONE Matching System Colors palette and the pop-up tint palette displaying the ten different tints available for the selected spot color. The tints are displayed on a flyout and range from 100 percent closest to the main palette to 0 percent at the left end of the tint palette.

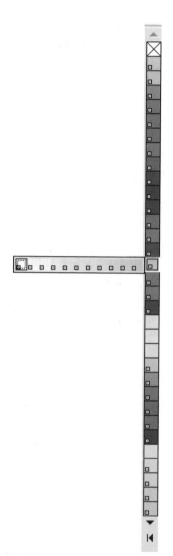

8

Using the Palette Editor

The Palette Editor in CorelDRAW 9 solves many past problems. Many designers asked for the ability to create custom palettes containing only a few colors. Although this capability has always been available, knowing how and where to create a custom palette was difficult. The Palette Editor's primary purpose (see Figure 8-4) is to let you create custom palettes. Creating a custom palette includes modifying an existing palette. You access the Palette Editor by choosing Tools | Palette Editor. You create a custom palette by choosing colors from the various models and palettes in the Select Color dialog box and adding them to the custom palette in the Palette Editor. This method requires having both the Palette Editor and Select Color dialog boxes open at the same time.

 NOTE *Having to use both the Palette Editor and Select Color dialog boxes when creating custom palettes is a change from the method used in CorelDRAW 8 where only the Palette Editor dialog box was used.*

Creating Custom Palettes

Practice creating a custom palette by Choosing Tools | Palette Editor. When the Palette Editor appears, click the New button at the top of the dialog box. The New Palette dialog box shown on the next page will appear. Choose a folder in which to store your custom palette (we chose the default Palettes folder). Name your palette

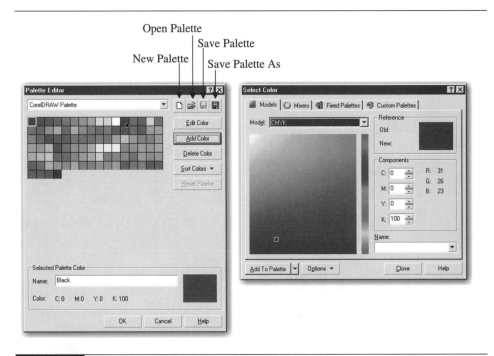

| FIGURE 8-4 | The Palette Editor and Select Color dialog boxes in their default configurations |

My First Palette, and click the Save button to save the palette. As soon as you save the name of your new palette, the Palette Editor will reappear, displaying the name of your custom palette. The palette area that will ultimately contain your custom colors will at first be empty.

```
┌─────────────────────────────────────────────────────┐
│ New Palette                                  [?][X]  │
├─────────────────────────────────────────────────────┤
│  Save in:   [📁] Palettes          [▼] [⬆] [📁*] [▦][▦] │
│                                                       │
│  [📁] Cmyk                                            │
│  [📁] Rgb                                             │
│  [📄] Gray100.cpl                                     │
│  [📄] Gray256.cpl                                     │
│  [📄] userinks.cpl                                    │
│                                                       │
│                                                       │
│  File name:   [My First Palette        ]    [ Save ] │
│  Save as type: [Custom palette (*.cpl)  ▼]  [Cancel] │
│  Description:  [                        ]             │
└─────────────────────────────────────────────────────┘
```

Adding Colors to a Custom Palette

While you're learning the process of adding colors to a custom palette, we will be asking you to choose colors from the various models, palettes, and mixers. In the real world, you would most likely create separate palettes from each source. There are four tabs at the top of the Select Color dialog box: Models, Mixers, Fixed Palettes, and Custom Palettes. Choosing each of these tabs reveals their respective dialog boxes.

Follow these steps to add color to the custom palette you created using the previous instructions:

1. Click the Add Color button in the Palette Editor dialog box. The Select Color dialog box will appear onscreen.

2. Choose the Models tab.

3. If the default RGB model is not selected, click on the down arrow of the Model list box and choose it.

4. Click anywhere in the color display window to choose a color.

5. Click the Add To Palette button, and the color you picked will be added to the new palette area of the Palette Editor dialog box. Pick several more colors, but remember to click the Add To Palette button each time. The Palette Editor should now resemble the one shown in Figure 8-5.

6. It's time to save your new palette. But before you can save the palette, you must first close the Select Color dialog box and click on the title bar of the Palette Editor dialog box to make it active. Then click on the Save button at the top of the dialog box.

7. If you want to give your new colors names, select a color square, and type the name in the Name box at the bottom of the Palette Editor. If you name your colors after you have saved the palette, be sure and click on the Save button again at the top of the Palette Editor dialog box.

Pretty easy so far, eh? Now let's add some more colors to your custom palette using the various other options in the Select Color dialog box.

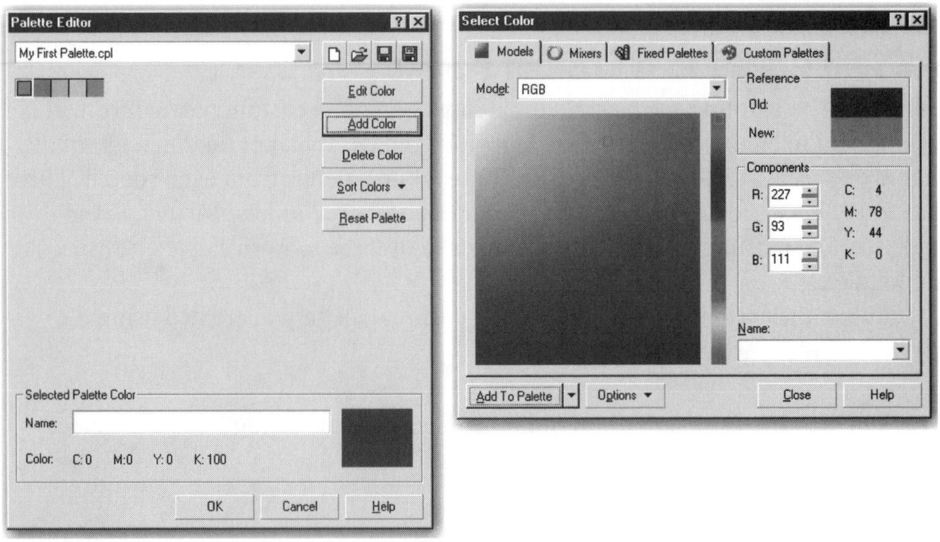

FIGURE 8-5   The Palette Editor with the palette "My First Palette" loaded and the RGB model selected in the Select Color dialog box

CHOOSING COLORS FROM THE COLOR HARMONIES DIALOG BOX   When
you choose the Mixers tab on the Select Color dialog box, color harmonies are
displayed. Color harmonies are a collection of colors that complement each other.
These harmonizing colors are displayed in a palette at the bottom of the Select
Color dialog box when the Mixers tab is selected. The default palette uses the
RGB color model selected from the Model drop-down list. In all, there are seven
color models to choose from: CMY, CMYK, RGB, HSB, HLS, LAB, and YIQ.
Each of the color models is displayed as a color wheel like the one shown in
Figure 8-6.

In addition to the seven color models, six different hue variations are available
in the Hue drop-down list. These hue variations determine the colors that display
in the color palette at the bottom of the Select Color dialog box. The hue variations
are Primary, Complement, Triangle 1, Triangle 2, Rectangle, and Pentagon. The

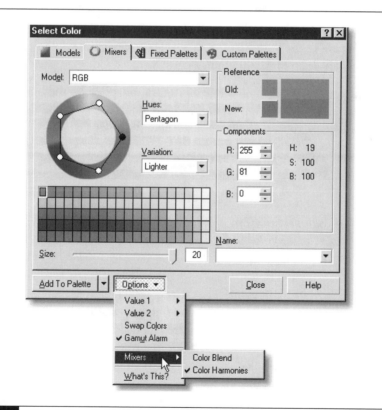

FIGURE 8-6   The Select Color dialog box displaying color harmonies

default is Pentagon. What makes these hue variations differ from each other is they each contain different sample points on the color wheel. The sample points determine the colors that harmonize with each other. For example the default Pentagon has five sample points where the rectangle has only four. You can click and drag on the black circle of any of the different hue configurations and rotate the sample points around the wheel. As you rotate, the colors will change in the palette below. If you click and drag on any of the other points, you can alter the placement of the points on the color wheel.

Choosing colors from color harmonies can be useful for those of you who need a little help choosing colors that complement each other. Practice choosing colors in the color harmonies dialog box using the following steps.

1. Open the Palette Editor.

2. Open the palette "My First Palette" you created earlier.

3. Click the Add Color button in the Palette Editor dialog box. Choose the Mixers tab in the Select Color dialog box to reveal the default color harmonies dialog box shown in Figure 8-6.

4. Using the default Pentagon hue configuration, click on the black circle, and drag in a circular motion on the color wheel. Notice the change in colors in the palette as you rotate the circle around the wheel.

5. If would like to alter the color's brightness or saturation or even to make the color cooler or warmer, click the down arrow in the Variation box, and choose one of the variations.

 TIP *If you select None from the Variation box, only the sample point colors will display in the color palette. For example, if you use the Rectangle hue configuration, only four colors would be displayed in the palette.*

6. When you're satisfied with the colors displayed in the palette, you can either add one color at a time as you did earlier in the chapter, or you can add a row of colors or even the entire palette. To add more than one color at a time, shift-click on the first color in a row and the last color in a row. This technique will select all colors between the two selected colors. With the colors selected, click on the Add To Palette button at the bottom of the dialog box, and they will be added to your custom palette in the Palette Editor. Remember to save the palette in the Palette Editor. To add non-contiguous colors, hold down the CTRL key as you select colors.

CHOOSING COLORS FROM THE COLOR BLEND DIALOG BOX   There is one more way of choosing colors using a similar technique to color harmonies called color blend. You can change the Mixers dialog box to display the color blend configuration by clicking on the drop-down arrow on the Options drop-down list and choosing Mixers | Color Blend. The Options child menu is shown in Figure 8-6. When you choose this option, the dialog box displays the color grid shown in Figure 8-7. The grid contains 256 blended colors comprised of the four colors located at each corner of the grid. To change the colors in the grid, you simply change the corner colors, which you can do by clicking and holding down the drop-down arrow next to the color to reveal the default CorelDRAW custom palette. When the palette is displayed, choose a new color. That color will now be blended with the other three colors. To completely change the blend, change all four corner colors. The default grid size is 16x16. To change the grid size, move the slider control beneath the grid. The minimum size is 3x3, and the maximum is 32x32. The greater the grid size the more blended colors are available.

8

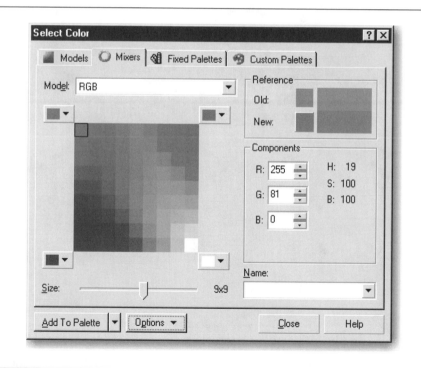

FIGURE 8-7   The Select Color dialog box displaying color blends

Practice changing colors in the blend, and then choose a few colors and add them to your custom palette.

CHOOSING COLORS FROM THE FIXED PALETTES DIALOG BOX   Choosing the Fixed Palette tab on the Select Color dialog box displays the Fixed Palettes configuration. It is here that you can choose spot colors to add to your custom palette. Click the down arrow on the Palette drop-down list to choose the Fixed Palette you wish to use. Figure 8-8 shows the Fixed Palette dialog box with the PANTONE Coated palette selected.

The default configuration shows the color names of each color directly on top of each color bar. If you prefer to see a larger palette of colors, click the Options

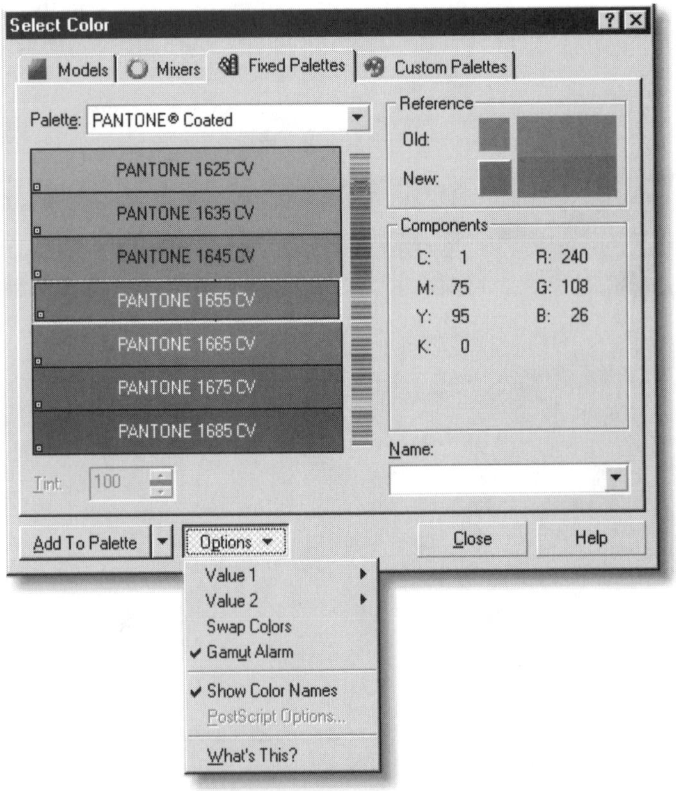

FIGURE 8-8   The Select Color dialog box displaying the Fixed Palette configuration

button, and Choose Show Color Names to toggle the name off. Repeat the procedure to toggle it on again.

Practice adding a few spot colors to your palette. Again don't forget to close the Select Color dialog box and save your newly added colors in the Palette Editor dialog box.

CHOOSING COLORS FROM THE CUSTOM PALETTES DIALOG BOX   Now, for the last stop in creating your custom palette, click the Custom Palettes tab to display the Custom Palette configuration shown in Figure 8-9. Here you can select any of the default custom palettes and any of the palettes you have previously created. The CorelDRAW Palette is the default palette. Choose a few colors from this palette each time, clicking the Add To Palette button to complete your custom palette.

If you haven't been saving your custom palette, now is the time to do it, or your added colors will be lost. Close the Select Color dialog box, and click the Save button at the top of the Palette Editor dialog box to save the palette. The Palette Editor should now resemble the one shown in Figure 8-10. Notice that the

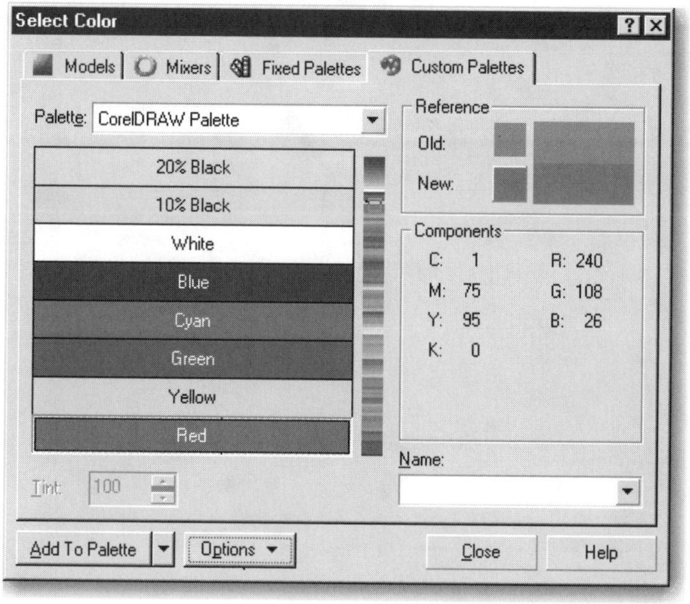

8

FIGURE 8-9   The Select Color dialog box with the Custom Palettes tab selected

Sort Colors drop-down list is also displayed in Figure 8-10. This list allows you to choose how the colors are arranged in the palette.

The next time you want to use your custom palette, simply choose <u>W</u>indow | Color Palettes | Color Palette <u>B</u>rowser. The Palette Docker will appear displaying your custom palette in the list of palettes available. Select your palette from the list, and it will be displayed next to the existing palette onscreen.

TIP   *If the Color Palette Browser Docker is already open and you are saving over a current palette, you can update the Color Palette by unchecking then rechecking the palette in the Docker.*

By now you should be an expert using the Palette Editor. You should find this ability to create custom palettes a real benefit when working in CorelDRAW.

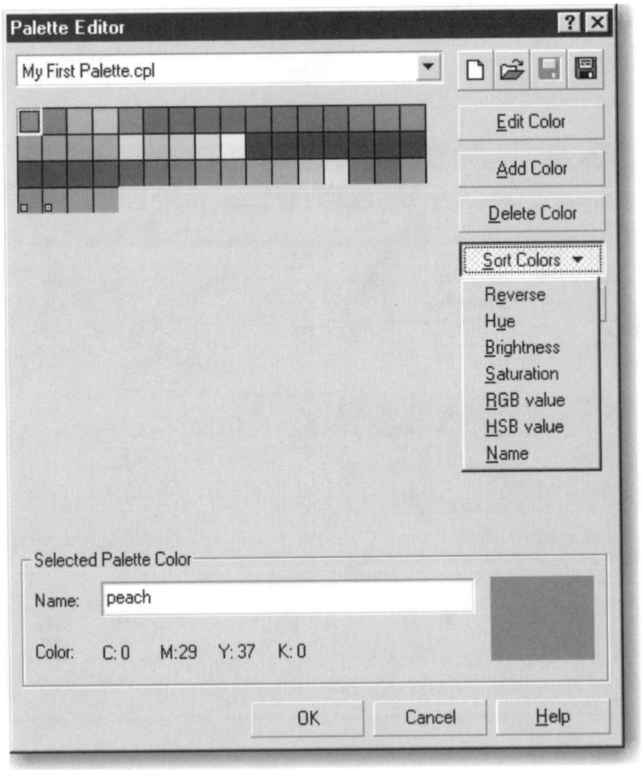

FIGURE 8-10   The Palette Editor dialog box displaying a custom palette

Creating Palettes from Open Documents and Selected Objects

We have just about reached the end of this interesting subject of color palettes. Before it can be considered complete, we have saved one of the best features for last.

For years, CorelDRAW users have asked to be able to create a custom palette using the colors in an existing document. Well, miracles do happen, and now you can. Not only can you create a palette using the colors from an existing document, but you can also create a palette using the colors from within a selection.

The process of creating these unique palettes is extremely simple. Follow these steps to create both of these palettes:

1. Open an existing drawing, or import a clipart image into a new document. We used a clipart image that coauthor Peter McCormick created several years ago. It can be found on the CD that came with your book. The path to the image is /Chap08/Pool.cdr.

2. Choose Window | Color Palettes | Create Palette from the Document menu.

3. The Save Palette As dialog box will appear (see Figure 8-11).

4. Give your new palette a name, and save it to a folder of your choice.

To use your new palette, choose Window | Color Palettes | Color Palette Browser. The Palette Docker will appear, magically displaying your custom palette in the list of palettes available. Select it from the list to display the palette next to the default palette. If you use the same image of a pool table as we did, your palette will look like Figure 8-12 at the left of the default palette. We have circled the new custom palette in the Color Palette Browser Docker.

Now that you've created a palette containing colors from a document, let's create a palette containing colors from only a selected portion of a document. Follow these steps:

1. Open an existing drawing, or import a clipart image into a new document. If you would like to use the image we used, it is also located on the CD that came with your book. The path to the file is Projects/Chap08/Jockey.cdr. Our goal is to capture only the colors used in creating the jockey.

2. Select the jockey. It is already a group of objects.

3. Choose Window | Color Palettes | Create Palette from Selection.

8

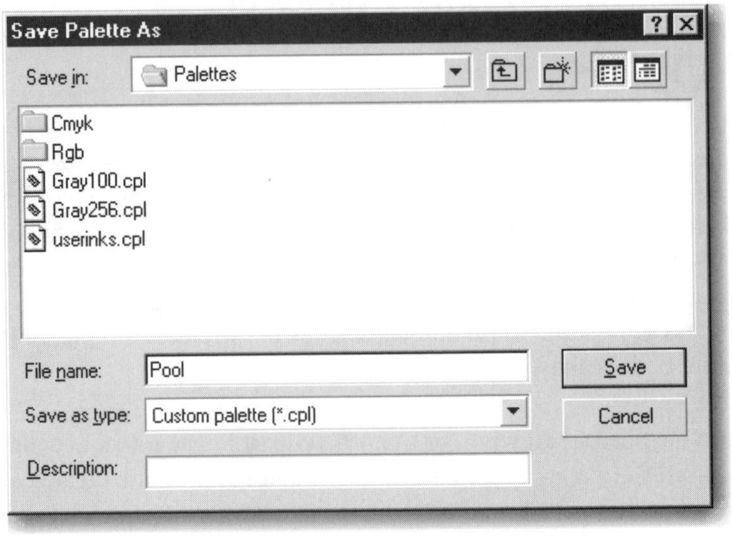

FIGURE 8-11 The Save Palette As dialog box

4. The New Palette dialog box will appear as before (see Figure 8-11).

5. Give your new palette a name, and save it to the default Palette folder.

6. Open your new palette as before by choosing Window I Color Palettes I Color Palette Browser. When the Color Palette Browser Docker appears, the new palette will be available. If you used the same file that we did, your new palette should look like the one in Figure 8-13 next to the Palette you created from the pool table document and the default palette.

In addition to learning about color models and color palettes and discovering how to create your own, you learned two important facts. One, you found out that your file will be printed in process color unless you specify spot colors. Two, you learned that it can be difficult to match the colors on your monitor to the printed

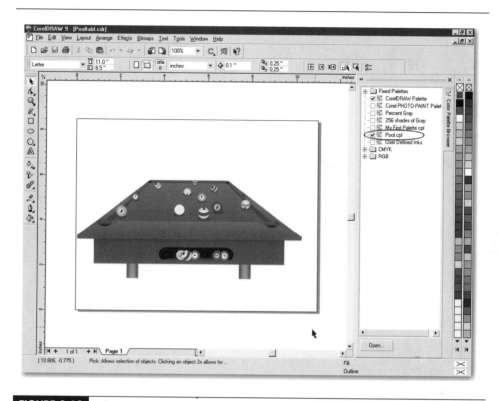

FIGURE 8-12   A custom palette created from the document displayed next to the
default palette

piece. The subjects of color and color printing can be confusing. If you want to
learn even more about color models and color palettes, refer to the online help files
in CorelDRAW.

Uniform Fills

If you are new to CorelDRAW and are looking for a way to fill an object with a
solid color, this is the place to start. If all you want to do is fill an object with a
color, simply select the object, and choose a color from the palette at the right of

FIGURE 8-13 A custom palette created from a selected object displayed next to the default palette

the CorelDRAW window. By default, objects must be closed shapes before you can fill them. However, you can fill open shapes with any of CorelDRAW's fills by choosing Tools | Options | Document | General. Once in the General dialog box, put a check mark in the Fill Open Curves box. The illustration shown here shows an open curve that has been filled with a solid fill. Notice that there is no outline at the top of the coffee cup. This ability to fill open curves is a long-awaited feature that is now a reality.

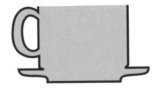

Uniform fills are considered solid fills. These are the colors found on the default color palette in the CorelDRAW window and in the color palettes and color models discussed earlier. The remainder of this chapter concentrates on uniform fills whereas Chapter 9 covers the special fills. Once you have learned how to use the uniform fills, it will be easier to create the special fills.

The Uniform Fill Dialog Box

You learned all about color models and palettes at the beginning of this chapter, and now you will learn how to use them. The Uniform Fill dialog box provides access to the various color models and palettes described in the beginning of this chapter. It is from these palettes that you choose colors to fill the objects you create in CorelDRAW. The Uniform Fill dialog box can be accessed from the Fill tool flyout or by choosing the edit button on the Property Bar when an object is selected with the interactive fill tool and the words "Uniform Fill" have been selected from the Fill type drop-down list. Color models but not color palettes can also be accessed from the Color Docker. Both the Property Bar and Color Docker methods will be discussed at the end of the chapter. In addition, you learned earlier that you can access dozens of color palettes by choosing Window | Color Palettes | Color Palette Browser. The default Uniform Fill dialog box is shown in Figure 8-14.

The Uniform Fill dialog box looks strikingly similar to the Select Color dialog box used with the Palette Editor described earlier in the chapter. In fact they are identical to each other. The only differences are the names of the dialog boxes themselves. If you have read the earlier part describing the Select Color dialog box, you will be able to easily follow along with the remainder of the chapter.

Setting the Default Uniform Fill Color

The first thing a user should learn is how to change the default uniform fill. It's important to know how to change the default setting in case a default value is changed accidentally (which happens more often than you might think). By default, No Fill is set for all objects, and Black (C=0, M=0, Y=0, K=100) is set for text. These values are recommended. If the defaults are changed, follow these steps to reset them:

1. Make sure no objects are selected. Then click the No Fill button (the one with the *X*) on the Fill Tool flyout.

2. The Uniform Fill message box shown here appears; check the Graphic check box, and leave the Artistic Text and Paragraph Text check boxes unchecked.

3. Click the OK button.

4. Click the Fill Color Dialog button on the Fill Tool flyout (the leftmost button on the flyout).

5. The Uniform Fill message box appears again; this time remove any check mark from the Graphics check box, and put check marks in the Artistic Text and Paragraph Text check boxes.

6. Click the OK button.

7. The Uniform Fill dialog box will now appear (see Figure 8-14).

8. Click the color Model button, and choose CMYK from the Model drop-down list.

9. Type in zeros in the num boxes marked C, M, and Y. Type in the number **100** in the K num box located in the Components section of the dialog box.

10. Click the OK button. That's it. You just reset the defaults to No Fill for graphic objects, a Black fill using 100 percent K, and zero percent of the other three colors for Artistic and Paragraph Text.

Using Color Models in the Uniform Fill Dialog Box

Before you open the Uniform Fill dialog box, you must have an object selected; otherwise, you will see the Uniform Fill message box asking you to change the defaults (see the section "Setting the Default Uniform Fill Color," earlier in this chapter). When you first open the Uniform Fill dialog box, one of the many color models or color palettes you learned about earlier will be displayed. The type of display depends on the uniform fill of the object selected. Depending on whether the object was filled with a color model or color palette, the palette or color model containing the color of the object will be displayed in a large view window to the left of the dialog box. If the object has no fill or is filled with a fill other than a solid color, the default CMYK color model is displayed.

The default CMYK color model view is HSB (hue, saturation, and brightness) Hue Based. When you click on the Options button at the bottom of the dialog box, a menu appears. Click on Color Viewers to reveal a child menu that offers a choice of five more visual representations of the visible color spectrum. Choose a color spectrum to select your colors. Figure 8-15 shows the CMYK color model with the CMYK-3D Subtractive view selected. If you wish to select colors from one of the

8

other color models, click the down arrow on the Model list box near the top of the dialog box, and select a model from the list.

When you select a color from any one of the color views, the color appears in a preview box in the upper-right corner of the dialog box adjacent to the word "New." If a smaller box displays a slightly different color next to the color, as shown in Figure 8-16, it means the color will not print exactly as it displays (see the section "Using the Color Gamut Alarm," later in this chapter). Figure 8-16 shows the Uniform Fill dialog box when the RGB color model is selected along

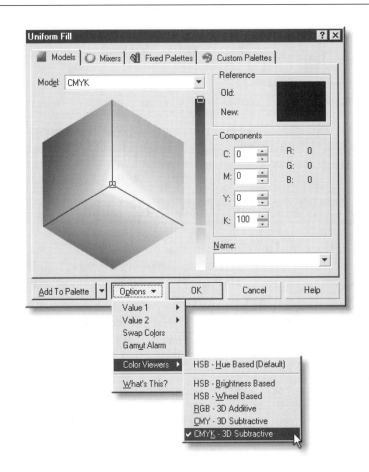

FIGURE 8-15   The Uniform Fill dialog box with the CMYK color model and CMYK-3D Subtractive view selected from the Color viewer child menu

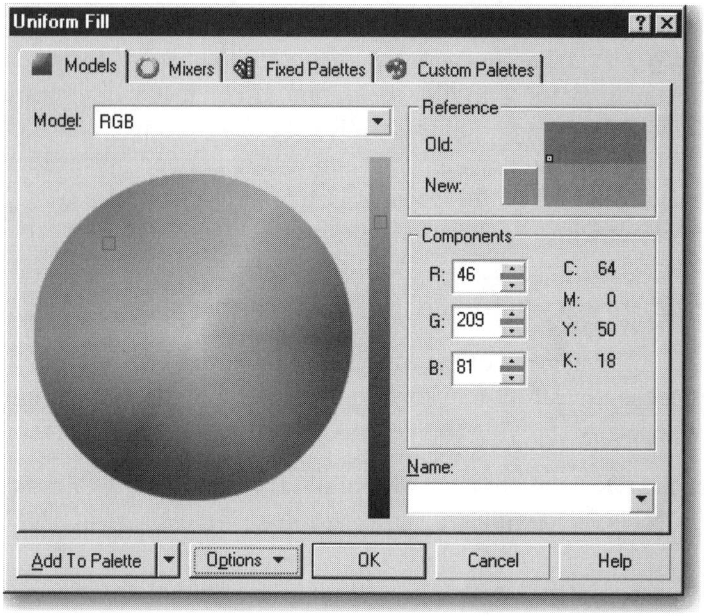

FIGURE 8-16   The Uniform Fill dialog box with an RGB color model and HSB
wheel-based color viewer displayed

with the HSB <u>W</u>heel Based color viewer. Notice too, the smaller square, indicating
the color will not print exactly as shown in this figure. When you are happy with
the color selection, click OK, and the selected object will be filled.

Using Registration Color

Registration marks are used to help the printer align the plates on the press. You
can have the default registration marks automatically placed on every plate of a
color separation when you enable the Print registration marks box in the Prepress
page of the Print dialog box.

Registration color refers to user-placed registration marks. At times you'll
want your own custom registration marks to print on each plate of the color
separation, in place of or in addition to default registration marks—for example,
dotted lines in the drawing that indicate a fold line. You may feel it's more
important to align the plates using these dotted lines than using the default

registration marks, or you might simply want to use your own registration marks instead of the default marks.

CorelDRAW lets you assign a registration color to objects in your drawings so they will print on all plates of a color separation. If you make up your own registration color containing all four CMYK colors, including plates containing spot colors, it will not print on plates containing user defined inks (see the section "Using User-Defined Inks to Fill Objects," later in this chapter).

To fill an object with a registration color, follow these steps:

1. Select the object you wish to fill with a registration color.

2. Click the down arrow of the Model list box in the Uniform Fill dialog box, and choose Registration Color. You will see a message explaining what will happen by applying this color.

3. Click the OK button to apply the color. The Status Bar will indicate that the object is filled with a registration color.

That's all there is to it. When the separations are printed, the object filled with the registered color will print on all plates, no matter how many plates are created. Figure 8-17 shows the Uniform Fill dialog box when Registration Color is selected from the Model drop-down list.

USING THE COLOR HARMONIES AND COLOR BLEND PALETTES   Color harmonies are custom palettes made up of colors that harmonize. These palettes are provided for the user who may have difficulty in choosing colors that work well together. To access these custom palettes, click on the Mixers tab in the Uniform Fill dialog box. Choosing the colors from one of the various harmony palettes is explained in detail in the section "Choosing Colors from the Color Harmonies Dialog Box," earlier in this chapter.

Color blends are accessed by clicking on the Options button at the bottom of the Uniform Fill dialog box and choosing Mixers | Color Blend. Color blends are also described in detail in the section "Creating Custom Palettes," earlier in this chapter. The Uniform Fill dialog box is shown in Figure 8-18 with the Mixers tab selected.

Using Fixed Palettes in the Uniform Fill Dialog Box

Choose the Fixed Palettes tab on the Uniform Color dialog box to access the fixed palettes. This is where you can choose spot colors for your projects. Click the

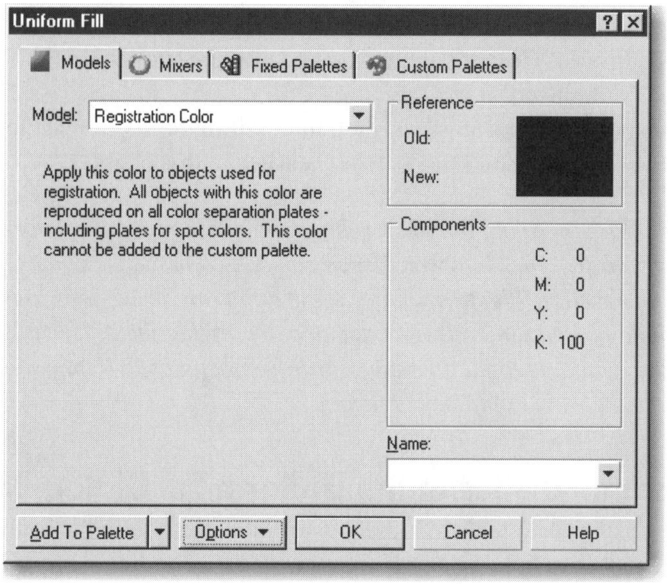

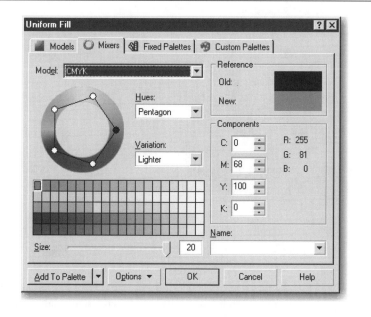

FIGURE 8-17   The Uniform Fill dialog box with Registration Color selected from the Model drop-down list

FIGURE 8-18   The Uniform Fill dialog box when the Mixers tab is selected down arrow on the Palette drop-down list to choose the fixed palette you wish to use. Figure 8-19 shows the Fixed Palettes tab of the Uniform Fill dialog box with the PANTONE Process Colors palette selected and the spot color PANTONE S78-7 selected from the color list.

The fixed palette options are described in detail in the section "Choosing Colors from the Fixed Palette Dialog Box," earlier in this chapter.

 NOTE   *We are trying not to be redundant by not repeating information about the various fill types that was already discussed in the section "Creating Custom Palettes." Just remember these different tab sections in the Uniform Fill dialog box are merely a means of categorizing the different kinds of fills that are available to fill the objects in your documents. If they were all in one drop-down list, it could be confusing.*

Using Custom Palettes in the Uniform Fill Dialog Box

To access the custom palettes, click the Custom Palettes tab in the Uniform Fill dialog box. When you click the down arrow of the Palette list box, you will be

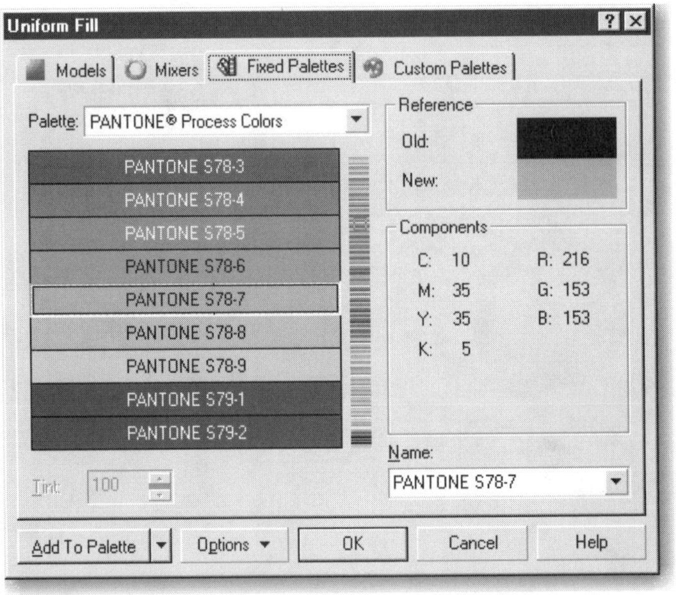

FIGURE 8-19   The Uniform Fill dialog box when the Fixed Palettes tab is selected

offered six choices. The first choice is CorelDRAW Palette, which is the default CMYK palette. The second choice is Corel PHOTO-PAINT Palette, which is the default RGB Corel PHOTO-PAINT palette. The third choice is Percent Gray, which allows you to choose from 0 to 100 percent gray in 1 percent increments. The fourth choice is 256 shades of Gray, which allows you to choose between all 256 shades of gray. The fifth choice is the User-Defined Inks palette discussed in this section that follows. The last choice is Open Palette. When you choose this option, you can open any of the CorelDRAW 9 custom palettes by choosing them from the Custom/Palettes folder. Figure 8-20 shows the Uniform Fill dialog box when the default CorelDRAW palette is selected while displaying the Palette drop-down list. The palettes Jockey.cpl, My First Palette.cpl, and Pool Table.cpl are the custom palettes we created earlier in this chapter. As you can see, this is yet another place to access any custom palettes you create.

8

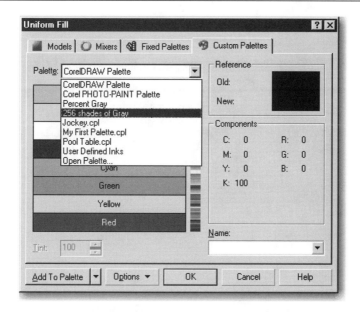

FIGURE 8-20 The Uniform Fill dialog box when the default CorelDRAW palette is selected

Using User Defined Inks to Fill Objects

Filling an object with the designation of User Defined Inks is a way to create a custom color plate in addition to any others created during the color separation process. The colors contained in this plate are used as "stand-in colors" for the colors that will actually be used when the project is printed. This means that if you want to use one of the more exotic inks, such as "Gold Foil," you fill the object with one of the User Defined Inks fills. When the printer gets to the plate containing the objects with the User Defined Inks, he or she simply uses the real Gold Foil ink on the press.

To fill an object with a User Defined Ink, follow these steps:

1. Click the Custom Palettes tab on the Uniform Fill dialog box.

2. Click the down arrow of the Palette list box, and choose User Defined Inks. Five User Defined Inks are displayed.

3. Choose among the inks offered. If you're going to use several, you might start at the top and choose Corel Black. (We used Corel Red in our example; see Figure 8-21.) Click the OK button to finish.

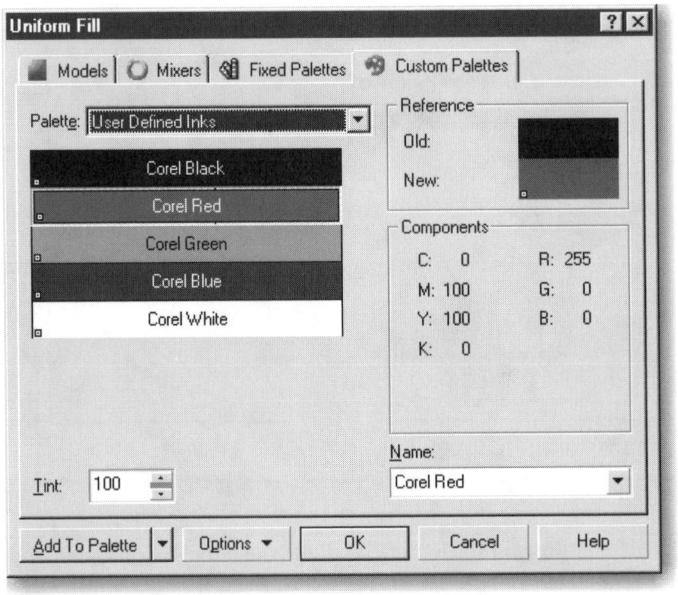

FIGURE 8-21   The Uniform Fill dialog box showing the User Defined Inks colors

Figure 8-22 shows the Separations page of the Print dialog box. Notice the user-defined ink color identified as Corel Red at the bottom of the Separations page.

If you are going to be using more than five custom inks, simply create additional ones by using the Palette Editor described earlier in the chapter.

Using the Color Docker Window

As mentioned earlier, solid fills are the single colors found in the many color palettes and color models available in CorelDRAW. The color palette at the right of the CorelDRAW window is the primary source for selecting colors to fill your objects. For many users, selecting colors from this palette is all they ever need. Others may prefer to use the Color Docker window to select their colors.

The Color Docker window provides a special convenience in that from this one Docker, you can access all the color models available in the Uniform Fill dialog box. An added bonus is that you can apply the selected color to the outline as well

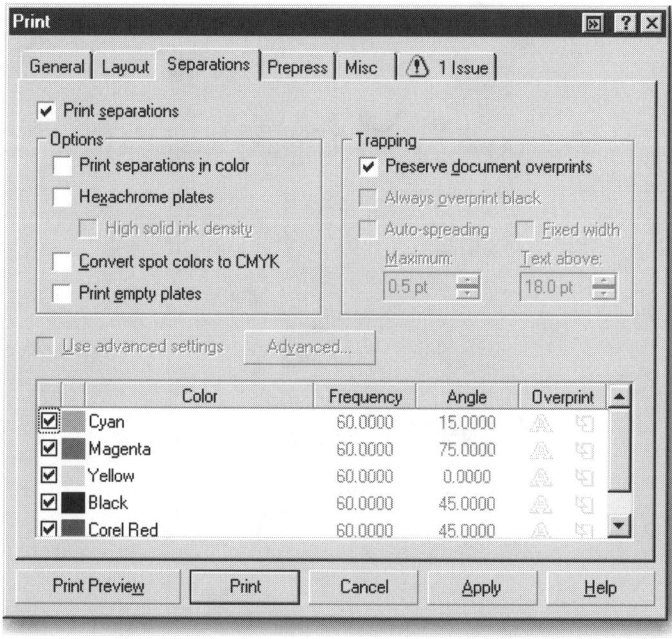

8

FIGURE 8-22   The Separations page of the Print dialog box showing a user-defined ink identified as Corel Red as to the fill. To open the Color Docker, click the Color Docker Window button on the Fill Tool flyout (it's the last one on the flyout).

 TIP *You can use the eyedropper in the Toolbox to select an existing object's fill or outline. When you left-click with the eyedropper on a object, the fill color and the color model corresponding to the selected color will automatically appear in the Docker window. If you left-click on the outline of the object, the outline color and the color model corresponding to the selected outline color will appear in the Docker window. (For more on the Eyedropper tool, see the section "Using the Eyedropper Sample and Fill Objects," later in this chapter.)*

Figure 8-23 shows the Color Docker window displaying the CMYK color model. Remember: to display a color model, click the down arrow on the list box at the top of the Color Docker window.

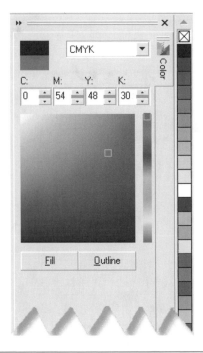

FIGURE 8-23 The Color Docker window with the CMYK color model selected

The color values displayed across the top of the model view window show the individual color values of the selected color depending on the color model selected. If you know the values for a specific color you would like to use, you can enter them in the appropriate num boxes.

If you wish to use one of the other color model views, right-click in an empty area of the Color Docker window, and select Color Viewers from the pop-up menu. Then make your selection from the five other choices. Figure 8-24 shows the color RGB color model with the RGB-3D Subtractive view selected.

Using the Color Gamut Alarm

No discussion of colors in the Color Docker window would be complete without mentioning the Color Gamut Alarm. But first we must define *color gamut*. Color gamut is the range of colors that a device can produce relative to what is normally discernible by the human eye. The human eye can discern millions of colors, while the film that color separations are made with can represent only a relative small

8

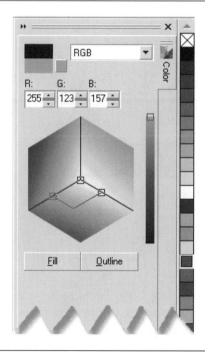

FIGURE 8-24 The Color Docker window with the RGB-3D Subtractive color model selected

percentage of those colors. Therefore, the function of the Gamut Alarm is to warn you if you have selected a color that won't print within the CMYK color range. This doesn't mean it won't print at all; it simply means the color you select is not in the printer's gamut, which means it will not print exactly like the color you see onscreen.

The alarm is not a sound; instead, it warns you by displaying a smaller preview box next to the selected color preview box at the top of the Color Docker window. To turn on the Gamut Alarm in the Color Docker window, right-click anywhere in the gray area of the Color Docker window, and select the Gamut Alarm from the pop-up menu. The Color Docker window is shown here with the pop-up menu displayed. Notice the Gamut Alarm is enabled.

 NOTE *There are two gamut alarms available, one in the Color Docker window and one in the Color Management dialog box discussed later on.*

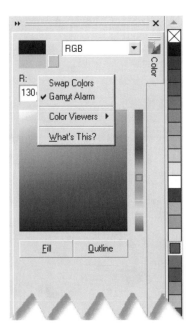

 NOTE *The only time the Color Gamut Alarm is active is when you are using RGB models or palettes. If you are using CMYK models or palettes, they will print more closely to the colors displayed.*

CAUTION   *We would be remiss if we did not warn you about enabling the Gamut Alarm in the Tools | Options | Global | Color Management dialog box. It plays a different role in letting you know if you have selected a color out of gamut. If you enable the Highlight colors out of printer gamut box, and then use an RGB color that is out of gamut, the color you used will display onscreen as bright green. Using the brightly colored green color instead of the color you chose is Corel's way of waving a big flag and telling you that you have used a color out of gamut. If your object turns green, you now know that you can turn off this gamut warning by removing the check mark from the Highlight colors out of printer gamut box in the Options menu. The Highlight colors out of printer gamut box is shown enabled in Figure 8-25.*

One final note about Gamut Alarm. If you remember to use only CMYK colors for the projects you create for print and RGB for projects you create for

8

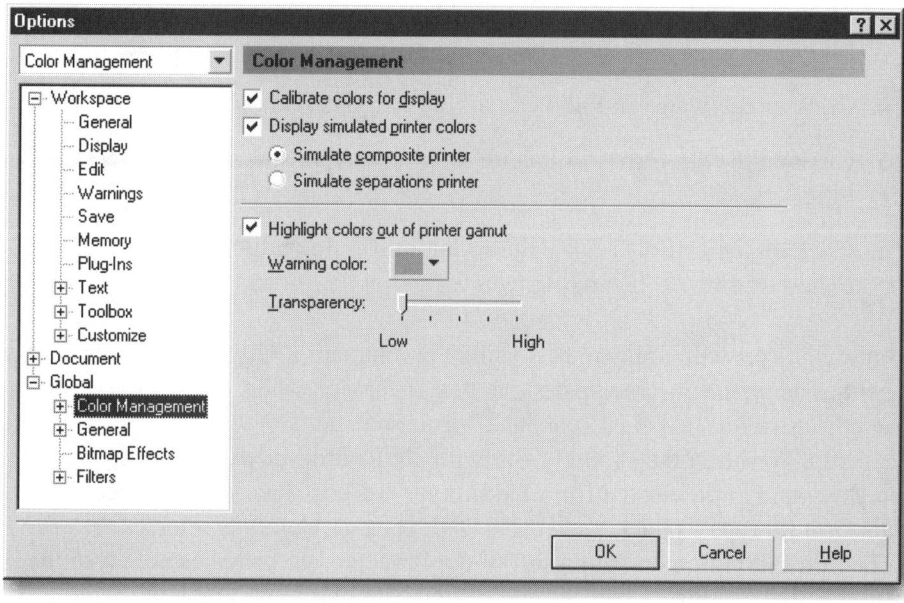

FIGURE 8-25   The Options | Color Management dialog box displaying the Highlight colors out of printer gamut box enabled

display, such as the Web or Corel Presentation files, you will never need to enable the Gamut Alarm.

Using the Property Bar to Apply Uniform Fills

After describing how to use both the Uniform Fill dialog box and the Color Docker to fill objects, we will end this section on uniform fills by showing you how to do many of the same things using the Interactive Fill tool and the Property Bar. We won't describe everything over again but will simply show you how the various color palettes can be accessed from the Property Bar.

To access the different color palettes from the Property Bar, follow these steps:

1. Select an object to fill.

2. Choose the Interactive Fill tool on the toolbox.

3. Click the down arrow on the Fill Type list box on the Property Bar, and choose Uniform Fill. If the object you selected had no fill or was filled with a fill other than a solid fill, it will be filled with the default fill of Black.

4. Click on the Uniform Fill Type drop-down list, and choose Palette.

5. Click on the Uniform Fill Palette drop-down list, and choose PANTONE Process Colors.

6. Click on the Uniform Fill Palette Color drop-down list, and choose Pantone S110-7.

Filling objects with uniform fills using the Interactive Fill tool method is not as efficient as using the onscreen palette but can be useful when you want to quickly fill an object with a special color from a special palette.

Figure 8-26 shows the Property Bar with all the drop-down menus displayed when Uniform Fill is selected from the fill type list box, Palette is selected from the uniform fill type list box, and PANTONE Process Colors is selected.

The Edit Fill button on the far left of the Property Bar provides access to the Uniform Fill dialog box, which should be very familiar to you by now.

Edit Fill Button

Fill Type

Uniform Fill Type

Uniform Fill Palette

Uniform Fill Palette Color

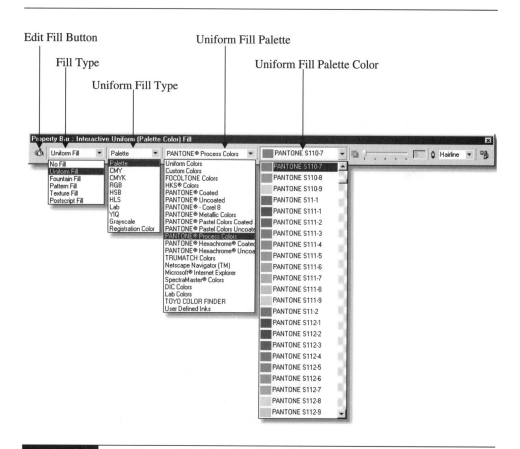

| FIGURE 8-26 | The Property Bar showing a list of the various Pantone colors |

Interactive Tints

A relative new feature in CorelDRAW lets you tint objects with colors from the onscreen color palette. As long as the object is not filled with a pattern, bitmap, or PostScript fill, it can be tinted. The benefit of being able to tint objects is twofold. You can alter an object's color slightly by adding tints of colors, and you can create the illusion of depth by tinting entire objects with the background color without having to recolor the entire image. Practice using this new feature by

8

following these steps. If you want to follow along, the file used in this exercise was created by coauthor Peter McCormick several years ago and is on the CD that comes with the book. The path to the file is /Chap08/Dolphin.cdr.

1. Open the clipart file Dolphin.cdr.

2. Select the background, and note the fill color as Kentucky Green.

3. Select the dolphin and seashell group.

4. Hold down the CTRL key, and click the color Kentucky Green in the color palette. Each time you click, the dolphin and sea shell will be given a 10 percent tint of the Kentucky Green color.

5. Continue holding down the CTRL key, and click a total of four times. The dolphin and seashell should now take on the appearance of being in the water instead of pasted on top of the water.

Figure 8-27 shows the original dolphin and seashell group on the left and the tinted version on the right.

FIGURE 8-27　The original dolphin and seashell group on the left and the tinted version on the right

CAUTION   _You can use this tinting technique on spot colors, but if you do, the spot color will be converted to RGB, which will separate to CMYK plates. By default, you'll see a warning dialog if you try to add tints to fixed colors._

Using the Eyedropper Sample and Fill Objects

The Eyedropper tool, new to CorelDRAW 9, is a long-awaited feature that has finally arrived. You will find it on the toolbox at the left of the screen. The Eyedropper tool lets you copy the fill and outline properties of one vector object and use those fill or outline properties to fill other objects on the page. The Eyedropper tool has a flyout that also contains a Bucket tool, which is used to drop fills and outline properties on other objects after the Eyedropper tool has taken a sample of the fill or outline properties of another object. The Eyedropper tool and its flyout, along with the Property Bar in the eyedropper configuration is shown here.

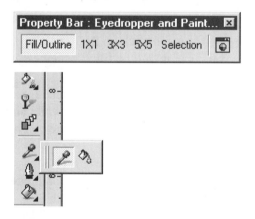

We have saved the best news of all about this great new tool for last. The Eyedropper tool lets you sample colors from bitmap images as well as vectors.

The easiest way to learn how to use this new tool is by practice. Use the following steps to get acquainted with the Eyedropper tool:

1. Draw an ellipse on the page, and fill it with the color red with a blue outline.

2. Draw a rectangle on the page, and fill it with yellow with a purple outline.

3. Choose the Eyedropper tool from the toolbox.

4. Using the Eyedropper tool, click on the fill of the red ellipse.

5. Select the Paint Bucket tool from the eyedropper flyout.

6. Use the Paint Bucket tool, click on the yellow rectangle to fill it with red.

What you just did was copy one fill to another. If you clicked on the outline of the ellipse, you would have sampled the outline color which you could have then applied to the outline of the rectangle. There is a shortcut method of copying and applying the color from one object to the next. If you hold down the SHIFT key with the Eyedropper tool still selected after sampling a color, it will turn into the Paint Bucket tool. This eliminates the extra step of selecting it from the flyout. Practice using this method by drawing four shapes on the page, filling each one with a different color. Fill one of the shapes with the color red and give it a blue outline color, then use the following steps.

1. With none of the shapes selected, choose the Eyedropper tool, and click on the red filled shape.

2. Hold down the SHIFT key and click on the remaining shapes. As you will see, each shape you click on will be filled with the color red.

Repeat the process, but this time instead of using the Eyedropper tool to click on the fill of the red object click on its outline. Then while holding down the SHIFT key click on the outlines of the other objects. This time you have copied the outline color of the red object.

Now comes the part that this author has waited for a long time, and that's the ability to copy a color from a bitmap image. If you would like to follow along using the same image as we use, the name of the file is Doll.tif located on the CD that comes with the book. The path to the file is /Chap08/Doll.tif. The doll image is shown in Figure 8-28.

1. Open a new file in CorelDRAW.

2. Choose File | Import and, using the path noted previously, import the file Doll.tif.

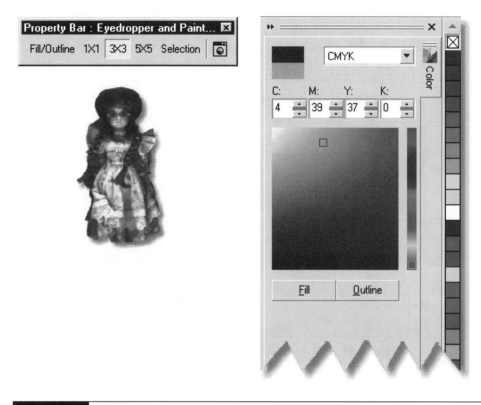

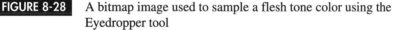

FIGURE 8-28   A bitmap image used to sample a flesh tone color using the
Eyedropper tool

3. Open the Color Docker window by clicking on its button on the end of the
   Fill tool flyout.

4. Choose the Eyedropper tool from the toolbox.

5. Click on the eyedropper 3X3 button on the Property Bar. The 3X3
   represents the number of pixels used when the color is sampled. If you
   chose Selection, you would draw a selection around the area you
   wished to sample.

6. Using the Eyedropper tool, click on the face of the doll.

7. If you clicked somewhere near where we did, you will see a flesh tone color displayed in the preview box of the Color Docker window. You can now use this sampled color to fill other objects in your drawing by clicking on either the Fill or Outline buttons at the bottom of the Color Docker window when a new object is selected.

Oftentimes the reason for sampling a color is to add it to an existing palette for future use. The process of saving a sampled color is as follows:

1. After sampling a color as you did in the previous steps, use that color to fill an object on the page.

2. Open the Color Palette Browser by choosing Window | Color Palettes | Color Palette Browser.

3. Click on the custom palette you made earlier in this chapter. If you don't have a custom palette that you've created, choose one of the other palettes.

4. Select this newly filled object, and click on the Uniform Fill button on the Fill tool flyout.

5. When the Uniform Fill dialog box appears, the new color will be displayed in the preview window shown in Figure 8-29.

6. Click the Add To Palette button at the bottom left of the dialog box. This will place the new color in the custom palette so you can use it over and over again.

You have learned throughout this chapter that the colors you see onscreen may not be the same when they are printed. Corel's color management system will go a long way toward correcting that problem. The purpose of color management is to allow you to calibrate your monitor, printer, and scanner so you can reach that elusive goal of "what you see is what you get." Corel knows that color management is difficult for the average user, so they have provided ICC profiles for dozens of different monitors, scanners, and printers, making it easy for most users to calibrate their systems. And with Windows 98's ICM color support, many manufacturers are now providing ICC profile files with their peripherals.

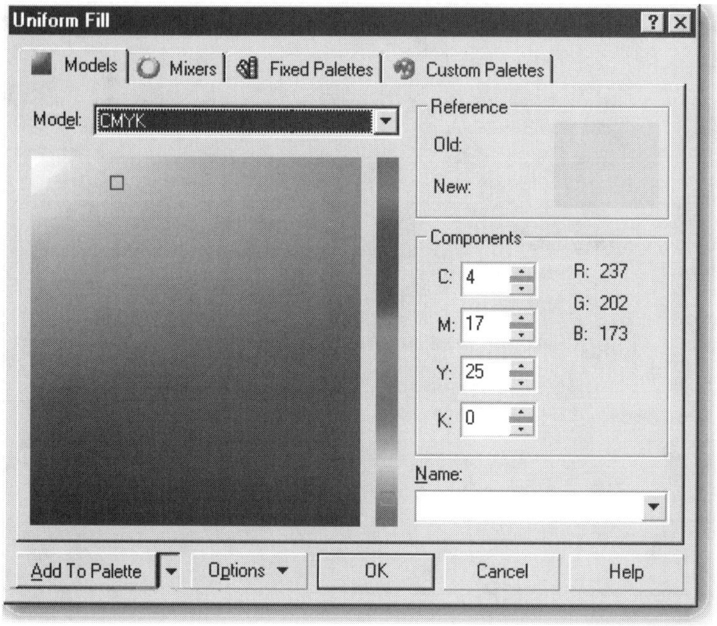

FIGURE 8-29   The Uniform Fill dialog box

NOTE   *It is recommended that you do not install color profiles during installation, as this will waste hard disk space needlessly. When you are ready to calibrate your devices, simply insert the install CD into your CD drive, choose the "Get profile from disk" option and browse to the Color folder on the CD.*

It's simply a matter of choosing your particular monitor, printer, and scanner from a list of profiles.

Choosing Profiles for Your System

To choose a profile for each of your devices, choose Tools | Color Management to display the Color Management screen. Then click Profiles at the bottom of the Color Management tree structure. The dialog box shown in Figure 8-30 will appear displaying generic profiles for each device.

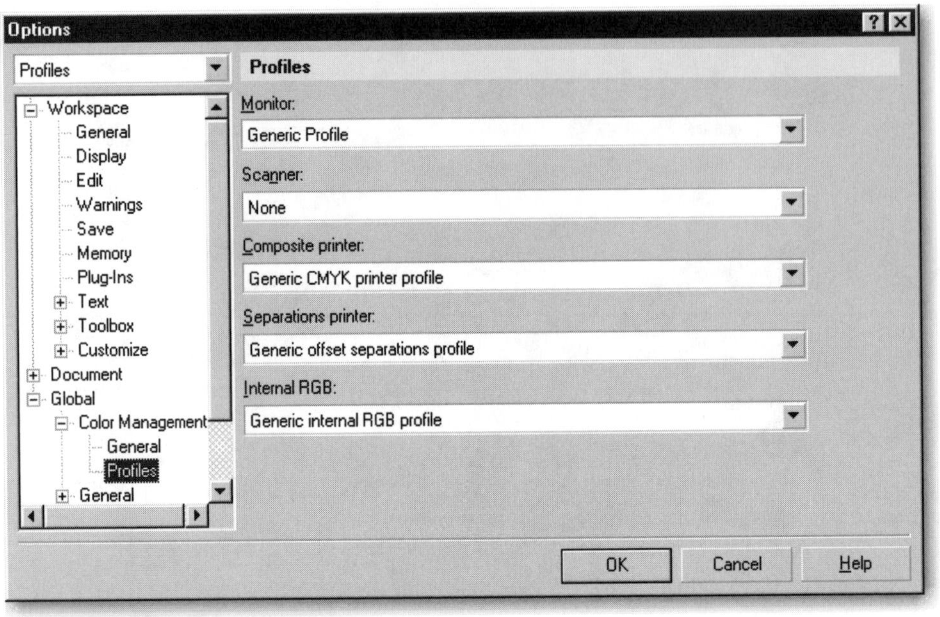

FIGURE 8-30   The Profile dialog box listing generic profiles

Follow these steps to calibrate your system.

1. Insert the install CD into your CD drive.

2. Click each device's list box and choose "Get profile from disk". The Browse for Folder dialog box shown here appears.

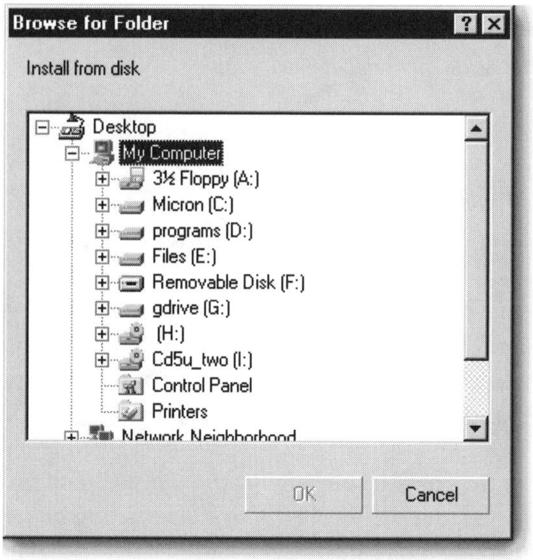

Browse for Folder   ? X

Install from disk

- Desktop
  - My Computer
    - 3½ Floppy (A:)
    - Micron (C:)
    - programs (D:)
    - Files (E:)
    - Removable Disk (F:)
    - gdrive (G:)
    - (H:)
    - Cd5u_two (I:)
    - Control Panel
    - Printers
  - Network Neighborhood

OK   Cancel

8

3. Change to the drive and folder where CorelDRAW 9 is installed, and click on the + icon to expand the folder. Choose the Color folder, and click the OK button. The Install From Disk dialog box shown here will appear.

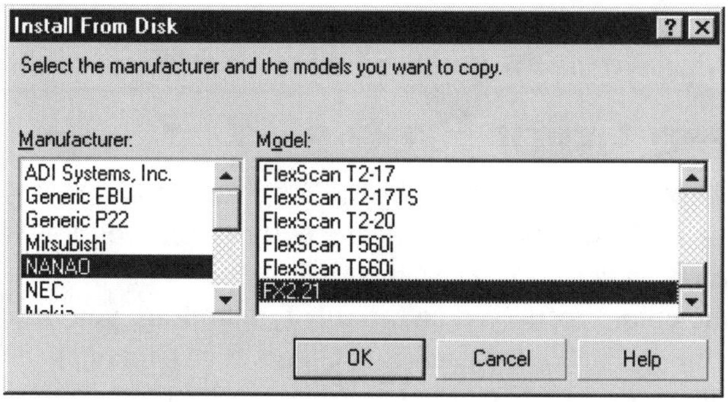

Install From Disk   ? X

Select the manufacturer and the models you want to copy.

Manufacturer:

Model:
FlexScan T2-17
FlexScan T2-17TS
FlexScan T2-20
FlexScan T560i
FlexScan T660i
FX2.21

- ADI Systems, Inc.
- Generic EBU
- Generic P22
- Mitsubishi
- NANAO
- NEC
- Nokia

OK   Cancel   Help

4. Choose the device you want to install and click OK. Repeat these steps for each device.

NOTE   *The Separations printer list contains the names of printers and image setters that are used for producing color separations. This list is usually used to select the name of the image setter your service bureau uses, but it can be used for any printer that outputs CMYK color.*

You really only have another option if the manufacturer of your device has provided you with an ICC color profile they have created. If you have such a profile, simply choose the Get profile from disk option, and change to the folder where the profile is stored. Select the profile, and it will be installed.

NOTE   *Generic profiles are selected by default. The fact that profiles are already selected, even though they are generic, means that Color correction is turned on.*

When you're done making your selections, click the OK button. That's all there is to it; you have just selected the color profiles for your system devices. If you change any of the devices, simply open the Profiles dialog box again to select different profiles.

How to Use a Color Profile

You've learned how to select a color profile for your system; now you need to know how to use it. Remember, you select a color profile for your system so you can view the colors in your images as they will be printed.

To ensure the color profile you selected is functioning, you must choose Tools I Color Management. Enable the Calibrate Colors for Display check box. You will be presented with three entries that you can check: Simulate Composite Printer, Simulate Separations Printer, and Highlight Colors Out of Printer Gamut. To get the most benefit from the color management system, you should check one of the printer options. The Simulate Composite Printer option should be checked when you're printing to your desktop printer. Check Simulate Separations Printer when printing to file to be sent to an image setter or service bureau where the job will be printed on an actual printing press. If you pay attention to which palette you use in your documents, you shouldn't need to enable the Highlight Colors Out of Printer Gamut box (see the section "Using the Color Gamut Alarm," earlier in this chapter). That's all there is to it. The colors onscreen should now closely match the colors that are printed. The Color Management dialog box is shown here.

Options   ? ×

Color Management ▼   **Color Management**

☐ Workspace
    General
    Display
    Edit
    Warnings
    Save
    Memory
    Plug-Ins
    ⊞ Text
    ⊞ Toolbox
    ⊞ Customize
    ⊞ Document
    ☐ Global
        ⊞ Color Management
        ⊞ General
        Bitmap Effects
        ⊞ Filters

☑ Calibrate colors for display
☑ Display simulated printer colors
    ⦿ Simulate composite printer
    ○ Simulate separations printer

☐ Highlight colors out of printer gamut
    Warning color: ☐ ▼
    Transparency: |———|———
                    Low   High

OK   Cancel   Help

8

NOTE   *Color Management is turned on by default using Generic profiles if you don't choose your own.*

In addition to learning about color models and color palettes and discovering how to create your own, you learned two important facts in this chapter. First, you found out that your file will be printed in process color unless you specify spot colors. Second, you learned that it can be difficult to match the colors on your monitor to the printed piece. The subjects of color and color printing can be confusing. If you want to learn more about color models and color palettes, refer to the online help files in CorelDRAW. There is also an excellent article on color management by Michael Cervantes that can be found at the www.unleash.com Web site. You learned how to fill objects using the Uniform Fill dialog box, the Color Docker window, and the Property Bar. Last, but not least, you learned about color management. Chapter 9 teaches you how to fill objects with fills other than solid colors.

CHAPTER 9

Special Fills

CorelDRAW 9

Y ou can design a great looking layout or draw an exquisite flower, but without a complementary fill, the objects remain nothing more than outlines. This chapter will teach you where to find the many special fill types and the methods for applying them.

There are many ways within CorelDRAW that you can apply a fill to an object. These include using dialog boxes, Dockers, and the Interactive Fill tool together with the Property Bar. In order to simplify the material and make you more productive, we will concentrate on one primary method for accessing the five fill types. It is the Interactive Fill tool used with the Property Bar.

The Fill Tool Types

CorelDRAW provides five fill types:

- Uniform fill (solid fill)
- Fountain fill
- Pattern fill (Two-color, Full-color, and Bitmap)
- Texture fill
- PostScript fill
- Interactive Mesh fill

All of the aforementioned fill types are covered in this chapter with the exception of the Uniform (solid) fills. Uniform fills are covered in Chapter 8.

Figure 9-1 shows the Fill Tool flyout with each of its fill type buttons. Each button's' corresponding dialog box or Docker window is also shown. These dialog boxes, with all their options, have in the past provided the primary means for filling objects with special fills. If you have used previous versions of CorelDRAW, you will recognize these dialog boxes and see little difference from one version to the next.

These reliable old dialog boxes will be visited throughout this chapter as you learn about each of the special fill types and how to create them using the Interactive Fill tool.

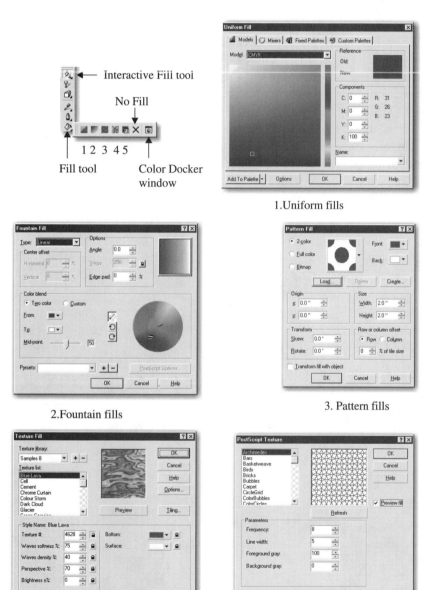

1. Uniform fills

2. Fountain fills

3. Pattern fills

4. Texture fills

5. PostScript fills

FIGURE 9-1 The toolbox, Fill flyout, and the corresponding dialog boxes and Docker

The Interactive Fill Tool

The best way to fill objects' is to use the Interactive Fill tool. The Interactive Fill tool is shown in Figure 9-2 in its selected state on the toolbox. Also shown in Figure 9-2 is the Property Bar with the Fill Type drop-down list in the upper left displaying the five different types of fills. To access this drop-down list, click on the down arrow in the list box on the Property Bar when the Interactive Fill tool is selected. Depending on the fill type selected, the Property Bar will display the options available for the specific fill type chosen.

In the following exercises, you will learn how to create each of the four major fill types using the Interactive Fill tool. They are Fountain, Pattern, Texture, and PostScript. We will begin with the Fountain fills.

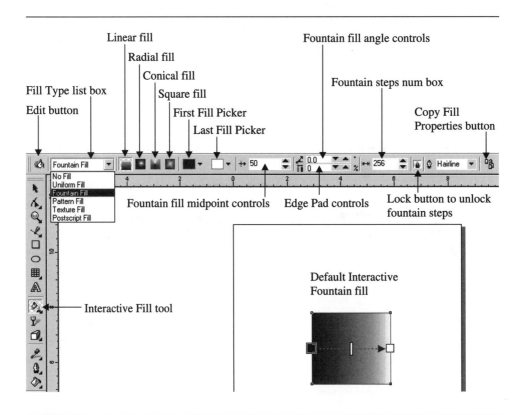

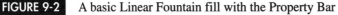
FIGURE 9-2 A basic Linear Fountain fill with the Property Bar

CAUTION *If you select the Interactive Fill tool and then select a fill type with no object selected, a message box appears just as it does when you select the Fill tool at the bottom of the toolbox without an object selected. This means you could set the default fill as a Fountain or Pattern fill instead of using the Fill tool at the bottom of the toolbox to set a solid fill (setting a solid color default fill is discussed in Chapter 8).*

 NOTE *The No Fill option at the top of the Fill Type list box removes the fill of any selected object just as its counterpart, the No Fill button on the Fill flyout, does.*

Fountain Fills

Fountain fills are gradient fills that blend one color into another. The angles at which the blended colors travel can be controlled, as well as the pattern that the blended colors produce. There are four different Fountain fill types. They are Linear, Radial, Conical, and Square. You can create all four of these fill types using the Interactive Fill tool, including custom Fountain fills that use more than two colors. The following steps will teach you how to create all four of the Fountain fills, beginning with the Linear Fountain fill.

CREATING LINEAR FOUNTAIN FILLS   Follow these steps to create a Linear Fountain fill:

1. Draw a rectangle on the page.

2. Click the Interactive Fill tool.

3. Using the Interactive Fill tool, click and drag inside the rectangle. By default, you will automatically create a Linear Fountain fill like the one shown in Figure 9-2. Because a Fountain fill is the default interactive fill, it is not necessary to choose it from the Fill Type list box on the Property Bar. Your rectangle should look like the one shown in Figure 9-2.

   The Linear Fountain fill is the default fill. Notice the dotted line with an arrow at the end points in the direction of the fill. At each end of the line are small squares that can be moved with the Interactive tool to change the angle. If you hold down the CTRL key when you move the squares, you constrain the angle to 15 degrees. In the middle of the dotted line is a midpoint slider. If you click and drag the slider, you can control the

9

position of the midpoint on the Fountain fill. For example, the default Fountain fill blends from black to white. At the center of the fill, the color is measured at 50 percent black. When you move the slider along the dotted line, you change the point where the value becomes 50 percent black. When you're dealing with colors other than black and white, the value at the midpoint is the average of the two end colors. This slider is present only when two colors are used in a Fountain fill.

4. Using the Fountain fill you just created, click the black square on the left, and drag it up and inside the rectangle. Click the white square on the right, and drag it down and inside the rectangle. Your Fountain fill should look like the one shown here, where the angle of the fill is diagonal from the upper-left corner to the lower-right corner of the rectangle. Also try moving the slider to change the midpoint.

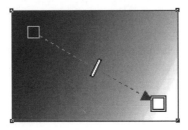

 TIP *If you hold down the CTRL key when you drag the black or white square, you can constrain the angles to 15 degree increments.*

5. Now comes the fun part. *(Read this entire paragraph before you begin the next step, or you will have to start over.)* Click the red color in the default Color palette at the right of the CorelDRAW window. Hold down the left mouse button, drag the color out onto the page, and place it directly on the dotted line of the interactive fill. If you don't click and drag in one continuous motion, you will fill the rectangle with solid red, and you will have to go back to step 1 and begin again. You'll know when to drop the new color onto the dotted line when your cursor shows a box with a plus sign.

6. Continue dragging additional colors and placing them on the dotted line. If you clicked and dragged correctly, your Fountain fill should look something like the following illustration. You can also replace the starting

and ending colors by dragging and dropping new colors onto their respective squares or by choosing a color from the First and Last Fill Picker drop-down color palettes on the Property Bar.

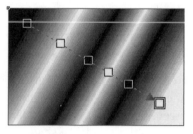

7. Now remove all the extra colors you just placed on the dotted line by right-clicking on each of the added squares. You're removing the added colors just to see how this is done.

That's it; you've just learned how to create a Linear Fountain fill using the Interactive Fill tool.

CREATING THE APPEARANCE OF METAL   Now that you have learned how to create a basic Linear Fountain fill, let's use one to create the look of metal. You can create the effect from scratch or get a head start by using the practice file found on the CD included with this book. The path to the practice file is: /Chapter 09/Metal.cdr. Using Figure 9-3 as a guide, complete the following steps to create this effect.

NOTE   *If you prefer to start from scratch, type the word SILVER on the page using a serif font. The font we used in Figure 9-3 is Bauer Bodoni Blk BT with a point size of 150. Contour the text to the outside using a .08 offset to the outside (to learn about contours, see Chapter 19). After you have contoured the text, use the Separate command to separate the text from the newly added contour shape. Select the text, and move it away from the contour shape. Now that you have two separate objects, you can apply a Linear Fountain fill to each object using the same steps used with the practice file.*

1. Open the file Metal.cdr (the path to the file is /Chapter 09/Metal.cdr).

2. Select the middle text object (it's colored blue).

3. Choose the Interactive Fill tool, and drag from left to right to create a horizontal Linear fill. Begin dragging at the beginning of the word and end at the end of the word.

4. Change the beginning and ending colors by dragging out a 60 percent black fill onto the beginning and ending squares.

5. Add additional shades of gray by dragging them from the palette and dropping them on the dotted line. Use alternating shades of black consisting of 20 percent black and 60 percent black until you end up with four shades of 20 percent black and five shades of 60 percent black.

6. Select the Pick tool, and reselect the middle object you just filled.

7. With the object selected, right-click and drag in a continuous motion until the cursor is over the top red object. The cursor will change into a circle with a crosshair. When you see this special cursor, release the right mouse button.

8. The Object pop-up menu will appear. Choose Copy Fill Here. The Linear fill you just created will be applied to the new object.

9. Select the Interactive Fill tool again. Click on the top object again to reveal the squares and dotted line.

10. Click on the square at the far right, and drag it to the bottom middle of the object.

11. Click on the square at the far left, and drag it to the top middle of the object. This action will change the Linear fill so that it blends from top to bottom.

12. Select both objects, and press the letter *C* to vertically center-align both objects. With the object still selected, press the letter *E* key to horizontally center-align both objects. This will place the middle object on top of the top object. Your finished metal effect should now look like the one at the bottom in Figure 9-3.

CREATING RADIAL FILLS   Now that you have mastered the art of creating a Linear Fountain fill, let's create a Radial Fountain fill:

FIGURE 9-3	Using horizontal and vertical Linear fills on contoured text to create the look of metal

1. Draw a circle on the page using the Ellipse tool.

2. Click the Interactive Fill tool, and click and drag inside the circle. Your circle will be filled from left to right with a black-to-white Linear fill, just as before.

3. With the Interactive Fill tool still selected, move the cursor up to the Property Bar, and click the Radial Fill button (refer back to Figure 9-2 to locate the button). Your circle should now look like the one shown here. Notice that because only two colors are used, the midpoint slider is present.

4. Click the straight dotted line of the interactive fill, and drag it to the upper-left corner of the circle. The reason you click and drag on the dotted

line is to maintain the relationship between the start and end points. Drag the midpoint slider a little closer to the white square to darken the lower portion of the circle. Your circle should now look like the one shown here.

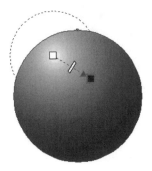

5. Click the black square on the right, and drag it down and to the right, toward the bottom of the circle.

6. With the Interactive Fill tool selected, click the red color on the Color palette, and drag it onto the page, placing it on the dotted line of the interactive fill. Using the example shown here as a guide, drag the new red square toward the white square. Your circle should now look like the three-dimensional sphere shown here. Practice dragging more colors onto the dotted line, and see if you can create a marble look, as you did earlier in this chapter.

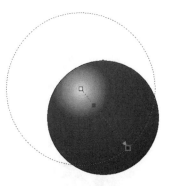

7. Remove any additional colors you may have added by right-clicking the unwanted squares. Leave the original black beginning square and white ending square in preparation for the following project.

ENHANCING INTERESTING SHAPES WITH RADIAL FILLS   The radial-filled shape in Figure 9-4 was begun by rotating and duplicating a custom drawn object filled with a solid fill. After the rotated objects were combined to form an eight-leaf pattern, a Radial fill was applied by copying the fill of a previously filled ellipse shown at the upper left of Figure 9-4. Another slightly smaller ellipse was drawn and filled with the same fill. This ellipse was placed behind the pattern to complete the effect. The practice file for this image is on the CD that comes with this book if you wish to duplicate the effect. The path to the file is /Chap09/Radial.cdr. Using the practice file, complete the following steps:

1. Open the practice file Radial.cdr, and draw a circle on the page using the Ellipse tool.

2. With the circle selected, select the Interactive Fill tool, and give the object a Radial fill.

3. Drag the color black from the palette, and drop it on the white square at the end of the dotted line.

4. Drag out five more colors from the palette, beginning with white and then alternating between black and white. The circle should now look like the one at the upper left in Figure 9-4.

5. With the Interactive Fill tool still selected, select the custom leaf pattern shape in the middle of the top row.

6. Click on the Copy Fill Properties button on the Property Bar (it's the last icon on the right when the Interactive Fill tool is selected). The cursor will change to large black arrow.

7. Using the black arrow cursor, click the radial-filled ellipse your created at the upper left of image in Figure 9-4. This action will copy the fill to the custom shape. The shape will now look like the one at the far right of the image in Figure 9-4.

8. Draw an ellipse slightly smaller than the circumference of the leaf pattern. The object is to let the points on the shape still remain visible (we have shown it as the middle object in the bottom row in Figure 9-4).

9. With the smaller ellipse selected, select the Interactive Fill tool. Click on the Copy Fill Properties button on the Property Bar again, and using the black arrow cursor, click the radial-filled ellipse again at the upper left of image in Figure 9-4. As before, this action will place the same fill in the smaller ellipse.

9

10. With the smaller ellipse still selected, choose the Pick tool. Click on the To Back button on the Property Bar.

11. Select both objects by shift-clicking or marquee selection, and press the C and E keys on the key board one at a time to center-align the two objects. Your finished image will look like the one at the bottom right in Figure 9-4.

CREATING CONICAL FILLS   Now that you are becoming an expert at creating Interactive Fountain fills, let's create a Conical Fountain fill:

1. Draw a circle on the page using the Ellipse tool.

2. Click the Interactive Fill tool, and click and drag inside the circle. Your circle will be filled from left to right with a black-to-white Linear fill, just as before.

3. With the Interactive Fill tool still selected, move the cursor up to the Property Bar, and click the Conical Fill button (refer back to Figure 9-2 to locate the button).

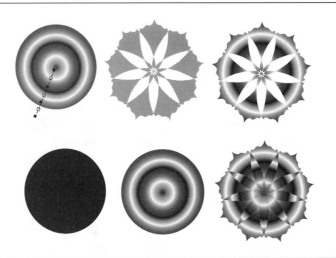

FIGURE 9-4   Using a custom Radial fill to further enhance an interesting shape

Your circle should now look like the one shown here. As before, because only two colors are used, the midpoint slider is present again.

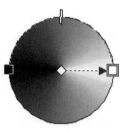

4. Click and drag the apex center square to the upper portion of the circle.

5. Drag the midpoint slider halfway to the right. Notice how the lighter color is now concentrated more on the right, giving the circle more of a cone appearance. Your new conical-filled circle should now look something like the one shown here.

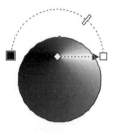

6. Using the above illustration as a guide, drag the color white from the palette, and place it left center on dotted line arc. Now drag the color black from the palette, and place it right center on the dotted line arc. Your conical-filled circle should now look like this illustration:

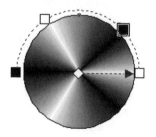

CREATING A RIBBON EFFECT USING CONICAL FILLS The conical-filled ribbon shape in Figure 9-5 was begun by rotating and duplicating an ellipse filled with a solid fill. After rotating the ellipses, they were welded together with the Weld command to form an outline of an award ribbon. A custom Conical fill was created by adding a total of 13 colors alternating between 50 percent black and white. Another smaller ellipse was drawn and filled with a solid fill. This ellipse was placed on the ribbon along with the text indicating first place to complete the effect. The practice file for this image is on the CD that comes with this book if you wish to duplicate the Radial Fill effect. The path to the file is /Chap09/Conical.cdr.

Using the practice file, complete the following steps:

1. Open the practice file Conical.cdr, and select the shape at the right in Figure 9-5. Give the object a fill of 50 percent gray and a black outline.

2. With the shape selected, select the Interactive Fill tool, and give the shape a Conical fill.

3. Click on the white square at the end of the dotted line, and drag it counter clockwise to about one o'clock on the outside of the circle.

4. Drag a 50 percent black from the palette, and drop it on the white square at the end of the dotted line.

5. Drag out a 50 percent black, and drop it on the black square at the other end of the dotted line.

6. Drag out 11 more colors from the palette beginning with white and then alternating between 50 percent black and white. The welded shape should now look like an award ribbon and be similar to the one in the middle in Figure 9-5.

7. Finish off the effect by selecting the ellipse tool, drawing a smaller circle than the ribbon, and placing it on top of the ribbon. Give it a Radial fill from 80 percent black to white.

8. Add the tails of the ribbon and the text (provided in the practice file), and you're finished.

FIGURE 9-5   Using a custom Conical fill to create an award ribbon

CREATING SQUARE FILLS   The last of the Fountain fills is the Square Fountain fill. Practice using this fill by completing the following steps:

1. Click the Rectangle tool in the toolbox, and draw a square on the page.

2. Rotate the rectangle 45 degrees so it looks like a diamond shape.

3. Select the Interactive Fill tool, and click and drag inside the rectangle. Your square will again be filled from left to right with a black-to-white Linear fill.

4. With the Interactive Fill tool selected, click the Square Fill button on the Property Bar. Your square should now look like the one shown here. Notice that the midpoint slider is again present because only two colors are used.

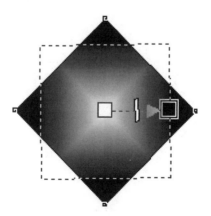

5. Referring to the next example, click the black square, and drag it down to the four o'clock position.

6. Drag out the color black, and place it on the dotted line next to the black square outside the rectangle. Drag three more colors from the palette, beginning with white and then alternating between black and white. The rectangle should now look like example shown here:

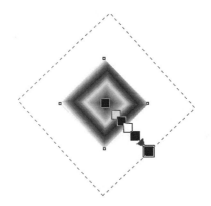

As we stated earlier, finding uses for Square fills is difficult, but Figure 9-6 shows how using duplicates of the fill in the last example and placing them next to each other to form a pattern could have a use when creating tiling patterns. To see how this pattern is used to create a tiling pattern, refer to Chapter 31.

EDITING FOUNTAIN FILLS   There will be times when you need to edit an existing Fountain fill, one you have just created or one that was created earlier by you or someone else. The easiest way to edit a Fountain fill is first to select the object with the Interactive Fill tool and then to click the Edit button on the far left of the Property Bar. This will display the Fountain Fill dialog box, shown in Figure 9-7. The dialog box on the right displays the custom configuration of the Fountain Fill dialog box. You can also display this box by selecting the object with the Pick tool and then clicking the Fill flyout. With the flyout displayed, click the Fountain Fill button.

FIGURE 9-6   Placing duplicate images together to form a pattern

9

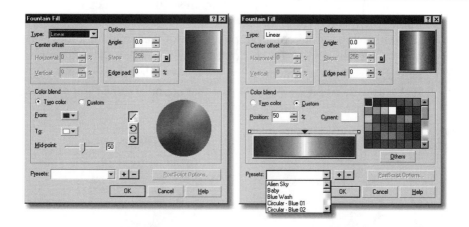

FIGURE 9-7   The Fountain Fill dialog box, displayed in both default and custom
configurations

The Fountain Fill dialog box lets you manually change all the attributes that can be applied to a Fountain fill. These attributes are described in the following list, beginning at the upper left of the dialog box.

- ■ *Fill Type*   Click the down arrow to choose from the four Fountain fill types.

- ■ *Center Offset*   These controls are active when all but the Linear fill are selected. Entering numbers in the num boxes will change the horizontal and vertical positioning of the center on Radial, Conical, and Square fills.

- ■ *Angle Num Box*   Entering numbers here will affect the directional angle of all but Radial fills. This takes the place of doing it interactively.

- ■ *Steps*   The Steps box defaults to 256 steps. This is the maximum number of steps allowable in a Fountain fill. If you wish to use a smaller number of steps, click the adjacent Lock button to enable the num box, and then enter your new number.

- ■ *Edge Pad*   The Edge Pad setting controls how long the first fill color and the last fill color in a Fountain fill remain solid before they begin blending into the next color. It can be used effectively on a circle filled with a Radial fill to maintain a solid color on the outside of the circle for a longer period of time, thereby giving the illusion of a darker shadow. The illustration here shows a standard radial-filled circle on the left and one with an Edge Pad setting of 20 on the right. Notice that the one on the right appears more spherical than the one on the left.

NOTE   *Adding an edge pad can be done using the Interactive Fill tool, but you have more control using the dialog. This is because the midpoint usually comes into play when adjusting the edge pad, so being able to set a specific midpoint value in the same dialog box comes in handy.*

■ *Preview Window*   The preview window at the upper left of the dialog box shows the direction of the Fountain fill. You can change the direction of a Linear fill interactively by placing the cursor in the window and dragging in a circular motion. When you click and drag in the window with a Radial, Conical, or Square Fountain fill, you change the position of the center of the fill. If you click and drag while holding down the SHIFT key, you change the angles of the highlights radiating from the center on Conical and Square Fountain fills.

■ *Color Blend*   The Color Blend section shows two radio buttons, Two Color and Custom. The default is Two Color. Below these radio buttons are the From and To color buttons, which, when you click them, reveal color palettes. It is from these color palettes that you choose the first and last colors of a two-color Fountain fill.

■ *Midpoint Slider*   The Midpoint slider control is beneath the color buttons. It functions in the same way described in step 3 of the section "Creating Linear Fountain Fills," earlier in this chapter. As you may remember, the position of the slider controls the point at which the two colors in the Fountain fill meet. This point represents the average of the two colors.

■ *Color Direction*   In the center of the Color Blend section of the Fountain Fill dialog box are three buttons. These buttons control the direction in which the two colors in the Fountain fill blend. The button at the top is the Straight Line blend. For example, if we blend red to blue, the Fountain fill will be composed of solid red, solid blue, and shades of red and blue. The second button is a rotation button. It directs the Fountain fill in a counterclockwise direction, using the color wheel at the right of the buttons. Using the same example, the colors contained in the Fountain fill would be solid red, solid blue, and shades of orange, yellow, and green because those are the colors the blending Fountain fill would pass through on the color wheel. A dark line is displayed on the color wheel, indicating the path of the Fountain fill when a rotation button is used. The last button is the clockwise button. Using the same colors as in the example, the blended colors of the Fountain fill would be solid red, solid blue, and shades of blue, purple, and pink.

■ *Presets*   The Presets list box at the bottom of the Fountain Fill dialog box contains many custom preset Fountain fills. To use one of these fills, click the down arrow, and select a custom fill from the drop-down list. The list box is empty by default so that if you have created a special Fountain fill

9

you can enter a custom name of your own and save it along with the other custom fills. Custom fills will be discussed later in this section.

■ *Custom*   When you click the Custom radio button in the Fountain Fill dialog box, the dialog box display changes to the configuration shown on the right in Figure 9-7. It is in this dialog box that you can create a Fountain fill containing more than two colors.

When you create custom fills interactively, you drag colors from the palette onto the dotted line of the interactive fill; here, you manually place markers on the color bar at the lower left of the Fountain Fill dialog box. Follow these steps to create a custom Fountain fill by adding colors to the color bar:

1. Draw a rectangle on the page.

2. Click the Fill tool in the toolbox to reveal the Fill flyout, and then click the Fountain Fill button (the second from the left).

3. When the Fountain Fill dialog box appears, click the Custom radio button. The dialog box should look like the one on the right in Figure 9-7.

4. Place the cursor on the color bar at the bottom of the dialog box, and double-click. When you double-click, a marker will be placed above the bar at the point you double-clicked. The position num box just above the color bar will indicate the marker's position by showing a percentage from 0 to 90. For example, if you want a new marker positioned along the bar at 20 percent, but when you double-clicked the marker was added at 34 percent, you could click the down arrow in the num box to move the marker to the desired 20 percent position. In the example shown in Figure 9-7, the added color was placed at the 50 percent position. You can add up to 99 new markers on the color bar. Each time you add a marker, you select the color for the desired position from the palette on the right of the color bar. The colors in the palette are the same as those in the currently used palette at the right of the CorelDRAW window. If you click the Others button, you can choose colors from other palettes or create custom colors. (For information on changing palettes, see Chapter 8.) If you would like to save your custom fill, give your fill a name by typing it in the empty Presets list box. With the name entered, click the plus (+) button next to the list box. Your new custom Fountain fill will be added, in alphabetical order, to the list of Presets.

TIP *The first and last colors of a custom Fountain fill are represented by the black and white squares at each end of the color bar. To change their colors, click one of the squares, and then click the Current color button above and to the right of the color bar. A palette will drop down, offering you the same choice of colors as the larger palette on the right of the dialog box.*

To end this section on Fountain fills, here is an image of a rose created by coauthor Peter McCormick using Fountain fills on both the petals and leaves.

9

Filling Objects with Pattern Fills Using the Interactive Fill Tool

Three types of Pattern fills are available on the Property Bar: Two-Color Bitmap Pattern Fill, Full-Color Pattern fill, and Bitmap Pattern fill, in that order. Pattern fills are useful when creating backgrounds that tile seamlessly or when creating realism, as in the case of the Bitmap fills. Each default fill is comprised of a relatively small square image that will tile seamlessly when applied. These image tiles can then be interactive resized and rotated to create completely different results from the original image.

The first Pattern fill is the Two-Color Bitmap fill. This fill lets you pick any two colors for the foreground and background colors for a variety patterns found on the First Fill Picker drop-down list shown beneath the Property Bar in Figure 9-8.

USING THE TWO-COLOR PATTERN FILLS Practice using the Two-Color Pattern fill by following these steps:

1. Open the practice file /Chap09/Bricks.cdr from the CD that comes with this book, or simply draw a rectangle on the page.

Two-Color Bitmap

Full-Color

Bitmap

First Fill Picker

Front Color

Edit button   Back Color   Transform Fill with Objects

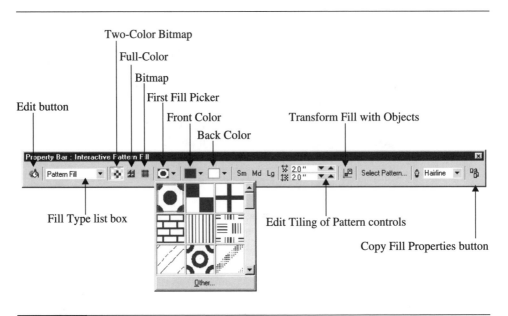

Fill Type list box   Edit Tiling of Pattern controls

Copy Fill Properties button

FIGURE 9-8   The Two-Color Pattern Fill Property Bar with the drop-down list

2. Select the object and choose the Interactive Fill tool from the toolbox, and select Pattern Fill from the Fill Type list box on the Property Bar.

3. Click on the Two-Color Bitmap Pattern button on the Property Bar.

4. Click on the First Fill Picker drop-down arrow on the Property Bar, and select the brick pattern from the pattern list box.

5. When the pattern fills the object, click the front color button on the Property Bar, and choose the color white from the drop-down palette.

6. Click the back color button, and choose the color red from the drop-down palette.

7. If you used the practice file, your object should now look like the one shown in Figure 9-9, displaying a red brick fill with white mortar joints.

TIP   You can drag a color from the onscreen color palette, and drop it on the either of the two square handles to change both the foreground and background colors instead of picking colors from the front and back color palettes on the Property Bar.

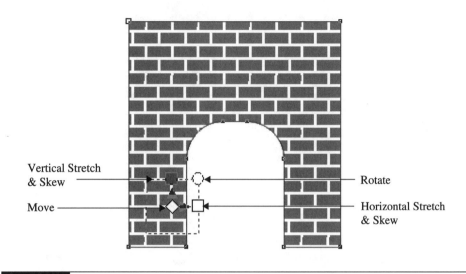

Vertical Stretch & Skew

Move

Rotate

Horizontal Stretch & Skew

FIGURE 9-9 Using a Two-Color Pattern fill to emulate a brick wall

9

Now it's time to learn how to interactively edit your new Pattern fill, using the Interactive Fill tool.

Follow these steps to interactively change the look of the default two-color Pattern fill:

1. With the Interactive Fill tool selected, select the object you just filled.

2. A dotted bounding box will be placed at the lower left of the fill. Click the diamond-shaped box in the center to move the bounding box. Click the top-center or middle-right handles to stretch or skew the bounding box. Click the circle handle to rotate the bounding box.

3. Practice moving the handles in various positions until you get the feel of interactively changing the pattern.

The next illustration shows two variations of the default Pattern fill that were accomplished by using the Interactive Fill tool.

TIP   *Holding down the CTRL key while rotating or skewing will constrain the angle to the default 15 degrees. Holding down the ALT key will allow rotations while locking the pattern size.*

USING THE TWO-COLOR PATTERN FILL DIALOG BOX   You have just learned that using the Interactive Fill tool lets you create some unusual two-color pattern variations. However, there will be times when you need to create a specific pattern. This is accomplished by clicking the Edit button on the Property Bar when an object with a Pattern fill is selected with the Interactive Fill tool. This action will display the Pattern Fill dialog box, shown in Figure 9-10.

NOTE   *When you're asked to click a specific area on the Property Bar, refer to the labels in Figure 9-8.*

Practice editing a file using this dialog box by completing the following steps:

1. Draw a rectangle, 2 inches square, on the page.

2. Click the Interactive Fill tool in the toolbox.

3. Click the down arrow on the Fill Type list box on the Property Bar, and choose Pattern (it will default to the Two-Color Pattern fill).

4. Click the First Fill Picker drop-down arrow, and choose the pattern of concentric squares shown in Figure 9-10.

5. Click the Edit button on the Property Bar to display the Pattern Fill dialog box.

6. Change the Width and Height settings to 0.5 inch in the Size section of the dialog box.

7. Look in the lower right of the dialog box for the Row or Column Offset section. Click the up arrow in the % of Tile Side num box until you reach the number *50*. Leave the radio button with the default setting of Row enabled.

8. Click the OK button to see the results on the right of the illustration shown here. The image on the left is the default fill, with the default two inch square Pattern fill. The image on the right contains smaller squares, based on the lower settings entered, and the squares are offset 50 percent, displaying the modified pattern.

TIP *When you enable the Transform Fill with Object button on the Property Bar, the tiling pattern will be stretched or reduced proportionately when you scale the pattern-filled object using a corner selection handle.*

NOTE *The Edit Tiling of Pattern controls on the Property Bar are used to stretch the pattern horizontally or vertically, not to offset the rows or columns.*

USING THE FULL COLOR PATTERN FILLS   You apply the Full-Color Pattern fills to objects in exactly the same way as the Two-Color fills, using the Interactive Fill tool and the Property Bar, with one exception. There are no Front and Back color drop-down color palettes on the Property Bar, because Full-Color Pattern fills are vector patterns that use more than two colors (see Chapter 31 on how to create vector patterns). Figure 9-11 shows the Pattern Fill dialog box when a Full-Color fill is selected. Figure 9-12 shows a Full-Color Pattern fill with basic Full-Color Pattern fill in the upper left and three variations created with the Interactive Fill tool.

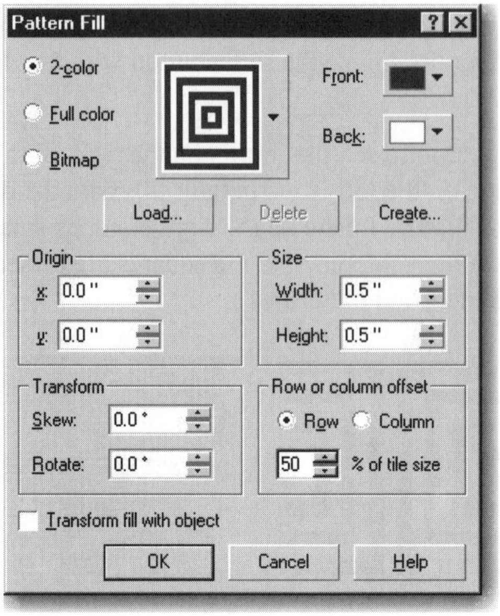

FIGURE 9-10 The Pattern Fill dialog box with 2-color Pattern fill selected

TIP *When scaling any of the Pattern fills, you might want to try choosing one of the preset buttons on the Property Bar. They are Sm, Md, and Lg. Selecting one of the presets will avoid any accidental skewing of the pattern when you're scaling. If the presets don't size your pattern to your liking, then you will have to either use the interactive method or make your size changes in the Pattern Fill dialog box. Click the Edit button on the Property Bar to access the dialog box shown in Figure 9-10.*

USING THE BITMAP PATTERN FILLS The Bitmap Pattern fills are used in the same way as Full-Color Pattern fills. For a little extra practice, complete the following steps to fill an object with a bitmap pattern:

1. Draw a rectangle on the page.

2. With the rectangle selected, click the Interactive Fill tool.

3. Select Pattern from the Fill Type list box on the Property Bar.

4. Click the Bitmap button on the Property Bar.

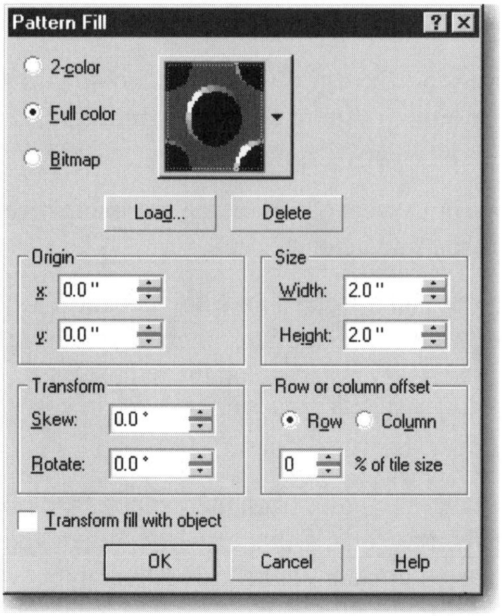

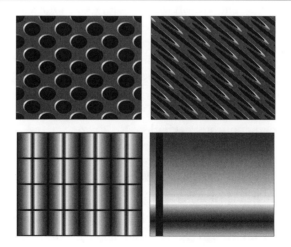

FIGURE 9-11 The Pattern Fill dialog box with a Full-Color Pattern fill selected

FIGURE 9-12 The original and three modified Full-Color Pattern fills

5. Click on the First Fill Picker button next to the Bitmap button on the Property Bar.

6. Click on the gold foil Bitmap fill from the drop-down palette. It gets easier each time. Your bitmap pattern should be similar to the one shown on the left in Figure 9-13.

7. Now rotate, size, and skew the fill using the Interactive Fill tool so that it looks similar to the middle object in Figure 9-13.

8. Open the Symbols and Special Character Docker (CTRL-F11), and choose the music category. Choose the Saxophone clipart symbol shown on the left in Figure 9-13, and drag it out on the page. (If you didn't install the symbols when you installed CorelDRAW 9, you will have to run the Install program and install them.)

9. Select the Interactive Fill tool from the toolbox, and click on the Copy Fill Properties From button on the Property Bar. When your cursor changes to a black arrow, use it to click on the gold-filled object you created earlier in step 6. The saxophone will now be filled with your modified Bitmap fill.

USING THE TRANSFORM FILL WITH OBJECT CONTROL   Figure 9-14 shows another bitmap pattern filling a rectangle. The larger rectangle on the left was filled using the Interactive Fill tool. Two duplicates of the rectangle were made and placed to the right of the original. The Transform Fill with Object button on the Property Bar was enabled, and the first duplicate was made smaller by dragging a corner selection handle inward. Notice that the pattern in the first duplicate (the center rectangle) was also scaled down proportionately. Nine droplets were in the original, and nine in the scaled down version. The Transform Fill with Object button was disabled when the third rectangle on the right was scaled down. The results are obvious: the droplets did not shrink in size and thereby allowed fewer droplets in the second duplicate rectangle.

Filling Objects with Texture Fills Using the Interactive Fill Tool

Texture fills are a special kind of bitmap know as *fractal images*. There are more than 100 default Texture fills to choose from, and each of these fills can be modified to look completely different from its default appearance. The number of variations that can be assigned to each texture can reach into the millions.

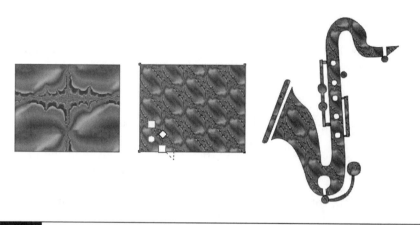

| FIGURE 9-13 | The original and modified Bitmap fill used to fill a musical clipart symbol |

9

Few CorelDRAW users take advantage of these truly unique fills. A common complaint is that Texture fills are jagged when printed. The jagged appearance is caused when the resolution and tile values are not set high enough. Read on, and you will get good results.

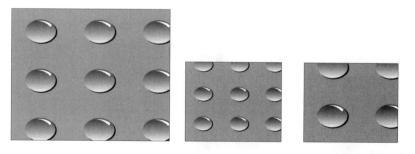

Original Full-Color
Pattern fill

Object size reduced with
the Transform Fill with
Objects button enabled

Object size reduced without
the Transform Fill with
Objects button enabled

| FIGURE 9-14 | Resizing objects filled with Bitmap Pattern fills using the Transform Fill with Object option |

To fill an object with a Texture fill using the Interactive Fill tool, follow these steps:

1. Click the Ellipse tool in the toolbox, and draw a circle on the page.

2. Select the Interactive Fill tool, and click the Fill Type list box on the Property Bar. Select Texture Fill from the drop-down list. Your ellipse will be filled with the default Texture fill Blue Lava. If your texture fill is different, don't worry; it's not important which fill appears first.

3. Click the down arrow on the Texture Library list box, and choose the Styles library.

4. Click the down arrow on the First Fill Picker button, shown in Figure 9-15, to display more of the Texture fills available in the library.

5. Click the thumbnail that looks like drapes located in the lower left of the first display. Your ellipse will now be filled with the Drapes texture, shown in Figure 9-15. Notice that the interactive controls are now available.

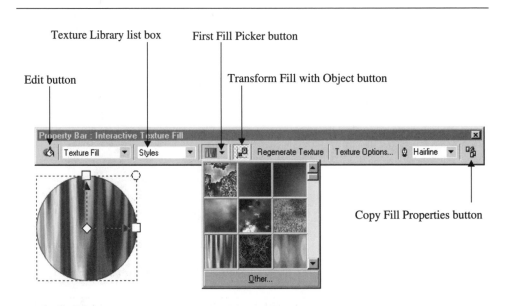

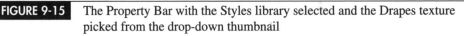

FIGURE 9-15   The Property Bar with the Styles library selected and the Drapes texture picked from the drop-down thumbnail

6. Click and drag with the square handles to stretch the fill horizontally and shrink the fill vertically. Then click the circle handle and rotate the fill. Your Texture fill should now look similar to the one shown here:

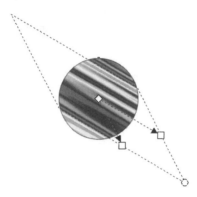

7. Click the Edit button on the Property Bar to display the Texture Fill dialog box shown in Figure 9-16. At the top left of the dialog box is the Texture Library list box. The same libraries are available that are provided in the Texture Library list box on the Property Bar. The Styles library contains original texture styles; the Samples libraries contain variations on the original styles.

8. Click the down arrow in the Texture Library list box, and choose the Samples 8 library. Directly below the Texture Library box is the Texture list box, containing the names of the individual textures within each library. To select a texture, scroll in the list box. When you click a name, a preview of the texture is displayed in the preview window. When you are satisfied with the texture, click OK. If you're following along, choose the texture Glacier.

The dialog box contains a number of parameter selection boxes that enable you to change various attributes of the selected texture. Each texture contains one common parameter box, called "Texture #." This box shows the identification number of the displayed texture. In it, you can scroll to or type any number from 1 to 32,767. Each change of the texture number will change the look of the texture to some degree. To see the effect of the changes made in the parameter boxes, you must click the Preview button.

9

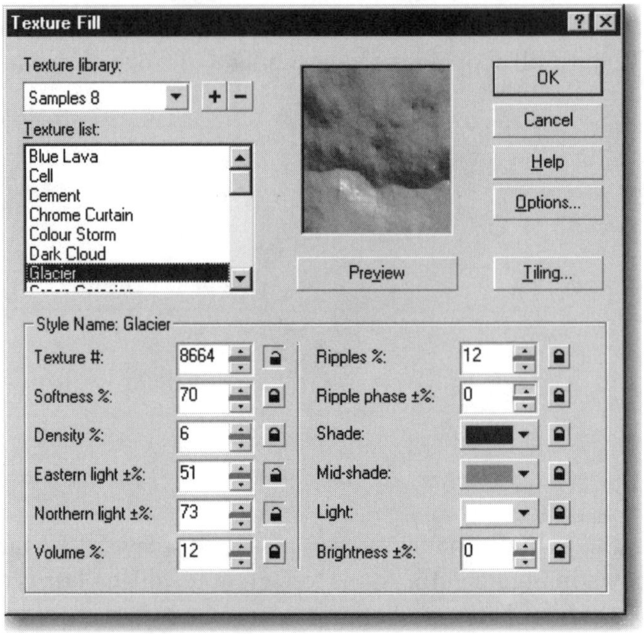

The Texture Fill dialog box, showing:

Texture library: Samples 8

Texture list:
Blue Lava
Cell
Cement
Chrome Curtain
Colour Storm
Dark Cloud
Glacier

Buttons: OK, Cancel, Help, Options..., Preview, Tiling...

Style Name: Glacier

Parameter	Value	Parameter	Value
Texture #:	8664	Ripples %:	12
Softness %:	70	Ripple phase ±%:	0
Density %:	6	Shade:	
Eastern light ±%:	51	Mid-shade:	
Northern light ±%:	73	Light:	
Volume %:	12	Brightness ±%:	0

FIGURE 9-16   The Texture Fill dialog box with the Glacier texture selected from the Samples 8 library

NOTE   *As with the other fills previously described, you can tile Texture fills in rows and columns by clicking on the Tiling button. See the section "Using the Two-Color Pattern Fill Dialog Box," earlier in this chapter.*

Practice making different Texture fills by changing the numbers in the various parameter boxes. Try changing the softness and density settings and then the brightness settings.

Notice the small lock buttons next to each parameter box. By default, most all but the Texture # parameter are locked. They default to the locked mode so that when you click the Preview button beneath the preview window without making any changes in the parameter boxes, the texture number will change in a random order. This behavior is helpful when you want to see other variations of a texture without manually typing a new number every time. Simply keep clicking the Preview button, and the numbers will change. If you click any of the lock buttons, you will unlock them. The next time you click the Preview button without making any changes, all the unlocked buttons and their respective settings will randomly change along with the texture number. A reverse variation on this method is to lock the texture number and unlock all the other parameters. This keeps the texture number the same but randomly changes all the other parameters.

 TIP *The Regenerate button of the Property Bar acts like the Preview button in the Texture Fill dialog box if no attribute changes have been made to the existing texture. This means that each time you click the Regenerate Texture button, the texture will randomly change.*

When you edit a particular texture and want to save it for future use, click the + button next to the texture library name. This will bring up the Save Texture As dialog box, where you can give your new texture a name and then save it in one of the Samples libraries or overwrite the library name to create a custom library of your own.

To delete a texture, simply select the texture, and click the minus (–) button next to the library name.

 CAUTION *You cannot save an edited texture in the Styles library.*

Clicking the Options button in the Texture Fill dialog box, or on the Property Bar, brings up the Texture Options dialog box, shown here. This dialog box allows you to set the resolution and maximum tile size of the Texture fill. The settings you make here are the key to creating Texture fills without jaggies.

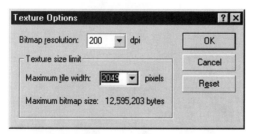

The following are options in the Texture Options dialog box:

- *Bitmap Resolution* The default setting is 120 dpi. Change the number for the resolution to twice the line screen of your final output device. For example, a common line screen used for outputting to a high-resolution image setter is 133 lpi. Therefore, in this case, you would set the resolution to 266.

■ *Maximum Tile Width*   This setting is as important as the resolution setting. The number you use is based on the size of the object you are filling. Use the following formula:

longest dimension of object (LDO) x lines per inch (LPI) = tile size.

When you have determined the tile size, type the value in the drop-down list box.

Suppose you are outputting an image measuring 3 x 5 inches with a 133-line screen. Using the preceding formula, the correct number to type in the Bitmap Resolution box is **266** (133 x 2). Then you multiply 5 (the longest dimension of the object) by 266 (the resolution), which gives you 1,330. Therefore, you type **1,330** in the Maximum Tile Width drop-down list box.

Coauthor Peter McCormick created the little scene in Figure 9-17 using the Texture fill Blue Lava for the water.

Creating Interactive PostScript Texture Fills

The last of the family of special fills are the Postscript fills. Postscript fills are another form of Pattern fills that use the PostScript page description language. To

FIGURE 9-17   Using the "Blue Lava" Texture fill to emulate water

put it simply, they are intricate vector fills that, when used to fill an object, will tile seamlessly.

To fill an object with a PostScript fill using the Interactive Fill tool, follow these steps:

1. Click the Ellipse tool in the toolbox, and draw a ellipse on the page.

2. Select the Interactive Fill tool, and click the Fill Type list box on the Property Bar. Select PostScript from the drop-down list. Your rectangle will be filled with the default fill called "Archimedes."

 NOTE *The view quality setting in the View menu defaults to Enhanced view. If you have changed the default to Normal view, a PostScript-filled object will display a series of PSs instead of the actual fill. The reason for this display mode in Normal view is that it can speed up redrawing the screen display. A sample of an image displaying a PostScript fill in Normal view is shown here:*

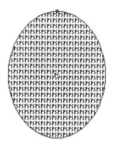

3. Click on the drop-down arrow in the PostScript Fill Textures list box, and choose the Color Circles fill from the list. The new fill will be updated automatically and will look like the one in Figure 9-18. As you can see from the list of fills in the drop-down list, quite a few PostScript fills are available.

 NOTE *PostScript fills in versions earlier than version 7 required a PostScript printer. They can now be printed on any printer that CorelDRAW supports. CorelDRAW 9 converts the PostScript fills to bitmaps for use in non-PostScript printers.*

Edit button   Postscript Fill Texture list box

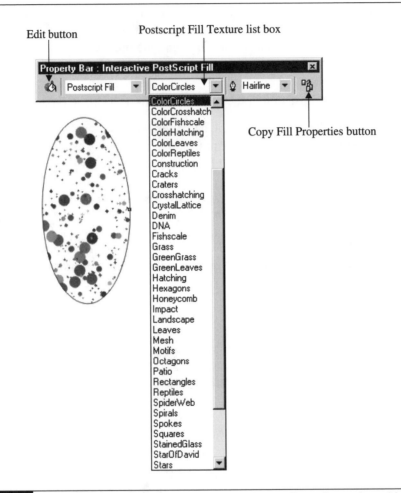

Copy Fill Properties button

FIGURE 9-18   The Property Bar displaying the PostScript configuration and an object
filled with the Color Circles PostScript fill

Clicking the Edit button brings up the PostScript Texture dialog box, shown
in Figure 9-19. Scroll through the list to quickly view the entire list of PostScript
fills. If you want to see what a PostScript fill looks like, click the Preview
Fill button in the dialog box. There are also various parameter settings you can
experiment with to vary the look of the PostScript texture. Use the Refresh
button under the preview window to see the results of any changes made in the
parameter boxes.

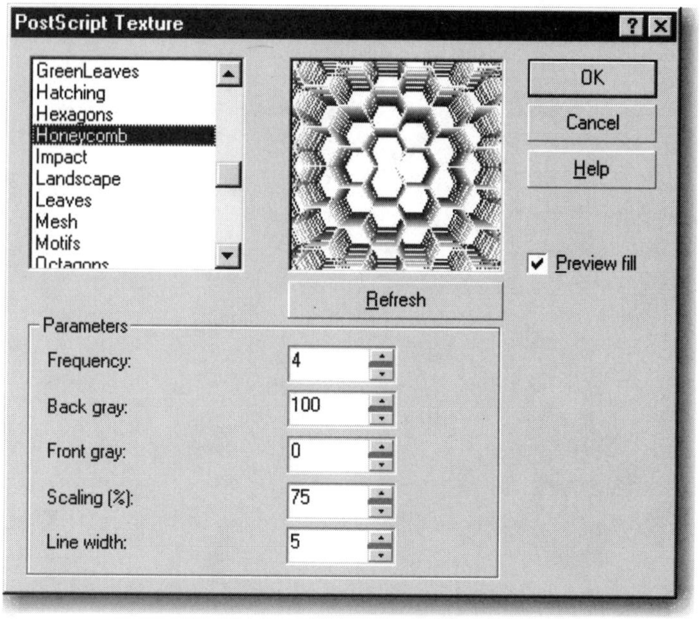

FIGURE 9-19   The Postscript Texture dialog box

Figure 9-20 shows several PostScript texture fills. These fills have been named so that you can locate them in the drop-down list if you wish to use them in your projects.

Using the Special Fill Dialog Box in Place of the Interactive Fill Tool

This entire chapter has been devoted to teaching you how to use the Interactive Fill tool together with the options on the Property Bar. Only when it was necessary did we discuss any extra options that might have been available in that particular fill's dialog box. Even though we strongly recommend you use the interactive method, everything you learned about special fills can be replicated in each special fill's corresponding dialog box. If you are a numbers person, you may find this method easier. To access any of the special fills dialog boxes, click and hold on the Fill tool in the Toolbox, and choose the button for the fill type from the Fill flyout (refer back to Figure 9-1 at the beginning of the chapter).

Honeycomb   SpiderWeb

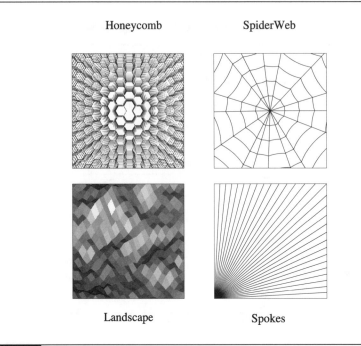

Landscape   Spokes

FIGURE 9-20   Four different PostScript Texture fills

The Interactive Mesh Fill Tool

We have saved the newest special fill for last. It's in a category of its own; it's the Interactive Mesh Fill tool. This unique tool lets you interactively fill objects with colors that blend together as you add them. The tool is accessed from the Interactive Fill tool flyout on the toolbox shown in Figure 9-21.

Also shown in the figure is the Property Bar displaying the options available when using the Mesh Fill tool. Each of the options are listed here:

- ■ *Grid size controls*   Use the up and down arrows to add or reduce the number of horizontal and vertical grid lines.

- ■ *Add intersection*   Left-clicking inside a section of the grid places a indicator mark on the Mesh fill. With the indicator mark placed, click the Add Intersection button. This action will add a new intersecting point that adds a set of both horizontally and vertically intersecting lines to the grid. Double-clicking on the indicator mark performs the same function as clicking the Add Intersection button.

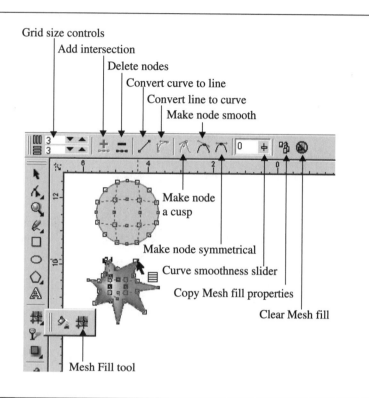

Grid size controls
Add intersection
Delete nodes
Convert curve to line
Convert line to curve
Make node smooth

Make node
a cusp

Make node symmetrical

Curve smoothness slider

Copy Mesh fill properties

Clear Mesh fill

9

Mesh Fill tool

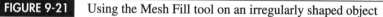

FIGURE 9-21   Using the Mesh Fill tool on an irregularly shaped object

- *Delete nodes*   When you select a node on the grid with the Mesh Fill tool, you can either click the Delete Nodes button on the Property Bar or double-click on the node to delete the node. If you place an indicator mark inside a grid section by left-clicking, you can delete an entire section either by clicking the Delete Nodes button or by double-clicking on the indicator marker.

- *Convert curve to line*   Clicking this button when a node is selected converts a curve node to a line node. This button and the next five buttons on the Property Bar all control node attributes. They function the same as the node attribute buttons found on the Property Bar when a curve object is selected with the Shape tool. For more on changing node attributes, see Chapter 7.

■ *Convert line to curve*   See preceding explanation on converting curve to line.

■ *Make node a cusp*   See preceding explanation on converting curve to line.

■ *Make node smooth*   See preceding explanation on converting curve to line.

■ *Make node symmetrical*   See preceding explanation on converting curve to line.

■ *Curve smoothness slider*   This control lets you reduce the number of nodes between intersecting points.

■ *Copy Properties*   Use this button to copy the Mesh fill of one object to another. You must have Mesh fills in both objects before you can copy from either of them.

■ *Clear mesh fill*   Use this command to remove the Mesh fill from the object.

Below the Property Bar in Figure 19-21 is an ellipse that has been selected with the Mesh Fill tool before any additional colors have been added. Below the ellipse is an irregularly shaped object that has had colors added to it and is being modified with the Mesh Fill tool.

Using the Interactive Mesh Fill Tool

When you select an object with the Mesh Fill tool, a grid of three horizontal sections and three vertical sections is created. This grid is displayed with dotted red lines. You can fill the object with color using either of two methods.

To use the first method, follow these steps:

1. Select the Mesh Fill tool, and left-click in a grid section to place an indicator mark. This action places selection handles around the marked section.

2. Left-click on a color of choice in the Color palette. The selected section will be filled with the selected color.

3. Select the Mesh Fill tool, and select a node at one of the intersections.

4. With the node selected, left-click on a color of choice in the color palette. The color you selected will be added to the fill and will radiate out from that point.

The second method lets you add the colors interactively by dragging them out from the Color palette. Follow these steps to practice using the Mesh Fill tool to create a shaded ball:

1. Draw an ellipse on the page, and fill it with cyan from the Color palette (it is not necessary to begin with a filled object).

2. With the ellipse selected, select the Mesh Fill tool from the Interactive Fill Tool flyout.

3. Click the color blue from the Color palette, drag it out onto the page, and drop it on the lower-middle section of the grid. This should begin to give the illusion of a shadow on a ball.

4. Continue dragging colors of blue and dropping them on either individual grid sections or nodes (you can drop color on the nodes on the perimeter of the ellipse as well).

5. At some point, drop the color white on the node at the upper-left intersecting nodes to place a highlight on the ball (you can move the nodes and the lines between the node as you are completing your shaded ball).

If you got as lucky as we did, you ended up with a ball like the one shown next. (We added a drop shadow for more realism. See Chapter 19 to learn how to create drop shadows.) The reason we say "lucky" is because using the Mesh Fill tool is not an exact science. You will experience many happy accidents while using this tool. It is for this reason that we won't have you complete any more exercises, but instead we encourage you to experiment on your own with this fascinating tool.

9

The following images were created using the Interactive Mesh Fill tool. Wayne Kaplan of Huntington Beach, California, created the apple shown here:

Debbie Cook of Valrico, Florida, created the burning match shown here. Not only the flames were created with the Mesh Fill tool, but the burned end of the match as well was created with the tool.

Coauthor Peter McCormick created the seascape shown on the next page using the Mesh Fill tool on the waves and water. The blending capabilities of the tool worked great when creating the eye of the main wave. Texture fills were used for the rocks and sky.

A Final Note

You have reached the end of a very long chapter. The most important part of this chapter for you to understand, if the Interactive Fill tools are new to you, is that the interactive method makes filling objects easy and intuitive. No more do you have to open a dialog box when you want to add a special fill to an object. And if that fill should need some adjusting, nine out of ten times you can do that by choosing options from the ever-present Property Bar. We recommend that you master the use of this tool so the only time you will need to use the dialog boxes is when it's absolutely necessary.

CHAPTER 10

Outlining Objects

CoreIDRAW 9

The settings you make in the Outline Pen dialog box control the look and style of the lines you draw and any outlines that are attached to objects and text. Outlines and lines can be changed into dotted and dashed lines and can even have arrowheads attached to them. This chapter describes how to set attributes with the Outline tool.

Methods of Setting Outline Attributes

As with the Fill tool, there is more than one way to change attributes with the Outline tool, and the same advice applies to keeping your sanity: choose one or two main methods for changing outline attributes, and use the others only when you need to. We recommend using the Property Bar to change outline attributes on ordinary lines and the Outline Pen dialog box when working with outlines applied to objects. We describe both methods in detail.

The Outline flyout shown here is accessed by clicking on the Outline tool on the Toolbox at the left of the screen. Here you can access the Outline Pen dialog box and the Outline Color dialog box. You can also quickly select a line width from six preset line widths.

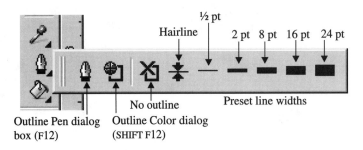

Setting the Outline Defaults

Before we get into the various outline settings available in the Outline dialog box and on the Property Bar, you should know how to set the default values for the outline width and color in case they are accidentally changed. If the defaults are accidentally changed, you could find yourself scratching your head at the unusual results on your screen.

Most users prefer not to use outlines when they enter text or import Paragraph Text because if the outline width is set too large, a black blob that looks something like this may be the result:

SETTING THE
OUTLINE DEFAULT
TOO WIDE

Worst of all, if the outline width is set too large and the default color is changed to white, the text on the page will not be visible.

By default, outlines for objects are set to a hairline width, with the color black and are not applied to Artistic Text or Paragraph Text. You should retain these default settings.

Setting Outline Defaults for Objects

Practice setting the outline defaults by following these steps:

1. Make sure no objects on the page are selected (press the ESC key to deselect anything that might be selected). Then click the Outline tool in the toolbox. When the Outline flyout appears, click the Pen icon (the first icon on the left). An Outline message box will appear on screen.

2. In the Outline Pen message box, check the Graphic check box, and leave the Artistic Text and Paragraph Text check boxes unchecked.

3. Click the OK button. The Outline Pen dialog box will appear.

4. In the Width parameter box, enter **0.216**.

5. In the units box, scroll to choose Points. Although the default setting is Points, you may prefer to use inches. If you choose inches, the setting in the Width parameter box will change to .003 inches.

10

6. Click the Color button in the upper-left corner of the dialog box, and choose the black well from the drop-down palette.

7. Click the OK button.

That's all there is to it. You just set the defaults so that when you draw a line or object on the page, it will have a black outline that is 0.216 points or .003 inches wide (depending on whether you chose points or inches).

Setting Outline Defaults for Text

The next step is to set the outline defaults for Artistic Text or Paragraph Text.

1. Make sure no objects on the page are selected (press the ESC key to deselect anything that might be selected), and then click the Outline tool in the toolbox. When the Outline flyout appears, click the No Outline icon on flyout (the third icon on the left). The Outline Pen message box will appear onscreen.

2. In the Outline Pen message box, check the Artistic Text and Paragraph Text check boxes, and leave the Graphic check box unchecked.

3. Click the OK button. The message box will disappear, and you're finished. Now when you type either Artistic or Paragraph Text, it will appear with no outline onscreen.

Using the Property Bar to Change Outline Attributes

When an object is selected, the Property Bar (shown in Figure 10-1), provides easy onscreen access for most of the outline attribute changes you will need to make. It contains most of the settings found in the Outline Pen dialog box discussed later. The one major difference between the Property Bar and the Outline Pen dialog box is that you can use the Property Bar to make outline settings only when you have ordinary lines or curves selected (see the following Note).

NOTE *The Property Bar provides no outline settings when objects such as rectangles, ellipses, and polygons are selected with the Pick tool. The exception to this rule is that when you convert an object to curves, the outline settings will appear on the Property Bar, and you can use them to make changes to the outline on the curve object.*

Figure 10-1 also displays the three drop-down list boxes that are available. These drop-down lists allow you to choose arrowheads, line style, and line widths. In addition to the drop-down list boxes, common settings such as position, size, and scale are also available. Using the settings is straightforward. Simply select the outline or curve, choose the attributes you wish to apply, and the attribute is applied instantly. This is the advantage to making outline changes using the Property Bar—the change is instant.

 NOTE *Arrowheads can only be applied to open path objects.*

10

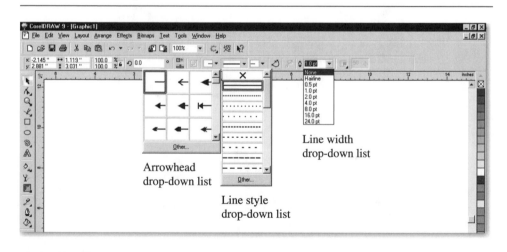

FIGURE 10-1   The Property Bar displaying the various drop-down lists and settings

Using the Outline Pen Dialog Box to Change Attributes

The Outline Pen dialog box, shown in Figure 10-2, contains all the attribute settings that can be applied to an outline. Although you should use the Property Bar for your everyday projects, when you need to choose special settings, the Outline Pen dialog box is the place to go.

The top half of the dialog box contains the settings found on the Property Bar. You already learned about the Color button and the Width and units boxes when you learned how to set the defaults. Editing the line style by selecting the Edit Style button, and choosing the options buttons to edit arrowheads, are covered completely in Chapter 31.

The bottom half of the dialog box contains the additional settings not available on the Pen Property Bar. (The Outline page of the Object Properties Docker also

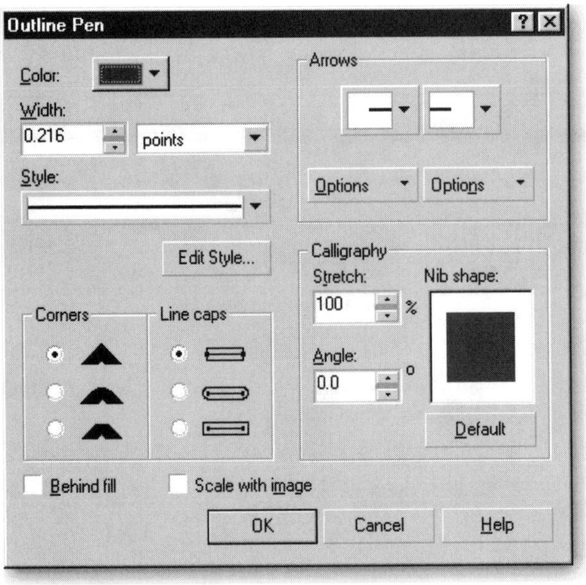

FIGURE 10-2   The Outline Pen dialog box

contains two of these additional settings, Behind Fill and Scale with Image, but for simplicity, stick to the Outline Pen dialog box because it contains all the settings available.) The following sections discuss these additional settings.

Corners

There are three corner attribute settings:

- ■ *Square corners*   This is the default setting and the most often used because it provides a look that fits most shapes.

- ■ *Rounded corners*   This setting can be used when you want a smoother look to lines that bend.

- ■ *Beveled corners*   This setting can be used when you want a more symmetrical look to your lines.

The rectangles shown here are examples of each type of corner setting applied to a single line:

Square corners   Rounded corners   Beveled corners

Line Caps

There are three line cap settings. The line cap settings determine how far the end of a line extends beyond the termination point of the line. Examples of the three different line cap styles are shown here: square, rounded, and extended square.

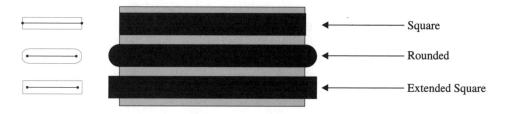

Square

Rounded

Extended Square

Behind Fill

Use the Behind Fill option when you want to apply an outline to a stylized font such as a script font. Normally, outlines are applied after the fill is applied. Half of the outline lies inside the object, and the other half lies outside the object. When you enable the Behind Fill check box, the outline is drawn first, and the fill is then placed on top of the outline. This method results in half of the outline being covered by the fill.

A good example of the use of the Behind Fill option is shown below. The font EnglischeSchT was used. The word "Chapel" on the left used a 3-point outline without the Behind Fill option checked. The word "Chapel" on the right used a 6-point outline with the Behind Fill option checked. You can see the obvious difference between the two examples. When the Behind Fill option was applied to the letters on the right, an outline width was used that is twice as wide as the one on the left, yet the quality is better. This is because the outline is behind the fill, thereby preserving the quality of the font.

Scale with Image

The Scale with Image option scales the size of the outline when you resize an object with an outline using any of the corner selection handles. This can be an important feature. For example, if an object has a 4-point outline and you later decide to reduce the size of the object by selecting a corner selection handle, you will probably want to reduce the outline width in proportion to the new size of the object. This will happen automatically if you place a check mark in the Scale with Image box. However, if you resize an object with any of the four middle selection handles, the outline will be distorted.

The following examples show the difference when the word "Chapel" and the outline on the rectangle behind it is reduced with and without the Scale with Image check box enabled. The top row displays the original word and rectangles. The word "Chapel" and the rectangle in the second row of the left column were scaled down by using a corner selection handle with the Scale with Image option checked. The word and rectangle in the second row of the right column were also scaled down, but without the Scale with Image option checked. Notice the outline on the word and smaller rectangle in the left column has been reduced proportionally. The outline on the word and smaller rectangle in the right column did not change in size and is out of proportion. In the case of the word "Chapel," the outline is overpowering the font much as it did when the Behind Fill option was not checked in the previous example.

The word and rectangle in the left column in the third row was scaled down using the top middle selection handle. Notice that the top and bottom outlines were scaled proportionally, but the outlines on the sides stayed the same. The word and rectangle in the right column in the third row was scaled down using the top middle selection handle as well, but because Scale with Image was not checked, all four sides, again, stayed the same.

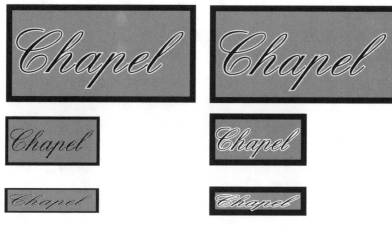

Left column, Scale with Image on   Right column, Scale with Image off

 CAUTION   *The Scale With image check box is not enabled by default. This could cause problems if you add outlines to objects and then stretch the objects proportionately.*

Calligraphy

The Calligraphy section of the Outline Pen dialog box provides settings to change the rectangular shape and angle of a line. You change the settings in the Stretch and Angle Num boxes. To the right of these boxes is a preview window that shows the size and angle of the line based on the settings in the Num boxes. The calligraphy examples shown here used point sizes of 16 and 8 and settings of 10 in the Stretch box and 45.0 degrees in the angle box.

You can interactively rotate the nib angle by placing the cursor inside the Nib shape preview box and dragging. The follwing illustration shows some examples of adjusting the Nib angle and Stretch amount on various objects. Figure 10-3 shows the Outline Pen dialog box with the Nib angle being changed interactively.

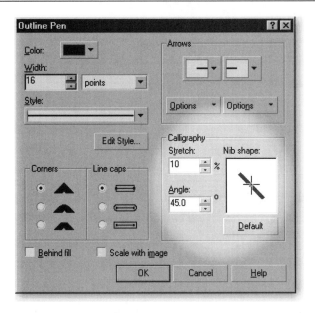

FIGURE 10-3   Interactively changing the Nib angle

Removing Outlines

There are a number of ways to remove an outline, but the three most basic methods are by using the outline flyout, the Property Bar, and by clicking on the No fill/No Outline swatch on the on screen color palette and choosing None from the Outline width drop-down list on the Property bar. The three methods are straightforward.

■ Click the No Outline button on the Outline flyout shown here:

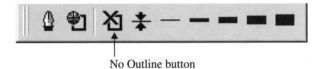

No Outline button

■ Right click the No fill/No outline swatch at the top of the Color palette shown here

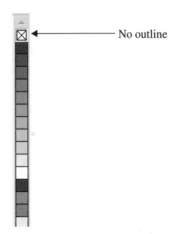

No outline

■ Click the Outline Width drop-down list on the Property Bar and choose None (refer back to Figure 10-1) to remove the outlines from open path objects. This last method's only practical purpose is to remove the outline from open paths. Interestingly enough, if you close an open path using the Auto-Close button on the Property Bar or manually close an open path using the Shape tool and clicking the Join Two Nodes button on the Property Bar, the None Outline option is also available.

As you have just seen, there's more to outlines than you might have thought. The most important lesson you can take away from this chapter is knowing how to set the default outline settings. With the default settings in place, you can now proceed without having to change the outline attributes on everything you draw.

Coloring Outlines

The quickest way to color an outline is to right-click the color you want on the onscreen color palette (on the right side of the drawing window). Realistically, the palette you use to fill an object is the same palette you use to color the object's outline most of the time. There is an Outline Color dialog box, shown here, which you access from the Outline flyout. Other than the name on the title bar, this dialog box is identical to the Uniform Fill dialog box, which is discussed in Chapter 8. This dialog box is where you can select special colors for lines and outlines, and where you can add a metallic spot color to an outline. To learn the intricacies of this dialog box, refer to Chapter 8.

At the end of this chapter, you will learn that you can convert outlines to objects, which you can then fill with all the special fills covered in Chapter 9.

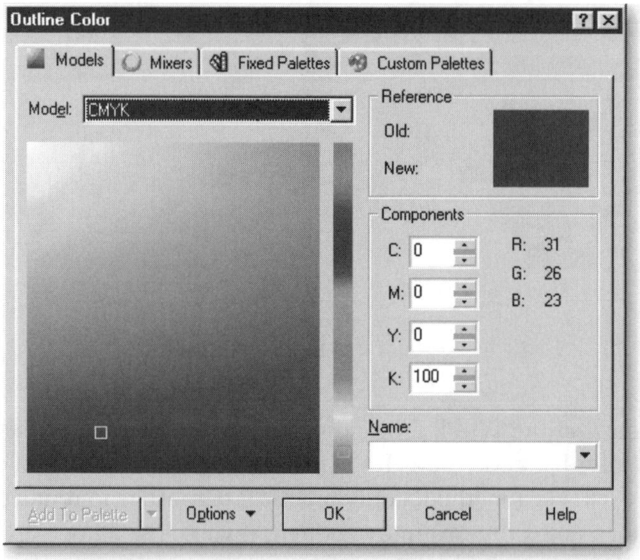

Using Preset Outline Attributes

Preset outline attributes are supplied in the Favorite Outlines folder found in the Scrapbook. You apply these preset attributes by dragging and dropping them onto the objects you want them applied to.

To access these presets, click <u>W</u>indow I Do<u>c</u>kers I <u>S</u>crapbook I Favorite <u>F</u>ills and Outlines. The Docker window will look like the one shown here:

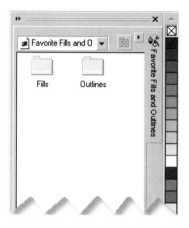

Double-click the Outlines folder in the Docker window. The Docker window will now display three Outlines folders and some basic styles, as shown here, along with four examples of the presets found in the default window.

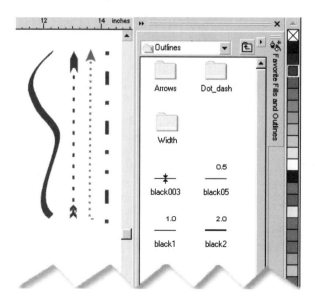

10

Besides the presets in the default Outline folder, there are subfolders containing specific outline attributes. To use any of the presets in the default folder or subfolders, simply select the one you wish to use by dragging it onto the object you wish to apply the outline attributes to. There is a second way to apply a preset outline. Select the object you want to apply the preset to and double-click on the preset in the Docker window. As you can see, there are lots of different outlines attributes to choose from—quite an array to make working in CorelDRAW easier.

Saving Your Own Presets

It's easy to save presets of outline attributes that you have created on your own. To save a custom outline attribute you have created, right-click and drag the object with the outline into the Favorite Fills and Outlines Docker window. When you're inside the window, a pop-up menu shown here will give you a choice of the attributes you wish to save. Using the right-click method gives you only one opportunity to save one of the attributes choices. However, if you left-click and drag the object into the window, the Save a Favorite dialog box appears, letting you pick more than one of the various attributes offered. The pop-up menu and Save a Favorite dialog box are shown here.

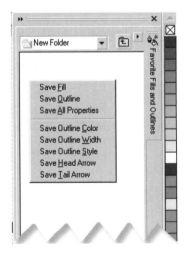

Save a Favorite   ☒

Which properties would you like to save with your favorite?

☑ Fill

☑ Outline color

☑ Outline width

☑ Outline style (dotting and dashing)

☑ Head arrow

☑ Tail arrow

Hint: You can quickly create a Favorite by dragging an object into the
      Scrapbook with the secondary mouse button, and selecting which
      properties to save from the menu which appears.

☑ Show this dialog again

        [OK   ]   [Cancel]   [Help]

After you have saved an outline preset, it will appear in its folder in the
Favorite Fills and Outlines Docker window. You can give your preset a name that
describes its attributes by right-clicking the default name and choosing Rename
from the pop-up menu. This action will highlight the preset name allowing you to
type in your own words.

As you have just seen, there is more to outlines than you may have thought.
Perhaps the most important lesson that's been covered here is knowing how to set
the default outline settings. With the default in place, you can proceed without
having to change the attributes on everything you draw.

Converting Outlines to Objects

You have learned a lot in this chapter, there's more. Beginning with CorelDRAW 9,
you can convert an outline to an object. Users have wanted this new feature for a
long time. The benefit of converting an outline to an object is that you can fill the
outline object with special fills, not just solid fills you were limited to before.

To convert an outline to an object, select any single line or an object with an outline applied to it, and choose Arrange | Convert Outline To Object. You can use this command on lines or outlined objects with widths larger than the default of .216 points or .003 inches. Practice using this command with the following steps:

1. Draw an ellipse on the page, and give it a yellow fill with an outline width of 24 points.

2. With the object selected, choose Arrange | Convert Outline To Object.

3. The new outline object will now be selected. Move the cursor to the palette, and left-click the color red. You will now have an ellipse filled with yellow and a red-filled outline object.

4. With the new outline object still selected, fill it with your favorite special fill. We replaced the yellow fill for the object with a conical fill from black to white and used a conical fill with multiple colors for the new outline object. The results are shown here.

We couldn't resist creating another object from an outline. This time we created a spiral with the Spiral tool and gave it a line width of 24 points. We then converted the spiral to an object using the command in the Arrange menu. With the spiral converted to an object, we filled it with another conical fill alternating between black and white a number of times. The results are shown next. The file is on the CD that comes with the book if you would like to see how this fill was accomplished. The path to the files is /Chap10/Spiral.cdr. If you're not sure how to create these conical fills, they're covered in detail in Chapter 9.

Filling Open Outline Shapes

The ability to fill open curves was a new feature introduced in CorelDRAW 8. It's a feature that lends itself to more abstract images. The image shown here is an example of this style. Notice that the outline on each of the objects does not go all the way around the objects, yet they have fills applied to them. These types of objects are referred to as *open curves* or *paths*. In order to use this feature, you must choose and enable the Fill open curves check box shown in Figure 10-4.

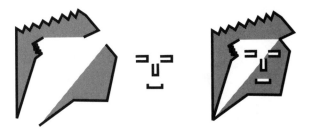

Just as with the spiral in the previous section on converting outlines to objects, we couldn't resist trying one more image using open curves filled with conical fills (shown next). Granted, we got a little carried away and went beyond the first step of duplicating and rotating the open curved triangle at the left in the figure. If you would like to dissect this image to see if you can duplicate it, you can find it on the CD that comes with the book. The path to the file is /Chap10/Hubcap.cdr. Chapters 9, 15, and 18 describe how to recreate this image.

FIGURE 10-4 The General dialog box with the Fill open curves check box enabled

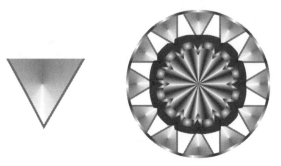

Having reached the end of this chapter, you now have the knowledge to count yourself among the few to have mastered the subject of outlines in CorelDRAW 9.

CHAPTER 11

Viewing, Zooming, and Panning

CoreIDRAW 9

If you are upgrading from an older version, you'll certainly notice that many more view types are available, the Zoom tool works differently, and the Pan tool is completely new. You'll find that these improvements will provide a higher-quality display in less time.

Viewing Types

Early versions of CorelDRAW had only two viewing types; now there are five: Simple Wireframe, Wireframe, Draft, Normal, and Enhanced. You'll examine each type here, from the crudest to the most detailed display. The quality can be selected from the View menu.

Simple Wireframe view does not show the fill of any objects but, rather, an outline. The outlines all appear in the layer color, regardless of the color of the outline. Normally, the layer color is black. For any effects such as extrusions, contours, and blends, only the control objects appear. All bitmaps are displayed in grayscale, except monochrome bitmaps, which are displayed in monochrome.

Wireframe view displays all objects as outlines using the layer color. Bitmaps are all displayed in grayscale, except monochrome bitmaps, which display in monochrome. Long-time CorelDRAW users know this view; this is the Wireframe view that has been around since the first version. The original Wireframe views show every object in the drawing, whereas the Simple Wireframe does not show intermediate objects in effects.

Draft view shows all objects. Solid fills are displayed normally. Fountain fills are displayed as solid colors. Texture fills, two-color pattern fills, full-color pattern fills, and bitmap pattern fills are all displayed with a distinguishing default pattern. Bitmaps are displayed in low resolution. Lenses are displayed as a solid color. The contents of PowerClips are not displayed at all.

Normal view displays all objects and fills without any changes. Bitmaps are displayed in high resolution. This full-color preview has been available since CorelDRAW 3. Note that PostScript fills are displayed as a series of PS characters.

Enhanced view creates a fully antialiased version of all objects using 2X Supersampling (Corel's official name for oversampling). Enhanced view can even display PostScript fills on the screen, but they will cause the display to take a long time to appear. The viewing of PostScript fills is turned on by default, but it can be turned off in the Tools | Options | Workspace | Display dialog box. Enhanced View is the default view in CorelDRAW 9.

When you want to see only your drawing and nothing else, you can select View | Full Screen Preview (F9), and the preview will cover your whole screen.

Even if CorelDRAW is not using the whole screen normally, other applications will now be covered. The view quality used by Full-Screen Preview can be set in Tools | Options | Workspace | Display. By default it is set to Enhanced.

Display Options

A number of options are related to the way an image is displayed on your screen, as shown in Figure 11-1. To get this dialog box, select Tools | Options | Workspace | Display.

Preview Colors

The colors used to display a drawing on screen can be dithered from either the Windows palette or Corel's own 256-color palette. If you are using a video adapter that displays only 256 colors, it is best to use Corel's palette. If your system can

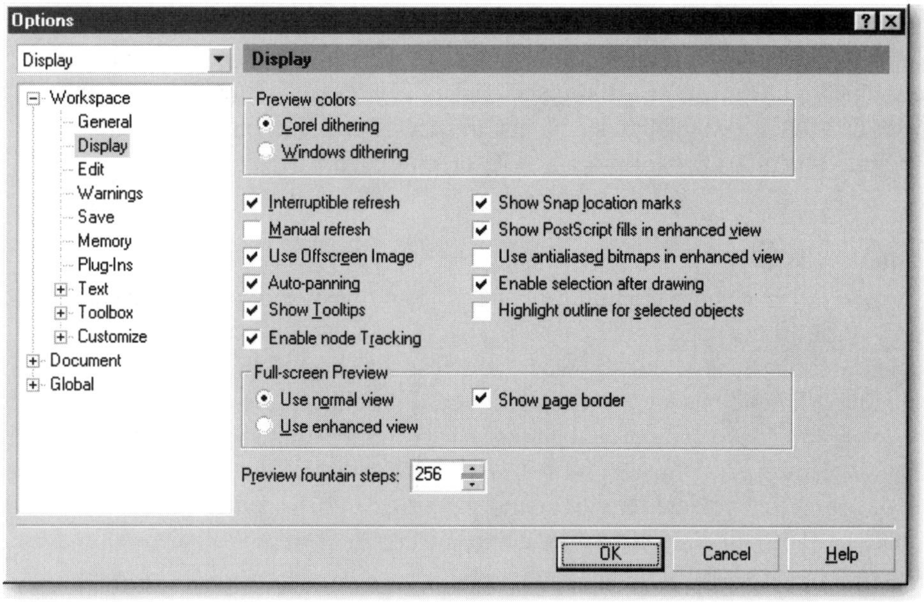

FIGURE 11-1   The Display Options dialog box

display 16-bit or 24-bit color, you'll notice that these options are grayed out since they are irrelevant.

Refresh

Any time you make changes to your drawing, CorelDRAW will attempt to redraw the screen, which sometimes can take a while. However, the part you want to see may have been the first thing drawn, or you may not even need to see a redrawn screen to continue your work. If you check the Interruptible refresh check box, you can stop screen redrawing by clicking anywhere on the screen or pressing any key. For example, suppose you've finished a drawing and are ready to print, but the drawing will take a minute to redraw. With this option checked, you can just use the CTRL-P shortcut and start printing right away.

If you don't want CorelDRAW to redraw the screen until you specifically tell it to, check the Manual refresh check box.

Offscreen Image

CorelDRAW 9 builds a bitmap version of your display off of the screen and then draws it all at once. So when you make changes to your drawing, only the parts that have changed will be redrawn. It will also instantly redraw after you've had a dialog box or roll-up onscreen above the image. By default this method is active because Use Offscreen image is checked. But if you want to return to the redraw methods used in previous versions, just uncheck this selection. Note that in the long run, it is much faster to use the Offscreen image.

Auto-Panning

Suppose you're right in the middle of moving an object and realize that it needs to end up just off the edge of your screen. If you have Auto-panning checked, the screen will scroll automatically when you near the edge of the drawing window. If you go too far and place your cursor above the scrollbars, the cursor will change to the international No symbol, indicating that you can't drag and drop to that location. However, if you stop just short of the scrollbars, the screen will scroll in the direction that you are moving. Auto-panning can help you in quite a few situations. The key is to move your cursor just short of the scrollbar (within about 7 pixels) so the screen is panned correctly.

Show ToolTips, Snaps, and PostScript Fills

A graphical user interface forces icons upon us. Sometimes icons are easy to understand, but some icons just can't be deciphered. Tool Tips can help solve this problem. If your cursor hovers over an icon, a little yellow textbox will pop up, providing the name of the icon's function. As long as the Show Tooltips check box is checked, this help will be provided. Note that a longer description of the command is also provided on the Status Bar, regardless of how the Tool Tips option is set.

When you are using Snap to Objects, Guidelines, or Grid, a blue marker will appear at the point where a snap occurs. By default, Show Snap location marks is activated, but you can eliminate these marks by unchecking this option.

You have the ability to display PostScript fills on the main screen when working in the Enhanced view. This provides great functionality, but the display can be very slow. By default, the Show PostScript fills in enhanced view option is activated, but those with slower systems may want to turn it off. Note that this option has an effect only when you use PostScript fills.

Node Tracking

One of the nice features in CorelDRAW 9 is the ability to manipulate objects and nodes when you have a drawing tool selected. If you do not want the ability to edit nodes with drawing tools, remove the check mark from the Enable Node Tracking check box. This is one of those options that you should create a custom keystroke for, as it is cumbersome to visit this box every time you wish to change the setting.

11

Antialiased Bitmaps

When you are using Enhanced view, you can have all bitmaps shown with antialiasing. Your bitmaps will have smoother edges and will generally look better this way. But they may look a tad blurry and will take longer to display. Check the Use antialiased bitmaps in enhanced view to enable this feature.

Enable Selection After Drawing

As you are drawing objects, you have the option of having the object immediately selected after you've drawn it. So if you draw an ellipse, the sizing and stretching handles will appear just after you finish drawing the object, even though you haven't selected the Pick tool. This option is on by default. You may wish to turn this option off if you are drawing objects in close proximity to one another and find that the bounding box handles get in the way.

Highlight Outline for Selected Objects

As a further visual indicator, you can have a dotted yellow outline added to selected objects. This option is especially helpful if you are selecting objects that do not have an outline; it has only a minor effect on objects that are already outlined. By default this option is off.

Full-Screen Preview

In Full-Screen Preview mode, only your document will be displayed, meaning that you won't see any menus, toolbars, etc. You have the choice of using Normal view or Enhanced view when you are in this mode. By default, the Enhanced view is used. Checking the Show page border check box will display the border of the page in this preview screen. This feature can be helpful when you want to know where objects are located in relation to the edge of the page.

Preview Fountain Steps

You want everything displayed on the screen with the maximum quality, but you also want it to get there as fast as possible. Gradient fills are one of the slowest fills to redraw. Their quality is controlled by the value in the Preview fountain steps box. The default in CorelDRAW 9 is the maximum value, 256 steps. Even at this maximum setting, the redraw speed is still much faster than in earlier versions. However, if you want to speed it up even more, lower the setting to 50, which provides good quality, although it leaves gradient fills visibly banded.

 NOTE *The value specified for the number of preview fountain steps is also used when you export to many different file formats. For the best exports, make sure to change this value to 256 before exporting. If you are converting to a bitmap, it is usually easier to just open a .cdr file in Corel PHOTO-PAINT, as the file will then always be created at the highest quality and you can select even more steps for your fountain fills. Note that this value does not affect printing. You control the number of fountain steps when printing in the Print dialog box as described in Chapter 26.*

Zooming

As you are creating a drawing, you'll want to zoom in to work on details and zoom out to see the whole image. You may change views hundreds of times before a particular drawing is finished, so using these tools efficiently is important.

Using the Zoom Flyout

You may remember the Zoom tool as having lots of different tools on its flyout. Now it simply contains the Zoom and Pan tools as shown here. Each of them can be used in many ways, and we'll go over each of those options.

The Zoom tool works just like the Zoom In tool of old. If you simply click with your left mouse button, the screen will zoom in by a factor of 2, centered around the point you clicked. The option is to drag a marquee box with the left mouse button. The drawing window will zoom to encompass as much of the marquee box as possible.

Clicking the right mouse button with the Zoom tool activated will zoom out to the last view by a factor of 2, or display a menu. You can change the behavior of the right mouse button in Tools | Options | Workspace | Toolbox | Zoom, Pan Tool as shown in Figure 11-2. If you select Context Menu, right-clicking will give you the menu shown here. Otherwise, you can select Zoom Out.

11

Zoom/Pan One-Shot		
Zoom Out	F3	
Zoom In		
Zoom	▶	400 %
		200 %
Zoom 1:1		100 %
Zoom To Page	Shift+F4	
Zoom To Width		75 %
Zoom To Height		50 %
Zoom To Selection	Shift+F2	25 %
Zoom To Fit	F4	10 %

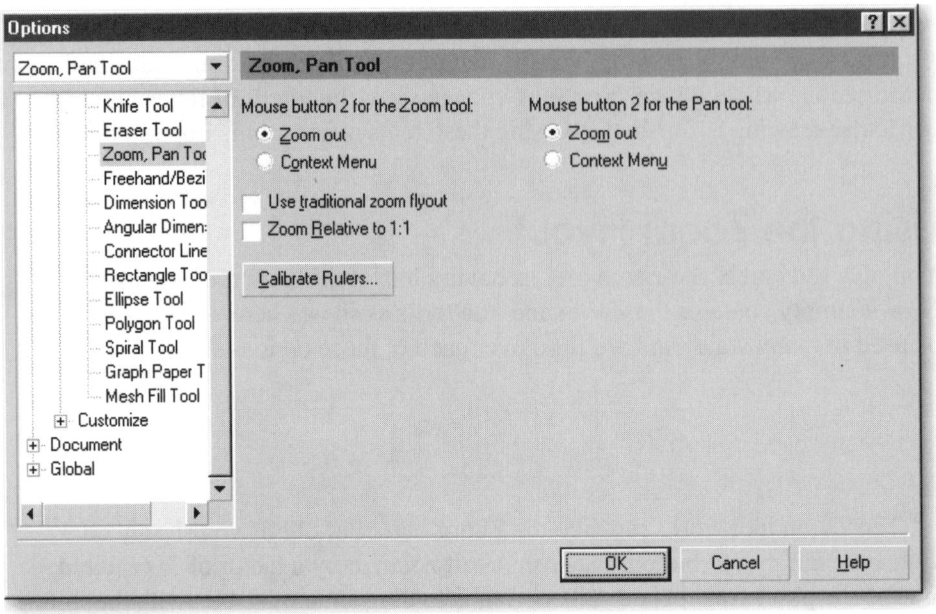

FIGURE 11-2   The Options Zoom, Pan Tool dialog box

An extra click or two will be required to zoom out, but this method gives you excellent control of the drawing window. The Zoom tool now has functionality that didn't exist in the "old" Zoom tool.

The right-hand tool on the flyout is the Pan tool; it will be discussed later in this chapter.

Using the Zoom Toolbar

The Zoom toolbar is available in several different places. You can display it as a toolbar by right-clicking the gray area around any existing toolbar and selecting Zoom from the pop-up menu. You can also make it the default Zoom flyout by checking Use traditional zoom flyout in the Zoom options dialog box shown in Figure 11-2. It is also available at the top of the View Manager Docker discussed later in this chapter. Regardless of how you choose to display it, it is by far the best method for using the Zoom tool. The Zoom toolbar is shown here.

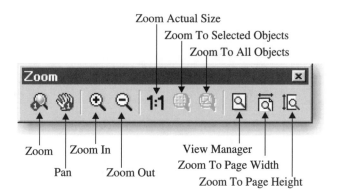

Zoom Actual Size
Zoom To Selected Objects
Zoom To All Objects

Zoom | Zoom In
Pan | Zoom Out
View Manager
Zoom To Page Width
Zoom To Page Height

Zoom In

The Zoom In tool works much like the Zoom tool described previously. The cursor will change to a magnifying glass with a + in the middle, just like on the tool itself. Clicking the screen with the left mouse button will zoom to 200 percent of the current view. Dragging a marquee box will zoom to the area within the marquee box. You can use the Zoom tool from the keyboard by using the F2 shortcut key, and you can marquee select the area you want.

Zoom Out

Selecting the Zoom Out tool will instantly zoom out to the previous zoom level or show twice as much information if there is no previous zoom level. Note that if you've made several slightly tighter zooms, the Zoom Out tool may seem to have little effect since there wasn't much change in views. You can also Zoom Out from the keyboard by using the F3 shortcut key.

Zoom Actual Size

To properly use the Zoom Actual Size tool, you need to calibrate your rulers. Click the Calibrate Rulers button shown in Figure 11-2 to get the screen shown in Figure 11-3.

You'll see two text entry boxes for inputting the horizontal and vertical resolution of the rulers. These numbers need to be adjusted until the rulers on the screen line up perfectly with a real-life ruler. The best way to do this is to get a plastic ruler (like the one that used to be supplied in the CorelDRAW box) and hold it up to the screen. Adjust the resolution values for each ruler separately until

11

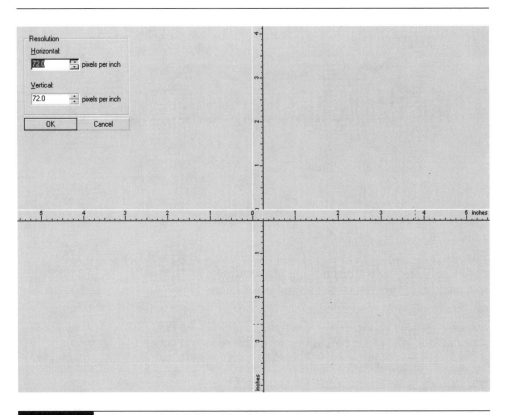

The screen used for calibrating the rulers

the onscreen rulers' tick marks line up with the ones on your plastic ruler (you did keep it, didn't you?). When everything is all set, click OK.

Now that you have the rulers calibrated, Zoom Actual Size will zoom your drawing in or out so that the units on the rulers are life size. Thus, if you are designing an ad that is 4.5 inches square, you'll see it on the screen in the exact size it will appear in print.

Zoom To Selected

Using the Zoom To Selected tool requires that you first select an object or objects. Otherwise, nothing will happen since there is not an object around which to zoom.

When you do have something selected, this tool will change the zoom level so the selected objects completely fill the drawing window. You can also access this tool from the keyboard using the SHIFT-F2 shortcut key.

Zoom To All Objects

The Zoom To All Objects tool zooms in or out until all objects in the drawing fill up the drawing window. Every now and then objects get placed quite a ways from the page itself and cause frustration when printing. You know they exist, but you can't find them. Using the Zoom to All Objects tool can help you to locate them so you can move or remove them. You may also see this command referred to as Zoom To Fit. It can be accessed from the keyboard using the F4 shortcut key.

Zoom To Page

In the drawing window is a graphical representation of the page size you've selected. Using the Zoom To Page tool will zoom the drawing in or out so that the page will be as large as possible in the drawing window. You can also access this tool from the keyboard using the SHIFT-F4 shortcut key.

Zoom To Page Width

Zoom To Page Width will zoom in or out so that the width of the onscreen page fills up the drawing window. You will not necessarily see the top of the page, but rather, a part of the page relative to the previous view. This means that if you zoom in near the bottom of the page, the bottom part of the page will be represented.

Zoom To Page Height

Zoom To Page Height works just the same as the Zoom To Page Width tool except that it will adjust the zoom so that the entire height of the page will fit in the drawing window. Note that in most cases you'll find that Zoom To Page Height works better than Zoom to Page.

Using the Standard Toolbar

The standard toolbar has a drop-down list of zoom levels, as shown.

11

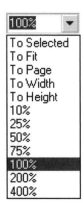

Many of these zoom levels have been previously described. Some of the other levels that are available here are common ones, such as 25%, 50%, 200%, and 400% of the page. The current zoom level will always be the first choice and will not necessarily be a round number. You can also type in any level you want, using a value as small as 1% or as large as 405651%. When zoomed to 1%, you can see nearly 100 feet in both the horizontal and vertical directions, while at 405651%, you can see only a few thousandths of an inch in both directions.

TIP *If you are at a zoom level you wish to save, type a name into the drop-down list window, and press ENTER. It will be saved in the list for later use with the current document.*

Zooming with an Intellimouse

You may have seen an Intellimouse. It is the latest variation of a rodent from Microsoft. Between the two buttons is a roller. Initially, the roller simply enabled you to scroll through a document in a word processor or Web page. But Corel has added support for the Intellimouse as a way to zoom in and out of your drawings.

If you roll the roller toward you, the display will zoom out by 10 percent for each "click" of the roller. For those who are unfamiliar with the Intellimouse, the roller will give a definite click after a certain amount of rotation. Roll the roller away from you, and the display will zoom out by a factor of 50 percent for each click of the roller. And if you roll it faster than half a second between clicks, the zoom will double itself. OK, so that is the technical description. But the best way to understand how it works is to roll the roller in each direction and watch what happens. Although a graphics tablet is still the best input medium for CorelDRAW users, for those using mice, the Intellimouse does have this cool feature.

Panning

Panning is used to move the drawing window so that the objects you are working with are displayed. If the screen is zoomed out for all objects, you won't need to pan, but if it is zoomed in tight, you'll frequently need to move around to see other objects or to move the object you are working with.

In older versions of CorelDRAW, panning was accomplished by moving the thumb buttons on the scrollbars or simply by zooming out and zooming back in on something else. Now you have the Pan tool, which provides the ability to pan with the keyboard and which supports panning with the Intellimouse.

Using the Pan Tool

The Pan tool (either the tool on the flyout or the one on the Zoom Property Bar) will change your cursor into a hand, which is appropriate. Simply use the hand to push (drag) the page where you want it. Thus, if you drag from the bottom of the screen toward the top, the drawing moves upward on the screen to show the part farther down on the actual page.

Using Keyboard Panning

If you are familiar with the nudge actions available in previous versions of CorelDRAW, keyboard panning will be extremely easy. Hold down the ALT key, and press one of the arrow keys on the keyboard. This will scroll the screen in the direction of the arrow you selected. You can even call it "nudging a whole page."

Panning with an Intellimouse

Again, the special roller on the Intellimouse will activate a special mode of panning. Remember, you can roll the special wheel in the middle of the Intellimouse to zoom in and out. To pan, depress the roller, just as with the other mouse buttons. Your cursor will change to a four-headed arrow. Now move the mouse in the direction you want the screen to pan. The four-headed arrow will change into an arrow pointing in the direction you are moving, and the screen will begin to pan.

Once you've moved to the desired view, click the roller wheel again, and the screen will stop panning. Basically, you're just treating this roller as a third mouse button that activates and deactivates the panning mode.

The View Manager

The View Manager provides an easy way to store the views of a drawing that you use often. The information stored includes the zoom level and page number. Figure 11-4 shows the View Manager floating in an undocked state with several saved views. The View Manager is accessed by choosing Window | Dockers | View Manager, by pressing CTRL-F2, or by clicking the rightmost icon on the Zoom Property Bar.

To create a new view, you first need to select the page and zoom to the magnification level you want to save. Then click the + icon in the View Manager roll-up, or select New from the flyout. The view will be added to the main display window of the roll-up. To delete a view, simply click the – icon, or select Delete from the flyout.

 TIP   *If you added a view by typing a name in the standard toolbar's drop-down list of zoom values, it will automatically appear in the View Manager.*

In the leftmost column in the View Manager is a Page icon. This controls where the specific page of the view will be applied when the view is selected. If the Page icon is dimmed, only the magnification of the view will be used. If you needed to zoom in on the lower-left corner of every page, you would definitely

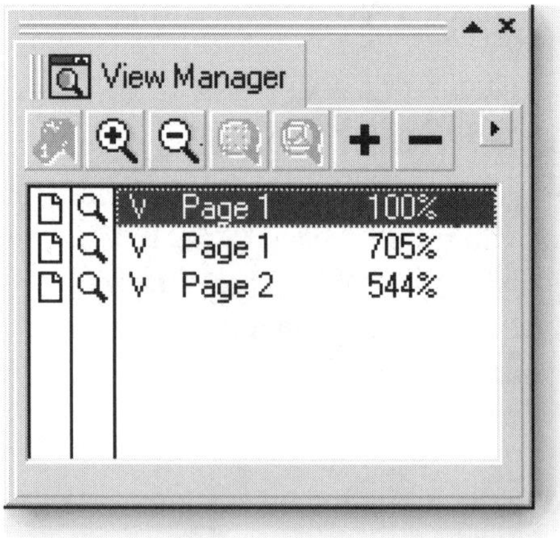

FIGURE 11-4   The View Manager Docker after several views have been saved

want to turn off the Page icon. Similarly, the Magnification icon controls whether the magnification information of the saved view is used. If all you need is a view of page 5, and you've saved a view of page 5, deselect the Magnification icon so that it is dimmed.

Initially, a new view will be named View *x-y*, where *x* represents the number of the view created and *y* is the magnification level. Click the name to highlight it or right-click and select Rename from the pop-up menu, and then type a more descriptive name, as in Figure 11-4. The next two columns show the page number and magnification level of the saved view.

By dragging a particular view, you can rearrange the order in which views are listed. Right-clicking any of the views displays the same menu as the flyout, except that it will appear right at your cursor. If you double-click a view or select Switch to View from the menu, your main display window will change to the selected view.

 TIP *If you will be sharing a drawing with others, creating saved views is a great way for you to point out certain items in the drawing.*

Without the Zoom tool, it would be very tough to work on a drawing. Sometimes you'd only see a tiny part of what you needed, and other times you'd see so much that you couldn't work with a detailed area. Understanding the Zoom tool will allow you to always work at exactly the view you need.

11

PART II

Manipulation

CorelDRAW 9

CHAPTER 12

Object Ordering, Layers, and the Object Manager

CorelDRAW 9

This chapter discusses the various methods for controlling and modifying the relationship of objects to each other. Object Ordering lets you change objects in their stacking order. Layers allow you to place objects on separate layers, which themselves can be placed in a stacking order. Object Manager provides a hierarchical display of the entire document, showing the stacking order of all the objects and layers within the document. Object Manager also lets you change the stacking order of objects and layers as well as allowing you to modify objects within Object Manger itself.

Ordering Objects

Remember that each time you draw a new object on the page, it is placed on top of the other objects on the page, in a *stacking order*. The last object you draw is considered to be at the top of the stacking order. Do not confuse stacking order with *layers* (discussed later in this chapter).

The Arrange | Order command allows you to select and move objects to different levels within your document. When you access the Arrange | Order child menu, you are given seven different choices for moving an object or objects in the stacking order:

- *To Front* Choose this option to move the selected object or objects to the front of all the other objects in the layer. This command comes in handy when you are rearranging objects in your document.

- *To Back* Choose this option to move a selected object or objects behind all other objects in the layer.

- *Forward One* Choose this option to move the selected object or objects forward one level at a time in the stacking order within the active layer.

- *Back One* Choose this option to move the selected object or objects backward one level at a time in the stacking order within the active layer.

- *In Front Of* Choose this option to move an object or objects in front of a specific object in the layer.

- *Behind* Choose this option to move an object or objects in back of a specific object in your active layer. The following illustration shows an example of the use of this option. Suppose you want to move the dog looking out the window in the back seat, to the front seat between the driver and the passenger. There are many objects in this document, and it would be hard to know where in the stacking order to move the dog so it is behind the driver's shoulder but in front of the passenger. To move the dog behind the shoulder, you first ungroup the clipart image and then select the group of elements that make up the dog. Now, move the dog between the driver and the passenger. Choose Arrange | Order | Behind. The cursor will change into an arrow. Use the arrow to point to the driver's shoulder; the dog will be placed behind his shoulder. If the dog is not in the perfect position, use the arrow keys on the keyboard to nudge the dog into the position of choice.

The dog in the back seat looking out the window

The dog in the front seat between the driver and passenger

■ *Reverse Order* Choose this option to reverse the order of two or more selected objects within the same layer. The following illustration shows an example of the use of the Reverse Order option. The positions of the car and gas pump on the left have been reversed in the image on the right. The gas pump is moved up in the stacking order, and the car is moved down in the stacking order.

Original images   Images in reverse order

12

There are other ways to move objects in their stacking order besides using the Order child menu accessed from the Arrange menu: you can use the Object menu or the Property Bar. You can also use the following shortcut keys:

- SHIFT + PGUP = To Front
- SHIFT+ PGDN = To Back
- CTRL + PGUP = Forward One
- CTRL + PGDN = Back One

You can access the Order options child menu by right-clicking an object or objects and choosing Order from the pop-up Object menu. The Order child menu will appear displaying all the various options, as shown in Figure 12-1. You may find using the Object pop-up menu a faster way to choose Order options than using the Arrange menu. The To Back and To Front commands found in the menus are also available on the Property Bar when objects are selected.

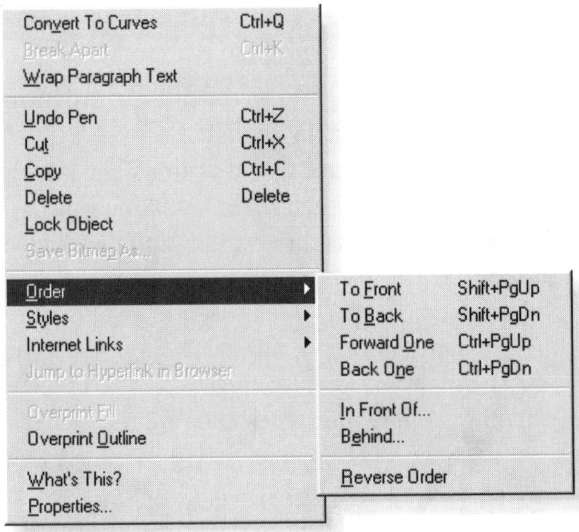

FIGURE 12-1   The Object menu and Order command child menu

CAUTION *If your document contains different layers, any changes in order will affect only the objects within their respective layers. For example, if you want to move an object on layer 1 behind an object on layer 2, you will first have to move the object on layer 1 to layer 2 (see the section "Working with Layers," later in the chapter).*

 TIP *If you move a small object behind a larger object so that it is completely hidden by the larger object, you will not be able to select the hidden object again. To solve this problem, use the new Digger functionality by* ALT*-clicking the object that is obscuring the hidden object until the hidden object is selected. Groups will be perceived as one object if you're using just the* ALT *key. Using the* CTRL-ALT *key combination will allow you to select a hidden object within a group. Using the* SHIFT-ALT *key combination will let you selected multiple hidden objects.*

The Object Manager

The Object Manager Docker displays the hierarchical tree structure of all objects, layers, and pages in your documents. Its Docker window displays the stacking order of objects and the layers on each page in the document. Each object in the document is represented by a small icon, along with a description of the object's fill and outline properties.

The Object Manager also includes information on individual layers within a document. This combining of objects and layers into a single Docker™ simplifies the organization of objects and layers.

12

Using Object Manager

To access Object Manager, choose Window | Dockers | Object Manager. Figure 12-2 shows the Object Manager dialog box when four objects are on the page. The first time you access Object Manager, it will display as a Docker window at the right side of the screen. If you have objects on the screen, they will not display in the Docker until you click on the + box directly under the Page 1 folder icon. Figure 12-2 shows the Docker after the + box was checked. Notice that each of the objects is listed below the upper row of icons. If there are groups of objects, the group will be listed with a + box at the left. Click the + box, and the objects within the group will be displayed in a list. In addition to objects, all the existing layers are shown beneath the Master Page folder. These include Grid, Guide, and Desktop because they are also considered layers.

Show Object Properties ——— ——— Edit across Layers

New Layer ——— ——— Layers Manager View

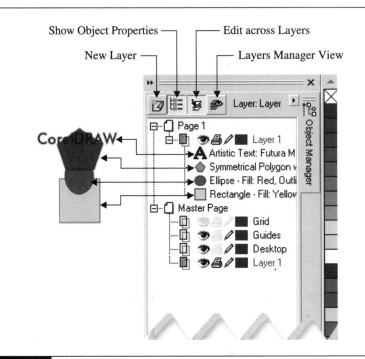

FIGURE 12-2   The Object Manager Docker with four objects on the page

The four icons across the very top of the Docker are (from left to right): New Layer, Show Object Properties, Edit Across Layers, and Layer Manager View. Choose the New Layer icon to add a new layer to the document. Each new layer is named in sequential order after the default layer 1.

The second icon toggles on or off the description of each object's properties within a document. Notice in Figure 12-2 that the fill and outline properties of the four objects in the document are partially displayed. If you toggle the icon off, only the words "Artistic Text, Symmetrical Polygon, Ellipse, and Rectangle" will appear.

 TIP   *The width of the Docker often prevents you from seeing the full descriptions. To see the complete properties description, place the cursor on the left edge of the Docker. When the cursor changes to a double-headed arrow, drag to the left to widen the Docker.*

The third icon toggles on and off the ability to edit across multiple layers. Toggling this function off prevents you from editing objects on a layer unless the layer is selected.

The fourth icon lets you turn off the Objects view so only the layers in the document are visible. Figure 12-3 shows the Docker with the Layer Manager View icon toggled on.

Although the Object Properties section appears above the Layers section in the dialog box, we will describe the Layers section first.

Working with Layers

Every time you draw an object in CorelDRAW, in effect you create a new layer on the page. Understanding this basic fact will help you understand the complex world of layers. The layers discussed in this section are not like the object layers you automatically create when you draw objects on the screen, but instead are special layers that can contain certain portions of your document. You can place one object or many objects on these special layers. This section describes layers and how you can use them to organize objects in your drawings. Organization can save you time and prevent accidental changes to your drawings.

Figure 12-4 illustrates the concept of layers. In the illustration the document is comprised of three layers with different objects placed on each layer.

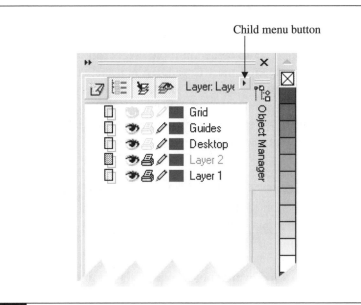

FIGURE 12-3   The Objects dialog box showing the layers in the document only

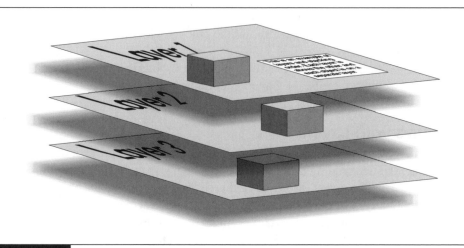

FIGURE 12-4   A cross-section of a page emulating a page with three layers

When you create separate layers, you create a subset of layers that can be stacked in any order. All objects placed on a layer can be moved relative to each other within that layer. All of these separate layers and the objects placed on them make up the completed document. This ability to create separate layers containing portions of the document provides the organizational flexibility referred to earlier.

Using the Object Manager to create multiple layers can be confusing and, therefore, counterproductive for many CorelDRAW users. If you take the time to learn how to work in a multiple-layer environment, however, you may find layers useful. Keep in mind that you don't need to use multiple layers for most projects. This author has created hundreds of complex drawings using only a single layer (the default layer 1) with great success.

Controlling the Layers in the Object Manager Dialog Box

The layers section of the Object Manager dialog box first shows the Master Page icon, and it is then divided into a tree of columns containing the various icons described in the following sections.

COLUMN 1   Right-click the overlapping rectangles icon to bring up the Layers pop-up menu shown in Figure 12-5. This menu lets you designate whether the layer is visible, printable, or editable, and whether it's a master layer. The remaining individual columns perform these same functions as well. You can also

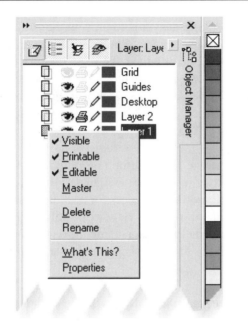

FIGURE 12-5   The Layers pop-up menu

delete or rename a layer in this menu. Choosing Properties at the bottom of the menu brings up the Layer Properties dialog box discussed later in this chapter.

COLUMN 2   The second column, filled with eye icons, controls whether a layer is visible or invisible. Click the icons to toggle between the two options. If the icon is dimmed, the objects on that layer will be invisible. Making a layer invisible eliminates the sometimes lengthy redraw time for an object. Making a layer invisible can also help if a layer overlaps other objects in your document, making them hard to work on. It also comes in handy when you want to view only one layer at a time.

COLUMN 3   The printer icons in column 3 can be toggled on and off to prevent or allow the printing of certain layers. The printer icons that are dimmed by default can be turned on, allowing you to print the guidelines in a document. Unless you are printing to a paper size larger than the page size, you shouldn't activate the printer icon for the Desktop layer (because objects on the desktop should not normally print).

12

COLUMN 4   The pencil icons in the fourth column are used to lock specific layers. The purpose of locking a layer is to prevent the accidental editing or moving of objects on the locked layer. When objects are on a layer that has been locked, they cannot be selected or edited. This can confuse the new user who has not worked with layers before. If you cannot select an object, first check whether the object is on a locked layer. A layer is locked if the all the objects on the layer are dimmed and the pencil icon is also dimmed. The Grid layer is locked by default and cannot be unlocked.

COLUMN 5   The icons in the fifth column represent layer colors. Double-clicking a color swatch lets you change the color assigned to the layer in the Object Manager dialog box. Using different colors for each layer can be helpful when viewing layers in a pseudo-Wireframe view while still in Preview mode. Using different colors can also be helpful when using the actual Wireframe mode. This technique is described in the section "Using the Layer Properties Dialog Box," later in this chapter.

COLUMN 6   The icons in the sixth column contain each layer's name. Master layers are repeating layers; therefore, any object placed on a master layer will appear on every page of a multiple-page document. The Grid, Guides, and Desktop layers are by default master layers and cannot be changed. This ability to place an object on a master layer allows you to use a masthead or any other object that you want to appear on every page without having to manually place it on each page. To make any layer a master layer, right-click a layer, and choose Master from the pop-up menu.

Selecting a Layer to Work on

When you are working with multiple layers, you must first select the layer you want to work on. You do so by clicking the actual name of the layer in the Object Manager Docker before drawing or placing an object. The area just to the right of the four icons at the top of the Docker also displays the layer that is currently selected. It's extremely important to always have the Docker open with the active layer displayed, or you could easily place your next object on a layer you didn't intend to use. The Status Bar at the bottom of the screen merely tells you which layer the currently selected object is placed on, not the layer you're working on.

Using the Object Manager Child Menu with Layers

You access the Object Manager child menu by clicking the button in the upper-right corner of the Object Manager Docker. Figure 12-6 shows this menu (the button is shown in Figure 12-4). The child menu contains ten commands beginning with the New Layer command. Choosing the command adds a new layer, just as if you clicked on the upper-left icon on the Object Manager dialog box. The second command lets you delete a layer.

The third and fourth commands let you either move or copy selected objects to a different layer. If you select Move To Layer, the cursor changes to an arrow that you can use to click the name of the layer you wish to move the object to. If you select Copy To Layer, you're presented with the same arrow, which you then use to place a duplicate copy of the selected objects on a different layer.

 NOTE   *The Move To Layer and Copy To Layer commands are only available when the Layer Manager View icon is enabled and only the layers are visible.*

 TIP   *Instead of using the Move To Layer command in the child menu, the quickest way to move an object from one layer to another is to use the drag-and-drop method from one layer to the next when the objects are visible.*

The next two commands, Hide Object Properties and Edit Across Layers, function the same as the second and third icons at the top on the Object Manager dialog box. Although the Show Object Properties icon sounds different, it functions the same in that it hides or shows the object properties in the Object dialog box.

The last three commands—Show Pages and Layers, Show Pages, and Show Layers—control which of the selected items is displayed.

USING THE LAYER PROPERTIES DIALOG BOX   The Layers Properties dialog box shown in Figure 12-7 provides additional controls over the layers in a document. To access the Layers Properties dialog box, right-click a layer name, and choose Properties from the pop-up menu. With the exception of the Override Full Color View and Apply all property changes to the current page only commands, the remaining options are duplicates of options discussed earlier. When you access the Layer Properties dialog box with either the Grid or Guides layer selected, the dialog box will display an extra Setup button. Clicking this Setup button brings up their respective Tools | Option dialog boxes, where you can control the Grid settings and Guideline placement.

12

FIGURE 12-6   The child menu displayed on top of the Object Manager Docker

The two options in the Layers Properties dialog box that are not found anywhere else in the Object Manager dialog box are described here:

- *Override Full Color View*   When you put a check mark in the Override Full Color View check box, the object fills are hidden for all the objects on a layer except the outline. You can change the color of the outline for easy identification of the objects by clicking the Layer Color button, just as you could in the Object Properties dialog box. Using Override Full Color View is another way of hiding an object without making it completely invisible. This method reduces the redraw time for complicated objects while still letting you see their location on the page.

- *Apply all property changes to the current page only*   Placing a check mark in this check box applies all the settings you have changed in the Layer Properties dialog box to the selected layer on the page you are working on. Use this special setting only if your document contains multiple pages.

 TIP   *You can choose either Simple Wireframe or Wireframe view from the Property Bar to view all layers at once with their assigned layer colors.*

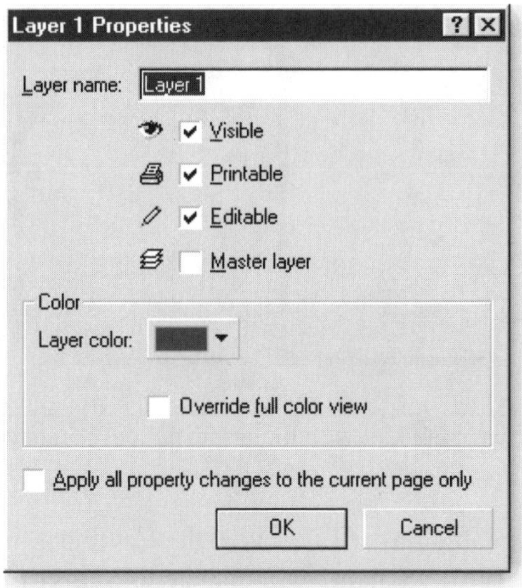

FIGURE 12-7   The Layer Properties dialog box indicating Layer 1 selected

HIDING LAYERS   There are times when you want to hide layers, such as when you want a masthead to appear on only odd numbered pages, as shown in Figure 12-8. This figure shows a four-page booklet. A masthead appears on the two left-hand (odd-numbered) pages, but it doesn't appear on the two right-hand (even numbered) pages. The masthead was placed only once on the first left-hand page. By changing the settings in the layers section of the Object Manager and Layer Properties dialog boxes, it was placed again on the second left-hand page without being placed in either of the right-hand pages.

Follow these steps to create the effect shown in Figure 12-8:

1. Open a new document.

2. Add three more pages by choosing <u>L</u>ayout | Insert Page. When the Insert Page dialog box appears, type **3** in the Insert Page parameter box, and then click the OK button. You can also add pages by clicking the + button in the navigation tools at the lower-left corner of the document window.

3. Open the Object Manager by choosing <u>W</u>indow | Dockers | Object Ma<u>n</u>ager.

4. Select Layer 1 at the bottom of the Object Manager in the Layers section.

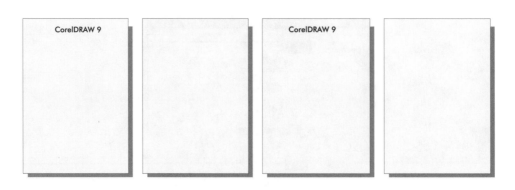

FIGURE 12-8   A four-page booklet with the masthead only on pages 1 and 3

5. Right-click the name Layer 1 to reveal the Layer pop-up menu, and choose Master Layer. The layer name will change to Master Layer 1.

6. Select the Text tool from the toolbox, and click the top of the page.

7. Type **CorelDRAW 9** on page 1.

8. Click the page 2 tab in the lower-left corner of the document window to move to page 2.

9. Click the layer name (Master Layer 1) to highlight it.

10. Right-click to bring up the Layer pop-up menu, and choose Properties.

11. Remove the check mark from the box next to the eye icon, and put a check mark in the <u>A</u>pply all property changes to the current page only box. Then click OK.

12. Click the page 4 tab at the bottom of the screen to move to page 4. Repeat steps 9 through 11.

Now click each page tab at the bottom of the screen. You will see that the masthead appears only on pages 1 and 3.

NOTE   *If your projects can benefit from using layers, you should spend some time exploring the various settings and commands until you know them. If you will be using layers only occasionally, pay careful attention to which layer you're working on. If you don't, you may find working with layers frustrating.*

TIP *You can click and drag on a layer name to change the stacking order of layers within the Layers section of the object manager. You can also move objects you have drawn on the page to the Guides layer as a way to create custom guidelines.*

Working with Objects in the Object Manager

The Object section at the top of the Docker combines, to some degree, everything you learned in the discussions of object ordering and layers, plus more. So what is the Object Manager? The Object Manager displays a complete visual representation of the active file you are working on. Because you can see every object in your document in a hierarchical structure, you can modify objects directly in the Object Manager. This hierarchical display shows the stacking order of each object and the individual layers on each page in the file. An icon is displayed next to each object in the list, followed by a brief description of the object's fill and outline properties. These icons are interactive. For example, if you select an icon in the list of objects, the corresponding object in the document will also be selected. Similarly, if you select an object in the document, the name of the object in the Object Manager will also be highlighted. When the object is selected in the Object Manager, you can modify the object within the document. In certain circumstances, you can edit the object right in the Object Manager itself, such as when changing the object's color. When modifying the objects from within in the document, the object will automatically be updated in the Object Manager if you have not previously renamed it.

12

The best way to learn how the Object Manager works is to practice using it. Follow these steps to learn some basic uses of the Object Manger:

1. Open a new document by choosing File | New.

2. Choose Window | Dockers | Object Manager.

3. Draw a rectangle on the page, and give it a red fill.

4. Draw an ellipse on the page, and give it an Ice Blue fill.

5. Type **Corel** on the page. Use a nice bold font with a size of 72 points. By default the text will be filled with Black.

The Object Manager Docker should now look something like the one in Figure 12-9. If the Docker is not wide enough to display all of the information, place the cursor on the left edge of the Docker. When the cursor changes to a double-headed arrow, drag to the left to widen the Docker. Notice that each of your objects is shown in its correct stacking order, and the object types are also named. The Artistic Text line shows the name of the font and font style. The Ellipse line indicates that the fill color is Ice Blue and that the outline is black with a hairline width. The Rectangle line indicates that the fill color is red and that this outline is also black with a hairline width.

NOTE *If none of this information is displayed, click the + icon under the Page icon labeled Page 1.*

TIP *You can change the name of an object by either clicking twice or double-clicking the name and description line and then typing in the new name. You may want to give an object a name that is more descriptive than Ellipse, Curve, and so on. Changing the name will only change the name of the object; it will not affect the description.*

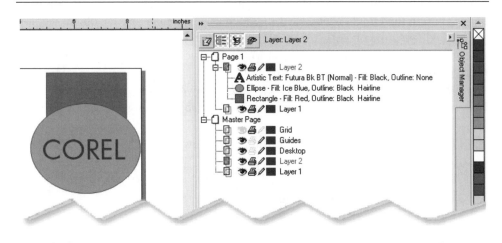

 FIGURE 12-9   The Object Manager Docker as it would appear with three objects in the document

Modifying Objects Using the Object Manager

One benefit of using the Object Manager is that you can modify objects by selecting them from within the Object Manager itself. Using the same objects you used in the previous exercise, follow these steps to learn how to modify objects from within the Object Manager:

1. Drag the color red from the color palette in the document window, and place the colored square on the letter A icon in the Object Manager. Your text on the page will now change to red.

2. Drag the color yellow from the color palette in the document window, and place the colored square on the ellipse icon in the Object Manager. Your ellipse on the page will now change to yellow.

As you can see, dragging colors from the palette directly onto the icon in the Object Manager changes the object's color on the page.

You may be wondering why you should learn how to change the color of objects using the Object Manager when you have been told throughout this book to color them in other ways. At times, certain objects in your document will be difficult to select because of their small size. When this situation occurs, locate the object in the object list in the Object Manager, and select it from there. With the object selected, you can proceed to edit the object in any way you wish.

12

Moving Objects in Their Stacking Order Within the Object Manager

You can also move objects and layers in their stacking order within the Object Manager. Again, using the same objects you used in the previous exercise, practice selecting and moving objects within the Object Manager by following these steps:

1. To emulate an object that would be hard to select, select the ellipse on the page, and drag it so that it is on top of the rectangle. Notice that the ellipse is also selected in the Object Manager.

2. Select the rectangle in the Object Manager.

3. Drag in an upward direction, and a solid black position line will appear. Place the line between the ellipse and the Artistic Text, and release the left mouse button. The rectangle will now be placed above the ellipse and beneath the text. Figure 12-10 shows the Object Manager with the black positioning line under the Artistic Text.

Figure 12-10 also shows the rectangle being placed on top of the ellipse and the objects after the move was completed.

 TIP *Besides moving objects within their stacking order, you can group objects by dragging the position line onto another object instead of in between objects. In fact, you must be careful that you don't group objects accidentally if your intention is only to move the object.*

Ellipse placed on top of rectangle   Position line

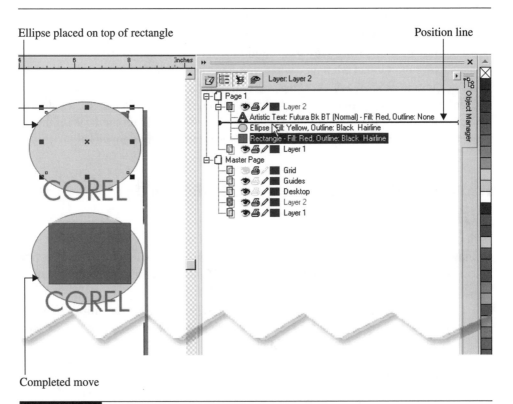

Completed move

FIGURE 12-10   Moving objects using the Object Manager

TIP   *There are other advantages to the Object Manager, such as being able to drag certain styles onto objects. Corel's Help menu can teach you some of the more unusual uses for the Object Manager. Another benefit is to use the Object Manager to locate problem objects such as ones that may contain a erroneous spot color.*

Figure 12-11 shows an image created by co-author Peter McCormick that was used in his company's ad campaign, along with the Object Manager on the right. Notice that all the objects that make up the image are listed in the order in which they appear on the page. You must be thinking we are nuts to think you can tell which object is which from the list of curve objects, and you are right. You can't tell which is which unless you select one of the name tags and change the color of the selected object to see which object on the page changes. It soon becomes clear

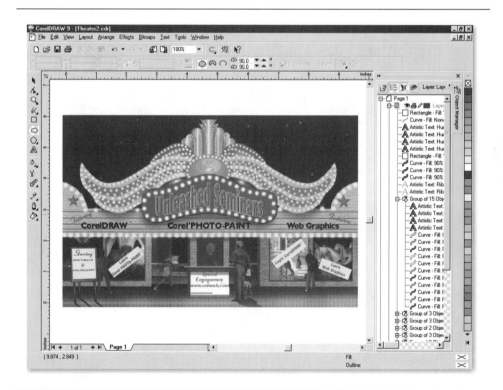

FIGURE 12-11   An original image with the various objects that make up the image listed in the Object Manager

that using the Object Manager for drawings you have already completed and for clipart images is not really practical unless you have a strong desire to spend a lot of time figuring out which object is which.

Advanced users of CorelDRAW, however, may find a benefit in using the Object Manager when creating new drawings because they can name the objects in Object Manager as they create them, thereby eliminating any confusion as to which object is which. This ability to keep track of each object using a hierarchical display of the document can be important when you're dealing with hundreds of objects.

You might ask if you are missing out if you don't use the Object Manager, but you probably are not. Although some may quibble with this viewpoint, the majority of users can work efficiently by relying on the more traditional tools and effects, including object ordering and layering, as discussed in this chapter.

CHAPTER 13

COREL.COM

CorelDRAW 9

Artists sometimes feel that rulers, guidelines, and grids only get in the way—that these are the tools of technical illustrators, and artists don't need them. However, this is definitely not true, and enlightened artists will wonder how they lived without these extremely useful tools.

Rulers

The rulers appear above and to the left of the drawing window. If you're upgrading from an older version, you'll notice that the rulers are now smaller, but they retain all of their functionality.

Measurement Systems

Many different units of measurement are available with the rulers. The following sections describe the units of measurement available.

Inches

Inches are the default unit of measurement. In versions shipped outside of the United States, the inch may not be the default unit, but it is still deeply ingrained in the product. The inch is the smallest unit in the measurement system used in the United States. It is equal to 2.54 centimeters.

Millimeters

A millimeter is a very small unit of measurement in the metric system. It is equal to one tenth of a centimeter.

Picas, Points

Picas and points are measures used in typography and design. Traditionally, there were just over 72 points to an inch, but this definition has been altered so that there are exactly 72 points in an inch. A pica is 12 points. Rather than a decimal point, a comma is used to mix these two measurements together. Thus, the measurement 1,3 means 1 pica and 3 points, which is the same as 15 points.

Points

Usually, points are used alone only when measuring type size and line spacing, as the numbers can get rather large in other situations.

Pixels

The word *pixel* is short for picture element. Simply put, when you are zoomed in very close to a bitmap, a pixel is one of those itty-bitty squares you see. It is the basic unit of all bitmaps. Pixels are extremely useful for creating drawings that will eventually be converted into bitmaps, such as Web graphics.

Ciceros, Didots

One didot is equal to 1.07 points, and 67.567 didots are in an inch. A cicero is 12 didots. This system is used by the French and is similar to the system of picas and points.

Didots

Didots are used alone, like points, to measure type size and line spacing. Each didot is equal to 1.07 points.

Feet

A foot is a larger unit of measurement in the measurement system used in the United States. One foot is equal to 12 inches.

13

Yards

There are 3 feet to a yard.

Miles

There are 5,280 feet to a mile.

Centimeters

A centimeter is a unit of measurement in the metric system. A centimeter is equal to 10 millimeters. It is also equal to .394 inches.

Meters

A meter is equal to 100 centimeters.

Kilometers

A kilometer is equal to 1,000 meters.

Working with the Rulers

You should see the rulers on your screen when you first start CorelDRAW. If they are not visible, choose View | Rulers. The origin point of the rulers—the point where each ruler equals zero—is the lower-left corner of the page by default.

 TIP   *You can drag the rulers into the drawing window by holding down the SHIFT key while pushing the ruler along. Hold down SHIFT while double-clicking the place where the rulers meet, and they will return to their docked positions.*

To make changes in the ruler defaults, you need to access the Options Ruler dialog box (shown in Figure 13-1) by double-clicking on the ruler. You can separately set the units of measurement used in the horizontal and vertical directions using any of the measurement units previously described. By default, the units will be the same, since the Same units for Horizontal and Vertical rulers check box is checked. If you want to use different units, simply uncheck this box.

You can also set the origin of the ruler by typing the exact coordinates on the drawing page where you want the origin to be. A positive horizontal value will move the horizontal point to the right, and a positive vertical value will move the origin up.

Another way to change the origin is to click the little box where the rulers meet, and drag the crosshairs that appear to the position where you want the origin to be. You'll notice that the rulers change as soon as you release the mouse button. Simply double-click the place where the rulers meet, and the origin will be reset to the default position.

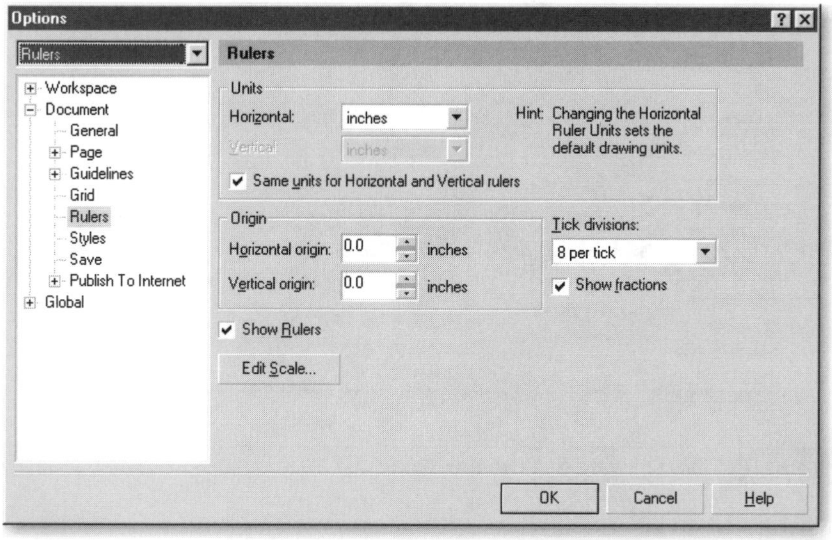

FIGURE 13-1   Options Ruler dialog box

The Options Ruler dialog box also allows you to change the tick divisions on the ruler to 6, 8, or 10. The number of ticks you want displayed may depend on the measurement system you are using. Just below the Tick Divisions box is the Show Fractions check box, which is checked to show fractions instead of decimals on the ruler. When you're working in inches, seeing the fractions on the rulers can be quite handy. This setting is especially useful when you're working with inches, as fractions such as "half an inch" or "quarter of an inch" are often used. With the metric system, the units all divide cleanly by 10, and therefore decimals make more sense.

Click the Edit Scale button to display the Drawing Scale dialog box shown in Figure 13-2.

The Typical Scales drop-down list provides drawing scales. For example, if you use the scale 1 inch equals 1 foot, the standard page of 8.5" x 11" equals 8.5' x 11'. The rulers will display measurements according to this scale, as will any dimension lines you draw.

Some of the drawing scales just have numbers such as 1:1 or 1:2. The first number indicates the size of the unit you are creating, and the second number indicates the size that will be indicated by the rulers. So with 1:1, a one-inch object

13

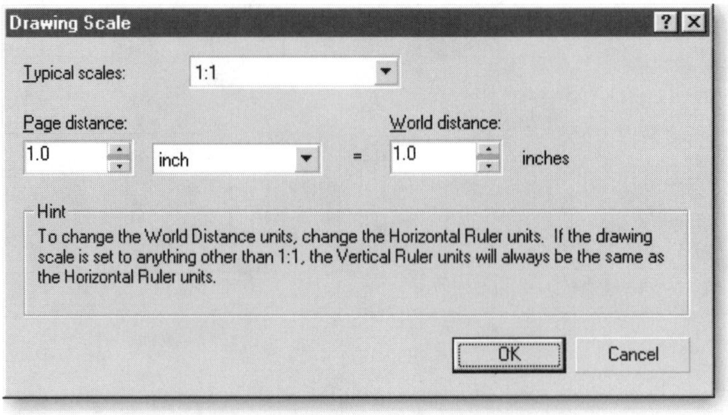

FIGURE 13-2   The Drawing Scale dialog box

is a one-inch object. With 1:2, a one inch object will be shown on the rulers to be two inches. In fact, a standard 8.5" x 11" page will be displayed as 17" x 22" if you choose the 1:2 scale. Other drawing scales follow this same formula.

If you can't find the scale you need in the Typical scales drop-down list, choose Custom (at the bottom of the list), and create your own scale. In the Page Distance boxes, type the number of units and the type of units. In the World distance box, type the value that you want the page distance to equal. Using the example where 1 inch equals 1 foot, you'd enter 1 inch as the page distance and 12 inches as the world distance. The world distance units are based on the units that are currently set for the rulers. If you're not happy with the units showing, simply change them in the Options Ruler dialog box.

Grids

Each page has an underlying grid of invisible lines. By default, the grid is invisible and will not affect your work. However, you can put the grid to work for you. Select View I Grid and Ruler Setup. This will display the dialog box shown in Figure 13-3.

The frequency of the grid specifies the number of invisible lines in the grid between each ruler unit. For very small ruler units, you may want to enter a fractional grid frequency. For example, if the ruler unit is a point, you might set the grid to 0.1 so that a gridline will appear at every tenth point.

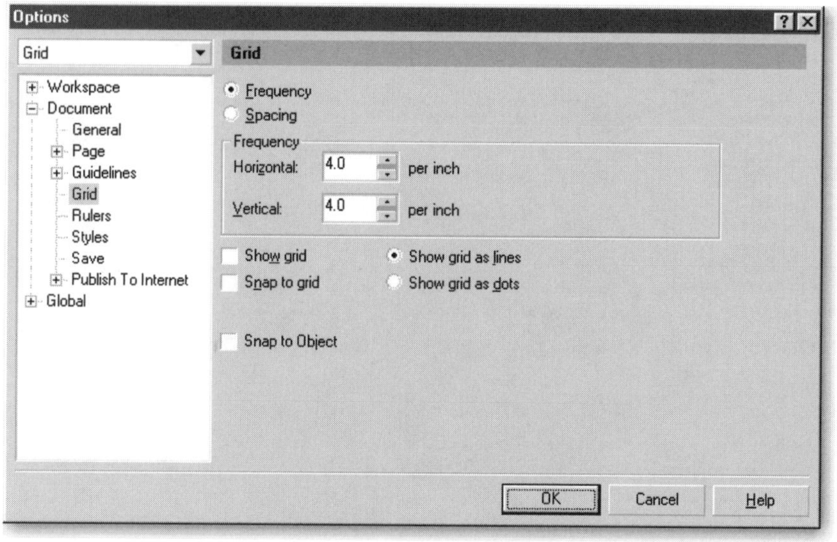

FIGURE 13-3   The Options Grid dialog box with Frequency selected

A new option allows you to specify the spacing between grid dots. Selecting the Spacing radio button displays the dialog box shown in Figure 13-4.

As with gridlines, you can specify the distance between grid dots in both the horizontal and vertical directions.

The Show Grid check box displays the grid on the screen. By default you'll see the actual gridlines as light gray lines. This differs from older version where the default was a blue dot where the lines intersect. You can switch back to the old method by selecting the Show grid as dots radio button. At times, you'll not see the grid at every position, because the lines are limited to a certain density. For example, if the ruler unit were pixels and a gridline appeared at every pixel, the whole screen would be gray. This is no help at all. As you zoom in, the gridlines will become increasingly dense until they appear at every position as they are specified. Also, if you really hate light gray, you can change the color in the Object Manager Docker window, described in Chapter 12.

Snap To Grid actually puts the grid to use. If you check this box, anything that you draw, distort, or drag will snap to the gridlines even if they aren't showing on screen. When you want to align things on the page or within an ad, for instance, the grid can be extremely useful, and it will certainly help you draw objects of precise sizes since the objects will snap to exact sizes.

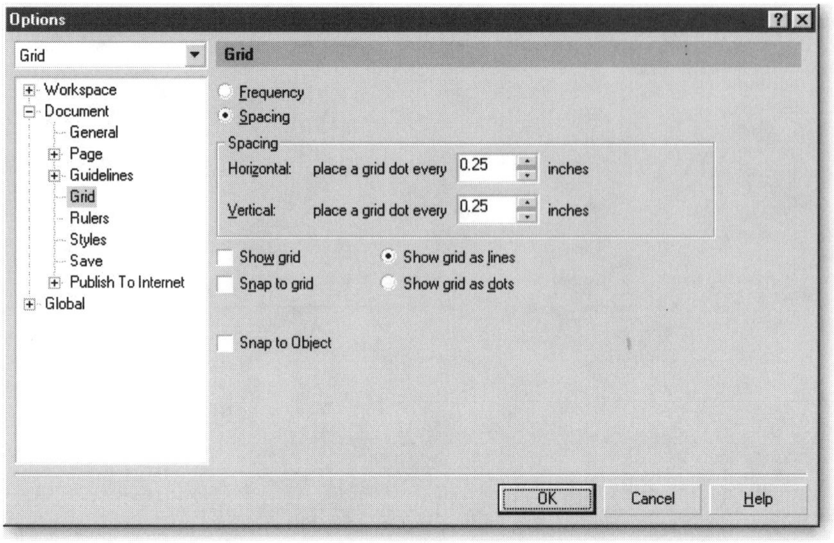

FIGURE 13-4   The Options Grid dialog box with Spacing selected

In the Guidelines dialog box, you can specify whether guidelines are shown and if the snap will be enabled. And the last option allows you to enable Snap to Object.

TIP   *You can also activate the Grid display by choosing View | Grid. You can turn on grid snapping with View | Snap To Grid (CTRL-Y). You'll also find icons on the Property Bar for Snap To Grid, Snap To Guideline, and Snap To Objects, as shown here. If you don't see them on your Property Bar, make sure the Pick tool is the active tool and that you have no objects selected.*

Guidelines

Guidelines are very similar to the invisible gridlines. You can put them anywhere in either the vertical, horizontal, or diagonal orientation. They are used just like the grid except that they appear only where you place them instead of at a particular frequency.

Create a guideline by clicking either of the rulers and dragging it onto the drawing window. A black dashed line will follow your cursor. When you release the mouse button, the guideline will be placed, and the color will temporarily change to red to indicate that it is selected. The ruler you drag from determines the orientation of the guideline. Thus, if you want a vertical guideline, drag from the vertical ruler.

 TIP   *Break the rules by holding down the ALT key while dragging guidelines. This will create a guideline perpendicular to the ruler it came from.*

To manually delete guidelines, select them, and press the DEL key.

Guidelines work like any other object you've drawn onscreen. If a guideline is currently selected, its color will change to red. You can drag guidelines to move them to a new location. If you click quickly, the handles will become rotation handles complete with a thumbtack. Use these handles and thumbtack to rotate the guideline to precisely the position you want. To recolor a guideline, select it, drag a color swatch from the palette, and drop it directly on the guideline. You'll see the swatch change to an outline when it becomes droppable. If the guideline is selected, you won't see the color change until after the guideline is deselected. This way, you can have different types of guidelines in different colors.

Now, let's try something else. Make sure you have two guidelines onscreen. Select the first one by clicking it. Now hold down the SHIFT key, and click the second one. Yes, they are both selected. You can now nudge them, move them as one, delete them, rotate them, cut them, copy them, paste them, or whatever you desire. You'll also notice that since they are both selected, they are both red. The key thing to remember is that selected guidelines are red and unselected guidelines are not. With all of these features, it is very easy to create parallel slanted guidelines without doing any math!

 TIP   *There's also a command that lets you select all of the guidelines. Choose Edit | Select All | Guidelines.*

Usually, you'll want guidelines at an exact position or exact angle. New to CorelDRAW 9 is the ability to change these settings on the Property Bar when the guideline is selected, as shown in Figure 13-5. At left is the location of the guideline. If the guideline is vertical, you'll only want to change the *x* value. If it is horizontal, change the *y* value. Next, you can enter a value of rotation and even the center of

13

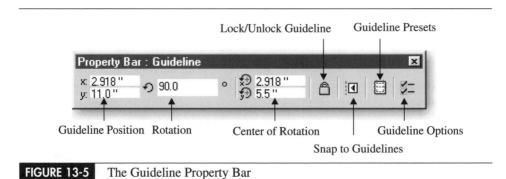

FIGURE 13-5 The Guideline Property Bar

rotation. Center of rotation defaults to the point on the guideline that is centered on the drawing page. Four more icons follow for locking the guideline, turning on guideline snap, guideline presets, and the Guideline Options dialog box. If you lock the guideline and then reselect the guideline, you will not receive the Guideline Property Bar. To unlock, right-click on the guideline, and choose Unlock Object from the pop-up menu that appears.

Display the Options Guidelines dialog box shown in Figure 13-6 by selecting View | Guidelines Setup, double-clicking any guideline, or right-clicking on a ruler and choosing Guidelines Setup. If you have a guideline selected, you may get another dialog box, so you'll need to select Guidelines in the tree list at the left of the dialog to get the dialog box shown in Figure 13-6. The first option is to Show Guidelines. By default, it is checked. If you do not want to see the guidelines, simply uncheck it. Next is the Snap to Guidelines check box. This determines if the objects you are creating or moving will magnetically snap to guidelines. You can also select a Default Guideline Color and a Default Preset Guideline Color using the color drop-down lists. Remember that you can recolor any guideline by dropping a color swatch on it.

There are numerous other settings you can set for guidelines. The first one is the Options Guidelines Horizontal Dialog box shown in Figure 13-7.

The Options Guidelines Vertical dialog box is identical in functionality to this dialog box and so it is not described separately. The left side lists the position of any existing guidelines. To add a guideline, type its position in the textbox at the top of the list, and click the Add button. To move an existing guideline, first select it from the list. Then type the desired position, and click Move. Select a guideline from the list, and click Delete to get rid of a guideline. Clicking Clear will remove all of the guidelines.

Slanted guidelines come in two flavors. Figure 13-8 shows the dialog box for Angle and 1 Point, and Figure 13-9 shows the dialog box for 2 Points.

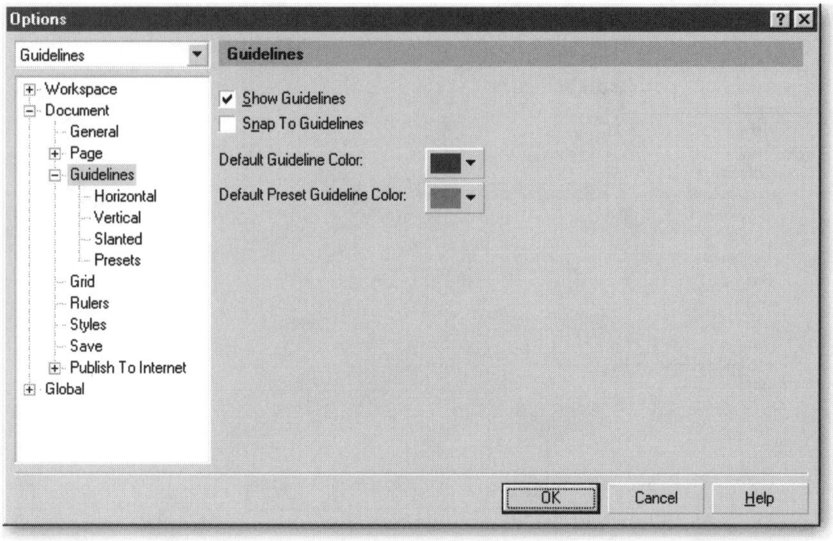

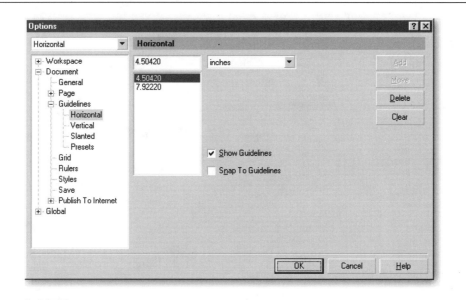

FIGURE 13-6   Options Guidelines dialog box

FIGURE 13-7   Options Guidelines Horizontal dialog box

13

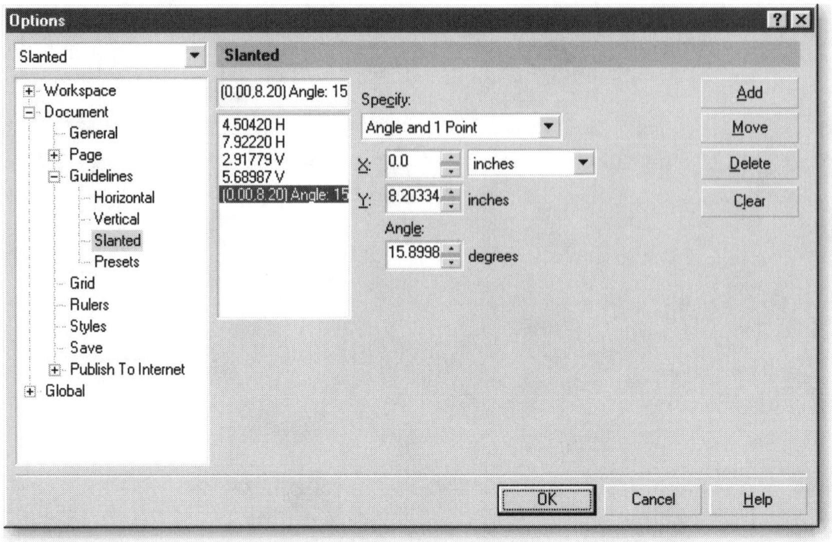

FIGURE 13-8   Options Guideline Slanted dialog box for Angle and 1 Point

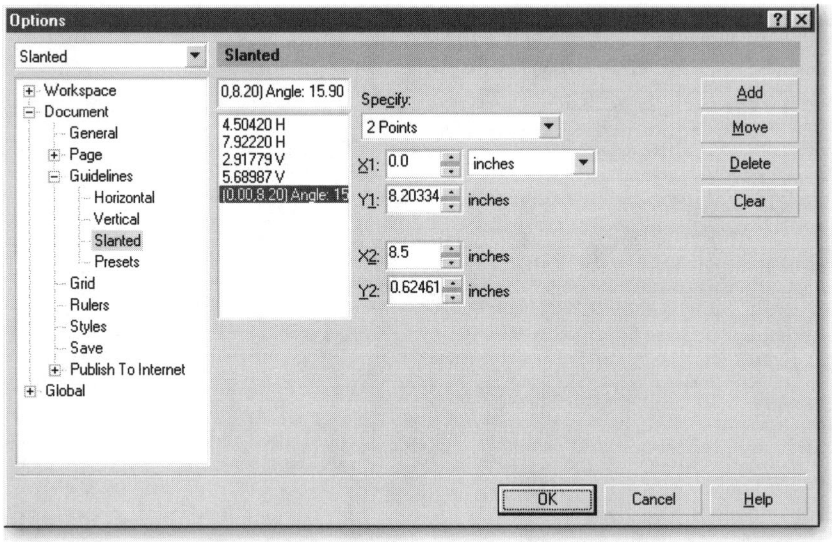

FIGURE 13-9   Options Guideline Slanted dialog box for 2 Points

The list box at the left side of both dialog boxes shows all of the guidelines. Horizontal guidelines are followed by an *H*, vertical guidelines by a *V*. Once a guideline has been slanted, it will be listed with either a single position and an angle, or with two positions, depending on how it was created.

With Angle and 1 Point, the x and y points are measured from the edge of the page closest to the ruler origins. By default, this will be the lower left corner. The angle is defined as the angle at which the guideline lays in relation to a completely horizontal line drawn across the page. With 2 Point, x and y points are measured first from the edge of the page closest to the ruler origins and then from the edge farthest from the ruler origin. It is a lot easier to understand all of this if you create a slanted guideline manually and watch the movement of it, relative to page edges, as you enter different coordinates into the Options dialog.

Guideline Presets

As you are working on a drawing, you will find certain sets of guidelines handy. New to CorelDRAW 9 are a series of guideline presets. Figure 13-10 shows the Corel Presets dialog box.

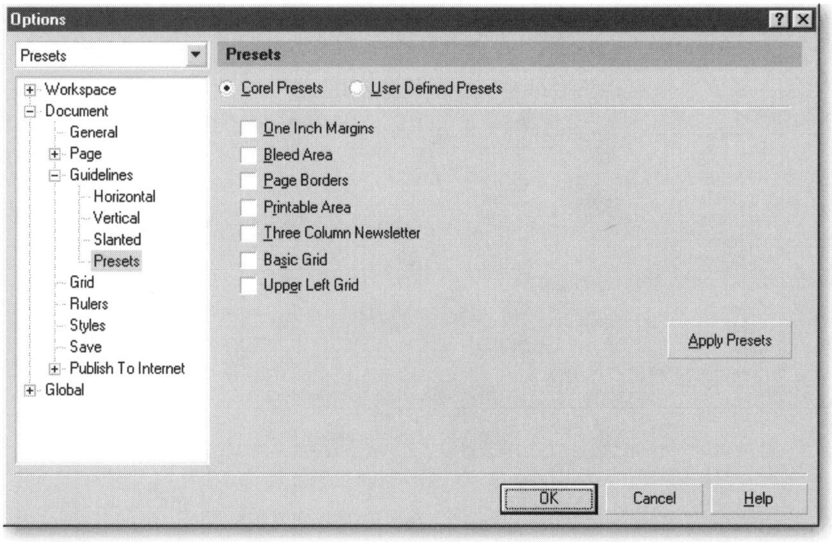

FIGURE 13-10   Options Guidelines Presets dialog box with Corel Presets selected

The various settings are fairly self-explanatory, and you can select more than one of the presets. When you click the Apply Presets, the guidelines will appear on the page behind the dialog box. If you want to "undo," simply uncheck the preset you don't want, and click Apply Presets again. If you don't find the preset you desire, click on the User Defined Presets radio button to get the dialog shown in Figure 13-11.

There are three sections, and you can choose to use one of them or all of them. In the Margins section are textboxes where you can enter Top, Bottom, Left, and Right margin values. If Mirror margins is checked, only the Top and Left boxes are available. Columns allows you to choose the number of columns and the distance between them. So if you were designing a newsletter with four columns of text, you'd use both Margins and Columns. The margins would be something like one-half inch, and you would have four columns with .25 inches between them. This is certainly easier than doing the math and placing them manually. The last section is used to create a grid. The settings here are very similar to those described in the Grid section of this chapter, but instead of having true grid lines, you have guidelines. Just like the Corel Presets, you click the Apply Presets button to apply your settings.

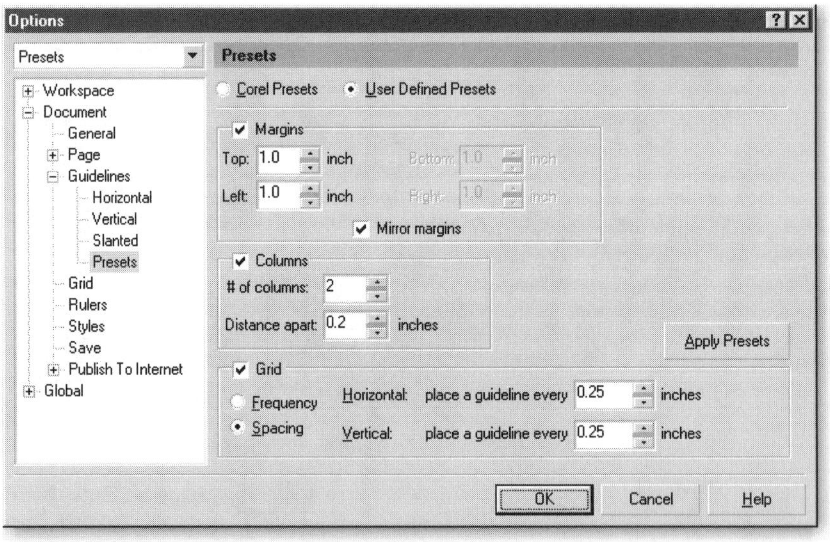

FIGURE 13-11 Options Guidelines Presets dialog box with User Defined Presets selected

Unfortunately, by default you cannot have both Corel preset guidelines and User Defined presets. To workaround this oversight, you will have to apply one set of presets (Corel or User Defined), close the dialog, and then manually recolor the guidelines to convert them to standard guidelines. Then apply the other set of preset guidelines. However, this is still easier than doing the math!

Using Objects as Guides

Any object that can be drawn can be used as a guideline. You simply need to place it on the Guides layer. Chapter 12 discussed how to move objects to another layer and how to draw on the Guides layer. Keep in mind that objects drawn on the Guides layer do not work the same as guidelines. Snapping will only occur at the object's snap points (usually nodes) and not along the entire path of the object.

This same effect can be achieved without putting objects on the Guides layer. Just choose View | Snap To Objects. Again, other objects will snap only to the snap points of the snap object and not to the object itself.

Guideline Wizard

The methods described previously will cover almost all of your guideline needs. But there is one more option—the Guideline Wizard. The Wizard has been around for a few versions now, and most of its functionality is part of the presets described earlier. But it does contain a few types of presets not included elsewhere. To access it, choose Window | Dockers | Script, and Preset Manager. When the Docker first appears, you'll see two folders in the Docker window, one labeled Scripts and one labeled Presets. Double-click the Scripts folder. Now scroll through the list of scripts until you find one called guidewiz, and double-click it. To explore further, just follow the steps in the Wizard. For those who want to learn more about scripts, see Chapter 35.

Now that you understand how to use guidelines and grids, give them a try on your next project; we think that you'll see just how useful they can be.

13

CHAPTER 14

Combining, Grouping, and Converting to Curves

CorelDRAW 9

The commands covered in this chapter share a common feature: they all work with multiple objects. There may be some who question whether this statement applies to the Convert to Curves command, but multiple objects are often involved when converting to curves as well.

When you are instructed to select a command in this chapter, you will use the Property Bar whenever possible. If the command is not on the Property Bar, you will use the Arrange drop-down menu.

Combining

The Combine command, located on the Property Bar (CTRL-L), is active only when two or more individual objects are selected. It is perhaps the least understood of all the commands. The function of this command is to combine two or more objects into one. The Weld command discussed in Chapter 15 also combines two or more objects into one, but in a different way. Differentiating between these two commands is important, but more important is understanding how the Combine command actually functions so you will know when to use it. It's also important to recognize when objects have been combined.

Knowing When Objects Are Combined

Knowing when objects have been combined can be a great help when working with clipart. To see the effect of combining objects, open the Symbols and Special Characters Docker by choosing Window | Dockers | Symbols and Special Characters. Choose the People category, and locate the two images shown in Figure 14-1. Drag the two symbols out on the page. Color the symbol of the girl pink and the man black. Now select the both objects by SHIFT-clicking on the girl and then the man. When the two objects are selected, look at the Status Bar at the bottom of the screen. The status line should indicate that you have two objects selected on layer 1. Click the Combine command on the Property Bar. Now look at the Status Bar again. This time it says that you have a curve selected on layer 1. You no longer have two separate symbols; instead, you have a single object, which is a considered to be a curve object. Also notice that the color of the combined object has changed to black. See the following Tip for an explanation as to why the color changed.

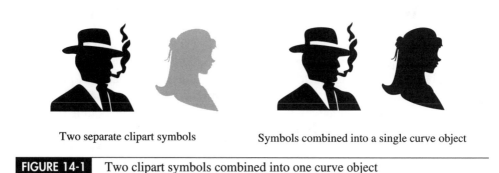

Two separate clipart symbols   Symbols combined into a single curve object

FIGURE 14-1   Two clipart symbols combined into one curve object

Now select the combined objects, and move them to a different location on the page. They look like two distinctly separate objects, but CorelDRAW sees them as one—as the status line tells you. This seemingly confusing set of circumstances is why the Combine command can be difficult to understand.

TIP   *If you are combining objects that are filled, the last object selected will determine the fill color. For example, if you select an object filled with a gradient fill and then an object filled with a solid color like red and combine the two, the resulting object will be red.*

Breaking Apart

The Break Apart command works hand in hand with the Combine command. It is accessed from the Arrange menu by clicking Arrange | Break Apart (CTRL-K). One of its functions is to undo the combining effect of the Combine command. It can also be used to break apart artistic text into individual letters and paragraph text into individual paragraphs as well as down to individual letters.

To see how Break Apart works, select the two clipart symbols you just combined, and then choose Arrange | Break Apart. Now select the girl. Notice that the selection handles now surround only the girl and not the man. With the girl now separated from the man, the objects can be modified separately.

Try the Break Apart command with artistic text. Type the word **COREL** on the page. Select the text and choose the Break Apart command. You can now select each individual letter in the word *COREL* and each letter is editable as text.

14

Using the Combine and Break Apart Commands Together

The fact that the Combine command works the way it does is what makes the command useful. One of the primary uses of the Combine command is to combine objects that share the same attributes. Two combined objects will take up less disk space and redraw more quickly. Corel's clipart provides the best example of this attribute sharing. Figure 14-2 shows a horse in the clipart collection. If you want to follow along, the filename is Horse329.cdr, and it's located on the Clipart CD that comes with the program in the Animals\Farm folder. We say it comes with the clipart that comes with the program because it has been there for several years. Hopefully it will be there again this year. If it's not, following along with the text and figures should teach you the technique quite well.

When you first import clipart, you should check the status line to determine whether the objects are grouped. If they are, you will need to ungroup them before you can work on individual parts of the image (see the section "Grouping and Ungrouping," later in this chapter). With the horse image ungrouped, select the tail of the horse. Notice the selection handles surround more than just the tail. The fact that the selection handles surround an area larger than the tail area should alert you

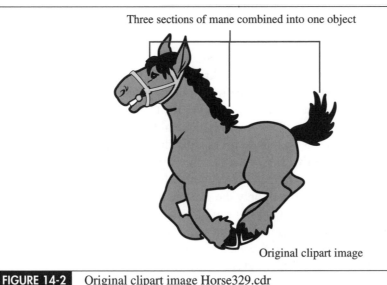

Three sections of mane combined into one object

Original clipart image

FIGURE 14-2   Original clipart image Horse329.cdr

that the tail is combined with another part of the horse. To find out what other parts of the horse are combined with the tail, simply change the color of the tail. When you change the color of the tail, any other object that has been combined with the tail will also change color. In the case of Horse329, the mane of the horse was combined with the tail. They were combined because they shared the same color and outline attributes. If you want to change the color of the tail without changing the color of the mane, you will need to use the Break Apart command. Figure 14-3 shows the mane and tail colored differently.

Remember, the function of the Break Apart command is to uncombine the combined objects into separate objects again. When the objects are no longer combined, they can be handled like any other single objects.

To convert the horse's tail into separate objects, select the tail, and then choose Arrange | Break Apart (CTRL-K). This action will separate the tail from the mane. Interestingly, the mane is composed of three separate objects, so when you originally clicked the tail, you actually selected three objects combined as one. Figure 14-3 shows the three separate parts of the mane each shaded differently.

All this information sounds a little confusing at first. If you practice using the Combine and Break Apart commands on simple clipart objects, you'll understand their functions more quickly.

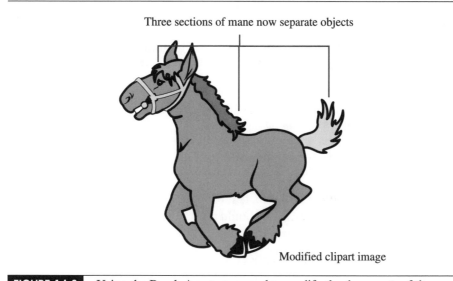

Three sections of mane now separate objects

Modified clipart image

FIGURE 14-3   Using the Break Apart command to modify the three parts of the mane

14

Using the Combine Command to Create Patterns and Masks

One of the more common uses of the Combine command used to be to create borders and masks. When the Trim command was introduced in an earlier version, it took the place of the Combine command for this role (see Chapter 15). However, the Combine command will function differently than the Trim command if an object partially overlaps another object or doesn't touch another selected object at all.

In the previous examples of the Combine command, the objects that were combined were separated from each other. If the objects being combined overlap, they behave in a completely different way. When objects overlap, a hole will be cut in the final combined object where the objects overlap. There aren't many times when this type of combining is particularly useful, but it can produce some beautiful patterns, as shown in Figure 14-4. Follow these steps to create this design:

1. Draw an ellipse on the page approximately .5" wide by 2" tall.

2. Give the ellipse a light blue fill with a red outline.

3. Press the + key on the numeric keypad to make a duplicate of the ellipse.

4. With the duplicate ellipse selected, click a second time to reveal the rotation arrows.

5. Drag the center of rotation thumbtack to the bottom of the ellipse (see the example on the left in Figure 14-4).

6. Holding down the CTRL key, click on the upper-left double-headed rotation arrows, and drag down and to the left. Holding down the CTRL key constrains your movement to 15 degree increments.

7. Look at the Status Bar, and when you have rotated the ellipse 15 degrees, release the mouse button.

8. With the rotated ellipse still selected, use the Smart Duplicate technique by pressing CTRL-D 22 times. You should now have 24 ellipses in a circle, as shown in the center of Figure 14-4.

9. Marquee select all 24 ellipses, and click the Combine button on the Property Bar. Your image should now look like the finished pattern at the right in Figure 14-4.

FIGURE 14-4   A pattern created using the Combine command

Using Combine to Create a Mask with Text

Another interesting use of the Combine command is creating an effect that appears as if you're looking through transparent text onto an image below. To create this effect, you begin by placing your bitmap image on the page and then drawing a rectangle large enough to cover the entire image. Type the text you wish to use on top of the rectangle. Use a wide font, and make it as big as you can without going outside the rectangle. Select the text and the rectangle, and combine them by clicking the Combine button on the Property Bar. Figure 14-5 shows the completed effect using a bitmap image of Hawaii as the underlying image.

 TIP   *Although this masking method is a tried-and-true way to fool the eye into thinking you are looking through text into a background, this same effect can be created by PowerClipping the background image into the text. For information on PowerClip, see Chapter 20.*

14

Grouping and Ungrouping

Grouping is a way to keep objects together as a unit. A good example of grouped objects is a clipart image. Usually a clipart image is made up of many individual objects. Grouping the objects prevents the accidental moving of a single object within the group. More important, it allows you to move a large number of objects at one time without adversely affecting the relationship of the objects within the group.

A group of objects can be blended from one group to another, and effects such as Perspective and Envelope can be applied to the group (see Chapter 17). Grouping

FIGURE 14-5   Text combined with a rectangle to create a mask allowing the underlying image to show through

several groups into a Nested group is also fairly common. The nested group is not called a "Nested group" on the status line; it is merely a group composed of several groups. For example, if you select a group that contains three separate groups, the Status Bar will tell you have a group of three objects; CorelDRAW doesn't know the three objects are groups. Form the habit of grouping objects that share commonalities as a means of organizing them.

Figure 14-6 shows individual groups outlined with dotted lines within a nested group.

The process of grouping is straightforward. Simply select the objects you want to group, and click the Group button on the Property Bar, or use the shortcut CTRL-G. Ungrouping is just as easy. To ungroup a group of objects, select the group, and then click the Ungroup button on the Property Bar, or use the shortcut CTRL-U.

There is also an Ungroup All button on the Property Bar. The Ungroup All command literally ungroups all groups that are selected. If you select single groups, master groups, or a combination of both, all the objects within these groups will revert to single-object status when you choose Ungroup All.

FIGURE 14-6   One nested group containing individual groups

Selecting Objects Within a Group

It is not always necessary to ungroup a group of objects to edit an individual object within the group. For example, you can change the color of a particular object or adjust the size or shape of an object without ungrouping the group.

To edit an individual object within a group, hold down the CTRL key, and select the object. Round selection handles will surround the object instead of the familiar square ones. Check the status line; it will tell you that you have selected a child object. A child object is a selected object within a group of objects. When a child object is selected, you can treat it just like any other object.

Figure 14-7 shows a group of objects on the left and a duplicate of this group on the right. The building in the left foreground has been selected and is a child object. It has been enlarged and the colors changed. In this case when the building was selected as a child object by CTRL-clicking, it was also a group. The status bar will indicate a child group. To change the colors within the child group, continue to click on the desired objects while holding down the CTRL key. This action will allow you to select individual child objects one at a time within the child group.

14

Child group

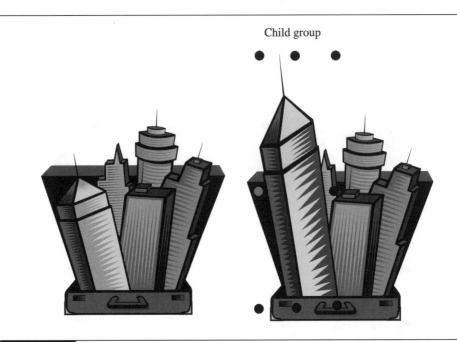

FIGURE 14-7   A child group and child objects modified within a master group

Separating

The Separate command, <u>A</u>rrange I <u>S</u>eparate, is used to take apart certain effects so that individual parts of the effect can be edited. Think of this process as an extra step that is required to edit individual objects within certain effects. The effects that you must separate prior to editing individual objects are Blend (including blends on a path), Clone, Contour, Extrude, Fit Text to Path, Dimension Lines, Connector Lines, and Drop Shadows. The Separate command separates the original object or objects from the objects created by these effects.

Consider the text on a Path effect (see Chapter 21). When the text is placed on a path like the one on the left in Figure 14-8, it is made up of the ellipse and the two text objects (the bear is a separate object and not part of the text on path effect). If you select any of the objects in the effect, the Status Bar will indicate that a compound object of three elements is selected. When you use the Separate command to separate the text on a Path effect, you are left with the original two text objects and the original ellipse, which can then be treated as individual objects again.

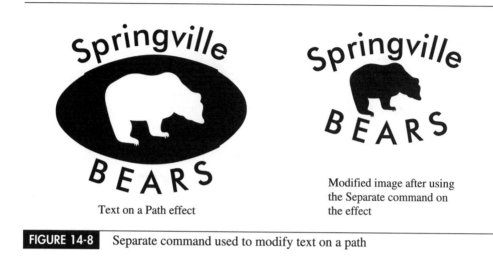

Text on a Path effect

Modified image after using
the Separate command on
the effect

FIGURE 14-8   Separate command used to modify text on a path

In Figure 14-8 we separated the text on a Path effect on the left, deleted the
ellipse, reduced the size of the bear, and moved the word *Bears* closer to the word
Springville.

Converting to Curves

The primary function of the Convert to Curves command is to convert rectangles,
ellipses, distortion effects, stars/polygons, and text into fully editable shapes. You will
use many different shapes when you create your projects in CorelDRAW, and most of
them, with the exception of clipart, will start out as rectangles, ellipses, or freehand
shapes. You will usually apply many CorelDRAW effects to these objects to achieve
your final image. In most cases, even though you use these effects, the original object
will still retain its original identity. For example, if you extrude an ellipse, the control
object is still an ellipse. If you apply an envelope to a rectangle, the new enveloped
shape is still a rectangle. If you add perspective to a word you've typed, the word
is still text.

You can have even greater control over all these objects if you convert them to
curves. This is not to say you should convert every rectangle you draw or text you
type to curves, but doing so gives you more artistic control over objects when you
need it.

14

How to Convert Single Objects to Curves

To convert a single object to curves, click the Convert to Curves icon on the Property Bar, or use the shortcut (CTRL-Q). For example, a basic ellipse has one node. When the ellipse is converted to curves, it will have four nodes. A basic rectangle has a node at each corner. When it is converted to curves, the nodes become editable. Text has a node at the base of each letter for kerning purposes. When text is converted to curves, many additional nodes are added to form the shape of the text. These nodes allow you to manipulate the text in a more artistic manner.

The right side of Figure 14-9 shows an ellipse that has been converted to curves. The figure shows where the four nodes will appear when the Shape tool is selected. The object on the right is the result of manipulating the four nodes into a different shape. A little more adjusting and it could fit on the shoes of a famous sports star. Just think: that logo could have been created with four nodes.

Using the Convert to Curves Command to Create Freehand Shapes

Converting an ellipse to curves is a way of creating freehand shapes without having to use the freehand tool. Unless you have the steady hand of a diamond cutter, using a mouse to draw freehand shapes can produce jaggy perimeters (Version 9 has added a Freehand smoothing control on the Property Bar that helps

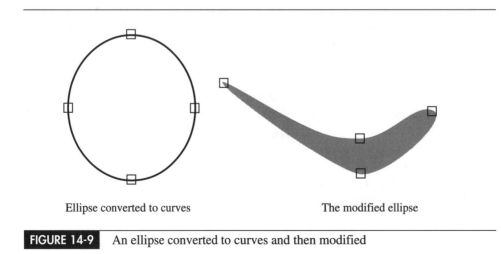

Ellipse converted to curves   The modified ellipse

FIGURE 14-9   An ellipse converted to curves and then modified to smooth out the jaggies, a great improvement over previous versions). When you convert an ellipse to curves, you can maintain smooth lines as you manipulate the shape with the Shape tool.

The dolphin in Figure 14-10 also began life as an ellipse. After it was converted to curves, the Shape tool was used to manipulate it into the silhouette of a dolphin. Additional ellipses were added and converted to curves to make the various shapes required for the final image. Think of it as shaping a lump of clay. It's really quite simple when you get used to it. To learn about adding nodes, changing from one type of node to another, and other Shape tool functions, see Chapter 7.

Using the Convert to Curves Command to Modify Text

When you want to create really unusual looking text, the Convert to Curves command is the command to use. The top of Figure 14-11 shows the word *CLOUDS* using the font Staccato555BT. The bottom of the figure shows the text

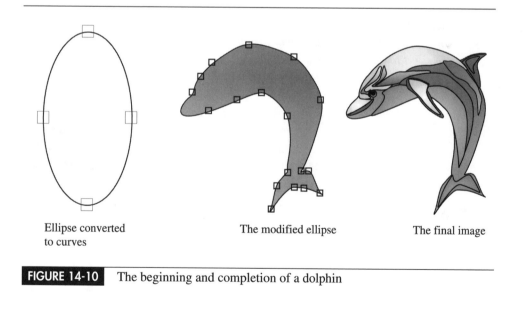

Ellipse converted
to curves

The modified ellipse

The final image

FIGURE 14-10   The beginning and completion of a dolphin

14

The original text

Text converted to curves and modified

FIGURE 14-11   Text modified with the Shape tool after it was converted to curves

modified with the Shape tool after it was converted to curves. As you can see, there are many artistic possibilities when you convert text to curves.

TIP   *If you add either the Perspective or Envelope effect to an object and then decide to modify the object with the Shape tool, you must first use the Convert to Curves command again before you can further modify the object. See Chapter 17 for information on the Envelope and Perspective effects.*

Having read how to use the various commands covered in this chapter, you have learned the relationship between the Combine and Break Apart commands as well as when to use the Separate command. Remember that the Group command is an excellent way to keep together objects that share a commonality. Understanding these basic concepts will go a long way in helping you master CorelDRAW.

CHAPTER 15

Weld, Trim, and Intersect

CoreIDRAW 9

COREL.COM

This chapter covers three different commands, all of which will help you draw shapes more quickly and easily than drawing them freehand. They also share one thing in common. Before any of these commands will work as designed, each object must overlap at least one other object in some fashion.

Note: Technically, you can use the Weld and Trim command on objects that don't overlap. In the case of Weld, the effect of welding objects that don't overlap would be the same as combining them (see Chapter 14). In the case of Trim the effect of trimming objects that don't overlap would be that the last object selected would be converted to a curve (see Chapter 14).

There are two ways to use the commands. You can either use the Quick commands on the Property Bar or the more complete commands in the Shaping Docker window. Before you use the Quick commands, you should learn how the individual commands work using the commands in the Docker window. Do this by clicking Window | Dockers | Shaping. Choose Weld from the flyout. This action will display the Shaping Docker with the Weld controls displayed. Also displayed at the top of the Docker are the three command buttons that can be used to alternate between the different command controls. This grouping of the Dockers allows you to quickly switch among the three commands as you work. As you learn how these commands work, you may find that using a Quick command on the Property Bar is faster than using the Dockers.

NOTE   *The Weld, Intersect, and Trim commands function differently when selected from the Property Bar. These differences are explained at the end of each command section.*

The Weld Command

The purpose of the Weld command is to create custom shapes by combining two or more objects together to form a single shape. The Docker window is accessed by choosing Window | Dockers | Shaping | Weld. Figure 15-1 shows the Shaping Docker with the Weld command controls displayed.

Welding is an additive process requiring that objects overlap each other before they can be welded. What actually happens when you weld objects together is the areas that overlap are thrown away and the outside perimeters of the objects are welded together to form one single object. Figure 15-2 shows before and after examples of the welding process. On the left are the individual objects overlapping each other to form the shapes. In the center are the objects after they have been

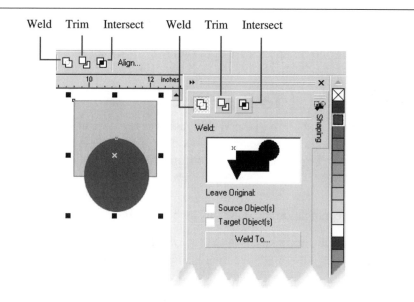

FIGURE 15-1   The Shaping Docker with the Weld controls

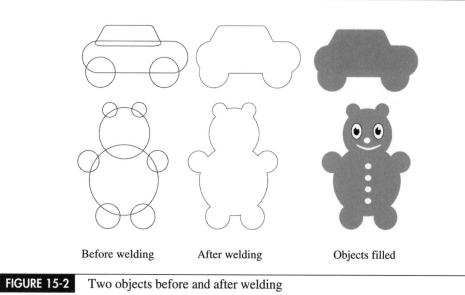

Before welding   After welding   Objects filled

FIGURE 15-2   Two objects before and after welding

welded. Notice how the intersecting lines of the overlapping objects have disappeared, and the objects have been transformed into a single shape. On the right, the objects are then filled with a solid fill. In the case of the teddy bear, we added a few details.

Using the Weld To Button

Clicking the Weld To button in the Weld Docker is the default method for welding when you use the controls in the Shaping Docker. To create the silhouette of the spray can shown in Figure 15-3, use the outline view on the left of the spray can as a guide and follow these steps:

1. Draw a rectangle on the page for the body of the can.

2. Draw a circle, and place it at the top of the rectangle, leaving about a fourth of the circle showing above the rectangle.

3. Draw two small rectangles like those shown in the figure, and place them so they overlap each other and so the bottom one overlaps the circle.

4. Select all of the objects except the largest rectangle by SHIFT-clicking (these objects are called the *source objects*; think of them as modifying objects), and then click the Weld To button.

5. A special weld cursor replaces the cursor. Use this cursor to select the large rectangle (this object is called the *target object*). When you select the second object with the cursor, all the objects will be welded together. You should have a silhouette of a spray can.

6. Color the silhouette with a fill of black. Your drawing should look like the right side of Figure 15-3.

 TIP *This method of welding several objects together at once can be confusing when you are welding many objects. In the preceding example, instead of selecting all but the largest rectangle, you could select all the objects at once by marquee selecting. Then, when you click the Weld To button, you can use the cursor to select any of the selected objects. The weld function will work just as if you had selected the first three objects and pointed to the fourth.*

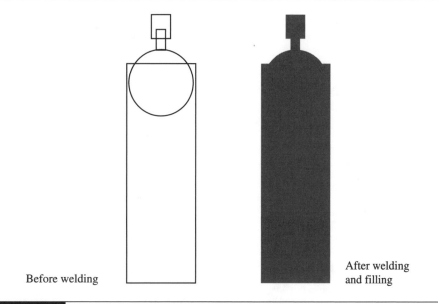

Before welding

After welding
and filling

FIGURE 15-3 Welding several objects to create a silhouette of a spray can

The other options in the Docker let you choose whether to leave the original of either the target objects or source objects after the weld function is executed. Put a check mark in the appropriate boxes to retain either the original or target objects, or both. When you use the Weld command, you will rarely leave any of the original objects behind.

There are many uses for the Weld command. Figure 15-4 shows a few examples of welding text to freehand objects and symbols to create drop caps. The examples shown were created by first creating the welded shapes as single shapes and then adding the remainder of the text afterwards.

Creating Street Maps with the Weld Command

Creating street maps can be frustrating without the use of the Weld command. Figure 15-5 shows a typical street map before and after the Weld command was used. To create street maps, you draw the streets using rectangles and then weld them together. If you need to add winding streets, try using the new Artistic Media tool. You can vary the width by changing the settings on the Property Bar.

15

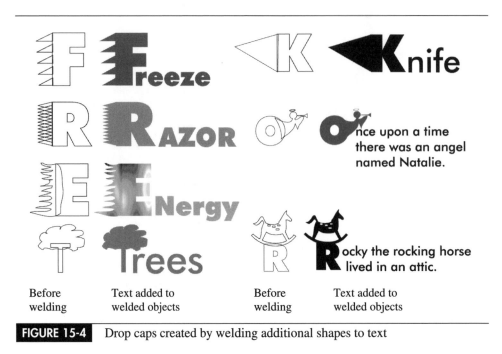

| Before welding | Text added to welded objects | Before welding | Text added to welded objects |

FIGURE 15-4   Drop caps created by welding additional shapes to text

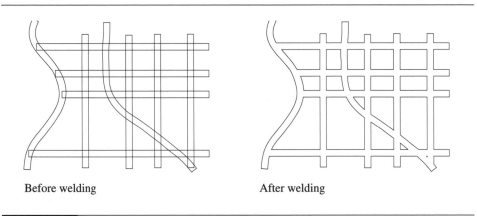

Before welding

After welding

FIGURE 15-5   These shapes were first drawn with the Rectangle and Artistic Media tools, and then they were welded together to create a street map.

Using the Weld Command with Groups of Objects

A new feature first introduced in CorelDRAW 8 allows you to weld groups of objects. There are two ways that you can use this feature. You can either weld all the objects within a single group of objects into one single curve object, or you can weld two different groups of objects together. Figure 15-6 illustrates the first method. A clipart image was selected from the Clipart library. The cocktail glass contains 72 objects and takes up 25K of disk space. The group of objects was selected, and the Weld button on the Property Bar was pressed. The result is a single curve object that can be used as a silhouette and a file size reduced to 15K.

The second method of welding two groups together is simply a matter of selecting two groups of objects that you have overlapped in some fashion and clicking the Weld button on the Property Bar. The result will be a single object with a perimeter encompassing the two overlapped groups.

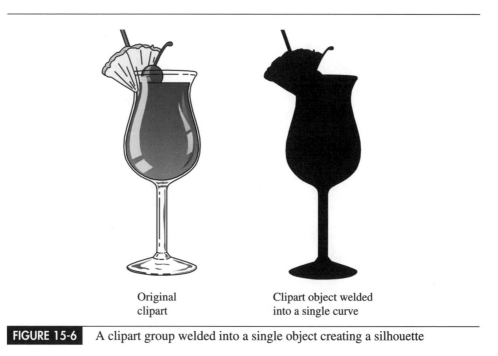

Original
clipart

Clipart object welded
into a single curve

FIGURE 15-6 A clipart group welded into a single object creating a silhouette

15

NOTE   *To avoid any problems when welding a single clipart object into a single curve, first ungroup the group by choosing the Ungroup button on the Property Bar, and then with all the objects selected, choose the Quick Weld button on the Property Bar.*

The Trim Command

The Trim command is another command that lets you create unique shapes quickly and easily. Like the Weld and Intersect commands, it requires at least two overlapping objects. To access the Trim command, choose Window I Dockers I Shaping. Choose Trim from the flyout. Figure 15-7 shows the Shaping Docker displaying the Trim controls. If the Docker is already open, you simply choose the Trim button at the top of the Docker.

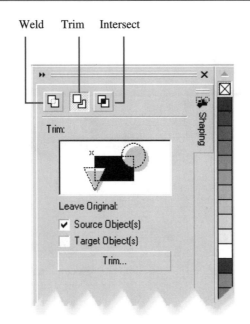

FIGURE 15-7   The Shaping Docker with the Trim controls

Using the Trim Command Like a Cookie Cutter

The Trim command works much like a cookie cutter. Instead of welding objects together like the Weld command, the Trim command removes sections of an object based on the shape of the trimming object. You can even trim an object with two or more objects.

To trim two overlapping objects, select the object you want to use as the trimming object, and then click the Trim button in the Shaping Docker. The cursor will change to a special trim cursor. Use this cursor to select the object you want to cut. When you click on the object, the trim is performed. The amount removed from the trimmed object will be in the shape created by the overlapping object that you first selected.

NOTE *By default the Source Object(s) check box is checked in the Shaping Docker. This means that after the trim is completed, you must move or delete the object you used to trim in order to see the results of the trimming action. If you don't want to have to take this extra step of moving or deleting the source object, uncheck the box.*

Figure 15-8 shows an example of a basic trim. The overlapping objects on the left have not been trimmed. The rectangle in the center with the hole in the shape of the overlapping ellipse is a result of using the ellipse to trim a hole out of the rectangle. The ellipse was selected first and then the rectangle. After the trim was

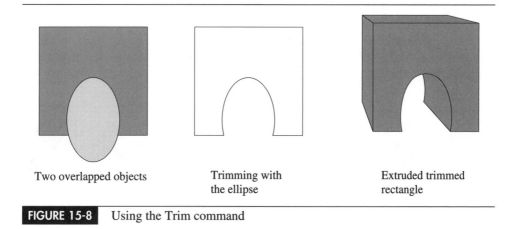

Two overlapped objects   Trimming with   Extruded trimmed
                                the ellipse   rectangle

FIGURE 15-8   Using the Trim command

completed, the ellipse was deleted. The object at the right is the result of extruding the trimmed rectangle. To learn more about extrudes, read Chapter 18. Can you see why Trim is described as the cookie cutter command?

Practice using the basic Trim command until you feel comfortable with the sequence of selection. Remember, the first object or objects you select are the cookie cutters, the last object selected is the object that gets cut. Then try to duplicate the example in Figure 15-9 by following these steps:

1. Draw a circle, and duplicate it six times.

2. Space the circles evenly apart in a straight line.

3. Draw a rectangle over the bottom half of the circles.

4. Remove any check marks from the Leave Original section of the Docker.

5. Select the circles either by marquee selection or by SHIFT-clicking.

6. Click the Trim button, and use the special trim cursor to select the rectangle.

7. Fill the remaining shape with a fill of your choice.

If you followed the steps correctly, your screen should look similar to Figure 15-9. Figure 15-10 takes this technique one step further by creating a postage stamp. Instead of placing circles on one side of a rectangle, they were placed around the entire circumference. Ask yourself how long it would take to create this stamp using traditional tools.

Many users think of the Trim command only as a way to trim closed objects by using other closed objects. Figure 15-11 shows that you can trim closed objects with open path lines as well.

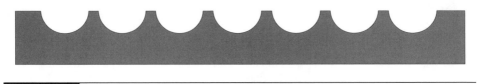

FIGURE 15-9   Example of trimming with multiple objects

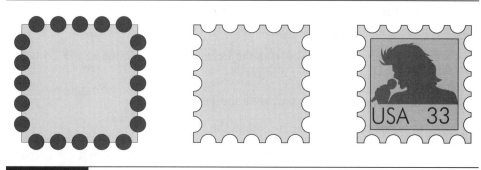

FIGURE 15-10 Using multiple objects to create a postage stamp

If you would like to try this trim method, follow these steps:

1. Using the Ellipse tool, draw a circle on the page. Fill the circle with a light gray color.

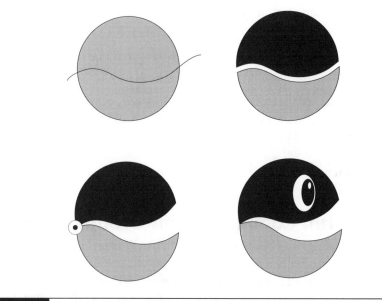

FIGURE 15-11 Trimming a circle with a single line and turning it into a fun image

15

2. Using the Freehand Pencil tool, draw a wavy line across the center of the circle like the one at the upper-left corner of Figure 15-11.

3. Remove any check marks from the Leave Original section of the Trim Docker.

4. With the wavy line selected, click the Trim button.

5. Using the special trim cursor, select the circle.

6. Now select the Pick tool and then select the circle again. Click the Break Apart command on the Arrange | Break Apart menu, or use the short cut CTRL-K.

7. Select the top half of the circle, and change its color to black. Move the two halves slightly apart. Your two halves of the circle should now look like the ones at the upper-right corner of the figure.

8. Select the top half of the circle, and click a second time to reveal the rotation arrows.

9. Move the center-of-rotation thumbtack to the lower-left corner of the selected half, as shown at the lower-left corner of Figure 15-11.

10. Click the upper-right corner rotation arrow, and rotate the top half of the circle to the left.

11. Add an ellipse for the eye, a second ellipse for the eyeball, and a third ellipse for the highlight in the eyeball, and you're finished. The finished image should look like the one shown at the lower-right corner of the figure.

What is it, you ask? We don't know, but it's cute.

Using the Trim Command with Groups of Objects

The ability to trim groups of objects was on CorelDRAW users' wish lists for years, and beginning with version 8, it became a reality. Figure 15-12 illustrates this wonderful feature. A clipart image of a cat containing 1,644 objects was opened, and a freehand shape covering all but the head of the cat was drawn. The freehand shape was selected first (the cookie cutter), and then the clipart group was selected. The

Source Object(s) check box was unchecked, and the trim button selected. The trim cursor was then used to click on the cat. The result was a group of 1,188 objects making up just the head of the cat. This one feature will save hours of image editing for anyone needing to modify clipart.

 TIP   *Many clipart images are not grouped when you first open them. However, if you import the clipart, it will be grouped. If you open an image that is not already grouped, select all the objects making up the image, and group them together using the Group command on the Property Bar.*

Using the Trim Command Together with the Weld Command

You learned how to use the Weld command earlier in this chapter. Now let's see how the Trim and Weld commands can be used together to create the gear shown in Figure 15-13. In order to complete this project, you should be familiar with

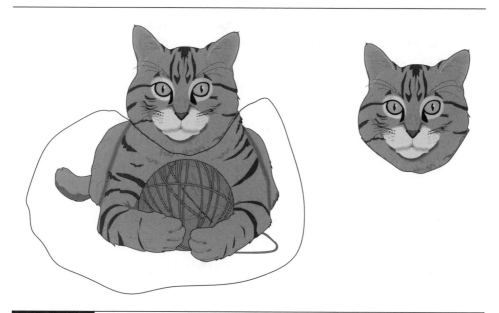

FIGURE 15-12   Trimming a group of objects

15

certain other functions in CorelDRAW. Use the Figure 15-13 as a guide as you follow these steps:

1. Draw a narrow rectangle like the one at the upper left in the figure.

2. Select the Pick tool.

3. Press the + key on the numeric key pad to make a duplicate of the rectangle.

4. With the rectangle still selected, click again to reveal the rotation and skew arrows.

5. Select the rotation arrow at the upper-left corner, and drag down and to the left while holding down the CTRL key. It's important that you hold down the CTRL key to constrain the rotation to 15 degree increments. Watch the Status Bar while you are rotating the rectangle. When you reach 30 degrees, release the mouse button.

6. With the duplicate rectangle still selected, use the Smart Duplicate command CTRL-D to make another duplicate that's also rotated another 30 degrees.

7. Continue to use the Smart Duplicate command until you have duplicated and rotated enough rectangles to complete the circle. You will end up with a total of six rectangles.

8. Draw an ellipse approximately the size of the one shown in step 8 of the figure, and place it on top of the rotated rectangles. Marquee select all the objects, then press the quick alignment keys C and E on the keyboard. This action will center the ellipse on the rotated rectangles.

9. With the objects still selected, weld them all together.

10. Using step 10 as a guide, draw another ellipse on top of the welded objects.

11. Marquee select the two objects, and center them using the C and E alignment keys you used in step 8.

12. Deselect the objects, and use the Trim command, selecting the ellipse first (the cookie cutter), to cut a hole in the welded rectangles.

13. Finish the gear by using the Interactive Extrude tool to extrude the shape in the direction of the gear in step 13. If you're not familiar with the interactive Extrude tool, see Chapter 18. We finished the gear by giving it a linear fountain fill.

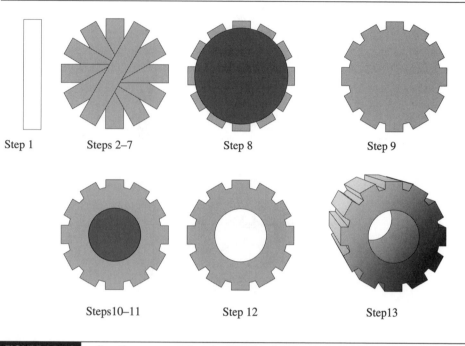

Step 1   Steps 2–7   Step 8   Step 9

Steps10–11   Step 12   Step13

FIGURE 15-13   Creating a gear using the Weld and Trim commands

The Intersect Command

The function of the Intersect command is to create a new object in the shape of the area of the overlapping objects. It is accessed by choosing Window | Dockers | Shaping | Intersect. The intersect controls are displayed by choosing the Intersect button at the top of the Shaping Docker window (see Figure 15-14). Notice that the Source Object(s) and Target Object(s) check boxes are checked by default. They are checked because in most cases you want the source and target objects to remain.

If the way the Intersect command works seems puzzling, look at Figure 15-15. The image at left consists of two overlapping circles. When the Intersect command is applied to the two circles, a shape of the area formed by the overlapping circles is created. This example may seem unimaginative, but think how long it would take you to create this intersected shape without the Intersect command. In this case, the new shape was colored differently to give the illusion of transparency between the two original circles. The point is that the Intersect command is a great way to create unusual shapes quickly.

15

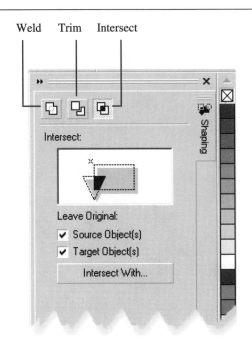

Weld   Trim   Intersect

FIGURE 15-14   The Intersect controls displayed in the Shaping Docker

Using the Intersect Command

Practice using the Intersect command to create the example in Figure 15-15 by following these steps:

1. Draw two circles that overlap each other as shown at the left in Figure 15-15. Color one circle red and the other blue.

2. Choose the Intersect button in the Docker window to display the Intersect controls.

3. Check to see that both the Source Object(s) and Target Object(s) boxes are enabled to leave the original objects.

4. Select one or both of the circles, and click the Intersect With button.

5. Use the special intersect cursor to select one of the circles. A third object will be created in the shape of the area created by your overlapping circles.

Color the new object purple. Your two intersecting circles, along with the newly created intersected object, should look something like the ones at the right in Figure 15-15, with the purple object giving the illusion of looking through one circle onto another.

Using the Intersect Command on Groups of Objects

One of the more practical uses for the Intersect command is to use it to crop clipart groups. Figure 15-16 shows an example of this technique. You might wonder why this project could be not be accomplished with the Trim command. It could, but it would take a little more setup and planning. Cropping could also be accomplished by using the PowerClip command discussed in Chapter 20, but doing so could make the resulting file more difficult to print. To create this example, open the Intersect Docker, and follow these steps:

1. Open a file similar to the bulldozer used in Figure 15-16.

2. Remove the check mark from the Target Object(s) check box in the Leave Original section of the Docker.

3. Using Figure 15-16 as a guide, draw a rectangle so that it intersects the bulldozer between the two wheels.

4. With the rectangle still selected, click the Intersect With button in the Docker.

15

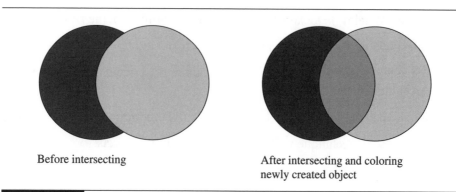

Before intersecting

After intersecting and coloring
newly created object

FIGURE 15-15   Two intersecting circles creating a shape to give the illusion of transparency

5. Use the special intersect cursor to select the bulldozer. The intersection will be performed, and the newly created intersected object will be cropped inside the lower-left corner of the rectangle. The original rectangle will still be visible.

6. Import a file similar to the trash cans using the File | Import command.

7. Using Figure 15-16 as a guide, place the imported file so that the lower-right corner of the rectangle intersects the cans. The imported cans will be on top of the rectangle, so you may want to bring the rectangle to the front by selecting the rectangle and choosing the To Front button on the Property Bar.

8. With the rectangle still selected, click the Intersect With button, and use the special intersect cursor to select the trash cans. The intersection will be completed, and the trash cans will be cropped inside the rectangle just as the bulldozer was.

9. To complete the project, add some text using your favorite font. The font used in this example is a specialty font called LowerEastSide.

Added Functionality for Trim and Intersection

CorelDRAW 9 has added more functionality to the Trim and Intersection Dockers. You can now perform Trim and Intersection on multiple objects without having to group them first.

For example:

■ Draw 4 rectangles on the page which overlap.

■ Choose Window | Dockers | Shaping. Choose Trim from the flyout.

■ Select two of the rectangles and press the Trim button.

■ When the cursor changes to the special cursor hold down the SHIFT key and select the remaining two rectangles.

■ When you release the SHIFT key the trim will be performed.

■ Use the same technique when intersecting multiple objects.

Before using the Intersect
command on clipart groups

The intersected objects
cropped inside the rectangle

FIGURE 15-16 Using the Intersect command to crop groups of objects

Using the Weld, Trim, and Intersect Buttons on the Property Bar

The Weld, Trim, and Intersect buttons on the Property Bar function independently of their respective Docker controls. Note that changing the settings in the Dockers does not change the commands on the Property Bar. That is, the commands on the Property Bar always use the default settings in regard to the Leave Original check box settings. The Property Bar with the Weld, Trim, and Intersect buttons is shown next:

15

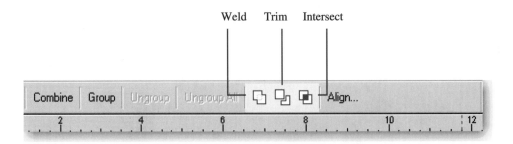

The Weld, Intersect, and Trim commands located on the Property Bar work as follows:

- ■ The Weld command welds all selected objects without leaving either the target object or other object(s) on the page.

- ■ The Trim command trims the last selected object (the target object) and leaves all other objects on the page.

- ■ The Intersect command leaves both the target and other object(s) on the page.

After having learned the different functions of the commands using the Dockers, you may find it quicker to use the commands on the Property Bar for the majority of your work. If the default leaves an object on the page you don't want, simply delete it.

CHAPTER 16

Align, Distribute, Copy, Paste, Clone

CoreIDRAW 9

COREL.COM

S ome CorelDRAW users have the eyes of an eagle and the steady hand of a diamond cutter. If you weren't born with these gifts, the Align and Distribute commands are the answers to your problems. Additionally, if you can remember a few simple keystrokes, you can use single-letter shortcut keys to align objects.

This chapter will also cover the Smart Duplicate command and a special Copy From command, in addition to explaining the difference between pasting objects using object linking versus object embedding. Finally, you will learn how cloning objects can save you time.

Aligning Objects

You access the Align command either by choosing Arrange | Align and Distribute or, when there are two or more objects selected by clicking the Align button on the Property Bar which is by far the quickest way. The Align command allows you to precisely align two or more objects to each other, to an edge of the page, or to the center of the page. If you marquee select the objects rather that selecting them one at a time, the lowest object in the stacking order is considered to be the last object selected (see Chapter 12).

TIP *When you marquee select the objects rather that selecting them one at a time, the lowest object in the stacking order is considered to be the last object selected. When you are aligning objects to other objects, the object to which all the other objects will be aligned is the object that is selected last.*

The Align and Distribute dialog box is shown in Figure 16-1. By default, it appears on the drawing page with the Align tab selected.

NOTE *At least one object must be selected before the Align and Distribute dialog box can be accessed from the Arrange | Align and Distribute menu. Two objects must be selected before you can select the Align command from the Property Bar.*

Lining Things Up

Figure 16-2 shows an Indy race car, a dragster, and a taxi, each randomly placed on a page. The stacking order of the three vehicles, starting at the back, is the race car, the dragster in the middle, and the taxi on top.

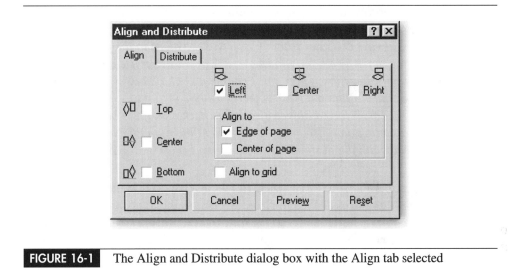

The Align and Distribute dialog box with the Align tab selected

16

Three objects randomly placed on the page

NOTE *Learning how the various settings affect the outcome is paramount in understanding how the Align command works. When aligning objects, you must always consider whether you want to align to the page or to another object. An easy way to keep track of what you are aligning objects to is to remember this: If you don't enable any of the boxes in the Align To section of the dialog box, your objects will line up with the designated edge of the last selected object. If you do check one of the boxes in the Align To section and also select a alignment location, the selected objects will line up with the designated edges or the center of the drawing page.*

You will now learn how to align objects to themselves and to the edges of the page. The three check boxes spaced horizontally across the top of the dialog box are used to align objects horizontally to the left, center, or right of the page or to the last selected object. The three check boxes spaced vertically down the left side of the dialog box are used to align objects vertically to the top, center, or bottom of the page or to the last selected object.

TIP *Note the underlined letters in the vertical and the horizontal check boxes. These are the shortcut keystrokes that you will learn about later in this chapter.*

Figures 16-3 through 16-5 all use different settings from the Align dialog box. To see how these various alignments are achieved, place three objects on a page, and follow along with the descriptions of the settings used for each figure. Remember that you can click the Preview button before you finalize any alignment. If you are not satisfied, click the Reset button, and try a different setting.

Figure 16-3 shows the results of selecting all the objects, enabling the Left box in the upper horizontal row, and choosing Edge of page in the Align to section. Notice how the left edge of each object aligns with the left edge of the page.

In Figure 16-4, the objects were again randomly placed and then individually selected using SHIFT-click, with the large taxi selected last (the wireframe silhouettes show the original object placement). Then the Right check box in the horizontal row of alignment boxes was enabled. This caused the right edges of the dragster and the race car to line up with the right edge of the taxi. If you are following along, and your objects moved to an object other than the one you expected, you probably marquee selected the objects instead of selecting them one at a time. Remember, marquee selection uses the object at the bottom of the stacking order as the alignment object.

Figure 16-5 uses Center, selected from the horizontal row of alignment boxes, and Center of Page, selected from the Align to section of the dialog box to align all

FIGURE 16-3   Aligning the left edge of objects to the left edge of the page by choosing
Left | Edge of page

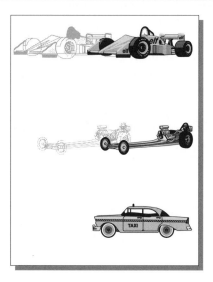

16

FIGURE 16-4   Aligning the right edge of the two top objects to the right edge of the
bottom object by choosing <u>R</u>ight in the upper row of alignment boxes

three vehicles to the center of the page while maintaining their vertical positions on the page. It's important to note that the Center box in the vertical row of alignment boxes was not checked.

 CAUTION   *Enabling the Center of Page check box also enables both the vertical and horizontal Center check boxes. In the case of Figure 16-5, it was necessary to remove the check mark from the vertical Center box to achieve the desired alignment.*

 TIP   *There is really no limit to the number of objects you can align at one time. However, don't overlook the benefit of aligning only one object to a specific place on the screen. For example, you may want to move an object to the center of the page by enabling the Center of Page check box. When aligning one object to the page, the Align button on the Property Bar is not available so you must choose Arrange | Align and Distribute to bring up the dialog box. Additionally, you can enable the Align to Grid check box if you want objects to snap to a grid when they are aligned. When the Grid box is enabled, the object will snap to the nearest grid point determined by the alignment check box selected.*

 NOTE   *The CTRL-A shortcut key that opens the Align and Distribute dialog box is no longer available in CorelDRAW 9.*

As you can see, you can use many combinations of alignment settings. You should practice using the different settings until you feel comfortable with them.

Aligning Objects Using Shortcut Keys

You have just learned how to align objects using the Align and Distribute dialog box, now you will learn how to accomplish the same thing using single key shortcut keys. The keys to use are:

- T for top
- B for bottom
- R for right

- L for left

- C for centering objects horizontally

- E for centering objects vertically

- P for center of page

Follow the same sequence rules as before for selecting objects that you want to align. Figure 16-6 shows a kitten in all the possible alignment positions on a rectangle. Next to each kitten are the keystrokes used to place the kitten in that position. Practice using these shortcut keys by drawing a rectangle and an ellipse on the page. Select the ellipse first, and then SHIFT-click to select the rectangle. With the two objects selected, see how the ellipse goes to the edges of the rectangle as you press each of the shortcut keys one at a time.

If you want to quickly place an object in the center of another object, select the objects and press the letter P key.

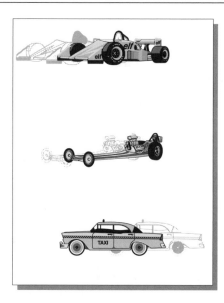

FIGURE 16-5   Aligning all three objects to the center of the page while maintaining their vertical positions on the page

16

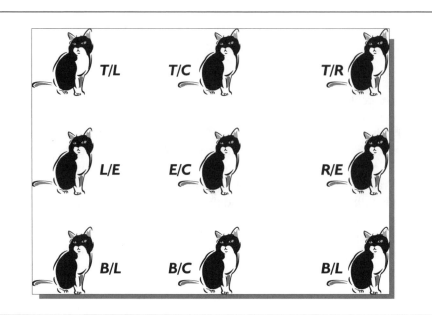

FIGURE 16-6   Aligning objects with shortcut keys

Distributing Objects

The Distribute command is used to evenly space objects on the page. It can distribute randomly spaced objects in a defined manner evenly across the page. However, before you can use the Distribute command, you must first use the Align command.

TIP   *If you are currently working on a project and have skipped over the Align command because you need to distribute only a few objects, we have bad news for you. The Align command plays a part in using the Distribute command. Review the Align command settings at the beginning of this chapter before you try to use the Distribute command.*

The Align and Distribute tabbed dialog box, shown in Figure 16-1, appears on the drawing page with the Align tab selected by default. Select the Distribute tab to display the Distribute page. The default Distribute page is shown in Figure 16-7.

The best way to become familiar with the Distribute command is to practice using it. The following sections provide examples for you to follow.

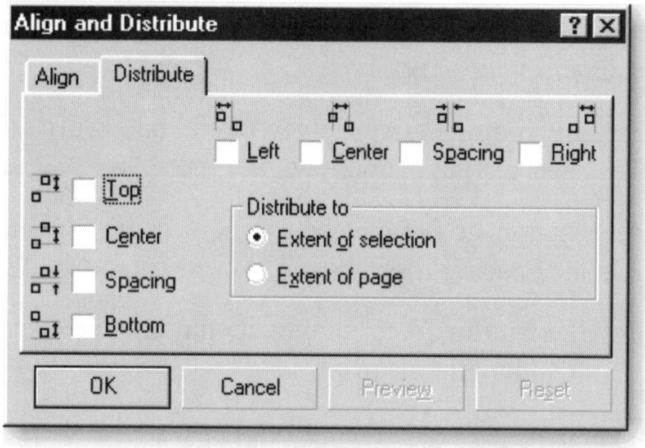

FIGURE 16-7   The Align and Distribute dialog box with the Distribute tab selected

Breaking the Rules: Distributing Objects Without Using Align

The example in this section contradicts what was said earlier about having to use the Align command prior to using the Distribute command. This method is the exception and not the rule. Follow these steps to distribute objects without using the Align command:

1. Choose Window I Dockers I Symbols and Special Characters (CTRL-F11), and select the Wingdings category. Scroll down the list of symbols until you find the phone shown in Figure 16-8.

2. Drag the symbol onto the page, and give it a black fill.

3. With the phone selected, choose Window I Dockers I Transformation to display the transformation Docker. Click on any of the tabs except the Skew tab and click the Apply to Duplicate button twice. This will create two copies of the phone on top of the original.

4. Click anywhere on the page to deselect the last duplicate object, and then marquee select all three copies of the phone.

16

5. Open the Align and Distribute dialog box, and click the Distribute tab. Enable the E<u>x</u>tent of Page radio button and the Sp<u>a</u>cing check box located in the horizontal row of check boxes.

6. Click the Previe<u>w</u> button. Your phones should be evenly distributed horizontally across the page, as shown in Figure 16-8.

7. Click the Re<u>s</u>et button, and enable the E<u>x</u>tent of Page radio button again. Put a check mark in the Sp<u>a</u>cing check box in the vertical row of check boxes.

8. Click the Previe<u>w</u> button. Your phones should now be evenly distributed vertically up and down the page.

You may be wondering how the phones would be distributed if any of the other horizontal or vertical check boxes were used with Extent of Page enabled. In fact, if any of the check boxes in the horizontal row are checked, the results will be the same as those in Figure 16-8. Additionally, if any of the check boxes in the vertical row are checked, the results will be the same as when you selected the Spacing check box in step 7 earlier. This is because all the objects were stacked on top of each other prior to using the Distribute command. If the objects were

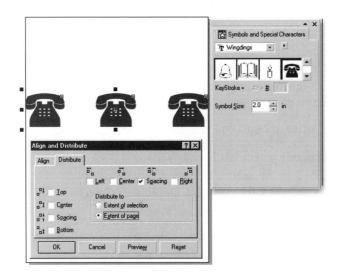

FIGURE 16-8   Three drawings of a phone distributed horizontally across the page

separated from each other when you chose the settings, you would get unpredictable results. This is why, in most cases, you need to use the Align command prior to using the Distribute command.

Using the Align Command Before the Distribute Command

For the example in this section, you need to use the Align command before performing the distribution.

1. Select the various food symbols shown in Figure 16-9 from the Food category in the Symbols and Special Characters Docker.

2. Drag the symbols onto the page and resize each to approximately one inch square.

3. Select the Pick tool and drag each of the symbols to separate places on the page. (If you're wondering why you need to do this, it's because this example attempts to simulate a real-world project, where you may have several objects

16

FIGURE 16-9   Five different drawings randomly placed on the page that were created at different times and that you now want to distribute across the page.) Your five symbols should be arranged something like those in Figure 16-9.

4. Marquee select all five symbols, and open the Align and Distribute dialog box by clicking the Align button on the Property Bar.

5. Enable the Center of Page box in the Align To section of the Align page, and then click OK. All the symbols should now be stacked on top of each other.

6. With all five symbols still selected, move them to the lower-left corner of the page.

7. Make sure the symbols are still selected, and open the Align and Distribute dialog box again. Select the Distribute tab, and enable the Extent of Page radio button and the horizontal Spacing box.

8. Click the Preview button. Your symbols should now be evenly distributed across the bottom of the page.

9. Disable the horizontal Spacing box, and enable the vertical Spacing box.

10. Click the Preview button again to see your food symbols evenly distributed vertically up and down on the left side of the page.

11. When you're satisfied with the results, click the OK button. Your symbols should be distributed as shown in Figure 16-10.

If you don't disable the horizontal Spacing box in step 9, your symbols will be distributed diagonally across the page.

Distributing Lines

A practical use of the Distribute command is to evenly space lines over the page. Imagine needing some ruled sheets of paper to take notes for a meeting and all you have is blank printer paper. Follow these steps to create a page with 20 evenly spaced lines on the paper:

1. Draw a straight line horizontally across the page using the Freehand tool (holding down the CTRL key when moving the cursor to the end of the line constrains the line, making it straight).

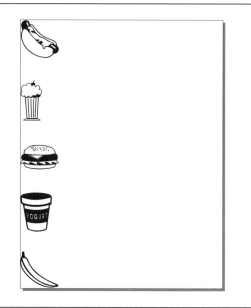

FIGURE 16-10   The five symbols evenly spaced vertically up and down the left side of
the page

2. Select the Pick tool and then choose Window | Dockers | Transformation to
display the transformation Docker. Click on any of the tabs, except the
Skew tab, and click the Apply to Duplicate button 21 times to add 21
duplicates of the original line.

3. Deselect the last duplicate line, and marquee select all 22 lines.

4. Open the Align and Distribute dialog box, and click the Distribute tab.

5. Enable the Extent of Page radio button and the Top check box, and click OK.

6. Remove the top and bottom lines, as they are aligned with the edges of the
page and serve no purpose, and you're left with 20 evenly spaced lines on
the page.

16

Smart Duplicating

Smart Duplicating could be considered in the same family as the Edit | Repeat
command (CTRL-R) and the Distribute command. The Repeat command repeats the

last transformation on an object, whereas the Smart Duplication remembers all transformations and properties edits and applies them to a duplicated object. Creating each additional duplicate applies the same transforms/properties edits to the new duplicates.

In order to use Smart Duplicating, you must first duplicate an object. Do this by using the keyboard shortcut CTRL+D. Follow these steps to learn how to use Smart Duplication:

1. Create an object on the page, and duplicate it.

2. Move the duplicate object to another position on the page.

3. Choose Edit | Duplicate (CTRL-D), and a second duplicate object will be placed the same distance from the first duplicate.

After reading this brief description of Smart Duplicating, you may wonder how you could use it in a real-world situation. Follow these steps:

1. Place an object at the upper-left corner of the page. Try using an object from the Symbols roll-up.

2. Duplicate the object by pressing CTRL-D.

3. Move the object one inch away horizontally from the original object.

4. With the duplicate object still selected, press CTRL-D.

5. Continue pressing CTRL-D until the objects reach the right side of the page.

If you followed the steps correctly, you just equally distributed copies of the original object across the top of the page. Depending on the object you used, you may have the beginnings of a decorative border.

 NOTE *The ability to use Smart Duplication will be lost once you deselect the object, select another object, or change tools. Smart Duplicate also retains the stretch, skew, and rotation relative to the last duplicate.*

Copying and Pasting

The Edit | Copy command (CTRL-C) is the same in CorelDRAW as it is in all Windows programs. It can be used in conjunction with the Edit | Paste command

(CTRL-V) to copy and paste whole images or parts of images from one application or file to another. An example of its use would be to copy an object from one .cdr file and paste it into another .cdr file.

 NOTE *If you copy and paste objects from another application into CorelDRAW it limits the clipboard contents to Windows defaults of RGB/low res.*

The Paste Special Command

The Edit I Paste Special command is a unique command that lets you copy an image from one application and paste it into CorelDRAW, while at the same time enabling you to edit the image in CorelDRAW or link directly back to the source application for editing. For example, if you want to use a Corel PHOTO-PAINT image in a CorelDRAW file, you first open the image in Corel PHOTO-PAINT and then copy it to the clipboard. You then use one of the options in the Edit I Paste Special dialog box in CorelDRAW to paste it onto the CorelDRAW page.

This method of copying objects is called *object linking and embedding*, or *OLE*. When you select Edit I Paste Special, a Paste Special dialog box appears (see Figure 16-11) giving you a choice of pasting the image as an embedded object or a

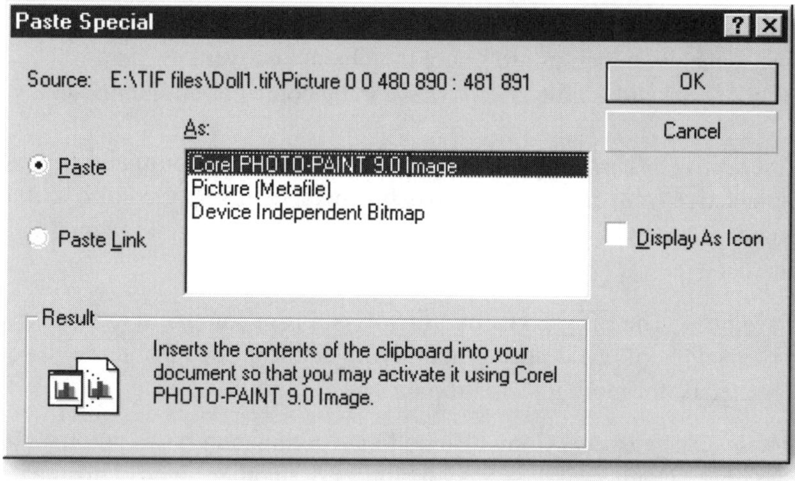

Paste Special `? X`

Source: E:\TIF files\Doll1.tif\Picture 0 0 480 890 : 481 891

               As:

- ○ **Paste** | Corel PHOTO-PAINT 9.0 Image |
                       Picture (Metafile)
                       Device Independent Bitmap

- ○ **Paste Link**

OK
Cancel

☐ Display As Icon

┌─ Result ─────────────────
Inserts the contents of the clipboard into your document so that you may activate it using Corel PHOTO-PAINT 9.0 Image.

16

FIGURE 16-11   The Paste Special dialog box in its default configuration linked object. The default is Paste, which is the embedded method. You can choose three types of embedded files: Corel PHOTO-PAINT 9.0 image (or the version number that it was created in), Picture (Metafile), and Device Independent Bitmap. When you paste a file using the embedded method, you can edit the file by choosing Edit | CorelPhotoPaint.Image.9 Object | Edit. This action replaces the CorelDRAW menus and tools with those of the source application. You can then edit the embedded object using the menus and tools of the source application. The editing does not affect the original image from which it was copied.

Because of the inherent unreliability and stability problems of the OLE technology, and the fact that CorelDRAW provides extensive bitmap-editing ability, we will not expand on the Paste Special command. If you can't find the necessary editing tool within CorelDRAW itself, we recommend editing your bitmap images in Corel PHOTO-PAINT and importing the finished bitmap back into CorelDRAW.

Effects Copy From Command

Whereas the Edit | Copy command copies objects and places them on the Windows clipboard, CorelDRAW's Effects | Copy command is a Copy From command that allows you to copy an effect from one object and apply it to another object.

To copy an effect to another object, you select the object, or in some cases, a group of objects, and then choose Effects | Copy to access the Copy child menu. From the child menu, select one of the Copy From commands. The cursor changes to an arrow, which you then use to select the object you want to copy.

CorelDRAW provides nine effects that can be copied to another object:

■ *Perspective*   The Effects | Copy | Perspective From command copies the perspective from an object that has had perspective applied to it to another object or group of objects. Refer to Chapter 17 for more information on perspective.

■ *Envelope*   The Effects | Copy | Envelope From command lets you copy the envelope of one object to another object or group of objects. Refer to Chapter 17 for more information on enveloping.

■ *Blend*   The Effects | Copy | Blend From command allows you to select two objects and copy the blend attributes of another blend. This means that attributes of the two selected objects will stay the same, but the attributes of the blend will be used when the blend is copied. For example, if you select a red square and a blue square and then use the Effects | Copy | Blend From command on an existing blend, the red and blue squares will be blended with the same number of steps and accelerations as the blend you used to copy from. If the blend is a compound blend composed of different steps and accelerations, the section of the blend you point to will be the section copied. Refer to Chapter 19 for more information on blends.

■ *Extrude*   The Effects | Copy | Extrude From command copies all the extrude attributes from an existing extrusion and applies them to another single object. To see how this copying effect works, draw a rectangle on the page and extrude it. Now draw a second rectangle on the page, and use the Effects | Copy | Extrude From command to copy the extruded rectangle. Refer to Chapter 18 for more information on extrusion.

■ *Contour*   The Effects | Copy | Contour From command copies the selected contour's attributes, including the outline and fill attributes of the contoured objects, while leaving the original fill and outline attributes of the original rectangle. For example, if you draw a rectangle on the page, fill it with yellow, give it a blue outline, and then copy a contour that uses a red fill with pink outlines for the control object and a green fill with orange outlines for the contoured objects, the attributes of the resulting new contour will be as follows: the control object will retain the original yellow fill and blue outline, the contoured objects will blend from yellow to green fills, and their outlines will blend from blue to orange. Refer to Chapter 19 for more information on contours.

■ *Lens*   The Effects | Copy | Lens From command copies the selected lens and all its attributes to another object. This command is intended to copy a lens to a single object, although it is capable of copying a lens to a group of objects. If you were to do this, each object in the group would have the lens copied to it. Refer to Chapter 20 for more information on lenses.

■ *PowerClip*   The Effects | Copy | Power Clip From command copies the contents of a PowerClip to a new container object. The fill and outline of the new container object will not be affected. If the original PowerClip was created with the default option Auto-center New PowerClip Contents disabled, the new container will not display the contents of the original PowerClip until you edit the new PowerClip container and move the contents inside the container. Refer to Chapter 20 for more information on PowerClips.

16

■ *Drop Shadow*   The Effects | Copy | Drop Shadow From command copies the drop shadow from one object to another. This command will copy drop shadows from single objects or groups of objects. You can also copy a drop shadow from a group of objects to a single object. When you use this command you must click with the pointing arrow on the drop shadow, not the object that has the shadow.

■ *Distortion*   The Effects | Copy | Distortion From command copies the distortion attributes of one object to another. The results can sometimes produce effects unlike the distortion of the object that was copied. The shape of the second object (the copied to object) will vary if the two objects are not identical and contain a disproportionate number of nodes. However, happy accidents sometime produce some amazing results.

Cloning Objects

Cloning objects can save a lot of time on a project when you are working with duplicate objects. When an object is cloned, a duplicate is made of the selected effect. The original object becomes the *control object*, and the duplicate object is called the *clone object*. For example, if you clone an ellipse, the Status Bar will call the clone a "clone ellipse." Clones can be created from single objects, groups of objects, and all Effect groups except Power Clips and Natural Media strokes. The benefit of using clones in your projects is that any attribute changes made to the control object are automatically made to the clone object. For example, if you used several duplicate objects in a project and they all had to be equally resized, you would have to individually resize each object without the Clone command. If you had planned ahead and created clones of the first object, you would need to resize only the original control object, and all the clones would be resized automatically.

The best way to learn a new command is to practice using it. Follow these steps to create a clone of a gorilla and modify the control object. Use Figure 16-12 as a guide.

1. Open the Symbols Docker by choosing Window | Dockers | Symbols and Special Characters (CTRL-F11), and choose the Animals 1 category. Select the gorilla (the center symbol on the second row), and drag it onto the page. Give it a black fill.

2. With the gorilla selected, choose <u>E</u>dit | Clo<u>n</u>e to create a clone of the gorilla. If you have not changed the default for Duplicate placement in <u>T</u>ools | <u>O</u>ptions | Edit, the clone will be created offset from the original object by 0.25 inch both horizontally and vertically. Select the clone gorilla, and move it away from the control gorilla.

3. Select the original object, which has now become a control curve, and change its color to orange. Notice that the clone gorilla also changes to orange.

4. With the gorilla still selected, select the interactive Envelope tool from the interactive tool flyout and move the side-middle nodes outward approximately 0.25 inch. See the gorillas gain weight.

5. Select the Shape tool, and marquee select the nodes making up the gorilla's hand and upper arm. Drag the nodes upward approximately two inches, and watch the arms of both gorillas grow longer.

As you can see from this short example, using the Clone command can be useful and time saving.

FIGURE 16-12   Modifying a control object and its clone

16

Using Clones in Conjunction With the Align and Distribute Commands

You can also use clones in conjunction with the Align and Distribute commands described earlier in this chapter. Practice this cloning technique with the Angel symbol shown in Figure 16-13:

1. Select the Angel shown in Figure 16-13 from the Festive category in the Symbols and Special Characters Docker.

2. Drag the symbol onto the page, give it a black fill, and resize it to approximately one inch square.

3. Choose Edit | Clone four separate times to create four clones of the angel. Remember that each time you use the Clone command, you must reselect the control angel to create another clone.

4. Marquee-select all five angels, and open the Align and Distribute dialog box by clicking the Align button on the Property Bar.

5. Enable the Center of Page box in the Align To section on the Align page, and then click the OK button. The angels should now be stacked on top of each other.

6. With all five angels still selected, move them to the top-left corner of the page.

7. Make sure the angels are still selected, and open the Align and Distribute dialog box again. Select the Distribute tab, and enable the Extent of Page radio button and the vertical Spacing box.

8. Click the Preview button. Your angels should now be evenly distributed up and down the left side of the page.

9. Click the OK button. Your angels should look like those in Figure 16-14.

10. Select the control object at the top of the page, and resize it to approximately one half of its original size (if the top object is not the control object, see the Tip that follows). The four clones will take on the new attributes.

As you can see, the Clone command can be quite useful.

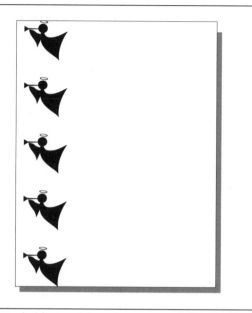

FIGURE 16-13   A control object and four clones spaced evenly down the page

TIP   If you use clones in a project and you want to find out which is the control object and which are the clone objects, right-click any one of the objects. If you selected a clone object, the Object menu will display the Select Master command at the top of the object menu. Select this command, and the control object will be automatically selected for you. If you got lucky and selected the control object the first time, the Object menu will display the Select Clones command. If you select this command, all the clones linked to the control object will automatically be selected together.

Rules Governing Clones

There are a few rules to keep in mind when working with clones:

- If you change any attributes of a single clone object, that particular attribute's link to the control object will be broken. For example, if you have a control object with four clones (like those in Figure 16-13) and you

16

change the color of one of the clones, you will break the color link between that clone and the control object. If you change the outline color of the same clone, you will then break the outline link to the control object. Any other modifications to the control object, other than the color and outline color will be applied to the modified clone object.

■   If you change the size of a clone, you will break all links between that clone and the control object.

■   The only effects that can be applied to control objects that will influence a clone object are the Interactive Envelope, Interactive Distortion, Transparency, and Lens effects.

■   If you delete a control object, all of its clones will also be deleted.

Cloning Other Effects

CorelDRAW's Effects | Clone Effect command gives you the ability to clone effects and works much like the Copy From command discussed earlier. You can clone four effects: Blend, Extrude, Contour, and Drop Shadow. The difference between cloning effects as described here and creating cloned objects as described earlier is that when you use the Clone Effect From command, only the effect is cloned. All other attributes such as fill and outlines are not cloned and will not be linked to child objects.

To clone an existing effect to an object or, in some cases, two objects, select the object or objects, and choose Effects | Clone Effect. From the flyout child menu, click the appropriate clone effect. When you select an effect, the cursor changes into an arrow. Use this arrow to select the effect (Blend, Extrude, Contour, or Drop Shadow) you want to clone.

The use of each effect is described here:

■   *Blend From*   To clone a blend, select two separate objects or two separate groups of objects on the page, and choose Effects | Clone Effect. From the child menu, choose Blend From. When the cursor changes to an arrow, click on the blend group you want to clone. When you clone a blend, all the attributes of the control blend will be applied to the clone blend except the color attributes. For example, if you create two objects on the page, one colored red and the other colored green, and then create a clone from a 20-step blend group that went from purple to white, the resulting clone will contain 20 steps, including any accelerations or rotations contained in the control blend, but the colors will stay the same, blending from red to green. If you change the number of steps in the control blend, the number will change in the clone blend.

■ *Extrude*   To clone an extrusion, select any single object (not a group), and choose Effects | Clone Effect. From the child menu, choose Extrude From. When the cursor changes to an arrow, select the extrusion you want to clone. The selected object will be extruded with the same attributes as the control extrusion.

■ *Contour*   To clone a contour, select any single object (not a group), and choose Effects | Clone Effect. From the child menu, choose Contour From. When the cursor changes to an arrow, select the contour you want to clone. The new clone will retain is original fill and outline color but will take on the attributes of the contour steps of the control contour.

■ *Drop Shadow*   To clone a Drop Shadow, select an object or group of objects, and then choose Effects | Clone Effect. From the child menu, choose Drop Shadow From. When the cursor changes to an arrow, use the arrow to click the drop shadow of the object you want to clone from. The new clone will be given a drop shadow like that of the original.

This chapter has covered features usually reserved for the advanced user. You could spend your entire life working in CorelDRAW and not be aware of the ability to do the things described here. For many users, this knowledge will be useful. For the casual user, the information is here when you're ready for it.

16

PART III

Adding Effects

CHAPTER 17

Enveloping, Distortion, and Perspective

COREL.COM

CorelDRAW 9

The effects discussed in this chapter share something in common: they each allow you to adjust the shape of an object or group of objects in a defined fashion. The Envelope effect allows you to force an image into a predefined shape or to warp the image into a free-form shape. The Distortion effect lets you unleash your creative powers or simply accept a Happy Accident or two. In either case, the results can be quite impressive. The Perspective effect lets you add perspective to portions of your drawings, giving viewers a sense of depth when they view the image.

Enveloping

The Envelope effect lets you warp an object's form into an irregular shape. You can also apply this effect to groups of objects with the following exception: before you can envelope a Blend, Contour, or Extrude group, you must first select the group and click Arrange | Group to group the individual parts of these effect groups. After they have been grouped, you can apply an Envelope effect to the new group.

The Envelope effect is applied by using the Interactive Envelope tool located on the Interactive Tools flyout. The button for the Interactive Envelope tool is the fourth from the left on the flyout, and the tool's icon looks like a bent rectangle with a node on each side. We have highlighted it on the Toolbox in Figure 17-1. When you select the tool with an object selected, a bounding box is automatically placed around the selected object. The bounding box has eight nodes around it. These nodes are similar to the nodes on ordinary objects. They also have handles like ordinary nodes that you use to control the warping effect. Clicking and dragging on these handles with the Interactive tool is what allows you to warp the image into different shapes. Figure 17-1 shows an example of applying an envelope to the word *WordPerfect*. The example shows the original text and the results of the envelope. We placed the enveloped text on a building-like object to give the illusion of perspective.

Choosing a Mode

Before you can begin to envelope an object, you must click a mode button. Modes influence the way an envelope is shaped. The mode buttons are located in the middle of the Property Bar (see Figure 17-1). The modes are named according to their functions. They are, from left to right, the Straight Line mode, Single Arc mode, Double Arc mode, and Unconstrained mode.

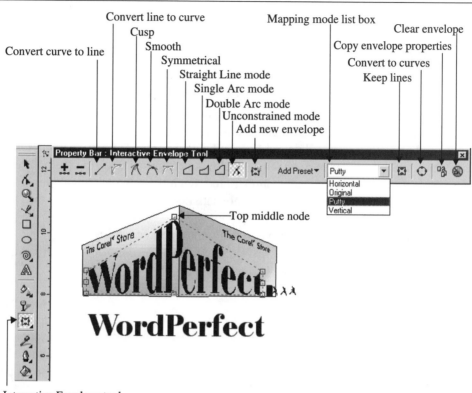

FIGURE 17-1 The Property Bar, toolbox, and an example of the Envelope effect applied to text

Using the Interactive Envelope Tool

The steps required to envelope an object are:

1. Select an object or a group of objects, and click the Interactive Envelope tool (a bounding box will automatically surround the object).

2. Click a mode button on the Property Bar.

3. Use the Interactive Envelope tool to select and move the nodes on the bounding box.

Practice this technique until you are comfortable manipulating the nodes.

The nodes attached to the bounding box are unlike the nodes on normal curves unless you chose the Unconstrained mode. The nodes in the Straight Line, Single Arc, and Double Arc modes are constrained to create the shapes for which the modes are named. For example, when the Straight Line mode is selected, the bounding box lines remain straight between the nodes when a node is moved in any direction. If you use the Unconstrained mode, two handles will be attached to each node. You won't see these handles until you select a node. When you move a node on the envelope, the red dotted lines indicate the intended new shape. You can move multiple nodes by first SHIFT-clicking or marquee selecting them. The number of moves you can make is unrestricted. Each time you move a node the shape is updated in real time. When you are satisfied with the shape, press the SPACEBAR, or click another tool in the toolbox.

The four modes are divided into two different types: constrained and unconstrained. The behavior of the Envelope effect can be controlled by choosing the appropriate mode.

Constrained Modes

The Straight Line, Single Arc, and Double Arc modes—all of the modes except the Unconstrained mode—can be constrained to perform in a specified manner when you hold down the CTRL and SHIFT keys separately or together. An envelope will be constrained, as follows, when you hold down one or both keys:

- If you hold down the CTRL key and drag a node, the node on the opposite side of the bounding box will move in the same direction.

- If you hold down the SHIFT key and drag a node, the node on the opposite side of the bounding box will move in the opposite direction.

- If you hold down the CTRL and SHIFT keys together and drag a node, the four opposing nodes on the bounding box will move in opposite directions from each other. For example, if you drag a center node in the "Envelope" example discussed previously, the other three center nodes will move away from each other. If you drag any corner node, the other three corner nodes will also move away from each other, but because they are corner nodes, the result will be simply that the object is enlarged proportionally.

The following enveloped text shows the results of dragging the top-center node on the bounding box upward and away from the text using the three methods just described. In the examples, the Single Arc mode was used.

Using the CTRL key   Using the SHIFT key   Using the CTRL-SHIFT keys

Unconstrained Mode

When you use the Unconstrained mode, the nodes on the dotted bounding box behave just as they do on normal curve objects (see Chapter 7). This means that you can change a smooth node to a cusp node or even add or remove nodes. The ability to control the number of nodes or change the type of node lets you create some interesting text shapes. Follow these steps to practice enveloping using the Unconstrained mode: The objective is not to create anything in particular, but merely to familiarize yourself with the technique of working with nodes.

1. Type a word on the page using any font.

2. With the text selected, click the Interactive Envelope tool.

3. Click the Unconstrained mode button on the Property Bar.

4. Using the Interactive Envelope tool, select the top-middle node.

5. Move the node upward and away from the text. You should now be able to see the control handles (and the blue dotted lines running between the handles and the node) on the node more clearly.

6. Drag the control handles to curve the red dotted line.

7. Continue distorting the text by dragging other nodes.

8. Try adding a few nodes by double-clicking the red dotted line. To add several nodes at once, marquee select more than one node with the Interactive Envelope tool, and click the + button on the Property Bar. This action will add a new node in between each node you selected.

9. Select a middle node, and change it to a cusp node by clicking the Cusp button on the Property Bar. Drag one of the control handles to change one side of the dotted line.

10. Select a corner node, and change it to a smooth node by clicking the Smooth button on the Property Bar. Move one of its control handles to move the lines on both sides of the node.

17

If you got carried away and ended up with a distorted mess, click the Clear Envelope button on the Property Bar to bring the text back to its original state.

Why did you select a middle node in step 9 and a corner node in step 10? The reason is that all middle nodes on an unconstrained envelope will, by default, be smooth nodes, and all corner nodes will be cusp nodes. Don't let this fact confuse you, because regardless of what the nodes are by default, you can always change them to accomplish the task at hand.

NOTE *Most of the examples in this chapter use Artistic Text to show the Envelope effect. This is because the effect works best on Artistic Text. You can envelope shapes such as rectangles and ellipses, but for the most part, creating unusual shapes with rectangles and ellipses can be better accomplished by converting these shapes to curves and using the Shape tool to create a distorted shape. You can also use the Weld and Trim commands (see Chapter 15) to create unusual shapes. If you decide to envelope shapes, the success or failure of getting what you expect is determined by how many nodes make up the shape. The more nodes (within reason), the better the envelope will shape the object based on the mode selected. For example, if you want to envelope a rectangle using the Straight Line mode, you need to add nodes between each corner node for the effect not to end up as a pregnant rectangle.*

The following text objects show the results of applying an envelope using the Unconstrained mode.

NOTE *The Add New button on the Property Bar is used to apply a new envelope on top of the first envelope. This means that a new bounding box will surround the previous enveloped object just as if you were beginning to envelope a new object. Be careful using a new envelope as you can end up with a pretty distorted shape.*

Although text objects are generally the best objects to envelope, grouped objects can sometimes provide interesting results. The illustration shown here of the before and after effect of two clipart images of a car and a face have separately had unconstrained envelopes applied to them. As you can see, adding an envelope to a clipart image can provide that extra effect that would be difficult to achieve in any other way.

Applying Preset Effects

The Add Preset button on the Property Bar lets you apply a predefined shape to an object. Preset effects are best suited to Artistic Text. When you click the Add Preset button, a drop-down list appears showing the available preset effects. To apply a preset effect, follow these steps:

1. Select the object to which you want the effect applied.

2. Click the Add Preset button, and then select a preset effect from the drop-down list. A dotted line in the shape of the preset effect will surround your selected object and the preset shape will be applied to your object.

When you first use these preset effects, you will probably be disappointed because the effect will likely not be what you expected. The reason is that most of

17

the shapes in the drop-down list are box-like, and the text to which you are applying these shapes is quite narrow. The way to solve this problem is to stretch the text vertically—and horizontally, if necessary—until it appears to be about the height and width of the preset effect you are using. In the real world, even this method rarely works well because of such factors as the numbers of letters in the word and the font used.

Preset effects really shouldn't be used on Paragraph Text because the same issues apply to Paragraph Text as to a single word: the height of the paragraph affects the result of the preset envelope. The problem in applying a preset effect Paragraph Text is that you can't stretch the characters within the paragraph to compensate for the height of the preset effect. If you want to place paragraph text inside an object, use the interactive text on a path method described in Chapter 21.

Sometimes you can get a happy accident by applying a preset envelope effect to a group of objects. In the example shown here, the original clipart is on the left, and a preset envelope in the shape of a octagon applied to the clipart is on the right. Here we have gone from a stock model to a concept car in one easy step.

Choosing a Mapping Mode

You access the four available mapping modes by clicking the down arrow of the Mapping Mode list box on the Property Bar. Mapping modes are not the same as the modes found in the Constrained and Unconstrained mode boxes. When you choose a mapping mode, you define how the object fits inside the envelope. As you saw in the previous examples, the text will look different depending on which mapping mode is selected. You have to select a mapping mode before selecting a preset shape, or you will create multiple envelopes.

The Mapping Mode list box offers four mapping modes:

- *Putty* The Putty mode maps the corner selection handles of the original object to the envelope's corner nodes only. When a circle is used as a target object, the nodes on the resulting envelope are at 12:00, 3:00, 6:00, and 9:00 o'clock. When the envelope is applied, the node at the upper-right corner of the original object is aligned with the node at 12:00 o'clock on the circle.

- ■ *Original*   The Original mode maps the corner selection handles of the original object to the envelope's corner nodes; it also maps the other nodes on the envelope to the edges of the original object's selection box. In some cases, the Original mode will produce a more exaggerated distortion than the Putty mode.

- ■ *Horizontal*   The Horizontal mode stretches the original object to fit the size of the envelope and then compresses it horizontally to fit the envelope's shape.

- ■ *Vertical*   The Vertical mode stretches the original object to fit the size of the envelope and then compresses it vertically to fit the envelope's shape.

Copying the Envelope

The Copy Envelope From command copies the envelope from one object and applies it to another object or objects. Look again at the example showing the words *Happy Accident* enveloped in an arc. If you wanted to envelope several words like that, you would use the Copy Envelope Properties button on the Property Bar. The actual process of copying an Envelope effect is as follows:

1. With the Interactive Envelope tool selected, select the objects to which you want to copy the Envelope effect.

2. Choose the Copy Envelope Properties button on the Property Bar, and the cursor will change to a large arrow. Use the arrow to click on the enveloped object you want to copy. The first objects you selected will now take on the envelope properties of objects you just selected.

Clearing an Envelope

Use the Clear Envelope button on the Property Bar to undo any and/or all changes made to the enveloped object. For example, if in the course of modifying the envelope in the Unconstrained mode, it became distorted to the point that you couldn't work with it anymore, you could click the Clear Envelope button to restore the object to the shape of the object before you applied the envelope. If the shape of the object was as a result of a previously applied Envelope effect, the

17

object would revert back to the last enveloped shape. Clicking the Clear Envelope button a second time will restore the object to its original shape.

 NOTE   *If you have added more than one envelope to an object, you can quickly revert to the original object's shape by choosing <u>A</u>rrange | Clear Transfor<u>m</u>ations.*

Using the Interactive Distortion Tool

The Interactive Distortion tool was first introduced in CorelDRAW 8. If you thought the Envelope tool distorted objects, you're in for an interesting and pleasant surprise. The Interactive Distortion tool can best be described as the ultimate "Happy Accident" tool. It is virtually impossible to recreate the same shape twice using the three variations of this tool. Therefore, we will merely show some examples and point out the various buttons on the Property Bar that can affect the distorted shape. The good news is that, although the shapes created with the distortion tool may be difficult to recreate, these distorted shapes could end up as truly unique logos that your peers will envy and never be able to duplicate.

The Interactive Distortion tool is located on the Interactive Tools flyout. The tool's icon resembles a wrinkled piece of paper. There are three different distortion modes you can use with the tool: Push and Pull, Zipper, and Twister. Figure 17-2 shows an example of using each of these distortion modes on a circle object. The figure also shows the highlighted tool selected from the flyout on the toolbox and the tool cursor applying the effect to the circle on the left.

The number and types of distortions you can apply to objects are endless. The final result depends on the distortion tool you select, which of the two control handles you select, the direction in which you drag the cursor, and the settings you make on the Property Bar. Draw an ellipse, and practice using the three different distortion tools by selecting their respective buttons on the Property Bar.

The other settings available on the Property Bar with this tool are:

■ *Add New button*   This button is not used to begin a distortion but instead is used to add a distortion on top of the existing one.

■ *Amplitude num box*   The number displayed in this box will change as you drag the object with the Interactive Distortion tool. You can enter different numbers, and the shape of the object will automatically update the amount of distortion using the new setting.

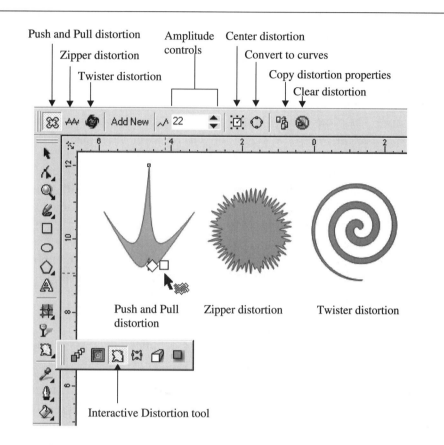

FIGURE 17-2   Three circles after being distorted with the Interactive Distortion tool

■ *Center Distortion button*   When this button is enabled, the left control handle is automatically placed in the center of the object.

■ *Convert to Curves*   This is the same Convert to Curves button that appears on the Property Bar when several other tools are selected. If you click this button when a distortion has been applied to an object, the distortion controls are removed, and the object becomes a normal curve that can be further manipulated with the Shape tool.

■ *Copy Distortion Properties*   The Copy Distortion Properties command copies the distortion from one distorted object and applies it to another object or objects. It works just like the Copy Envelope command discussed earlier.

17

■ *Clear Distortion* Choose this command when you want to clear the last distortion you applied. Like the Clear Envelope command, if you have multiple distortions applied to the same object, use the Clear Transformations command in the Arrange menu.

Figure 17-3 shows three before and after examples of using the Zipper Distortion tool. The same rules of handle and cursor placement, and direction of dragging apply here as well. The Zipper tool has an added slider control that allows you to control the number of lines generated. Moving the slider toward the square handle increases the number of points.

The first example used a distortion frequency of 100 and a amplitude setting of 20. The second and third examples use straight lines as the original objects. The settings used on the horizontal line were Amplitude of 98, Distortion 35, with the Random Distortion and Smooth distortion buttons enabled on the Property Bar. The settings used on the vertical line were Amplitude 91 and Distortion 60. Practice using this tool until you feel comfortable creating effects with it.

There are more settings available on the Property Bar when the Zipper tool is selected:

■ *Add New button* As described earlier, this button is not used to begin a distortion, but to add a distortion on top of the existing one.

■ *Amplitude num box* The number displayed in this box will change as you drag the object with the Interactive Distortion tool. You can enter different numbers, and the shape of the object will automatically update the amount of distortion using the new setting.

■ *Frequency num box* The number displayed in this box will change when you drag the slider between the left and right control handles. You can also enter numbers directly in this box, and the frequency of the zipper lines will automatically update.

■ *Random Distortion* When you enable this button, the zipper lines will be distributed randomly around the object's shape.

■ *Smooth Distortion* Clicking this button will round off the sharp corners of the zipper lines.

■ *Local Distortion* Local distortion emphasizes the distortion over a particular area of the object, rather than randomly or from the center out.

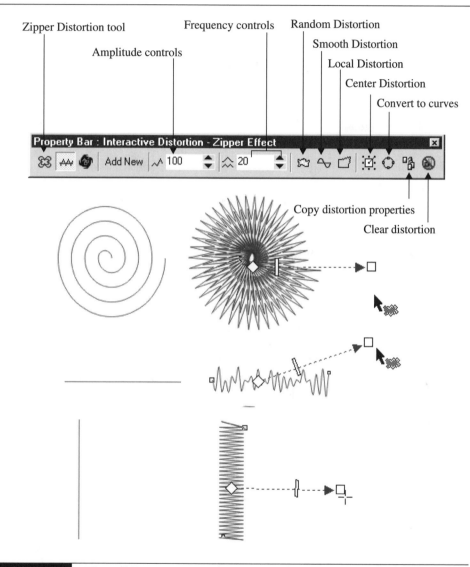

FIGURE 17-3   Three different objects distorted with the Zipper Distortion tool

- *Center Distortion*   If Center Distortion is enabled, the object is distorted evenly around the distortion control handle. When Center Distortion is disabled, the object distortion "moves" toward the direction of the control pointer.

- *Convert to Curves*   As described earlier, if you click this button when a distortion has been applied to an object, the distortion controls are removed, and the object becomes a normal curve that can be further manipulated with the Shape tool.

- *Copy Distortion Properties*   The Copy Distortion Properties command copies the distortion from one distorted object and applies it to another object or objects. It works just like the Copy Envelope command discussed earlier.

- *Clear Distortion*   Choose this command when you want to clear the last distortion you applied. Like the Clear Envelope command, if you have multiple distortions applied to the same object, use the Clear Transformations command in the Arrange menu.

 TIP   *You can enable any combination of the Random, Smooth, and Local buttons to increase the number of zipper variations.*

Figure 17-4 shows examples of using the Twister Distortion tool on three different objects. As before, the positioning of the cursor when you drag will determine the distortion results. The first and third examples shown in Figure 17-4 use clipart taken from on the Symbols and Special Characters Docker. The middle example used a straight line to create a double-ended spiral. The technique used in creating Twister effects is to click and drag in circular motions around the selected object. Each time you complete a full rotation, a higher number will appear in the Complete Rotations num box. You can also manually type a figure in the num box. Of the three distortion types, the Twister mode is probably the most predictable. Pretty much whatever object you choose to apply the effect to ends up in a circular shape.

As with the other distortion tools, other adjustment settings are available on the Property Bar when the Twister tool is selected:

- *Add New button*   As with the first two distortion tools, this button is not used to begin a distortion but instead is used to add a distortion on top of the existing one.

- *Clockwise Rotation*   Use this button to move your distortions in a clockwise direction.

- *Counterclockwise Rotation*   Use this button to move your distortions in a counterclockwise direction.

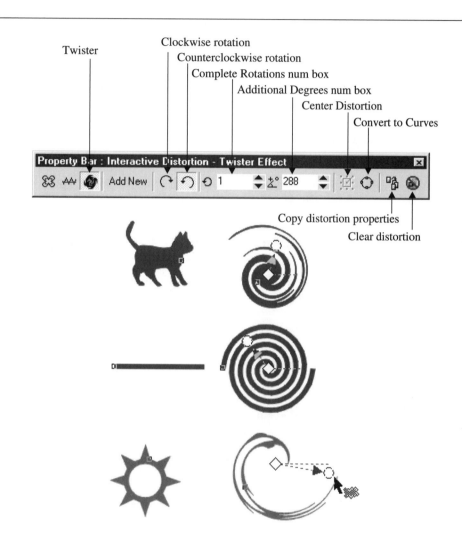

FIGURE 17-4   Three different objects distorted with the Twister Distortion tool

17

- *Complete Rotations num box*   Use this num box to enter the number of complete rotations you want your distortion to have.

- *Additional Degrees num box*   This num box allows you to enter additional degrees to a complete rotation. For example, if you used one complete rotation, you could add 20 degrees more for a total of 380 degrees.

- *Center Distortion button*   When this button is enabled, the left control handle is automatically placed in the center of the object, and the distortion will flow outward from that center point.

- *Convert to Curves*   As described before, if you click this button when a distortion has been applied to an object, the distortion controls are removed, and the object becomes a normal curve that can be further manipulated with the Shape tool.

- *Copy Distortion Properties*   The Copy Distortion Properties command copies the distortion from one distorted object and applies it to another object or objects. It works just like the Copy Envelope command discussed earlier.

- *Clear Distortion*   Choose this command when you want to clear the last distortion you applied. Like the Clear Envelope command, if multiple distortions are applied to the same object, use the Clear Transformations command in the Arrange menu.

We hope that you will find some unique uses for these amazing new tools.

 CAUTION   *The distortion tool can create some incredibly complex objects, which can cause problems when printing. There's a warning dialog box that will display on extremely complex distortions, offering you a chance to cancel out because the effect will take "several minutes" to complete.*

 TIP   *Using the Interactive Distortion tool on text will usually produce less-than-desirable results. Try applying the effect to one letter at a time. A sample of using the Zipper distortion tool on the letter S is shown here.*

Perspective

Perspective adds a sense of depth and dimension to an object relative to the angle from which it is viewed. When you add perspective to an object in CorelDRAW, you create the illusion that an object is receding into the background. Almost everyone has stood in the middle of a road and observed the road narrowing into the distance, or has noticed that the telephone poles alongside the road look smaller as you move away from them. Most of us don't pay much attention to the fact that objects appear to become smaller as they get farther away because we live in a three-dimensional world. The problem we face when working on a flat surface like a computer screen is there is no third dimension. We can, however, trick the viewer's eye into believing that a third dimension exists by using one or more of CorelDRAW's effects—in particular, the Perspective effect.

The Perspective effect can be used on single objects or groups of objects. It cannot be used on several objects at once; you can, however, copy the perspective from one object to another (see the section "Copying Perspectives," later in this chapter).

Choosing One-Point versus Two-Point Perspective

There are two types of perspective: one point and two point. The word *point* here refers to the vanishing point. Therefore, a one-point perspective uses one vanishing point, and a two-point perspective uses two vanishing points.

One-point perspective gives the illusion that an object is receding, and two-point perspective provides the added illusion that the object is leaning or twisted. The following illustration shows a one-point perspective and a two-point perspective.

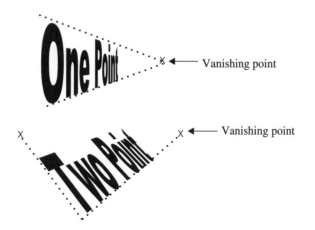

Vanishing point

Vanishing point

17

Adding the Perspective Effect

To add perspective to an object, first select the object or group of objects to which you want to apply the effect. Then choose Effects | Add Perspective. After you have done so, the object or group will be surrounded by a rectangular selection box outlined with a dotted line and four nodes at each corner. Filling the entire selection box will be horizontal and vertical dotted gridlines. The Shape tool will automatically be selected for you. Use the Shape tool to apply perspective to the object by clicking a corner node and dragging. Whether you apply a one-point or two-point perspective is determined by the direction you drag. As you drag the nodes, the vanishing points will appear on the page.

Here are the results you can expect when dragging any of the corner nodes or the vanishing points:

- If you hold down the CTRL key and drag any node horizontally or vertically, you will apply a one-point perspective. If you don't hold down the CTRL key to constrain the node as you drag so that it moves in a perfectly straight line either horizontally or vertically, you will create a two-point perspective.

- If you drag a node while holding down CTRL-SHIFT, the opposing node will either move away from or toward the other. For example, if you click on the upper-left node and hold down the CTRL-SHIFT keys while dragging horizontally to the left, the node at the upper-right moves the same distance in the opposite direction. If you drag the upper-left node to the right, the upper-right node moves inward toward the upper-left node an equal distance. Holding CTRL-SHIFT while dragging vertically on a node does the same thing as dragging horizontally, but in the vertical direction instead. If you drag any node in a vertical direction after you have dragged a node in a horizontal direction, you will apply a two-point perspective.

- If you drag any node in a horizontal direction after you have dragged a node in a vertical direction, you will apply a two-point perspective.

- If you drag any node diagonally, you will apply a two-point perspective.

- When vanishing points become visible, you can move the vanishing points instead of the nodes to adjust the perspective, thereby retaining the overall size of the object.

TIP   *If you can't see the vanishing points, zoom out on the page. It may be necessary to zoom out twice in certain situations.*

Creating a Simple One-Point Perspective

The before and after illustrations in Figure 17-5 show a simple example of one-point perspective. You can use this technique on any object or group of objects to show them receding away from the viewer's eye. You can practice using this technique by drawing two rectangles to represent a road, and one with black and the other with white. Now follow these steps.

1. Select the two objects, and group them together using the Group button on the Property Bar.

FIGURE 17-5   Adding perspective to a group of two objects to give the illusion of a receding road

17

2. With the group selected, choose Effects | Add perspective.

3. While holding down the CTRL and SHIFT keys, click and drag toward the center on the upper-left node. Drag inward until you're satisfied with the results.

That's all there is to it. You're already an expert at adding perspective. We added the telephone poles for a little extra realism.

Creating a Two-Point Perspective

Two-point perspective involves the use of two vanishing points. Figure 17-6 shows the use of two-point perspective on letters placed on a block. You may want to practice placing perspective on letters to match an extruded shape. Use the following steps to recreate the effect shown in Figure 17-6:

1. Separately type the letters *A*, *B*, and *C*.

2. Draw a perfect square on the page.

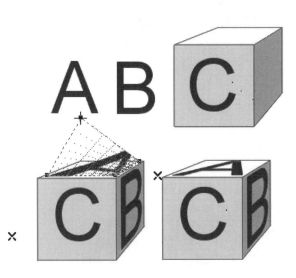

FIGURE 17-6   Placing letters on a block using perspective

3. Fill the square with a color, and extrude it to approximately the size of the one in the figure. If you need to learn how to extrude objects, refer to Chapter 18.

4. With the extruded object selected, choose Arrange | Separate. This will break the extruded object down into two objects.

5. Select the back extruded object, which will be a group of four objects, and click the Ungroup button on the Property Bar.

6. Color the top and side objects with different colors, which should be different from the color of the original square. The objective is to make the cube look like a three-dimensional cube.

7. Select the letter *C*, and place it on the front of the cube. Resize it to fit.

8. Move the letter *A*, near the top of the cube.

9. With the letter *A* selected, choose Effects | Add Perspective. The Shape tool will automatically be selected.

10. Using the Shape tool, click on the upper-left node on the grid, and drag it to the upper-left corner of the top cube.

11. Select the upper-right node on the grid, and drag it to the upper-right corner of the top cube.

12. Now do the same thing with the lower nodes, aligning them to their respective corners.

13. Select the letter *B*, and repeat the steps you just used, but this time align the letter *B* to the right side of the cube.

That's it. You've created a real-world example with the Perspective effect.

Copying Perspectives

The Effects | Copy Effect | Perspective From command works by copying the perspective from one object and applying it to another object or objects. If this sounds familiar, it's because this command works just like the Copy Envelope command discussed earlier in this chapter. This command can be useful when creating an object that you want to place on top of another object that has had perspective applied to it. The example here shows the perspective copied from the right side of the building and applied to the sign. The original clipart used in this example did not have perspective applied to it. We added the perspective to demonstrate the effect.

 NOTE   *Copying the perspective from one object to another does not mean that the objects will share the same vanishing point. They will however, share the same plane. In addition, you cannot apply perspective to Paragraph Text or bitmaps.*

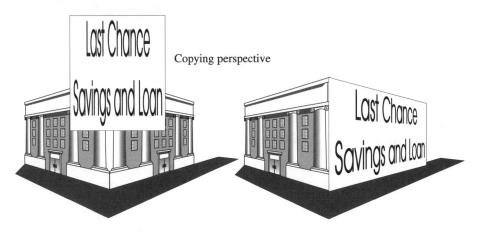

Copying perspective

Clearing Perspectives

Using the Effects | Clear Perspective command completely removes the Perspective effect and returns the object to its original state.

This chapter has given you some knowledge that will help you improve your drawings. Now you can use your own talents to implement what you have learned.

CHAPTER 18

Extruding

CoreIDRAW 9

The Extrude effect lets you visually add a third dimension to two-dimensional objects. When an object is extruded, CorelDRAW creates projecting surfaces away from the original object in the direction of the vanishing point. In addition to extruding objects of various shapes and sizes, the Extrude effect can produce some pleasing results when applied to text. CorelDRAW 9 now includes a bitmap extrude option that lets you create three-dimensional objects or text. The difference between the bitmap extrude option and the basic Extrude effect is that the bitmap option renders the object as a true three-dimensional bitmap image while the basic Extrude effect creates the three-dimensional illusion as a vector object. If you are striving for crisp edges and lines, you should stay with the Extrude effect. The great thing about using the interactive method is that it lets you create extrudes interactively in real time.

The Extrude effect is achieved by using the Interactive Extrude tool found on the Interactive tool flyout along with the various extrude options on the Property Bar. Figure 18-1 shows the Interactive Extrude tool selected from the Interactive tool flyout and the Property Bar when an extruded object is selected.

Using the Interactive Extrude Tool

The best way to learn this tool is to jump right in and practice using it. Follow these steps to learn how this fascinating tool works:

1. Type **3D** on the page (we used the font Arial black). Fill the text with a 50 percent black and apply a white outline.

2. Select the Interactive Extrude tool from the Interactive tool flyout shown in Figure 18-1.

3. Click inside the text, and drag up and to the right. Notice that a white square is placed in the center of the text with a dotted line pointing in the direction in which you dragged. The X at the end of the dotted line is the vanishing point. This means you can interactively place the vanishing point

Bitmap Extrude mode

Vanishing point relative to page origin

Vector Extrude mode

Vanishing point relative
to object center

X&Y Object position on page

Extrude rotation drop down

Extrusion Type drop down

Reset rotation button

Depth setting

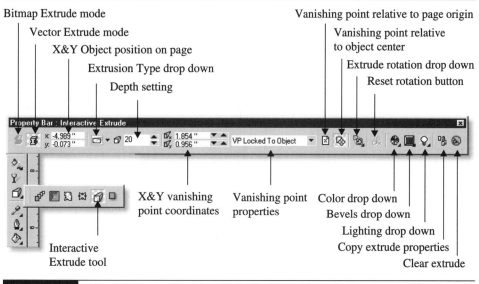

X&Y vanishing
point coordinates

Vanishing point
properties

Color drop down

Bevels drop down

Lighting drop down

Copy extrude properties

Clear extrude

Interactive
Extrude tool

FIGURE 18-1 The Interactive Extrude tool selected from the Interactive tool flyout and
the Property Bar displaying the various options available

in any position when creating the extrude. Your extruded text should look
similar to that shown here:

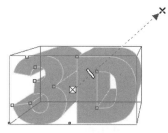

4. With the Interactive Extrude tool still selected, click the Depth slider (the
white bar on the dotted line), and drag it toward the vanishing point. Use
the last illustration as a guide. Sliding this bar along the dotted line allows
you to control the depth of the extrude. Practice moving this slider to see
how it works.

18

5. Click and drag on the vanishing point X, and drag to the left to change the direction of extrude. Your text should now look similar to the text shown here:

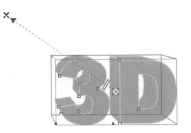

6. Now comes the fun part. Click on the extruded text (not the slider) to reveal the rotate cursor controls. Place the cursor inside the dotted circle. The cursor will change to the one shown in the following illustration. This cursor lets you move the object in the X and Y axes. Practice rotating the extrude in both axes by dragging the cursor until it looks similar to the one shown here:

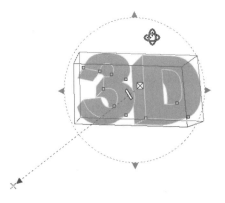

7. Place the cursor on the dotted lines of the circle, and the cursor changes to the one shown in the following illustration. It is important than you keep the cursor on the dotted lines and not inside them. This cursor lets you rotate the object in the Z axis. Again, practice rotating the object until it looks similar to the one shown next:

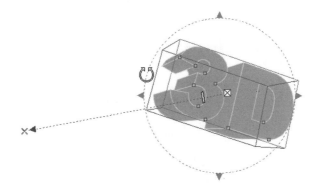

8. Place the cursor inside the dotted circle again, and rotate the object on the X and Y axes until it looks similar to the one shown in the following illustration. (If necessary adjust the Z axis as well.) As you drag, try to end up with the object looking like the one shown here. Interactively moving the rotation cursor is a trial-and-error process, so don't get discouraged. Just keep dragging the cursor in different directions until your object resembles the one we have created. You may need to undo some of your steps and try again. It is not as important to replicate the figure as it is to learn the process of interactively rotating an extruded object.

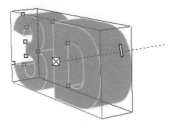

The extrude type of the extrude you just created is called Small Back. There are a total of six extrude types available from the Extrusion Type drop-down menu shown next. Each type produces a different 3-D effect. The default extrude is Small Back. To change to any of the other types, select a type from the list after a default extrude had been created.

 NOTE *There is no depth control slider on parallel extrudes. To increase the length of a parallel extrude, move the vanishing point in or out.*

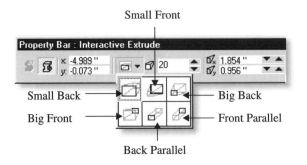

The six rectangles shown here have had each of the extrude types applied to them.

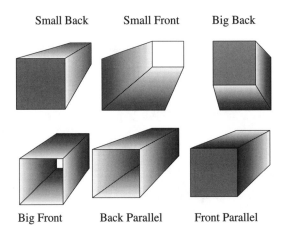

Now that you've seen how to create a basic extrude and learned that there are six types to choose from, let's continue learning how to use the other options on the Property Bar.

Locking the Vanishing Point

The first extrude you created had the vanishing point locked to the object. That means if you move the extrude object to a different location on the page, the vanishing point does not change, and the direction of the extrude will look the same as it did in its original position.

If you click on the down arrow of the Vanishing Point Properties drop-down list on the Property Bar and select VP Locked to Page, the vanishing point will be determined by its location on the page rather than the object. When you move an extruded object that has its vanishing point locked to the page, the extruded object will be updated automatically based on the location of the locked vanishing point. The drop-down list is shown here:

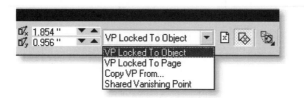

The image shown here shows an extruded text object at the lower left and three duplicates placed at different locations on the page. Notice that the duplicate objects use the same vanishing point as the original object. The vanishing point was locked to the page when the first text object was extruded.

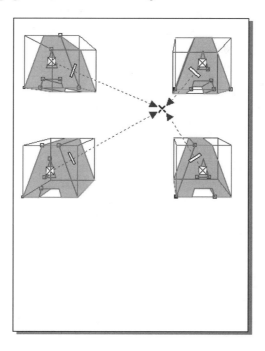

Copying the Vanishing Point

To copy a vanishing point from another extruded object, click on a existing extruded object, and then select Copy VP From from the vanishing point properties drop-down list. The cursor will change to a cursor with a question mark. Use this cursor to click on the extruded object you want to copy. The object you first selected will now have the same vanishing point as the object you clicked on. If this object was created with the default VP Locked to Object and then moved, its vanishing point will remain locked to the object and will not move like it did earlier when the vanishing point was locked to the page.

Shared Vanishing Point

The Shared Vanishing Point command is a combination of the VP Locked to Page and the Copy VP From commands. This is how it works. When you select an extruded object that was created with the default Locked to Object and then select the Shared Vanishing Point command from the Vanishing point drop-down list, the cursor changes to a question mark. Use this cursor to click on the extruded object that you want to share the vanishing point with. After the command is completed, the vanishing point of the first object will share the vanishing point of the second object regardless of where on the page the object is moved. The difference between this option and the Vanishing Point Locked to the Page is when the vanishing point of the second object (target object) is moved, the vanishing point of the first object is updated automatically, similar to the Clone effect (see Chapter 16).

Vanishing Point Coordinates

The next two buttons on the Property Bar are Vanishing Point Relative to Page Origin and Vanishing Point Relative to Object Center, in that order. These two buttons indicate which type of extrude you have clicked on.

NOTE   *You cannot rotate an extruded object if the vanishing point is locked to the page.*

Manually Rotating an Extrude

You learned how to interactively rotate an extruded object earlier using the Interactive Extrude tool. If you prefer to be more exact in your rotations, enter the exact coordinates in the Rotation values box shown next:

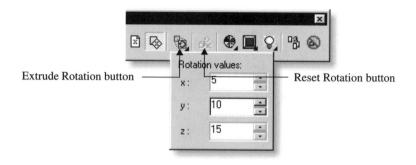

Extrude Rotation button —————   ————— Reset Rotation button

Practice using this method by typing **Rotate** on the page. Using the Interactive Extrude tool, extrude the text with the default Small Back setting. Use the example on the left shown here as a guide (we used the font Playbill, but you can use your favorite font). After you have extruded the text, click on the Extrude Rotation button on the Property Bar to display the Rotation values box. Enter **5** in the X value box, 10 in the Y value box, and 15 in the Z value box. Your extruded text should now look similar to the one on the right in the example.

 NOTE   *If you are not satisfied with the rotation of this or any extrude you have created, click on the Reset Rotation button on the Property Bar.*

Dissecting an Extrude

Before we continue with the rest of the options on the Property Bar, we should examine the different elements that make up extrudes. An extrude is made up of two basic parts: the original object and the group of objects created in the extrude process. The original object, after it has been used to create the extrude, is the control object. Depending on the shape of the original object, the control object will then be called "Control Text," "Control Rectangle," "Control Curve," and so on. The added objects created by the extrude process are called the "extrude group." The extrude group can be colored separately from the control object with solid fountain fills. The control object can be filled with any of CorelDRAW's fills. This ability to change the color of both the control object and the extrude group gives you greater control over the final look of the extruded object.

Coloring Extrudes

So far you have learned how to create various types of extrudes and how to rotate them. Now it's time to learn how to color the two components of extrudes. Three types of fill methods are available from the Color drop-down box shown here. They are: Use Object Fill, Use Solid Color, and Use Color Shading. It's important to understand the differences between the three methods.

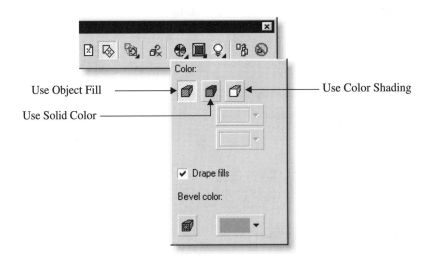

The best way to learn the differences between the three color options is to practice using them. The following instructions describe how to complete the exercises.

Use Object Fill

1. Draw a rectangle on the page, and fill it with your favorite color.

2. Using the extrude shown here as a guide, select the Interactive Fill tool, and extrude the rectangle so it looks like the one shown here:

3. With the extruded rectangle selected, click on the Color drop-down button to reveal the three color options. Notice that the default Use Object Fill button is highlighted. When you choose this option, the color of the extrude group is colored the same as the color you selected for the original rectangle you drew in step 1. This is the simplest of the three fill options. As you can see, the extruded portion of the rectangle is the same color as the original rectangle.

NOTE   *Notice that you cannot choose another fill from the drop-down box when the Use Object Fill icon is checked. If you want to change the fill of the extruded object, you must use either the color palette or any of the fill types available using the Interactive Fill tool or from the Fill Tool flyout (see Chapter 9).*

DRAPED FILLS   The Drape Fills option is also available with the Use Object Fill option. This option is useful when using fountain fills and pattern or bitmap fills. When you enable this check box, the chosen fill is used to fill both the control object and extrude group as a single fill rather than filling each separate component of the extruded object. If this box is not checked, the chosen fill will fill each individual component of the extruded object. An example of using the Drape Fills option is shown here. The image on the left is the bitmap fill used to fill the original rectangle before it was extruded. The extruded rectangle in the center used the Drape Fills option. The Drape Fills check box was not enabled for the extruded rectangle on the right. Notice the difference between the two extruded objects. The fill is stretched over the control object and two sides of the extrude in the center so it looks like a single image. The extrude on the right contains three images of the bitmap, one for the control object and one each for the two sides of the extrude. You can't see much of the image in the extruded sides because there isn't enough space to show the entire image.

Use Solid Fill

This fill option often gets confused with the first option. When the Solid Fill option is selected from the drop-down color box, a color bar is displayed, and when it's clicked on, the color bar displays the default color palette shown here. When you select a color from the palette, the color you selected is used to fill only the extruded portion of the object. The color of the control object retains its original color.

If you wish to access any of the other color models or palettes, click on the Other button at the bottom of the palette.

On the left of the example shown here is a rectangle filled with a light gray that was extruded with the Use Solid Color fill button checked. The extruded portion of the extrude is filled with the default color white. The extrude on the right shows the same extrude, but the extruded portion was filled with a darker color by choosing a color from the Use Solid Color fill drop-down palette.

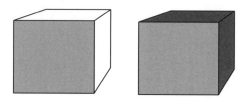

NOTE   *To recap the Use Solid Color fill option, use it to fill extrudes when you want only a solid color fill on the extruded portion of the extruded object. You can still fill the control object with any of CorelDRAW's other fills using either the Interactive Fill tool or the fill available from the Fill Tool flyout.*

Use Color Shading

The Color Shading option lets you fill the extruded portion of the extrude with a two-color fountain fill. This allows you to emulate a sense of light and shadow or just to give the extruded portion a pretty color scheme. You choose the colors for these fountain fills by selecting them from the drop-down color palettes displayed when you click on either of the two color bars. The colors selected from the palette accessed from the From: color bar control the color nearest the control object. Once a color is selected, the color bar takes on that color. Prior to selecting a color from the drop-down palette, the color for this color bar is the color of the control object. If the control object has no fill, the color of the bar is white.

The color selected from the palette accessed from the To: color bar controls the color at the back of the extrude group. These two colors then blend together to form the fountain fill. The Color drop-down box is shown here with the Use Color Shading option selected. Also shown is a spokelike image that has been extruded to look like a gear. If you would like to practice using the shading option with this image, it can be found on the CD that comes with the book. The path to the file is Projects/chap18/Gear.cdr.

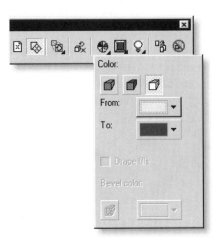

NOTE *Remember, the color of the control object is also the color of the first color bar. If you change the color of the control object by selecting it with the Pick tool and choosing a color from the onscreen color palette, the color you picked will replace the front color used in the extrude group.*

Bevels

You can add a bevel to the control object of an extruded object for an added effect. To add a bevel, click on the Bevel button on the Property Bar to reveal the following drop-down dialog box:

Learning to use the bevel effect will also teach you the benefits of typing in values to achieve a certain look instead of trying to create the effect interactively. Follow these steps to create a bevel on an extruded rectangle:

1. Draw a rectangle on the page approximately two inches square, and give it a 50 percent black fill.

2. Select the Interactive Extrude tool from the interactive toolbox, and create any kind of basic extrude.

3. With the extrude selected, click on the Extrude Type drop-down button, and choose Big Back (it's the icon on the right in the top row).

4. Type **0.0** in the both the X and Y vanishing points coordinates boxes on the Property Bar, and press the ENTER key for the changes to take effect. Your extrude should now look like the one shown here:

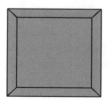

18

5. Click on the Color drop-down button on the Property Bar, and choose the Color Shading button. Select the color black from the From: color bar and the color white from the To: color bar. Your extrude should now look like the one shown here:

6. With the extrude still selected, click on the Bevels button to display the Bevels dialog box.

7. Enter **1.0** in the Bevels Depth num box. Enter **11** in the Bevel Angle num box. Click anywhere on the page for the changes to take effect. The dialog box will disappear.

8. Click on the Color drop-down button on the Property Bar again, and choose the Color Shading button. Click on the Use Extrude fill for bevel button at the lower left of the color box. Click on the color bar, and choose 20 percent black from the Color palette. Your extrude with the bevel should now look like the one shown here:

9. Now click on the Bevel drop-down button on the Property Bar, and enable the Show Bevel Only check box. This action will remove the extruded portion of the extrude and display only the bevel portion looking like the one shown next:

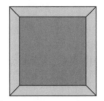

Figure 18-2 shows the progression from extruding a text object using Small Back to placing a bevel on the extrude in the middle object, then finally showing just the bevel at the bottom of the figure. The font used was Futura XBlk BT. The Depth of the bevel is 1 inch with an angle of 5 degrees.

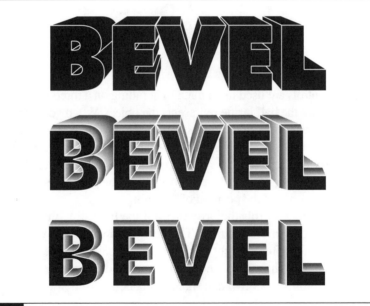

FIGURE 18-2   An ordinary extruded text object, an extruded text object with bevel attached, and an extruded text object with only the bevel showing

18

Lighting Effects

When you click the Lighting button on the Property Bar, the lighting control box shown here is displayed. The default shows the display with no lights turned on.

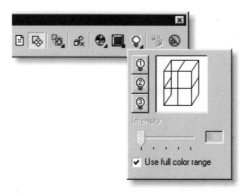

The lighting controls are used to emulate light falling on a three-dimensional extrude. The grid with the ball inside represents the object. When you click on a light, a black circle with the number of the light is placed on the upper-front-right corner of the grid. To change the position of a light, click on the circle, and move it anywhere on the grid where two lines intersect. You can use all three lights when lighting the object. As you move the lights to different locations on the grid, the shadow under the ball will change to reflect the position of the light.

The Intensity slider controls the brightness of the light. Enabling Use full color range makes the shading more realistic. The best way to acquaint yourself with the lighting effect is to try different light positions and intensities. The first of the two illustrations shown next show only one light being used on an extruded text object. The second illustration shows two and three lights being used.

 NOTE *All of the examples of lighting were done on extrudes filled using the Object Fill mode. The shading was created by the placement of the lights, not from using the Color Shading mode.*

18

Extruding Lines

This entire chapter has dealt with extruding objects. Many users are unaware that you can extrude lines as well. Here is an example of extruding lines. Extruding the shape shown at the top of the illustration created the two extruded objects. That original shape was created using the Bezier tool from the Drawing Tools flyout.

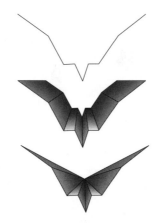

The settings for the two extrudes are as follows:
Middle extrude

- An Extrude Type of Small Back

- A Depth setting of 45

- An X Vanishing coordinate of 0.0

- A Y Vanishing coordinate of 1.4

- The vanishing point was locked to the object

- And finally, a color shading of black to white

Bottom extrude

- An Extrude Type of Small Back

- A Depth setting of 99

- An X Vanishing coordinate of 0.0

- A Y Vanishing coordinate of 0.0

- The vanishing point was locked to the object

- And again, a color shading of black to white

What do these shapes look like to you? Could they be paper airplanes, or birds, or petals of a flower? Whatever they are, they look great. Experiment by extruding other line art. You might just get some happy accidents. Here is one more example of extruding lines. This time we extruded a spiral.

Copying Extrudes

Now that you have learned how to create various types of extrudes, you may someday want to copy one rather than recreate it from scratch. To copy the extrude effect from one extrude object to another extrude object or to a single object, select the object you want to copy the extrude to, and then select the Copy Extrude button on the Property Bar. Use the pointing arrow to click on the extruded object you want to copy. The properties of the extrude you clicked on will be transferred to the new object. Pretty simple, eh?

 NOTE *You cannot copy an extrude to groups of objects.*

Bitmap Extrusions

The ability to convert vector objects to bitmap objects and extrude them is now possible. This ability to make three-dimensional bitmap objects is accomplished by using the Interactive Extrude tool along with the settings on the Property Bar. Figure 18-3 shows the Property Bar with a symbols clipart object in the process of being extruded.

18

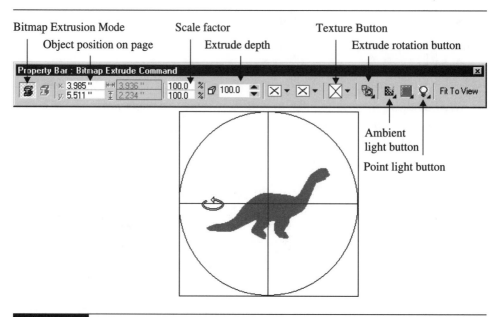

Bitmap Extrusion Mode

Object position on page

Scale factor

Extrude depth

Texture Button

Extrude rotation button

Ambient light button

Point light button

Using the bitmap extrusion mode on a symbols clipart object

Follow these steps to convert a vector object into a bitmap and then extrude and add lighting to it:

1. Type a letter on the page, or use an object from symbols clipart. We used the dinosaur from Animals 1 symbols clipart. If you wish to use the same clipart, simply type the capital letter *A* on the page, and then change the font to Animals 1. Fill the object with a light color.

2. With the object selected, select the Interactive Extrude tool and then click the Bitmap Extrusion Mode button at the far left of the Property Bar.

3. Double-click on the object to convert the object into a bitmap.

4. Double-click the new bitmap object to reveal the rotation controls shown on the object in Figure 18-4.

5. Place the cursor on the center horizontal line, and drag to the right to rotate the object on the Y axis.

6. Place the cursor on the center vertical line, and drag upward, rotating the object on the X axis.

7. Place the cursor on the perimeter of the circle, and drag up or down, rotating the object on the Z axis.

8. When you are done experimenting, try to end up with the object in the extruded position shown here. The shading won't look like that shown here until you apply the lighting to the object.

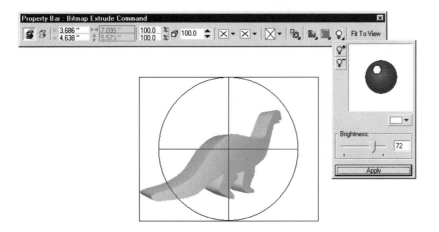

9. With the object still selected, click on the Point light button on the Property Bar to display the Lighting dialog box.

10. Click on the light bulb icon with the + on it to place a white dot on the black sphere. Position the dot where you want the light to fall on the object.

11. Adjust the brightness slider, and click the Apply button. Your dinosaur should now look like one shown in at step 8.

18

12. Click on the Texture button, and select the texture from the drop-down palette shown here. Your dinosaur will now look like this:

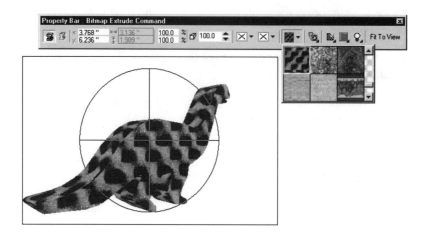

13. As a final touch, let's adjust the ambient light. Click on the ambient light button on the Property Bar to reveal its dialog box.

14. Click on the color bar, and choose a color from the drop-down palette. Changing the color of the ambient light can be used to tint the texture you just added with a different color. We used a blue color in the example shown here. Because you're seeing it in grayscale, it doesn't mean much but it does improve the image.

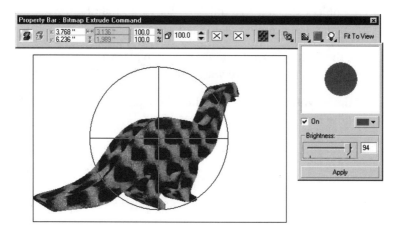

Click anywhere on the desktop to deselect the bitmap extrude when you finished creating your 3-D image.

 NOTE *To change the resolution of bitmap extrudes, choose Tools | Options | Document | General and enter the resolution value in the resolution number box in the Rendering section.*

 TIP *After you have created a bitmap extrude, you can create some great effects by converting the bitmap extrude into an ordinary bitmap by choosing Bitmaps | Convert to Bitmap. Choose the Transparent background option in the Convert to Bitmap dialog box when converting the bitmap extrude. Once the bitmap extrude has been converted to an ordinary bitmap add some transparency or even a drop shadow.*

A Third-Party Extrusion Script

By itself, CorelDRAW is a powerful program, but it lacks some features required by technical illustrators. EZ Metrics, a third-party utility, fills that void. Now it just takes a few clicks to convert an orthographic drawing into one of five different axonometric drawings such as isometric, dimetric, two forms of trimetric, and axonometric. EZ Metrics also makes it easy to move and extrude objects in the third dimension based on the type of drawing you are creating. It simply automates features that already exist in CorelDRAW. Functions that require a number of steps and lots of math in CorelDRAW are reduced to a single click. What this means is that you will be saving time while creating some fantastic technical illustrations. A 15-day fully working evaluation version of the software is found on the CD that accompanies this book. Figure 18-4 shows an example of the orthographic view created in CorelDRAW and the isometric view after using EZ Metrics. Converting the three orthographic views to a finishing isometric view took less than five minutes thanks to EZ Metrics.

Creating extrudes can give your work a three-dimensional look, but don't overdo it. Simple is often better when trying to get your message across. Sometimes just adding perspective (see Chapter 17) to an object can give the viewer the sense of depth you're trying to convey.

18

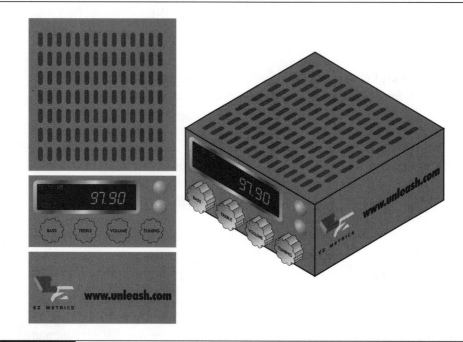

FIGURE 18-4   On the left are the three orthographic views with the finished isometric view on the right

CHAPTER 19

Blending, Contouring, and Drop Shadows

The Blend and Contour effects are covered in the same chapter because in some ways they share what appear to be common attributes. For example, the group of objects on the left here is a Blend group, and the group of objects on the right is a Contour group. As you can see, they look identical. However, except in this one particular use of the two effects, they are completely different. The Blend effect is used to morph one object into another, using a series of intermediate steps. The Contour effect creates duplicates of the original object on either the inside or outside of the original object. The difference between the two effects will become obvious as you learn more about them.

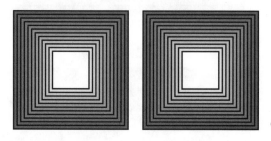

Blend group   Contour group

The Blend Effect

The Blend effect can be used in a number of different ways, and it all begins with two objects. These objects can be as simple as a rectangle or an ellipse or as complicated as a clipart group containing hundreds of objects. Blends can be used to create the illusion of perspective or mimic the look of neon. Blends can also be used for practical purposes such as spacing objects around another object or just on the page itself.

Before you jump right in and start creating blends, it is important to understand the parts of a blend. To begin, a blend is called a *blend group*, not just a *blend*. The blend group consists of three parts: two control objects (the start and end objects) and a group of objects containing the objects created when the Blend effect is applied. The following illustration shows a five-step blend using a symbols clipart image. The image at the far left is one control object, and the image at the far right is the second control object. The objects in between the control objects are a group of five objects created by the Blend effect.

Dynamically Linked Blends

All objects in a blend group are dynamically linked. This means that if you move one of the control objects to a different location on the page, the blend will automatically be updated according to the new control object position. The next illustration shows the same blend as before, but this time the larger control object on the right has been moved downward to give the illusion of perspective that the men are on standing on stairs. When the control object was moved, the blend was updated to the new location. Notice also that the spacing between the men has increased slightly in the second illustration. This is because the blend effect, by default, always spaces the intermediate steps equally between the two control objects. You will learn later in this chapter that you can control the distance between the intermediate steps by accelerating or decelerating the steps.

19

Creating Your First Blend

Now that you know how the Blend effect works, it's time to learn how to create one using the Interactive Blend tool. The best way to learn how to use this tool is to jump right in and try it. Follow the steps here to create a simple blend:

1. Draw one large circle and one small circle on the page, and space them apart horizontally by about two inches. Fill each circle with a different color.

2. Click the Interactive tool flyout in the toolbox, and select the Interactive Blend tool, which is shown highlighted here:

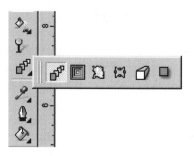

3. Using the Interactive Blend tool, click and drag from the large circle to the small circle.

4. Release the mouse button to see the results of your first interactive blend. It should look like the one shown here:

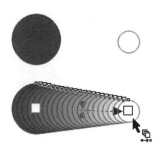

Now lets try an interesting feature of this tool. Create two more circles as you did in step 1 of the last exercise, and select the Interactive Blend tool again. This time hold down the ALT key, and draw an irregular shaped path from one circle to the next. End on the second circle, and release the ALT key and mouse button. Your blend should look similar to the one shown here. This shape has possibilities, perhaps an elephant's trunk?

Once a blend is created and the blend group is selected, the Property Bar shown here will display the many controls that let you to make modifications to the blend. The controls are described here, beginning at the left of the Property Bar.

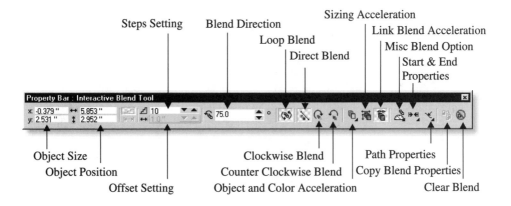

■ *Objects position*   Like the size controls, the position tools are the same as on the default Property Bar. In the case of a blend, you would most often move to a different location on the page.

■ *Objects size*   The size controls are the same as on the default Property Bar. They allow you to manually enter the coordinates for the size of an object. In the case of a blend, you most often would resize a control object.

■ *Steps setting*   This num box lets you enter the number of steps you want in your blend.

19

- *Offset setting*   This num box lets you enter a fixed amount of spacing between the steps.

- *Blend direction*   This numb box lets you enter the angle of direction for the blend. This means if you use any number other than zero, the intermediate objects within the blend will begin to rotate progressively as they blend from one control object to the next. An example of this feature is shown here. The control objects are the same size and orientation. The center objects making up the blend are rotating 180 degrees from one control object to the next.

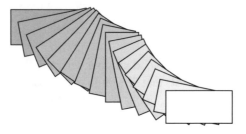

- *Loop blend*   This option is available only if you have entered a number in the Blend Direction num box. When activated, the rotating blend will loop upward or downward based on the positive or negative degree of rotation. An example of this feature is shown here, looping the rotated blend just shown. Notice that the intermediate objects almost disappear in the middle of the loop. This happens because the nodes on the two control objects don't match. You will learn how to correct this problem later in the chapter.

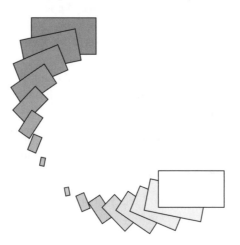

■ *Direct blend*   This button and the next two buttons relate to color. The direct blend button blends the color of the first control object to the color of the second control object in a straight line through the color wheel spectrum. For example, if one control object was colored red and the second control object was colored yellow, the colors of the different intermediate objects within the blend would range from red to shades of orange and then to yellow again.

■ *Clockwise blend*   This button blends the color of the first control object to the color of the second control object in a clockwise direction through the color wheel spectrum. If you used the red for the first control object and blue for the second control object, the intermediate colors would be made up of magentas, purples, and blues.

■ *Counterclockwise blend*   This button blends the color of the first control object to the color of the second control object in a counterclockwise direction through the color wheel spectrum. If you used the same as the second example, the colors of the intermediate objects within the blend would consist of orange, yellows, greens, and blues.

■ *Object and color acceleration*   When you choose this button, a drop-down control box appears displaying slider controls for the object and color acceleration within the blend.

■ *Sizing acceleration*   When this button is enabled, the size of the intermediate objects are accelerated between the two control objects.

■ *Link blend accelerations*   When this button is enabled, the Object and Color acceleration sliders move together rather than independently.

■ *Misc blend option*   When you click this button, a drop-down menu displays six different options that control how a blend behaves. The options contained in this menu will be discussed later in the chapter.

■ *Start and end properties*   When you click on this button, a drop-down menu displays four different options that relate to the control objects at the start and end of the blend or at the intermediate blend of a compound blend. These options will also be discussed later in the chapter.

■ *Path properties*   When you click this button, a drop-down menu displays three path options that relate to blends on a path. Blends on a path will be discussed in detail later in the chapter.

19

■ *Copy blend properties*   This option lets you copy all properties, except the fill and outline properties, from one blend to another.

■ *Clear blend*   Click this button to remove the intermediate parts of the blend. The only parts left will be the control objects.

Now that you learned what all those buttons on the Property Bar are, let's create a blend using text as the control objects. Use the following steps to create the three blends shown here.

1. Select the text tool from the tool box, and type the word "Blend". We used the font Harlow Solid Italic, but you can use your favorite font.

2. With the word selected, press the + key on the keyboard to make a duplicate. Fill the second copy of the word with the color white, and give it a black outline.

3. Using the example as a guide, move the duplicate up and to the right.

4. Select the interactive blend tool, click on the first text object filled with the default fill color black, and drag it to over to the second text object to create the blend. Your blend should now look like the one at the lower left in the example.

5. Draw an rectangle over the entire blend, and give it a 20 percent black fill. Move it to the back by clicking on the To Back button on the Property Bar.

6. Now remove the outline from the white-filled text. Your blend should now look like the one at the upper right in the example.

7. Delete the rectangle in the back, and give the front control object a fill of 50 percent black with a black outline.

8. Select the back control object, and give it white fill with no outline. You blend will now look like the one at the lower right in the example.

This last exercise demonstrated how blends can be used to give the illusion of three dimensions. The example shown here uses the same technique, but instead of having the text the same size and offset from each other, the back text object is made much smaller and placed directly behind the larger front text object. The objects were then blended in the same way as in the previous exercise, but this time the illusion is different.

The set of barbells shown here is an example of another way of blending objects.

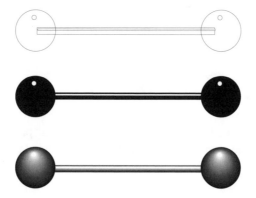

If you would like to follow along use these steps:

1. Using the example as a guide, draw an narrow rectangle approximately four inches long.

2. Press the + key on the keyboard to make a duplicate of the rectangle, and scale it vertically upward until it looks like the example.

3. Draw two circles on the page and place them on the end of the rectangles.

4. Select one of the circles, and press the + key on the keyboard to make a duplicate.

19

5. Using the examples as guides again, scale this duplicate circle down to a very small circle, and place it near the top of the larger circle.

6. Make a duplicate of this small circle, move it over to the second larger circle, and place it near the top.

7. Fill the smaller circles with the color white and the large circles with the color black.

8. Fill the smaller rectangle with white and the larger one with black. Your barbells should now look like the one in the middle of the example.

9. Using the interactive blend tool, blend the large circle on the left to the smaller circle on the left.

10. Marquee select the blend group and right click on the X at the top of the color palette to remove the outlines.

11. Repeat this with the circles on the right.

12. To finish your barbells, blend the large rectangle to the small rectangle. Don't forget to remove the outlines from the blended rectangles.

Putting Blends on a Path

Placing blends on paths can create some interesting effects. When you place a blend on a path, you force the blend to follow a particular path that you have previously created. The example shown here contains the elements of a blend on a path. If you would like to follow along, use these steps. Because you probably won't have the clipart we used in the final piece, draw a larger circle in step 2.

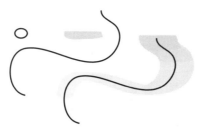

1. Using the example as a guide, draw a ellipse on the page.

2. Select the Pencil tool, and draw a shape similar to the one in the example (draw a larger circle if you don't have the clipart).

3. Select the Pencil tool again, and draw an curved line like the one in the example.

4. Select the Interactive Blend tool, and blend together the ellipse and shape (or larger circle).

5. Enter **200** in the Steps num box on the Property Bar, and then press the ENTER key for the change to take effect.

6. With the blend group selected, click on the Path Properties button on the Property Bar, and choose New Path. The cursor will change to a crooked arrow. Use this arrow to click on the path. The blend will now follow the path, but it won't travel the entire length of the path.

7. Click on the Miscellaneous Blend Options button on the Property Bar, and choose Blend along full path. This will force the blend to follow the entire length of the path. If you did everything right, your blend should look similar to the one at the right in the example.

8. Select the Pick tool, and then select the path curve you used for the path.

9. With the curve selected, right-click on the X at the top of the color palette to remove the color from the outline, making it invisible.

If you used a larger circle in step 2, your blend should resemble a tornado. We used two pieces of clipart to place at the top and bottom of the blend to create the genie coming out of a lamp shown here.

19

Another interesting effect can be achieved by using the blend on a path technique on text. In the example shown here, we used a font Ribbon and converted it to curves. Once it was converted to curves, we broke it apart and saved only the outer perimeter of the letters' shapes. We then combined all the separate parts back together using the Combine command on the Property Bar. You can use the font without breaking it apart and throwing away pieces as we did, but the results will be slightly different.

The example shown here shows the components that went into completing the effect. If you would like to practice this technique, use the following steps:

1. Using the example as a guide, draw an ellipse on the page, and give it a radial fill.

2. Scale the ellipse down to a very small size.

3. Make a duplicate of the small ellipse, and blend the two ellipses together using the Interactive Blend tool.

4. Enter **400** in the Steps num box on the Property Bar, and then press the ENTER key for the change to take effect.

5. Type the word "sail" on the page using a script font like Ribbon.

6. Select the Interactive Blend tool, and select the blend group.

7. Repeat steps 6 through 9 of the last exercise to complete the effect. Try changing the number of steps in the blend if you're not satisfied with the appearance.

The finished effect should look something like the one show in the example.

Creating an ID Chain

We have one last exercise that you might like to try using blends on a path. The CDR file is on the CD that comes with the book. The path to the file is Projects/Chap19/ID bracelet. In this exercise, you will also learn how to blend lines to lines. Use the following steps to complete the effect shown here.

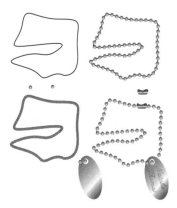

1. Open the file Bracelet.cdr.

2. Choose View | Enhanced so you can see the irregular shape more easily.

3. Select the irregular shape at the upper left, and make a duplicate by pressing the + key on the keyboard. This shape has an outline of 2 points and is colored with a 50 percent black.

4. Move the duplicate shape down below the original.

5. Select the Interactive Blend tool. Make sure that none of the accelerator buttons are enabled.

6. Using the Interactive Blend tool, click and drag from one ball to the other to create a blend.

7. Enter **50** in the steps num box, and press the ENTER key.

8. With the blend group selected, click on the Path Properties button on the Property Bar, and choose New Path. The cursor will change to a crooked arrow. Use this arrow to click on the path. The blend will now follow the path, but again, it won't travel the entire length of the path.

19

9. Click on the Miscellaneous Blend Options button on the Property Bar, and choose Blend along full path. This will force the blend to follow the entire length of the path. If you did everything right, your blend should look similar to the one at the upper right in the example.

10. Select the Pick tool, and then select the path curve you used for the path.

11. With the curve selected, right-click on the X at the top of the color palette to remove the color from the outline, making it invisible.

12. Select the duplicate you made of the irregular shape, and press the + key on the keyboard to make a duplicate right on top of the original shape.

13. With the duplicate shape selected, click on the down arrow on the Outline Width box on the Property Bar, and choose Hairline from the drop-down list.

14. With the outline still selected, right-click on the color white in the default color palette.

15. Select the Zoom tool from the toolbox, and zoom in on the outlines about 5000 percent (you need to zoom this much so you can see the distinction between the two lines and use the Interactive Blend tool correctly).

16. Select the Interactive Blend tool, and drag from the narrow white outline to the larger outline.

17. Enter **15** in the steps num box, and press the ENTER key. This blending of the two lines creates the three-dimensional looking string on which the balls are attached.

18. Marque select the blend group containing the 50 balls, and the blended lines you just created.

19. Press the letters C and E keys to center the balls on the line.

20. Now select the back portion fastener we created for you in the CDR file, and place it behind two of the balls at the top of the bracelet.

21. Select the front half of the fastener, and place it in front of the same two balls. Move them around until it appears the balls are inside the fastener.

22. Using the example as a guide, select the ID tag, and place it on top of the bracelet so that one of the balls shows through the hole in the tag.

23. Select the extra balls and string we created for you in the CDR file, and place them on top of the ball that appears in the hole and the ball to the left of it. This will give the illusion that the ball and string are going through the hole in the tag.

That's all there is to it. You're finished with another fun project, and you learned how to blend line to lines.

To finish this section on blends on a path, Figure 19-1 is a real-world image created by Gary and Linda Rapson of South Africa. The image was created as an entry for a logo contest for Rick Altman's upcoming CorelWORLD 99 User Conference in Orlando Florida Oct 3-8, 1999. The Rapsons can be contacted at info@regals.co.za.

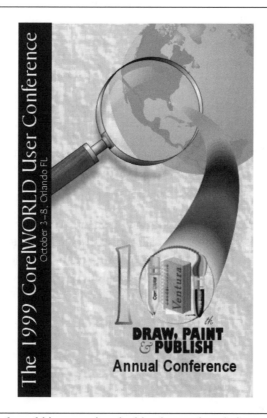

FIGURE 19-1   Real-world image using the blend on path technique

Creating a Neon Effect

Creating a neon effect is accomplished by either blending lines to lines or outlines to outlines. You learned how to blend lines to lines in the exercise on creating an ID bracelet. This exercise will blend the outlines on two text objects to each other. Use the following steps to create this effect:

1. Type the word **OPEN** on the page using the font Futura Md BT. If you don't have this font installed, use a similar font like Arial Black.

2. Size the text to 150 points, and give it a 60 percent black fill.

3. Place an outline on the text of 8 points, and color the outline black.

4. Press the + key on the keyboard to place a duplicate of the text directly on top of the first text object.

5. Remove the fill from the duplicate text object by left-clicking on the X at the top of the color palette.

6. Change the outline color of the selected duplicate text object to white by right-clicking on the color white in the color palette.

7. Change the outline on the duplicate text object to a hairline width. You can do this by clicking on the Outline tool in the toolbox and selecting the hairline button on the outline tool flyout.

8. Select the Zoom tool, and zoom in on the outlines of the two text objects.

9. Select the Interactive Blend tool, and drag from the wider black outline to the white hairline outline. Change the number of blend steps to 15 in the Steps settings num box, and press the ENTER key to complete the blend. Your neon text should look like the one shown here except for the drop-shadow. Save this file for when you will learn all about drop shadows later in the chapter.

Miscellaneous Blend Options

When you click the Miscellaneous Blend Options button of the Property Bar a drop-down box shown here is displayed displaying several options.

These are the options on the drop-down box:

- *Map Nodes*   When you blend two objects together, CorelDRAW uses the first node on both the start and end objects to create the intermediate objects based on their relative locations. If you are blending two completely different shapes, the intermediate shapes created may not give you the results you expected. When you click the Map Nodes button, the cursor changes to a pointing arrow, and one of the blends control objects is selected Use the pointing arrow to select one node on the selected control object. After you select a node, the second control object is selected. Use the pointing arrow to select a node that corresponds to the node on the first object you selected. By experimenting with different nodes, you can alter the way the intermediate shapes look. The following illustration shows a swimming duck blended to a flying goose. A node at the front of the beak of the swimming duck was mapped to the node at the front of the beak of the flying goose. As you can see, a pleasing morphing effect was achieved.

19

- *Split*   This option lets you add a new control object to a blend by converting one of the intermediate objects into a third control object. To spilt a blend, click on an existing blend with the Interactive Blend tool, and then click on the Split button on the drop-down menu. The cursor will change to a crooked arrow. Use this arrow to click on an object within the original blend. This action changes the object you clicked on into a new control object, and the original blend becomes a compound blend. The compound blend is now composed of the starting object of the original blend blending to the newly added control object. The newly created control object then blends to the ending object of the original blend. Remember that blends are dynamically linked objects; thus, you can move the newly created control object to a different location on the page, and thereby create a bend on the blend. An example of a split blend where the added control object has been moved is shown here:

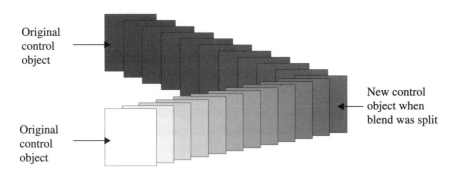

Original control object

Original control object

New control object when blend was split

- *Fuse Start*   This option removes any additional control objects from a compound blend and converts it back to a single blend.

- *Fuse End*   This option removes any additional control objects from a compound blend and converts it back to a single blend.

To fuse a blend, click the compound blend with the Interactive Blend tool selected while holding down the CTRL key. Either the Fuse Start or Fuse End button will become active, depending on which half of the blend you clicked. If there are several control objects as a result of splitting a blend more than once, you have to click the Fuse End button once for every extra control object before the blend completely reverts to the original blend.

The last two options in the drop-down are the Blend along a full path and Rotate all objects check boxes. You have already learned how to use the Blend along a full path option. When you enable the Rotate all objects box, the objects within the blend rotate along the path.

Start and End Options

■ *New Start*   When you click the Start and End Object Properties button on the Property Bar , a drop-down menu offers four options. The first option is New Start. This option lets you define a new control object to blend to. For example, suppose there are three objects on the page: one orange, one blue, and one green. If you blend the orange object to the blue object and then decide you should have blended the orange object to the green object, you can do the following: Select the blend containing the orange and blue control objects. Click the Start button, and select New Start. Use the funny-looking arrow that will replace your cursor to select the green object. Click the Apply button to make the change take effect. The blue object will now be blended to the green object.

 CAUTION   *If the green object is in front of the blue object, you will get a message saying "Cannot use current control; Use Reverse Order to invert." To correct this situation, simply select both control objects with the Pick tool and reverse their stacking order by right-clicking and selecting Order | Reverse Order from the Object menu.*

■ *Show Start*   The second option displayed in the drop-down menu is Show Start. When you select this option, the first control object in the blend is selected, and the selection handles appear. This option can be handy when you want to identify the starting and ending control objects when you are working with compound blends.

■ *New End*   The New End and Show End options work like the New Start and Show Start options. (Note that the preceding Caution also pertains to the New End option.)

Path Options

When you click the Path button on the Property Bar, a drop-down menu appears with three options. The first option is New Path. This option lets you point to the path where the blend will be placed. You have already learned how to use this

19

option in earlier exercises. The second option is Show Path. This option selects the path displaying the selection handles so you can identify or edit the path. The third option lets you detach the blend from the path. Detaching the blend from the path returns the blend group to its original state.

Separating Blends

At times you'll need to separate a blend group. For example, you may want to take apart a blend to use one of the intermediate objects in a blend group. To separate a blend, click the blend group (not one of the control objects), and select Arrange | Separate. Once a blend group is separated, you will be left with the original control objects and the group of objects containing the intermediate steps created by the blend. To ungroup the group containing the intermediate objects, click the Ungroup button on the Property Bar.

Using the Interactive Contour Tool

The Interactive Contour tool adds concentric duplicates of the selected object that are either smaller and inside the original object or larger and outside the original object. The fill and outline colors assigned to the duplicate objects blend into the fill and outline colors of the original object. You can interactively control the number of duplicate objects created and the distance between the objects, or you can enter the settings in the Contour Steps and Contour Offset num boxes on the Property Bar. Three types of contours are available from the Property Bar. They are To center, Inside, and Outside. An example of these three contour types is shown here:

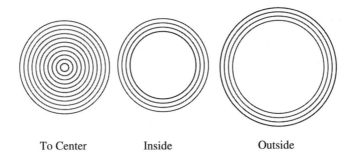

To Center   Inside   Outside

NOTE   *Contours can be applied only to single objects and Artistic Text. Single objects can be objects that have been combined or something as simple as a single line.*

Figure 19-2 shows the Property Bar with the Interactive Contour tool selected. Described here are the options on the Property Bar when the Interactive Contour tool is selected:

■ *To Center*   This setting ignores the Steps value and adds as many concentric duplicate objects as possible inside the original object based on the Offset value entered. For example, if you contoured a 2-inch-diameter circle using the To Center option using a 0.1-inch offset, there would be 9 additional concentric circles placed inside the original circle. Remember that the distance between each object is being reduced both horizontally and vertically, so you end up with 10 circles instead of 19.
The contour on the left of the earlier example is a 2-inch-diameter circle that has been contoured using To Center with a 0.1-inch offset.

■ *Inside*   Inside is the default setting. It also adds concentric duplicate objects inside the original object, but instead of adding as many duplicates as possible, it lets you control the offset and the number of steps. The total number of steps is limited by the size of the original object and the size of the offset distance you use. If you try to enter too many steps for the offset, the steps value will change to the maximum steps allowed for the size of the offset. The contour in

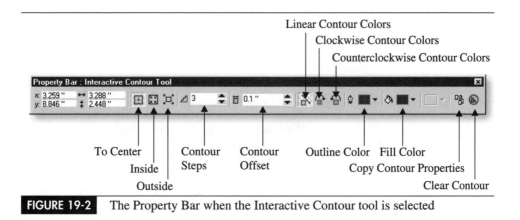

FIGURE 19-2   The Property Bar when the Interactive Contour tool is selected

19

the middle of the earlier example is a 2-inch-diameter circle contoured using Inside with a 0.1-inch offset using three steps.

■ *Outside* This setting adds concentric duplicate objects outside the original object, but unlike the first two options, you are not limited by the number of steps or the offset distance. The outside contour expands the duplicate objects as opposed to contracting them as the Inside option does. Keep in mind that the numbers you enter in the Steps and Offset num boxes greatly affect the look of the contour. The example at the right of the earlier example shows a 2-inch circle contoured to the outside using an offset of 0.1 inch and three steps.

■ *Contour Steps* The number of steps you enter here determines the number of steps in a Inside and Outside contour (see exception to Inside contours described previously).

■ *Contour Offset* This number determines the distance between each contour step.

■ *Linear Ccontour Colors* Choosing this button blends the fill color of the original object to the fill color of the last object in the contour group. This color is determined by the contour fill color selected from the drop-down palette when you click on the down arrow of the Fill Color button of the Property Bar.

■ *Clockwise Contour Colors* This button blends the first and last color of the contour through the color spectrum wheel in a clockwise direction.

■ *Counterclockwise Contour Colors* This button blends the first and last color of the contour through the color spectrum wheel in a counterclockwise direction.

■ *Outline Color* Click on the down arrow of this button to choose an outline color for the last object in the contour group.

■ *Fill Color* Click on the down arrow of this button to choose the fill color for the last object in the contour group.

■ *Copy Contour Properties* Use this button to copy the properties of another contour effect. For example, if you already have a contour on the page, you can draw a new shape, and then with the shape still selected, select the Copy Contour Properties button. When the cursor changes to a

"Contemplation" was the Best of Show winner of Corel's 1999 World Design Contest. It was created by **Adauto Machado dos Santos** of Brazil using only CorelDRAW. The majority of the design was creating using the Blend effect which produced the smooth transitions. In other areas, the Freehand, Bézier and Natural Pen (now known as the Natural Media tool) tools were used to draw curves of the blends to make the transitions more natural. This was especially helpful in creating the wrinkles in the skin. Smoke was creating by combining curves, converting it to a bitmap, applying a Gaussian Blur and using the Interactive Transparency tool to make it transparent. The artist can be reached by e-mail at adauto@sergipe.com.br.

"Arequipa" was a monthly winner of Corel's 1999 World Design Contest in the Landscapes and Landmarks category. It was created by **Paola Angelotti** of Italy using mostly CorelDRAW 7 with a little help from Corel PHOTO-PAINT 7. It is a poster depicting the church of the Society of Jesus built in 1698 in Arequipa, Peru. It mixes the colonial baroque style of the face with a typical European composition and South-American shapes. The image was originally scanned and manipulated in Corel PHOTO-PAINT before importing into CorelDRAW for vectorization. Tools used include the Freehand tool, Shape tool, Rectangle tool and the Ellipse tool. The image isn't exactly symmetrical, but it was drawn and mirrored. So that it isn't perfectly symmetrical, the lines were again edited with the Shape tool. The image was finished in CorelDRAW 8. The artist can be reached by e-mail at ilgatto@tin.it.

"St. Tropez Harbor" was the Grand Prize World winner of Corel's 1999 World Design Contest in the Landscapes and Landmarks category. It was created by **Hans Jaochim Kardinal** *of Germany using only CorelDRAW 8. It is based on an original watercolor painting of the St. Tropez harbor in France. The basic elements like houses, windows, boats and people were created using mostly the Freehand tool, Shape tool, Fill tool, Interactive Fill tool and Interactive Blend tool. Colorization of the objects was adjusted on screen using the Interactive Fill tool. The file consists of approximately 5700 objects on 16 layers. The artist can be reached by e-mail at hjk@mailcity.com.*

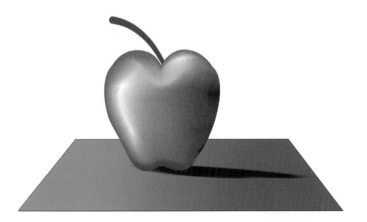

Each of these images was created mainly with the new Mesh Fill tool in CorelDRAW 9. **Wayne Kaplan** *of California created the apple,* **Debbie Cook** *of Florida created the match, and* **Peter McCormick** *of Arizona created the seascape. You can learn more about the Mesh Fill tool in Chapter 9.*

This image was submitted by **Linda Rapson** of South Africa as an entry in a brochure contest held by Rick Altman for the 1999 CorelWORLD Conference in Orlando, Florida. One of the highlights in the image is the use of the Blend effect to create the link between the logo and the state of Florida.

The 1999 CorelWORLD User Conference
October 3–8, Orlando FL

DRAW, PAINT & PUBLISH
Annual Conference

Peter McCormick created this image to show off the Interactive Extrude tool in CorelDRAW 9.

Ruth Huking of Arizona drew "Backyard" as an image of her own backyard using CorelDRAW and Corel PHOTO-PAINT. Each of the elements was first created in CorelDRAW and then converted into a bitmap and placed as a floating object in Corel PHOTO-PAINT. The only part of the image that isn't in her yard is the snake!

In this image, **Ruth Huking** *drew "Hilda with the Birds" based on a fountain on her patio. It was drawn in CorelDRAW and then exported into Corel PHOTO-PAINT to add the texture and shadows. The rest of the picture was done in CorelDRAW and then Hilda was imported back into the picture. Ruth can be contacted by e-mail at rhuking@juno.com.*

Ruth Huking drew "Algorta" from a photograph she had taken of the town of Algorta on the North coast of Spain. The entire image was drawn in CorelDRAW with the people being modified clipart. After the image was drawn, it was imported into Corel PHOTO-PAINT to add some texture.

"Spanish Arch" is another picture from Spain which was drawn in CorelDRAW and then imported into Corel PHOTO-PAINT to add the foliage and texture. When it was all finished, Ruth used the Impressionist filter to give it the feel of a painting.

"Indian Basket Weaver" is another image by **Ruth Huking**. The Indian woman and child along with the background were drawn completely in Corel PHOTO-PAINT. The baskets in the picture were made in CorelDRAW using a custom fill for the baskets. They were then exported to bitmap for use in Corel PHOTO-PAINT. A tutorial explaining how to create the baskets can be found at http://www.unleash.com/ruth.

"Returning Home" features two figures modeled after pictures taken of 12-inch high papier maché figurines. They were scanned so that they could be used within the image. The cat was also scanned from a picture of Ruth's cat and the cow came from Corel's clipart collection. All of the other elements in this image were created from scratch in CorelDRAW. A filter was used on the mountains to give them the hazy look.

"Madera Canyon" was a monthly winner in the Landmarks and Landscapes category of Corel's 1997 World Design Contest. The image was drawn by **Ruth Huking** *in CorelDRAW and the leaves, flowers and shadows were added in Corel PHOTO-PAINT.*

"Springdale Farms Market" is another of **Ruth Huking's** *images. It recreates a market in New Jersey that belonged to her daughter-in-law's family. It was "torched" back in the mid 1980's. Ruth took a photo of it and created this image for her son and his wife for Christmas in 1995. The image was drawn in CorelDRAW with the flowers and leaves added in Corel PHOTO-PAINT.*

"The Stamp" was a monthly winner of Corel's 1999 World Design Contest in the People, Plants and Animals category. It was created by **Ljubomir B. Penov** of Bulgaria. The idea for "The Stamp" came when the artist was unexpectedly impressed by the picture of an old airplane. The difficulty was in creating a realistic image. This was accomplished with the Interactive Transparency tool, Fill tool, Interactive Drop Shadow tool, Bitmap Color Mask, Intersect, Weld, Trim and many more of CorelDRAW 8's features. The artist's aim was not to literally copy the originals, but rather to enhance them and to create something new. For the face, he used an image from one of Corel's CD-ROMs as inspiration. Again, a Corel CD-ROM was used to create the sky. The work is created in ten different layers such as background, face, jacket, hat, glasses and shawl that were later combined on export. One of the toughest parts was the pilot's cap and glasses. For this, the artist visited several museums and took pictures with his digital camera. From those pictures, he was able to recreate the image in CorelDRAW. The artist can be contacted by e-mail at ljupen@hotmail.com.

"Sunset on the Pond" was a monthly winner of Corel's 1999 World Design Contest in the People, Plants and Animals category. It was created by **Giuseppe Mariotti** of Italy. This image was created using CorelDRAW and Corel PHOTO-PAINT. Features used in CorelDRAW include fountain fills, Blend and Interactive Transparency. Once exported to a bitmap, several filters were applied in Corel PHOTO-PAINT. The list of filters used include CSI PseudoColor, CSI Photo Filter, CSI Grad Tone, KPT3 Texture Explorer, Emboss and Lens Flare. The artist can be contacted by e-mail at diandzie@internit.it.

KINDERGARDEN

PLAYGROUND

GYMNASTIC HALL

CLASSES

EMERGENCY EXIT

GREENHOUSE

KITCHEN

"Kindergarten" was a monthly winner of Corel's 1999 World Design Contest in the Corporate ID category. It was created by **Tomasz Wawrzyczek** *of Poland. Each of the images was drawn in CorelDRAW using a Wacom ArtPad. The artist can be contacted by e-mail at tomis@pik.gliwice.pl.*

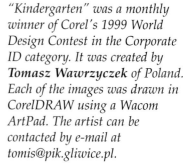

"The Unit" was a monthly winner of Corel's 1999 World Design Contest in the Corporate ID category. It was created by **Tamas Hajas** *of Hungary. The majority of this image was created in Corel PHOTO-PAINT 7. But there were portions created in CorelDRAW and exported to Corel PHOTO-PAINT. The artist can be contacted by e-mail at softcontact@tiszanet.hu.*

*"MTH Challenger" was a monthly winner of Corel's 1999 World Design Contest in the Technical Drawings category. It was created by **Stephen Schaffner** of Maryland. This image was created entirely in CorelDRAW. The tough part was converting pieces into an isometric view for which script was used. Once objects were in the isometric view, they were Extruded to give them depth. The artist can be contacted by e-mail at lazaruswolf@hotmail.com.*

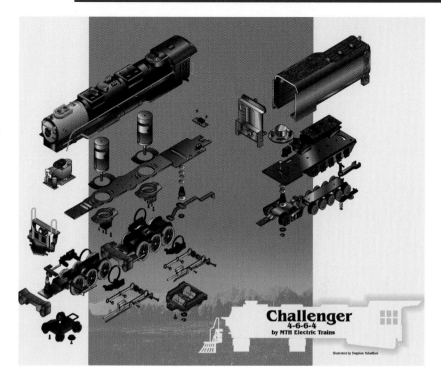

EZ · METRICS

*The EZ Metrics logo was designed by **Gary Priester** of California for Unleashed Productions with EZ Metrics software. It was created entirely in CorelDRAW 8. To get the 3D look, he used an early beta of the EZ Metrics software which made creating isometric faces and extrudes very easy.*

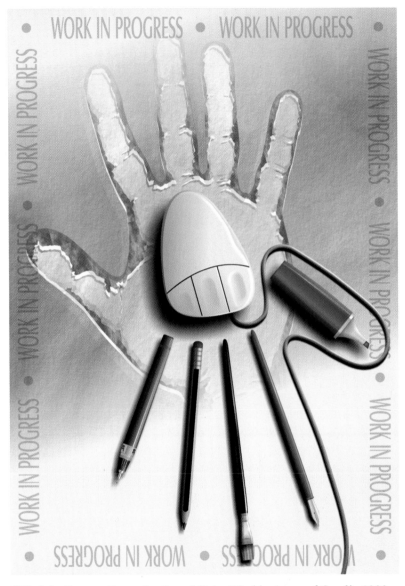

"Work In Progress" was the Grand Prize World winner of Corel's 1999 World Design Contest in the Page Layout category. It was created by **Franchini Flavio** of Italy. This image was created in CorelDRAW 8 with the exception of the mouse cable which was done in Corel DREAM 3D 8. The hand was recreated from a scan with the Zipper Distortion added to it. Various layers were added with transparency to give the hand texture. All of the other shapes were simple polygons modified with Weld, Intersect and Trim. The artist can be contacted by e-mail at premier@numerica.it.

*"Mountain Bike" was the Grand Prize World winner of Corel's 1999 World Design Contest in the Technical Drawings category. It was created by **Dennis Koutylov** of Russia. The image of the bike was created in CorelDRAW 7 and then exported for use in Corel PHOTO-PAINT 7. The artist can be contacted by e-mail at koutylov@hotmail.com.*

"Unleashed Theater" was created by **Peter McCormick** of Arizona to promote Unleashed Productions Seminars and Boot Camps. The original design was created completely in CorelDRAW 8 with the lights all being created using Blends on a path. Each of the people was designed using MetaCreations Poser. All of the elements were then combined in Corel PHOTO-PAINT 8 to get the finished image.

large black arrow, click on the existing contour. The properties of the existing contour will be applied to the new shape with the exception of the colors. If you filled your new shape with a color, that color will blend with the last color in the contour object you copied from. If your new object had no fill, none of the objects in the new contour would have fills.

■ *Clear Contour*   Choose this button to remove all contour objects that were added by the contour effect. This will leave you with the original object.

Interactively Changing the Steps and Offset Amounts

When you create a contour on an object with the Interactive Contour tool, you will notice a dotted line with an arrow at the end. At the end of the line that has the arrow attached is a rectangle. The color of the rectangle depends on the color you choose from Outline color drop down palette on the Property Bar. At the other end of the line is a diamond-shaped polygon. Its color is determined by the color you choose from the Fill Color drop down palette on the Property Bar (see "Using the Color Settings," later in the chapter). Attached to the dotted line itself is a slider control. Depending on which way you drag when you begin the contour determines the direction of the contour, and the arrow will point in that direction. Seeing the direction of the arrow tells you if the contour is an Inside or Outside contour. If it's a To Center contour, the arrow will point in the same direction of an Inside contour.

The slider control on the dotted line lets you set the number of offsets. The closer you move the slider to the diamond shape, the more offsets you create.

Being able to interactively change the number of steps and offsets may have its benefits, but in the real world of creating contours, most users are better served by entering the exact numbers for the number of steps and the amount of offset for the contours they create. In the following exercises, we instruct you to use the direct parameter-entering method.

Creating a Button

For your first Contour effect, you will create a button that could be used for a Web site:

1. Draw a circle that is about 2 inches in diameter.

2. Select the Interactive Contour tool from the Interactive tool flyout shown here (we have circled it for you).

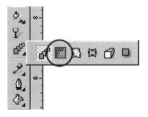

3. Click and drag inside the circle toward the center of the circle. An Inside contour will be created.

4. Click the Outside button on the Property Bar to create an Outside contour. We have you do this as practice in case you forget which way you should drag, so you can always change the setting on the Property Bar.

5. Enter **1** in the Steps num box on the Property Bar.

6. Enter the value **0.25** in the Offset num box.

7. Press the Enter key for the changes to take effect.

8. Select <u>A</u>rrange | <u>S</u>eparate. The original object and the outer circle will remain.

9. Fill each of the objects with gradient fills to simulate a three-dimensional look. Try using a conical fill on the outer ring and a linear fill on the face of the button itself.

10. Remove the outlines, or color them with a complementary color.

11. Add artwork or text to the front of the button to complete the effect.

Your button should look similar to the one shown here.

Using the Color Settings

The color controls on the Property Bar let you choose the fill and outline colors for the last object created by the Contour effect. These colors will then blend with the fill and outline colors of the original object.

To see how the colors blend together, follow these steps:

1. Draw a circle on the page approximately 2 inches in diameter, and give it a red fill. Leave the default black outline on the circle.

2. Select the Interactive Contour tool, click just inside the circle, and drag outward away from the circle. This will create a contour to the outside.

3. Enter **0.1** in the Offset parameter box.

4. Enter **7** in the Steps parameter box.

5. Click the Fill button (the paint bucket) on the Property Bar, and select one of the blues in the drop-down palette.

6. Click the Linear contour colors button on the Property Bar. It's the one depicting a straight diagonal line with a small square at the bottom left.

7. Press the Enter key to see the results.

Notice that the last outside object created by the Contour effect is filled with the color blue you selected in step 6. This object then blends with the original red object, thereby creating the colors seen in the middle six offset steps.

If you select the Clockwise Direction button on the Property Bar, the blended colors will be colors made up of magentas and purples, because these are the colors between blue and red in the color wheel when you travel in a clockwise direction.

If you select the Counterclockwise Direction button, the blended colors will be made up of yellows and green, because these are the colors between blue and red in the color wheel when you travel in a counterclockwise direction. We have not shown an example of using color because all the examples in the book are printed in grayscale, making color distinction meaningless.

Contouring Text

One important use of the Contour effect is to create a font that is either a bolder or lighter weight than what is available from your font list. You can contour a word to the inside to create a lighter weight font or to the outside to create a bolder weight font. When you are through contouring, simply separate the contour group and delete the original text, and you'll be left with your new font. Technically, this is not really a font but a curve object.

The examples shown here use the Britannic Bold font. The *A* on the left shows a lighter weight version of the font created by contouring to the inside. The *A* on the right is a bolder weight version created by contouring to the outside.

   NOTE   *When you click and drag toward the center of a small object like text, you may get a warning message that says "Contour offset too large." When this happens, change the settings in the Offset num box until the size of the offset is acceptable, and then press the ENTER key.*

Contouring Irregular Shapes

Figure 19-3 shows an irregular shape contoured to the inside. Notice the colors blend from the darker original color of the outside object to the lighter color in the center of the last shape created by the inside Contour effect. The concentric shapes created by the Contour effect could be used to illustrate contour lines depicting an elevation change in an architectural drawing. However, with the introductions of fillable outlines in CorelDRAW 9 (see Chapter 10), a more representative drawing showing elevation change could be done by varying the width of shapes with different filled outline widths.

Creating a Neon Effect with Contour

A neon effect similar to the ones created with the blend effect can be created with the Contour effect. Figure 19-4 shows the word *NEON* using the font Arial Rounded at

FIGURE 19-3   A before and an after example of contouring a irregular shape to the inside

150 points. To create the effect shown underneath the original font in Figure 19-4, follow these steps:

1. Type **NEON** on the page using Arial Rounded (or your favorite font) at 150 points.

2. Fill the text with the color red.

3. With the text selected, choose the Interactive Contour tool from the interactive tool flyout, and click and drag on the text. A default contour using the To Center mode will be created.

4. Click the Inside button on the Property Bar.

5. Enter **12** in the Contour Steps num box.

6. Enter **0.01** in the Contour Offset num box.

7. Click the linear contour colors button on the Property Bar.

8. Choose the color red from the Outline color drop-down palette.

9. Choose the color white from the Fill color drop-down palette.

10. Press the ENTER key to apply the changes. Your neon text should look that in Figure 19-4.

19

NEON
NEON

FIGURE 19-4 Creating a neon effect using contour

Creating Interactive Drop Shadows

A drop shadow is a transparent bitmap object that casts a shadow from the original object. You control the transparency of the shadow, allowing any underlying image to show through the shadow. The ability to create transparent drop shadows interactively has been greatly expanded upon in CorelDRAW 9. It is now possible to create drop shadows with perspective.

Before you learn how the new features work, let's start with a plain flat drop shadow. Follow these steps to learn how to create this great effect:

1. Click on the Text tool, and type **Drop Shadows** on the page. We used the font Futura Md Bt at 72 points.

2. Click on the Interactive Drop Shadow tool on the interactive tool flyout shown here (we have circled it for you).

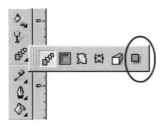

3. Click and drag on the text object to create the shadow. Figure 19-5 shows the actual process. The direction you draw the black rectangle determines where the shadow falls. The farther you drag the black rectangle away from the object, the greater the offset. If you move the slider on the dotted line closer to the black rectangle, the shadows' opacity is decreased, and it becomes darker. If you move the slider closer to the white rectangle, the opacity is increased, and the shadow becomes lighter.

Congratulate yourself, you just created your first drop shadow.

FIGURE 19-5   A basic flat drop shadow

Drop Shadow Options

Now that you've seen how easy it is to create drop shadows, let's review the various options on the Property Bar shown here.

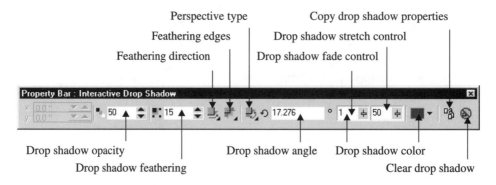

- *Drop shadow opacity* Enter a number from 0 to 100 in the num box to control the amount of transparency you want for your drop shadow.

- *Drop shadow feathering* Enter a number from 0 to 100 in the num box to control the amount of feathering. Entering zero produces a solid shadow with no feathering. Entering numbers between 40 and 100 produces shadows with no discernible edges.

- *Feathering direction* Clicking this button displays a drop-down menu shown here. This menu offers four feathering options, Inside, Middle, Outside, and Average. Depending somewhat on the shape of the object, you will see a different feather pattern.

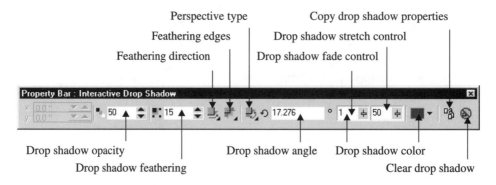

- *Feathering edges* Clicking this option displays the drop-down menu shown here. This menu lets you choose an edge style. The styles are Linear, Squared, Inverse Squared, and Flat.

Feathering Edges:

☐ Linear

☐ Squared

☐ Inverse Squared

☐ Flat

■ *Perspective Type*   Choosing this option displays the Perspective Type drop-down menu. This menu lets you choose a flat drop shadow or one of the four perspective types of drop shadows. They are Bottom, Top, Left, and Right. An example of each of the five types and the drop down menu are shown in Figure 19-6.

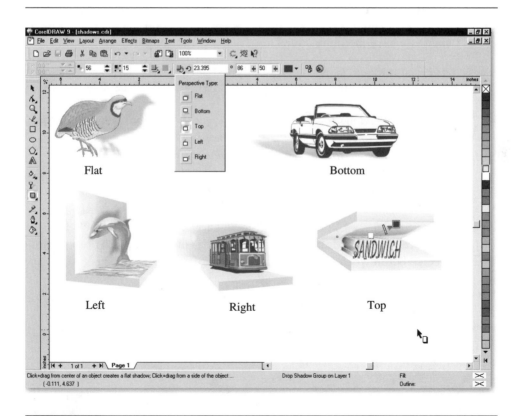

FIGURE 19-6   The five types of drop shadows

- *Drop Shadow Angle*   This number reflects the angle of the drop shadow you create interactively. If you want to change the angle, manually enter a new number in the num box.

- *Fade Control*   This option is available only for perspective type drop shadows. It allows you to fade the end of the drop shadow into the background. To use the slider control, click on the slider icon on the Property Bar to reveal the slider control shown here just under the Fade Control num box. Drag the slider left or right to control the amount of fade.

- *Stretch Control*   This option is also available only for perspective type drop shadows. It allows you to stretch the shadow to lengthen or shorten it. You can also do this interactively by dragging in or out on the black square when you have the Interactive Drop Shadow tool selected.

- *Drop Shadow Color*   Click on this button to reveal a color palette. Choose any of the colors from this palette to change the color of the drop shadow.

TIP   *Drop shadows are 32- bit CMYK images. If you want only a grayscale drop shadow, you can reduce the size of the file by using the Arrange | Separate command to separate the drop shadow from the shadow's object and then converting the default CMYK drop shadow to grayscale using Bitmap | Mode | Grayscale 8-bit.*

- *Copy Properties*   Choose this button when you want to copy the properties from one drop shadow to another. You must have a drop shadow selected before you can copy the properties of another drop shadow.

- *Clear Drop Shadow*   Click this button to remove the drop shadow from the original object or group of objects.

Your ability to vary the basic drop shadow types is almost limitless using the options just described.

Creating Drop Shadows with Perspective

Your ability to create drop shadows with perspective opens up thousands of possibilities. Some of the ways you might use the effect is with bitmap images of people and objects or groups of objects. Here are two examples using perspective drop shadows. If you would like to practice placing a perspective drop shadow on the doll image shown here, it is located on the CD that comes with the book. The path to the file is given in step 2.

1. Open a new file in CorelDRAW 9.

2. Choose File | Import, and use the following path to select the file: /Chap19/doll.CPT. The file will appear as a group of two objects.

3. With the imported image selected, choose Ungroup from the Property Bar.

4. Click anywhere on the desktop area to deselect the objects, then click on the doll again to select it.

5. With the doll selected, drag it to the right of the page

6. Marquee select or click in the area where the doll was to select the white background that was part of the imported group. It will be invisible because it is the same color as the background.

7. Delete this object.

8. Select the Interactive Drop Shadow tool from the interactive tool flyout.

9. Click at the bottom left of the doll, and drag up and to the left. This action will automatically create a Bottom type perspective drop shadow. Drag the black square control handle up, down, or sideways to tweak the shadow until you are comfortable with the way it looks. If you clicked in the wrong place when you began the drop shadow, go to step 9.

10. Click on the Drop Shadow Perspective type button, and choose Bottom from the drop-down menu. This choice will place the drop shadow in the proper position. Go back to step 8 to tweak the shadow.

The image of the art gallery uses the same techniques on the doll except the shadow was made to go to the front of the objects by dragging the black control handle down and to the side.

Practice using this tool to discover the many different types of drop shadows you can create. Try changing the color of the shadow, or experiment by dragging the Offset handle and the Opacity slider with the interactive tool to see the change in the shadow. Then try the various controls on the Property Bar. In the image shown here, a drop shadow is applied to the neon looking image we created earlier in the chapter using the Contour effect. This is a good example of applying a drop shadow to a group of objects. If this image were in color, you could use a colored drop shadow to create the glow around the neon tubes. Here are the settings used for this particular effect: Opacity was set to 80, Drop shadow feathering set to 30, Feathering edges set to Linear, feathering direction set to Middle, Drop shadow type to Flat.

NOTE   *You must be aware that when applying drop shadows to named groups like contour groups or blend groups you must first separate the named group with the Arrange | Separate command and then regroup all the objects making up the previously named group. This action creates an ordinary group that you can then apply a drop shadow to.*

This chapter has taught you how to create blends using the Interactive Blend tool so you can create dozens of special effects. Experienced CorelDRAW users continually find new ways to use this fascinating feature. You have also learned how to use the Contour effect to make concentric objects from a source object to create everything from the look of neon to lighter or bolder weight fonts. And finally, you have learned how to interactively place transparent drop shadows with perspective beneath various objects. Experimenting with all of these effects can produce very interesting results.

19

CHAPTER 20

Lens, Transparency, and PowerClip

COREL.COM

CorelDRAW 9

The effects in this chapter produce radically different effects, yet they also have many similarities. One of the biggest problems you'll find with any of these effects is that they can cause serious printing problems. You may need to convert the resulting effect into a bitmap for it to print properly. The whys and wherefores of these problems will be detailed as each effect is described.

Lens

You should think of the Lens effect by considering the effect it has not on the object it is applied to, but rather on the objects behind it. Objects that have a lens applied are important only for their shape and their positioning. When you apply a lens, the fill that was in the object will no longer be present, but the outline will remain. Each object can have only one lens, but you can duplicate the object on top of itself and apply another type of lens to the duplicate. A lens can be applied only to a closed path.

CAUTION   *Although you can place a lens over anything, beware of how lenses are placed. We heard from a user who scanned a map and then placed 118 lenses over the top of the map to indicate various types of businesses. When it came time to print, the print file created was well over 1 gigabyte. This was because each lens required that the whole bitmap be printed again—and if any of the lenses had been stacked on top of each other, the problem would have been even worse. In these situations, select all of the objects, and convert them to a bitmap within CorelDRAW, which compresses all of the lenses into a single bitmap again. This will print much more easily and smaller.*

To bring up the Lens Docker, choose Effects | Lens, or use the ALT-F3 shortcut key. The following illustration shows it in an undocked state with the Brighten lens selected.

At the top of the Docker is a crude depiction of what the Lens will create. The preview objects will always be a rectangle and a square rather than the real objects in your drawing. Once you learn how each of the lenses works, you'll probably not use the preview very often.

Three other options—the Frozen, Viewpoint, and Remove Face check boxes—are available to all lenses. Each of these options will be demonstrated later in this chapter.

Several types of lenses can be selected from the Lens Docker: Brighten, Color Add, Color Limit, Custom Color Map, Fish Eye, Heat Map, Invert, Magnify, Tinted Grayscale, Transparency, and Wireframe.

Brighten

Have you ever played with the Brighten knob on your monitor or television? Of course you have, because you wanted to adjust the picture so that it was just right. The Brighten lens works in a similar matter except the changes apply only to objects below the Lens object in the stacking order.

When you select Brighten from the drop-down list in the Docker, you'll also see that the parameter box is now labeled "Rate." Whatever percentage you type, from 0 to 100, will increase the brightness of the objects behind the lens object. If you set the percentage to 100 percent, everything will become white, so this value is not really desirable. Clearly, the higher the number, the brighter the lens.

You can also type a negative percentage, and the lens will behave as a Darken lens. Using a value of –100 percent will make the lens black. Figure 20-1 shows the effects of using both the Brighten and Darken lenses.

FIGURE 20-1   The Brighten and Darken lens used on an image to create a simple ad

Color Add

The Color Add lens is probably the most difficult to understand. It is based on the additive light model, where the more color you have, the closer you get to white. The best way to understand what is happening is to create the effect manually:

1. Create two objects, coloring one red and one green.

2. Create another object off to the side and leave it unfilled for now.

3. Draw another object that covers the red and green objects.

4. Apply a Color Add lens with a rate of 50 percent red to the last object you created. The object that was originally red should be unchanged. Because the background is white, adding light will not change its color at all, but you'll see that the formerly green object is now a yellowish green.

5. Fill the object that was created off to the side with an RGB fill of 128 red, 255 green, and 0 blue. The fill simulates a green object that has been covered by a 50 percent red Color Add lens. Notice that the color is the same as in the lens you created earlier.

6. Change the lens so that its rate is 100 percent. The green object should now be completely yellow, and if you left a black outline on the object, you'll notice that it has changed to red. Black is no light, and you have added red light to it; thus, the result is red.

7. To see this effect in the object off to the side, change the RGB fill to 255 red, 255 green, and 0 blue. That is the exact formula for creating yellow, and so this object should look the same as the "green" object under the lens.

An example file containing the examples described in these steps can be found on the CD as coloradd.cdr.

Color Limit

If you've ever done photographic work, you are familiar with the various color filters you can use. The Color Limit lens is similar to a camera filter. It allows only the color you select and black to show through the lens.

When you select Color Limit from the drop-down list in the Docker, you'll be presented with two other choices. You can select the rate and the color that will be limited. The rate can be anything from 0 to 100 percent. The higher the rate, the less color that is allowed through the lens. If the rate is 100, only black and the color selected will remain.

Suppose you have several objects on the page that are solid red and solid green:

1. Draw another object that surrounds all of the existing objects.

2. Apply a Color Limit lens of 50 percent strength and the color red. You'll see that the red objects are unchanged, but the green objects are now closer to a forest green. If any areas of the white page are showing, they are pink. You might say that this effect is like looking at the world through rose-colored glasses.

3. Change the rate to 80 percent, and click Apply. Now the green objects are a very dark green that is nearly black. The page will be almost red, and the red objects themselves are still unchanged.

 TIP   *If you don't want the lens to affect the blank parts of the page, check the Remove Face check box described later in this chapter.*

An example file for this project can be found on the CD as Colrlimt.cdr.

Custom Color Map

The Custom Color Map lens is similar to the Tinted Grayscale lens described later, except that you choose the colors and their order. Everything within the lens will become a shade of the two colors you select. For truly colorful effects, you can even use the rainbow options.

When you select Custom Color Map from the drop-down list in the Docker, you are presented with three choices. The colors can be mapped in a direct palette, forward rainbow, and reverse rainbow. You can also choose two colors for the beginning and end of the lens. A Direct Palette maps directly from one color to the other. Each of the rainbow options defines the direction of the rainbow as it moves around the color wheel.

Two separate color pickers are provided. They work like all the other color pickers in CorelDRAW. Between them is a small button. Click it, and the colors reverse their order. There is nothing more frustrating than picking the colors and finding that they are at the wrong ends of the fill. This little button solves the problem in a heartbeat.

In areas behind the fill where nothing appears, the To color will be used. The possibilities with this fill are really awesome. An example file using this effect can be found on the CD as colormap.cdr.

Fisheye

You've seen a fisheye lens in action before. Through a fisheye lens, the whole world seems to exist in a spheroid. This same effect can be applied to objects in CorelDRAW. Note that the Fisheye lens works only on vector objects and has no effect on bitmaps. Similar effects are possible in Corel PHOTO-PAINT if you need to work with bitmaps.

The best way to envision this lens is to imagine that you are going to place the objects behind the lens on a ball. If you use a positive value for the rate, the objects will appear to be on the front curved surface of the ball. Negative values will make the objects look as if they are on the back side of the ball. The smaller the number, the smaller the area of the ball you will be working with; if you use a large value for the rate, the objects can wrap all the way around the ball. Rates can be anything from –1,000 to 1,000, with a value of zero having no effect at all.

To see the Fisheye lens in action, try the following:

1. Draw some graph paper with five cells in either direction.

2. Ungroup the rectangles, and fill every other one with black.

3. Regroup the rectangles.

4. Draw a circle that is about one and a half times larger than the rectangles and perfectly centered around them.

5. Apply a Fisheye lens with various rates to see exactly how they affect the objects.

Figure 20-2 shows two examples of this experiment. This file can be found on the CD as fisheye.cdr.

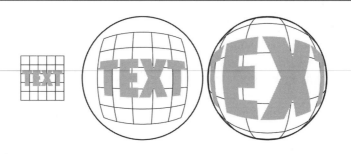

FIGURE 20-2   The original on the left and two examples of the Fisheye lens on the right

Heat Map

Heat Map is just another name for "infrared." Using this lens allows you to measure the level of "heat" in an image. A very limited palette of white, yellow, orange, red, blue, violet, and cyan are used to indicate the various levels of heat. The "hot" colors in an image are mapped to red and orange, and the "cool" colors are mapped to violet and cyan.

When you select Heat Map from the drop-down list in the Docker, you'll also get the chance to choose a value for the palette rotation. With the rotation set to 0 percent, the effect is exactly as just described, but if you change it to 50 percent, the cool colors are represented as hot and vice versa.

Using the Heat Map lens is a great way to get a very abstract image from a photograph. Most of the time, you can't even recognize the original image. A file showing several examples of Heat Map lenses is on the CD as heatmap.cdr.

Invert

Look through those old photos you hid in a shoebox, but instead of looking at the prints, look at the negatives. Some of them are quite bizarre, yet graphically appealing. We don't expect you to want a negative of Uncle Harry in your projects, but some of the textures can be fascinating.

20

This effect is quite easy to create within CorelDRAW using the Invert lens. When applied, it will display the objects behind it in their complementary CMYK colors—basically it is very similar to a photographic negative.

To create an inversion lens, choose Invert from the drop-down list, and click the Apply button. Unlike the other lenses, the Invert lens has no other parameters to set.

One interesting side effect that you should be aware of is that when the lens object is over the drawing page, it will invert the background as well. This usually means that you get black since the page is most often white.

The Remove Face Option

You just saw that the Invert lens can create a problem when placed over a blank page since it also inverts the page. Corel added an extra feature to solve this problem. If you check the Remove Face check box, the lens will be applied only to areas with "stuff" behind them. This means that the Invert lens won't try to invert a naked page. Figure 20-3 shows an example of the Invert lens used with and without the Remove Face option checked. The difference is quite noticeable. You'll also find a copy of this file on the CD as invert.cdr.

Remove Face option not checked   Remove Face option checked

FIGURE 20-3   The Invert lens used on a photograph with and without the Remove Face option checked

Magnify

With the Magnify lens, only one parameter is available, which is the amount of magnification. Any value from .1 to 100 can be used. Using .1 will actually shrink the objects behind the lens rather than magnify them as the name of the lens suggests. Setting the magnification all the way to 100 will enlarge the object by 100 times, to a gigantic size. Most of the time, you'll use a much smaller number, probably between 2 and 10.

One of the most interesting uses for this lens is in working with maps. Suppose you have a map of an entire area or city, and you want to magnify the area directly surrounding a particular landmark. If you just place an ellipse or rectangle above the area you wish to magnify, it will also cover up part of the map, which can cause problems, as shown in Figure 20-4. Luckily, the Frozen and Viewpoint options can help correct this problem.

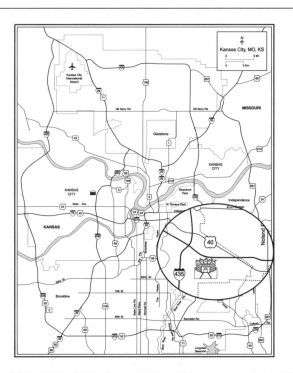

FIGURE 20-4   An area on the map magnified using a lens, which covers an important area of the map

20

The Frozen Option

The problem with the map shown in Figure 20-4 is that you can't see the area near the magnified area because it is covered by the lens. You might think that the obvious solution is to just move the lens out of the way. Go ahead and try it. Notice that the lens changes as it is moved. Remember that a lens does nothing more than affect the objects behind it. When you move the lens, the objects behind it change.

If you check Frozen in the Docker and then click Apply, the lens will become a snapshot of what is behind it. Then you can move it anywhere you like, and it will not change. So this is one way to solve the problem with the map: simply freeze the lens, and move it someplace where it isn't covering anything important. But there is another solution.

The Viewpoint Option

Another way to solve the problem is to use the Viewpoint option. Normally, a lens affects what is directly behind it, so the viewpoint is directly behind it as well. If you check the Viewpoint check box in the Lens Docker, however, you can move the viewpoint. As soon as you check this box, an Edit button will appear. Click the Edit button, and an X will appear at the center of the lens object. Drag the X anywhere in your drawing. Wherever it is placed will become the reference point for the lens. To finish the effect, click the End button in the Docker. Then click Apply, and the lens will be complete.

 NOTE   *If you use Viewpoint, what you see in the Lens object isn't affected by what is behind the Lens. It is instead affected by what is "behind" the X of the viewpoint.*

So with both the Frozen and Viewpoint options available, which one should you use? This really depends on the drawing. If you expect the objects that the lens affects to change, you'll probably want to use the Viewpoint option because it will be updated automatically. Using Frozen gives you a static view that will change only if you update the lens.

 CAUTION   *It must be stressed once again that a lens affects what is behind it, so if you create new objects that are above the lens object in the stacking order, they will not be affected by the lens. This applies to the Viewpoint option as well. If you draw a new object and the lens doesn't change, make sure to move the new object down in the stacking order until it is below the lens object. A great way to do so is by using the Object Manager because it gives you a visual representation of the stacking order.*

Now that you've seen how the Frozen and Viewpoint options can help you, take a look at Figure 20-5 to see the same map using the Viewpoint option to move the highlighted area off to the side. Note that we've added a light-gray transparency over the area that is magnified so that the viewer can easily see what the magnified portion is taken from.

Tinted Grayscale

How many times have you wanted to convert something from color to grayscale? This is exactly what the Tinted Grayscale lens will do. Place an object around some clipart or a photograph, and apply a Tinted Grayscale lens. Instantly, the original image will be converted. Normally, when you visualize this scenario, you think about black and white, but the "grayscale" can be any color you like.

Select Tinted Grayscale from the drop-down list in the Docker. Choose the color you desire for the darkest shade, and click Apply. Everything in the original image will be a shade of the color you chose.

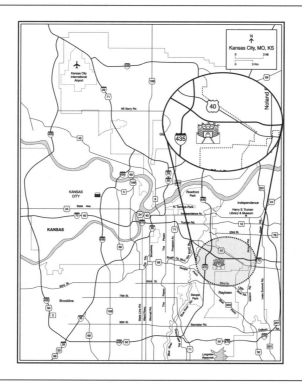

FIGURE 20-5   The Magnify lens used in conjunction with the Viewpoint option

20

One of the best ways to use this lens is with a photograph, but remember that you don't have to apply the lens to the whole photograph. Create smaller objects that will highlight a certain part of a black-and-white photograph in color, or use the Combine command to cut the shape out of a larger rectangle to leave only a small portion of the photograph in color and convert the rest to grayscale.

An example of a Tinted Grayscale lens is supplied on the CD as tinted.cdr.

Transparency

With the Transparency lens, you can select the rate of transparency and the color or shade of the object. If the selected object has already been filled, the color will be the same as that fill. If the rate is set to 0%, nothing will happen since the object will have no transparency. If the object is set to 100%, the resulting effect will be the same as giving the object no fill at all. With any percentage between the two extremes, the object will become uniformly transparent. If the number is low, you will be able to see the objects behind the transparency object only faintly.

In earlier versions, this Docker selection was the only way to add transparency to an object. Now it can be done in another way, through the use of the Interactive Transparency tool described later in this chapter. You'll find that the Interactive Transparency tool provides many more options, and you'll prefer it in almost all situations.

Wireframe

Since the beginning of CorelDRAW, there has always been a Wireframe view, but to get the wireframe look on a particular area of the drawing was difficult. Using the Wireframe lens, it is easy to get the look with the colors of your choice for the outline and fill. All objects behind the lens will take on the fill and outline colors that you specify.

Select Wireframe from the drop-down list in the Docker. Again two color selectors will appear. Next to each color selector is a check box. If you want to change only one of the colors and leave the other untouched, simply uncheck the appropriate check box. Note that objects behind the lens that have no fill will now be filled with the color you choose. Figure 20-6 shows an example of a Wireframe lens.

 NOTE *Applying a Wireframe lens over a bitmap will treat the bitmap as a rectangle.*

FIGURE 20-6 The Wireframe lens in action

Interactive Transparency Tool

The Interactive Transparency tool is found in the toolbox. To use it, you must apply the transparency to an existing object or group of objects.

We'll walk you through several small projects so that you can see how the tool works. Suffice it to say that once you understand what is happening, it is much easier to use the tool properly.

The Interactive Transparency tool creates a grayscale bitmap that acts as a transparency mask on an object. If you have used Corel PHOTO-PAINT extensively, this concept will make perfect sense. The rest of you should read on.

In a grayscale bitmap, you can have up to 256 shades of gray, ranging from solid white to solid black. Where the bitmap is solid black, the object will have full transparency. The white areas provide no transparency. The gray levels in between provide transparency relative to their shade of gray.

When you use the Interactive Transparency tool, you are doing nothing more than creating this grayscale bitmap using the same fill types and methods that are used with the Interactive Fill tool that was described in Chapter 9. Now that you understand the basics of how this tool works, let's try a few examples. For a quick look at how transparency works, we'll create a red ball.

1. Draw a simple green circle. It looks very flat, but with some shading it can look three-dimensional.

2. Make a copy of the circle using CTRL-C.

3. Paste the copy on top of the original using CTRL-V.

20

4. Change the color of the copy to black.

5. Select the Interactive Transparency tool, and choose Fountain from the Property Bar.

6. Click the Radial Fill icon.

7. Move the center of the fill towards the upper-left part of the circle.

8. Adjust the size of the transparency circle until the ball looks real to you.

What we did was take the green circle and add black shading through the use of the Interactive Transparency tool. To make the ball look more realistic, we'll make it look like a bright light is shining on the ball.

1. Select the top ball with the transparency, and copy it to the clipboard with CTRL-C.

2. Paste in another copy with CTRL-V.

3. Change the fill color of this new transparent object to white.

4. Select the Interactive Transparency tool so that you can edit the transparency.

5. Drag the color White from the color palette, and drop it on the black square of the transparent object.

6. Drag Black onto the original white square of the transparent object.

7. Adjust the outside edge of the transparency until you think it looks good.

Now you've seen a quick example of how to use transparency to create shadows and highlighting so that the green ball looks more realistic. You could have done this by creating a custom fountain fill, but it probably would have taken a little longer. One benefit to this method is that it works with any type of fill and not just a solid color. So you've got one more step to finalize this little project.

1. Select the original green circle. A quick way to do so is by using the Digger tool. Click on the topmost object, and then ALT-click until the green object is selected. Watch the Status Bar until it shows that the selected object has a green fill.

2. Use the Interactive Fill tool to fill the circle with the maple.tif bitmap fill found on the book's CD.

Now you should see a beautiful wooden ball. Figure 20-7 shows the progression of these steps from the original green circle through our wooden ball. You'll find the example file on the CD as balls.cdr.

This first example showed you how transparency could be used to add highlights and shadows to objects. There certainly was nothing fancy about how it worked. You just need to observe how light affects objects and recreate that effect with transparent objects.

Now we're going to merge two photographs. This technique is useful for combining two pictures that each contain an element that you would like to use. Getting this effect has traditionally been something that you would do in an image editing package like Corel PHOTO-PAINT. Now you have a choice.

1. Import the files bootcamp.tif and kapalua.tif from the CD supplied with the book.

2. Select the picture of our CorelDRAW Boot Camp class, right-click, and choose <u>O</u>rder | To <u>F</u>ront from the pop-up menu. (For those interested in Boot Camps, details can be found at http://www.unleash.com/training/bootcamp.html.)

3. Place the two pictures so that they sit on top of each other and the bottom quarter of the golf course sticks out below the picture of the Boot Campers. We want to get the Boot Camp picture so that the desert dirt is replaced by nice green grass. Remember that you can use the single key shortcut "L" to align the left side of the images.

4. Select the Interactive Transparency tool, click just below the feet, and drag down just a little bit.

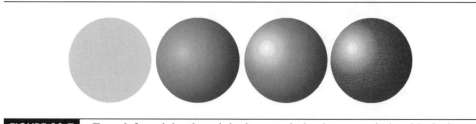

FIGURE 20-7   From left to right, the original green circle, the green circle with shadow applied, the green circle with shadow and highlight, and the wooden ball

You should now see the two images seem to merge together. You may need to adjust the transparency somewhat until the picture looks just right. The finished image looks similar to the one shown in Figure 20-8.

NOTE *Remember that you must have the Interactive Transparency tool selected to see the tools on the Property Bar.*

Our last project will introduce you to some of the other settings on the Property Bar. Let's first discuss some of these settings.

The Property Bar shown on the next page is the initial Property Bar shown when the Fountain Transparency type is selected. Clicking the Edit Transparency button will bring up the familiar Fountain Fill dialog box that was discussed in Chapter 9. Remember that when you create a transparency, you are creating a

FIGURE 20-8 On the top are pictures of the Boot Campers and golf course before they are merged to create the finished image on the bottom.

grayscale transparency mask. With the Fountain Transparency, you are using the Fountain Fill to create a gradient from black to white.

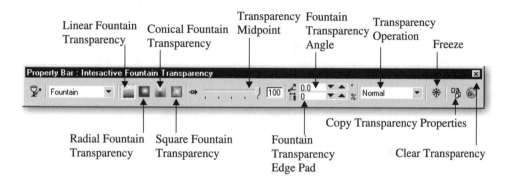

Linear Fountain Transparency   Conical Fountain Transparency   Transparency Midpoint   Fountain Transparency Angle   Transparency Operation   Freeze

Radial Fountain Transparency   Square Fountain Transparency   Fountain Transparency Edge Pad   Copy Transparency Properties   Clear Transparency

In the case of Fountain Transparency, the Property Bar contains a series of four buttons: for linear, radial, conical, and square fills. These can be changed right on the Property Bar or within the Fountain Fill dialog box.

To the right of the four buttons is a slider control that controls the transparency level at the selected point. It is initially set to 100 percent.

CAUTION *When you are editing the fill, you can choose any colors you want. The darker the color, the more transparency, regardless of what appears on the slider. Unfortunately, the sliders and dialog boxes do not change to reflect each other in this regard. All of the colors will be converted to grayscale for the final transparency.*

The next series of settings control the angle of the fill and the edge padding. These settings are set to change with the Fountain Fill dialog box. You can also make the changes manually. Click the object that has the transparent fill, and you'll see two rectangles with a dotted line between them. The angle on the Property Bar is the angle of this line. Note that there is no angle for radial transparencies. Click and drag either of the rectangles to change the angle. The farther the rectangles are inside the edge of the object, the larger the value for the edge pad. If the rectangles are outside the object, there will be no edge pad, and this option will be reset to zero on the Property Bar. If you manually type in a value, the start/end indicators will move back inside of the object.

Another drop-down list just to the right of the textboxes for the angle and edge pad provides all of the different Transparency Operations that are available. These are the same modes that are available in Corel PHOTO-PAINT. The best way to understand these operations is to simply experiment. While they always work in the same manner, the results are dependent on the objects beneath the object you have selected, so describing them is like trying to hit a moving target. The modes include Normal, Add, Subtract, Difference, Multiply, Divide, If Lighter, If Darker, Texturize, Hue, Saturation, Lightness, Invert, And, Or, Xor, Red, Green, and Blue. We'll show you an example of using a Transparency Operation in our next project.

If you've finished creating and want to convert your objects into something permanent, click the Freeze icon. This will freeze the transparent object exactly as shown when the Freeze button is selected, and any objects that were showing through will show in the result as well. However, if you move the object, you'll notice that things look strange, since the transparency will not change. Thus, this option is certainly something you should do after everything else is finished. If you need to get back to editing the transparency, you can try using the Undo (CTRL-Z) command. If you click on the Freeze button a second time, it will toggle back to an unfrozen state and you can continue to edit the object.

 NOTE   *The resolution of the bitmaps created by the transparency tool are dependent on the new rendering resolution setting. Select Tools | Options | Document | General to change the resolution.*

The last two options on the Property Bar allow you to Copy the transparency to another object or to Clear Transparency. These buttons are self-explanatory. You may also notice that the Status Bar reports that the objects with transparency have a lens applied; after all, consider that Transparency is just a special form of a lens.

So far, the only transparency we've discussed is adding a Fountain Fill transparency. You can also add several other kinds of transparencies. The Uniform transparency gives the same level to the whole object; this is very similar to what the Transparency lens traditionally offered. You can also use Pattern and Texture transparencies.

Pattern transparencies allow you to choose any of the two-color bitmaps, full-color vectors, or color bitmaps for your transparencies. You can then create some really awesome effects. The Texture transparencies allow you to use any of the many texture fills that were described in Chapter 9.

Our next project will be a picture of graffiti painted on a stucco wall.

1. Draw a rectangle that is approximately 4 inches by 2 inches.

2. Using the Full Color Bitmap Pattern fill, fill the rectangle with the Stucco.tif fill found on this book's CD.

3. Enter **www.unleash.com** as Artistic Text. Select the font Staccato 555 BT at 48 points, and move the text so that it is approximately centered in the "stucco wall."

4. Rotate the text 10 to 15 degrees so that it is angled up and to the right. And give it a fill of green.

5. Convert the text to a bitmap. Choose <u>B</u>itmap | <u>C</u>onvert to Bitmap, and choose 24-bit RGB, Transparent Background with a resolution of 200 dpi.

6. Now blur the text by choosing <u>B</u>itmap | <u>B</u>lur | <u>G</u>aussian Blur. We used a radius of 5 for the blur, but feel free to adjust it until you are happy with it.

 NOTE *You need to have Auto inflate bitmaps for bitmap effects enabled in <u>T</u>ools | <u>O</u>ptions | Document | General for this effect to work properly.*

Already the text is starting to look as if it were spray painted onto the wall. But we want to take the texture of the stucco into consideration. So let's apply some transparency to the text.

1. With the Interactive Transparency Tool selected, choose a Uniform Transparency, and adjust the Starting Transparency slider to 0.

2. Now select Multiply from the Transparency Operation drop-down box, and you'll see the stucco pattern emerge from the text; it is starting to look realistic.

3. Change the Transparency Operation to Difference. The text will change to purple, and there will be very little paint in the area inside the text. There's quite a difference just from changing this one option.

Figure 20-9 shows the last two versions of our stucco wall. You'll also find this image on the CD as Thewall.cdr so that you can see the colors.

FIGURE 20-9   The top stucco wall has the Transparency Operation of Multiply on the text while the bottom version uses Difference.

PowerClip

A PowerClip sounds like a heavy-duty hedge trimmer or the latest style in hair styling, but the name is just a fancy marketing term for the ability to paste an object inside of another object. Anything you create in CorelDRAW can be pasted inside any other object or group of objects.

When using a PowerClip, you need to become familiar with two basic terms: artwork that will be pasted inside of another object is called the *contents*, and the object in which the contents are placed is called the *container*. The container does not have to be a closed path, but the contents will not be displayed until the container path is closed. The container can be a group, but in that case, separate copies of the contents will be pasted inside each object within the container group.

A PowerClip can create a complex clipping path, and complex clipping paths can generate problems when printing. Therefore, attempt to keep the path of the container object fairly simple. If problems arise, you may have to convert the whole object to a bitmap, or use the instructions described at the end of this lesson to export and reimport the PowerClip objects.

Creating a PowerClip

Before you begin creating a PowerClip, you need to set an option. Choose Tools | Options | Workspace | Miscellaneous, and find the Auto-center New PowerClip contents check box. Make sure that a check is *not* in this box. Checking this box can cause a tremendous amount of confusion.

 NOTE *The main reason that the Auto-center new PowerClip Contents option is checked by default is so that a PowerClip will always result in a visible object within the container object. However, when you create a PowerClip, you will usually place the container in the exact position that you need. Therefore, this option does not need to be checked for these situations.*

Now you need your content object and your container object. Place the container in relation to the contents, knowing that any part of the contents outside of the container will be clipped—it will still exist, but it won't be visible. Once you have everything placed correctly, choose Effects | PowerClip | Place Inside Container. This tells CorelDRAW that you want to put anything that is selected inside a container, but the program has no idea what to use for a container. Therefore, you'll see a large arrow on the screen. Use the arrow to point to and click the container object.

Let's work through a simple example so you'll understand a little better how PowerClip works:

1. Open the file Powrclip.cdr from CD in the book.

2. We want to use a series of triangles to fill the letter B.

3. Select all the triangles, and choose Effects | PowerClip | Place Inside Container.

You'll now see that the parts of the triangles that extended beyond the letter B are no longer visible.

Here is an illustration of the letter B and the triangles before and after PowerClipping. Note that the outline on the leftmost B is exaggerated so that you can see the letter.

 TIP   *If you right-click and drag the "triangles" and drop them onto the letter, you will receive a pop-up menu when you release the mouse button. That menu contains the option PowerClip Inside. Select that option, and you get an interactive method for PowerClipping.*

If you had tried to draw this same object freehand, you would have had to worry about trimming each triangle to line up perfectly with the edge of the letter. You can certainly do that, but it's not nearly as easy as using PowerClip.

Now that you have an idea of what PowerClip does, imagine the many ways it can be used. One of the more popular uses is for cropping bitmaps. We've been asked thousands of times how to get rid of those stupid white squares around bitmaps. It can be done with the Bitmap Color Mask quite easily if the background is a single solid color that isn't used elsewhere, but it can be quite difficult with a busy background. Using PowerClip, however, it is as simple as drawing an outline around the part of the photograph that you wish to cut out. Drawing that shape can be time consuming, but it is not a difficult process.

Editing PowerClips

You've just finished PowerClipping something, and it didn't turn out the way you expected. Maybe something was left out, or maybe the positioning was out of whack. No need to undo the PowerClip and start over—you can edit the existing PowerClip.

Select the PowerClip object, and choose the Effects | PowerClip | Edit Contents command. The contents will now appear in their entirety, and the container will be displayed as a gray outline. At this point, you can make any changes that you desire. Move things around, recolor them, draw new objects, or do whatever you need to do to make things just right. When you've made all the necessary changes, choose Effects | PowerClip | Finish Editing This Level, which will put the PowerClip back together for you with all of the changes.

The other option you have is to just take the PowerClip completely apart. Simply choose Effects | PowerClip | Extract Contents, and the PowerClip will be broken into the contents and the container object.

Working with Complex PowerClips

If you find that a PowerClip you've created is causing you problems, you can simplify it by exporting and reimporting the pieces:

1. Select the PowerClip objects.

2. Choose File | Export.

3. Select Encapsulated PostScript (EPS) from the Files of Type drop-down list.

4. Check the Selected only check box, and click the Export button.

5. In the EPS Export dialog box, just click OK.

6. Choose File | Import.

7. Find the file you just created, and highlight it.

8. Select the PostScript Interpreted (PS, PRN, EPS) file type, and click Import. You'll get an Import PostScript dialog box. Just click OK, and the file will be imported.

 NOTE   *To get information on the File Export dialog box, see Chapter 24.*

Now you should have the original PowerClipped objects back in your drawing. However, the container object no longer hides objects; it actually trimmed them. Now there is no longer a clipping path, and the file should be much easier to print.

Lens, Transparency, and PowerClips are some of the most "flashy" features in CorelDRAW. They also can present the most difficulties in printing. All of these features should be used carefully, not only because of their complexity but also from a design standpoint. The best way to output these complex effects is to convert them to bitmaps. And if you're creating the images for the Internet, you're going to convert them into bitmaps anyway.

CHAPTER 21

Fitting Text to a Path

COREL.COM

CorelDRAW 9

The Fit Text to Path effect is probably one of the least understood features in CorelDRAW. Like most of CorelDRAW's features, understanding it boils down to understanding what takes place when you apply the effect to a path. When you understand how it works, using it becomes easy. If you want to unravel the mystery of the Fit Text to Path feature, take the time to read this chapter from beginning to end. Previous users of CorelDRAW will notice that the Fit Text to Path roll-up is gone. Everything is now done interactively.

Dynamically Linked Paths

Fitting text to a path dynamically links the text to the path so that the text flows along the path. "Dynamically linked" means that the text is affixed to the path, and the relationship between the text and the path will remain the same even if you modify the text or the path.

For example, if you use the Fit Text to Path feature to place a word or a string of words on a path, you can change the words or you can change the path, and the words and the path still stay together. CorelDRAW recognizes two types of paths: closed paths and open paths. We will explore the various ways you can use this unique effect in your projects.

Fitting Text to a Path Interactively

Placing text on paths interactively requires using the Text tool in combination with the Property Bar. This technique considerably speeds up the process of placing text on a path from earlier versions of CorelDRAW. Figure 21-1 shows the Property Bar when text on an open path is selected.

Placing Text on an Open Path Interactively

Practice placing text on an open path by following the steps here:

1. Draw a curved line on the page using the Freehand tool.

2. With the line still selected, click the Text tool in the toolbox.

3. Place the text cursor directly on the first node at the beginning of the line. When the text cursor changes to an I-beam cursor with the letter A attached,

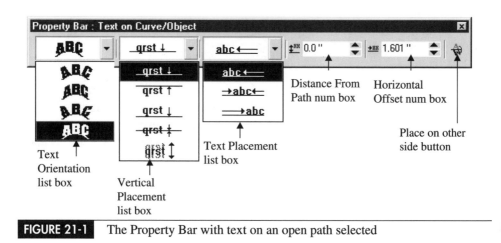

FIGURE 21-1   The Property Bar with text on an open path selected

click to place a text insertion bar on the line. It is important that you place the insertion point on the first node of the line so that you can justify it correctly in step 7.

4. Type **This seems easy**. The text will automatically be placed on the path.

5. Select the Pick tool, and then click the desktop area to deselect the text.

6. Using the Pick tool, click on the text again. This action selects the text and the path.

7. Click the down arrow of the Text Placement list box, and select the Center Justification option from the drop-down list (the center option in the list). Your text on a path should look similar to the text on a path shown here.

8. With the text on the path selected, click four times on the up arrow of the Distance From Path num box until you reach 0.2 inch. Your text should move upward away from the line by 0.2 inch as shown here.

21

Now repeat the previous steps but instead of placing the insertion bar at the beginning of the line, place it anywhere on the line you want. Proceed to type as before. Notice that you are now allowed to begin the text at any point along the line that you choose. You have just learned a new feature in CorelDRAW 9, which is that you can start typing anywhere on the path you desire. One caveat about not starting text input at the beginning of a line: you can't take advantage of the settings in the Text Placement list box. The reason for this is that the text placement, more commonly called *justification*, is relative to where you start typing. If you started typing at the right side of the line and then choose right justification, the text would "pile up" on itself at the end of the line. If you chose Left justification, the text would fall somewhere between the far left of the line and the center.

Having said that, if you do have justification problems when typing randomly on the line, you can manually justify the text by changing the settings in the Horizontal Offset num box. Practice this by following these steps:

1. Draw a straight line on the page; make it exactly five inches from start to end.

2. With the line still selected, click the Text tool in the toolbox.

3. Place the text cursor directly on the line somewhere to the right of center. When the text cursor changes to the I-beam cursor, click to place a text insertion bar on the line.

4. Type **COREL**. As before, the text will automatically be placed on the path.

5. Select the Pick tool, and then click the desktop area to deselect the text.

6. Using the Pick tool, click on the text again. This action selects the text and the path.

7. Click the down arrow of the Horizontal Offset num box until the numbers reach 2.5. The left edge of the letter *C* in the word *COREL* will now be centered on the path and should look similar to the text on a path shown here.

COREL

COREL

The alignment of the word on the line was actually based on the node on the letter *C*. Therefore, instead of center-justifying the text as you might have expected, you justified it based on the first letter of the word. Realistically you would continue clicking the down arrow to move the text still farther left so that it was completely center justified.

NOTE   *Had you drawn a curved line in the exercise just completed, the word COREL would have been center justified closer to the letter E than the letter C, depending on how curved the line was.*

These two exercises have taught you an important lesson. That is, if you are concerned about perfect justification, you should always begin typing by placing the insertion bar on the first node of the path and then choosing the justification from the Text Placement list box on the Property Bar.

Manually Editing Text on an Open Path

There are several things you can do to text on a path. You can change the words. You can change the font and the font size. You can change the way the text "stands" on the line. You can change the spacing between letters or words. You can move letters or words anywhere on the path. You can place the text on the line or beneath it. And finally, you can move the path itself.

- To make any changes to the text, select the text while holding down the CTRL key. This action isolates the text from the path.

- To change the font or the font size, select the text using the method previously described. Then choose a new font or font size from their respective list boxes on the Property Bar.

- To change the way the text "stands" on the line, select the text without holding down the CTRL key, and choose one of the options from the Text Orientation list box.

21

- To change words, select the Text tool from the toolbox, and place the insertion bar in the text string. With the insertion bar in the text string, you can then deleted or add words (you can also press CTRL-SHIFT-T to bring up the Edit Text dialog box and make your changes there).

- To change the spacing between letters and words in a text string, select the Shape tool from the toolbox, and select the text. Still using the Shape tool, click on the horizontal spacing arrow, and drag to the right. This action will increase the percentage of spacing between each letter and the space between each word in the text string. Dragging to the left will decrease the percentage of spacing.

- To change the spacing between words in a text string without changing the spacing between letters, hold down the SHIFT key while dragging the horizontal spacing arrow to the right or left. This action will change the percentage of spacing between the words only in the text string.

- To change the direction of the path, select the Shape tool, and then select the path. The nodes of the path will appear on the line. Click and drag on any of the nodes to change the direction of the path.

Applying What You've Learned

The best way to learn how the various Fit Text to Path options work is to practice. Using the following illustrations as a guide, follow these steps to apply text a curved open path:

1. Select the pencil tool, and draw a wavy line completely across the page

2. Select the Text tool, and place the insertion bar on the line at the top of the first hump.

3. Type **Counting sheep helps one sleep**. Depending on the font you used, the text should look like the example shown here.

4. Select the Shape tool from the toolbox, and use it to select the text.

5. Click on the horizontal Spacing arrow on the right, and then hold down the SHIFT key while dragging to the right about one-half inch. This will put additional spacing between the words.

6. Click again on the Spacing arrow, and drag another one-half inch to the right without holding down any keys. This will put a little extra space between each letter and each word. If there is a letter or two that is crawling on top of an adjacent letter, use the Shape tool, and click on the offending letter's node. Drag the node until the letter looks correctly spaced.

7. Click four times on the up arrow on the Distance From Path num box to move the text away from the path by 0.2 of an inch. Your text on a path should now look similar to the example shown here.

Now let's put the text on the other side of the line. If you're thinking here is where you use the Place on Other Side button on the Property Bar, you're wrong. That button is most often used for placing text on closed paths.

8. With the text above the path by 0.2 of an inch, select the Pick tool, and then select the text.

9. Click on the down arrow of the Vertical placement list box (refer to Figure 21-1), and choose the second option showing the text under the line. This will place the text under the line. The top portion of the text will be touching the line. We want to have it offset from the line like it was when it was above the line. To do this, continue with the next step.

10. Click the down arrow of the Distance From Path num box a total of 12 times. This will place the text 0.2 below the line. When you first click the down arrow in the num box, the text will jump to the top of the line. As you continue clicking the down arrow, the text will start moving down until it reaches 0.2 below the line position after the twelfth click. Why it functions this way is a mystery to us as it functioned the same way in version 8. Ours is not to question why but simply to know that this is how it works. Your text on a path should now look like the example shown next.

21

In the course of moving the text to below the line, it may have shifted to the right. We want to center justify it anyhow, so do the following to center-justify the text.

11. Select the Shape tool, and click on the text to select it. Marquee select the entire text string. Notice that the nodes on each letter are highlighted.

12. With the nodes selected, use the Shape tool, and click on any one of the selected nodes and drag to the left. Notice the entire text string is moving to the left as you drag. Stop dragging when you feel you have the text center justified. The example shown here shows the nodes highlighted and the text being moved.

FITTING TEXT TO AN OPEN PATH USING THE TEXT MENU   No chapter on fitting text to a path would be complete without placing a text string on a spiral. This time you won't use the full interactive method, but instead you will choose the Fit Text to Path command from the menu. Follow the steps here to place a string of text on a spiral:

1. Draw a three-revolution spiral on the page (if you don't know how to draw a spiral, see Chapter 3).

2. Type **Going down the drain** on the page using a bold font.

3. Select the text and the spiral.

4. Click on the <u>T</u>ext menu, and choose Fit <u>T</u>ext To Path. The text will be justified at the beginning of the spiral in the center.

5. Use the default options in both the Orientation and Vertical Placement list boxes.

6. Select the right justification setting in the Text Placement list box. The text will now be justified at the open end of the spiral.

7. Select the Shape tool, and use it to drag the right spacing handle to the right while holding down the SHIFT keys until the text is approximately in the configuration shown here:

MOVING THE PATH   You have learned how to place text on a open path; now let's see how simple it is to move the path, and while we're at it, let's change the text. Using the last example of placing the text on a spiral, do the following:

1. Select the Pick tool from the toolbox, and CTRL-click on the text.

2. Place the insertion bar in front of the word *down*.

3. Press the Delete key four times to delete the word *down*.

4. With the insertion bar still in the text string, type the word *up*.

5. Select the Pick tool again, and click somewhere on the desktop to deselect the text.

6. Select the Shape tool from the toolbox.

7. Click on the end node at the right of the spiral.

8. Drag out and down to the right. Use the node handles if necessary to adjust the line. Your spiral should now look like the one shown next.

21

 NOTE   *We didn't discuss the settings offered in the Horizontal Offset num box when talking about placing text on a open path. This num box lets you enter a positive or negative value that will move the line in either a left or right direction. This method of moving the text along the line replaces the interactive method of manually dragging the spacer arrow or text nodes. It could be useful for moving a text string or individual words a specific distance.*

You should now be familiar enough with the technique of placing text on an open path that no project will be too difficult.

Placing Text on a Closed Path

Now that you learned the rules for placing text on an open path, let's explore how you use the various options on the Property Bar to place text on a closed path. Figure 21-2 shows the Property Bar in its configuration when text on a closed path is selected. Each of the options is described next.

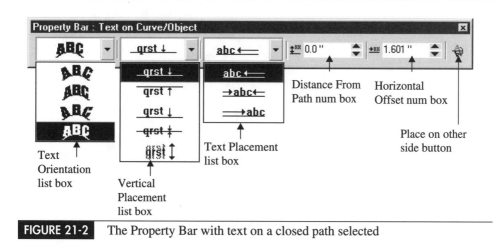

FIGURE 21-2   The Property Bar with text on a closed path selected

Using the Settings in the Text Orientation List Box

The first set of options on the Property Bar is the Text Orientation list box. The orientation you choose from the list determines how the text "stands" on the line. If the line is straight, as on a rectangle, little visible change takes place. The orientation options work best on curved lines. The following list describes how each orientation option affects the way the text stands on the line.

- If you choose the first option, the default, the text will follow the contour of the line whether it's curved or straight.

- If you choose the second option, the text will appear to be standing upright as it travels around a curved line.

- The third option horizontally skews the text so that it appears to be turning inward toward the screen when placed on a curved line.

- The final option vertically skews the text so as it travels around a curved line, the letters remain in a vertical position.

The following illustration shows the four different options applied to four different ellipses.

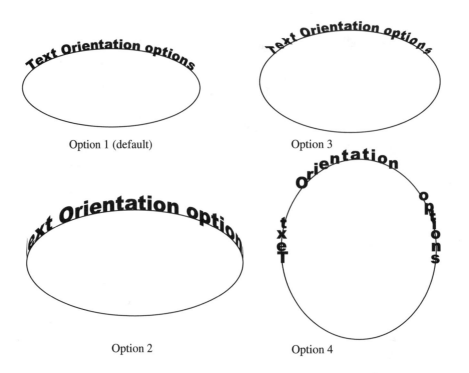

Option 1 (default)   Option 3

Option 2   Option 4

Using the Settings in the Vertical Placement List Box

The next set of options is found in the Vertical Placement list box. These are the same options offered when placing text on an open path. The choices you make here determine if the text is on top of the line, below the line, in the center of the line, or in a custom setting. The descriptions for each of the settings follow.

- The first option places the text on the line with the descenders below the line.

- The second option places the text below the line.

- The third option places the text on top of the line with the descenders resting on the line.

- The fourth option centers the text on the line.

- The fifth option allows you to manually adjust the position of the text to the line. This custom option will appear in the list box window if you move the text after choosing any of the other options. For example, if you began with the default option and then moved the text away from the line using the settings in the Offset num box, the Custom designation would then appear in the Vertical Placement window.

Using the Settings in the Text Placement Options List Box

The last set of options on the Property Bar in list format is the Text Placement options. These four options affect the placement of the text in the following manner:

- The first option places the text at the top of the closed path.

- The second option places the text on the right side of the closed path.

- The third option places the text at the bottom of the closed path.

- The fourth option places the text on the left of the closed path.

 NOTE   *In order for the text to be placed correctly in the locations just described, the alternate method of placing text on a path must be used. This method was used in the last exercise when placing text on a spiral. As a reminder, type the text on the page that you want placed on a path. Create the shape you will be placing the text on. Select the text and the path, and choose Text | Fit Text to Path. The text will automatically be placed on the top of the shape. Now when you choose a specific placement, such as on the right side of a shape, it will be placed there. Using the interactive method instead of the method just described will produce unpredictable results.*

Two of the last thee options on the Property Bar have been covered in the section covering fitting text to an open path. They are, in the order they are placed, the distance from Path num box and the Horizontal Offset num box. The last option on the Property Bar is the Place on Other side button. This button will be used in the next exercise when you learn how to place text on a closed path.

Applying What You Have Learned

Placing text on a closed path is not quite the same with the interactive method as when you use the alternate method of using the Fit Text to Path command in the Text menu. To begin with, as you learned earlier, CorelDRAW 9 now lets us place the insertion bar anywhere on the path. This feature was helpful when you were typing text on an open path because you could begin the word at specific location on the line. If you use this technique on a closed path and want to center justify the text after you have placed it on the path, enter 0.0 in the Horizontal offset box on the Property Bar. To understand the interactive technique, do the following:

1. Draw an ellipse on the page.

2. Select the Text tool, and place the insertion bar at approximately two o'clock on the ellipse.

3. Type **I'm going backwards**. Notice as you type, the text moves to the left on the ellipse as if it were backing up. This phenomenon prevents you from placing the text in an exact location on the path without taking the extra step of either manually moving it to the desired location or typing in the coordinates in the Horizontal offset box on the Property Bar. If you followed the steps correctly, your ellipse with the words *I'm going backwards* should look like this.

Now let's try an exercise that will allow you to place text on a closed path in exact locations. Follow the steps here to place two strings of text on an ellipse using the Fit Text to Path command in the Text menu along with choosing certain options on the Property Bar:

1. Select the ellipse tool from the toolbox, and draw an circle on the page.

2. Type **CYCLING CLUB** in caps on the page. Use the default size of 24 points.

3. Select the text and the ellipse.

4. Choose Text | Fit Text to Path. The text will be placed on top of the circle, and the Property Bar will now display the Fit Text to Path options.

5. Click the down arrow of the Vertical Placement list box, and choose the second option down, which shows the text beneath the line. Notice that the text immediately moves inside the ellipse, following the contour of the inside of the ellipse.

6. Click the down arrow of the Text Placement list box, and choose the third option down, which shows the text underneath an arc. Notice that the text immediately moves to the inside bottom of the ellipse and the text is backward.

7. Click the Place on Other Side button on the Property Bar. The text is moved from the inside of the ellipse to the outside bottom of the ellipse and is no longer backward. The text and ellipse should now look something like this.

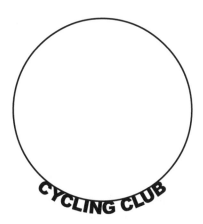

8. Now you are ready to place the next string of text on the top of the ellipse. Type **SUN CITY WEST** in caps on the page using the same point size.

9. Select the words you just typed, and SHIFT-click on the ellipse to select it along with the text.

10. Choose Text | Fit Text to Path again. The text will be placed on top of the circle.

Your text and ellipse should now look like the example shown here. We added a little extra touch by filling the ellipse with a radial fill and adding a symbols clipart of an old-fashioned bicycle.

Congratulate yourself on placing two strings of text on an ellipse using the Fit Text to Path command.

USING THE PLACE ON OTHER SIDE OPTION   We've already talked about the Place on Other Side button; now let's put it to use again. Use the following steps to place text on a path inside the shape:

1. Select the ellipse tool, and draw a circle on the page.

2. Type **Stuck in** on the page.

3. Select both the circle and the words, and choose <u>T</u>ext | Fit <u>T</u>ext to Path. The text will be placed on the top of the circle.

4. Click on the down arrow of the Vertical placement list box, and choose the second option showing the text beneath the line. The text will now be inside the circle at the top.

5. With the text on the path still selected, select the Text tool from the Toolbox, and place the cursor at the bottom of the ellipse. Then click to place the insertion bar on the path.

6. Type **The middle**. As you type, the letters will appear backwards and at the bottom of the circle.

7. After you've finished typing, select the Pick tool from the toolbox.

8. Click the text you just typed, and look at the status line. It will tell you that you have selected a Compound Object of 3 Elements on Layer 1. Notice no options are available for text on a path on the Property Bar.

9. Hold down the CTRL key, and click the text a second time. The status line will now read: Text on a Path on Layer 1. The text on a path options will be now available on the Property Bar.

10. Click on the Fit Text on Other Side button on the Property Bar. The text will now be placed inside the circle and be right reading.

11. Because you interactively placed the text at the bottom of the circle, the text most likely was not center justified. If this is the case, select the Shape tool from the Toolbox, and select the text. Click and drag a marquee selection completely around the words so that the nodes on the letters are selected. You will know if they are selected if the nodes become filled with black.

12. With all the nodes selected, click on any one of them, and drag left or right to justify the text. You may want to adjust the spacing as well at this time. To learn how this is done, refer to the earlier section "Manually Editing Text on an Open Path." The spacing technique is the same.

13. As a final touch, fill the circle with a radial fill. If you did everything correctly, your circle and text should look like the one shown here.

TIP   *Before we finish the sections on fitting text to a path, it should be pointed out that at times you won't want the shape used as the path or its outline to be visible, whether or not the shape is filled. Instead of using the Arrange | Separate command to separate the text from the path so you can delete the shape, simply remove the fill from the shape and outline. The shape and outline will become invisible. This is the preferred method, and it allows you to keep the effect "live" if you ever need to edit again.*

Placing Text Within a Closed Path

One of the more interesting uses of the new interactive method is typing text directly inside a closed path. This method differs from placing text inside a closed path where the text is dynamically linked to the outside or inside of the path. Typing text directly inside a closed path actually forces the paragraph text within a shape you select. Practice placing text within a closed path by following these steps:

1. Draw an ellipse on the page.

2. Select the Text tool from the toolbox.

3. Place the crosshairs of the text cursor just inside the outline at the top of the ellipse (the text cursor will change to an I-beam with the letters *AB* in a box next to it). Your ellipse should now look like this:

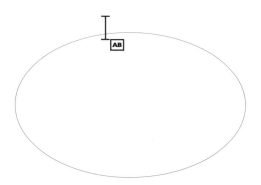

4. With the I-beam still displayed, click once with the left mouse button. A text insertion point will be placed at the top middle portion of the ellipse, and a dotted line will flow around the inside of the ellipse, as shown next.

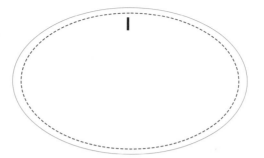

5. Begin typing inside the ellipse, and your text will automatically flow from one side of the ellipse to the other. Fill the entire ellipse with text.

6. When you're finished typing, click the Pick tool to complete the task. You will now see your text inside the ellipse, as shown here. You can fill the ellipse with any of CorelDRAW's fills as a background to the text.

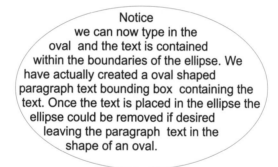

7. You may make the ellipse invisible so that only the text is visible in the shape of the ellipse. To do this, hold down the CTRL key, and select the Ellipse. Now left-click on the X at the top of the color palette to remove the outline color Your text should look similar to the text shown here.

Notice
we can now type in the
oval and the text is contained
within the boundaries of the ellipse. We
have actually created a oval shaped
paragraph text bounding box containing the
text. Once the text is placed in the ellipse the
ellipse could be removed if desired
leaving the paragraph text in the
shape of an oval.

21

8. Now select the text again, and the status line will indicate that you have selected only Paragraph Text (see Figure 21-3). Notice the window shade handles attached to the top and bottom of the ellipse. By clicking and dragging on these handles, you can resize the shape of the Paragraph Text.

CAUTION   *If you try to place more text inside a shape than it will physically handle, it will get cut off. To solve this problem, you either change the point size of the text so that all the text fits or make the shape larger. If this is not an option because of the design of the page, try flowing the text into a new shape (see the next section).*

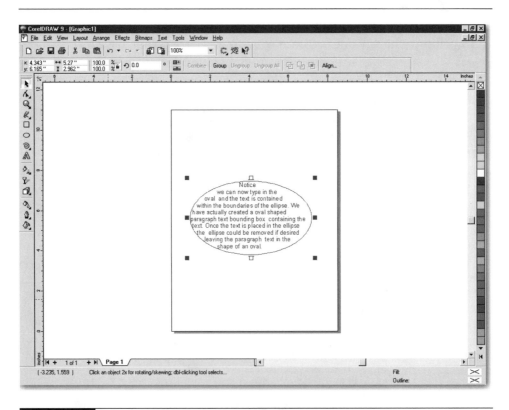

FIGURE 21-3   Paragraph Text selected after being shaped to a path

FLOWING TEXT FROM ONE SHAPE TO ANOTHER   You can flow Paragraph Text to another shape if you run out of room in the first shape and don't want to enlarge it because of design issues. If there is more text than will fit in the shape you are using to contain the paragraph text, a black arrow will appear in the window shade handle at the bottom of the shape. This tells you that you either enlarge the shape to allow room for all the text to fit or flow it into another shape. If you want to practice this technique, you can use the same file we used. It is located on the CD that comes with the book. The path to the file is /Chapt21/flowtext.cdr. To practice flowing the text into another shape, do the following:

1. Open the file on the CD. If will contain the ellipse with the text you need.

2. Draw a new shape on the page.

3. Select the first shape with the text, and click on the window shade handle at the bottom of the ellipse with the Pick tool. The cursor will change into a small page icon with an arrow sticking out of the lower-right corner.

4. Place this cursor inside the new shape. The cursor will now change to a large black arrow.

5. Click with the arrow inside the shape. The remainder of the text from the first shape will flow into the second shape, and a blue dotted line will indicate the connection.

6. Select the new shape, and drag it to a new location on the page. Notice the connection line travels to the second shape and the connection remains.

   If you used the sample file we provided on the CD, your page should now look like the illustration shown here.

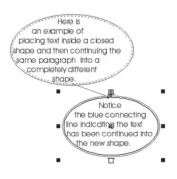

Using What You've Learned in a Real-World Example

A real-world example of interactively typing text inside a shape is shown in the following illustrations. A symbols clipart image of a plaque was used as the shape. This type of shape posed a small problem in that the text flowed straight across the plaque correctly but lower than expected. The bounding box controlling the placement of the text prevented the text from being placed higher. To solve this design problem, we added a small symbol at the top.

This chapter has taught you several different ways to place text on a path using both the Fit Text to Path command in the Text menu and the interactive method. You may be wondering which method is best to use. We suggest the interactive method for open paths and the command method together with the controls on the Property Bar for closed paths.

CHAPTER 22

Color Adjustments and Bitmap Effects

COREL.COM

CorelDRAW 9

This chapter covers the color adjustment features for vector and bitmap objects in CorelDRAW 9. It also covers bitmap effects and how to use them correctly in CorelDRAW itself. The bitmap features can eliminate the need to open Corel PHOTO-PAINT to use its effects.

Color Adjustments

The ability to make global color adjustments to an entire drawing or to individual parts of a drawing can greatly improve the look of the final image. There are four color adjustments for vector and bitmap images and seven additional ones just for bitmap images. These adjustment controls are accessed by choosing Effects | Color Adjustment. The Effects | Color Adjustment child menu is shown here:

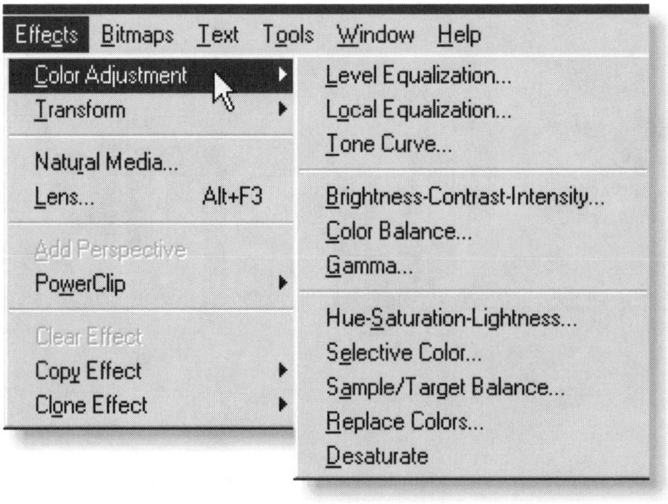

The four color adjustment dialog boxes, shown in Figure 22-1, can be used to modify both vector images and bitmap images.

The color adjustments are described next:

Brightness-Contrast-Intensity	Allows you to make individual adjustments to the brightness, contrast, and intensity of the selected objects or the entire image.
Color Balance	Allows you to make adjustments to the color values in the image. The controls are arranged in complementary pairs of the primary (RGB) and secondary (CMY) colors. Notice that the RGB values are on the right and the CMY values are on the left. Basically, these controls allow you to replace certain colors with their complements in varying degrees.

Gamma	Enhances the detail in low contrast images without greatly affecting the shadows or highlights. The slider control darkens or lightens a normal image while maintaining the contrast relationship between colors in the image.
Hue/Saturation/Lightness	Allows you to individually control the hue, saturation, and lightness of an object or the entire image. Use the slider controls or enter values directly in the parameter boxes.

Figure 22-2 shows a CorelDRAW vector image of a calendar on the left, and a duplicate calendar on the right. The cartoon image of the donkey sweeping leaves has been lightened by moving the Lightness slider to a setting of 70 in the Hue/Saturation/Lightness dialog box. Making the image lighter gives it a watermark effect and makes the calendar more readable where it overlays the cartoon. Using this lightness control on your images can produce some pleasing results.

Figure 22-3 shows the effects of using the Hue adjustments on duplicate clipart images of a flower. Changing the hue allows you to change the overall color of the flower from the original blue to pinks, purples, and yellows by entering positive and negative numbers using the slider control. With this simple control, you can change the colors of your images to fit the overall look and feel of the project. Think about it; what easier way is there to change a simple blue flower into a beautiful bouquet of different colored flowers?

FIGURE 22-1   The four color adjustments dialog boxes

FIGURE 22-2 Using the Lightness slider on a portion of the calendar

Figure 22-4 shows the results of using the Tone Curve on a scanned painting of a golf course. If you're a golf enthusiast, this is the signature fifteenth hole at Troon North in Scottsdale, Arizona. The painting is acrylic on canvas and was painted by coauthor Peter McCormick. The image on the left is the scan of the original painting. The image on the right was color corrected to enhance the tonal values in the shadows and highlights using the Tone Curve. The Tone Curve

FIGURE 22-3 Changing the color of flowers using the Hue adjustment control

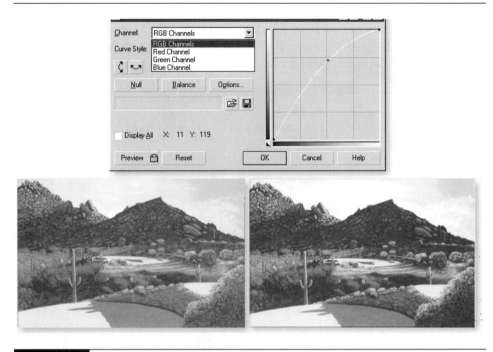

FIGURE 22-4 Using the Tone Curve to color correct a scanned painting

dialog box lets you adjust the individual colors in the image in addition to
controlling the gamma setting.

Bitmap Effects

The ability to edit bitmaps within CorelDRAW itself has grown with each new
version. Version 9 now offers virtually every bitmap-editing feature that you find in
Corel PHOTO-PAINT with the exception of masks and painting tools. This ability to
apply an effect to a bitmap object in CorelDRAW without have to export or open the
file in PHOTO-PAINT makes for a more seamless and efficient way to work.
Having said this, we still recommend that you use Corel PHOTO-PAINT as your
primary application for the more extensive editing and bitmap image creation. We
cannot possibly cover all the effects available in the Bitmap drop-down menu. To do
so would require another 1,000 pages. Instead we will show you a few of the more
interesting effects that you may find useful in your projects. If you want to learn

more about these controls and effects, pick up a copy of *Corel PHOTO-PAINT 9: The Official Guide* by David Huss (Osborne/McGraw-Hill, 1999).

The Bitmaps drop-down menu, shown here, contains five bitmap-editing controls, nine bitmap effects categories, and three plug-in filters.

Four of the most commonly used commands in the drop-down menu are described here. A few of the other options are described a bit later.

Convert to Bitmap	Use this command to convert a vector image to a bitmap image. You must use this command on vector images before you can use any of the bitmap effects.
Edit Bitmap	Use this command to edit bitmaps in CorelDRAW that can't be edited using the effects available in the Bitmap drop-down menu. For example, if you want to paint the image with Corel PHOTO-PAINT's Airbrush tool, you have to do it in Corel PHOTO-PAINT, not in CorelDRAW. When you choose this command, Corel PHOTO-PAINT is opened with your bitmap displayed. After making the necessary changes, click Save in Corel PHOTO-PAINT's File menu, and then exit PHOTO-PAINT. The CorelDRAW screen will reappear showing your modified bitmap image.

Resample   Choose the Resample command to change the size or resolution of the bitmap image using the Resample dialog box.

Mode   The Mode command lets you change the bitmap image from one type to another. For example, you can convert an RGB 22-bit image to a grayscale 8-bit image (you can convert a color image to grayscale, but you can't convert grayscale to color). More important, if you are incorporating bitmap images into your CorelDRAW files and those files will be output with process colors, you should always convert color bitmaps to CMYK 32-bit images so they will print correctly. Conversely, if you're designing for the Web, you want to convert to a 24-bit or 8-bit paletted image.

Using the Bitmap Color Mask

When you choose Bitmaps | Bitmap Color Mask from the Bitmaps drop-down menu, its Docker appears at the side of the screen (see Figure 22-5). The bitmap color mask is most frequently used to make certain colors transparent in a bitmap. For example, when you import bitmaps, they often appear using a rectangular background filled with white. Making the white background transparent so the underlying image shows through is the job of the bitmap color mask. Figure 22-5 is a good example of how the color mask works. This image was imported into CorelDRAW as a 32-bit bitmap image. You can see the white background of the bitmap image against the gray background of the page. The image at the right is missing the white background after using the bitmap color mask. The white background color has been made transparent, allowing the gray background of the page to show through.

NOTE   *When using the Bitmap Color mask, remember that it masks the sampled color wherever that color exists in the image. This means, in the case of a person's face, the whites of the eyes or teeth could very well drop out, allowing the background color to show through. You could end up with a person with green spots on their eyes and teeth. Or just as bad, you may get a green shirt if the original shirt was white and the background was white as well.*

The actual process of making a color transparent in a bitmap is as follows:

1. Select the imported bitmap image.

2. Choose Bitmap | Bitmap Color Mask to display its Docker.

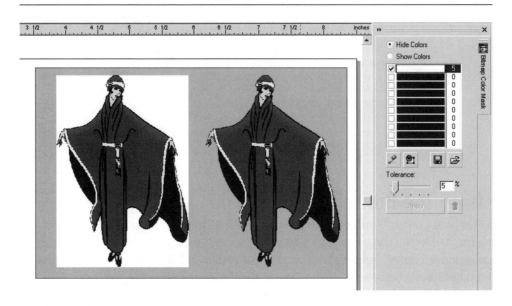

FIGURE 22-5	Using the bitmap color mask to eliminate the white background of a bitmap image

3. Click the Eyedropper tool. The cursor will change to an eyedropper.

4. Use the eyedropper to sample the color you want to make transparent (in this case, the white background). A check mark will be placed next to the top color bar, and the color you sampled will appear in the color bar.

5. Move the Tolerance slider to the right until you reach 5%. The Tolerance slider controls the range of color hues that will be made transparent. In the case of white, setting the slider to 5% simply allows for any slight variation or imperfection in the color white.

6. Click the Apply button to see the results.

The bitmap color mask works great on most bitmap images with solid background colors, but it is not the answer to all your masking needs. For the best results, you should import bitmap images that require the backgrounds to be removed as masked, such as TIF or CPT images containing a floating object. For information on how to create masks and floating objects, refer to

Corel PHOTO-PAINT 9: The Official Guide by David Huss (Osborne/McGraw-Hill, 1999).

Bitmap Effects Filters

Before you can use any of the Bitmap effects filters, you must either import a bitmap image into CorelDRAW or convert an existing vector image into a bitmap. You notice we mention converted bitmaps. Yes, you can convert an existing vector image into a bitmap right in CorelDRAW itself. Simply select the vector object or group of objects, and click on <u>B</u>itmaps | <u>C</u>onvert to Bitmap. The Convert to Bitmap dialog box shown below will appear. The best news of all is that when you convert a vector object to a bitmap, you have the option of making the background transparent, thereby removing the need to use the bitmap color mask.

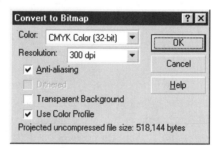

The options available in the dialog box are:

- *Color*   Click on the down arrow, and choose the color depth that fits the way the image will be used. The default is 32-Bit CMYK because generally you will be outputting to a printer that supports CMYK.

- *Resolution*   Click on the down arrow to choose from several different resolutions. If you don't see the one you want, enter it directly in the num box.

- *Anti-aliasing*   Choose this option to eliminate the jaggies created by the square edges of bitmap images. Intermediate colors are created along the edges of the image giving the illusion of a smooth line. Generally you would want to check this box.

- *Dithered*   This option is available only if you are converting the image with 256 colors or less. If this option is used, the colors will be randomly mixed together as opposed to seeing them a individual colors.

- *Transparent Background* Choose this option to eliminate the white box around an irregularly shaped vector image.

- *Use Color Profile* Choose this option if your using a color profile for the rest of the document.

Basically, all the bitmap effects in Corel PHOTO-PAINT are available with the exception of those effects that require the bitmap image to be masked before the effect can be applied. Masking is a Corel PHOTO-PAINT procedure and cannot be done in CorelDRAW.

Exploring the Effects

As mentioned earlier, the large number of bitmap effects prevents us from covering them all, but a few of the more spectacular ones are covered in the following sections.

Page Curl

Page Curl is one of the most popular effects. The Page Curl dialog box, along with an image of a golf hole with the effect applied to the lower-right corner, is shown in Figure 22-6. It's the fifteenth hole at the Makena Golf and Country Club in Maui, Hawaii. The original is an acrylic on canvas painted by coauthor Peter McCormick. It was scanned in on a flatbed scanner. If you didn't know you could scan objects larger than the scanner's platen, you can learn how to do so by visiting McCormick's Web site at http://www.happyaccident.com.

To use the Page Curl effect, follow these steps:

1. Select the bitmap.

2. Choose <u>B</u>itmaps | <u>3</u>D Effects | <u>P</u>age Curl to bring up the Page Curl dialog box.

3. Select the corner that you want to curl from the corner grid at the left of the dialog box.

4. Use the slider controls for both the width and height of the curl.

5. Choose either <u>V</u>ertical or <u>H</u>orizontal orientation.

6. Choose either <u>O</u>paque or <u>T</u>ransparent for the curl.

7. Click on a color button for the back of the curl. If you want to use a color from the image, use the Eyedropper tool to sample a color

FIGURE 22-6   The Page Curl effect applied to a scanned painting

in the image. The background color box and Eyedropper are unavailable in CorelDRAW. If you use this filter in PHOTO-PAINT, they will be available.

8. Click the Preview button to see the effect. If you are not satisfied, continue to change settings.

9. When you are satisfied with the results using either of the dialog boxes, click the OK button.

Using Plug-in Filters

CorelDRAW 9 supports plug-in filters, including many third-party filters. The four plug-in filters included with CorelDRAW 9 are:

- Digamarc's Watermark filter to protect the copyrights of your work

- Julia Set Explorer 2.0, a filter that produces fractal images

- Terrazzo, a unique filter that creates seamless pattern tiles from bitmap images

- Squizz, a distortion filter that lets you do some outrageous things to images of people or any other bitmap you use

The Squizz and Terrazzo filters are covered in the following sections.

The Squizz Filter

Use the following steps to practice with the Squizz filter:

1. Choose File | Import, and choose your favorite bitmap image of yourself or a relative from wherever it is stored on your system.

2. With the bitmap image selected, choose Bitmaps | Plug-ins | Hsoft | Squizz to open the Squizz dialog box shown at the left in Figure 22-7.

3. Choose Brush as the method of distortion. The Brush configuration dialog box is shown at the left in Figure 22-7.

4. Use the brush to click and drag on the image. Depending on the direction you drag, the images will be distorted in that direction. For smaller areas like the eyes or mouth, reduce the brush size by changing the number in the Size num box.

5. Experiment with the other controls as well.

6. When you're happy with the results, click the Apply button.

7. Try choosing the Grid method offered in the opening Squizz screen on the same or a different image.

8. Drag on the intersecting line of the grid to distort the image.

9. Experiment with the preset options in the center portion of the dialog box. Click Apply when you are finished.

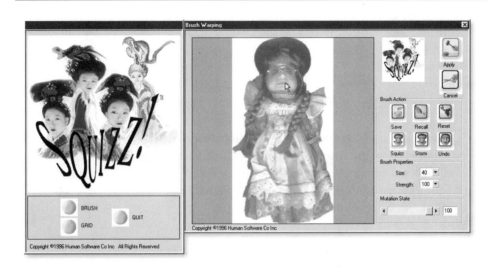

FIGURE 22-7   The Squizz opening screen and the Brush configuration dialog box

Here are the results of using both the Brush and Grid methods for distorting an image of at doll that was scanned in on a flatbed scanner. Yes, you can scan objects as big as dolls with a flatbed scanner. What names would you give the three young ladies?

The Terrazzo Filter

The Terrazzo filter definitely falls in the "happy accident" category—you never know what you will get with it. The good news is that you usually will be happy with everything you try. The problem is trying to choose which choice is best. The patterns you create are based on quilting patterns.

To practice using this incredible filter, follow these steps:

1. Open any file you want. If it is not already a bitmap, convert it into a 24-bit bitmap using the Bitmap I Convert to Bitmap command. You must use the 24-bit option, or the filter will not work. Trust us when we say any file will do. You are about to be surprised. This image was created by coauthor Peter McCormick several years ago.

2. With the bitmap image selected, choose Bitmap I Plug-ins I Fancy I Terrazzo to reveal the Terrazzo dialog box. The default symmetry is Pinwheel.

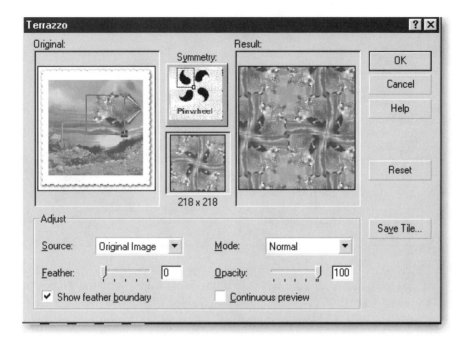

3. Move the rectangular selection tool around in the original image window on the left. The pattern created from the sampled area within the selection tool will appear in the Results window on the right of the dialog box. If you like the pattern created, click the OK button, and the original bitmap you started with will be filled with the pattern.

   The main purpose of this filter is not to fill the original bitmap with the new pattern, but to create a tile pattern that will tile seamlessly when used as a fill. The small preview window between the larger Original and Result windows is a preview of the tile that will be created from the sample area within the Original window.

4. When you're happy with what you see in the center preview window, click on the Save Tile button to bring up the Save Tile dialog box. The default folder is the Programs folder off the folder name you used to install CorelDRAW 9. We always install in a folder called "Corel90".

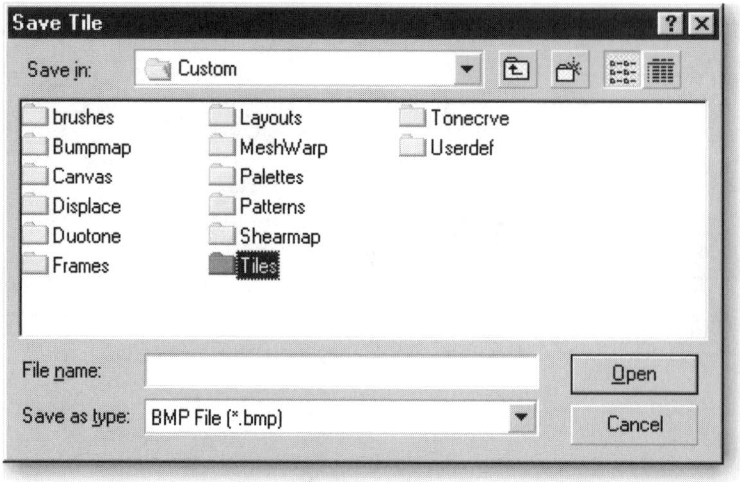

If you want to install your new tile in the same folder with the Tiles that
ship with CorelDRAW 9, change to the folder where you installed
CorelDRAW 9, and then choose the Custom folder. From the Custom
folder, choose Tiles. Give your tile a name with a .bmp extension. When
we saved our tile, it was necessary to manually type in the .bmp extension.
Click the Save button, and you're ready to use your new tile. If you aren't
familiar with tiling bitmap patterns, read the section on bitmap fills in
Chapter 9.

5. OK, now it's time to try a different symmetry. Click on the Symmetry box
   at the top of the Terrazzo dialog box between the Original and Result
   windows to reveal the Symmetry dialog box shown here.

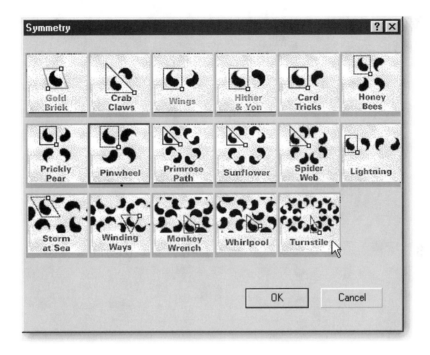

6. Click on any of the 17 symmetries, and then click the OK button to get back to the Terrazzo dialog box. We used the symmetry Turnstiles to create the pattern shown next.

```
Terrazzo                                                    ? X

Original:                      Result:
                    Symmetry:
                                                          OK

                                                        Cancel

                    Turnstile                            Help

                                                        Reset
                    636 x 368

Adjust                                                 Save Tile...

Source:  Original Image  ▼    Mode:  Normal  ▼

Feather:  |----·-·-·-  0      Opacity:  -·-·-·-|  100

☑ Show feather boundary        ☐ Continuous preview
```

7. We liked the results and saved the tile. The final tile is shown, next to the original bitmap image.

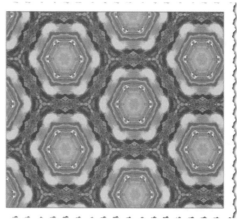

Creating Duotones

Many designers use duotones in place of CMYK images. The advantage of using duotones is that only two separations have to be made, instead of the usual four when working in CMYK colors. Two plates mean lower cost to the client. Using only two colors can sometimes improve what otherwise would be a mediocre image. Selecting certain colors can create a mood in the image. Figure 22-8 shows a duotone being applied to the image on the right. It's difficult to see the change

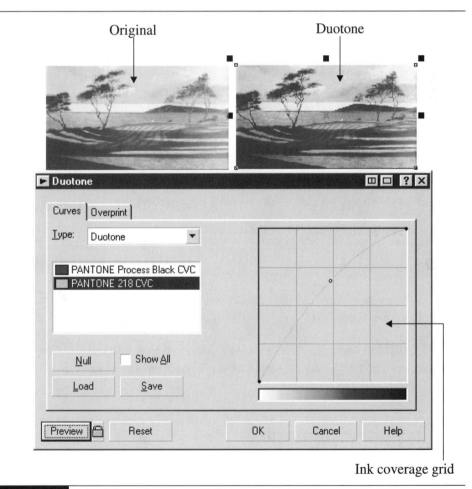

FIGURE 22-8   Applying a duotone to an image

take place in the grayscale figure, but the duotone on the right used black and a PANTONE magenta to give a overall medium-to-dark pink tone to the image. It worked well for this particular image because the location is in Hawaii where the sunsets are pink due to the lack of dust in the air.

To create a duotone, use the following steps:

1. Import a bitmap image.

2. Click on Bitmaps | Mode | Duotone.

3. When the Duotone dialog box appears, select Duotone from the Type list box.

4. Double-click on the PANTONE process yellow color button to reveal the Select Color dialog box.

5. Choose the PANTONE color you want to use. If you wish to use another spot color system, select it from the Type list box in the Select Color dialog box.

6. Don't change the PANTONE Process Black CV color for a standard duotone. Black is commonly used to enhance the shadows in the image. You could use another color to create a special effect.

7. Adjust the ink coverage on each color by first clicking on each color button and then dragging the curve in the grid at the right of the dialog box.

8. Click on the preview button to see the results.

9. When you're satisfied with the results, click on the OK button in the Duotone dialog box.

 CAUTION   *Any plug-in filter that requires a mask will not work in CorelDRAW. To use filters requiring a mask, you must use Corel PHOTO-PAINT.*

Linking Bitmap Images

CorelDRAW lets you link bitmaps when importing them into CorelDRAW. This feature lets you add bitmaps to your drawing while reducing the size of your file.

What actually takes place is that the bitmap file you import into your CDR file remains in the folder where it was originally stored. Instead of the file being imported, a low-resolution preview header file is used for placement only in the CDR file. The real image stays in the folder where it is stored. When it comes time to print the CDR file with the image, the real file is retrieved for printing. Included in the Bitmaps menu are options on updating the bitmap and resolving the link to a bitmap. These options are discussed later in this chapter.

To link a bitmap to your drawing, follow these steps:

1.   Click File | Import to bring up the Import dialog box.

2.   Change to the drive and folder where your bitmap is stored.

3.   Enable the Link bitmap externally box at the top of the list of various options at the middle right of the Import dialog box.

4.   Click on the Import button at the top of the dialog box.

5.   Position the import placement cursor on the page where you want the image to display.

6.   Click once to place the bitmap in its original size, or press the SPACEBAR to place the image in the center of page. Use can also use the placement cursor and drag to define a custom size for the image. If you hold down the ALT key while dragging, you can resize the image to any dimension, but the image will be distorted.

Updating a Linked Bitmap

When you update a linked bitmap, you're telling CorelDRAW to reimport the preview header file. You do so when you know changes have been made to the file since it was originally imported as a linked file. Because the linked file that is displayed on the page is merely pointing to the original file, updating the link is a simple thing to do. The changed preview header is now displayed in place of the old one. The actual process of updating a linked bitmap is as follows:

1.   Select the linked bitmap with the Pick tool.

2.   Click Bitmaps | Update From Link.

Resolving a Linked Bitmap

Resolving a linked bitmap removes the link between the bitmap header file that points to the original bitmap. When you resolve the bitmap, the low-resolution header is replaced with the actual high resolution file. The bitmap is no longer linked and behaves like any other bitmap file.

To resolve a linked bitmap, do the following:

1. Select the linked bitmap with the Pick tool.

2. Click <u>B</u>itmaps | Resolve Lin<u>k</u>.

 NOTE *You cannot use any effects on a linked bitmap.*

Saving Bitmaps in CorelDRAW

CorelDRAW 9 now lets you save a bitmap you have created in CorelDRAW by using the <u>B</u>itmap | Convert To Bitmap command or one you have imported and perhaps made changes to.

To save a bitmap within CorelDRAW, right-click on the bitmap, and choose Save Bitmap As from the object pop-up menu. This action will display the Export dialog box. Choose a file type such as .TIF or JPG from the Files of <u>t</u>ype drop-down list. Give the bitmap image you're saving a name, and choose a folder to save it in. Then click the Export button at the top of the Export dialog box.

This chapter has covered how to make adjustments to the colors of vector and bitmap images. It has also discussed how to take advantage of several of the bitmap effects directly in CorelDRAW, eliminating the need to take the extra time to open and use Corel PHOTO-PAINT when you are not making extensive edits to a bitmap.

PART IV

Input and Output

CorelDRAW 9

CHAPTER 23

COREL.COM

Scanning and Tracing Bitmaps

As the cost of scanners goes down, it is becoming more commonplace to find a scanner on the average user's desktop. Now that they can apply effects to bitmap images within CorelDRAW 9 itself, many users will discover the benefits of using scanned images in their projects.

Scanners

Scanners are available in four types: hand-held, flatbed, Sheet-fed, and drum. The most commonly used scanner type is the flatbed. Hand-held scanners are very inexpensive, but they require a steady hand to operate. They do have their place in the world of scanning, even though they're not used often. One important use of a hand-held scanner is to scan a fragile document that can't be removed from its binding. Drum scanners are very expensive and therefore reserved for high-end users such as service bureaus and companies such as Corel Corporation.

A flatbed scanner is much like an office copy machine. A traveling light bar illuminates the work placed on the glass plate. The reflected light from the image is passed through a lens onto the charged couple device (CCD) sensors. The red, green, and blue light information is collected from the sensors and sent to the computer.

Unlike a photographer, who spends a great deal of time in the darkroom developing and enlarging film, a person using scanning software can process an image in minutes and can adjust the size, resolution, contrast, brightness, tonal control, and saturation of the image. Professional photographers go to great pains to get the lighting and exposure just right so they spend less time in the darkroom. Similarly, you should spend the extra time to make the necessary software settings and adjustments prior to committing to the final scan.

You must first determine the correct resolution to scan your image. The resolution is determined by the quality you are seeking and the requirements of the printer. (The printer may mean the physical printer that sits on your desktop or the person who will print the job.) A good rule of thumb is to scan your image at one and one-half times the line screen of your printer.

The Basics of Scanning

You can scan many kinds of things on a flatbed scanner, ranging from images on paper to a pair of pants. You can scan small three-dimensional objects or even artwork that exceeds the size of the scanner surface. If you think we are joking about the pants reference, we're not. We once needed a denim texture fill so we scanned the pocket of a pair of Levis. Candy wrapped in cellophane looks great when scanned. The reflections off the cellophane really sparkle.

Before you scan an image, you should determine how you will be using the image. If the image will be used only for screen display, you can scan at a relatively low resolution such as 100 dpi (dots per inch). However, if you plan on using the image for a display ad as well, then you should scan the image at a higher resolution and lower the resolution for the screen image in an application such as Corel PHOTO-PAINT. If your scanned image will be printed in grayscale, you may decide to scan it in color as well for future use. Once you discard original information (the color values when you convert a 24-bit color scan to grayscale, for example), they are lost to the file forever.

The images you can scan are grouped into three basic categories: line art, halftones, and continuous-tone images (full-color and black-and-white photographs).

Scanning Line Art

Line art is considered to be a black-and-white image. If you are planning on converting a scanned black-and-white bitmap image into a vector image using either CorelDRAW's Auto-Trace feature or the standalone application CorelTRACE, you should scan the image at a minimum of 300 dpi for best results. If the line art image contains very fine lines, scan it as a grayscale image instead of as a black-and-white image.

If you are planning to leave scanned line art as a bitmap image for printing on commercial presses, you should scan at the output resolution (dpi) of the press but not exceeding the maximum optical resolution of the scanner.

Scanning Halftones

When discussing halftones, you need to differentiate between scanning an image using the Halftone setting in your scanner software and scanning an image that has been previously printed as a halftone (pictures in magazines, for example).

You should avoid scanning images using the Halftone setting in the software in most cases. Use this setting only if you are planning to print on a printer that cannot generate its own halftone dots, such as a dot-matrix printer.

The second form of halftone is a grayscale or color image that has been previously printed in a magazine or book. Scanning this type of halftone presents a problem because its image is made up of tiny halftone dots created by the printing process. Before you even attempt to scan an image that has been previously printed, make sure you have the right to do so. Copyright laws are very specific on this subject.

The best way to ensure good results when scanning an image that has been printed with the four-color process, is to first scan the image at the proper resolution. (See the formulas for determining correct scanning resolutions later in this chapter.) Once the image is scanned, open it in a paint program such as Corel PHOTO-PAINT to remove the moiré pattern that results from scanning the halftone dots. Corel PHOTO-PAINT has a Remove Moiré filter you can use just for that purpose. When the moiré pattern has been removed, use the Unsharp Mask filter in PHOTO-PAINT to return the image to its original sharpness. CorelDRAW 9 also has a Remove Moiré and Unsharp Mask filter you can use without having to use Corel PHOTO-PAINT if the image doesn't require any extra work.

Scanning Continuous-Tone Images

Continuous-tone images can be either grayscale or color. The images that fall in this category are black-and-white or color photographs and original artwork such as oil paintings. Other than adjusting for hue and saturation, you should treat a grayscale image like a color image.

Scanning Issues

It is extremely important to scan at the proper resolution. If you scan an image at too low a resolution, it will become pixelated. If you scan using a resolution that is too high, the image-editing program has to throw away information that it can't use when you manually resize the image to fit on the page. The effect of this on the final image is a loss of subtle detail.

To produce the best-quality prints or film, use the rule of thumb for scanning an image by using a dpi setting of one and a half times the line screen (screen frequency).

There are two methods for determining the correct scanning resolution. The first measures in pixels, and the second measures in inches. Before you begin scanning using either of these methods, you must determine the optimum resolution by asking your printer what line screen will be used to create the film. This is extremely important if you want a high-quality scan.

23

Using Pixels as the Measurement Unit

Measuring in pixels can be less complicated than using inches. For example, if your printer tells you that he or she will be using a line screen of 133 on your project, which is a common line screen used in commercial printing, multiply that number by 1.5 and round up to the nearest value. In this case, 1.5x133 equals 189.5, so you would round up to 190 dpi.

The next thing you need to determine is the final output size. If the size of the output image will be the same as the original, use the resolution that the formula calls for (in this case, 190 dpi), enter that number in your scanning software, and proceed to scan the image. If the output image will be smaller or larger than the original, use the scaling adjustment in your scanning software to scale the image to the desired size. For example, if you are scanning an image that is 5x7 inches and you have determined that the correct scanning resolution is 200 dpi, the image will measure 1000x1400 pixels. If you decide to output the image at twice the original size, at 10x14 inches, you will need to use the scaling adjustments in the scanning software to increase the size of the image by 200 percent, making the final scanned image 2000x2800 pixels. If this scaling exceeds the scanner's resolution, the image will be increased using interpolation (a sophisticated algorithm for guessing what pixels to add as filler, which doesn't always give accurate results). Remember that once you know the correct resolution at which to scan your image, it's simply a matter of multiplying that number by the size of the final output image.

Using Inches as the Measurement Unit

The second method is to determine the size of the output image using inches as the unit of measure. You can use the formula ((LDO x LS) x 1.5) divided by LDI = OSR, where

- LDO is the longest dimension of the output image

- LS is the line screen to be used in the final output

- LDI is the longest dimension of the input image

- OSR is the optimum scanning resolution in DPI

For example, suppose you are scanning a photo that is 8x10 inches, and you want to output your image at a size of 4x5 inches with a 150-line screen. Use these values: LDO=5, LS=150, and LDI=10. Plug these numbers into the following formula:

((5 x 150) x 1.5) divided by 10 = 112.5 dpi (round up to 120 dpi)

Here is another example. Suppose you are scanning a photo that is 5x7 inches, and you want to output your image at a size of 10x14 inches with a 100-line screen. Use these values: LDO=14, LS=100, LDI=7. Plug these numbers into the following formula:

((14 x 100) x 1.5) divided by 7 = 300 dpi

The following table shows the default line screen of output devices rated by dpi. (For example, a 600 dpi laser printer produces a default line screen of 80.) This table will help you determine the correct resolution for scanning.

Maximum dpi of the printer	Default line screen
300	60
600	80
1000	100
1200	133
1270	133
1693	150
3386	200

Using a Script to Calculate dpi

If you have difficulty with math like many of us, a script can automatically calculate the correct dpi to scan your images. The script shown here is called "Scanning

Calculator" and is included on the CD that comes with this book. The filename is ScanCalc.csb. Use the following steps to install the script in CorelDRAW:

1. Copy the file ScanCalc.csb from the book CD. The path to the file is: /Chap23/ScanCalc.csb.

2. Paste the file in the Scripts folder of CorelDRAW. We have shown the path to the folder here. The only difference between your path and the path shown here is that the folder named "Corel90" is where we have CorelDRAW 9 installed. The name of your folder may be different.

3. Once the file is pasted into the Scripts folder, select Tools | Corel SCRIPT | Run Script to reveal the Run Script dialog box shown here.

Run Script		? X
Look in: Scripts		
Presets		
Scripts		
File name:		Open
Files of type: Script Files (*.csc)		Cancel
Description:		

4. Double-click on the Script folder in the Run Script dialog box to reveal the default scripts shown here. These scripts will have a .csc extension.

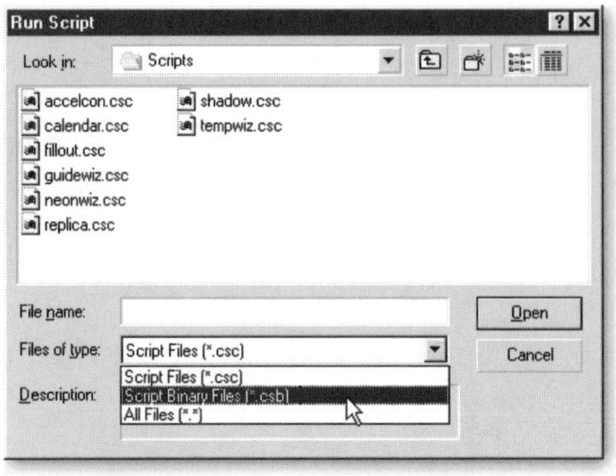

5. Click the down arrow of the Files of Type list box, and choose Script Binary Files (*csb) to reveal the ScanCalc.csb script shown here:

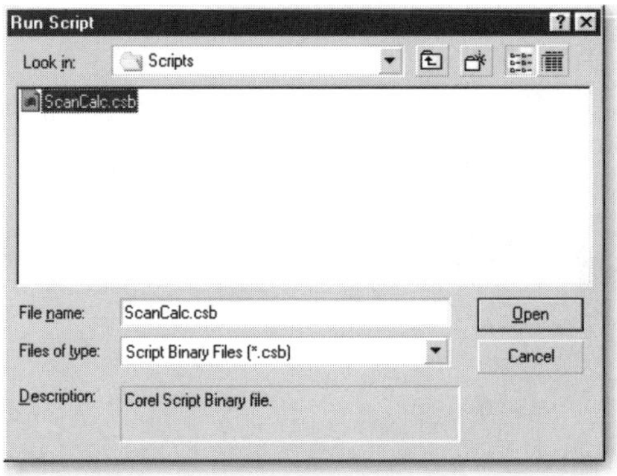

6. Select the script, and click on the Open button to reveal the Scanning Calculator dialog box shown at the top of the three dialog boxes:

7. Enter the number for the line screen your printer will be using to output your job in the LPI box.

8. Enter the width size of the image you will be scanning in the Original Width box.

9. Enter the width size of the final output image in the Width of the Printed Image box.

10. Enter the number **1.5** in the Quality Coefficient box (you will use 1.5 most of the time).

11. When all the boxes have been filled with data, look at the bottom left of the dialog box to see the correct dpi to scan your image.

12. Click the OK button to exit the script.

We have shown two different possible scenarios in the middle and lower dialog boxes, each using the same line screen.

The first example using the middle dialog box makes the following assumption: The number in the Original Width box represents a typical 8.5x11-inch letter size image. The number in the Width of Printed Image box was based on the assumption that the output image would be 5x7. The Scanning Calculator displays the correct scanning resolution of 117dpi at the lower-left corner of the dialog box.

The second example using the bottom box makes the following assumption: The number in the Original Width box represents a typical 2x3.5 business card image. The number in the Width of Printed Image box was based on the assumption that the output image would be twice the size of the original or 4x7. The Scanning Calculator displays the correct scanning resolution of 465 dpi at the lower-left corner of the dialog box.

Now that you have both the mathematical formulas and the Scanning Calculator, you should never make another mistake when deciding the correct resolution to scan your image.

Using Your Scanning Software

You have just learned the importance of scanning at the proper resolution, but that's only half of the story. The second most important thing you need to know is what to do next. Any good scanner will have its own proprietary software that ships with it. This software allows you to make adjustment to things like brightness and contrast, color corrections like hue and saturation, and tone curve correction for shadows and highlights. All of these controls are vital to achieving a good scan.

You may have been told or read in a book that you don't have to concern yourself with the software the scanner manufacturer ships with their product. You may have been told that all you need to do is scan an image and make the necessary corrections in a good image-editing program like Corel PHOTO-PAINT. If you have been operating under these misconceptions, you have been making your image-editing life much more difficult than necessary.

It is imperative to select the proper settings in the scanning software prior to the final scan if you want good results. You should make every effort to adjust the scanner software settings so your final scan produces the best-quality image possible. The rationale behind this advice is the old saying that goes something like this: "You can't make a silk purse out of a sow's ear"; that is, you can't expect to improve an image if the data is not present in the scan. Figure 23-1 shows the

23

interface of the Deskscan software supplied with Hewlett Packard scanners. Notice the object being scanned. Your eyes are not deceiving you. It is a real teddy bear. If you have never tried scanning three-dimensional objects, you are missing many scanning possibilities.

Scanning Directly into CorelDRAW

CorelDRAW provides a File | Acquire Image | Acquire command that lets you scan directly into CorelDRAW. This method takes you directly to your scanner's software, where you can make the necessary adjustments, and then when you press your scanner's scan button, it places the image on the page in CorelDRAW. This method works very well and is quick and easy to do. Having said this, we recommend that you don't do it. Our reason is that although your scanner software can be helpful in

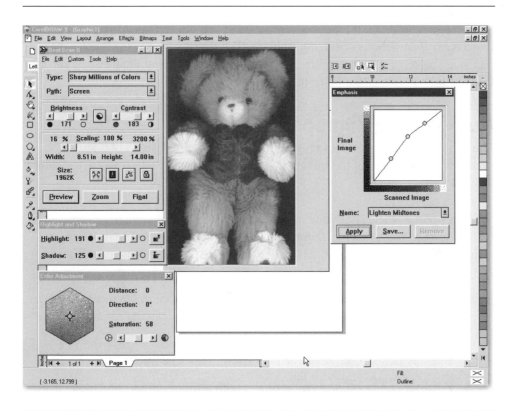

FIGURE 23-1   A scan of a three-dimensional object

producing a good scan as stated earlier, you usually need to make further adjustments to the image in an image-editing program like PHOTO-PAINT. The teddy bear shown earlier is a good example. The scan of the teddy bear, while it turned out very well, still needs some "fine tuning" to get it perfect. That can be done best in PHOTO-PAINT because it will require masking, which is not available in CorelDRAW.

Tracing Bitmaps

Tracing bitmaps has become commonplace in the desktop publishing community. Perhaps the most frequent reason for tracing bitmaps is to turn customers' scanned logos into scalable vector graphics. The CorelDRAW 9 suite includes the standalone program, CorelTRACE, which can be used to convert bitmaps to vectors. It's a robust program that provides numerous ways of tracing bitmaps from line art to colored photos. It can even be accessed within CorelDRAW itself by choosing Bitmaps | Trace Bitmap when a bitmap is selected. Because it is such a feature-rich program, it's beyond the scope of this book. Instead you will learn two alternative methods of tracing bitmaps. The first method is the Auto-Trace method. The second is by physically tracing the bitmap using the Bézier tool. Let's begin with the Auto-Trace method.

Auto-Tracing Bitmaps

The Auto-Trace feature works only with black-and-white line art. At best, it produces a crude trace of the image. If you would like to practice using the feature, follow these steps:

1. Import a black-and-white bitmap image. (If you just want to see what kind of trace you can expect, draw an octagon on the page using the Polygon tool, and convert it into a bitmap using the Bitmaps | Convert to Bitmap command.)

2. With the bitmap selected, click on the Freehand tool in the toolbox (the cursor will change to a crosshair with a dotted line on the right end of the horizontal line of the crosshair).

3. Use this cursor to click on the selected bitmap. The trace will be created.

4. Fill your newly created vector object with a fill of choice, and move it away from the bitmap.

In the illustration shown here, you see the original octagon bitmap at the top right and the results of the auto-trace at the top middle. We have also traced a portion of the bitmap image of the CorelXARA logo on the bottom left and have shown the results of the auto-trace at the bottom middle of the illustration. As you can see, the auto-trace results leave a lot to be desired. The vector images on the right, both top and bottom, were manually traced using the Bézier tool from the toolbox. We think you would agree that the manually traced bitmap images look superior.

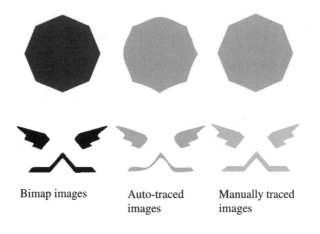

Bimap images   Auto-traced   Manually traced
                    images   images

NOTE   *You might ask why the Auto-Trace works so poorly; we can only say that the feature has been in CorelDRAW since version one and has never been improved upon or removed. We have covered this tool and shown you the results you might expect, so you don't think you are doing anything wrong.*

Having seen the Auto-Trace method, it's time to learn how to trace bitmap images manually using the Bézier tool.

Tracing Bitmap Images Manually

In the many years we have taught users how to trace bitmap images using the Bézier tool, we have found that the first reaction is one of "that sounds too difficult." We only ask that you give the technique an honest try, and if you do, you will be counting yourself among the many professional users that have been using this "dot-to-dot" method for years with excellent results.

Use the following steps to practice learning how to trace a bitmap image using the Bézier tool. We will start out with an easy one for your first try. Draw an octagon on the page using the Polygon tool, and give it a 50 percent black fill.

1. Convert the polygon into a bitmap by choosing Bitmaps | Convert to Bitmap.

2. With the bitmap still selected, right-click and choose Lock Object from the pop-up menu. This action will lock the bitmap image to the page and prevent the Auto-Trace function from occurring when you click on the image with the Bézier tool to trace the image. You will know that the bitmap is locked when the square selection handles turn into little locks. The pop-up menu and the lock handles around the bitmap are shown here.

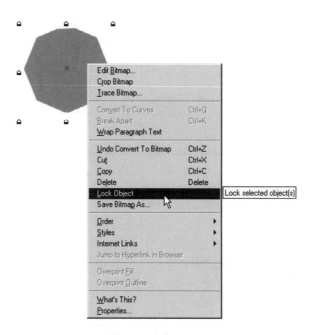

3. With the bitmap selected, select the Bézier tool from the Curve flyout menu of the toolbox.

4. Click once on any of the points of the octagon.

5. Continue clicking on the remaining seven points. After you have clicked on the eighth point, click again on the point you started with to complete the shape.

6. Select your new shape, move it away from the bitmap image, and give it a 50 percent black fill. That's it, you're done.

You have just learned the secrete to manually tracing a bitmap image. It was easy, and you ended up with a perfect vector graphic. They won't all be that easy, but with practice using the Bézier tool, you will be tracing bitmaps with the best of them.

NOTE *It isn't necessary that the bitmap be black-and-white line art if you use the manual technique because it's used only as a pattern to trace.*

TIP *When you need to trace a logo in bitmap form that contains text, try finding the original font used in the logo from the many fonts supplied with CorelDRAW. If that is not possible, find one that's close, convert it to curves, and tweak it into the shape of the font you need.*

Let's try a more difficult image. If you want to use the image we use, you can find it on the CD that comes with the book. The path to the file is /Chap23/ PCC.cdr and is shown here:

This graphic is a typical representation of a logo you might get from a client. This particular logo is Philipp's Communications' logo in Las Vegas, Nevada. It has several curves plus the letter *P* that will require using the Combine command to cut a hole in the center.

Practice the Bézier tool technique on this logo using the following steps:

1. Open the file PCC.cdr from the CD that came with this book. The logo is already in TIF format.

2. Select the bitmap image, and right-click in the color palette on 20 percent black. You are changing to a lighter color so that you can better see the lines and handles as you trace the bitmap. Black-and-white bitmap images let you

change the foreground and background colors by left- or right-clicking in the color palette. If you're paying attention, this should tell you that you can change the colors of black-and-white bitmap images into any two solid colors or make either color transparent by clicking the No Fill swatch at the top of the color palette.

3. With the bitmap still selected, right-click and choose <u>L</u>ock Object from the pop-up menu just as you did in the first exercise.

4. Select the Bézier tool from the Curve flyout menu. Using the example below as a guide, begin tracing the logo by starting at the upper left.

5. Click once to begin the trace.

6. Click a second time to draw the straight line across the top of the logo, just as you did in the first exercise.

7. Click a third time along the upper-right side of the logo, but this time but don't release the left mouse button. Instead, as you click, drag downward along the vertical line of the image. Handles will appear on either side of the node, and the line between the second click and third click will begin to curve. Because you dragged downward, your cursor will be controlling the lower handle.

8. Move the handle in and out to control the amount of the curve, all the while keeping the handle aligned to the vertical line. Your trace should now look like this:

9. When you're pleased with the results, move to the next point, and click to create another straight line.

10. If you're using the sample logo we provided, you should be in a position to make a turn to the left. Do this by simply clicking once with the left mouse button to create another straight line to the corner.

11. Now move up to the point where the line curves to the left, and click. This will create the next short straight line.

12. Click again where the curve starts to straighten out, and drag to the left along the horizontal line. Move the left handle in and out to control the curve, while keeping it horizontally aligned. Your trace should now be looking like this.

13. Continue tracing the outside shape using this modified dot-to-dot method. To complete the shape, click a final time on the node which began the trace. Your trace should now look like the example here:

Before you start tracing the rest of the image, check that you have performed an accurate trace. If you missed making a curve match the original bitmap, you will need to adjust the curve using the Shape tool. The Shape tool and its many uses is covered in Chapter 7. When you are satisfied with the shape, fill it with black.

Now continue the trace by starting with the next inside shape using the same techniques you used on the first shape. There will be times when no matter how you try, you can't get a square corner to come out with a straight line. We have shown an example of this problem here; notice the pronounced curve on what should have been a straight vertical line at the lower-left of the inside shape:

When this problem occurs, follow these steps to turn the curve into a straight vertical line:

1. With the Shape tool selected, select the two nodes on either side of the offending curve by SHIFT-clicking or marquee selecting the nodes.

2. With the nodes selected, click on the Convert Curve to Line button on the Property Bar. We have highlighted and circled it for you in the illustration shown here. This action creates a straight line between the two nodes.

Convert curve to line   Convert line to curve

3. When the curved line is converted to a straight line, it can also make one of the adjacent curved line segments straight like the example shown here:

4. To correct this problem, selected the two nodes on either side of the line, and click on the Convert line to Curve button on the Property Bar.

5. Click on the line itself with the Shape tool, and pull out to recreate the curve. When you're happy with the results, fill this second shape with black.

   It's now time to trace the inside shape of the image. The center section of the letter *P* will be the final component of the trace.

6. Select the Bézier tool again, and start tracing this final shape. As you trace you may end up with two curved segments where they should have been straight, as in this illustration:

7. Use the same steps you used in steps 3 through 5 to correct the problem.

8. When you're finished tracing the inside shape, select the Bézier tool again, and trace the center of the letter *P*.

9. With the final shape traced, it's time to cut the hole in the letter *P*.

10. Select the inside shape and the center of the letter *P* shape, and click on the Combine button on the Property Bar. This action will finalize the inside shape and it should now look like the one shown here:

11. Adjust any curves that need adjusting, and fill the last shape with black.

The final trace is shown here, below the scanned image of the actual business card.

 TIP *To aid you in keeping the straight lines straight, use guidelines with Snap to Guidelines turned on. This will keep all vertical and horizontal lines perfectly straight. If you're not familiar with guidelines, see Chapter 13.*

If you're wondering how a trace of this image would have turned out using the auto-trace method, the answer is shown here:

Finally we want to show you an image of a computer monitor that was traced using the manual trace method. A user in Norway sent this before-and-after example of how he uses the Bézier tool technique. This illustration is created in CorelDRAW 8 from a digital photo by Håvard Bartnes, © Data Power AS, Norway.

We hope this exercise has taught you a technique that you can use for years to come. All that it takes to be an expert is practice, practice, practice.

Digital Camera Support

CorelDRAW 9 now allows you to bring your digital camera images directly into CorelDRAW. It's really quite simple. After connecting your camera's flash card to your computer's serial port, use the following steps to open a image from your digital camera:

1. Choose File I Digital Camera I Select Camera to bring up the dialog box shown here:

2. Click on the down arrows of the Communications Port and Port Settings textboxes, and choose the options that meet your system requirements.

3. Click the down arrow of the Import As Type box, and choose the format that your camera outputs. Click OK to exit the dialog box.

4. Now that your settings are correct, choose File | Digital Camera | Get Image to access the images from your camera.

CHAPTER 24

Importing, Opening, Saving, and Exporting Files

CoreIDRAW 9

With most software, opening files is very straightforward, and the import options are very limited. CorelDRAW is just the opposite. With most projects, you'll need to use many different files. Text will come from a word processor, bitmaps will come from your favorite bitmap editing program (Corel PHOTO-PAINT, right?), and some elements may come from other CorelDRAW files or even from a Macintosh Illustrator user. With each type of file that you open or import, the procedures may be slightly different. This chapter explores the many aspects of opening and importing files so that you'll know exactly how to work with the files you need.

Once you've spent lots of time working on an image, you don't want to throw it away—so you save the file for future use. This used to be a fairly straightforward operation, but now there are many useful options to choose from. A .cdr file isn't always what you want, so you also need to know about the various export filters that are available. This chapter doesn't cover all of them, but it explains the most important ones.

The Open/Import Dialog Box

You use the same dialog box to both open and import files. However, the list of file types is much more extensive when you are importing files. This dialog box is what is called a common dialog box, as it is used throughout most Windows programs. An example is shown in Figure 24-1.

You may see a similarity here with Windows Explorer, which makes sense because this dialog box works just like Windows Explorer in many ways. The main part of the dialog box lists the files by name, with a small icon on their left. You can change this view with the buttons above the main window. The rightmost button changes the view to Details, which shows the file size, type, and date to the right of the filename. If you choose Details, you will see only a single column of filenames rather than the multiple columns you see in the default List view. You can change back to List view with the List button just to the left of the Details button.

In the upper-left corner of the dialog box is the Look in drop-down list box, which lets you choose the computer, drive, and folder for which information will be displayed. To change to a folder lower than the one currently displayed, double-click the folder in the main window. To move one folder up in the hierarchy, click the button just to the right of the drop-down list. The next button to the right automatically creates a new folder. Of course, you can also create a new folder by right-clicking in the main

Create New Folder   List

Up One Level

Details

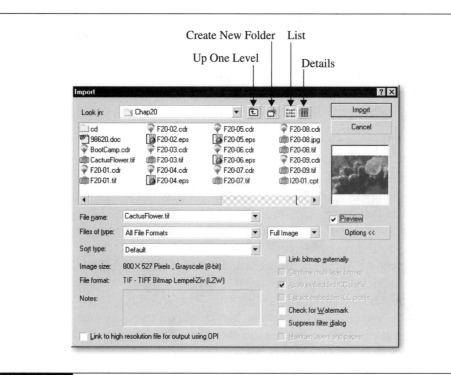

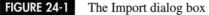
FIGURE 24-1   The Import dialog box

window and choosing New | Folder from the pop-up menu. On that same menu you'll find numerous other options just like those in Windows Explorer.

Someone once asked how to delete a file in CorelDRAW. We all got this weird look on our faces since that was not something you'd even think of trying to do in CorelDRAW. Wasn't that the purpose of Window's File Manager? Now you can delete a file by simply clicking the filename and pressing the DEL key. You can even rename a file by clicking the name twice (not a double-click, which will just open or import the file), just as in Explorer. These small enhancements are one of the main productivity benefits provided by the Windows 9x interface.

The name of the selected file is shown in the File name list box just below the main window. You'll also notice that there is now a most recently used list of the last five files and/or paths accessed. If you want to see only files of a certain format, select that format from the Files of type drop-down list. For some file formats, this is the only way to reliably open or import files. If you've selected a bitmap to import, another drop-down list is available (just to the right of the File name drop-down list) that allows you to choose which part of the image to import. This process will be discussed later in this chapter. New to CorelDRAW 9 is a Sort type drop-down list that lets you choose how the various file types will be sorted. You can choose from a list alphabetized by Extension, alphabetized by Description, organized by the Most Recently used filter, or listing just the Vector, bitmap or animation formats.

 TIP *You can select multiple files for opening or importing by holding down the CTRL key while clicking on each filename.*

To the right of the main display window, a preview of the selected file will be displayed if the Preview check box is checked. Some file formats do not provide a preview, and those that do can sometimes be saved without a preview header. In those cases, you'll just see a large X in the preview window.

If you've chosen not to see all options, the dialog box will be empty except for the Open or Import and Cancel buttons. However, if the Options button shows two arrows pointed inward (<<), the dialog box contains the maximum amount of information, and clicking the Options button will decrease the amount of information shown. If the arrows are instead pointing outward (>>), click the Options button to expand the dialog box.

The first additional option is the Image Size information box. Any time you have a bitmap selected (or a file with a bitmap header), this area will show you the image size in pixels and the color depth. Note that this information will appear only in the Import dialog box as you cannot open a bitmap in CorelDRAW.

 TIP *If you want to work with a bitmap, you'll have to either import it into CorelDRAW or use Corel PHOTO-PAINT to open it.*

Below the image size information is another information area that shows the file format. This information can be especially helpful when you have not specified a particular file format. If the format contains subformats that can be identified, they will be shown as well.

Some file formats allow notes to be stored with the file. If a file with stored notes is selected, they will be displayed in the large Notes textbox.

At the lower-left corner of the dialog box is a check box labeled Link to high-resolution file for output using OPI. OPI stands for Open Prepress Interface.

This feature will commonly be used when you have a service bureau scan files for you at a high resolution. The bureau will give you a low-resolution version of the file for placement within your document. If you import with this option checked, the larger file can be substituted by the service bureau when they output your file.

The first option gives you the ability to import a bitmap but to Link Bitmap Externally. If the external file changes, so will the image inside of CorelDRAW. And since CorelDRAW saves only a small proxy image, your CorelDRAW files will be much smaller than if you imported the bitmap without linking. On bitmap formats and files where linking is available, the Link Bitmap Externally check box will be available. Chapter 22 supplies more information on working with externally linked bitmaps.

If a bitmap contains several different layers or floating objects, you can flatten the image by checking the Combine multi-layer bitmap. Remember: if you want to have irregularly shaped bitmaps, do not check this option. You also have the ability to either Apply embedded ICC profile or Extract embedded ICC profile. This gives you the choice of keeping any color profiles that were used in saving the image. This will usually be a bitmap file saved from either CorelDRAW, Corel PHOTO-PAINT, or Adobe Photoshop.

Several other options are available. When you are importing files that contain multiple layers or pages, you have the option to Maintain layers and pages. This is turned on by default. Note that it is grayed out for file formats when it doesn't apply. Bitmaps can have a watermark stored within their data so that the creator of the image can be identified. When you've selected a bitmap for import, the Check for Watermark option is available. If you would like CorelDRAW to look inside the bitmap for a watermark, select this option.

A few filters will bring up another dialog box after the original Open/Import dialog box. If you find that all you are doing is accepting the default settings, you may want to avoid this extra dialog box. Simply check the Suppress Filter Dialog check box, and the file will be imported using the default settings.

There are a few slight differences between the Open and Import dialog box. Figure 24-2 shows the Open dialog.

In the lower-right of the dialog, you'll notice that several of the options from the Import dialog box have disappeared, and they are replaced by information about the file you are opening. In Figure 24-2 you can see that the selected file is a CorelDRAW 9 file, the amount that the file was compressed, the exact version of CorelDRAW that saved the file, and the language version of the software that saved it. This can be helpful in finding potential problems.

Open Drawing				? X

Look in: Chap20

cd	F20-02.cdr	F20-05.cdr	F20-08.cdr
98620.doc	F20-02.eps	F20-05.eps	F20-08.jpg
BootCamp.cdr	F20-03.cdr	F20-06.cdr	F20-08.tif
CactusFlower.tif	F20-03.tif	F20-06.eps	F20-09.cdr
F20-01.cdr	F20-04.cdr	F20-07.cdr	F20-09.tif
F20-01.tif	F20-04.eps	F20-07.tif	I20-01.cpt

File name: BootCamp.cdr

Files of type: All File Formats

Sort type: Default

Keywords:

Notes:

☐ Open

Cancel

☑ Preview

File Version: Version 9
Compression ratio: 45.6%
Last saved by: CorelDRAW 9 (pc)
                  build 301
Last saved in: English (United
                  States)

☐ Extract embedded ICC profile
☑ Apply embedded ICC profile
☐ Maintain layers and pages

FIGURE 24-2   The Open dialog box

Placing Imported Files

In earlier versions of CorelDRAW, an imported file would automatically be placed on the page. Now you get a special cursor with an attached filename that allows you to precisely place the file. It works much like the Rectangle tool in that you draw from one corner to another. By default, the image will be constrained to its original aspect ratio. Holding down the ALT key will allow you to distort the image.

 TIP   *A good way to import a file and retain its placement on the page is to right-click on the filename in either the Import dialog box or the Scrapbook, and select Import from the pop-up menu. If you press the SPACEBAR or ENTER key, the file will be placed and sized automatically, just like in the older versions of CorelDRAW.*

If you have chosen to import multiple files, the process of placing files will continue until all files have been imported. For those who would rather just see the images, a double-click will import the file in its original size, as in previous versions. Dragging the file from the Scrapbook with the left mouse button will place the file in the position in which you drop it.

Special Considerations for Particular Formats

Many of the file formats are straightforward. Others require special attention when you import them. This section describes the most commonly used formats that require special handling. The other formats are described in the help files, should you require further information.

CorelDRAW CDR and CDX Formats

The CDR format is CorelDRAW's native format, but each version of CorelDRAW that has been released includes a new format. CorelDRAW 9 can read only files created in version 3 and higher. If you need to access older files, you'll need CorelDRAW 5 or earlier. A CDR file will occasionally become corrupted and cause errors during opening or importing. If CorelDRAW 9 encounters a corrupt object, it will try to skip that object and continue opening the file. Most of the time this will allow you to open a file that previously could not be opened. Then you'll just need to find out which object was skipped and recreate it.

 NOTE   *You may have trouble opening some files from CorelDRAW 3 and 4. It is a good idea to keep a copy of CorelDRAW 5 around just in case you need to convert these files.*

CDX files are simply compressed CDR files. Files in this format are used on some of Corel's Artshow CDs.

Corel CMX and CPX Formats

The CMX format was used for the clipart that was supplied with CorelDRAW in past versions. You can also save files in this format, but it does have some limitations. Effects are not kept live. This means that if you have a Blend effect in your file, it will be saved as a group of objects rather than as a blend. Clipart that was originally created with blends can then be difficult to edit since the blends become just a group of objects. Since CorelDRAW 8 provides clipart in CDR format, this should be less of a issue than in the past. CMX is useful for files that you want to load in Corel PHOTO-PAINT or Corel VENTURA. One benefit of CMX files is that layers will be retained, whereas the layers in imported CDR files will not be used.

CPX is just a compressed version of CMX.

Adobe Illustrator, PostScript Interpreted, and EPS Formats

You'll come across files in EPS format quite often. How you handle them can vary greatly, however, because there are several variations of EPS, and each is quite different from the next.

Adobe Illustrator files are sometimes given the .eps extension, and sometimes they're given the .ai extension. However, the contents are the same. The Illustrator format is actually a small subset of EPS.

Since Illustrator has been one of the most popular design packages on the Macintosh, the AI format has been one of the best ways to share files across platforms. Early versions of CorelDRAW do a poor job of accurately importing AI files, but much has been done to improve the filter in CorelDRAW 9, so you should be able to import AI files with few problems. You must make sure, however, to select the AI format so the files don't get confused with the other variations of EPS.

The worst problem you'll now find in working with AI files is the differences in font names. Panose should help you solve the problem, but it still won't always choose the right font for you. As long as you haven't chosen to suppress the Filters dialog box, you'll have the opportunity to choose the fonts that are substituted.

True EPS files are normally treated like a black box. When they are imported by a program, the data is basically just stored, and a low-resolution header is displayed on the screen if a header is stored in the file. Then when the document is printed, the actual EPS data is sent to the printer. If you don't print to a PostScript printer, the low-resolution header is printed instead. This is how CorelDRAW handles an EPS file if you choose Encapsulated PostScript (EPS). But there is another way.

The PostScript Interpreted filter will actually convert the contents of the file into editable objects. Note that this won't magically convert bitmaps into vector objects, it will just store the bitmap in the CorelDRAW file. Most of the time, this process works fairly well. The main problem is that a large number of objects can be created. This is not a bug in CorelDRAW, but rather is the result of the way the data is stored in the EPS file. You'll also notice that the PostScript Interpreted filter is resource intensive. If your system is low on memory, it could crash. The more complex the information in the EPS file, the harder it is to interpret the file, and the longer it takes to interpret. So if it seems to be taking a long time to import a file, just wait. If something goes wrong, you'll definitely know it.

CorelDRAW 9 enables the PostScript Interpreted filter to handle multiple-page files including color separations.

Which PostScript Filter Should You Use?

Since there are three different PostScript filters to choose from, many users are confused as to which one they should use. If you know the file came from Illustrator, use the Adobe Illustrator filter. If you want to edit any other type of file, or if the origin is unknown, use the PostScript Interpreted filter. Lastly, if you just want to place the image and print it, use the Encapsulated PostScript filter.

Bitmap Formats

Bitmaps work differently from vector files. They are always rectangular, even though they may seem not to be. Areas that are white in the bitmap really consist of white pixels, and they will cover up objects behind them. There are ways to make bitmaps into odd shapes. PowerClips are discussed in Chapter 20, and the Bitmap Color Mask is discussed in Chapter 22. With these effects, you can eliminate the parts of a bitmap you don't want. You can also use the Shape tool to crop a bitmap into an odd shape, as described in Chapter 7. The best way to get an odd-shaped bitmap is to work with the image in PHOTO-PAINT and save the file in CPT format with a mask or as floating objects. Complete instructions on how to do this can be found at the companion Web site, http://www.unleash.com.

When you import a bitmap, CorelDRAW looks at the size of the bitmap in pixels and the resolution in dots per inch. It then sizes the bitmap based on those numbers. So if you have a bitmap that is 600 pixels by 400 pixels at 200 dpi, it will be sized to 3 inches by 2 inches in CorelDRAW. You can easily enlarge or reduce the bitmap by grabbing the handles as with any other object, but remember that the exact number of pixels will not change. Therefore, if you make the object larger, it may look very pixelated, and if you make it smaller, extra data will be stored unnecessarily, so the best thing to do is to size the bitmap appropriately in Corel PHOTO-PAINT before importing it into CorelDRAW. You can also do some of this from the Bitmap menu which is described in Chapter 22.

If you will be outputting the file to a CMYK printer, you'll want to convert it to CMYK in Corel PHOTO-PAINT. If the destination is a grayscale device, convert the file into a grayscale bitmap. The important thing is that you will most likely need to prepare the file in Corel PHOTO-PAINT before using it in CorelDRAW. Although CorelDRAW 9 has capabilities for working with bitmaps (see Chapter 22), this kind of editing is still best done in Corel PHOTO-PAINT. Remember that at its heart, CorelDRAW is designed for editing vector images and Corel PHOTO-PAINT is designed for editing bitmap images. You are best served by using the tool that is designed for the job.

Cropping Bitmaps

At times, you'll want to import a bitmap, but you'll want only a certain area of it instead of the whole thing. In this case, you'll want to crop the image. You can do this prior to importing in Corel PHOTO-PAINT, but you can also crop the image when it is imported into CorelDRAW. After you select the bitmap you wish to import, select Crop from the drop-down list to the right of the filename. After you click the Import button, you'll be presented with another dialog box, shown in Figure 24-3.

There are two ways to crop an image. You can grab the handles surrounding the image and drag them so they surround the area you wish to keep. You can also specify the size to keep by entering the Top, Left, Width, and Height values for the image. By default, the Units value will be pixels, but you can change to any measurement system that CorelDRAW supports. If you want to bring in the whole image, simply click the Select All button. The new size of the image in bytes is listed near the bottom of the dialog box. Note that this is the uncompressed size.

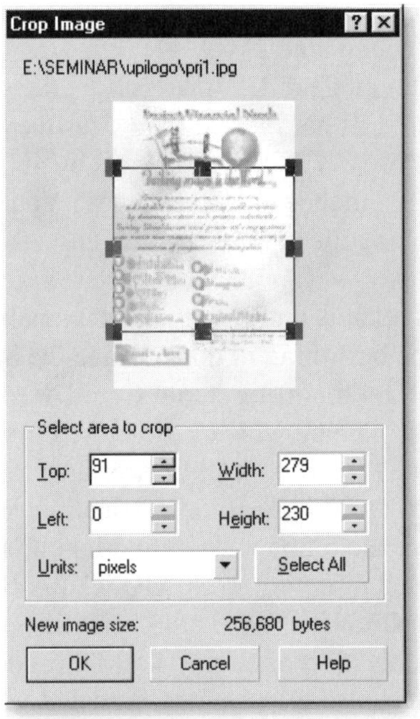

FIGURE 24-3   The Crop Image dialog box

NOTE   *Cropping an image during import will reduce the size of the file, while cropping an image with the Shape tool only hides portions of the image. If you use the Crop Bitmap command after cropping the image with the Shape tool, the extra data will truly be thrown out.*

Resampling Bitmaps

Sometimes the bitmap you wish to import will not be the correct size. If it is too small, you may want to find a way to get a larger original without resampling, since resampling will degrade the quality of the image. You can use resampling to reduce the size and still retain a good-quality image, at least to a point.

When you select a bitmap to import, choose Resample from the drop-down list to the right of the filename. Once you click Import, you'll be presented with a dialog box similar to that shown in Figure 24-4.

The first section allows you to change the width or height of the image either using the specified units or specifying a percentage of the current size. If you check the Maintain Aspect Ratio check box, any changes made to one of the values will also affect the other value.

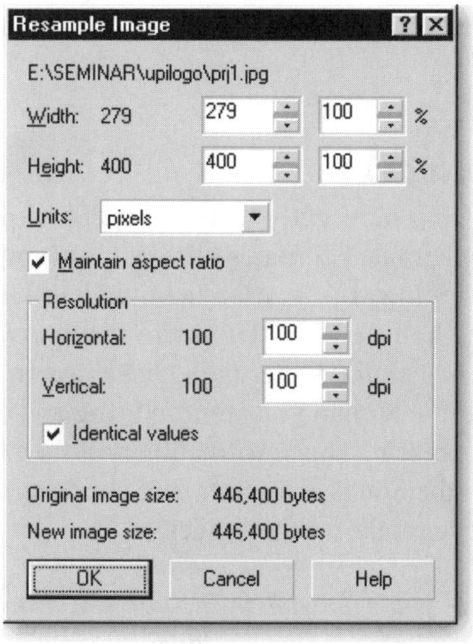

Resample Image   ? ✕

E:\SEMINAR\upilogo\prj1.jpg

Width: 279   279   100   %

Height: 400   400   100   %

Units: pixels

✔ Maintain aspect ratio

Resolution

Horizontal: 100   100   dpi

Vertical: 100   100   dpi

✔ Identical values

Original image size: 446,400 bytes

New image size: 446,400 bytes

OK   Cancel   Help

FIGURE 24-4   The Resample Image dialog box

The next section lets you set the resolution of the image. You learned in Chapter 23 that the resolution of an image is, for the most part, a meaningless number. Changing the resolution does not necessarily change the size of the bitmap. This setting is meaningful only when you know the output resolution (the line screen, not the dpi) that will be used to print the image. If you do wish to change the resolution, you can do so in both the horizontal and vertical directions. If you want both values to be the same—and rarely would you not want this—then check the Identical Values check box.

You are informed of the original and new sizes of the image in bytes at the bottom of the dialog box. Note that these are uncompressed values, and the saved file may be much smaller.

Corel PHOTO-PAINT CPT Format

When you import a .cpt file containing floating objects, you'll notice that you have a group of objects on the page. The floating objects remain floating and cut out in CorelDRAW. This provides a fantastic way to touch up artwork with the precision of CorelDRAW. It is also a great way to delete an unwanted background from a photograph. You'll need to ungroup the various objects and delete the background object if you want to eliminate the "white box" or other unwanted background images. Remember that this only works if you have created floating objects in Corel PHOTO-PAINT first.

Embedding Watermarks

A new technology has emerged recently that allows digital photographs to have a watermark embedded in them that contains copyright information. If you'd like to learn more about the technology that is used in both CorelDRAW and Corel PHOTO-PAINT, visit the home page of Digimarc at http://www.digimarc.com.

When you check the Check for Watermark check box in the Import dialog box, CorelDRAW will look at the bitmap you are importing and extract any copyright information that may be present. This information will then be displayed as part of the object's properties in the Status Bar. Note that checking for this information will make the import process take a little longer.

 TIP *For those of you who wish to include watermarks on your own images, a plug-in filter has been included that works in both CorelDRAW and Corel PHOTO-PAINT. Note that you'll need to contact Digimarc to purchase a serial number to embed.*

PhotoCD (PCD) Format

Kodak created the PhotoCD format for storing 35mm photographs on a compact disc that can be viewed on television. The consumer market never really caught on to Photo CDs, but the graphics market soon found that this was a great way to store photographs. The problem with the files is that since they were developed for viewing on television screens, they are not really optimized for a printing press. With the controls provided by CorelDRAW, this limitation can be overcome.

After you select a PhotoCD file for import, you'll see a dialog box similar to the one in Figure 24-5. The PhotoCD image shown is stored on the book's CD as julia.pcd.

You'll see the original image and a preview of the image to be imported at the top of the dialog box. Below the preview, at the right, is a drop-down list for selecting the size of the image you want to import. PhotoCD files can store up to six resolutions of the image within a single file, from the tiny Wallet size (192 x 128 pixels) to the huge Billboard size (6,144 x 4,096 pixels). Most files contain only five sizes, with the largest being the Poster size (3,072 x 2,048 pixels).

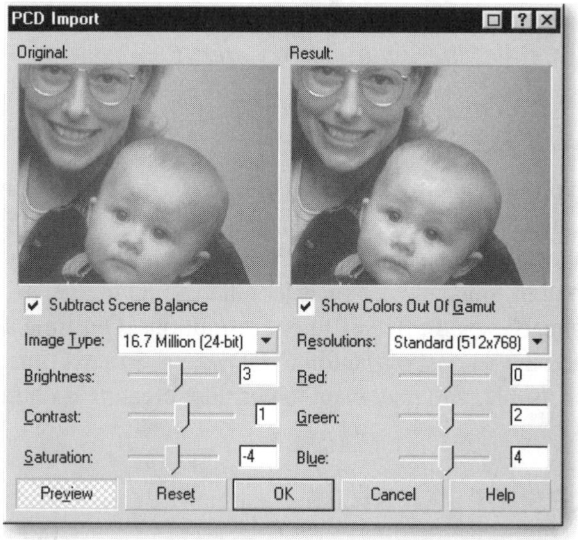

FIGURE 24-5 The PCD Import dialog box

Another drop-down list below the original image lets you choose the color depth of the file, from 16.7 million colors to 256 colors to 256 grayscale. Sometimes it is best to choose 16.7 million colors even if you will be using fewer colors in the final image. This way all manipulations you make to the file will be performed using the highest quality.

Now you can make adjustments to the color. You can adjust the red, green, and blue tints in the image as well as the brightness, saturation, and contrast. All of these changes require you to enter a number. Note that the levels of contrast are much more limited than the other sliders.

When the image was originally scanned, the scanner operator included information to balance the scene. By checking the Subtract Scene Balance check box, you can remove this information. Check the Show Colors Out Of Gamut check box to make sure that the adjustments you've made are valid. When you click Preview, any colors that are out of gamut (that is, they can't be displayed correctly on your screen) will change to blue or red. Continue to make adjustments until no colors are out of gamut.

When you click OK, the image will be brought into CorelDRAW with all adjustments made. Since some of these adjustments are very processor intensive, it may take a little while for the import process to complete on slower systems.

 TIP *You might want to import the PhotoCD file into Corel PHOTO-PAINT first and adjust the colors so that they are just perfect. Then save the file as a TIF or CPT file, and import it into CorelDRAW.*

Creating Your Own Photo CDs

We recently had a project where we needed to scan 30 images for a brochure. We were given slides, negatives, and transparencies. Because we don't have a slide or transparency scanner, we chose to create a Photo CD instead. This was a great solution to the problem, since the cost was less than $3 an image, and we now have a permanent copy of each scan in five different resolutions. Our time alone for a scan would easily exceed the $3 cost of the Photo CD scans. So next time you're faced with a project such as this, you may want to consider creating a Photo CD.

Word Processor Formats

The Import dialog box lists a number of text and word processing filters, including all of the modern word processor formats and many long-gone formats as well. When you import the text from these formats, most of the original formatting is retained. We suggest that the person who creates the word processor file should not do any formatting. Do the formatting in the final destination for the text, which is now CorelDRAW.

When the file is imported, it will be placed on the page so that it fills the page size. If the text won't fit on the current page, more pages will be created until there are enough to hold all of the text. These text boxes will be automatically linked to flow from one frame to the next. Unfortunately, there is no way to tell CorelDRAW not to create these extra pages, and often you will need to delete the extra frames, and recreate them where you need them using a different size.

A way around this problem is to first create a paragraph text frame and then import the text from the Edit Text dialog box. If you use this method, the text will be placed into the frame you drew, and no other frames or pages will be created. This new method makes page layout in CorelDRAW 9 much easier than in past versions. Chapter 5 contains a project that will teach you how to do page layout.

We've explained each of the common types of import filters. The individual filters may have specific limitations. Check the Help | Technical Support section of the help files to get detailed information on any of the filters.

Saving Files

When you choose File | Save (CTRL-S), the Save Drawing dialog box you see will be nearly identical to the Open/Import dialog box you explored earlier in this chapter. All of the features of the Windows Explorer are just as applicable here as in the Open/Import dialog box. An example of the Save Drawing dialog box is shown in Figure 24-6.

Below the main window is the File name textbox. Type in name for your file, and feel free to make it as long as 255 characters. You can either add the .cdr extension yourself or leave it blank and let CorelDRAW do it for you.

 TIP   *If you want to give a file a name that doesn't include a .cdr extension or that includes another extension, place the entire name in double quotation marks.*

By default, the file will be saved as a CorelDRAW (.cdr) file, but you can choose other types from the Files of type drop-down list. Note that in previous versions, you had to export files if you wanted a format other than .cdr, which is no longer necessary. You also have the same Sort type drop-down list as in the Open and Import dialog boxes.

The Save Drawing dialog box

The Keywords and Notes sections allow you to specify information about the files. Keywords are words that you can use to search for a particular topic. Thus, if you had a picture of a German Shepherd, you might want to enter **German Shepherd, Dog**, and **Animal** as keywords. In the Notes box, you can enter a more detailed description of the image. These notes will be displayed in the Open Drawing dialog box and can be especially helpful when you have a number of files with similar names or when you want to pass a file to another user.

At the right side of the dialog box are two drop-down lists for choosing which version of the CorelDRAW file format to use and how big of a thumbnail to include. Only versions 5, 6, 7, 8, and 9 of CorelDRAW are supported. If you need to save to an older format, you'll need a copy of CorelDRAW 5. First you'll have to save to CorelDRAW 5 format and then use CorelDRAW 5 to save to an older format. There are a number of features not supported in older versions, so going back any further than CorelDRAW 5 is a bad idea if you want the file to look the same. Thumbnails are small bitmaps of the file that can help you to identify the file in the File Open dialog box or the Scrapbook. They are not required, and leaving them out makes the file slightly smaller.

Four other options are available in this main dialog box. You can save only those objects that are currently selected by checking the Selected only check box.

This can be handy if you have a certain element in your drawing that you wish to save for future use. Just make sure to change the name so you don't overwrite the file containing the whole drawing. And you need to select the objects before attempting to save the file, or the Selected only check box will not be available. If you've used a color profile and you're saving to a format that supports embedding of the color profile, check the Embed ICC profile. The No White Spaces, Special Characters check box will make sure that the filename doesn't contain either white spaces or special characters that could cause problems for web servers. Last, you have the ability to embed the fonts you've used in the .cdr file itself (using the TrueDoc technology discussed in Chapter 32). Just check the Embed Fonts using TrueDoc check box.

There are more options that are considered advanced functions; click the Advanced button to access these additional features. Note that all of the features apply to CorelDRAW 9 files but not necessarily to older formats. The Options Save dialog box is shown in Figure 24-7.

The first option in this dialog box is Save Presentation Exchange (CMX). You'll learn more about the CMX format a little later, but for now note that having this extra data is useful if you plan to use the .cdr file in other Corel products such

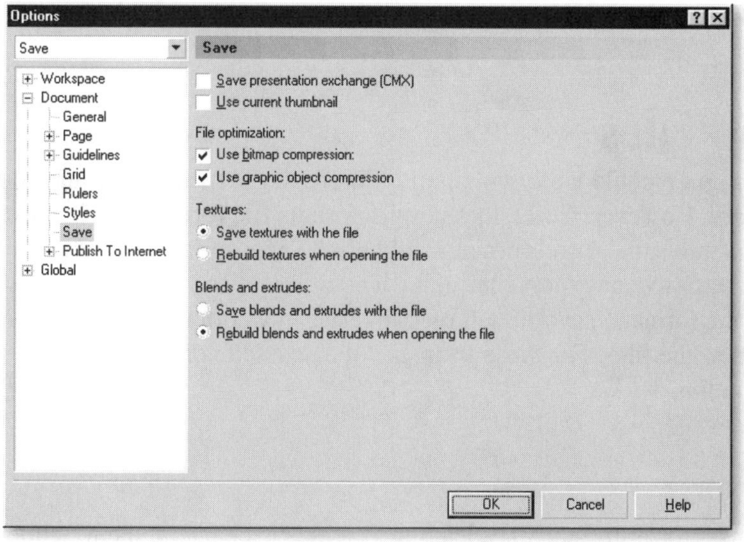

FIGURE 24-7   The Options Save dialog box

as Corel PHOTO-PAINT or Corel VENTURA. Otherwise, it just enlarges the file by a factor of 1.5 or 2.

If the Use current thumbnail option is checked, CorelDRAW will not generate a new thumbnail each time you save a file. By default, this option is turned off.

With each release of CorelDRAW, the file format has produced files that were larger than those in the previous version. This expansion was especially noticeable in the move from CorelDRAW 5 to CorelDRAW 6. Going from a 16-bit file format to a 32-bit file format nearly doubled the file sizes.

Both bitmaps and vector objects can be compressed using LZW technology. This is the same compression format that is used by the PKZIP program and .tif files. With only this type of compression, you should see a significant reduction in file size. Texture fills are nothing more than bitmaps. You can have them saved as bitmaps in the file or have them regenerated when the file is opened. Obviously, regenerating them can take some time, but it can save a significant amount of space on your hard drive. Similarly, blends and extrudes can create a large number of new objects; now you can save just the original objects with the information to rebuild the effect when you open the file. Again, this is a great way to save space if you have the extra time.

 NOTE *There is one other option that can appear. If you have done anything in the VBA editor, you will see the Save With Embedded VBA Project option. If it appears, it will be checked by default.*

Exporting Files

If every program could work with native CorelDRAW files, exporting wouldn't be necessary. However, Corel does not disclose its file format, and in addition, in some applications the Corel format would not be appropriate. Therefore, Corel enables you to save or export files in a wide variety of formats. This section describes the formats that you will probably use most often, and explains how to best optimize the files. For those formats not discussed here, check the help files for information.

AI Format

Adobe Illustrator is currently the leading graphics package on the Macintosh (but Corel is now chasing close behind). The AI format is also used in many other applications, especially in sign-cutting and graphics software. Corel's export filter

24

for AI was poor in past versions, but they've taken great pains to rewrite the filter for maximum compatibility.

When you select Exporting to AI, you'll see the dialog box shown in Figure 24-8.

The Compatibility drop-down list shows each version of Adobe Illustrator that was released prior to CorelDRAW 9. By default, it selects Adobe Illustrator 7.0, but if you are creating files for users with an earlier version, simply select that version from the list. You can also select whether the destination is a PC or Macintosh platform.

You can leave text as text or have it converted to curves when you export. Remember that font compatibility may be a problem if the file is opened on the Macintosh. Spot colors can be automatically converted to their process equivalents. Remember that these colors will be quite different than they would be if they were printed with the true spot color inks. If effects, such as dotted lines, have been used "as" or "for" outlines, you can select Simulate outline effects to get a close approximation. Similarly, some types of fills do not have an equivalent feature in Illustrator. So checking Simulate complex filled curves will try to match the fills as closely as possible. If you have included bitmap images in your file, they can be

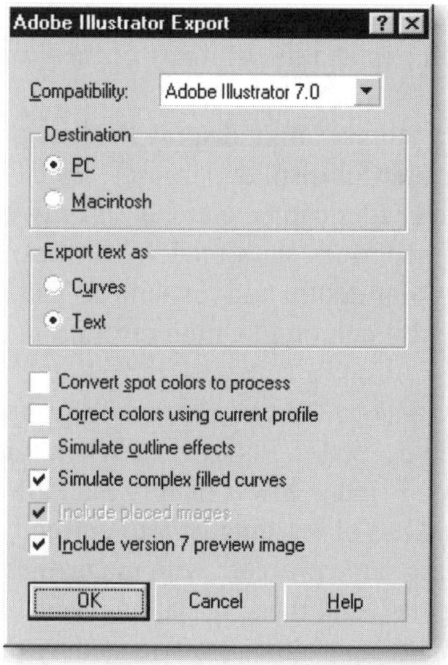

FIGURE 24-8   The Adobe Illustrator Export dialog box

included in the Illustrator file, but note that this is supported only in newer versions of Illustrator. Lastly, you have the choice of including a preview image if you are exporting to Illustrator 7.0 format.

EPS Format

Encapsulated PostScript, or EPS, is the best file format to use for maximum compatibility with all of the features contained in CorelDRAW. It can be used by almost all programs on the PC and the Macintosh, but it does require a PostScript printer to print correctly.

Many Macintosh-biased service bureaus may ask you to convert your .cdr files to EPS format for output. This is not a good idea because it means that the service bureau is going to place the file in another program to print them. There may be limitations in the program where the EPS file is placed. For example, some page layout programs will not color separate an EPS file containing RGB bitmaps. So the service bureau may blame Corel's EPS filter when the problem is a limitation of the page layout program. Instead of creating an EPS file, you could also print to a PostScript file and provide that to your service bureau for direct output.

When you choose EPS, you'll see the dialog box shown in Figure 24-9. Notice that many of the options are the same as when printing to a PostScript printer. You'll find a more detailed explanation of many of these options in Chapter 26 when we discuss printing.

Since most operating systems cannot display PostScript files on the screen, EPS files can contain a header for display purposes. By default, the Include header check box is checked. The header can be either a .tif or .wmf file. TIF files provide maximum compatibility since Macs can't read WMF files. When you use them, you can specify the type (color depth) and resolution. The bitmap display can be quite good if you choose 8-bit color and a high resolution, although doing so is not always a good idea.

We've had bad luck with some so-called graphics professionals who assume that all EPS files should be opened in Photoshop. When this is done, all they get is the bitmap header, which is much lower quality than the embedded PostScript data. They blame Corel instead of learning how to correctly use their software. We've also experienced this same problem with magazines for which we've written. If we are the "experts" and these so-called professionals aren't willing to listen, we can only imagine the problems experienced by the average users. We just can't stress enough that the header is supposed to be used only for a low-resolution screen preview.

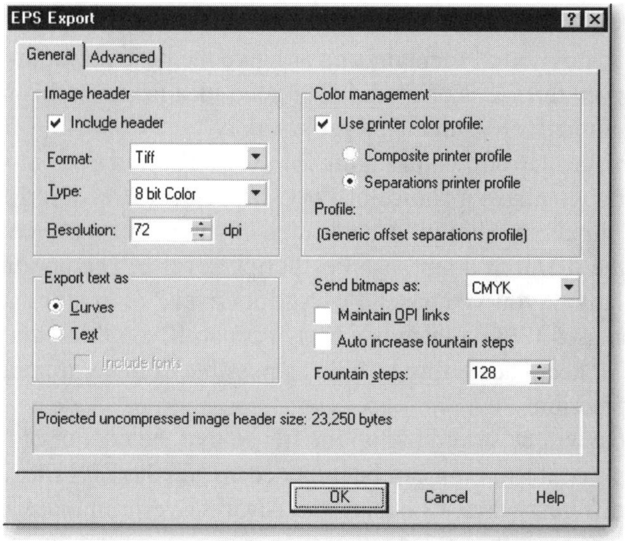

FIGURE 24-9   The EPS Export dialog box

The header you include is also used when the file is printed to a non-PostScript printer. Because the TIF header may look crude, you can also specify a WMF header. This approach provides the best onscreen display and printing since WMF is a vector format, but since it is a Windows-only format, these files have limited compatibility with layout software and should be used with caution.

Just as with the Adobe Illustrator filter, you can convert text to curves or leave it as text. If you choose Text, the fonts can be embedded within the file so that the recipient doesn't need them, but this does increase file size. In most instances, it is best to leave the text as text, but if you have very short blocks of text and numerous fonts, converting to curves is a good idea.

In the upper-right of the dialog is the choice of color management. You can choose to use a color profile and if so, either the composite or the separations profile. More information on these color profiles can be found in Chapter 8.

If the file contains bitmaps, you can choose to send them to the EPS file as CMYK, RGB, or Grayscale. Your choice should be determined by how the file will be output. For example, we created all of the artwork for this book in color. But it will be output in grayscale, so we exported the bitmaps as grayscale. If you were exporting the EPS to be used to create a PDF file, you'd want everything stored as RGB. If you've placed bitmaps that were scanned by the service bureau and given to use as low-resolution OPI images, make sure to check the Maintain OPI links check box. The Auto increase fountain steps check box will automatically create enough fountain steps to give the best output on the selected output device when the file is printed. It is a good idea to check this box. Lastly, you can set the number of Fountain steps manually.

On the Advanced tab shown in Figure 24-10, you'll find even more options. For compatibility, you have a choice of PostScript Level 1, PostScript Level 2, or PostScript 3. Your choice should be determined by the output device that will be used to output the file. If in doubt, use PostScript Level 1! The option to compress bitmaps is available if you've chosen PostScript Level 2 or PostScript 3. Note that the compression uses JPEG, which is a lossy format. If you think that you must compress the file, keep the quality as high as possible (a lower number). It is best to not use compression.

The username will be stored within the file so that the creator of the file is recorded. Trapping information can be included within the EPS file, and is applied in two different ways. Choosing the Always overprint black option prints black ink on top of any other color rather than trying to cut out the text or other

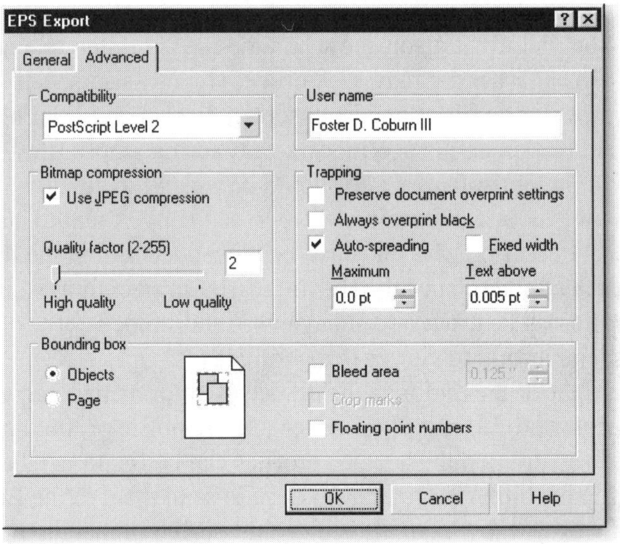

FIGURE 24-10   EPS Export Advanced dialog box

detailed object. Since adding black does not change the color much, this is the best way to trap small black text on a colored background. Spread traps are also supported, through the Auto-spreading option. You can specify the maximum width of the trap and the point at which text will begin to be trapped. The first option, Preserve Document Overprint Settings, will keep any manual trapping you've done when checked. For more information on trapping options, see Chapter 26.

The size of the .eps file is stored in the first few lines of data as the bounding box. You can store the size as the size of the whole page or just the objects on the page. You can also specify that a bleed area of a certain size and crop marks are used. Typically the bounding box size is an integer, but by checking Floating point numbers, you can store it as a floating-point value. Several other options are also available in the Print dialog box, as described in Chapter 26. Since printing to a PostScript printer and printing EPS files are similar, it is no surprise that these options are in both dialog boxes. See Chapter 26 for a full discussion on these features.

CMX Format

Earlier you saw how .cmx files can be embedded within a .cdr file. You can also save them as standalone files. The thing to remember about .cmx files is that any effects in the file will not be saved as live effects. Thus, Blend effects will still look the same when a .cmx file is opened, but they will be difficult to change. The same is true for Extrude, Fit Text to Path, and other effects—so whenever you save a file in .cmx, you should make sure you have a .cdr file as well.

PDF Format

Corel has added a great new filter for exporting to PDF. As it is quite in-depth, we have devoted Chapter 27 to describing the process. Please note that there are two ways to create PDF files. Do not use the export filter! Use the Publish to PDF process described in Chapter 27.

Corel Image Map and HTML Formats

These filters are used to create special items for inclusion on a Web page. They will be covered in depth in Chapter 33.

TTF and PFB Formats

CorelDRAW is a great program for font creation, although this feature is hidden
from obvious view. CorelDRAW doesn't contain many of the high-end features
found in programs such as Macromedia's Fontographer, but it is great at creating
the font characters. The help files contain extensive information on how to prepare
a proper character for export. Search the Index tab for "font conventions,
becoming familiar with."

NOTE   *These filters are not installed by default. If you are not seeing
them in the list of supported types, you'll need to do a custom installation
and add them.*

Once you've created a character (you can create only one at a time), select
either the PFB (PostScript) or TTF (TrueType) export filter. When you click
Export, you'll see the Options dialog box shown in Figure 24-11.

The Family name entry is the main name of the font, without any weight
attributes. If the font contains symbol characters rather than alphabetical characters,
check the Symbol Font check box. Only four styles are available in the Style
drop-down list.

This dialog box also provides Grid size and Space width settings. These values
will differ between the PostScript (1000) and TrueType (2048) formats. Only in
rare circumstances will you want to change these values.

Click OK, and a second dialog box appears, as shown in Figure 24-12.

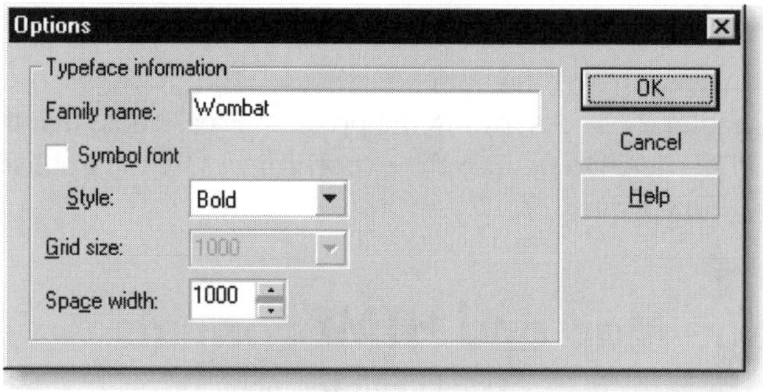

FIGURE 24-11   The Options dialog box

24

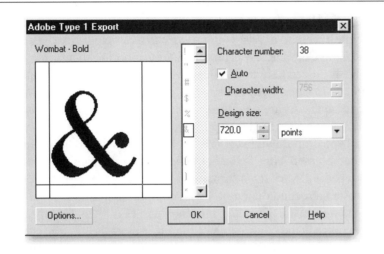

FIGURE 24-12   The Adobe Type 1 Export dialog box

The left side of the dialog box displays the character and three lines. The two vertical lines represent the left and right sidebearings of the character. You cannot move the left sidebearing, but you can adjust the right one numerically. To do so, uncheck the Auto check box, and modify the Character width value. You'll notice that the right sidebearing moves to the left when you enter low numbers and to the right when you enter high numbers.

You also need to assign the character a position in the font. You can do so either through the scrolling list of characters or by entering the ASCII code in the Character number box.

Last, you need to specify a design size. The default value is to 720 points, and if you've followed the instructions provided in the help file, you should leave this value unchanged. Click OK to write the changes to the font file.

You'll need to repeat this process for each character of the font, making sure to use the same names each time. Also ensure that you place every new character in a different ASCII position so one doesn't overwrite an existing character. When you are finished, install the font using the processes described in Chapter 32, and then start using your new font.

Bitmap Format

Quite often, you'll want to export your artwork to a bitmap format. You can do so in two ways. Using CorelDRAW, you can simply export to that format; this method will be discussed here in detail. However, the best way is to open a .cdr (or .cmx) file directly in Corel PHOTO-PAINT. The dialog boxes in both instances are similar, but the results are not always the same.

When you select one of the bitmap formats, you may be presented with the Compression Type drop-down list if it is applicable to that flavor of bitmap. If you want the file compressed, choose the compression format from that list. The compression types will vary from format to format, and some formats, such as JPEG, will present a second dialog box with compression information.

For all bitmap formats, the dialog box shown in Figure 24-13 appears.

Your first choice is the color depth of the file. Select the appropriate choice from the drop-down list. Remember that your choice should reflect the palette you have used. Therefore, if you want to export to RGB, you should use an RGB palette to select your colors in CorelDRAW. For color depths other than 16 million or CMYK, the Dithered option is available. This helps to retain the look of the original image in the lower color formats. However, this option is not always desirable, such as when creating a GIF of the smallest size. You also have the option of using the color profile to convert RGB colors to CMYK or vice versa.

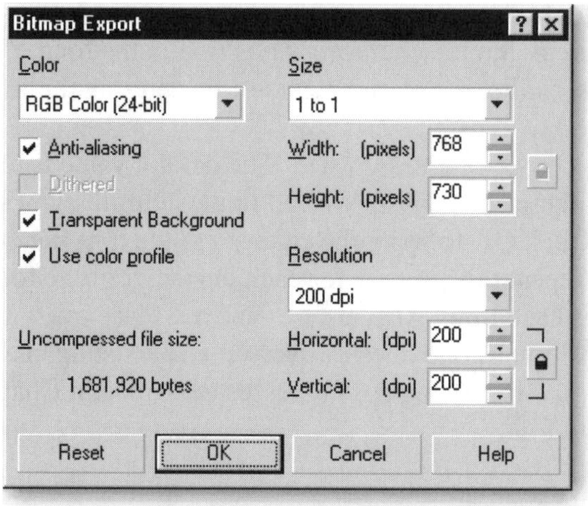

FIGURE 24-13   The Bitmap Export dialog box

You can also choose the size of the image from a drop-down list. Several popular monitor resolutions are in the list, as are 1 to 1 and Custom. Most of the time, you'll want to use 1 to 1. The fixed monitor sizes are of little use unless you want your images to fit that aspect ratio. Also, you really need to design your images with exporting in mind so that you use the correct aspect ratio in CorelDRAW. When using the Custom option, make sure that you keep the lock locked so that the aspect ratio is retained. If you want the image to be distorted, unlock the lock. If you select Keep The Lock Locked, entering a value in either the Width or Height box will automatically change the value in both boxes.

Resolution rears its ugly head again in this dialog box. We can't stress often enough that this value is quite often deceptive. Several of the popular resolutions are listed in the drop-down list, and Custom can be found at the bottom. With Custom, you can type any resolution you like, down to 1 dpi. Again there is a lock so that the resolution will be the same in both Horizontal and Vertical. Unless you have a very good reason to have mixed resolutions, leave this locked.

Just below the Color drop-down list is the Anti-aliasing check box. If you don't want to introduce any more colors into your image, make sure to leave it unchecked. Adding anti-aliasing can improve the look of line art, but it can hamper the creation of transparent GIF files. You also have the option of having the image Dithered if you are exporting with a color depth less than 24-bit color. Dithering will put two colors close together to simulate other colors. If you are trying to keep files small, it is a bad idea to use dithering because the file compression will not work as well. Transparent Background will retain the irregular shape of the objects being exported if the file format supports the feature. Thus you don't get the dreaded "white box." Lastly, you can choose to Use color profile. Again, the profile is discussed in Chapter 8.

As you are making changes, you'll notice that the projected size of the file is shown at the bottom of the dialog box. Note that this size is for uncompressed files, so if you compress your bitmap, the actual file size should be much smaller.

GIF, JPEG, and PNG Formats

The GIF, JPEG, and PNG formats are all variations on bitmaps. Since they are mainly used when creating artwork for the Internet, they are discussed fully in Chapter 33.

Exporting files properly is the key to using your CorelDRAW artwork in other applications. If the file isn't exported properly, the appearance of the graphics in the file may be changed, or you may not be able to import the file into the application of your choice.

CHAPTER 25

Page Setup

COREL.COM

CorelDRAW 9

CorelDRAW offers a wide variety of paper sizes, including foreign paper sizes. It also includes sizes for envelopes and labels. With the exception of labels, all of the paper sizes can be selected directly from the Property Bar, which is quicker than selecting them from the Options dialog box.

Using the Property Bar to Set Up the Page

The paper size and orientation can be selected directly from the Property Bar. The page setup options are available on the Property Bar only when nothing is selected on the page and the Pick tool is selected from the toolbox. The Paper Size list box is at the far left of the Property Bar. The default page setup is Letter 8.5x11-inch Portrait mode. The Paper Width and Height boxes are to the right of the list box followed by the Portrait and Landscape Orientation buttons. To select a paper size, select the down arrow, and choose a type from the drop-down list. Then choose the orientation you want by clicking the appropriate button. Figure 25-1 shows the Property Bar in its default mode. If you prefer to measure your page in units other than inches, click the down arrow on the Drawing units list box, and pick a unit of measurement.

 NOTE   *If your operating system is in a country which uses units of measurement other than inches then your default unit of measurement will reflect that.*

The only paper sizes missing from the drop-down list on the Property Bar are those for labels. These are not included in this list because of the vast number of label styles available. You can select labels from an Options dialog box that is discussed later in this chapter.

Adding Multiple Pages

Many CorelDRAW users create projects requiring more the one page. Adding pages is easily accomplished by using the Navigator controls at the lower left of the CorelDRAW window. The Navigator shows the total number of pages in your

Paper Size drop-down list   Portrait Orientation button

      Paper Width and   Landscape Orientation button
      Height boxes   Current Page Size Orientation buttons

                    Drawing Units drop-down list

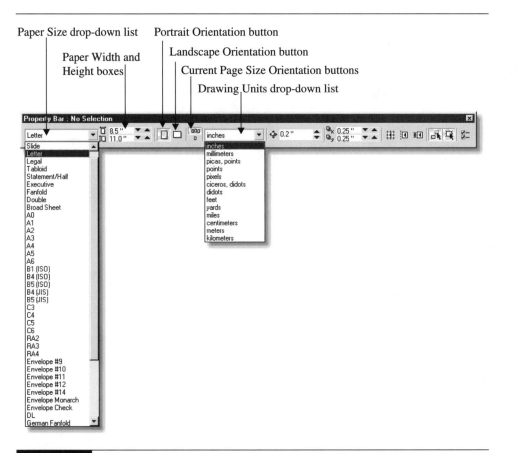

25

FIGURE 25-1   The default Property Bar with nothing selected and the Paper Size and
Drawing Units drop-down lists displayed

document as well as the page you are currently working on. If you're working with
a single page, the Navigator will look like this.

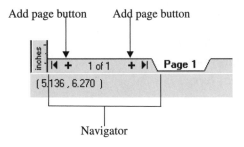

Navigator

Clicking either of the two plus buttons on the Navigator will add a page. If you click the left plus button, a new page will be added before the original page, with the last added page being the one displayed. If you click the right plus button, a page will be added after the original page, and the added page will then display. After you have added a second page to the original, the left plus button will not appear. You can continue adding pages when needed by clicking the right plus button.

Each time you add a page, a new number button appears next to the Navigator with the number of the page displayed. After you have added a page, two more buttons appear at the left of the Navigator. They are called First Page and Last Page buttons. These buttons let you quickly go to either the first or last page of a multiple page document. When you right-click on a page tab, a pop-up menu appears that offers six page options. Listed here are the six options and the functions they perform:

Option	Function
Rename Page	This options displays the Rename Page dialog box that you use to name the page. Naming pages can help you better identify what's on a page. This feature comes in handy when working with documents containing multiple page sizes (see the section called "Adding Custom Size Pages Within a Multi-Page Document," later in the chapter).
Insert Page After	This command is the same as clicking the right plus button on the Navigator. It adds a page after the currently selected page.
Insert Page Before	This command adds a page before the currently selected page. It is also the same as clicking the left plus button on the Navigator when there is a single page.
Delete Page	This option deletes the currently selected page.
Switch Page Orientation	This option switches a portrait page to a landscape page and vice versa and it only changes the current page.
Resize page	This option displays the Resize Page dialog box, allowing you to choose a different page size for current page only.

Figure 25-2 shows the Navigator when three pages have been added to the document. Also shown is the pop-up menu displaying the six options just described.

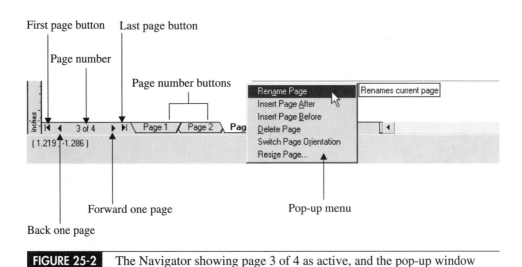

First page button   Last page button

Page number

Page number buttons

Rename Page
Insert Page After
Insert Page Before
Delete Page
Switch Page Orientation
Resize Page...

Renames current page

inches

I◀ ◀ 3 of 4 ▶ ▶I \ Page 1 / Page 2 \ Pag

(1.219 , -1.286)

Forward one page   Pop-up menu

Back one page

FIGURE 25-2   The Navigator showing page 3 of 4 as active, and the pop-up window

Using the Options Dialog Box to Set Up the Page

Five dialog boxes are available for setting up the page. These include page layout styles such as Booklet and Tent Cards, numerous labels styles, and a category called Backgrounds. There are two ways to access these new dialog boxes: The easiest method is to double-click the open document's page border. Figure 25-3 shows the default dialog box as it appears when you double-click the border. The second method involves choosing Layout | Page Setup to get to the same dialog box shown in Figure 25-3. Use Figure 25-3 as a guide to the expanding tree structure as we cover each of the dialog boxes.

Using the Page | Size Dialog Box

Figure 25-3 shows the Page | Size dialog box. Keep in mind that several of the settings in this dialog box are also on the Property Bar. The page options for size are as follows:

■ *Normal Paper/Labels*   The default is Normal Paper. Selecting Labels will take you directly down the directory structure to the Options | Label dialog box. Labels will be disabled if any page has been individually resized or reoriented.

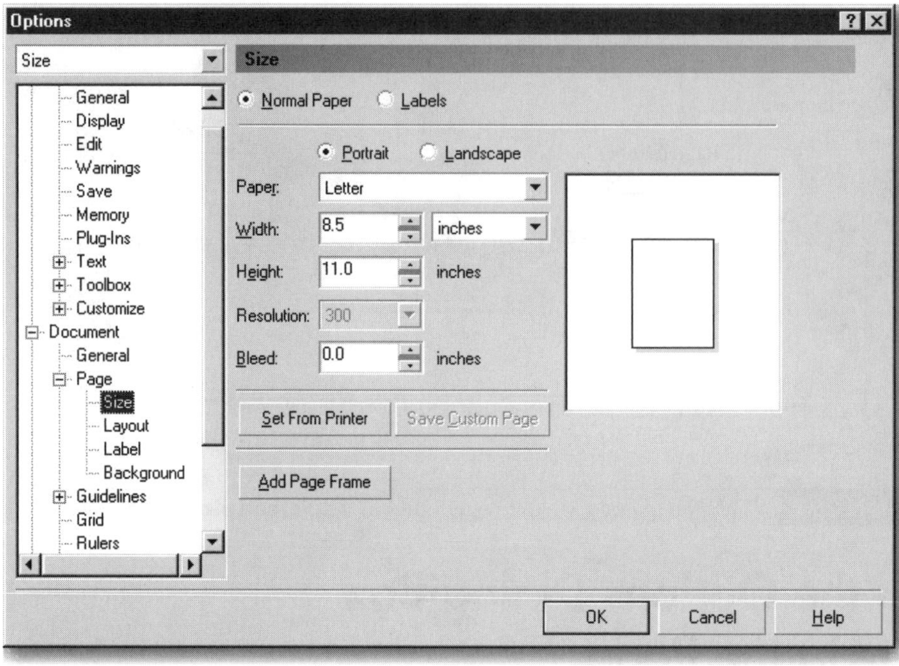

FIGURE 25-3   The Options dialog box with Page I Size selected

■ *Portrait/Landscape*   Enable either of the radio buttons to select the orientation of the page. The preview window at the right displays the orientation selected.

■ *Paper*   Select the down arrow on the list box to scroll through the list of paper sizes.

■ *Width/Height*   The Width and Height boxes are automatically updated to reflect the paper size selected. When you select Custom at the top of the list, you can enter values directly in the number boxes. Measurements are shown in inches by default. You can change to various other measurement systems by selecting them from the drop-down list.

■ *Resolution*   This setting is grayed out unless you have used pixels for page units. If you have used pixels, the resolution you choose controls the Publish to Internet settings when publishing your files to the Internet (see Chapter 33). To set the page resolution for page sizes other than pixels, go to the Options I Document I General page.

■ *Bleed*   This setting allows you to set the amount of page bleed for your documents. Setting a bleed is important only if any part of the drawing goes all the way to an edge of the page. This would include backgrounds (see the section "Using the Page | Background Dialog Box," later in this chapter).

■ *Set From Printer*   This button sets the paper size to the default setting of your default printer. The current setting is not necessarily the default printer setting.

■ *Save Custom Page*   If you use a custom Width or Height setting, click this button to display the Custom page type dialog box. Here you can give your custom page a name, and it will appear in the page size drop-down list along with all the other page sizes. This button will change to "Delete Custom" page when a custom page or any other custom setting is selected in this dialog box.

■ *Add Page Frame*   Click this button to place a rectangle on the page that is the size of the paper in your printer. The page frame is created as the lower-most object on the current layer. This rectangle is an object just like any other object and will be filled with the default fill and outline colors. Remember, it will print just like any other object; therefore, if you are printing on colored paper, you do not use the page frame to represent the paper (see Background Options). You can also quickly add a page frame anytime by double clicking on the Rectangle tool.

Using the Page | Layout Dialog Box

Six different layout styles are available in the Page | Layout dialog box. The default style is Full Page. When you select the down arrow on the list box, you'll get a choice of five additional styles. Do not confuse these styles with CorelDRAW's Graphic and Text styles or the Color styles. These are layout styles, and as the name implies, they allow you to design your projects so the images print in the proper orientation on the sheet. When you select a particular style, the preview window shows a graphical representation of the style. Below the list box are two context-sensitive description lines that change whenever you select a new style. These descriptive lines tell you the number of pages per sheet required (see the section "Adding More Pages," later in this chapter) and the size of each page. Each available style is listed here, along with the finishing method (e.g. folded or trimmed):

■ *Full Page*   This is the default style. One full page is printed per sheet.

- *Book*   Two pages per sheet are printed so the document can be cut in half.

- *Booklet*   Two pages per sheet are printed so the document can be folded vertically in the middle.

- *Tent Card*   Two pages per sheet are printed so the document can be folded horizontally for a top fold.

- *Side-Fold Card*   Four pages per sheet are printed so the document can be folded horizontally for the top fold and vertically for the side fold.

- *Top-Fold Card*   Four pages per sheet are printed so the document can be folded vertically for the side fold and horizontally for the top fold.

Figure 25-4 shows the preview window with a graphical representation of the Top-Fold Card option.

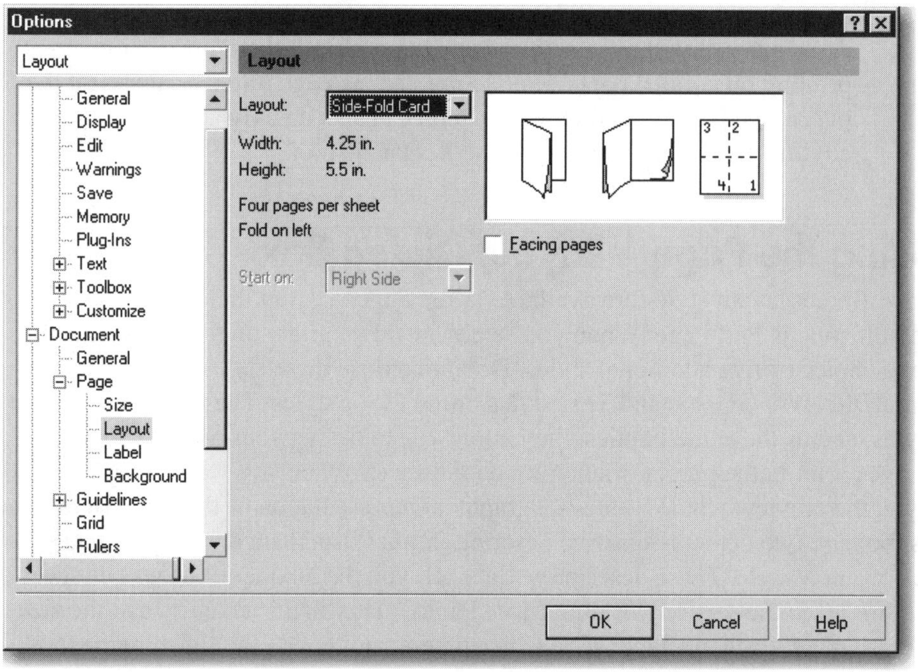

FIGURE 25-4   The Options dialog box with Page | Layout selected

The remaining options in the Layout section are:

- *Facing Pages*   Enabling this option allows you to see facing pages if your document contains multiple pages.

- *Start On*   This list box lets you choose which page to start with if your document has multiple pages and you have enabled the Facing Pages check box.

 NOTE   *If any page has been individually sized or oriented, only the full page layout is available.*

Using the Page | Label Dialog Box

Labels are handled differently than the other layout styles. They are not included in the Paper Size drop-down list on the Property Bar because an additional list box is required to show all the various styles. You instead select a label style from the Label Types list box in the Page | Label dialog box. After you select a label from the dialog box, the word "Label" will appear in the Paper type/Size drop-down list box on the Property Bar to let you know a label style is currently being used.

The label list box contains folders for all the popular brands (and brand styles) of labels. When you expand a folder by selecting the plus button next to the folder, a list of all the labels available for that particular brand's styles appears. Figure 25-5 shows the Avery Laser 5371-2x3.5 Business Card style selected. Notice that the preview window displays the labels as they would actually appear on a real sheet of labels.

 NOTE   *If you don't see a list of labels in the Page | Label dialog box, like that shown in Figure 25-5, click on the Labels radio button at the top of the dialog box.*

After you select the label style and click OK, the first label with a page border the size of the label will be displayed. For example, suppose you select the business card label shown in Figure 25-5, which is set up with ten cards per page. If you need to enter different information for each card, you can enter the information on page 1 and then click the + button in the navigation tools at the bottom of the drawing window to add a second page. When the second page is displayed, you can enter the new information. You can continue adding pages until you reach the total number of cards or labels required for the project.

25

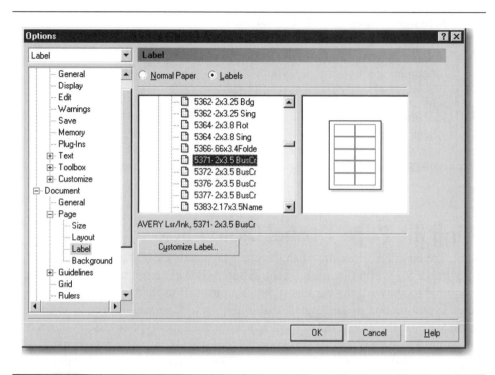

FIGURE 25-5 The Page I Label dialog box showing an Avery label selected from the list box

Printing Labels with the Same Information

If you want to print labels with the same information on each label, you use a different process. Follow these steps to place the same information on every label:

1. Select a label style from the Label type list box.

2. Select Layout I Insert Page to bring up the Insert Page dialog box. Enter the number of extra pages required for the number of labels you will be printing. For example, if you want to print 50 labels, enter 49 in the Insert Page num box, and click on OK.

3. Select Window I Dockers I Object Manager to bring up the Object Manager dialog box.

25

4. Right-click Layer 1, and click Master Layer in the pop-up menu shown here. This action will place the information from the first page on every page (label) in the document.

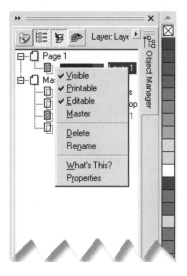

That's all there is to it. When it comes time to print the labels, CorelDRAW knows you're printing labels and will automatically add the number of label sheets required for the number of labels (pages) created. All you have to remember to do is load the required number of label sheets in the printer.

Using the Page | Background Dialog Box

You can control the fill properties of the backgrounds, which is similar to creating a page frame as discussed earlier, except that you do not create an object the size of the background as you do when creating a page frame. Instead, the entire page area is simply filled with the color or bitmap you select. This feature comes in handy when creating ads for the yellow pages, for example, and you want to see how your ad looks on a yellow background.

To fill the page with a color, click Background at the bottom of the page tree structure to display the Background dialog box shown in Figure 25-6. Across the top of the dialog box are three radio buttons: No Background (the default), Solid, and Bitmap. To fill the background with a solid color, enable the Solid radio button, and click on the down arrow of the palette box to reveal the default custom palette. Choose a color from the palette. If you want something other than a color

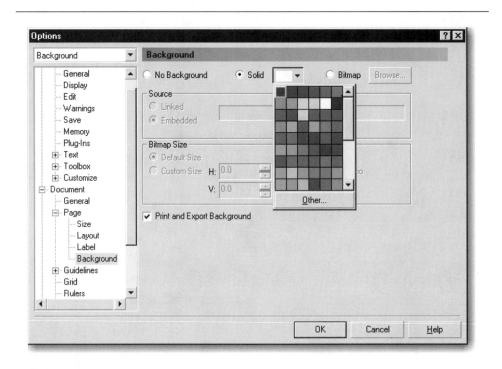

FIGURE 25-6   The Background dialog box with the default custom palette displayed

from the custom palette, click on the Other button at the bottom of the palette to reveal the Select Color dialog box. From this dialog box, you can choose any of the color models including a spot color.

When you enable the Bitmap radio button, as shown in Figure 25-7, the Browse button is activated. Clicking this button allows you to select a bitmap image from anywhere on your hard drive. When you use a bitmap as a background, the dialog box reveals other options. The first is the Source option; it lets you choose whether the bitmap file is linked to the file or embedded in the file. (For more on object linking and embedding, see Chapter 22.)

The second option is Bitmap Size. Enabling the Default Size radio button uses the actual size of the selected bitmap image. If the image is smaller than the paper size, it will be tiled into the background. If it is larger than the paper size, only a portion of the image will display. When you enable the Custom Size radio button, enter custom horizontal and vertical dimensions for the selected bitmap image in the num boxes. When you use a custom setting, the selected bitmap will be resized

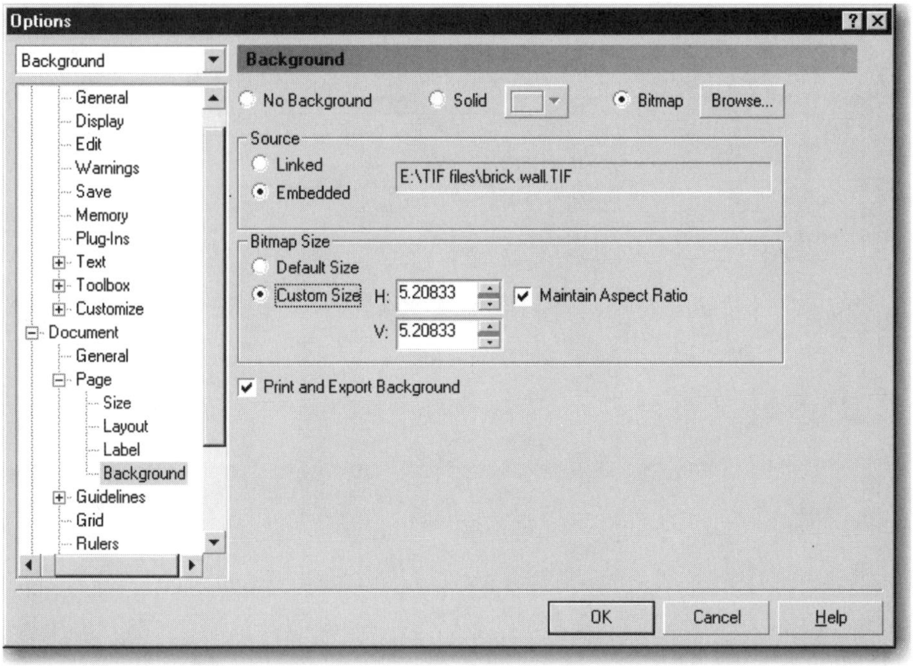

FIGURE 25-7   The Page | Background dialog box when a bitmap image has been used

to fit the dimensions. Figure 25-8 shows a small bitmap image that was tiled to fit the background.

The third option in the Page | Background dialog box is the Print and Export Background check box. If you enable this check box, the background fill will print. If you export the document to another format, the background fill will be exported as part of the document. It will also be published as the background image color or pattern when publishing your files to Internet. If the default of none is selected, the web page background will be white (see Chapter 33).

Adding More Pages

There are two ways to add more pages to your documents: you can add pages one at a time, or you can add several pages all at once. To add pages one at time, click the + button on the navigation toolbar at the bottom of the drawing window. To add several pages at once, select Layout | Insert Page, and enter the number of

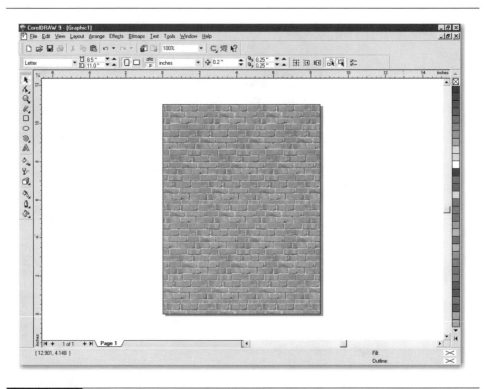

FIGURE 25-8   Using a bitmap image as a background fill

pages in the Insert Page dialog box. You have the option of adding the pages before or after the currently selected page. You can also right-click on a page tab at the bottom of the window and choose one of the insert page options.

Adding Custom Size Pages Within a Multipage Document

A new feature in CorelDRAW 9 lets you change page sizes within multipage documents. This can be accomplished by using a combination of the Navigator and the Property Bar, or by entering the number of pages and sizes in the Layout | Insert Page dialog box shown here.

Although we usually recommend using the Property Bar whenever you can, the Insert Page dialog box method may be quicker and easier to use than the Navigator and Property Bar combination. In either case, the follow instructions take you through the steps for choosing custom page sizes within the same document using both methods.

Adding Custom Page Sizes Using the Dialog Box Method

To add multiple pages of different sizes using the Insert Page dialog box, do the following:

1. Click Layout | Insert Page to reveal the Insert Page dialog box.

2. Enter the number of pages you wish to add of a particular size.

3. Click either the Before or After radio buttons to designate where the pages will be added.

4. Click either Portrait or Landscape mode for the added pages.

5. Choose the paper size from the Paper drop-down list for the added pages.

6. If you want to add a custom page size, enter the sizes in the Width and Height num boxes.

7. When you're finished making changes, click OK.

Adding Custom Page Sizes Using the Navigator and Property Bar Method

To add multiple pages of different sizes using the Navigator and Property Bar, do the following:

1. Click the + button on the Navigator to add a page.

2. Click the bottom button of the Current Page Size and Orientation buttons shown circled in the illustration here. This applies the page size for an individual page within a multipage document. You can enable this button once, and it will remain selected until you select the top button.

3. Choose a page size from the Page Size drop-down list, or enter a custom size in the paper width and height num boxes. If you manually enter a page size by typing in the numbers, you must press the Enter key for the settings to take effect.

4. Repeat steps 1–3 for each new page you add.

The biggest difference between the Insert Page dialog box method and the Navigator and Property Bar method is that using the first method allows you to add more than one page at a time.

NOTE *When switching between pages that contain varying sizes, the pages will not all display in the default view for each page size. For example, if you begin the document with a letter-size page and then add a larger page size, it will be displayed correctly, but when you return to the first page, it will be displayed smaller. To view the first page in its default view, click on the down arrow on the Zoom Levels drop-down list, and choose To Page. When you return to the larger second page, it will display in a zoomed in state, and you will not be able to see the entire page. Choose To Page again from the Zoom Levels drop-down list to view this page in its default view. Choosing To Page from the Zoom Levels drop-down list is required each time you switch between pages of different size if you want to see the entire page in its default view.*

More Page Setup Options

One more dialog box affects page setup. It's the Options | Page dialog box shown in Figure 25-9. The dialog box is accessed by clicking the page button at the top of the Page tree structure. The dialog box offers the following three choices:

- *Show Page Border*   This option lets you choose whether to show a page border (the outline and drop shadow around the page). If you do not show a page border, any objects outside the page border area will not be visible on all pages. So, the desktop area becomes useless. Also, Fit to Page in the print options will fit all objects, both on and off the page. With a page border visible, only objects actually on the page are fitted to the page with this print option.

- *Show Printable Area*   This option will show a dotted line on the page indicating the printable area based on the default printer and its settings (e.g. landscape / portrait) selected from the File | Print Setup dialog box.

- *Show Bleed area*   This option will show a dotted line around the page based on the bleed amount selected in the Options | Page | Size dialog box (see Figure 25-3).

Moving Between Pages

There are two ways to move between pages one page at a time. One method is to click either the left or right arrowhead on the navigation toolbar at the bottom of the drawing window. Another method is to click the PGUP or PGDN key to move forward or backward one page.

To go directly to the first or last page, move to the navigation toolbar again and click the First page button to go to the first page, or click the Last page button to go to the last page (see Figure 25-2).

If you want to go to a specific page, click on the page tab number. If there is a large number of pages, making it difficult to click on a page tab, choose Layout | Go To Page. Enter the page number in the num box in the Go To Page dialog box, and click OK.

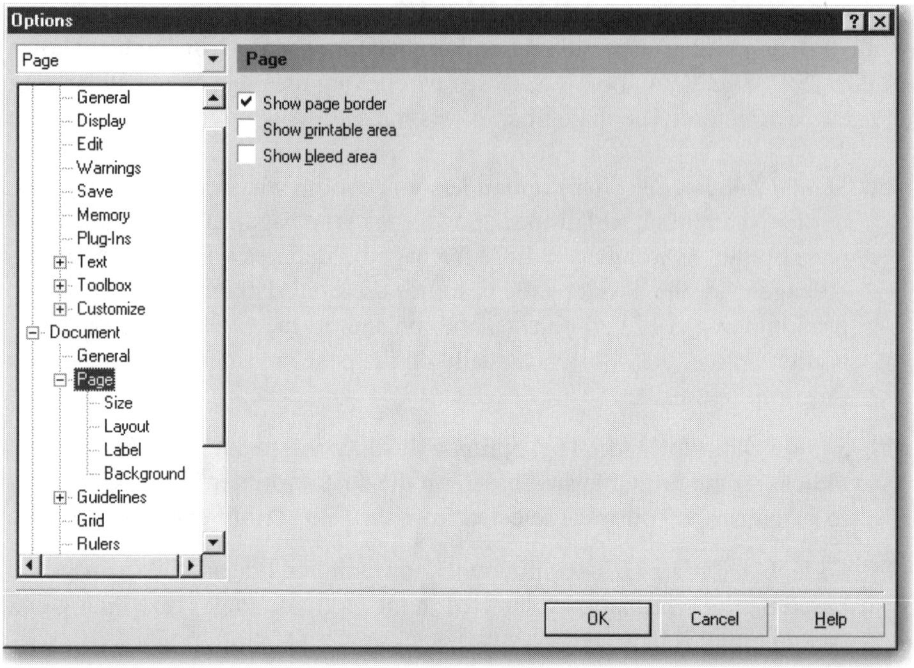

FIGURE 25-9 The Options | Page dialog box showing the three options available

In summary, you have learned that setting up a page can involve more than you might have thought. You have also learned how to add pages of varying sizes within a single document and how to create labels.

CHAPTER 26

Printing

CorelDRAW 9

Printing is probably the most important topic of all when you're working with CorelDRAW. Unfortunately, it is also one of the most difficult to master. This chapter discusses everything from printing the simplest drawing to producing a color separation. The interesting thing about a color separation is that the techniques used are essentially the same as those for creating a high-quality black-and-white image, with one or two extra steps. Even if you don't work with color you'll gain valuable information from this chapter that you can use to improve the quality of your output.

Many of the printing problems that people experience are actually design problems. It is easy to create artwork that just won't print or causes difficulty in printing. In almost every case, there's a workaround to solve the problem. Throughout this book, you'll find information on printing problems and how to solve them. Just remember: if it doesn't print, it's just a video game!

 NOTE *Some of the printing problems you'll encounter will be problems with your printer driver. Check with your hardware vendor to make sure you have the latest driver. Sometimes the latest driver will be the one causing problems so you might want to keep copies of previous drivers in case you need them.*

The Print Dialog Box

Earlier versions of CorelDRAW always displayed the Print dialog box before anything was printed. Now you can avoid this dialog box, but it contains too much important information for you to skip it completely.

To bring up the Print dialog box, shown in Figure 26-1, choose File | Print (CTRL-P) from any view of the document, including Print Preview. This initial dialog box is divided into four major sections: Destination, Print range, Copies, and Print style.

 NOTE *If you are already in the Print Preview screen, selecting File | Print (CTRL-P) will automatically print the document. Click the Options button to bring up the dialog box in Figure 26-1.*

For those who want to see a small preview of the page along with the Print dialog box, click the >> button just to the left of the ? button in the Print dialog's title bar. This will give you a preview window to the right of the dialog box.

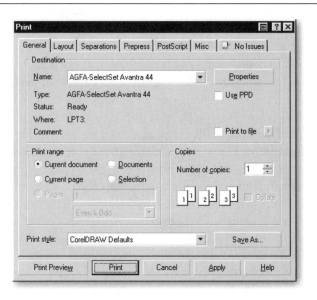

FIGURE 26-1   The Print dialog box

Destination

The Destination section of the Print dialog box is where you choose the printer to which the file will be sent. At the top is a drop-down list of all of the printers currently installed. Note that these names are not the names of the printer models, but rather the names they were given by whoever installed them. This means that sometimes you won't know your printer by the name displayed here.

After you select a printer, information about it will be listed just below its name. Status indicates the current status of the printer: it may be unavailable, busy, or ready to go. Type tells you exactly what model of printer you are working with, since the name can be misleading. Where tells you how the printer is connected to your computer: via a network, a local port, or even a file. The Comment field may contain a comment about the printer; the comment is supplied by the printer driver, but this field is rarely used.

In the right side of the Destination section are two check boxes. The top check box allows you to use a PPD file for outputting your job instead of a printer driver. When the box is first checked, you'll be asked for the location of the PPD file. After selecting a PPD, you'll see "(PPD)" at the beginning of the Type description. The next check box enables printing to a file. If you'll be preparing a file for a service bureau or for Adobe Acrobat Distiller, this feature is extremely important. It allows you to print using the features of a printer at a distant location, then supply the finished print file to that location. If you plan to use Print to file, it is a good idea not to connect the printer to the file port, because doing so can create conflicts. Instead, connect the printer to a "phantom port," such as LPT2 or LPT3, and then check the Print to file check box. Check this box only if you will be preparing a PostScript file for a service bureau or for Acrobat Distiller. Otherwise, you can just print directly to the printer.

Just to the right of the Print to file check box is a flyout arrow that gives several more choices. When the For Mac option is checked, the CTRL-D characters normally included at the beginning and end of the print stream are replaced by spaces. This function is extremely important if the file will be output from a Macintosh computer since Macintosh computers interpret CTRL-D as the end-of-file character. Even though this feature is specifically designed to help in outputting files on a Macintosh, it doesn't do any harm if the file is output on a PC. Therefore, it is a good idea to check For Mac whenever you are creating a file for service bureau output. You'll also find options on the flyout for choosing whether everything goes into a single file, each page is sent to a separate file, or each plate is sent to a separate file. If you are dealing with large files or several pages, you may want to use one of the latter options.

In the upper-right of the Print dialog box is the Properties button. Click it, and you'll be presented with all the options available on the printer or PPD you've selected. The dialog boxes that follow are completely dependent on the printer selected, the operating system you use, and/or the PPD you've chosen. The dialog boxes are supplied by the operating system itself and not by CorelDRAW, with the exception of the PPD dialog. Thus, this section discusses what you can, in general, expect to find in these dialog boxes, but it does not go into specific details.

Figure 26-2 shows the Properties dialog box for an AGFA Avantra image setter under Windows NT 4. Figure 26-3 shows a similar dialog box for this image setter using a PPD, and Figure 26-4 shows a Lexmark 5700 inkjet printer under Windows 95.

The most important settings to verify are the paper size, number of copies, and page orientation. Paper size is especially important when you're printing to film. Make sure you select a paper size larger than the document you've created if you need to print the various printer's marks, such as crop marks, registration marks, color bars, or densitometer scales. The number of copies can be set either in this dialog box or in the Print dialog box itself; it makes no difference which one you use. Note that changing the number of copies in the driver will be reflected in all applications, not just CorelDRAW. If you specify a large number of copies, make sure you reset the copy count before printing another file for which you want only one copy. Most of the time, the orientation is automatically adjusted by

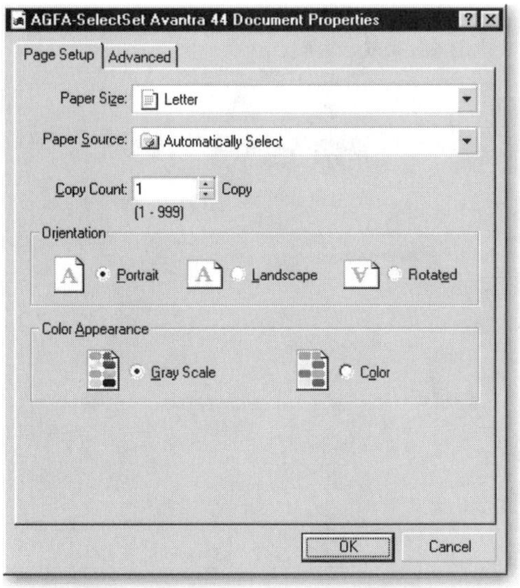

FIGURE 26-2   Printer Properties dialog box for an image setter operating under Windows NT 4

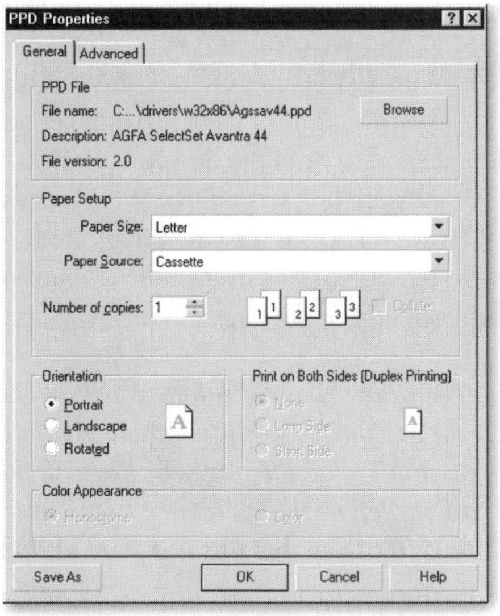

FIGURE 26-3   PPD Properties dialog box for an image setter

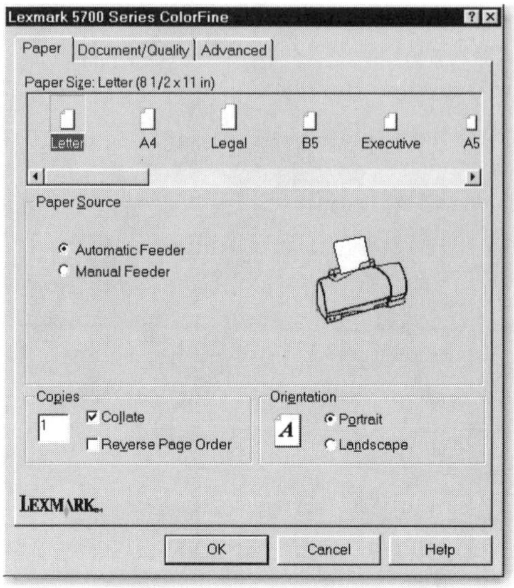

Lexmark 5700 Series ColorFine

Paper | Document/Quality | Advanced

Paper Size: Letter (8 1/2 x 11 in)

Letter   A4   Legal   B5   Executive   A5

Paper Source

    • Automatic Feeder
    ○ Manual Feeder

Copies
1   ☑ Collate
    ☐ Reverse Page Order

Orientation
A   • Portrait
    ○ Landscape

LEXMARK.

OK   Cancel   Help

FIGURE 26-4   Printer Properties dialog box for a Lexmark 5700 inkjet printer under Windows 95

CorelDRAW after it displays a message asking if it is all right to make the change. In most cases, you'll want to allow CorelDRAW to change the orientation for you, but in some situations you won't. You can change the orientation to whatever you need.

For example, we often needed to print the dialog boxes you see in this book. If these files are wider than they are tall, CorelDRAW will ask to change the page orientation to Landscape. However, since we wanted all the screen shots to be oriented the same way, we choose to leave the page in Portrait orientation. If we hadn't done this, we would've had to frequently rotate pages to read the text in the dialog boxes.

TIP   *When you're printing files for Adobe Acrobat Distiller, you'll almost always want to print in Portrait orientation, even though the paper is wider than it is tall. If you don't print the pages in Portrait mode, Acrobat will rotate them on your screen so that you have to tip your head sideways to read anything. Suffice it to say that this is a pain in the neck.*

You'll notice that other tabs are in each of the dialog boxes shown. Because each printer will contain different options, we'll leave it to your printer manufacturer to explain all of the settings available. The good news is that you can change the settings from within CorelDRAW.

Print Range

The Print range section of the Print dialog box allows you to choose exactly the pages or objects you wish to print. By default, it is set to print all the pages in the current document and everything on those pages. You have the option of printing only the current page or the current selection. The Selection option is dimmed if nothing is selected in your file. You can also select Documents to get a list of all open documents. Then you can select which documents you want printed in their entirety.

 TIP *If you select Tools | Options | Global | Printing, there is a check box for printing the current page only by default.*

You can also print only certain pages if your document contains more than one page. Type the page numbers you want to print in the textbox to the right of the Pages radio button. If you want to print nonconsecutive pages, place commas between the page numbers. To print a range of consecutive pages, type the beginning number followed by a hyphen and the ending number. These two methods can also be mixed together.

Below the page numbers is a drop-down list containing three choices: Odd Pages, Even Pages, and Even & Odd. You can use this list to select pages without having to type the page numbers manually.

Copies

As we've already discussed, you can specify the printing of multiple copies in the Printer Properties dialog box or in the Copies section of the Print dialog box. You can also specify whether the copies should be collated. If you choose Collate, printing will take much longer because each copy of the document will be sent to the printer separately, rather than all of them at once with the instruction to print each page multiple times. This means that the complete set of data will be sent for each copy that you request. If you don't collate the pages, the data is sent once with an instruction to print multiple copies of each page.

Print Styles

At the bottom of the Print dialog box, you can select a set of printing defaults from the Print style drop-down list. When you first install CorelDRAW, the only style available will be CorelDRAW defaults, but you can add more styles. This process is described later in this chapter.

If Print Preview is not already displayed, a Print Preview button will be shown at the lower left of the Print dialog box. If you already have Print Preview displayed in the background, the button won't be there.

To start printing using the current options, click the OK button. Clicking Cancel will return you to the view you had before you entered the Print dialog box. If Print Preview is displayed, the Apply button will apply the changes you've made to the Print Options. Note that there is now also a mini-preview available at the right side of the Print dialog box; unique to version 9.

Print Layout

The Layout tab of the Print Options dialog box controls the location of the image on the page. Figure 26-5 shows the Print Layout dialog box.

Image Position Within Page

At the top of the dialog box are options for sizing and positioning the image on the page. The default setting is As in document. This means simply that everything will be sized and positioned based on your document. Next is Fit to page, which will resize the original image so that you get the largest possible image that fits within the page. Your third option is Reposition images to, which gives you a drop-down list of nine different positions around the edge of the page and the exact center. If you elect to reposition the image, you can also resize the image.

Before you start changing the size of pages, note that you can select the page for which you want to change settings. You can then select the position of the upper-left corner of the image, the size, and the scale factor. By default, the lock icon at the far right is locked, which will maintain the aspect ratio of the image. You can unlock it, which allows you to change more settings. Note that this practice will distort the image and should thus be used cautiously.

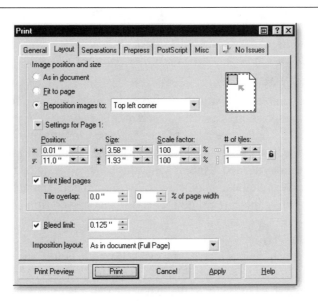

FIGURE 26-5 The Print Layout dialog box

Tiling

If your artwork extends beyond one page, you can have it tiled across as many pages as you need. Check the Print tiled pages check box; the dialog box will change slightly so that you can define a tile overlap. The overlap can be specified as either a measurement or a percentage of the page width. You can also select the number of tiles.

Other

The last few options span various categories. First, there is a check box that allows you to limit the bleed. Bleed allows your artwork to extend beyond the drawing page when it is printed. Bleed is extremely important for offset printing because it allows your artwork to extend all the way to the edge of the page in the finished piece. If you check Bleed limit, you can type in a maximum amount of bleed that will be printed. Normally, this won't be necessary since most artists create the bleed objects to the exact size their printers require. This is useful when you print labels—you can keep the artwork from one label from bleeding onto another one.

Imposition Layout

Imposition layout combines the signature layout and N-up functions from previous versions. Imposition is a method used in offset printing for printing several document pages on a single large sheet of paper. If you carefully arrange the document pages, the larger sheet of paper can be folded or cut so that the pages will be in the exact positions needed. Traditionally, this has been done by the "stripper" (this stripper does wear clothes), but the age of electronic publishing allows you to impose the pages before they are printed. This saves money on film and labor, not to mention saving time.

Several signature layout styles have been predefined for you and can be selected from the drop-down list. For example, you can select Side Fold-Card, which is a style set up to work with a four-page CorelDRAW document. Each of the pages will be arranged on a single sheet of paper so that when the paper is folded, it will create a greeting card that opens from the side. Page 1 in your CorelDRAW document will be the front of the card, pages 2 and 3 will be the inside portion, and page 4 will be the back. The first time you use this feature, you may find it a little frustrating, but once you see how it automatically arranges and rotates the pages to create the proper layout, you'll use it quite often.

The real power of layout styles lies in the capability they afford for creating your own styles. This can be done visually in the Print Preview screen; it will be described later in this chapter.

The previous example showed a way to print multiple pages on a single sheet with powerful control over how the image will appear, but you can also print the same page multiple times on a single sheet or just print multiple pages on a sheet. Some of the more popular choices are listed in the drop-down list. If you've chosen a particular type of labels in Tools | Options | Document | Labels, the name of that label style will appear in the drop-down list. If you don't find the desired option in the drop-down list, you can create your own. This will be discussed later in this chapter.

Separations

If you want to print large quantities of a color document to an offset printer, color separations will probably be necessary. Color separations are nothing more than black-and-white images of each of the spot, or process, colors used in your document. But getting these black-and-white images correct is something of an art form. By following the instructions described in this section, you'll be able to step into the world of color printing in no time.

The first option on the Separations tab, shown in Figure 26-6, is Print separations. If you are creating a separation, you should check this box.

Options

In the Options section, you have the option of printing separations in their own colors rather than in black, but you will rarely want to do this because the majority of color separations are printed in black. Note that this option is available only when you've selected a color printer for the output device. The actual color is added when the paper is on the printing press. You might, however, use this option to print each separation in color on a sheet of film, or overlay. When all the overlays are stacked together, they will show you an approximation of the final output.

You can also choose to print hexachrome plates, a type of separation that uses six colors instead of four to provide more vibrant color. Of course, when six colors are being used, you need more than the normal four sheets of separations. Before

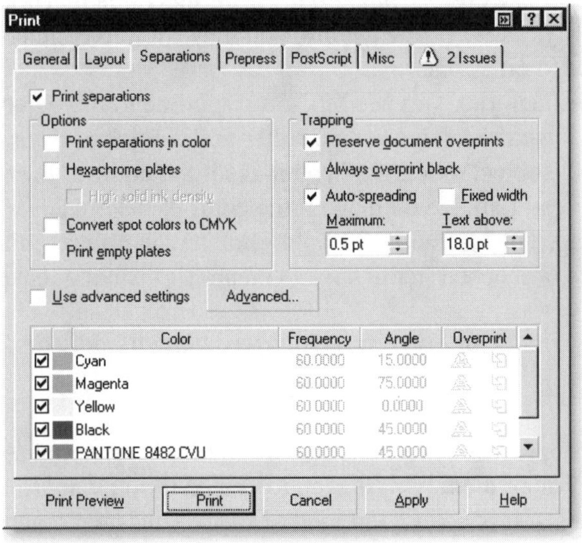

FIGURE 26-6   The Print Separations dialog box

using this technology, you should discuss it in detail with your printer and service bureau as they may not be familiar with this type of printing. It is fairly new and not in widespread use. One of the main problems is that there is no way to proof a hexachrome print job without actually proofing it on press. Some devices use a high solid ink density. If that is the case with the device you will be printing on, you should check the High solid ink density check box. Your service bureau should be able to tell you whether this is necessary.

Spot colors can be converted to process colors when you are creating a separation, but this is not ordinarily a good idea. If you are expecting an exact color that you have chosen from a swatch book of spot colors, you will be disappointed. Spot colors are meant to be printed with an ink that has been premixed. Trying to recreate that color with process colors can lead to disastrous results.

The last option is Print empty plates. If you want to pay for a blank piece of film, check this box—though this is almost never a good idea.

Trapping

When you're printing colors that touch, getting the two colors to register (line up) correctly is often problematic. This is because of the mechanical limitations of the printing press. To compensate for these limitations, it is sometimes necessary to "trap" the artwork so that the colors will overlap slightly. A detailed explanation of trapping is found in Corel's *Commercial Printing Guide* that was provided with CorelDRAW 8. If you don't have a copy, you may want to contact Corel Customer Service to order one.

To create a manual trap, you need to add an outline to the object that is to be trapped. Change the color of the outline either to the color of the selected object or to the color that the object touches. If you make it the color of the selected object, you'll create a spread trap. If you make it the color of the outside object, you'll create a choke trap. The last step is to right-click on the object, and make sure that Overprint Outline is checked in the pop-up menu. If it is not checked, click on it.

 NOTE   *Printing an overprinted outline will work only on a PostScript printer.*

CorelDRAW 9 provides two tools for automatically trapping a document. Before choosing one of them, you'll need to decide if you want to Preserve document overprints. It is not a good idea to create your own manual traps and then have autotrapping applied. The Always overprint black check box makes any black fill or outline overprint any color hidden beneath it. The idea is that black on top of another color is still black. Be aware, though, that black printed this way will actually be a bit shinier and darker than plain black.

Check Auto-spreading to use artificial intelligence to add spread traps wherever CorelDRAW deems them necessary. The maximum amount of the trap is controlled by the number in the Maximum textbox. You can also specify trapping for text only if it is above a specified point size. By default, trapping is performed only on text that is larger than 18 points. You should either leave this default setting alone or make it applicable to even larger text. When trapping is performed, outlines are added to the letters. This can destroy the look of small text.

The last option is Fixed width auto-spreading. When this check box is selected, the Maximum parameter box changes to the Width parameter box. Normally the spread is a variable amount not exceeding the value specified in the Maximum box; with this box checked, it is a fixed amount, as specified in the Width box.

 NOTE *Do not use the Auto-spreading function if you have created manual traps in your document. If you do, CorelDRAW will try to create traps of the traps you've created. All you need to do is uncheck the Preserve document overprints check box to remove any trapping that you created manually.*

By using the various auto-spreading methods in the Print Options Separations dialog box, you can spare yourself the trouble of creating the traps manually. But to get the best results, you will want to create the traps manually because it gives you much more control.

Advanced Settings

Custom halftone angles and screens can be controlled by checking the Use advanced settings box and then clicking the Advanced button. This control is especially important if you want to change the screen angles of spot colors. The Advanced Separations Settings dialog box will be discussed a little later in this chapter.

 NOTE *The Use advanced settings checkbox is available only if you are printing to a PostScript device. Other settings also require a PostScript device, so if something is currently unavailable to you, that is probably why.*

The Advanced Separations Settings dialog box, shown in Figure 26-7, allows you to choose from several predefined screening technologies or to enter your own custom frequencies and angles. Most frequently, an image setter will automatically change the frequencies and angles from the generic settings shown in Figure 26-7 to those appropriate for that image setter. That means this box is usually not necessary. Ask your service bureau if you are in doubt.

For each screening technology listed, several different resolutions and screens are available. When you're changing these values, you should be in close contact with both your service bureau and your printer to make sure that you choose the correct settings.

With some screening technologies, you will see CrlRaster or HQS listed in the Basic screen box or Screening technology box. These listings indicate AGFA's Cristal Raster or Linotronic's HQS technology. Cristal Raster produce stochastic, or frequency-modulated, screens. The results that they create can be incredible, but you should use this technology carefully. Contact your printer and service bureau before using it. A major problem is that the service bureau may not be able to provide you with proofs of your image. This will force you to go to press without ever seeing a proof. Another problem is that sometimes an excess amount of ink will be laid down. If you do choose to use stochastic screening, make sure you choose a service bureau and printer that are familiar with the pitfalls you may encounter.

The middle of the dialog box shows each of the colors used in the document. You can change the screen frequency, angle, and overprinting of any color individually.

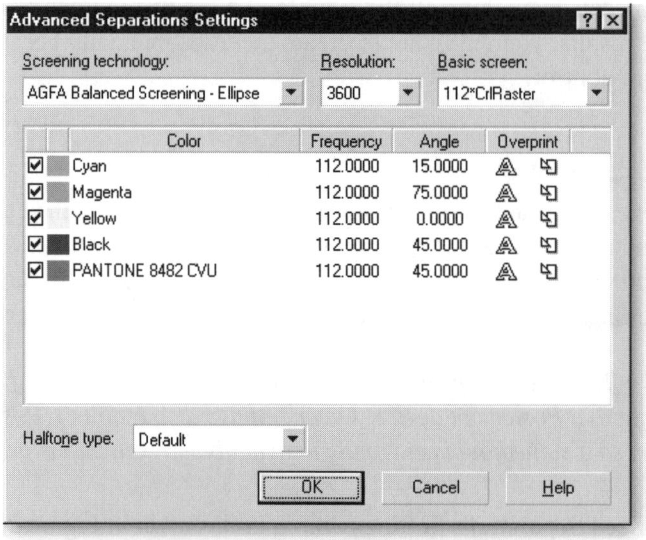

FIGURE 26-7   The Advanced Separations Settings dialog box

Simply select the color you wish to change, and use the Frequency and Angle textboxes to enter new values. If you click the text or graphics icon, you can choose whether the text or graphics will overprint. Note that changing any of these values can create severe problems if it is not done carefully.

At the bottom of the dialog box is a drop-down list of halftone types. The default halftone type is usually a dot or an ellipse, depending on the technology chosen. A number of specialty dots are shown in this list. The results of using an alternative halftone type can be quite interesting, but problems can occur if the printer or service bureau is not prepared to work with these alternative types. More importantly, they can take a long time to print, and your service bureau will charge you for that extra time.

When you exit the Advanced Settings dialog box, the changes you have made will be reflected at the bottom of the Print Separations dialog box. If you chose not to use Advanced Settings, you can see the colors used in the document, along with the settings for their frequencies, angles, and overprints. The only change you can make is to select the colors that you wish to print. By default, the colors used in the document will be selected.

Prepress

The Prepress tab brings you to the Print Options Prepress dialog box, shown in Figure 26-8. This contains many important settings that you'll need when outputting film for offset printing.

Paper/Film Settings

The first two settings can usually be left turned off (not checked). The first setting, (Invert), controls whether the image is printed as a positive or a negative, and (Mirror) controls whether the job is printed with the emulsion side of the film up or down. You will need to ask your printer what type of film to use. Then ask your service bureau what type of file it needs to give your printer the correct film.

Here is why it is often best to leave these two settings unchecked: Suppose your printer asks for negative film and you therefore check the Invert check box. Your service bureau may change this same setting in the image setter, and it is common for service bureaus to make everything a negative. In this case, however, your file will then be output as a positive. The same sort of problem can occur if you choose the Mirror option. Therefore, speak with both your printer and your service bureau before setting either of these options.

26

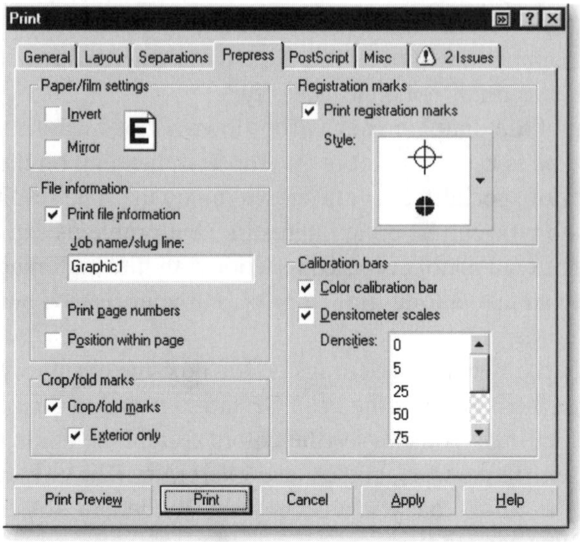

FIGURE 26-8 The Print Prepress dialog box

Here is a specific example of the situation we have just described: The printer of this book wants to receive right-reading emulsion-down negative film. This means that both of these options need to be checked to get the file correct in the preview window. However, our service bureau prefers that we send it a file without these settings activated. Thus, we just output our file as if we were printing a plain positive image on paper, and the service bureau does the rest for us.

TIP *The Mirror option can be very useful if you are creating t-shirt transfers.*

File Information

The next setting turns on Print File information. Any job output from an image setter should have this setting activated. You can print the information within the document by checking the Position within page check box. This is handy for stamping a printout with the filename, time and date printed, and more. You can also add a page number to the bottom of each page if you like. Note that this information is outside the page and therefore will not affect the look of your document (unless you check Position within page). Another option in CorelDRAW 9 allows you to specify the job name or slugline that will be printed. This setting defaults to the name of the current file, but you can type any name you wish.

Crop/Fold Marks

The next two settings are related to crop and fold marks. Crop and fold marks should always be present when you are outputting a job for a service bureau. They show the service bureau the page boundaries and give your printer valuable information on how to finish the job. If you check Exterior only, any crop and fold marks within the page boundaries will not be printed. This option is especially useful when you've created impositions. Most important, crop marks are used by the printer to determine where to crop (cut) the page.

Registration Marks

Registration marks are just as important as crop marks when you're creating a color separation. Turn them on by placing a check in the Print registration marks check box. Registration marks give your printer a way to accurately line up the multiple sheets of film. The style of registration marks can be chosen graphically by clicking the sample shown and selecting your choice from the graphical drop-down list.

Calibration Bars

The next two settings are related to the calibration bar and the densitometer scale. These allow your printer and service bureau to make sure their equipment is working properly. Both of these should be activated for service bureau output. To turn them on, place checks in both the Color calibration bar and Densitometer scales check boxes. When you select Densitometer scales, a list of the densities that will be printed appears. You can change these values by clicking any of the numbers. The number will then be editable, and you can change it to anything you wish. However, before doing so, contact your service bureau because the defaults are the standard densities that the service bureau will likely expect.

PostScript

If you are outputting to a PostScript printer, setting various options in the Print PostScript dialog box, shown in Figure 26-9, is a necessity. If you are not printing to a PostScript printer, you will not see this dialog box.

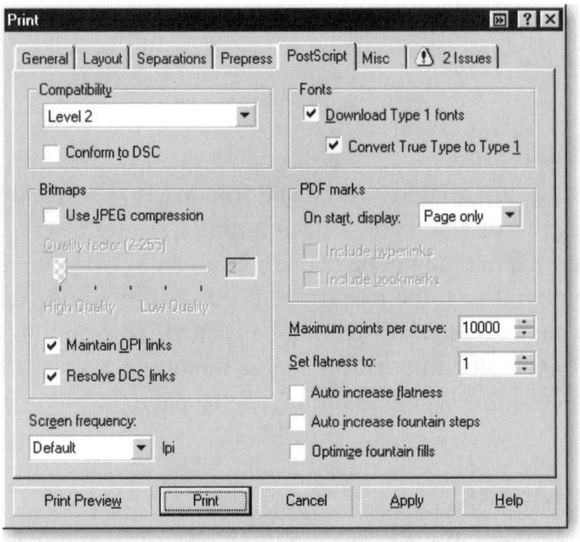

FIGURE 26-9   The Print PostScript dialog box

Compatibility

Select the version of PostScript used in your printer from the drop-down list. If you use an older version than those your printer supports, it can make your files larger and slower than necessary. However, it is helpful only if you are truly using a PostScript device that supports the new features. Most PostScript printers released in the past few years use PostScript Level 2, and PostScript 3 printers have just started to appear. Check the user manual for your printer to find out what it supports.

> **TIP**   *If you are having problems printing and you currently have PostScript Level 2 or PostScript 3 selected, try printing with PostScript Level 1.*

Bitmaps

If you selected PostScript Level 2 or PostScript 3, you can use JPEG compression on any included bitmaps. Remember that JPEG is lossy compression (see Chapter 33 for a more complete description of JPEG) and that it may decrease the quality of your output. The slider lets you choose the level of the quality. The lower the quality, the more compression you get. Be sure to use this option with caution.

Another check box lets you maintain OPI links—OPI stands for Open Prepress Interface. If you receive files scanned at your service bureau, they will quite often be low-resolution copies for you to place in your document. The service bureau keeps the high-resolution files and swaps them for the low-resolution copies when the files are output. The most common format used is OPI, so this option is needed if you want your service bureau to be able to swap in the correct image for you. Another related option is Resolve DCS links. You should check with your service bureau to find out whether it wants you to resolve the links or whether it will do that for you.

Below the bitmaps section is the setting for Screen frequency. If you are outputting separations, you have probably already changed this setting in the Separations tab. Otherwise, you'll want to set it here. To set an appropriate screen frequency, you'll want to ask your printer (the person) what is required for the job. If the job will not be printed on a printing press, the limits of your desktop printer (the machine) should be considered. The value depends on many factors, such as the printing press, the paper (or fabric) type, and the quality you desire. Higher frequencies are great if they will work with all the other factors.

Fonts

If you are using a PostScript printer, which you obviously are or this option wouldn't be available, make sure you check both the Download Type 1 fonts and Convert True Type to Type 1 check boxes. This will ensure that any needed fonts (other than the fonts stored within the printer) will be downloaded to the printer or output file. More information on each of these font formats is given in Chapter 32. If you have used a large numbers of fonts on a page, you may want to uncheck these boxes so that the text will be sent to the printer as curves. Sending too many fonts may exceed the memory limits of your printer.

PDF Marks

If you are preparing a file to be processed by Adobe Acrobat Distiller, you'll want to choose the settings most appropriate for your needs. The initial drop-down allows you to choose what is displayed in Adobe Acrobat Reader when you first open the file. You can choose for your document to be shown full screen, as a page with the Acrobat interface, or with thumbnails along the left side of the screen. If you have created hyperlinks and bookmarks, you have the option of including them in the PostScript data generated by CorelDRAW.

Other

The flatness setting controls how smoothly each curve is drawn. The best setting is always 1, but complex jobs may not be able to print with this setting. Your best bet is to leave the setting at 1 and check the Auto increase flatness check box. This will cause CorelDRAW to try the flatness at 1, then 3, then 5, and so on until it reaches 11 (assuming that 1 is specified in the Set flatness to box). CorelDRAW will try values up to 10, plus the number you type in. Anything higher than 11 will probably cause changes that will be visible to the naked eye, and thus may cause problems. One way to avoid changing the flatness is to change the number of points in the curve from the default value to a lower value, such as 400. This is necessary only if you have a PostScript Level 1 device. Lower numbers are allowed, but they can cause printing to take much longer. If a file will not print, you can attempt a maximum number of curves as low as 20.

Several check boxes help you optimize the fountain steps and fountain fills. It can be helpful to check these in case you made a mistake elsewhere when you were setting the number of fountain steps. These boxes will correct those mistakes based on the selected device.

Miscellaneous

The Print Misc dialog box, shown in Figure 26-10, contains all the settings that don't belong in any of the other tabs.

At the top of the dialog box is a check box for using a Color Profile for output. It is available only if you are outputting to a color device or are printing color separations. If you wish to change the settings for your color profile, click the Set Profiles button. Now you can select profiles for your monitor, scanner, composite printer, and/or separations printer. For more information on choosing and using color profiles, see Chapter 22.

Job Information Sheet

If you want to make your service bureau operator happy, be sure to check the Print job information sheet check box. To see what will be printed, click the Info Settings button. It will bring up the dialog box shown in Figure 26-11.

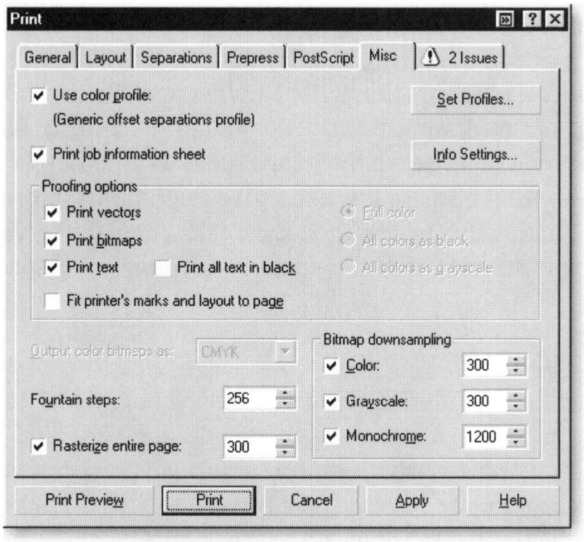

FIGURE 26-10 The Print Misc dialog box

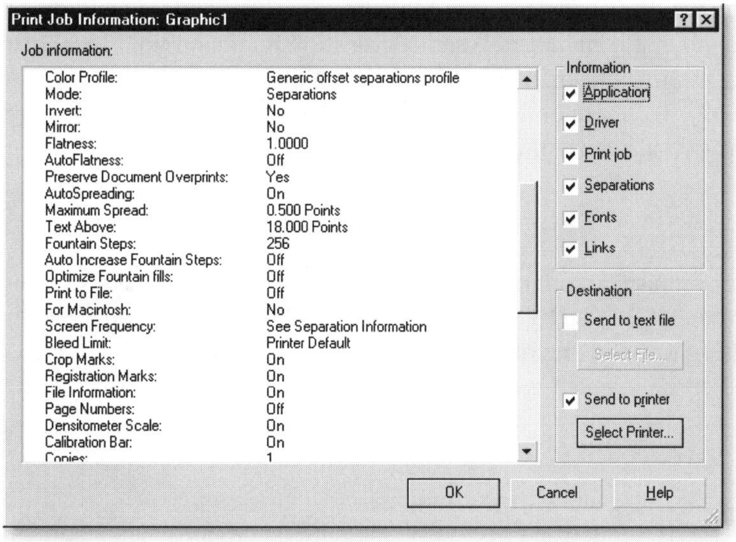

FIGURE 26-11 The Print Job Information dialog box

26

The figure shows some of the details of the Print Job Information dialog box. You can choose the options that will be printed by checking the appropriate check boxes on the right side of the dialog box. By default, they are all checked. You can also choose whether the information will be output as a file or to a specific printer. This information is printed immediately after you print the main file.

Make sure that you don't select the image setter as your output destination for the job information sheet because it is expensive to print this information to film. The idea behind printing this information sheet is to show the service bureau what is contained in the PostScript PRN file you are providing for output.

Proofing Options

In the Proofing options section of the Print Misc dialog box, you'll find many options that can assist you in printing quick proofs of your design. The first three options allow you to choose whether vectors, bitmaps, or text are printed. If you know that a large bitmap is correct, simply uncheck Print bitmaps to save the time it would take to print the bitmap. If you choose to print text, you can print it entirely in black, which can be helpful if you have very light-colored text that may be difficult to proof if it is printed on white paper.

On the right side of this section, you can choose whether the document is printed in color, with all colors converted to black, or with all colors as levels of grayscale.

The last option in this section is Fit printer's marks and layout to page. Proofing a job that contains crop and registration marks on your local printer can sometimes be difficult, since these marks often are outside of an 8.5x11-inch page. The availability of these options is dependent on custom page positioning and the separations options chosen.

Color Bitmaps

When color bitmaps are included in a document, you have several options. They can be output in CMYK, RGB, or grayscale. RGB is especially useful when you are outputting to a slide recorder or for an Acrobat file that is meant to be viewed onscreen. For the majority of color jobs, you'll want CMYK. And for those occasions where color isn't involved, you'll want grayscale.

Fountain Steps

For the highest quality output, set Fountain steps to 256. This is the maximum allowed in PostScript Level 1 and 2 devices. If you are using a PostScript 3 device, it supports up to 1,024 levels, but that is certainly an extreme value. The number of fountain steps (levels of gray that can be printed) that are possible on any given printer at any given line screen can be calculated with the following formula:

$$\text{Fountain steps} = [(\text{DPI})/(\text{LPI})]^2$$

DPI (dots per inch) refers to the printer resolution. LPI (lines per inch) refers to the screen frequency.

Rasterize Entire Page

Some files are just plain complex, and are thus difficult to print. With files such as these, you can choose Rasterize entire page and convert everything to a bitmap when you print. If you choose this option, you can choose the resolution. For those using non-PostScript printers, it can also be useful to create bitmaps instead of relying on the Windows GDI.

Bitmap Downsampling

Users will commonly scan images at too high a resolution. We've provided some guidelines for you in Chapter 23. A new option in CorelDRAW 9 will allow you to downsample bitmaps to a lower resolution. For example, users with inkjet printers see that the printer can print 720 dpi and thus scan everything at this resolution. Sadly, this is a waste of disk space. Anything over 200 dpi is unused. This problem can be solved by choosing 200 dpi in the Bitmap downsampling section. You can choose separate resolutions for color, grayscale, and monochrome images. This can also be handy when you create files to be used in Acrobat Distiller. Another use for this feature is printing proofs. If you design artwork for high-resolution output, downsampling when printing to your local laser printer will save you time in proofing the file.

Issues

Because of the many cool effects in CorelDRAW, it is easy to create things that can cause printing problems. The Issues tab, shown in Figure 26-12, lists a number of potential problems, along with explanations to help you find and fix problems. Or, you can just ignore them.

The top part of the dialog box lists each of the issues that has been identified. Clicking on the issue will display a detailed description of the problem and possible solutions at the bottom of the dialog box. If you get messages that you don't want to see in the future, check the Don't check for this issue in the future check box.

26

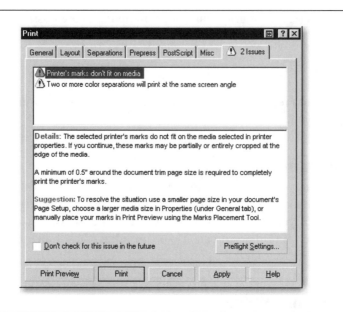

FIGURE 26-12   The Print Issues dialog box

Preflight Settings

A complete list of issues that are checked can be seen by clicking the Preflight Settings button to reveal the dialog box shown in Figure 26-13.

If there are issues that you don't want CorelDRAW to check, simply uncheck that option, and you won't be prevented with warning messages in the future. These same options can be found by choosing Tools | Options | Global | Printing | Preflight outside of the Print dialog box.

Special Settings

Even with all the options we've presented, some settings are included to solve particular printing problems. These can be found by select Tools | Options | Global | Printing outside of the Print dialog box. You'll see the dialog box shown in Figure 26-14.

Here, you'll see a list of each of the Special settings options on the left and the setting itself on the right. One of the most important settings is for users running Windows NT and printing to inkjet printers. Make sure the setting for Send Large Bitmaps in Chunks is set to Yes, if larger than threshold. If you don't do this, you

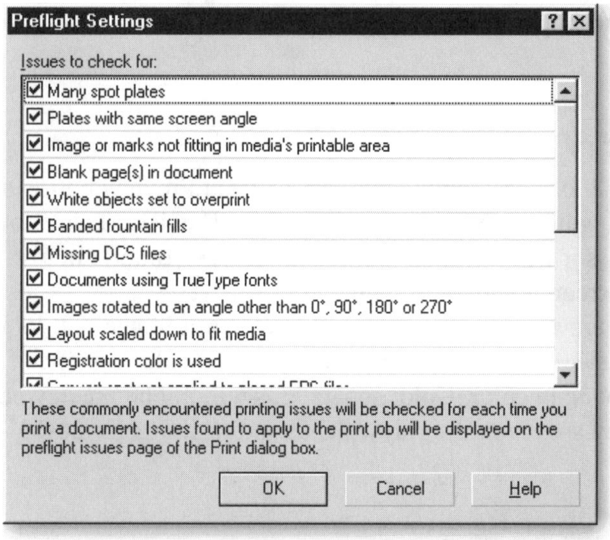

FIGURE 26-13 The Preflight Settings dialog box

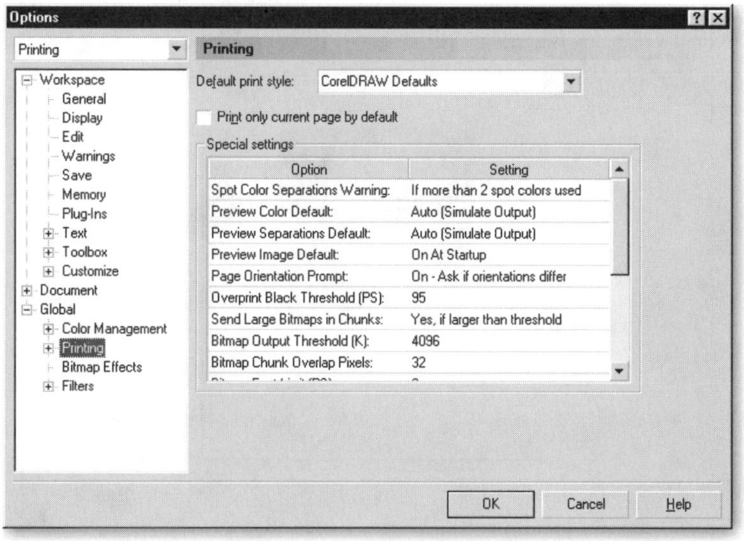

FIGURE 26-14 The Options Printing dialog box

probably will not be able to get any large bitmaps to print. Most of these settings are used by technical support to solve specific problems. Contact Corel for more details.

Print Preview

Print Preview can be accessed by clicking the Print Preview button at the bottom of the Print dialog box or by selecting File | Print Preview. This allows you to see the file exactly as it will print, including the various printer's marks. The Print Preview main screen is shown in Figure 26-15.

The default preview shows you exactly how your image will look when it is printed on the selected printer. If the printer is not a color printer, of course the preview will not be in color. Color separations will not be previewed in color either, since they are output as grayscale, as shown in Figure 26-15. The default

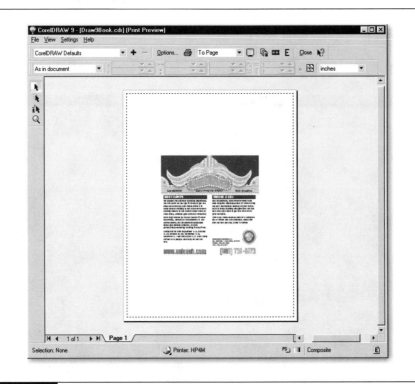

FIGURE 26-15 The Print Preview screen

preview can be changed with the View | Preview Color | Color command. You'll also see several other options that can be set for the preview.

Unlike the preview screens of old, this one allows you to zoom to any level you wish, with either the Zoom tool or the drop-down list of zoom levels. The bottom of the screen contains tabs for each page to be printed, including separations. You can also use the navigation buttons to move between pages.

You can use the Options button to activate the dialog boxes discussed previously to make further changes. You'll also notice that many of the dialog boxes discussed in this chapter can be accessed directly from the Settings menu.

Creating Imposition Layouts

When a printed piece is created, multiple pages of the document will often be output on the same sheet of film. After printing, the paper is carefully folded and cut to produce the finished multiple-page document. Each of these large sheets of film is called a *signature*; creating them in CorelDRAW 9 is accomplished in the Print Preview screen. When you select the Imposition Layout tool (the second tool down in the Print Preview toolbox), your screen will show how the pages will be laid out. The controls for changing the signature are located on the Property Bar, as shown in Figure 26-16.

To fully understand how to use this tool, we need to look more closely at the Property Bar. It will initially look similar to the one shown here with the Edit Basic Settings button depressed:

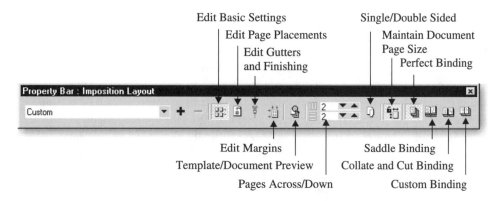

The first four buttons, Edit Basic Settings, Edit Page Placements, Edits Gutters and Finishing, and Edit Margins control which buttons are shown on the right half of the Property Bar. Let's first look at the options made available when Edit Basic Settings is selected.

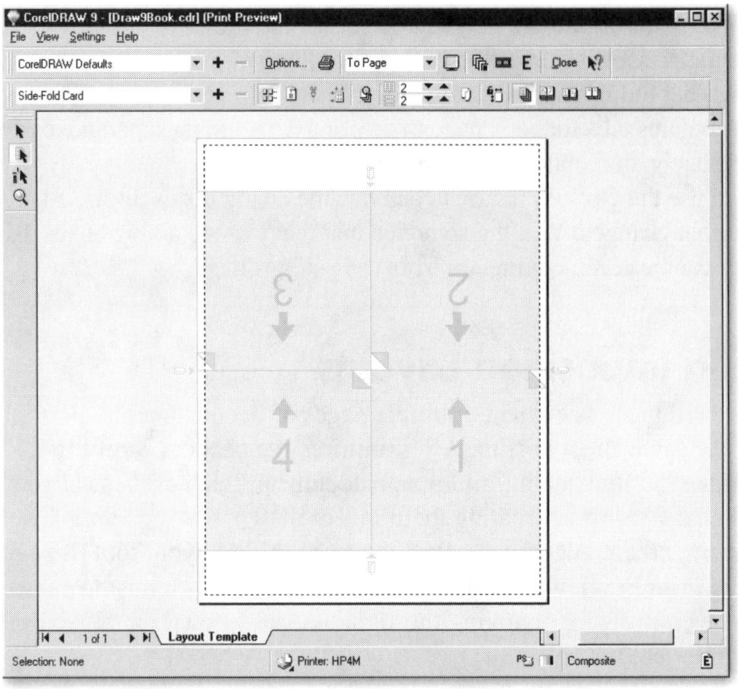

FIGURE 26-16   The Print Preview screen for previewing a signature layout

Edit Basic Settings

You can toggle between a preview of the template and the document by clicking
the Template/Document Preview button. This is handy for seeing if your layout
looks correct with the data in the document. Next are the numbers of pages across
and down. In the sample we have chosen, there are two pages in each direction.
The last button in this section toggles between single and double sided.

By default, the size of the page will automatically change to fit the imposition
layout, but you can lock the page to its current size. If the layout doesn't fit, you'll
see the edges of the imposed pages outside of the margins.

The last four buttons on this Property Bar control the method of binding you
plan on using. First is the button for perfect binding. In this method, all of the
pages are cut apart and glued together at the spine of the book. This book is perfect
bound. When perfect binding is used, all of the pages will be printed in order.

Next is the button for saddle binding. A simple example of this type of binding is when you have two pages printed on one side of each sheet. You fold the pages in half and staple them down the middle. A glossy magazine is a good example of saddle binding. When you select Saddle Binding, the Property Bar will expand to give you the Pages Per Group selection box. Here you choose the numbers of pages that are grouped. The first choice is to not group, and then the number increases in increments of four.

Collate and Cut Binding is the third binding option. Let's again use the example of having four pages per signature. If the document is 32 pages, you'll have a total of eight signatures. The first signature contains pages 1, 9, 17, and 25. The next signature contains pages 2, 10, 18, and 26. This continues until the last signature contains pages 8, 16, 24, and 32. Then you collate the signatures and cut them into stacks containing the pages in order.

The last option is Custom Binding. In this method, you define each signature separately. When the option is selected, you'll get a box for entering the number of signatures. This allows you to have signatures that are not the same.

Edit Page Placements

Once you've got the basics out of the way, it is time to decide where the pages will be placed on the signature. When you select the Edit Page Placements button, the Property Bar will change to the one shown here:

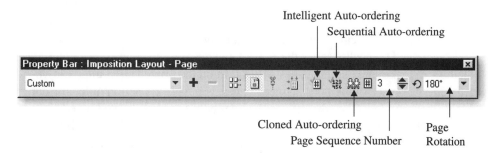

Intelligent Auto-ordering
Sequential Auto-ordering

Cloned Auto-ordering
Page Sequence Number
Page Rotation

If you select Intelligent Auto-ordering, CorelDRAW will choose the page ordering that seems most logical based on your document. You can then decide which page is placed in each of the positions. To do this, click on the page in the preview window that you wish to edit. You'll know it is selected because it will have a red border. You can then use the Page Sequence Number box to choose which page will go in that position. The Page Rotation can also be set to either 0 where the top of the page is printed up or 180 so that the top of the page is printed down.

When you choose Sequential Auto-ordering, the pages are automatically arranged on the sheet in a logical order. You can still override these settings by adjusting the Page Sequence Number and Page Rotation as described earlier. Cloned Auto-ordering assumes that you want the same page repeated multiple times on the page. The best example of this is printing eight or ten business cards on a single sheet of paper.

Edit Gutters and Finishing

Now that you've got the pages in place, you may need to provide a gutter between the pages. You may also want to add cut and fold lines. When you select Edit Gutters and Finishing, you'll have access to these controls on the Property Bar, as shown here:

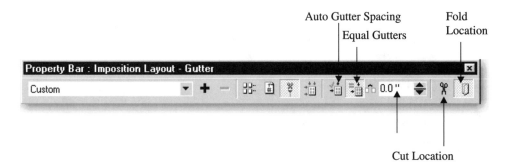

The Auto Gutter Spacing icon will automatically space the gutters. If you would rather adjust them manually, select the Equal Gutters icon, and change the Gutter Size. Remember to make sure that the pages will still fit on the printed sheet after you've added gutters. At each of the lines between pages, you have the option of having cut and fold marks printed. Click directly on the line so that it is highlighted in red, and then click either the Cut Location or the Fold Location icon on the Property Bar. When you do this, you'll see either a pair of scissors, indicating cut, or a folded piece of paper, indicating fold, appear at the ends of the line.

Edit Margins

Just when you thought you were finished, one more adjustment can be made. When you select the Edit Margins icon, you'll get the Property Bar shown here:

Equal Margins

Auto Margins

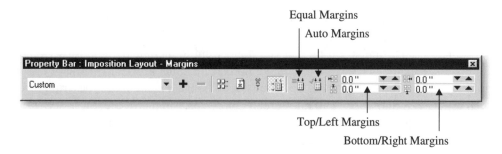

Top/Left Margins

Bottom/Right Margins

The margins determine where the imposition will sit on the printed page. By default it is set to be in the upper-left of the page. Your first choice is the Equal Margins icon. When this is depressed, you can only change the Top/Left Margins settings. The values you use will be duplicated for the Bottom/Right Margins. If you would prefer to adjust all four manually, make sure that the Equal Margins button is not depressed. For those of you who want the margins calculated automatically, just depress the Auto Margins button, and let CorelDRAW do the work for you.

Adding Prepress Marks

The third icon down in the Print Preview toolbox allows you to set the prepress marks visually. For the most part, the Property Bar simply allows you to select icons, as opposed to selecting check boxes in the Print Prepress dialog box we discussed earlier.

Saving Print Styles

With the myriad settings in the Print dialog boxes, remembering which check box and buttons to press can be daunting. But if you can get through it just once, you'll be able to save the settings for future use.

For example, we used this feature often during the production of this book. We are required to print any images to be used and supply them to the publisher. Some of the dialog boxes print rather small, so we want them fitted to the page. We also want the file information on the page so that the name of the file is on every image. Neither of these settings is difficult to specify, but it can be a nuisance to set them every single time you need to print. Thus, we created a print style for this purpose.

Select File | Save Print Style (CTRL-S) to overwrite the default style or File | Save Print Style As (F12) to create a new one. You can also select the Save As button in the Print General dialog box. Either way, you'll be presented with the dialog box shown in Figure 26-17.

If there is a particular setting that you don't want to include in the print style, simply uncheck the box next to the name. In the File name box is the name of the print style itself followed by the .prs extension. Choose a name that is descriptive, such as "Screen Shots" or "150 line-screen color seps." In the future, these styles will be listed in the main Print dialog box. Choose them from the drop-down list, and print. You can also share these styles with other users who don't fully understand the Print dialog boxes.

Using the Duplexing Setup Wizard

Most users have a reliable printer for printing on one side of the page. However, you'll often need to print something on both sides of the page. By using the Duplexing Setup Wizard, you can print on both sides of the paper with ease.

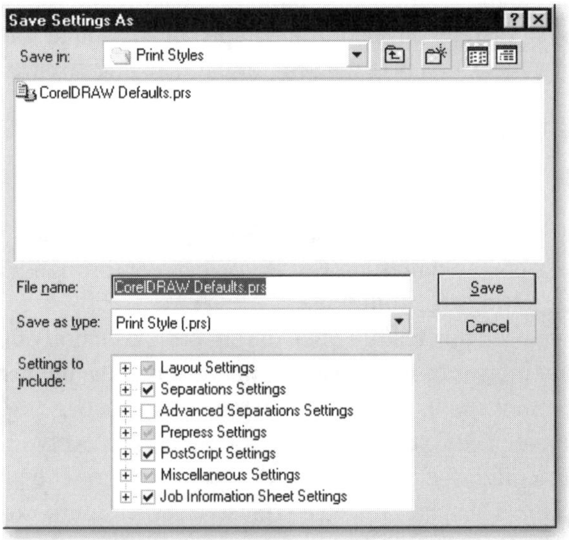

FIGURE 26-17   The Save Print Style dialog box

To begin the process, select Settings | Duplexing Setup Wizard (CTRL-D) while you're at the Print Preview screen. You'll see a series of dialog boxes that walk you through the printing of sample pages. At the end, you'll be presented with instructions on how to accurately print double-sided pages from CorelDRAW.

Prepare for Service Bureau Wizard

As a CorelDRAW user, one of your most difficult tasks can be dealing with service bureaus. This is largely because service bureaus have a bias for the Macintosh platform. Each new release of CorelDRAW has added features to make this task a little bit easier. We'll walk you through the Prepare for Service Bureau Wizard to prepare a CorelDRAW file for delivery to your service bureau.

Service Bureaus

For those of you who are not familiar with service bureaus, we'll describe them briefly. Most users can't afford, or have no desire to work with, the equipment needed to produce the film for color separations, color slides, posters, and various other projects. A service bureau purchases and maintains this expensive equipment and lets you pay only for the services you need. If you need film for color separations, you pay the service bureau for each set of film they output. The main problem you'll find is that not all service bureaus will work with CorelDRAW files. This usually results from a heavy bias for the Macintosh platform, for which CorelDRAW became only recently available.

Finding a good service bureau can be really tough. When you do find a good one, be sure to cooperate with it because it can be a valuable partner in many of your projects. It can also be a good source of information. And you can help the people who work with you by keeping them informed as to the status of your project and anything that they may need to know before outputting the job.

Corel provides a list of its authorized service bureaus on its Web site. To get to this site, select Help | Corel on the Web | Approved Service Bureaus, or select the Approved Service Bureaus item in the CorelDRAW 9 | Setup and Notes subfolder of your Start menu. The Web site is a good starting point, but you should still do more research to make sure you choose someone who is willing to really work with you. Ask other CorelDRAW users in your area what service bureau they are using and whether they know anything about the ones you've located. Ask the people at the service bureau for the names of its clients who use CorelDRAW. If they hesitate, you may want to look elsewhere.

26

You certainly shouldn't start this search process on the eve of an important project. If you wait until the last minute, you may make a hasty (and costly) decision. Before sending that important rush project to a service bureau, test the firm by sending a simple file with no time constraints. You may need to spend a little money up front to test several service bureaus, but in the long run, this experimenting will pay you back many times over.

Prepare for Service Bureau Wizard

In order to use the Wizard, you must have an open document containing at least one object. Although the Wizard will help you to create a file for the service bureau, it is still a good idea to consult with both your printer and service bureau in advance to meet their desired specifications for the file.

To start the Prepare for Service Bureau Wizard, choose File | Prepare for Service Bureau. The first screen of the Wizard is shown in Figure 26-18. You have two choices. You can have all the files used by your project gathered into a folder for delivery to the service bureau, or you can use a profile created by your service bureau to give them exactly what you want.

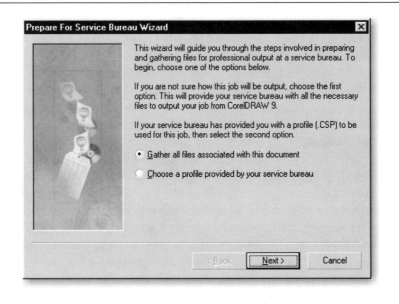

FIGURE 26-18   The initial Prepare for Service Bureau Wizard dialog box

We're going to describe only the method of gathering files because this will be sufficient for most users. To begin, select <u>G</u>ather all files associated with this document, and then press <u>N</u>ext to get the screen shown in Figure 26-19. Note that this screen is not shown if there is no text in the document.

On this screen you will see a list of all the fonts used in your document. You have the option to copy the fonts for delivery to the service bureau. Before doing so, you should carefully read the license agreement for the fonts. It is rarely legal to give the fonts to anyone under any circumstances. If the service bureau has CorelDRAW, then they should also have all the fonts that come with the program. You'll also find that most service bureaus have the complete Adobe library of fonts. So it is a rare occasion that they would even need you to supply fonts since they'll have the most commonly used fonts. The list of fonts needed will be provided in a file named fonts.txt, and this should be sufficient. Click <u>N</u>ext to continue. Those who must supply fonts, supply the file as a PostScript print file or a PDF file with fonts embedded.

A good way to soft-proof your file is by creating a PDF file. The next screen of the Wizard, shown in Figure 26-20, allows you to create PDF file to send to the service bureau.

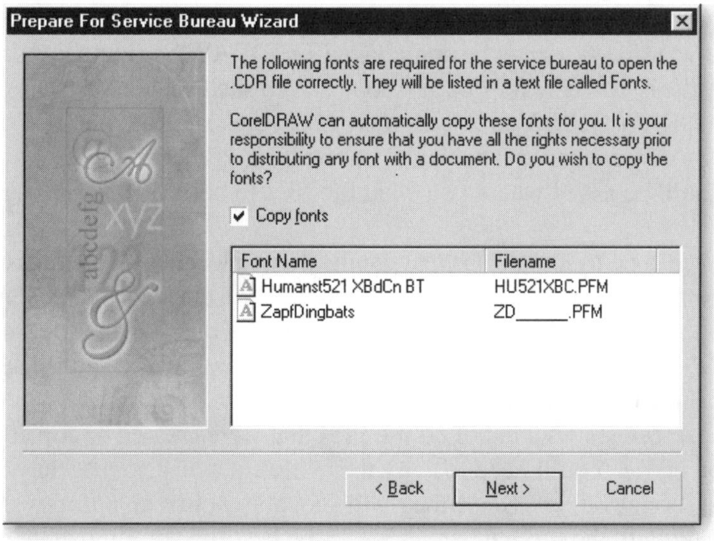

Prepare For Service Bureau Wizard

The following fonts are required for the service bureau to open the .CDR file correctly. They will be listed in a text file called Fonts.

CorelDRAW can automatically copy these fonts for you. It is your responsibility to ensure that you have all the rights necessary prior to distributing any font with a document. Do you wish to copy the fonts?

☑ Copy <u>f</u>onts

Font Name	Filename
Humanst521 XBdCn BT	HU521XBC.PFM
ZapfDingbats	ZD_____.PFM

\< <u>B</u>ack   <u>N</u>ext \>   Cancel

FIGURE 26-19   The Prepare for Service Bureau Wizard fonts dialog box

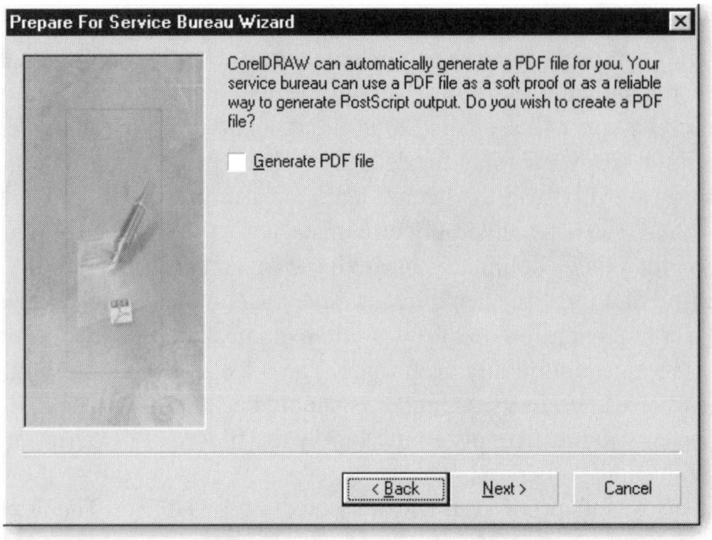

FIGURE 26-20   The Prepare for Service Bureau Wizard PDF dialog box

Just in case there are problems with the CDR file you provide, it is a good idea to provide a PDF file since PDF is a more universal file format. It can also be a good way to send your file to users who don't have CorelDRAW because the Adobe Acrobat Reader is available for free at Adobe's Web site. Note that it is also supplied on the CorelDRAW 9 CD. You'll learn more about creating PDF files in Chapter 27 so we won't worry any more about it now. Click Next to continue.

Next, you'll be asked where you want the files to be copied, as shown in Figure 26-21.

This screen is pretty simple. Either type the desired location of the files or use the Browse button to find an existing folder. When finished, click Next to continue.

The next screen you see will show the progress of copying the files, creating the PDF file, and other operations. When everything is finished, you'll see the dialog box shown in Figure 26-22.

The last screen shows a list of all the files that were created or copied to the location you chose. You'll need to copy these files to a disk so that they can be taken to the service bureau. Since they will probably not fit on a floppy disk, it is best to consult with the service bureau about the best type of removable media to use. Our favorite media is a writable CD-ROM as it holds over 600MB of data,

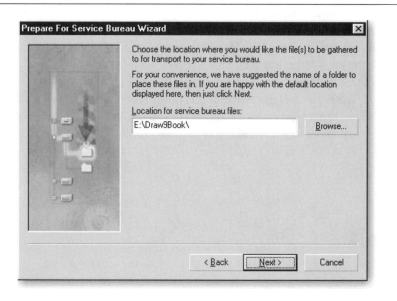

FIGURE 26-21   Prepare for Service Bureau Wizard file location dialog box

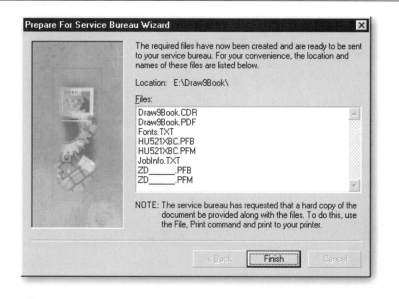

FIGURE 26-22   The Prepare for Service Bureau Wizard file list dialog box

and all computer users can read a CD. When you click Finish, the Wizard will be all finished, and you'll return to the main CorelDRAW screen.

With this Wizard, creating files for a service bureau has been greatly simplified. Armed with the knowledge learned in this chapter, you should now be ready to tackle almost any type of printing job, from the simplest flyer to a full-color brochure. Just keep in mind, when you feel that some of this information is unnecessary, that "if it doesn't print, it's just a video game." And when you think that color printing seems difficult, just remember that it's nothing more than printing several sheets of black and white.

CHAPTER 27

Publishing Portable Document Format (PDF) Files

CorelDRAW 9

Just a few years ago, it was difficult to share files with users unless they had the same software as you. And even then, the documents could change if the recipient didn't have the same fonts installed on their computer. Users also desire to create WYSIWYG on the Web. One format for meeting all these needs is PDF. PDF has also come to be a standard for the publishing world.

PDF is not a single product, but rather a file format that can be created, viewed, and edited by a range of products. Some of these products that work with PDF files are distributed at no cost, and others can cost thousands of dollars. CorelDRAW 9 can create documents in PDF format, complete with hyperlinks and other advanced features.

People wanting to look at PDF files will need the Adobe® Acrobat® Reader. The Mac and Windows versions of the Reader can be distributed free of charge and can be easily downloaded from Adobe's Web site (http://www.adobe.com). You'll find the Windows version of Acrobat Reader on the CorelDRAW 9 CD. UNIX and DOS readers are also available from Adobe. The Reader is what allows someone to view a PDF file. The latest version of the Reader also works as a plug-in to the Netscape Navigator and Internet Explorer Web browsers, which means that any PDF file stored on a Web site can be viewed just as all other Web content. Since PDF files can retain formatting and font information, the limitations imposed by HTML code can slowly be removed.

The next step up the Acrobat chain is Acrobat Exchange. With Exchange, you can open PDF files and make modifications to the hyperlinks and various other attributes associated with them. There is also the capability to put sticky notes into the document so that workgroups can easily group-edit a file. There are some other features found in the Exchange product, but they are mainly useful for working with some of the third-party tools available. The features in CorelDRAW 9 alleviate the need of having Acrobat Exchange for most users. It is necessary only if you will need to edit the PDF files after creating them in CorelDRAW.

The last part of Acrobat is Acrobat Distiller. By using CorelDRAW 9's Publish to PDF feature, you can avoid the need for Acrobat Distiller completely.

Designing for PDF

Creating a PDF File

Once you have a file created, select File | Publish To PDF to get the dialog box shown in Figure 27-1. You'll notice that it has some similarities to the Print dialog box discussed in Chapter 26.

Your first choice is to provide a name for the PDF file that will be created. Next, you need to select which parts of the document will be exported. Choices include All, Current Page, Pages, and Selection. If you select Pages, you can

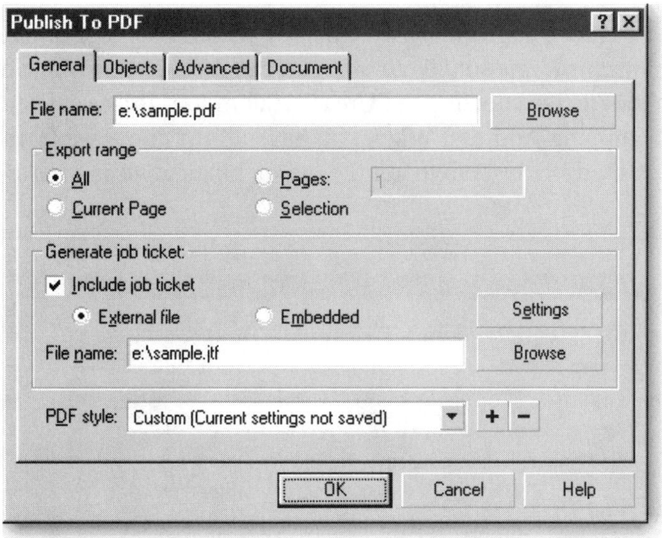

27

FIGURE 27-1   The initial Publish To PDF dialog box

specify the page numbers to be included. Selection will include only the objects you currently have selected.

Job Tickets

Since one of the benefits of creating PDF files is to create a file for service bureau output, a "job ticket" can be created that describes the file for the service bureau. Your first choice is whether or not you wish to Include job ticket. If you choose to include it, you can have it created as an External file or Embedded in the PDF file. Job tickets that are stored externally will have to be named, and the common extension used is .jtf. After you've decided to create a job ticket and specified where it is stored, you need to fill out the job ticket (or PJTF—Portable Job Ticket Format) by clicking the Settings button. This will bring up the dialog box shown in Figure 27-2.

Fill out the requested information with your account number, job name, and the various contact information. Note that you can include up to four different contacts with the file by selecting the Creator/Submitter, Primary Contact, Billing Address, and Shipping Address. When you have all the contact information complete, click the Delivery tab to get the dialog box shown in Figure 27-3.

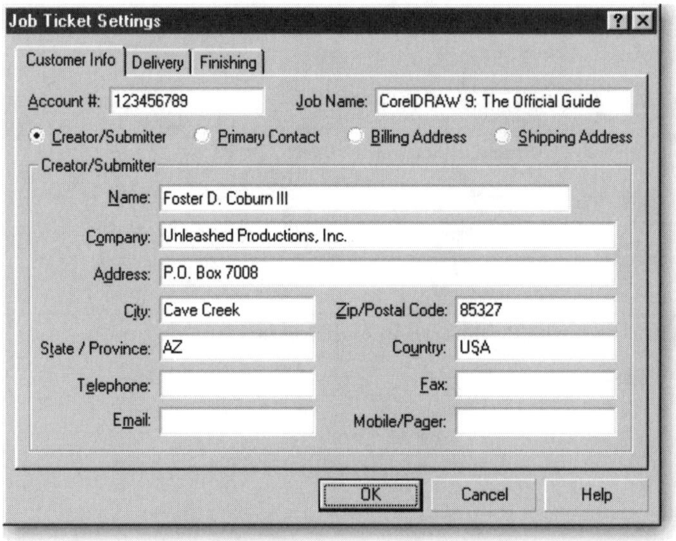

FIGURE 27-2   Job Ticket Settings for Customer Info dialog box

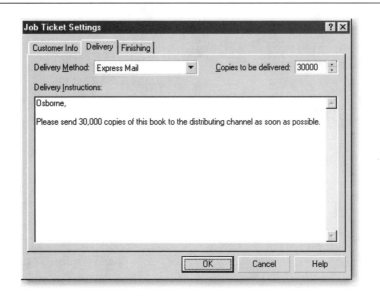

FIGURE 27-3   Job Ticket Settings for Delivery information dialog box

First, you'll need to choose how you want the job delivered. The Delivery Method drop-down list gives you a number of choices. Next, you need to enter the number of copies that you want delivered. This is limited to no more than 32,767. Finally, you can include specific instructions. Since you are limited to a low number of copies, you might want to include a larger number of copies in these instructions. When you've finished with the delivery information, click the Finishing tab to get the dialog box shown in Figure 27-4.

On the left side of the dialog box are the various finishing operations that can be performed. Select the options you want, and click the Add button. If you get something and later decide you don't need it, select it, and click Remove. You can also reorder the options using the Move Up and Move Down buttons. More information can be added in the Job Note section if you need to give specific instructions.

When you are all finished with the job ticket information, click OK to return to the Publish To PDF dialog box. At the bottom of the dialog box is a list of PDF styles. Corel has predefined several styles for you, and you can add to the list if you like. So if you use certain settings often, just save them as a style so that you don't have to reenter the information each time. To save a style, type in a new name, and click the + button. Now that you've seen the basic settings, let's look at the many

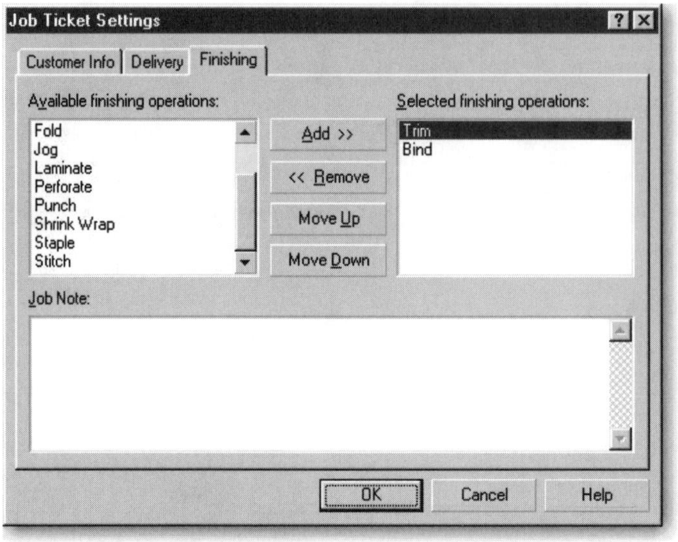

FIGURE 27-4 Job Ticket Settings for Finishing information dialog box

ways that you can optimize your PDF files. Select the Objects tab to get the dialog box shown in Figure 27-5.

Any bitmaps in your file can be stored in a compressed format in the resulting PDF file. In the Compression type drop-down list, you can choose between None, LZW, and JPEG compression. LZW is a lossless form of compression that will give you the best quality with less compression. JPEG is a lossy compression that can create very small files at a loss of image quality. If you choose JPEG, you get a slider for Quality factor that ranges from 2 through 255. A lower value will provide less compression but higher quality. If you have text or crisp lines in your artwork, LZW is the better choice. For full-color photos, JPEG is the better choice at a medium level of quality. You might have to try several values to see which works best for you. Keep in mind if the PDF file is destined for output at the service bureau, you will probably want to avoid JPEG altogether as it does degrade the quality of the images.

Another way to make files smaller is by downsampling the bitmaps. This should be used only if the resulting PDF file is designed to be viewed onscreen or distributed electronically. You wouldn't want to downsample bitmaps if the PDF file was headed for the service bureau. There are three checkboxes for Color, Grayscale, and Monochrome bitmaps followed by a resolution for each. If the check box is checked, then that type of bitmap will be downsampled to the

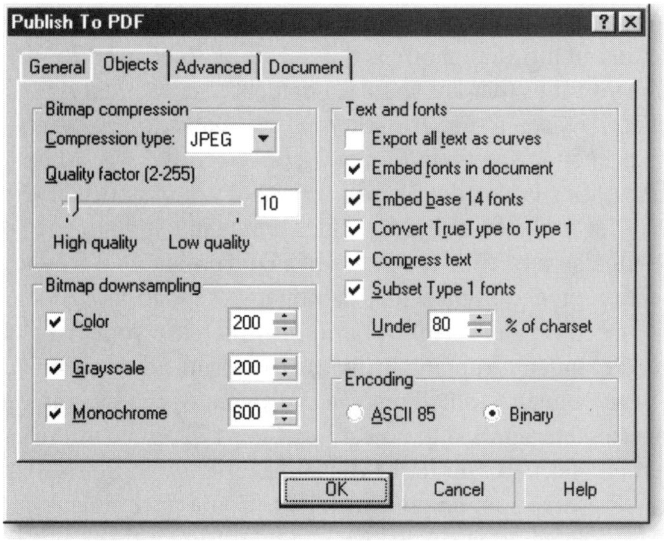

FIGURE 27-5 Publish To PDF Objects dialog box

resolution provided. Keep in mind the destination when choosing the resolution, as the right value is dependent on the job.

One of the benefits of PDF files is that fonts can be embedded inside the file. This means that the person receiving the file does not have to have the same fonts as the person creating the file. The Text and fonts section contains a number of settings that give you control of how the text in the file will be stored. For simple files with only a small amount of text, it may be better to Export all text as curves. In this case the text is converted to a graphic and is no longer text. Embed fonts in document will store any needed fonts inside of the PDF file. Embed base 14 fonts will also store the most common fonts such as Times and Helvetica in the file. To ensure that the file will not change, this is a good idea if you've used one of the basic fonts. The problem is that two fonts may have the same name, but different character widths, which could lead to a reflow of the text. Convert TrueType to Type 1 will convert any TrueType format fonts into a PostScript Type 1 font. For the best results, you'll want to leave this checked if you've used TrueType fonts. Compress text will store the text in a compressed format so that the file is smaller. Finally, you can store only a subset of a font within the PDF file. If you only use 30 characters of the font, then only those characters are stored, which makes the file smaller. You can also specify the percentage at which the fonts are subsetted.

This setting will apply only to PostScript Type 1 fonts. Many times it will be best to embed the whole font, especially if the PDF file is destined for a service bureau.

The last setting in this dialog box is the encoding to be used for the PDF file. Binary will give you files that are about 20 percent smaller than ASCII. So unless you have a specific reason to use ASCII, your best bet is to use binary. Now let's look at the Advanced tab shown in Figure 27-6.

Most of the options in this dialog box are important only if you will be supplying PDF files to a service bureau. Files that take a long time to redraw in CorelDRAW will also take time to redraw in PDF format. One way to overcome this problem is to Render complex fills as bitmaps. Rendering these complex fills as bitmaps will speed up their display, but it may increase your file size a bit. If you have created manually trapping using the overprint fill or outline options, you'll probably want to check the Preserve document overprints option. Files that contain halftone screens applied to objects will most likely want Preserve halftone screen information checked. Similarly you can keep information about spot colors by checking the Preserve spot colors check box. If you have linked images to your file using OPI, make sure to check the Maintain OPI links check box.

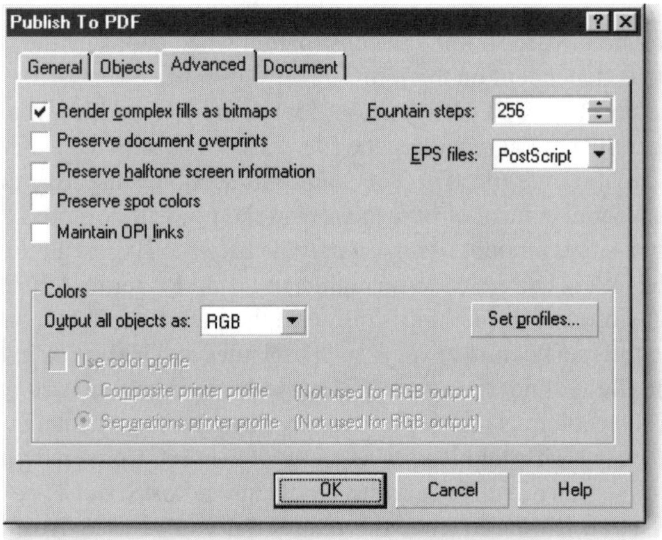

FIGURE 27-6   Publish To PDF Advanced dialog box

Fountain steps was discussed in Chapter 26. For high-quality output, you'll probably want this setting at 256, which is the maximum, but for output to devices like laser printers or ink jet printers, you can probably use a much lower value to simplify the file. If EPS files have been used in your CorelDRAW file, the bitmap preview can be included in the PDF file, or you can have the actual PostScript data included. In most cases, you'll want the actual PostScript data and not a low-resolution bitmap.

Just as when printing, you can specify to output in RGB, CMYK, or grayscale. If the file is meant for the Web, you'll probably want RGB. Files to be printed should be either CMYK or grayscale, depending on the desired output device. You can specify to use either the composite or separations color profile as they are currently defined. To change profiles, click the Set profiles button, and select the appropriate devices.

The last options for PDF files are found on the Document tab shown in Figure 27-7. You have the option of including hyperlinks within the file. If you have created hyperlinks in CorelDRAW, then you'll probably want this option checked. For files destined for service bureau output, you'll want to disable the hyperlinks.

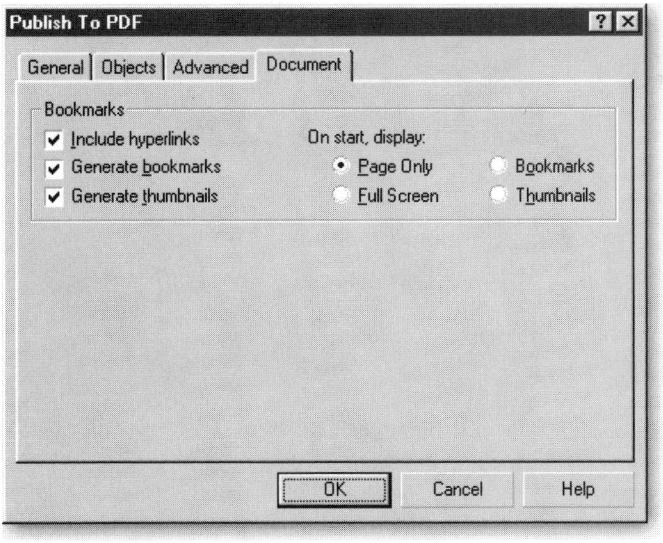

FIGURE 27-7   Publish To PDF Document dialog box

You can also generate both bookmarks and thumbnails. Doing so will create a larger file. To best understand exactly what these options do, you may want to try a file with and without them to compare. Then you can decide which best meets your needs. In the On start, display section, you have four options. These relate to the look of the file when it is first opened in Acrobat Reader or Acrobat Exchange. If you have not included bookmarks or thumbnails in the file, you certainly wouldn't want to choose the last two options. Page Only will show the full page in the Acrobat screen while Full Screen will zoom the page to fill the screen. Again, you may want to test the various views in Acrobat to decide the best choice for your document.

The new Publish To PDF functionality makes it much easier for CorelDRAW users to provide files to the service bureau or to distribute fully formatted documents on the Web. Best of all, the tools you need are all included, and you don't have to buy anything extra. This is the easiest way to create a PDF file for the service bureau and there are features that can be included using Publish To PDF that couldn't be created if you used Adobe Acrobat Distiller.

PART V

Advanced Topics

CHAPTER 28

Word Processing Features

COREL.COM

CorelDRAW 9

CorelDRAW is by no means a word processor, but there are many times when you need the functions of a word processing program. For example, nothing is more embarrassing than misspelling a word in an ad, and using inch marks for quotations is a sure sign of someone who hasn't been in the graphic design business for long. With the writing tools included with CorelDRAW 9, these problems can be minimized.

Find and Replace

CorelDRAW 9 has two types of Find and Replace commands. The first type is for graphical objects and is described in Chapter 30. This chapter is concerned with finding and replacing text. Either the find or the replace commands will find all occurrences of text within your drawing, even if the text is on multiple pages.

Bring up the Find Text dialog box with the Edit | Find and Replace | Find Text command. Note that if you don't have text on the page, then the command isn't available. The dialog box is shown here.

Type the text you want to find in the Find what textbox. If you want the search to be case sensitive, check the Match case check box. This means that if the word you typed has a capital letter, the search will match the desired word only if it has the same capital letter. When you're ready, click the Find Next button. This will highlight the next text block that contains the desired text. It will not highlight the word within that text block, however, so if the text is contained within a full page of Paragraph Text, you will have to manually search for it.

Clicking the Find Next button again will move forward in the document to the next text block containing the desired text. If multiple instances of the desired text are within one Paragraph Text block, the search feature will highlight the block only once and then move on to the next block. If the text cannot be found, a message will appear telling you that the text can't be found.

To take the search one step further, use the Edit | Find and Replace | Replace Text command. It will present the Replace Text dialog box shown here:

Replace Text	? X
Find what:	CorelDRAW 5	**Find Next**
Replace with:	CorelDRAW 9	Replace
		Replace All
☐ Match case		Close

Now after the desired text is found, it can be replaced. Type the replacement text in the Replace with textbox. To replace the text in only the first text block encountered, use the Replace button. Note that this option replaces every occurrence within the highlighted text block, so if you replace "the" within a large block of Paragraph Text, there will undoubtedly be lots of changes. The Replace All button replaces every occurrence of the specified text within every text block in the document.

When using the Replace Text dialog box, you must be careful how you search for text. Remember that Find Text will also find the characters you specify within other words. In those cases, you may want to type the desired word followed by a space and possibly preceded by a space so that only whole words will be found.

 TIP *One of the most common mistakes of typists new to word processing is to add extra spaces between sentences. Use Find and Replace to replace all occurrences of two spaces with a single space. Repeat this process until all extra spaces have been eliminated. If you are using fixed width fonts, this process should not be used.*

Type Assist

If you've used any modern word processor, Type Assist should look familiar. It made its debut in CorelDRAW 5, but most long-time users are unaware that it exists. It can be quite useful, and in CorelDRAW 9, all of its features are set by default to work without any user intervention.

To access the Type Assist dialog box, choose Text | Writing Tools | Type Assist. The Type Assist Options dialog box shown in Figure 28-1 will appear.

The first option is Capitalize first letter of sentences. This works similarly to the Sentence case option of the Change Case command discussed in Chapter 5.

28

The first letter following sentence punctuation will automatically be capitalized. Sentence punctuation includes the period (.), exclamation point (!), question mark (?), and the Spanish-language symbols ¿ and ¡. Other marks such as the colon (:), semicolon (;), and comma (,) will not be affected.

One of the most common mistakes made by desktop publishing rookies—and many veterans—is using the inch and feet marks as quotation marks. With Type Assist, there is no need to remember weird ASCII codes in order to type the correct quotation marks. Simply check the Change straight quotes to typographic quotes check box. With Type Assist, you just type the "wrong" quotation marks, and it will convert them to curly quotation marks for you.

When you are typing really fast and use the SHIFT key, you sometimes may hold it down a little bit too long. Then you may end up with more than one capital letter at the beginning of a word. Check the Correct two initial, consecutive capitals check box, and the extra capital letters will be changed back to lowercase.

CAUTION   *Do you need to type abbreviations like PC, CD, and DTP often? If you type them, they will be converted to Pc, Cd and Dtp if you enable the Correct two initial, consecutive capitals check box. In this situation, you'll need to disable the Type Assist feature for converting initial consecutive capitals.*

Proper grammar says that the names of the days of the week should be capitalized. We all forget to do this from time to time, but Type Assist can be set to remember for you. Check the Capitalize names of days check box.

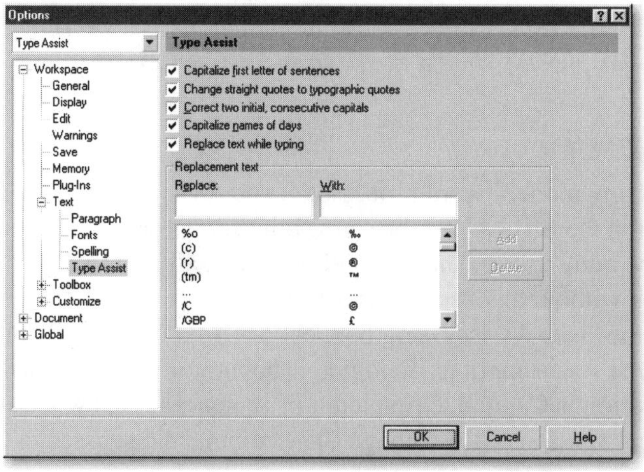

FIGURE 28-1   The Type Assist Options dialog box

The last option is Replace text while typing. When this option is checked, the replacement table at the bottom of the dialog box is used. The left side of the table shows what you type, and the right side of the table displays the text that will appear on the screen. For example, you can type (**c**) to get the © symbol. You'll notice that quite a few commonly misspelled and mistyped words are in the table with their incorrect and correct spellings.

Another great use for the Replacement text table is for abbreviations. Since we're talking about CorelDRAW 9, wouldn't it be great to type CD9 and have CorelDRAW 9 appear? Click the cursor in the Replace textbox, and type **CD9**. Now TAB to the With textbox, and type **CorelDRAW 9**. Click the Add button. Now every time you type CD9 using Artistic or Paragraph Text, it will automatically be converted to CorelDRAW 9.

If you would like to remove a particular entry from the table, highlight it, and click the Delete button. If you used previous versions and you typed the letter *s* followed by a space, you saw the word "sincerely" appear, and if you typed the letter *j* followed by a space, the word "gentlemen" appeared. This was Type Assist in action. Corel has removed those entries, but you will probably find another entry that interrupts your work. So rather than turn it off, simply scroll down through the list until you find the entry that bothers you, highlight it, and press the Delete button. Repeat the process for any other problem entries.

Spell Checker

When Corel purchased WordPerfect a while back, many users wondered what was going to happen. One immediate result is that CorelDRAW now includes the spell checker, grammar checker, and thesaurus that WordPerfect developed. This strengthens the effectiveness of CorelDRAW's other tools.

To spell check text, choose Text | Writing Tools | Spell Check, or simply use the CTRL-F12 shortcut key. If you have text selected when you bring up the spell checker, the selected text will be checked; otherwise, the whole document is checked.

When a misspelled word is found, you'll be presented with the dialog box shown here.

The top box will display the word that the spell checker doesn't understand. Just below it will be the best suggestion for a replacement, and below that will be a list of other possible replacements. On the drawing page, you'll notice that the word is highlighted so you can see it in context with the rest of the text. If none of the words suggested are correct, type the correct text in the Replace with textbox, and then click the Replace or Auto Replace button. If you don't want any changes made to the word, use the Skip Once or Skip All button, depending on how many more times the word may appear. If the word is a frequent thorn in your side or a word that you use often, use the Add button to add it to the list. If you make a mistake, simply click the Undo button.

Many more options are available when spell checking. Click the Options button to display the menu shown here:

With these options, you can customize the spell checker so that it works exactly as you want. For more information on these functions, click the ? button in the title bar of the Spell Checker dialog box.

Automatic Spell Checking

All of the latest word processors have a great feature that puts a red squiggly line under any misspelled words. Since Corel is now in the word processing business, that functionality has been added to CorelDRAW as well. By default, this feature is turned on, but if it's off, you can access it by choosing Tools | Options | Text | Spelling. This will bring up the dialog box shown in Figure 28-2.

Checking the Perform automatic spell checking check box will activate the new spell checking feature. You can also choose to show errors in all text frames or only the selected text frame. The latter provides the fastest performance if you

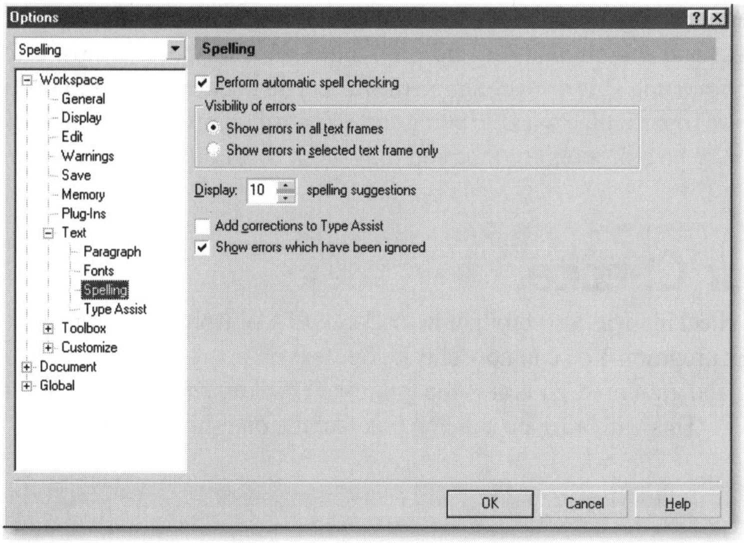

FIGURE 28-2   The Spelling Options dialog box

have large quantities of text onscreen. Note that it doesn't automatically change the spelling, it just gives you a visual cue to which words might be misspelled.

When a word is highlighted, simply right-click it with the Text tool, and you will be presented with a pop-up menu like the one shown here. This menu lists proposed correct words. The number of words depends on how many corrections are found in the spell checker word list and the number you specify in the Options dialog box.

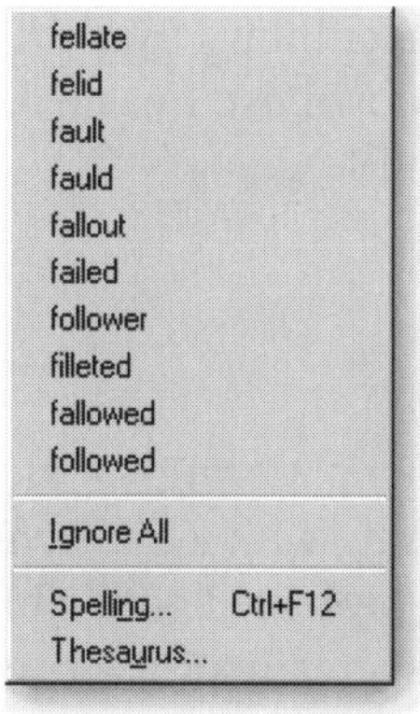

When you correct a word, you can have it automatically added to Type Assist if you check the Add Corrections to Type Assist check box. Note that this may add many words and should be used carefully. You can also specify Show errors which have been ignored. This option can be useful if you accidentally skip making a correction of a particular word. Having the error still shown will remind you that the word may be a problem or that you may want to add it to your user word list.

Grammar Checker

Grammar checking was also brought in to CorelDRAW from WordPerfect's Grammatik program. You can now check your text on many different levels for errors in spelling and grammar. To access the grammar checker, choose Text | Writing Tools | Grammatik. This will bring up a dialog box like the one shown here.

You'll notice that the right side of the dialog box is similar to the Spell Checker dialog box. The dialog box describes the error and suggests how best to correct the problem. If replacements are suggested, they will be shown in the Replacements box, and the corrected sentence that Grammatik suggests will be shown in the New sentence box. You can either use the correction or ignore it, but there is no way that you can edit the change to be made.

You can check quite a few other things by clicking the Options button and selecting an item from the drop-down list. For more information on each of these items, see the CorelDRAW Help file.

Thesaurus

Suppose you're working (or is that puttering?) really hard on a document, and you want to find a way to say something with a different word. Choose Text | Writing Tools | Thesaurus, and you'll be presented with a blank dialog box similar to the one shown next. Note that we've already proceeded with the next step so that the image shown is not empty. You can also right-click on a word and choose Thesaurus from the pop-up menu.

Type a word in the textbox at the upper left (if it is blank), or use the word that is already found. Click the Look Up button if you don't already have suggestions in the lower part of the dialog box. The lower part should now be filled with suggested words or phrases along with definitions of each suggested replacement. The results of the search depend on the choices you make in the Options drop-down menu shown here. If you don't understand any of these choices, click the ? on the title bar of the dialog box, and it will provide information to help you understand.

You can have the Thesaurus find many different types of words or phrases related to the word you specify. From the Options menu, you can decide which of these types will be shown in the lower-right and lower-left list boxes.

If you highlight a word in your document before bringing up the Thesaurus, you can automatically replace it with a new word or phrase. Select the new word or phrase in the lower-left list box, and click the Insert button. Your original word or phrase will now be gone, and the new one will be in its place.

TIP *Make sure that you only select the word and not the spaces surrounding the word, as it may affect the results.*

Text Statistics

As you work on a document, you will often find it handy to know certain information about the text within the document. The Text | Text Statistics command will give you information about either the selected text block or all the text in the document (if no text is selected). The Statistics dialog box is shown here.

```
Statistics                                          ? X

Selection: Paragraph Text Frame

Statistics:

  Not all of the text fits in the frame.
  Paragraphs:                    10
  Lines:                         24
  Words:                         490
  Characters:                    2705
  Fonts used:                    Times New Roman
                                 Arial
  Number of styles used:         1
     Default Paragraph Text      1

  ✔ Show style statistics

                              [ Close ]      Help
```

This dialog box lists the types of objects and the number of each object. The types of objects that may be listed include Paragraph Text frames, Paragraphs, Artistic Text objects, Lines, Words, Characters, and Fonts. Knowing the fonts used in a document can be extremely important when it comes time to share the document with another user or a service bureau.

If you check the Show style statistics check box, more information related to text styles will be displayed. This information includes the number of styles used, a list of the styles, and the number of times each style was used.

Document Information

A similar option gives you even more detailed information about the entire CorelDRAW file. Select File | Document Information to get the dialog box shown next.

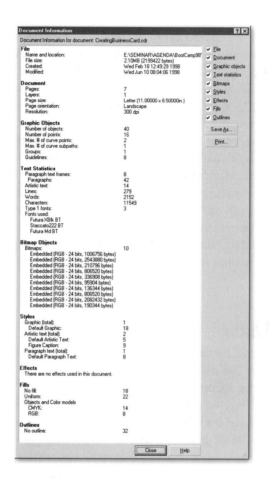

In addition to the text statistics described earlier, you will also learn information about where the file is located, the number of pages and their orientation, the number of objects, a list of bitmaps, the number of styles and their types, the effects, the types of fills, and the types of outlines. You can either save this information to a separate file or print it for future reference. This can be a handy tool if you are troubleshooting a problem file.

Extracting and Merging Text

Somewhere in the world is a user of CorelDRAW who thinks this program is a word processor. Well, it isn't, and you will sometimes find it easier to edit text with a word processor than with CorelDRAW. To do so, you will need to get the text out of CorelDRAW and into a format your word processor can read (extract it), and then you must get the edited text back into CorelDRAW (merge it back).

The methods for doing this are the same for both Artistic and Paragraph Text. Just create your drawing with all the text you want. Then when it comes time to edit the text outside of CorelDRAW, follow the instructions in the sections that follow.

As CorelDRAW has grown, it has added more and more features that were once the domain of word processors. Now it can spell check, grammar check, and much more. So there is less need to use the Extract and Merge Back commands, and Corel has removed the commands from the default menus that come with CorelDRAW 9. But all is not lost. You can fully customize the menus to do exactly what you need. And the commands do still exist. In Chapter 34, we describe how to customize CorelDRAW. When we get to the section in Chapter 34 on customizing menus, we show how to add these two commands since it is a somewhat lengthy explanation. For those who aren't familiar with this process, turn to Chapter 34. The rest of you, continue on.

Extracting Text

When you extract text, first save your CorelDRAW file. Otherwise, a message asking you to save the file will be displayed. You don't need to select the text, since all text within the document will be extracted. You next just choose the Text | Extract command, if you've customized your menus as explained in Chapter 34, and you will be prompted for a filename and location. The text will be converted to an ASCII file with various markers so that CorelDRAW can accurately remerge the file.

Open the text file in your favorite word processor, and make the necessary changes. You'll notice the symbols @PTXT prefacing any Paragraph text and @ATXT prefacing any Artistic text. Many of the other markers will be contained with angle brackets (< and >). Make sure that you edit only the text and that these markers remain unchanged; otherwise, the file will not remerge correctly, if at all.

When you are done editing the file, save the file as plain ASCII text. If you save the file in the format of the word processor, CorelDRAW will not be able to use it.

 TIP *Another great use for this feature is to just extract all of the text so that you can use it elsewhere—maybe for page layout or even a Web page.*

Merging Text

To bring the text back into your CorelDRAW document, you'll need to have the document loaded. Select Te_x_t I Merge Bac_k_, assuming that you've customized your menus as described in Chapter 34, and choose the text file that you edited. Your edited text will be brought into your document so that it replaces the existing text. Some attributes such as font, font size, character spacing, and alignment will be retained. Attributes that affect individual characters such as the character angle, baseline shift, and font style will not be maintained, since the text they refer to may have changed. If an effect has been applied to the text, you may notice that there are alterations. You can reapply the effect to the text to correct any problems.

The abilities to extract and merge text are more important when you are working with large blocks of Paragraph Text. In that case, you might want to explore a different method. Create the text in your favorite word processor, and perform any editing in the word processor. When the text has your final approval, import it into CorelDRAW. This will eliminate the need to worry about the markup codes within the text and the need to reapply attributes.

28

Using Print Merge

If you've used a word processor for any length of time, you've probably performed a mail merge operation. Mail merge is great for producing plain old form letters, but suppose you want to create a really great looking document that can be merged with a set of data? You can do this with CorelDRAW if you carefully prepare your CorelDRAW document and the data that is to be merged.

Preparing the Drawing

When preparing a drawing to be merged, you must observe several restrictions. You can create anything you want in the document, but any text that is to be replaced must be Artistic Text. Within that Artistic Text string, you can enter any text you want, but it must be unique from other strings. For example, you can use the text "Name," where a person's name would be substituted. Just keep in mind that the name being substituted may be substantially longer than the four characters in the word "Name." Any of the attributes applied to the original text string, such as font, size, and alignment, will also be applied to the substituted text. The only effects that will not be applied to the merged data are Blend and Extrude.

Once you've designed the drawing to your liking, simply save it as a .cdr file just like any other file.

Now it is time to prepare the data that will be merged with your drawing.

Preparing the Text

The hardest part to the whole merging process is creating a data file, since this is a very exacting process. You can create the file in your favorite word processor, but it may be easier to just use Windows Notepad. Advanced users may want to use the Database Publisher utility that comes with Corel VENTURA to automate the process.

The first item in the file should be the number of text blocks that will be merged. For example, if there are three items that are going to be replaced, insert the number 3.

Next, you need to list each of the text blocks that will be replaced. The text must be preceded and followed by the backslash (\) character. Make sure that the text is typed exactly as it appears in the CorelDRAW document, including its spelling and punctuation. The last character must not be a space, or the process will not work. Each of the data elements can appear on a separate line, or all of the elements can be grouped together on a single line.

Now you need to enter the data that will be merged into your document. Again, it must be preceded and followed by the \ character. Here are two examples of the data file, one with each set of data on a single line and the other with the data on separate lines.

Data on one line:

```
3
\Name\\Class\\Date\
\Joe Q. User\\CorelDRAW 9 Boot Camp\\October 28-30, 1999\
\Jane Artist\\Corel PHOTO-PAINT 9 Boot Camp\\November 11-13, 1999\
```

Data on separate lines:

```
3
\Name\
\Class\
\Date\
\Joe Q. User\
\CorelDRAW 9 Boot Camp\
\October 28-30, 1999\
\Jane Artist\
\Corel PHOTO-PAINT 9 Boot Camp\
\November 11-13, 1999\
```

Once the data has been entered properly, save it in plain ASCII format.

Merging the Document with the Text

When you execute the merge operation, the text file cannot be opened, so make sure you've closed the file in your text editor. You will not see any of the pages onscreen before they are printed, so take a second to look at the data file to make sure it is correct before you precede.

 CAUTION *A common problem that users may encounter is that the original text in CorelDRAW may contain invisible characters such as a space or a carriage return. So if you're having problems, check the text carefully!*

Print Merge is yet another command that has been removed from the default menu structure. So you'll also have to customize your menus (as described in Chapter 34) to add it to the File menu where it used to be located. Once you've done that and opened your drawing, simply select File | Print Merge. You will be prompted to select the text file containing the merge data. Click OK, and your merged documents will soon come out of your printer. If things don't look right on the document, the data file probably contains errors that need to be corrected.

Figure 28-3 shows a sample certificate before the data file is merged. Figure 28-4 shows an example of what the certificate looks like after the Print Merge operation.

The ability to merge a data file into CorelDRAW lets you create some really awesome documents that just aren't possible in your word processor or database. Getting the correct syntax can be daunting at first, but once you master it, the process is quite simple.

Limitations of Print Merge

Let's look at a common task that CorelDRAW users may want to perform. Suppose you want to create a set of name tags for an event. You've gone down to your office supply store and purchased some premade tags that you can run through your laser printer. They come eight to a sheet, and CorelDRAW even has a label template that works perfectly. So far, so good. The problem is that the Print Merge operation only works on one document at a time rather than the multiple pages within the same document that would be required to print the name tag labels. There is a workaround, but it is extremely tedious. You will need to create

FIGURE 28-3   Certificate template to be merged with a data file

FIGURE 28-4   The certificate after the Print Merge operation

variables titled "Name1," "Name2," "Name3," and so on and more variables if you want to include other data such as the company name on the label. Suffice it to say that this process is not very smooth.

To accomplish the name tag project, it is probably easier to create the graphic portion of your name tag and use it in conjunction with Corel VENTURA or a database program. This gives you the graphic power of CorelDRAW and the mail merge power of the other programs.

With the various word processing tools that are provided, CorelDRAW has the capability to work with all of the text in your ad, flyer, or newsletter. And since these tools are common to many Corel applications, the learning curve for using each application is much smaller. Just keep in mind that longer text-intensive projects are best handled in a true page layout package such as Corel VENTURA.

28

CHAPTER 29

Styles, Templates, and Scrapbooks

CorelDRAW 9

One of the best ways to improve your productivity is to take advantage of the features described in this chapter. Styles come in many flavors, and they allow you to easily create reusable elements. Radical color changes are simple to make when using color styles. Templates give you a good starting point for creating documents. Scrapbooks make it easy to manage the plethora of clipart and stock photos that are included with CorelDRAW.

Graphic and Text Styles

Graphic and text styles have been available for many versions, but few users know of their existence. By understanding how styles work, you'll be able to produce work faster. You'll also avoid receiving the messages telling you that you are missing fonts even though your file contains no text.

When you load CorelDRAW the very first time, you will be working with the default template CORELDRW.cdt. As you'll see later, some templates contain actual objects. However, the default template contains only the default styles. To see the styles in the current document, select Tools | Graphic and Text Styles (CTRL-F5). By default, they will be displayed as a Docker. If you drag the Docker onto the desktop, it will look similar to the one shown here.

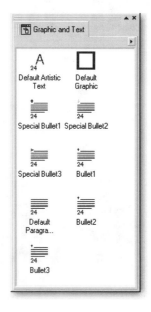

You'll notice that there are three types of styles: Artistic Text, Graphic, and Paragraph Text. The default template includes several styles for Paragraph Text, including many with bullets, but there is only one style each for Artistic Text and Graphic.

Applying any of these styles to an object is simple. Select the style you wish to apply, and drag it onto the object to which you want it applied. The cursor will change to indicate that you can drop the style. The other way to apply a style is to right-click any object and choose the appropriate style from the pop-up menu that appears.

When you first see the Docker, the icons may all be rather large. You have the option of changing the view so that it is in list format instead. Right-click the white area inside the Docker window, and select Ⅴiew | Ⅾetails from the pop-up menu. This will change the list of styles so that they look similar to the ones shown here.

29

Name	Type	Hotkey
A Default Artistic Text	Artistic Text	
Default Graphic	Graphic	
Special Bullet1	Paragraph Text	
Special Bullet2	Paragraph Text	
Special Bullet3	Paragraph Text	
Bullet1	Paragraph Text	
Default Paragraph Text	Paragraph Text	
Bullet2	Paragraph Text	
Bullet3	Paragraph Text	

Creating Styles

You can create new styles in two ways. By far the easiest method is to drag an object (text or graphic) that contains the attributes you want onto the Styles window. It will be automatically added to the list and named. You can change the name simply by clicking the name twice (do not double-click) and typing the new name. If you wish to make more extensive changes, highlight the name, right-click it, and choose Properties from the pop-up menu. The dialog box shown here will be displayed.

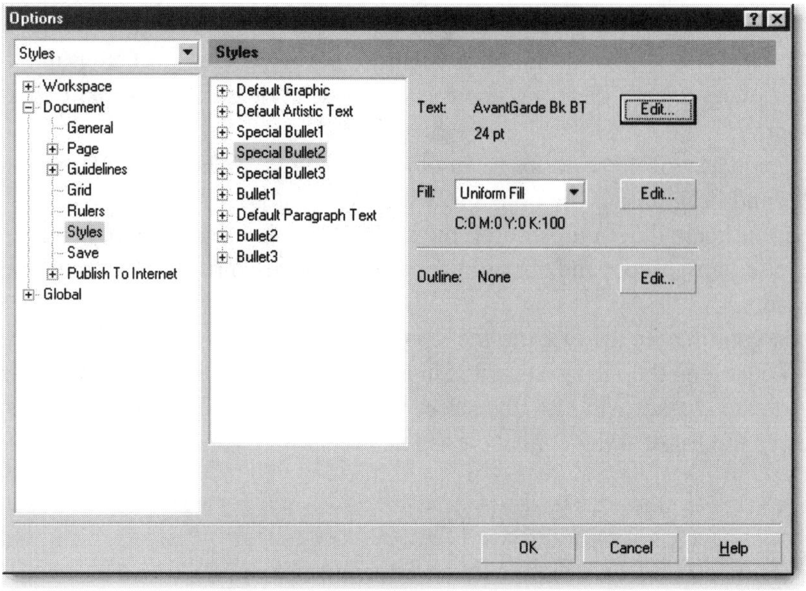

By navigating through the tree structure of the style you wish to change, you can edit all attributes of the style. Each of the major attributes has an Edit button; by clicking this button, you will be taken to the appropriate dialog box for changing the attribute. If you don't want a certain attribute to be part of the style, just deselect that option.

The other way to create a new style (or modify an existing style) is to right-click an object (text or graphic) that contains the attributes you want in your style. Choose Styles | Save Style Properties from the pop-up menu, and you will be presented with the dialog box shown here.

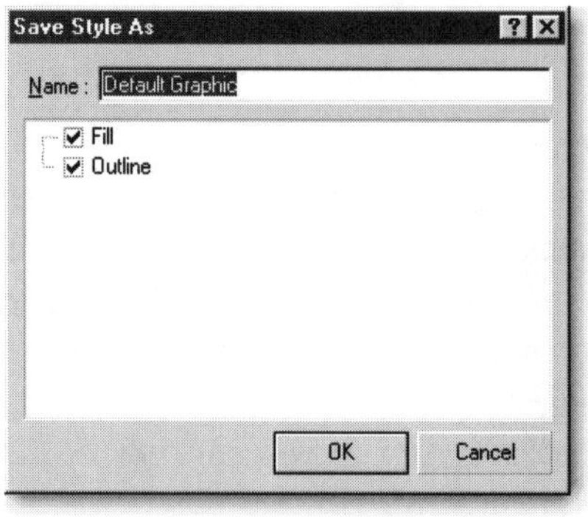

Give the style a new name if you don't want to override the attributes of the selection's current style. Note that if you don't change the style name, all other objects with the selected style will be affected by your changes—which can be desirable. If you don't want certain attributes to be part of the style, deselect them in this dialog box before you click OK.

A Simple Project

In Chapter 5, we worked on a project that involved laying out a newsletter. We supplied a template that already included several styles to be used on the text. Now let's walk through how a couple of those styles were created.

Let's start by changing the existing style named Default Paragraph Text.

1. Select Tools | Options to bring up the Options dialog box, and then choose Document | Styles in the tree structure on the left side of the dialog box.

2. Select Default Paragraph Text in the list of styles, and click the Edit button.

3. You should now see the Format Text dialog box that was described in detail in Chapter 5. For the newsletter example, we chose Futura Md BT for the Font and 8 points for the Size. On the Space tab, we changed the Line spacing to 9 points and the Before paragraph spacing to 12 points.

4. Click OK, and the style will be updated.

We could certainly have changed many other options, but those were the only changes needed for our newsletter. That method works great if the style already exists. Now let's work through creating a new style. In our newsletter, we have another style of Paragraph Text called Level 2 Heading.

1. First, you need to create a Paragraph Text frame, and type some text.

2. Highlight a full paragraph of text, and format it as you desire. You can do the formatting with the Property Bar or the Format Text dialog box.

3. While the text is still selected, right-click and select Styles | Save Style Properties.

4. In the Save Style As dialog box, type **Level 2 Heading** for the Name.

29

You've now seen how to create a brand new style. Note that the styles you created will exist only in the current document. If you would like to use them elsewhere, you'll need to return to the Options dialog box and choose Document from the tree structure at left. Check the Save options as defaults for new documents check box, and make sure that Styles is also checked. This will make the styles in the current document into the default for any new document you create. Another option is to click the flyout button at the top of the Styles Docker and choose Template I Save As. This lets you save the set of styles for use as a template for other documents. You'll learn more about templates later.

Color Styles

Have you ever created a really intricate design based on a single color or two colors and then decided that you would really prefer the design to be a different color? Changing every single object is time consuming, so you just leave things as they are. With the new color styles, such a change can be made nearly instantly.

First you will start with an existing design to see how color styles can be created automatically. Use the file FLWRCART.cdr provided on the book's CD. The flower cart and the flower are pink and red. We want to change these colors to various shades of yellow.

1. Choose Tools I Color Styles to bring up the Color Styles Docker. We dragged it out onto the page so that it is floating as shown here.

2. You'll see five buttons in the window. Choose the one on the far right, Auto Create Color Styles. If it is dimmed, remember that you must have the objects selected that are to become your new color styles. By double-clicking on the Pick tool, you can easily select all the objects in the drawing.

3. The dialog box shown here will appear. Just to make sure that everything will work properly for this image, click the Preview button, and the right window of the dialog box will show the color styles that will be created.

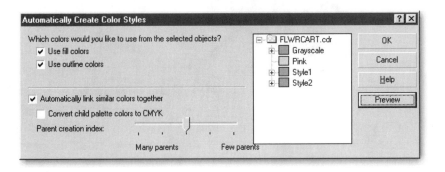

4. You should see that four styles will be created. One of them contains various shades of gray, and there will be three separate styles for reds and pinks. We want the red and pink to be part of one single style.

5. Slide the slider at the bottom of the dialog box one notch to the right, and click Preview again. There should only be two styles now. One will be grayscale, and one reddish in color.

6. Click the OK button, and the styles will be created.

7. You'll now see a + next to FLWRCART.cdr in the Color Styles Docker. Click on it so that the list of styles is visible. Then select the red swatch, which should be named Style1.

8. Click the Color Wheel icon along the top of the Docker window to get the dialog box shown next.

29

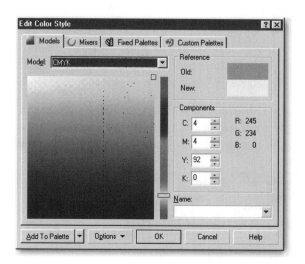

9. You'll see that this is same as the Uniform Fill dialog box described in Chapter 8. Remember that we want a shade of yellow. Select the new color, and press OK.

See how easy it is to change the entire color scheme of a complex image? Now let's take a closer look at the dialog box you just used to create the color styles.

The first choice you can make is whether to create the styles from fill colors or from outline colors. In the example, you didn't need to worry about outline colors, since the colors were all black and you didn't want to change them.

Be sure to choose the Automatically link similar colors together option. If this is not chosen, you'll get many more styles, and therefore changing the color of a whole drawing won't be nearly so easy. You can also choose to convert any child color from its current color scheme to CMYK as the styles are created.

The last option is a slider that controls the number of parent colors created. If you slide the pointer to the far left, there will be little tolerance between color shades. Sliding it to the right provides a wide range of tolerance. Your best bet is to leave the slider at the default (middle) position for most drawings. By clicking the Preview button, you can see exactly what styles will be created, and you can adjust the slider accordingly to get the styles you need.

That is the automated way to create color styles; in our opinion, it is the best way. Create your drawing, then have the styles created from the drawing. However, there is another way that lets you create your own styles.

NOTE   *You can also use color styles for images that use spot colors.*

The button at the far left of the Color Styles Docker will create a new color style. It brings up the New Color Style dialog box, just like the Uniform Fill dialog box discussed in Chapter 8. Whatever color you choose will become your new parent color. While you're in the New Color Style dialog box, you can give your new style a name, or you can click the name twice (don't double-click) in the Docker and then change the name. If you have a parent color selected, you can create a child for that parent by clicking the next button in the Docker. It will provide you with the dialog box shown here.

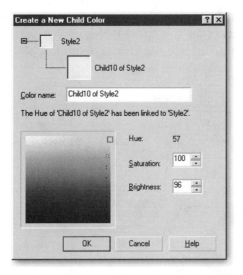

In the Create a New Child Color dialog box, you can enter a name for the child color. Most of the time, it is best to leave the name alone so that it shows the link to the parent. You can change only the saturation and brightness values for the child color, because changing the hue value would make it a distant cousin instead of a child!

Instead of manually creating child colors, click the fourth button in the Color Styles Docker. This will automatically generate shades of the parent color, as shown in the following dialog box.

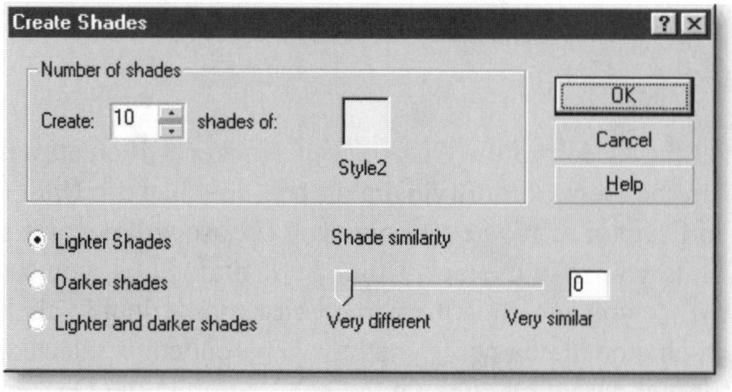

Up to 20 different shades can be created. With the radio button, you can specify whether the shades should be lighter, darker, or both in relation to the parent. You can also control the similarity of the new colors to the original ones with the slider control.

Another way to get to the commands is to right-click any of the color styles. This will bring up the menu shown here.

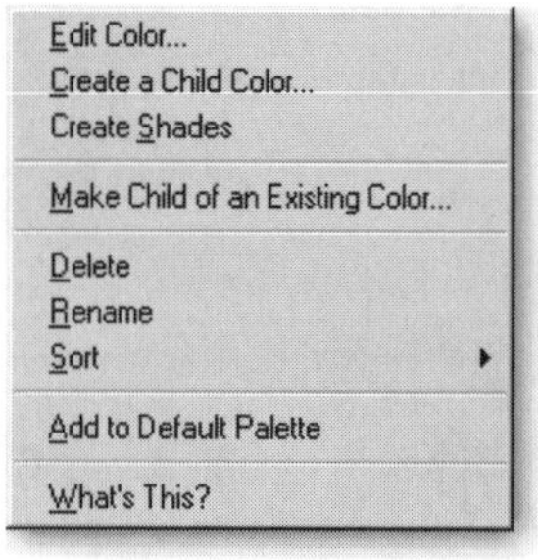

Templates

In essence, a template is nothing more than a CorelDRAW file with a different extension. Templates can be repositories for predesigned work; they can store styles you've created as well as content.

A number of templates are provided with CorelDRAW; examples of each are shown in the clipart manual. Note that the PaperDirect templates are not shown in the clipart manual, but they are shown in each of the PaperDirect catalogs. These templates are divided into CorelDRAW templates and PaperDirect templates, which are meant to be used with paper supplied by PaperDirect.

If you know exactly which template you want, choose File | Open, and open the file you want. To find a template appropriate for your job, choose File | New

From Template, and you'll be presented with the Template Wizard, shown here. Select the set of templates you want to choose from. You can choose from CorelDRAW templates, PaperDirect templates (text and paper samples), and PaperDirect templates (text only). Then click Next.

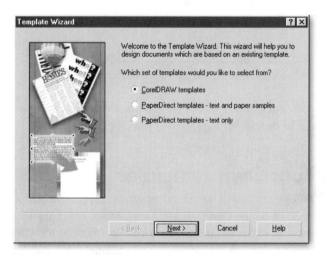

Now you'll be presented with a list of template types as shown here. Make a selection, and then click Next.

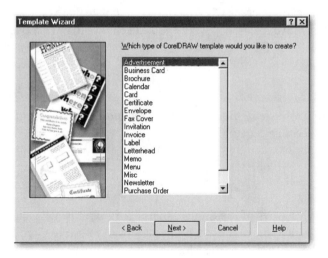

You can now choose a subtype of a template based on your previous selection. Again, make your choice, and then click Next.

The next screen lists individual templates.

In the upper right, you'll see a small preview of the template, just as in CorelDRAW's File Open dialog box. You'll also see the option Open with contents. You can either bring in only the styles from the template or include any text and graphics that may be in the file.

Once you've made all your selections, click Finish. The file will be opened in CorelDRAW.

You'll soon see that templates are similar to clipart, but instead of being just one graphic, a template contains a whole document.

 NOTE *You must select the Open with contents option if you want guidelines to be loaded from a template file.*

Creating Your Own Templates

Any documents that you regularly create are good candidates for templates. To create your own template, choose the CorelDRAW Template (CDT) File Type in the Save As dialog box. Since all of the templates are normally stored in the \Draw\Template folder below the main folder where CorelDRAW was installed, you can even add your own templates to the Wizard by putting them in that folder and running the Tempwiz script to add them to the template list..

If you don't want to go through the Wizard each time you want to use a template, select File | Open, and select the CDT file for the template that you want to open. You will be presented with a dialog box where you can choose to open the template for editing the template itself or to use it as a template for a new document, with or without contents.

 TIP *To learn more about how to create your own templates, you may want to open one of the PaperDirect templates and dissect it using the Object Manager.*

Scrapbooks

Scrapbooks provide ways of looking at your clipart, photos, fills and outlines, 3D models, FTP sites, and other files that you may want to use in CorelDRAW. The Scrapbook Docker is similar to the Mosaic roll-up that was featured in older versions of CorelDRAW, but it has much more functionality.

Each of the sections of the Scrapbook can be opened from the Tools | Scrapbook drop-down child menu. Let's begin with the Clipart Scrapbook by selecting Tools | Scrapbook | Clipart. The only thing it contains is a folder labeled "Clipart." If you don't already have the clipart CD in your CD-ROM drive, you will be asked to insert it. Double-click the folder (just as in Explorer), and you'll see a list of all the folders on the Clipart CD. Africa will be the first item listed. Double-click it to see the contents. Again, you'll see a long list of folders. Double-click Art. Now you should see a number of files shown as small icons with the filename below each. The icons are rather small, but you can enlarge them. Right-click the white space in the roll-up, and choose View | Thumbnail Size from the pop-up menu. This brings up the following dialog box.

Change the Size value to Large, and click OK. All the icons should be much larger and easier to interpret, as shown here.

Now you simply need to locate the file you wish to add to your drawing. Drag it onto the drawing page. This will automatically import the file at the point where you release your mouse button.

Many times you'll have a few pieces of your own "clipart" that is reused quite often in a project. A quick way to create such files is to simply drag the object or objects that you wish to save directly into the Browse window. This will save the image as a "Scrap." You can rename the file after dropping it in the Scrapbook, but it will not generate a thumbnail. A better idea is to create a folder on your hard drive where all such files will be located. Save each of the "clipart" images in this folder, and then use the Scrapbook to access the files. This way they will all have a thumbnail associated with them.

At first, the features discussed in this chapter may not seem to be as impressive as some others, but templates can help increase your productivity by giving you a starting point for a project. Moreover, once you have experienced the need to make drastic changes in a project late in the design cycle, you'll learn to appreciate the use of styles.

CHAPTER 30

Find and Replace Wizards

CorelDRAW 9

You've just imported some clipart, you resize it, and all of the outlines go crazy; or it comes time to print, and an extra spot color shows up somewhere in your drawing. These are some of the common situations that make you wish that there was an easy way to globally change attributes of objects.

Early versions of CorelDRAW required you to step through a drawing, object by object, until you found what you were looking for and then change the setting. Now with the Find and Replace Wizards, this task is much simpler.

Find Wizard

If you choose Edit I Find and Replace I Find Objects, you'll be presented with the Find Wizard's initial screen, shown in Figure 30-1.

Notice that there are three options. The simplest option for most operations is Find objects that match the currently selected object. Create an object containing the attributes you wish to find, and then use this option. Just remember that it will

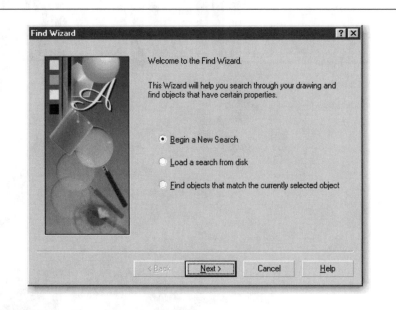

FIGURE 30-1   The initial Find Wizard screen

only find objects exactly like the one you created. However, the nice thing is that you can edit the attributes before the search begins, so this option is a great way to make sure all of the relevant attributes are included.

Using Preset Finds

Because the Find Wizard can be somewhat overwhelming to the first-time user, Corel provides preset options for several of the most common attributes you may want to find. These include PANTONE fills, PANTONE outlines, overprinted outlines, scale with image off, and text with RGB fills.

Choosing Load a search from disk displays a standard File Open dialog box, where you can select any searches you previously saved. The five types of searches previously mentioned will always be listed in this dialog box. Since each of these searches is a separate file, you can share your favorites with other users.

Once you've made your choice, the first object of that type will be found and selected. If no such object exists, a message will let you know. If such an object is found, the following dialog box appears.

The controls here are similar to those in a spell checker. Find Next finds and selects the next object, if there is one, and Find Previous finds and selects the previous object, if there is one. Find All finds and selects all objects that match your specification. The Edit Search button takes you back to the Find Wizard so you can specify different attributes.

Whenever an object is selected, you can make any changes you desire. With this particular option, there is no way to easily replace the attributes you find with different attributes. However, a few search and replace functions are included, as discussed later in this chapter.

Conducting New Searches

The real power of the Find feature lies in the Begin a New Search option. If you choose this option and click Next, you'll be presented with the dialog box shown in Figure 30-2.

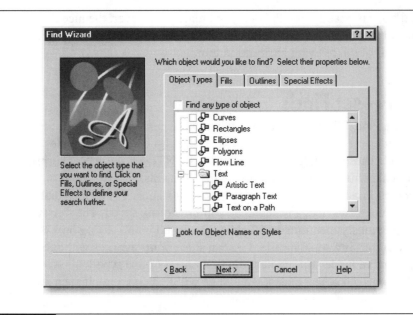

FIGURE 30-2   The second Find Wizard screen

Here, each type of object is listed individually as well as by general type, such as Text. Place a check mark next to each type of object that you want to find. Sometimes the type of object is not important because you want to find every object with a certain property. In that case, make sure to check Find any type of object at the top of the list box. For now, just select Ellipses for a sample search.

Three other tabs in this dialog box allow you to choose specific types of fills, outlines, and special effects for inclusion in your search criteria. These tabs each provide a list similar to that shown for the Object Types tab. For a sample search, go to the Fills tab, and select Uniform Color. Then go to the Outlines tab, and select Outline properties. Finally, go to the Special Effects tab, and select Blend. At the bottom of the dialog box is a check box labeled Look for Object Names or Styles. If this is checked, all other parts of the dialog box will be dimmed. If you choose this option and click Next, you'll see the dialog box shown in Figure 30-3.

In the Object Manager, you can name each of your objects. If you have named objects and want to search on those names, check the Object name check box, and type the name you wish to find. If you can't remember whether you used names with uppercase or lowercase letters, make sure not to check the Match case check box.

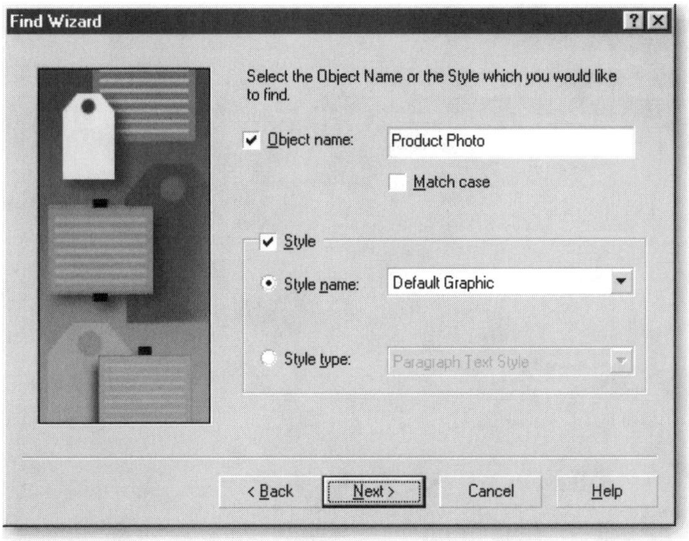

FIGURE 30-3   Find Wizard screen for selecting an object by name or style name

When searching for styles, you have the choice of searching for a specific style name or a style type. You can even search for both an object name and a style if you so desire.

Clicking Next now displays a dialog that summarizes all of your search criteria and allows you to begin finding objects. This dialog box will be discussed later in this chapter after the rest of the Find options have been discussed.

As long as you haven't chosen Look for Object Names or Styles, clicking the Next button will display a series of dialog boxes asking for more information on the options you have selected. The first dialog box you will see is shown in Figure 30-4.

The example selection criteria looked only for ellipses. In the upper-left corner of the dialog box, all of the types of objects you've selected are listed. At the bottom of the dialog box is a complete description of the search criteria. This information is provided just to show you your choices and cannot be changed directly.

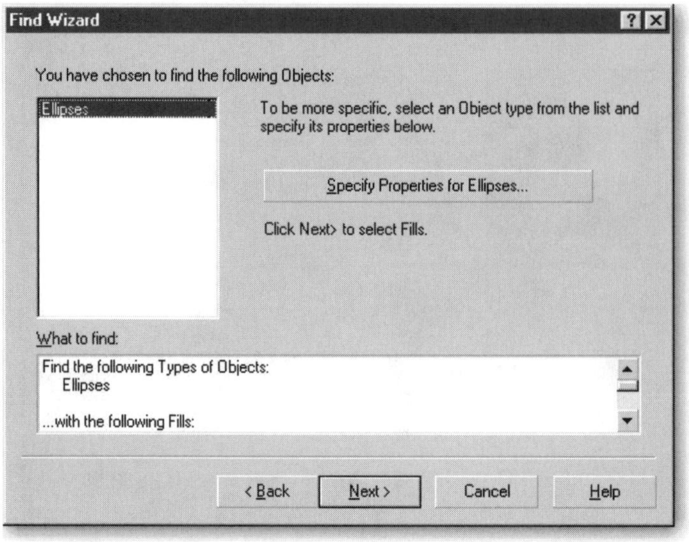

FIGURE 30-4   Find Wizard dialog box for more detailed information on ellipses

This example searches for ellipses, so you can choose Specify Properties for Ellipses. This brings up the dialog box shown in Figure 30-5.

This dialog box includes all of the parameters that can be set for ellipses. If there are any specific parameters that you don't understand, refer to Chapter 3 for more information. Note that you can also search for ellipses of a specific width and height. Doing this will narrow the search considerably; you should use these criteria with caution. Click the OK button to return to the previous dialog box.

If you choose to find other types of objects, you will be able to specify properties for those types individually. When you've finished specifying properties for all the object types selected, click the Next button to display the dialog box shown in Figure 30-6.

This dialog box searches for objects with a uniform fill. You can specify that you want to find any objects with a uniform color fill or only those objects with a specific uniform color fill. If you want to find a specific color, click the color picker, and find the exact color you need. Another check box lets you specify whether the overprint attribute of the fill is important. If you check Overprint fill, you can specify whether the attribute should be turned on or off. Again you'll see a complete description of your search criteria at the bottom of the dialog box.

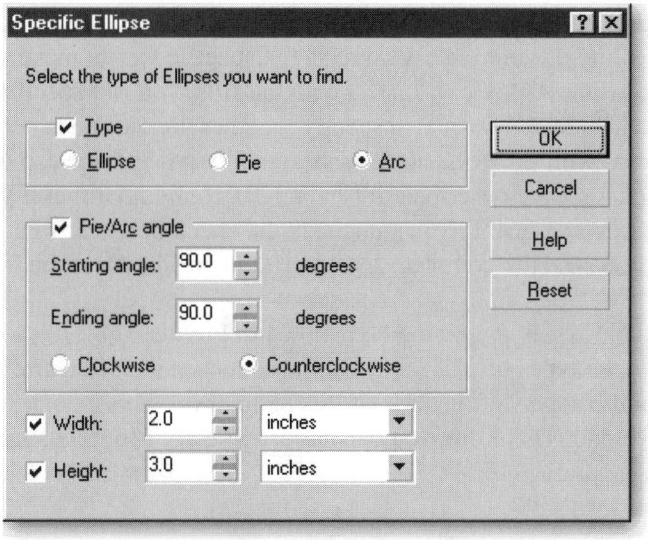

FIGURE 30-5 The Specific Ellipse dialog box

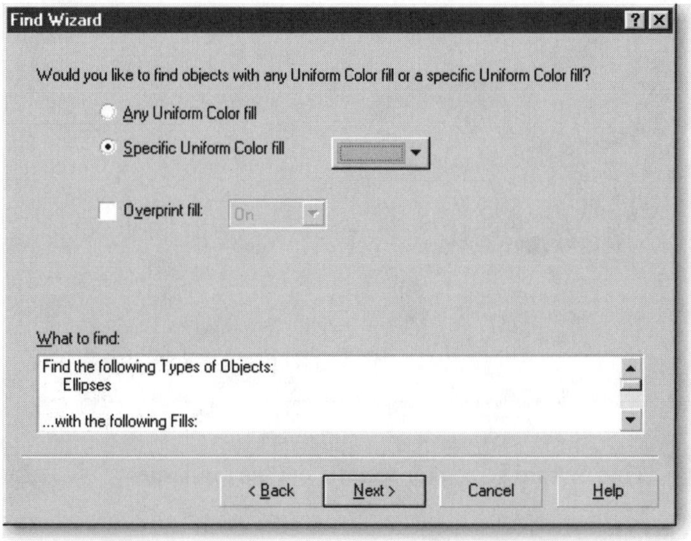

FIGURE 30-6 Find Wizard screen for finding objects with a uniform fill

Click Next to go to the dialog box shown in Figure 30-7. Now come all of the specific properties of outlines you wish to find. The first option lets you choose the width of the outline. If you don't want to find a specific width, make sure that the Width check box is not checked. Just as with the fills, you can specify a color or the overprint attribute. You can also specify whether the outline is behind the fill, whether the scale with image attribute is set, and the type of line cap on the line. All of these options were described in Chapter 10. Remember that if you don't care about a particular attribute, just uncheck the check box next to it. As with the previous dialog boxes, the complete search criteria are shown at the bottom of the dialog.

Click Next to display the dialog box shown in Figure 30-8.

Just as with the types of objects, if you have chosen a particular effect, it will be indicated in the upper-left list box of this dialog box. This example searches for objects with a blend. Therefore, you can choose Specify Properties for Blend to see the following dialog box.

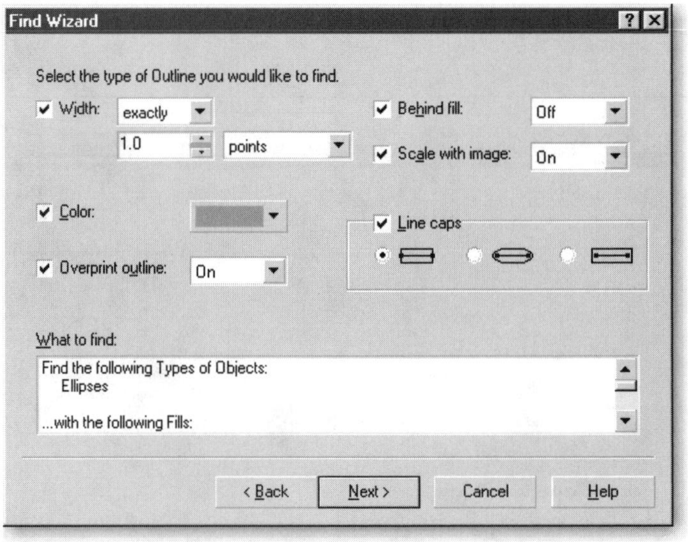

FIGURE 30-7   Find Wizard screen for specific outline properties

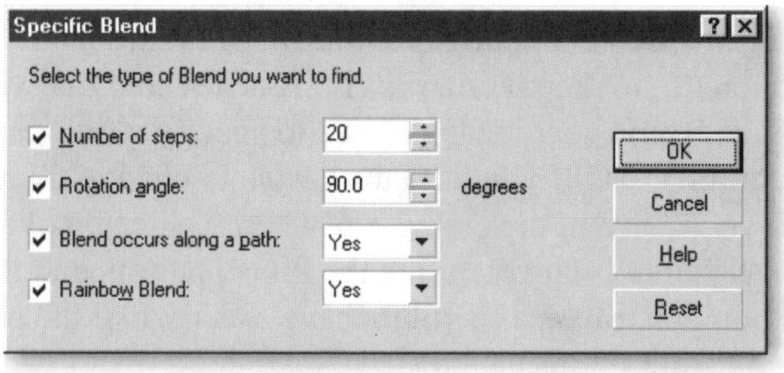

For blends, you can specify only the number of steps, rotation angle, whether the blend occurs along a path, and whether the blend is a rainbow blend. Once you've specified all of the attributes for blends and other effects you may have chosen, click the OK button to return to the previous dialog box. As before, a complete description of the search criteria is shown at the bottom of the dialog box.

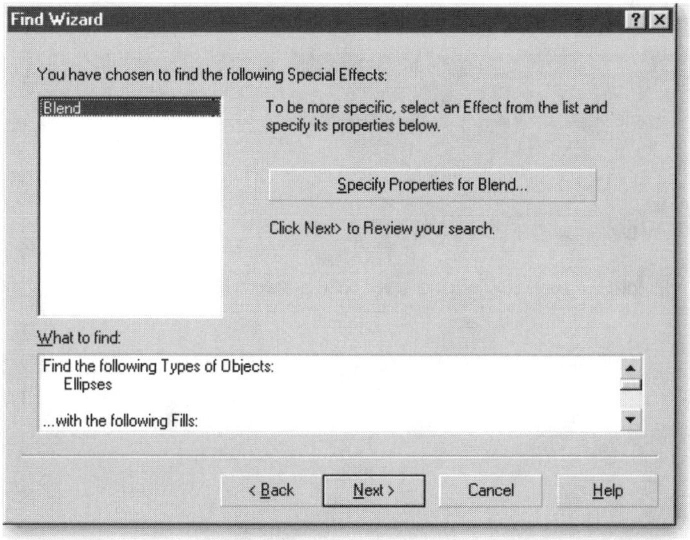

FIGURE 30-8   Find Wizard screen for special effects

Click Next to go to the next dialog box, shown in Figure 30-9. It provides a complete description of the search criteria. If this is a search that you will perform again, click the Save button so you won't have to specify all of the attributes again. Check the criteria, and if you left out or wish to change something, use the Back button until you return to the dialog box where you can make the desired changes. When everything is correct, click the Finish button, and the search will begin. From this point on, the search will behave exactly like the predefined searches discussed earlier in this chapter.

Replace Wizard

The Replace Wizard lets you search for a limited set of attributes and replace them with something else. Access the Replace Wizard by choosing Edit | Find and Replace | Replace Objects. You'll be presented with the initial Replace Wizard dialog box, shown in Figure 30-10.

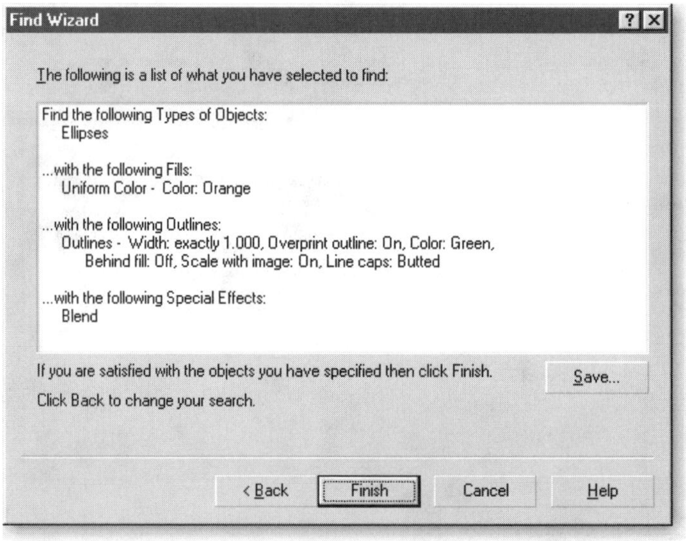

FIGURE 30-9   Final Find Wizard screen

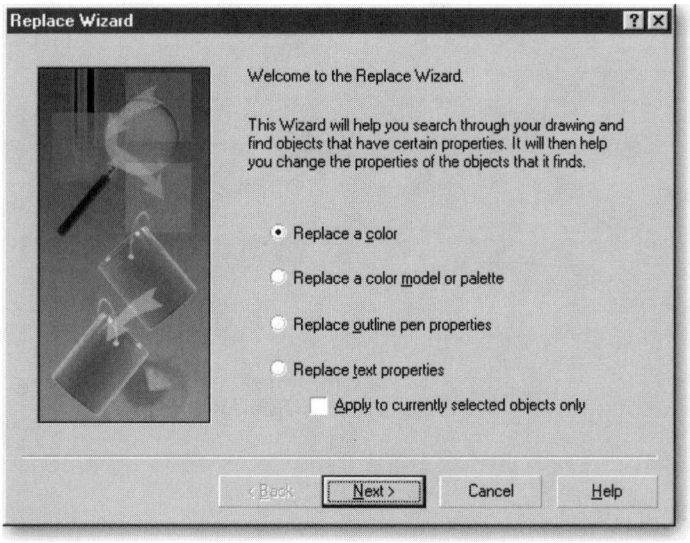

FIGURE 30-10   The initial Replace Wizard screen

Normally the Replace Wizard will search through all the objects in your drawing, but if you specify Apply to currently selected objects only, it will search only the selected objects.

Replace a Color

If you select Replace a color and click the Next button on the initial screen of the Replace Wizard, you'll see the dialog box shown in Figure 30-11.

Two color pickers appear at the top of the dialog box. The top one specifies the color that you want to find, and the bottom one specifies the replacement color. These color pickers show the default palette in a drop-down box. But by clicking "other," you can access the Uniform Fill dialog box discussed in Chapter 8 to select any color from any palette. You can choose whether to replace the colors in outlines or fills, but you cannot do both at the same time.

The standard way of searching for colors is to look only at objects that have a uniform fill. However, you can also choose three other fill types by checking their

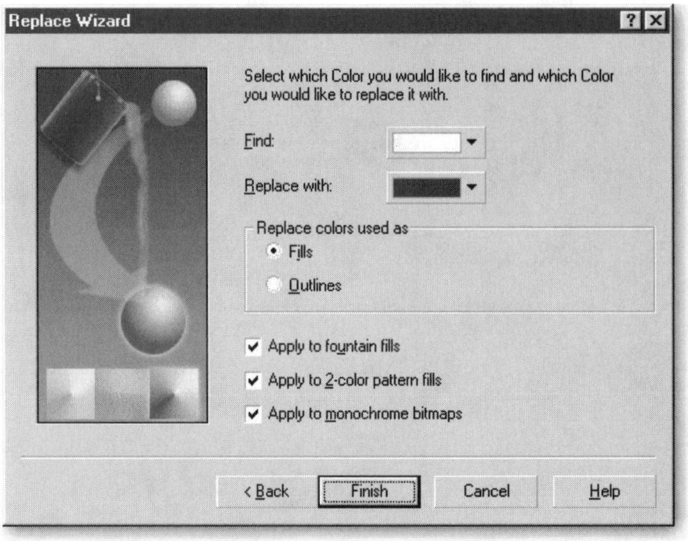

FIGURE 30-11   Replace Wizard screen for replacing one color with another

check boxes: Apply to fountain fills, Apply to 2-color pattern fills, and Apply to monochrome bitmaps. These options don't cover all of the fill types, but they cover the ones used most often.

Replace a Color Model or Palette

If you select Replace a color model or palette and click the Next button on the initial Replace Wizard screen, the dialog box shown in Figure 30-12 will appear.

You have three choices for the search. You can Find any color model or palette, Find a color model, or Find a color palette. If you choose to find a specific color model or palette, you can choose which of the models or palettes to find. Then you need to choose which color model to use for the replace operation. Note that you can't choose a palette here since there is no way to map colors into a palette. For that, you'll need to use the Replace Color Wizard shown earlier and replace each color one by one. Another option would be to use Color Styles, which are discussed in Chapter 29.

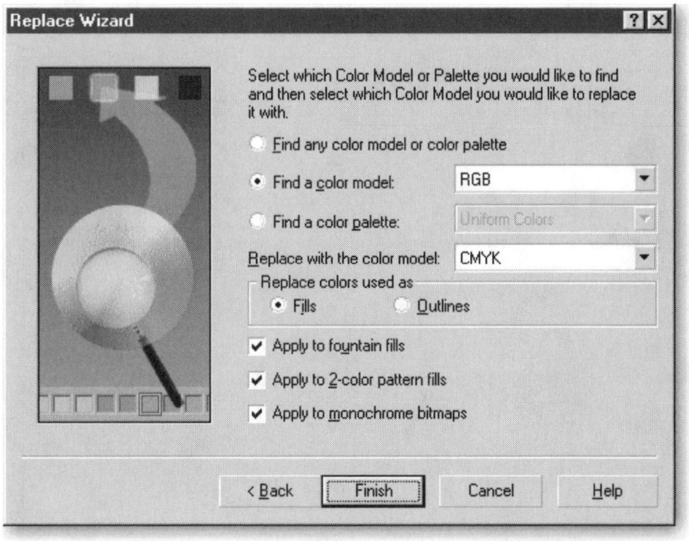

FIGURE 30-12   Replace Wizard screen for replacing a specific color model or palette

As with the Replace Colors Wizard, you have the option of replacing Fills or Outlines, but not both at the same time. You can also replace the colors within fountain fills, two-color pattern fills, and monochrome bitmaps.

Replace Outline Pen Properties

If you select Replace outline pen properties and click the Next button on the initial Replace Wizard screen, you'll see the dialog box shown in Figure 30-13.

You can search for and replace three properties of outlines: Outline width, Scale outline with image, and Outline Overprint. Searching for objects that have the Scale outline with image feature turned off and then turning it on again can be very useful when editing the clipart supplied with CorelDRAW. The appearance of art in the clipart library can change dramatically since the scale outline attribute is not turned on in most of the clipart. Changing the outline width could come in handy if you've used the default of hairline for your outlines. This is extremely

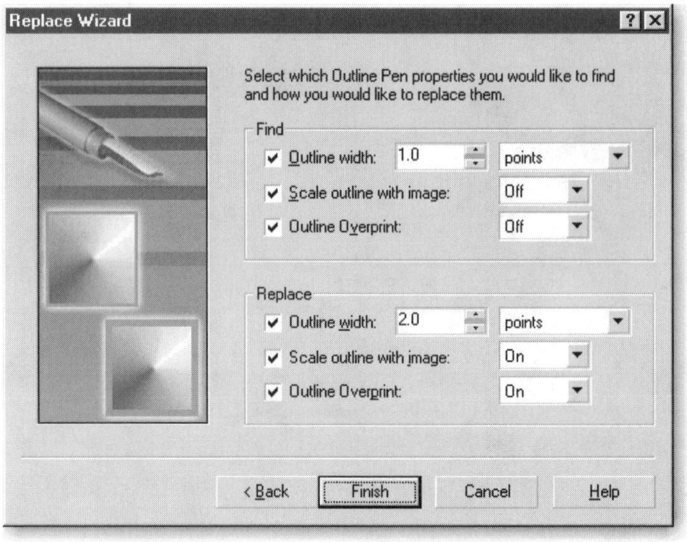

FIGURE 30-13   Replace Wizard screen for replacing outline properties

small, especially when outputting at high resolutions. For this reason, you may want to globally replace the outlines with a thicker outline. Making changes to the overprint setting will only affect the output to a PostScript device and should be used carefully. This option is discussed in more detail in Chapter 26.

Replace Text Properties

You can select Replace text properties and click the Next button on the initial Replace Wizard dialog box to display the dialog box shown in Figure 30-14.

Text has three properties that can be searched for and replaced: the font name, weight, and size. The Replace Wizard lists only the currently installed weights in the Weight drop-down list. This way, you can't choose any weights that do not exist.

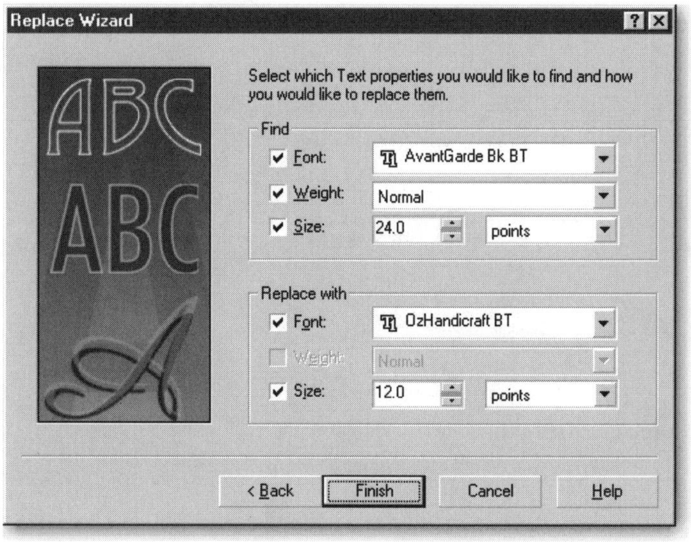

FIGURE 30-14   Replace Wizard screen for replacing text properties

We remember the many times that we've had to change the outline properties of an object so that they were all set to scale with image, or the last-minute color changes when a picky client couldn't stand our choice, or even the times when a drawing contained a single spot color that we just couldn't find. Now with the Find and Replace Wizards, all of these tasks are extremely simple. Just don't tell your clients (or your boss) how easy these changes can be!

CorelDRAW 9

CorelDRAW provides the tools to create custom arrowheads, symbols, patterns, and line styles. When you see the word "custom," you may think, "Here we go again; another learning curve to conquer." However, the good news is that creating custom arrowheads, symbols, patterns, and line styles is really quite easy.

Creating Custom Arrowheads

Although there are dozens of arrowheads to choose from, there never seems to be the one you need for that special project. When you find yourself in this situation, it's time to create your own. If you follow three simple rules, you will be creating arrowheads with the best of them. First, the object used to create the arrowhead must be a single object; this can include objects that have been combined or welded together. Second, the object you create should fill an area approximately 6 inches in either direction and be in a left-to-right or right-to-left orientation. This means if the shape of the object naturally points to a specific orientation such as a flying bird, it should point to either the left or right. The reason for the size requirement is that if you begin with an object much smaller than the recommended six inches, the arrowhead will be too small. Third, you are limited to a total of 200 arrowheads in the drop-down list at any given time.

To create a custom arrowhead, follow these steps:

1. Either draw an object on the page, or use any of CorelDRAW's symbols. These can include the Symbols clipart found on the CorelDRAW 9 CD. Remember that the object must be a single object; you can't use groups, for example. The example here uses a car found in the Transportation category of the Symbols and Special Characters Docker window. To open this Docker, click on Window | Dockers | Symbols and Special Characters.

2. Scale the object so that the longest dimension is approximately 6 inches.

3. Choose Tools | Create. When the flyout appears, choose Arrow.

4. You will see a message that asks if you want to create an arrowhead from the selected object. Click the OK button.

In the wink of an eye, you have just created your first custom arrowhead. To see if you did indeed create an arrowhead, follow these steps:

1. Using the Pencil tool, draw a line on the page.

2. Click on the down arrow on the outline width box on the Property Bar, and choose a width of 8pts.

3. Click the End Arrowhead selector on the Property Bar. When the drop-down list appears, scroll down the list of arrowheads. When you reach the bottom, your new custom arrowhead will magically appear.

4. Click on your new arrowhead to apply it to the line.

5. If your arrowhead isn't pointing as if it were coming off the end of the line, choose the Shape tool, and select the node at the end of the line. Use the node control handle to adjust the direction of the arrowhead.

6. Figure 31-1 shows the Arrowhead drop-down list from the Property Bar with the car arrowhead at the bottom of the list. This figure also shows the original symbols clipart along with the line drawn on the page with the new arrowhead placed on the right end. We have also displayed the view of the end node being edited with the control handle.

31

TIP   *To remove an arrowhead that has been applied to a line, click the upper-left or upper-right thumbnail image (depending on which end of the line the arrowhead is attached to) in the Arrowhead selector drop-down list.*

Editing Arrowheads

At times you may want to change an existing arrowhead just a little. To edit an existing arrowhead, select the line with the arrowhead, and open the Outline Pen dialog box shown in Figure 31-2 by clicking the Outline Pen button on the Outline Tool flyout. Choose any of the five options by clicking the Options button and choosing from the drop-down menu. We have circled the Options drop-down menu in the figure.

NOTE   *Even though there is an Options button for both ends of the line, if you make a change to the right end of an arrowhead, the left end will be modified as well.*

Start Arrowhead selector   End Arrowhead selector
Outline width box

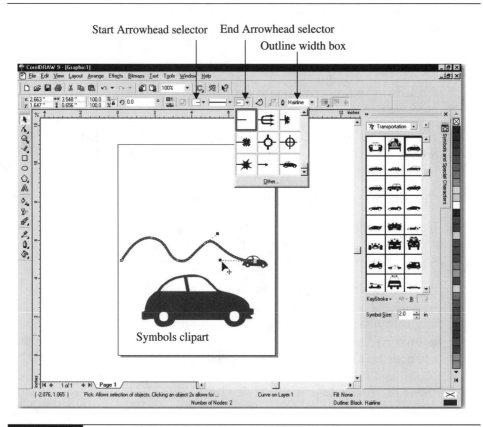

A custom arrowhead created by using a symbol from the Symbols roll-up

The five options on the menu are None, Swap, New, Edit, and Delete.

- *None*   Select this option to remove any existing arrowhead from the selected line.

- *Swap*   Select this option to move the existing arrowhead to the opposite end of the line.

- *New*   Select this option to modify and save a new arrowhead without affecting the original arrowhead. This can now be done using the Edit Arrowhead dialog box accessed from the Arrowhead drop-down list on the Property Bar (see the next section).

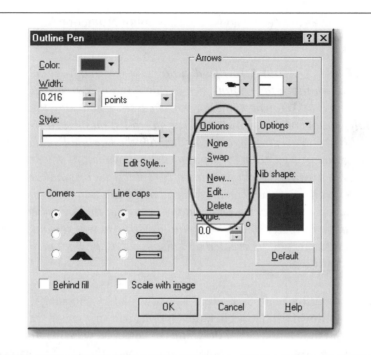

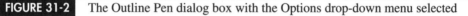

FIGURE 31-2   The Outline Pen dialog box with the Options drop-down menu selected

- *Edit*   Select this option to permanently modify an existing arrowhead. When you modify an arrowhead using this option, the modified arrowhead will permanently replace the original arrowhead.

- *Delete*   Select this option to permanently delete an arrowhead from the drop-down list. Because there's a limit of 200, you may want to delete arrowheads you will never use.

Modifying Existing Arrowheads

CorelDRAW lets you modify existing arrowheads by changing their placement in relation to the end of the line. You can also scale them horizontally, vertically, or proportionally. You can even create mirror images either horizontally or vertically. If you use the New option in the Option drop-down list, you can modify an existing arrowhead and save it as a new arrowhead. This new arrowhead will appear at the bottom of the arrowhead drop-down list. If you want to permanently change an existing arrowhead, choose the Edit option. Either option brings up the Edit Arrowhead dialog box shown in Figure 31-3.

CAUTION   *The Edit Arrowhead dialog box selected from the Options drop-down list in the Outline Pen dialog box saves arrowheads differently than the Edit Arrowhead dialog box accessed by clicking the Other button at the bottom of the Arrowhead drop-down list on the Property Bar. When modifying an existing arrowhead through the Outline Pen dialog box, always select New from the Options drop-down list. If you select Edit, the changed arrowhead will permanently replace the original arrowhead. However, if you modify an arrowhead using the Edit Arrowhead dialog box accessed by clicking Other at the bottom of the Arrowhead drop-down list on the Property Bar, the original arrowhead will remain unchanged, and a new one will be created and displayed at the bottom of the drop-down list.*

To modify an arrowhead, first select an arrowhead by choosing it from the Arrowhead drop-down list. Now click the Options button beneath the selected arrowhead. From the Options drop-down menu, select New. When the Edit Arrowhead dialog box (shown in Figure 31-3) appears, the selected arrowhead will appear in the edit window with eight selection handles surrounding it.

Here are the editing tools available in the Edit Arrowhead dialog box:

- *Selection Handles*   The selection handles surrounding the arrowhead are used to change its size or shape. Using one of the corner selection handles will proportionally resize the arrowhead. Using a middle selection handle will stretch the arrowhead inward toward the center or outward away from the center.

- *Nodes*   There are nodes at various points along the outline of the arrowhead. If you select any of these nodes, you can move the entire arrowhead in any direction. This ability to move the arrowhead allows you to position the arrowhead above or below the line. It even lets you move the arrowhead horizontally away from the line. There is also a node at the end of the line that appears in the Edit Arrowhead dialog box. It can be difficult to see because the arrowhead sometimes conceals it. However, if you place the cursor at the very end of the line and drag to the left, you should see the line getting shorter. Making the line shorter is another way of separating the arrowhead from the line.

■ *Reflect in X*   This button mirrors the arrowhead horizontally, which can be useful when you want the arrowhead to follow the line rather than point away from the line.

■ *Reflect in Y*   This button mirrors the arrowhead vertically.

■ *Center in X*   This button centers the arrowhead vertically relative to the center X in the middle of the edit window.

■ *Center in Y*   This button centers the arrowhead horizontally relative to the center X in the middle of the edit window. To position the center of your arrowhead directly in the middle of the edit window, you select both the Center in X and Center in Y buttons.

■ *4X Zoom*   Check the 4X Zoom box to magnify the edit window by the power of four.

The arrowhead shown being edited in Figure 31-3 is one of the arrowheads that ship with CorelDRAW 9. We simply made the pointing hand a little fatter.

31

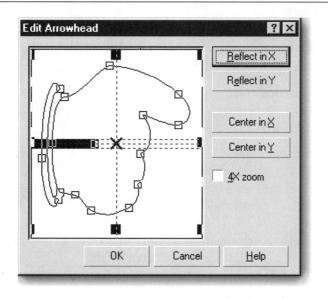

FIGURE 31-3   The Edit Arrowhead dialog box with an arrowhead selected

Creating Custom Patterns

CorelDRAW gives you the ability to create custom pattern fills from vector or bitmap images. Pattern fills are image tiles that are repeated over and over as they fill the selected object. A good pattern fill is one that tiles seamlessly. This means the viewer should not be able to see where the individual tiles begin or end.

There are two types of pattern fills: two-color and full-color. Full-color pattern fills are also broken into two categories: vector and bitmap. The bitmap category is considered to be anything other than two-color bitmaps, which are monotones. The easiest of these fills to create are the two-color and vector pattern fills. You will see later in this section that you don't create bitmap fills in the way you create the two-color and vector fills.

Creating Vector Patterns

To create a custom vector pattern, you must first define an area on the page to serve as a template. The template should be of equal length on all sides.

Creating a Template

Follow these steps to create a template:

1. Click the top ruler, and drag down two horizontal guidelines, placing one at 8 inches and the other at 4 inches vertically.

2. Click the vertical ruler, and drag out two vertical guidelines, placing one at 2 inches and the other at 6 inches horizontally. The guidelines should now form an area 4 inches square inside the lines.

3. It is usually difficult to place the guidelines at exactly the right place. To avoid creating a template that is not square, double-click a guideline, and manually set the position of both the horizontal and vertical guidelines in the Guideline options dialog box. While you're in the Guidelines dialog box, enable the Snap to Guidelines check box. (Even though we recommend a 4-inch square area, you can make your area any size you wish as long as the sides are all of equal length.)

TIP *Remember that when you change the position designation in the Guideline Setup dialog box, you must click the Move button prior to clicking the OK button for the change to take effect. Refer to Chapter 13 if you need to brush up on guidelines.*

4. You will be creating a diamond pattern using a group of four diamonds we created in Chapter 9. If you want to learn how to create the square fountain filled with diamond shapes, read the section on square fountain fills in Chapter 9. If you want to follow along in this exercise, you can open the .cdr file containing these diamonds shapes on the CD that comes with the book. The path to the file is /Chap31/Diamond.cdr.

5. Open the file Diamond.cdr using the path noted in the previous step.

6. The first thing to do is accurately place a group of four diamonds and four others at specific locations at the corners of the square created by the intersecting guidelines. Open the Position roll-up by choosing Arrange | Transformation to open the Transformation Docker window.

7. Select the group of diamonds, and click on the Position button (double-headed crossed arrows) at the top of the Transformation Docker.

8. Remove the check mark from the Relative Position check box.

9. With the group of diamonds selected, type the coordinates of the upper-left intersecting guidelines in the Horizontal and Vertical parameter boxes located in the Position roll-up. The correct numbers using the example shown here are 2.0 inches (Horizontal) and 8.0 inches (Vertical).

10. Click the Apply button to move the group of diamonds to the designated coordinates.

11. With the group of diamonds still selected, press CTRL-D to create a duplicate.

12. With the duplicate diamonds selected, enter the coordinates for the upper-right intersecting guidelines, just as you did in step 9. The correct numbers for these coordinates are 6.0 (Horizontal) and 8.0 (Vertical).

31

13. Click Apply to move the group of diamonds to the designated coordinates.

14. Make a duplicate of the second group of diamonds just as you did in step 11.

15. With this duplicate selected, repeat step 9 using new coordinates of 6.0 (Horizontal) and 4.0 (Vertical). These coordinates will position the third group of diamonds at the lower-right intersecting guidelines.

16. Now make a duplicate of the third group of diamonds, and use the coordinates 2.0 (Horizontal) and 4.0 (Vertical) to place the fourth group of diamonds at the lower-left intersecting guidelines. As before, click the Apply button to make the move take effect.

17. Make a duplicate of the fourth group of diamonds, and set the coordinates at 4.0 (Horizontal) and 6.0 (Vertical). These coordinates will place the fifth group of diamonds in the center of the template. Click Apply to complete the move.

If your template looks like the one in Figure 31-4, you followed the instructions correctly.

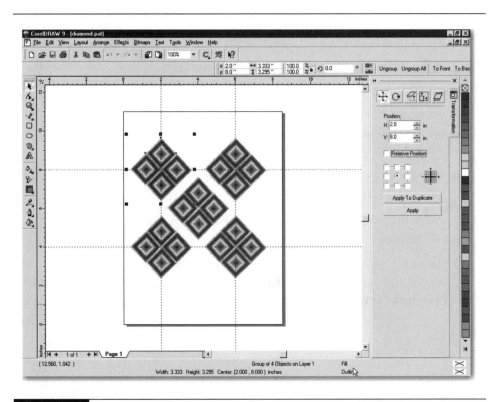

FIGURE 31-4   The new pattern template with the five groups of diamonds

Creating the Pattern

Be patient; you are almost finished. You have finally reached the stage where you can actually create the pattern.

1. Choose <u>T</u>ools | Cre<u>a</u>te, and from the flyout, choose <u>P</u>attern. The Create Pattern dialog box will appear. Click the Full Color radio button.

2. Click the OK button. The cursor will change to a crosshair extending the full length and breadth of the screen.

3. Use the point of the intersecting crosshairs to click and drag a bounding box beginning at the upper-left corner of the template and ending at the lower-right corner. With Snap to Guidelines still turned on, it should be easy to create a bounding box in the shape of the square. If you're not sure whether you have accurately delineated the square, watch the color of the guidelines as you drag out the square. When you are exactly over the edges of the rectangle, the guideline will change to yellow, and you can release the mouse button.

4. When you have finished dragging out the bounding box, the Create Pattern message box will be displayed on top of your pattern, asking if you want to create a pattern from the selected area. Click the OK button to bring up the Save Vector Pattern dialog box.

5. Give your custom pattern a name (the .pat extension will be added automatically). You should store your custom patterns in a folder you have created expressly for custom patterns. However, if you store them in the default folder, Graphics9\Custom\Patterns, they will appear in the Pattern drop-down list when you choose it. Figure 31-5 shows the Save Vector Pattern dialog box.

Congratulate yourself. You have created your first custom pattern.

 NOTE   *If you selected the <u>T</u>wo-color option from the Create Pattern dialog box in step 1, the pattern will be added to the existing two-color patterns, and you will not be able to give your pattern a name or store it in a separate folder.*

31

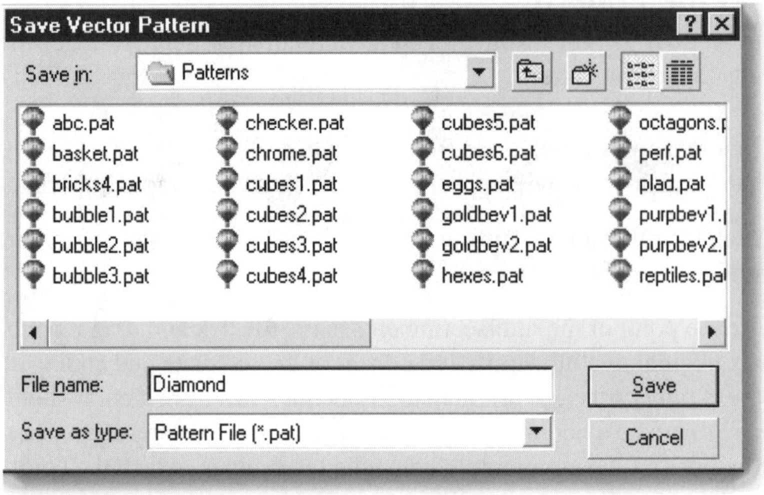

Save Vector Pattern	? X

Save in: 📁 Patterns   ▼ 🗁 🗋 🔳 🔳

abc.pat   checker.pat   cubes5.pat   octagons.p
basket.pat   chrome.pat   cubes6.pat   perf.pat
bricks4.pat   cubes1.pat   eggs.pat   plad.pat
bubble1.pat   cubes2.pat   goldbev1.pat   purpbev1.p
bubble2.pat   cubes3.pat   goldbev2.pat   purpbev2.p
bubble3.pat   cubes4.pat   hexes.pat   reptiles.pa

File name: Diamond   Save

Save as type: Pattern File (*.pat)   ▼   Cancel

FIGURE 31-5   The Save Vector Pattern dialog box

Using Your New Pattern

Now it's time to see if the pattern you created will indeed create a diamond pattern. Follow these steps to fill an object with your new pattern:

1. Draw a large rectangle on the page.

2. Select the Pattern fill button on the Fill flyout.

3. When the Pattern Fill dialog box appears, click the Full Color radio button.

4. Click the Load button. The Import dialog box will appear. Change to the folder where you stored your custom pattern, and select it from the folder (if you stored your pattern in the default folder, it will appear in the Pattern drop-down list).

5. When you have selected your custom pattern from within the Import dialog box, click the Import button. Your custom pattern will appear in the preview window shown in Figure 31-6.

6. Enter **2.0** in the Width and Height num boxes in the Size section of the roll-up.

FIGURE 31-6   The Pattern Fill dialog box selected from the Fill flyout with the custom pattern loaded

7. Click the OK button to see the results.

If you followed all the steps, you should see the pattern shown here.

You may wonder why you placed the four outside group of diamonds so they were centered on the point of the intersecting guidelines. The reason for this unusual placement is to ensure that the pattern will tile seamlessly.

The tiling pattern shown here was created in the same way as the diamonds. The Eggs were placed at the corners, and the rooster was placed in the middle. If you would like to create this pattern using the same coordinates as the diamonds, the file is on the CD that comes with the book. The path to the file is /Chap31/Eggs.cdr.

Editing Patterns

You can change the color schemes of vector patterns by editing the .pat file. Suppose you like a particular default pattern or even a custom pattern you have created, but the colors don't work with the project you are working on. When you are faced with this situation, you can simply open the pattern file with the .pat extension from Graphics9\Custom Patterns, make the necessary color changes, and then save the modified file with a new name. You don't have to draw a bounding box prior to saving the modified file.

 CAUTION *When saving a modified .pat file, you cannot move the pattern from the place on the page where it first appears on opening, and you must save the file with the Selected Only box enabled.*

 TIP *If you are filling an object with a pattern fill that requires trapping, simply trap the objects in the pattern file. Then when you fill the object, the entire pattern fill will be trapped.*

Creating Two-Color Pattern Fills

You create two-color pattern fills using the same steps you used to create a vector pattern. The difference is that after you have created the images you want to use as a pattern, you select the Two-Color radio button instead of the Full Color radio button from the Create Pattern dialog box that appears when you select Tools | Create | Pattern. Your images used for the pattern area will automatically be converted to a monochrome bitmap image and will appear at the bottom of the Two-Color drop-down list in the Pattern Fill dialog box when accessed from the Fill flyout. Your new pattern will also be available from the Two-Color drop-down list on the Property Bar when the Interactive Fill tool is selected.

 NOTE *Technically, you don't have to create a perfect square when beginning to create two-color and vector pattern fills. You can delineate any area you wish of your image, and a tile will be created. The caveat is that it probably will not tile seamlessly.*

Creating Bitmap Pattern Fills

You don't create bitmap pattern fills the same way that you create two-color and vector pattern fills. You create them by using an existing bitmap image. This bitmap image could be a photograph or simply an abstract bitmap background.

   The way to fill an object with a bitmap fill is to click the pattern fill icon on the Fill flyout to reveal the Pattern Fill dialog box, choose Bitmap, and click the Load button. The Import dialog box will appear with Patterns listed in the dialog box. Click the folder icon (with the arrow) next to the Look In drop-down list. The word "Custom" will appear in the Look In drop-down list. Double-click the Tiles folder in the dialog box below the Look In drop-down list, and choose a bitmap fill from the available fills. Creating new bitmap fills is fully covered in Chapter 9.

   When you use a bitmap image as a fill, you have virtually no control over how the edges of the image will tile together, unlike with two-color and vector fills. As a result, bitmap pattern fills often show the telltale lines where the sides don't match on all four corners of the tiles when the object is filled.

   Unless you are a genius at using Corel PHOTO-PAINT, the only sure way of creating seamless bitmap pattern fills is to use the Terrazzo filter found in Bitmap | Plug-Ins | Fancy | Terrazzo. To learn how to use this unique filter, refer to Chapter 22. You can also use Corel Texture, a stand-alone application included with CorelDRAW 9.

31

TIP *You can convert any bitmap file into a monochrome tiling pattern fill. Click the pattern fill icon on the Fill flyout to reveal the Pattern Fill dialog box. Select 2-color and click the Load button. Browse to the desired bitmap file to be used as the fill pattern, make the foreground/ background color changes as desired, and click OK to exit the dialog box. You can create some really interesting fills and textures with this trick, and still create spot color separations.*

Creating Custom Symbols

Hundreds of symbols are available in the Symbols and Special Characters Docker, but invariably the symbol you need is not in the Docker. Corel's development team knew they couldn't make a symbol for every situation, so they made it possible for you to create your own. Creating symbols is even easier than creating arrowheads because you don't have to be concerned with how big to make the original object.

You can create a custom symbol from any single curve object, including objects that are combined or welded into one object. This means you can make your company's logo into a symbol as long as it has been combined or welded into a single curve object. For information on combining objects, see Chapter 14.

Follow these steps to create the symbol shown in Figure 31-7.

1. Open the Symbols and Special Character Docker window by choosing Tools | Symbols and Special Characters (CTRL-F11).

Original symbol   Symbol and modified rectangle   New symbol
                    covering body of wolf

FIGURE 31-7   Creating a new symbol from an existing symbol

2. Select the Animals 2 category, and drag the wolf shown in Figure 31-7 onto the page.

3. Using the Rectangle tool, draw a rectangle over the body of the wolf.

4. Convert the rectangle to curves by selecting the Convert to Curves button on the Property Bar.

5. Use the Shape tool to modify the rectangle until the box covers all but the head and neck of the wolf.

6. Select the box, then SHIFT-click on the wolf to select both objects (the sequence is important), and click on the Trim tool on the Property Bar.

7. Delete the box; you will be left with just the head and neck of the wolf.

8. Select the newly created symbol, and rotate it to the right until it looks like the one on the right in Figure 31-7. Then choose Tools | Create | Symbol.

9. When the Create Symbol dialog box shown here appears, choose a category from the list. You may want to type a custom name in the Symbol category box so all your custom symbols will be together.

That's all there is to it. You just created a symbol. Select the category where you saved your new symbol, and drag it onto the page. If you created a new category for your new symbol, as was done here, all the preview boxes in the Docker window will display the new symbol, as shown in Figure 31-8. As you create new symbols and add them to your custom category, the preview boxes will update accordingly. You can add up to 255 symbols in each new category.

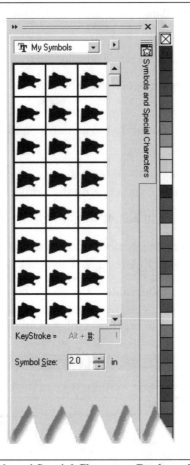

FIGURE 31-8 The Symbols and Special Characters Docker window displaying the custom category and symbol created in the previous steps

Creating Custom Line Styles

Creating custom line styles in CorelDRAW is as easy as pointing to and clicking a style bar. Follow the steps here to create a custom line style:

1. Select the Freehand tool from the toolbox, and draw a line on the page.

2. With the line still selected, click the Outline Style Selector on the Property Bar. The Line Style drop-down list shown next will appear.

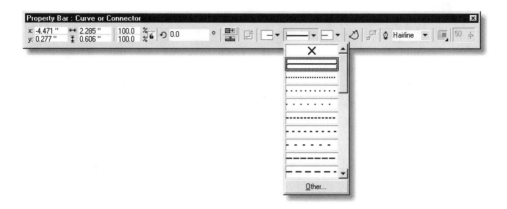

3. Click the Other button at the bottom of the list.

4. The Edit Line Style dialog box shown here will appear in its default configuration. The instructions in the dialog box are very good. Refer to them in the future if you are not certain what to do.

31

5. The slider bar is positioned so that only two squares are visible. The first square must always be turned on. The second square is blank. This combination of the first square highlighted and the second square left blank produces the pattern shown in the preview window at the lower-right corner of the dialog box.

6. Drag the slider bar to the right until ten squares are revealed.

7. Turn on the second through seventh square by clicking the squares (to turn off a square that has been turned on, click it a second time). Skip a square,

and turn on the ninth square, leaving the tenth square blank (turned off). Your outline style should now look like the one in Figure 31-9. Notice that the squares that are turned on next to each other form a dash, and the single highlighted square forms a dot.

8. Move the slider until 35 squares are revealed.

9. Turn on the first seven squares. Leave the eighth and ninth squares blank, and turn on the tenth.

10. Leave the remaining 25 squares blank. Your line style should now look like the one shown in Figure 31-10.

If you want to save your custom line styles, click the Add button. Your custom outline style will be added to the bottom of the drop-down on the Property Bar.

 NOTE   *You can have a total of 39 line styles at once. If you try to add more than that, you will be prompted to delete current styles to make room for new custom line styles. If you have lines styles you want to back up, you can save the styles in the coreldrw.dot file. Copy this file to a safe backup location for future recall of your custom line styles.*

Edit Line Style   ⊠

Click on the squares to turn dots in the line style on and off:

Hint: The first dot in the line style must be black, and the last dot must be a space. You can adjust the end of the line style by moving the bar on the right side of the line. There is a limit of 5 dashes per outline style.

[Add]   [Replace]   [Cancel]   [Help]

FIGURE 31-9   A custom line style using dashes and dots in a repeating pattern

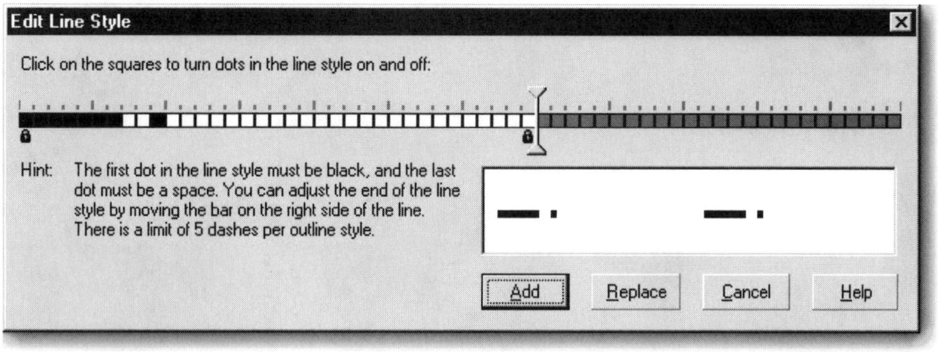

Edit Line Style

Click on the squares to turn dots in the line style on and off:

Hint: The first dot in the line style must be black, and the last dot must be a space. You can adjust the end of the line style by moving the bar on the right side of the line. There is a limit of 5 dashes per outline style.

Add   Replace   Cancel   Help

FIGURE 31-10 A second custom outline style using one dash and one dot in a repeating pattern

Now that you're at the end of the chapter, you can see that it's not as difficult to create custom effects as you may have thought. Having this ability to create custom effects can give you an edge over your peers that makes your work stand out from theirs.

31

CHAPTER 32

Fonts, Font Formats, Panose, and Font Management

CorelDRAW 9

When Corel first started as a company, it introduced a product called "Corel Headline." Headline was able to apply numerous special effects to one of the many fonts that were included with the Corel program. Back in 1988, "many" fonts meant less than 50. Corel Headline later became known as CorelDRAW, and the number of fonts included in the product is now well over 1,000. Working with a large number of fonts provides great freedom for a designer, but managing the fonts can be tricky.

We find that most users don't understand the various formats of fonts that currently exist in the marketplace. So we'll explain each of the formats and give you some guidelines on how each format is best used. With the plethora of fonts available, the problem of font substitution crops up quite often. CorelDRAW includes Panose, which is a semi-intelligent method of substitution. We'll explain how it works and how to put it to use. CorelDRAW users will often install all of the included fonts and find that their system screeches to a halt. We'll explain the correct way to use the fonts that come with CorelDRAW.

What Is a Font?

The definition of a font has changed since type became available on computers. A font used to be a specific size and weight of a specific font family. For example, Times Roman 12 point was a single font, Times Roman 14 point was another font, and Times Bold 12 point was yet another font.

Now a font is a specific weight of a specific font family. The point size isn't part of the definition because digital fonts are fully scalable to any point size. No longer are fonts metal blocks of a specific size. Now most fonts are stored as mathematical equations that can be reproduced on the screen and in print. Note that there are a few bitmap fonts that are not scalable, but you can't use those type of fonts within CorelDRAW.

Font Formats

When you purchase a computer, you choose which operating system to install. There are several popular operating systems to choose from, each with its pros and cons. Likewise, you can choose among fonts. There are two major formats in the world of fonts—PostScript and TrueType—and a third format is being introduced soon to replace the existing two. A few other fonts and technologies are available as well. Most people are aware that these different formats are available, but they don't understand the benefits of each and how to make an intelligent choice between the two. The result is that most users choose a font format to use without considering the consequences of that choice. Many times this misinformed choice will cause problems that can get very expensive.

WFN

The WFN format is a proprietary format created by Corel for use with early versions of CorelDRAW. It became unnecessary in CorelDRAW 3 when support for PostScript and TrueType fonts was added, and it was eliminated completely in CorelDRAW 6. If you still have WFN fonts that you'd like to use in your work, you'll either have to use an older version of CorelDRAW or convert them using Ares FontMonger, which is now very hard to find.

PostScript Type 1

The PostScript Type 1 font format was invented by Adobe Systems in the 1980s and became the worldwide standard for digital type software. Although it is the font format used in the PostScript page description language, it does not require a PostScript printer to be used. When used with a PostScript printer, the font is directly downloaded to the printer rather than being rasterized (converted to a bitmap) and then sent to the printer.

Characters in a PostScript font are constructed using bézier curves, which just happens to be the same method CorelDRAW uses to create curves. This approach is especially beneficial when you convert a font to curves, as fewer nodes are needed to accurately describe the shape. For example, Figure 32-1 shows two versions of the same ampersand character (&) from the Las Vegas fonts supplied with CorelDRAW. Each has been converted to curves, and the nodes are indicated with boxes on the characters. The character on the right is from the PostScript version of the font and contains 53 nodes. The version on the left is the TrueType character, and it contains 73 nodes. This is a very significant difference for just a single character. Note that the difference may not always be as great in number but will be similar in percentage.

If you were dealing with only a single character, this problem would be minimal. But multiply that difference by a word or sentence of text, and you can see that it becomes quite significant. Remember that each node increases the complexity of the object and makes the file a little bit bigger. In this case, the extra nodes provide no

32

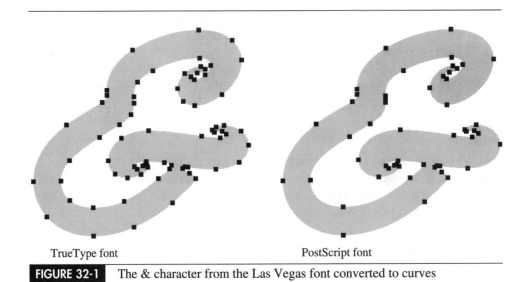

TrueType font   PostScript font

FIGURE 32-1   The & character from the Las Vegas font converted to curves

benefits. They could cause the file to take longer to output at the service bureau which could cost you more money.

To display PostScript fonts on the screen (and print them on non-PostScript printers), the Adobe Type Manager (ATM) utility is required for Windows 9x. ATM is an inexpensive utility that is frequently included with software and new fonts. Windows NT directly supports PostScript fonts, although a version of ATM was made available in May 1997 that provides a much more reliable screen display. The direct support of PostScript fonts by Windows NT 4 is very poor because it simply converts the fonts to TrueType as they are installed, and the conversion process can be error-prone. This problem should be eliminated in Windows 2000, which will include the ATM technology. If you need a copy of ATM, you can order ATM Lite from Adobe for a minimal shipping charge.

PostScript fonts are supported across many different operating systems, and more than 30,000 different fonts are available. Some of these fonts are what are called "expert sets" that include extra characters such as old-style figures, small caps, ligatures, and other variations. Expert sets are useful for professional typography.

A subset of PostScript fonts are multiple master fonts. These fonts contain at least two design axes such as weight, width, style, and optical size. Many different variations can be created from the base font to assist in copy fitting and the creation of special effects without compromising the type by artificially squeezing and stretching.

TrueType

TrueType was invented by Apple Computer to compete with the PostScript technology. (For historians, the original name was "Royal Type.") It was less expensive for Apple to create its own font format than to license the PostScript technology from Adobe. TrueType was later licensed by Microsoft to include in Microsoft's operating systems. Unlike PostScript fonts, TrueType fonts have no corresponding page description language.

TrueType characters are created using quadratic B-splines. Thus, when a TrueType character is converted to curves in CorelDRAW, it has more nodes than the same character in a PostScript font, as you saw in Figure 32-1.

TrueType support is built in to Windows 3.1, Windows 9x, Windows NT, and the Macintosh OS. It has become the default standard on Windows platforms because of Microsoft's influence but has been very poorly received on the Macintosh.

TrueType fonts are rasterized by the operating system except when they are printed on a PostScript printer. In that case, they are converted to a PostScript font and then downloaded. This conversion process causes a degradation in quality and a slight delay in printing. Windows NT uses a TrueType font to display PostScript fonts on the screen; however, it downloads the actual PostScript data when printing on a PostScript printer.

When TrueType fonts were released, the market was flooded with new fonts. Many of these fonts were of extremely low quality and bundled in large quantities. While the temptation to purchase these font packages is very high, be very careful as they can cause problems when you use them. This is true of any of the font formats bundled in large quantities for a very low price. Remember that the cost of a font for a major project is minimal compared to the cost of having to reprint film.

32

OpenType

After years of battling over font formats, Microsoft and Adobe called a truce in the spring of 1996. The result of the truce is the OpenType font format. In essence, it combines the PostScript and TrueType formats into one single format. This means that both font formats will be fully supported by future versions of Windows.

This new format is really an extension of TrueType called "TrueType Open v2." Fonts designed for TrueType Open will support much larger character sets, and applications will be able to perform great typographical tricks with them. Strangely, TrueType Open does not include typographic characters such as ligatures in the thousands of characters it supports. Note that while the technical name is "TrueType

Open," the more common name is "OpenType." This latter name avoids the bad reputation that TrueType has earned among graphics professionals. OpenType may be the solution to many of the type problems that users currently face. But OpenType support is not included in any currently released operating system, and no fonts have been released as of mid-1999. Since there is no operating system support and no fonts, the level of support within CorelDRAW 9 is relatively unknown.

TrueDoc

TrueDoc is not so much a font format as a technology. It works with the other formats to create a synthetic variation on the font that can be embedded in your CorelDRAW file.

When you embed a font in your file, the character shape recorder (CSR) is invoked, and it creates a synthetic glyph for each character necessary. This synthetic font is called a *portable font resource* (PFR). The recipient of your file can load it, and the character shape player (CSP) will recreate the font data from the PFR. It can be recreated as either a bitmap or a vector. When sent to the printer, it can even be sent in PostScript format so no printing problems are associated with it. In addition, you should see no degradation in quality, although, because of the conversions, the conversion may not be exact.

Font embedding using TrueDoc is available in the File Save dialog box of CorelDRAW, as described in Chapter 24. You can find methods for font embedding using TrueDoc on the Web; visit Bitstream's Web site at http://www.bitstream.com.

Choosing Which Format to Use

Most users do not make a conscious decision regarding which format to use. Instead they just use the format that is forced upon them. As you are installing CorelDRAW, you will be offered the option to install fonts—in this case, TrueType fonts, even though both formats are supplied on the CorelDRAW CD.

Before deciding which format to use, keep the following points in mind: Both TrueType and PostScript are just as easy to install and use when you use the Adobe Type Manager Deluxe or Font Navigator utility programs described later in this chapter. All of the fonts included with CorelDRAW are supplied in both TrueType and PostScript format. There is no extra cost to use either format. You can even use both formats at the same time and in the same document. Or you can begin a document with one format and finish it with the other just by loading the other font format—the fonts have exactly the same internal names. The only issue that you may face is that the text could reflow because of slight spacing differences between the two formats.

If you will be using a PostScript printer at any time, either in your own office or at a service bureau, you really should use PostScript fonts. Many service bureaus will refuse jobs that use TrueType—and for good reason. Files that use only a single TrueType font can cause output errors and can even cause the image setter to crash in rare instances.

If you will be using Adobe Acrobat Distiller to create PDF files, this program will behave much better if you use PostScript fonts. TrueType fonts generally become embedded under a really obscure font name that will not always be recognized by other machines.

If you have other software that supports only TrueType, you may need to use TrueType. An example of such software is fax software and 3D rendering programs. Many of these do support both formats, but there are exceptions.

Even after considering these issues, many users may still be tempted to use TrueType no matter what since it is endorsed by Microsoft and it just seems easier. We've worked with several clients in the sign cutting industry who complained about the quality of the lettering in the signs they generated with CorelDRAW. The problem was more noticeable to sign cutters because they commonly output letters that are several feet high. After researching the problem, we realized that it was TrueType that was causing the awful output. The clients switched immediately to PostScript and saw a dramatic change in the quality of their signs. Note that the fonts in question are from the same foundry and are the fonts supplied with CorelDRAW.

 TIP   *We've noticed that PostScript fonts redraw significantly faster than TrueType fonts. This is especially evident if you are using large blocks of Paragraph Text.*

Storing the Fonts

A few years ago, it was quite easy to keep track of the 100 to 200 fonts that most users owned. Now with CorelDRAW supplying over 1,000 fonts and users typically having many more, it can be very important to manage them properly. The first step in font management is learning how to properly store them on your system. If you follow the instructions provided in this chapter, you will have well over 1,000 fonts available to you without causing serious problems to your operating system.

Some users prefer to keep their fonts on the CorelDRAW CD-ROM, which is a really bad idea because at some point you'll remove the CD and therefore you'll remove all of the fonts. We suggest that you copy the fonts to your hard drive. This will take approximately 60MB of space, but with the current low prices for huge hard drives, that amount is minimal. If you are using a FAT partition table on your hard drive, you'll want to copy the fonts to a small partition since the files are typically fairly small and would waste unnecessary space on drives with a large cluster size. Follow these instructions to copy the files:

1. Create a folder entitled TT, PS, or both in the root of the drive to which you will copy the files. It is very important that the names be as short as possible because the longer names take up more space in the Windows Registry.

2. On the CorelDRAW CD, locate the Fonts folder. This folder contains several other folders entitled Symbols, Ttf, Type1, and Windows95. Go into either the Ttf or Type1 folder, depending on which type of font you wish to use.

3. Copy all of the folders from within the Ttf folder to your newly created TT folder or from the Type1 folder to your PS folder. This may take a few minutes.

4. Now change to the Symbols folder on the CorelDRAW CD-ROM. In it you will find both Ttf and Type1 folders. Copy the contents of your desired font type to a Symbols folder within your TT or PS folder on your hard drive.

5. Lastly, copy the Windows95 folder to your hard drive. All of these fonts are TrueType and so for clarity's sake should go into a TT folder.

You've now copied all of the fonts to your hard drive. Unfortunately, there are a couple of steps remaining. All of the files you copied from the CD-ROM are still marked as read-only. So you'll want to remove the Read-Only attribute, which will take a few minutes, but you only have to do it once. The main reason for turning off the Read-Only attribute is so that you will have the ability to completely manage the fonts within Font Navigator. Without doing this, you will not be able to delete the files.

1. Go into one of the folders that you copied. For example, the first folder inside of TT or PS should be A. Select all of the files inside of that folder by clicking on the first one, scrolling to the end of the list, and SHIFT-clicking on the last one.

2. Press ALT-ENTER to bring up the Properties dialog box shown in Figure 32-2. You'll probably notice a check mark in the Read-Only check box in Figure 32-2. If it isn't there, great. But if so, click on it, and remove it.

You'll have to repeat these last two steps for each folder that you copied. It isn't fun, but it should only take five to ten minutes. The last step is necessary only if you chose to copy the PostScript fonts and only if you wish to save some hard disk space. Along with the fonts, an AFM file was copied for each font, which is not necessary to use with CorelDRAW or most other Windows applications. So go into each of the folders one last time, and delete all of the AFM files. Again, this is a bit of a hassle, but should take only a few minutes.

You've now got all of the fonts on your hard drive and available for use. Note that they are not installed and will not drain your system resources other than the small amount of hard drive space that they occupy. And if you ever need the font files, you'll know exactly where to find them.

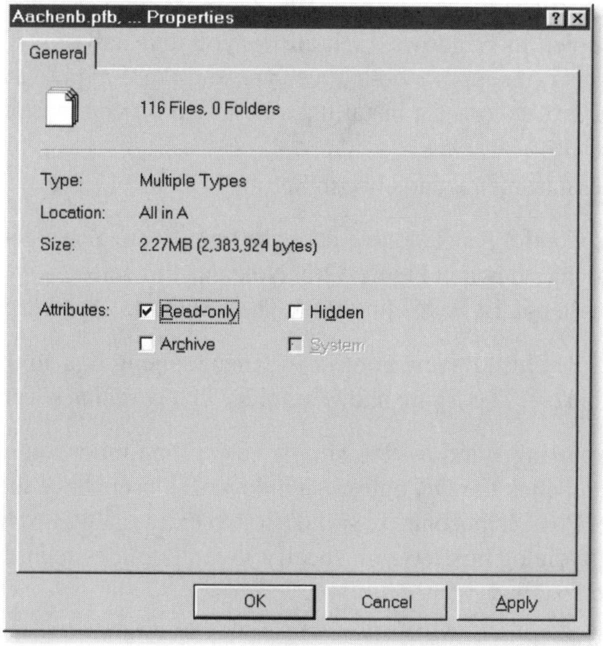

FIGURE 32-2 Properties dialog box for font files

TIP   *If other programs provide fonts, just follow these same steps so that you can keep all of your fonts under control. Microsoft maintains a list of which fonts came with which of their programs. Since the Web page containing this information tends to move, we recommend that you visit http://www.unleash.com/articles/fonts where we maintain a link to that page.*

Installing Fonts

The standard way of installing fonts can be difficult and certainly does not allow you to easily manage the large number of fonts that are included with CorelDRAW. Thus, this section briefly describes the method built into Windows. We suggest that you do not use this method, but rather one of two utility programs that can assist you in dealing with your fonts.

Using the Control Panel

To install fonts in either Windows 9x or Windows NT, you can use the built-in Control Panel applet. In Windows 95, it allows you to install only TrueType fonts, and in Windows NT, it supports both TrueType and PostScript to a certain extent. Here are a set of instructions for installing a new font on your system:

1. Open the Start menu, and choose Settings | Control Panel.

2. From the Control Panel, double-click the Fonts icon. You'll see a folder similar to that shown in Figure 32-3. Note that this screen is from Windows 95, so it will not list PostScript fonts. These fonts do appear in Windows NT.

3. Choose File | Install New Font. You'll see a dialog box similar to the one in Figure 32-4. The figure shows a folder that contains several fonts.

4. If you are using Windows 9x, simply select the font or fonts you wish to install, and click the OK button. Windows NT users have the option of selecting PostScript fonts. If you do so, an extra dialog box will appear. This extra dialog box lets you specify several options regarding how the fonts are installed.

 NOTE   *If you want your PostScript fonts to be downloaded accurately, make sure that you allow them to be copied to the Windows folder. This is not a problem if you are using Font Navigator or ATM for Windows NT.*

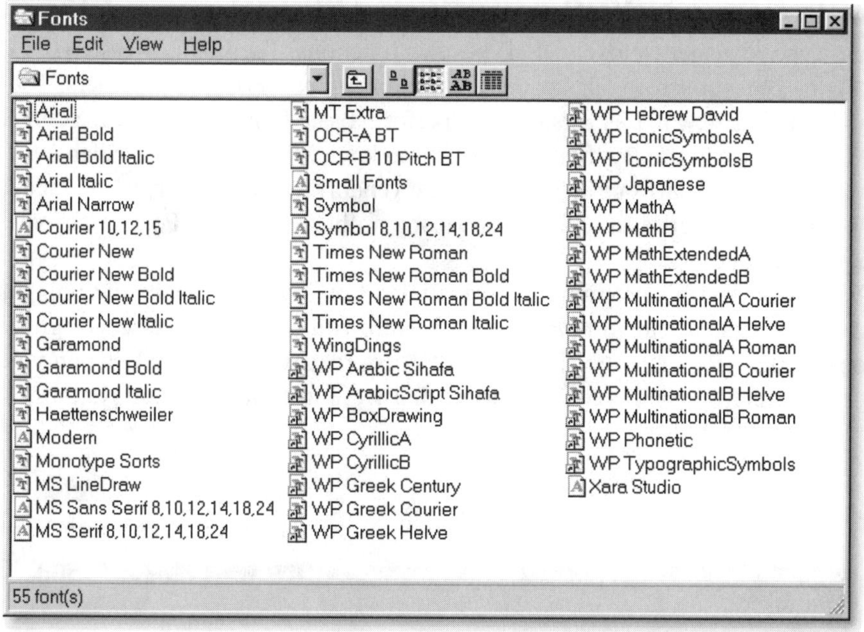

FIGURE 32-3   Control Panel Fonts dialog box

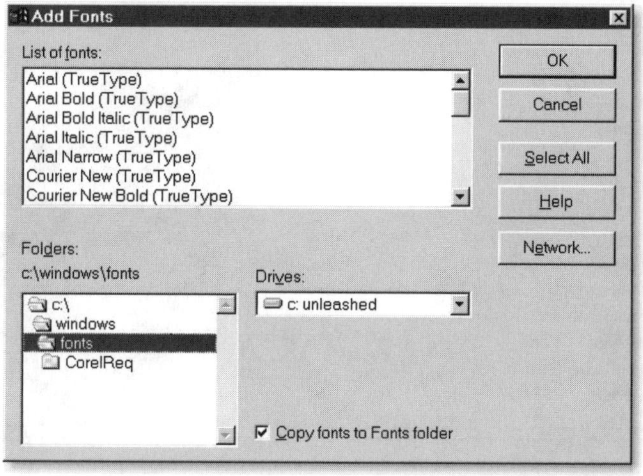

FIGURE 32-4   The Add Fonts dialog box

Using Adobe Type Manager Deluxe

Adobe Type Manager Deluxe (ATM) has two functions. The first is to rasterize PostScript fonts for screen display and for printing on non-PostScript printers. The second function, new to this version, is to perform basic font management. You need ATM if you wish to use PostScript fonts in Windows 9x; it should be available for around 50 dollars from your favorite software vendor. It is also highly recommended for Windows NT users as it will alleviate many problems of using PostScript fonts with just the built-in support.

When you use this program, the first dialog box that you'll encounter displays a list of font sets, as shown in Figure 32-5. Here you can select the sets or groups of fonts you wish to activate. The Starter Set is created automatically when you first install ATM. It will contain all fonts that were installed on your system when you added ATM.

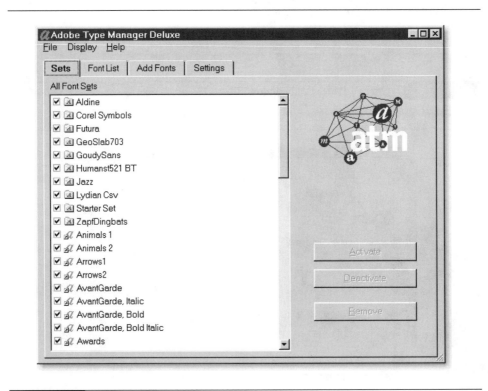

FIGURE 32-5   The ATM Sets tab

You can also view all of your fonts on the Font List tab, shown in Figure 32-6, where the fonts are all shown individually. You can control what is displayed by choosing All Installed Fonts or Only Active Fonts. You can select a font in the list and click the Remove button to delete it from the list if it is no longer necessary. Note that this list shows only the fonts that ATM knows about and not every font on your system. There is no easy way to have it search for all the fonts, as there is in Font Navigator.

You can add fonts using the Add Fonts tab, shown in Figure 32-7. Again, the currently installed fonts are shown on the left, and the folder where the new fonts are located is displayed on the right.

You can use the Settings tab, shown in Figure 32-8, to turn ATM off or on. You can also assign a certain amount of memory to a font cache. This memory will then save the prebuilt font glyphs so they do not have to be recreated each time you use the font. The default setting of 256K is normally adequate unless you use a large number of fonts in a single project. You can specify a particular directory where new fonts will

32

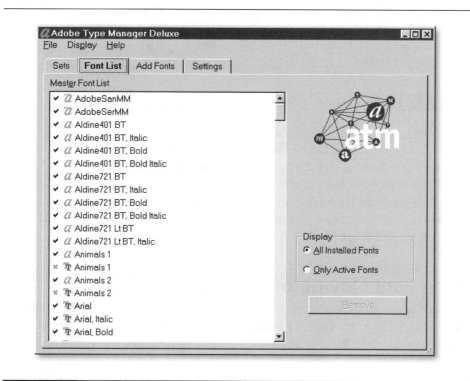

FIGURE 32-6   The ATM Font List tab

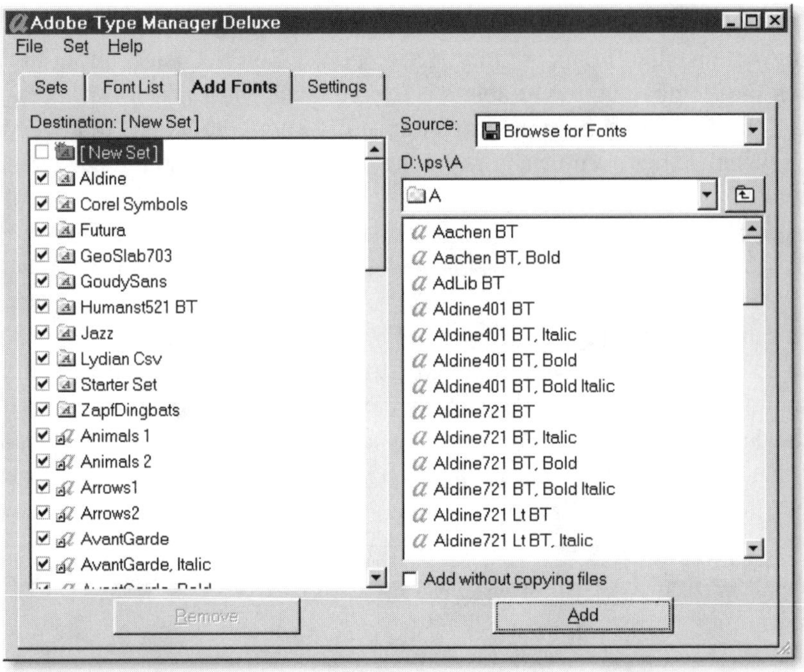

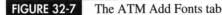

FIGURE 32-7   The ATM Add Fonts tab

be stored. Such directories can quickly become filled, so you may want to do some planning before arbitrarily placing all your fonts in a single directory.

ATM also provides a number of settings related to font display, font substitution, and sample sheets, as shown in Figure 32-9. You access these settings by clicking Advanced on the Settings tab. These settings are explained in detail in the ATM manual or the online help files.

Using Font Navigator

Font Navigator is to fonts what slices are to bread. This program makes it extremely easy to manage large numbers of fonts. It is included with CorelDRAW 9 but is not installed if you choose the default install. You must do a custom installation and specifically ask that it be installed. For more information on the installation process, see Chapter 1.

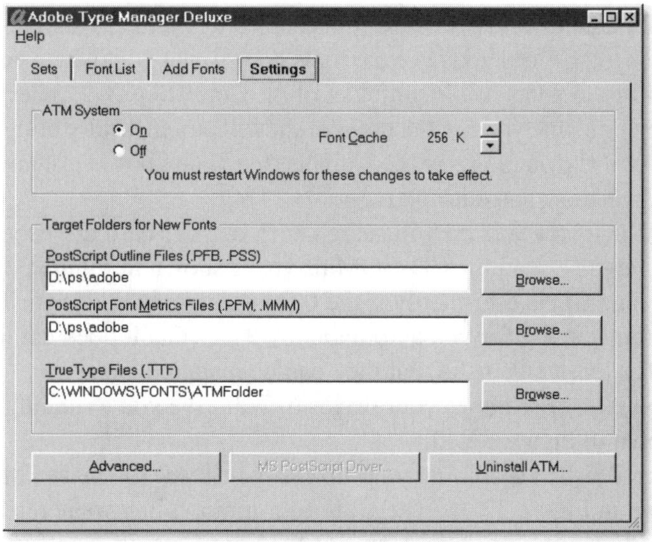

FIGURE 32-8 The ATM Settings tab

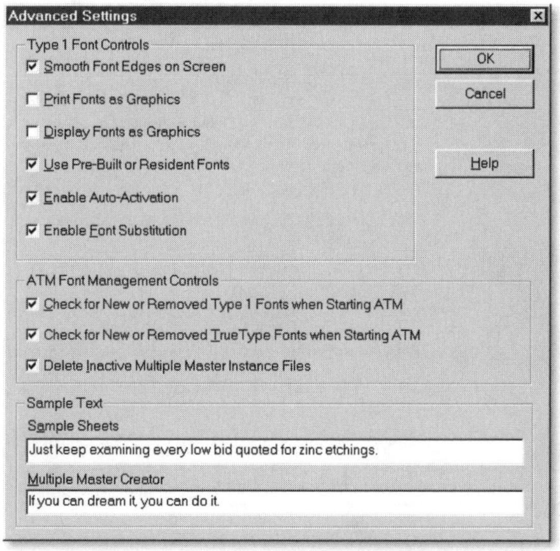

FIGURE 32-9 The ATM Advanced Settings dialog box

Font Navigator will automatically find all of the fonts on your system. So before you run it, you might as well get all the fonts copied to your hard drive as described earlier in this chapter. Once you have the fonts copied, run Font Navigator. Note that it is found in the Productivity Tools subfolder of the CorelDRAW 9 folder in the Start menu. The first time that you run the program, it will automatically bring up the Font Navigator Wizard shown in Figure 32-10. This first dialog box is just an introduction, so read the information, and click <u>N</u>ext.

The Font Navigator Wizard will search each of your hard drives you specify for fonts and can also search a CD-ROM drive, as shown in Figure 32-11. But finding fonts on a CD is useful only if the CD is *always* in the drive. This Wizard will create a font catalog for you automatically. Note that it does not install any fonts, but rather locates them so that they can be installed later.

As Font Navigator searches your drives, it will give you a running progress report, as shown in Figure 32-12.

Once it has finished searching your drives, you'll see the main Font Navigator window shown in Figure 32-13. There are four major windows here. The upper-left window contains the contents of the Font Catalog. Fonts with TT are TrueType fonts, and T1 indicates a PostScript font. A check mark indicates that the font is currently installed.

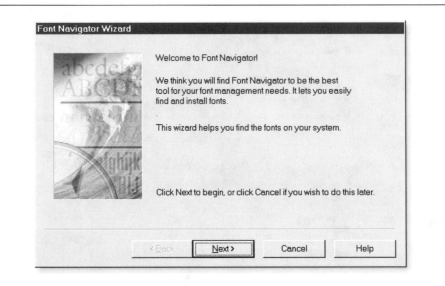

FIGURE 32-10   Font Navigator Wizard

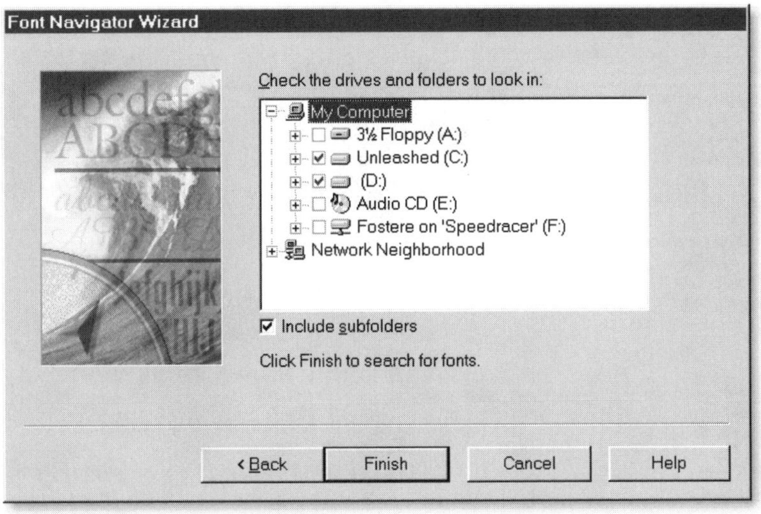

FIGURE 32-11   Font Navigator Wizard Font Location dialog box

The upper-right window lists the currently installed fonts and font groups. To install a font, you simply drag it from the Font Catalog window into the Installed Fonts window. And to uninstall, you simply drag the font from the Installed Fonts window back into the Font Catalog window, or right-click and select Uninstall Fonts from the pop-up menu. It just doesn't get any easier than that.

The lower-right window is the Font Sample window. Drag any font into this window to see a quick sample. If the font contains more than one weight, the

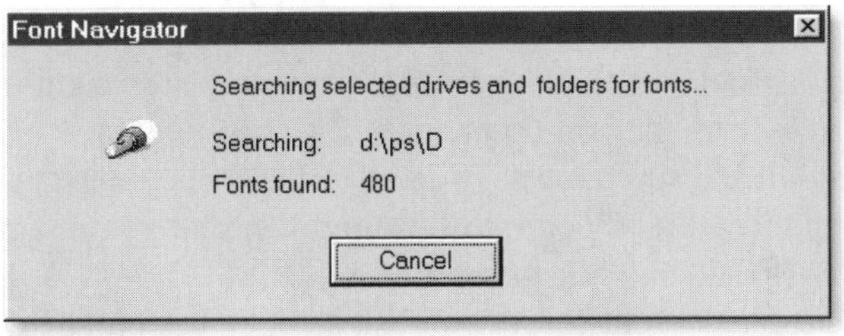

FIGURE 32-12   Font Navigator Searching dialog box

32

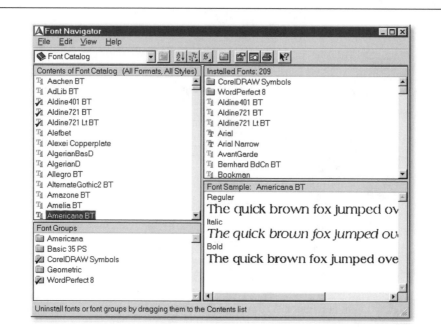

FIGURE 32-13   The Font Navigator main window

preview will show each one of them. And as with installed fonts, dragging a font
out will remove its display.

The real power of the application lies in the lower-left window, where the font
groups are shown. You can create as many groups as you like. So creating groups
for a particular job or client will help you work with any related jobs in the future.
When the current job is finished, uninstall the font group until it is needed again.

To create a new group, right-click the Font Groups window, and choose New
Group from the pop-up menu. If you wish to rename the group, just type in a new
name as soon as the folder is displayed. Or to rename it later, right-click the group,
and choose Rename from the pop-up menu.

Now you need to add some fonts. Drag all of the fonts you want from the Font
Catalog, and drop them directly onto the group folder that you just created. They
will automatically be added to the group.

Once you've created a font group, you can install the group by dragging the
group into the Installed Fonts window and uninstall the group by dragging it out of
the Installed Fonts window. So font groups are just as easy to work with as
individual fonts.

Some of the font groups that we'll create are for the symbols supplied with CorelDRAW and for the WordPerfect symbols. Creating groups for the symbols makes it easy to uninstall them when you no longer need them. Then we'll create groups based upon a particular client or project. This way we can install the fonts when needed and take them out when a project is done. You can even share your group files with other users.

This discussion only scratches the surface of Font Navigator's power. To fully understand how this program works, look at its online help file, which includes detailed descriptions of how everything works.

OK, so Font Navigator is a great way to manage your fonts, but it gets even better now that Corel has integrated it into CorelDRAW 9. After Font Navigator has cataloged the fonts on your hard drive, select Tools | Options | Workspace | Text | Fonts, and click the radio button to Use Font Navigator Catalog on Open. Then click the Panose Font Matching button, and be sure that the Allow font matching box is checked. Now when you open a CorelDRAW document that uses fonts that are not currently installed, you will see the Panose dialog box, but you now have the option to let Font Navigator install the missing fonts permanently or temporarily for use only in the current CorelDRAW session. The font list within CorelDRAW 9 displays permanently installed fonts in black type and temporarily installed fonts in gray type as shown in Figure 32-14.

Panose substitution is still available as used in previous versions. Details on Panose substitution are covered later in this chapter.

 NOTE *This will not work properly unless Font Navigator is closed.*

How many times have you gotten a Panose message warning that a particular font was needed, but not currently installed? Panose is discussed in the next section.

Font Substitution

You've spent hours on a project using just the right font to get your message across, and at the last minute, someone changes the font and prints the project without your knowledge. You'd probably be pretty upset if this were to happen. Guess what—it happens all the time, and most users aren't aware of it. This operation is called *font substitution*, and it is built into CorelDRAW and Windows.

Font substitution can be harmless if all you need to do is read a document. When it alters your design, changes line or page breaks, and causes text to overlap, however, it is evil.

32

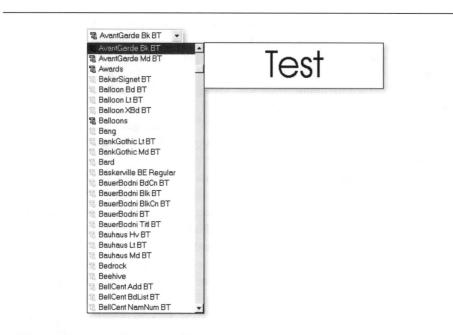

FIGURE 32-14 CorelDRAW 9 Font List Combo box

A classic example of font substitution may occur quite often when you print. The default font in CorelDRAW is Avant Garde Bk BT. This font is very similar to the Avant Garde font that is built into PostScript printers. The characters are nearly the same, but the spacing and kerning are not even close. Thus, often the Avant Garde in the printer will be used to print when Avant Garde Bk BT was used onscreen, and what you get out of the printer will not look the same as what you see onscreen. This sort of substitution happens quite often with Arial and Helvetica as well. Windows has a built-in font substitution list in the PostScript print drivers. Make sure that you disable all substitution. You might even want to ask your service bureau to do the same to avoid any problems.

 NOTE *We mentioned earlier how often the two variations on Avant Garde get substituted. We've seen many documents that were identifiable as something done in CorelDRAW simply because of this substitution, which is so obvious when printed. It can not be stressed enough that substitution should be avoided at all costs if a document is to be printed.*

Using Panose for Font Substitution

The Panose system tries to substitute fonts according to font attributes rather than using a random approach. It was developed by ElseWhere and has been incorporated into Windows as well as CorelDRAW.

Panose can substitute fonts in several ways. Because of the way trademarks apply to fonts, some fonts are nearly identical except for their names. A font may basically have been copied and assigned a different name that was not trademarked. Thus, you'll find that CG Omega, Optima, and Zapf Humanist have characters that look alike. Panose can help you to substitute fonts in cases like this. Remember, though, that even if the characters are identical (and they won't be), the spacing and kerning can be quite different.

TIP *Font Navigator will allow you to see the names of fonts that are very similar to a particular font. Right-click any font name within Font Navigator, and choose Properties. In the Properties dialog box, select Analog Names, and you'll see a list of names of all fonts similar to the one you've chosen. If the Analog Names tab isn't visible, no other names are stored with the font.*

Another common situation when Panose is useful is when files are being shared between Macintosh computers and PCs. PC font names do not contain spaces, whereas their Macintosh counterparts do. Panose keeps a database of font names to spot these differences across platforms. In most cases, the font substituted will be identical because it is from the same font foundry.

The most interesting feature of Panose is its ability to assign a number to fonts based upon characteristics of the characters. This substitution uses a font that is similar in characteristics rather than just a font with the same name but different spacing in the name. It uses x-height, midline, letter form, arm style, stroke variation, contrast, proportion, weight, serif style, and family type to determine the ten-digit number assigned. Panose will find a font with a similar classification number to substitute for a missing font assuming that a similar font is installed. If there is not a similar font, AvantGarde will be used. Just keep this in mind if you see a font being substituted that doesn't seem to be at all similar in name to the missing font.

Setting Panose Preferences

To change the Panose preferences, you must dig deep to find them. Choose Tools |
Options (CTRL-J) | Workspace | Text | Fonts, and then click the Panose Font
Matching button to display the dialog box shown in Figure 32-15.

If you want font matching turned off completely, simply make sure that Allow
font matching is unchecked. Since there will then be no "intelligent" way to
substitute for missing fonts, the default font will be used for all missing fonts.

If you check the Show mapping results check box, you will see a list of
substitutions made when you open a file that is missing fonts. The Panose Font
Matching Results dialog box will be discussed later in this chapter.

NOTE   *You cannot disable Font Matching if you are using Font Navigator
to automatically install missing fonts.*

Earlier you learned how Panose assigns a ten-digit number to a font. This
number is used with the Substitution tolerance slider. This slider controls how
close a font's number must be to the missing font. If it doesn't fall within that
range, the default font is substituted instead. If you move the slider all of the way
to the left, only an exact match will be made for the font. If you slide it all of the
way to the right, the substituted font may not be very close to the original font.
By default, the slider is left in the middle to provide a chance for "similar" fonts
to be substituted.

If no match is found, the font in the Default Font box at the bottom of the
dialog box is used. This defaults to AvantGarde Bk BT-Normal, one of the fonts

---

PANOSE Font Matching Preferences

☑ Allow font matching

☑ Show mapping results

Substitution tolerance: 30

Exact   Normal   Loose

OK

Cancel

Spellings...

Exceptions...

Default font: Czar-Normal

FIGURE 32-15   Panose Font Matching Preferences dialog box supplied with CorelDRAW 9. However, you may want to use a symbol font of some sort instead. Then when substitution occurs, you'll be able to spot it instantly so you can make any appropriate changes.

 TIP *The Alefbet and Czar fonts that come with CorelDRAW are a great choice for the default font because most users have no need for these alternative alphabets.*

If you click the Spellings button, the Alternate Spellings dialog box shown in Figure 32-16 appears.

You'll see two columns of font names. The left column contains the common Windows name of a font, and the right column contains the Macintosh name. Notice that the Macintosh names contain spaces, and the Windows names do not. If a particular name is not on the list, you can add it by clicking the Add button. If you want to change a listing, select the font name in the list, and click the Edit button.

You can also specify certain font-matching exceptions that will be used. Back in the Panose Font Matching Preferences dialog box, click the Exceptions button. It will bring up the dialog box shown in Figure 32-17.

Initially, the dialog box will be blank since no exceptions have been made. You can modify this list directly by clicking the Add button and entering a new

32

Windows name:	Macintosh name:	
AmericanTypewriter	American Typewriter	OK
BrushScript	Brush Script	Cancel
CenturyOldStyle	Century Old Style	
CooperBlack	Cooper Black	Add...
FreestyleScript	Freestyle Script	
FrizQuadrata	Friz Quadrata	Edit...
Heavy FrGothHeavy	H Franklin Gothic	
LetterGothic	Letter Gothic	Remove

FIGURE 32-16   The Panose Alternate Spellings dialog box

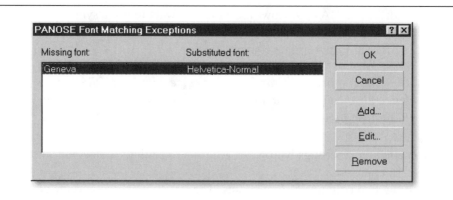

FIGURE 32-17   The Panose Font Matching Exceptions dialog box

exception. You can also add fonts to the list when a file is opened that is missing fonts. If you change the suggested font substitution to another font, you'll be asked if you want to save the change as a permanent exception.

Panose in Action

So now that you understand all of this Panose stuff, what does it do? Hopefully, it won't do anything because font substitution won't be necessary. However, if you open or import a file that is missing fonts, you'll see a dialog box, as in Figure 32-18, that lists each font that is missing and allows you to substitute the font of your choice.

The dialog box displays three columns of text. The first column lists any fonts that are missing. Some of the fonts in this list are not used in the file and are listed here simply to drive you nuts. The list doesn't show the fonts *used* in the file, but rather the fonts stored in the file's style sheet. Because of the way CorelDRAW manages styles, you'll frequently have lots of extra fonts in the style sheet that are never actually used in a file. It is a good idea to create a style sheet that is devoid of extra fonts. Style sheets are described in Chapter 29.

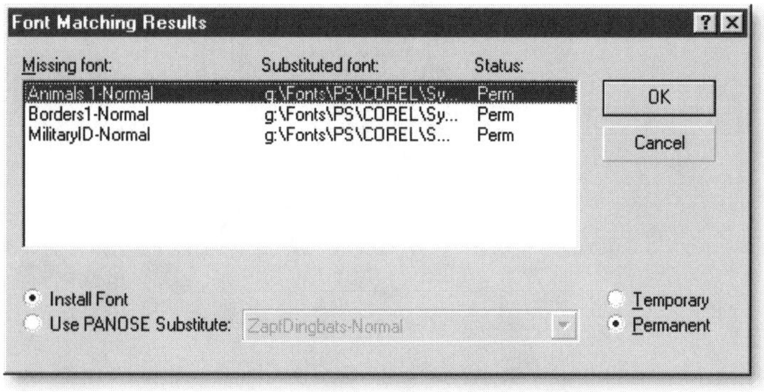

FIGURE 32-18   Font Matching Results dialog box

In the middle column is the font that will be substituted for the missing font. The last column states whether the substitution will make a permanent change in the file or will apply only to this drawing session.

To change any of the proposed substitutions, select the missing font listing, and select the font you'd like substituted from the Substituted font drop-down list. Again, if you think the missing font warning is bogus, make sure to substitute some weird-looking symbol font. If the font is truly missing, you'll find it really quickly. To change the status of a font substitution from temporary to permanent or vice versa, simply select the Temporary or Permanent radio button.

When you're done, click OK, cross your fingers, and clutch your voodoo doll tightly! Hopefully everything will come out to your liking.

Quite often fonts are taken for granted. Hopefully, now that you understand the many pitfalls that you may encounter, you'll spend a little bit more time making sure that they are used correctly. In the long run, your documents will thank you and so will your clients and your service bureau.

32

CHAPTER 33

CorelDRAW and the Internet

CorelDRAW 9

COREL.COM

In the past five years, we've taught thousands of people how to use CorelDRAW and Corel PHOTO-PAINT at our seminars and Boot Camps. Two of the most frequent complaints we've heard are that what appears on the screen doesn't look anything like what prints on the printer, and that the files required to create professional-quality work are too big. So what if we were to tell you that we can solve both of these problems, and you can use this knowledge to make a quite a comfortable living in creating graphics? Welcome to the World Wide Web!

Because the Web is viewed on the screen, just like the tools you use for design, the final product looks exactly as you expected, and because the graphics must pass through a slow communication device, such as a modem, files must be small or their transmission won't succeed. In addition, every company is madly rushing to have its own presence in cyberspace—which creates a tremendous demand for designers of Web graphics.

We'll briefly discuss the features in CorelDRAW that allow you to create Web pages, but we must caution you that CorelDRAW is best used to create a quick sample to show a client and nothing more. The Web pages it creates tend to be very complex, and you would be better served by creating these pages in a program dedicated to Web site creation. CorelDRAW is great for creating Web graphics, just not the whole page or the whole site.

Web Design Basics

Designing for the Web means putting everything you possibly can into a very small area. Figure 33-1 shows the Netscape Navigator browser in its standard configuration on a 640x480 monitor. You must assume a screen this small since the average user works at that resolution, and you must cater to the lowest common denominator. The gray area in the center is the area where the Web page will be displayed, and you can see that there is a space of only 630x364 pixels for content. Note that the exact window size can vary depending on which toolbars are open and which browser is used. To get an idea of how small that actually is, the icons on the Windows desktop are 32x32 pixels.

Sizing Your Image

When you create graphics, you must keep in mind the small area you have to work with. We're also going to round this size down in case someone has lots of

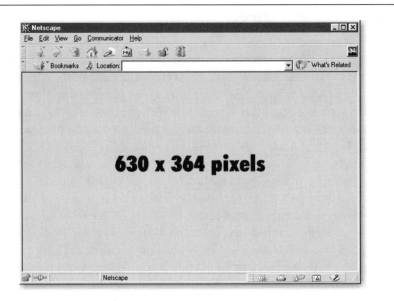

FIGURE 33-1   The Netscape Navigator screen showing the available design area

toolbars open. So let's assume a viewable area of 600x300. That means no graphic should exceed 600 pixels in width and 300 pixels in height, and even that size can create a file that takes too long to download. Also note that many Web surfers can see only 256 colors on their monitors. Therefore, designing everything in 24-bit color (16.7 million colors) makes no sense for these people. Not only can people not see all the colors, but the display may be worse, and the file will take longer to download.

Coloring Your Image

Using the right colors is extremely important in all types of design. For jobs that go to print, you should use CMYK colors, which can look quite different onscreen than in print. For Web graphics, you should use RGB colors. Since the final output device is the screen, when you design for the Web, what you see is generally what you get. Note that everyone's monitor is slightly different, and that is why we say "generally."

33

Determining the Right File Size

One of the most common questions asked by budding Web designers is, "How big should my files be?" We've heard this question answered in many different ways, but we don't feel it has an exact answer. Instead, you need to learn how to determine for yourself the file size that is appropriate for the Web site you are designing.

Again, you need to assume that visitors to a Web site have 14.4 baud modems, even though these are outdated; you must assume the lowest common denominator. On a 14.4 baud modem, it takes about 1 second to download 1K of data, so if you have a 30K graphic, it will take 30 seconds to download. The real question thus becomes, "How long will the visitors to the Web site be willing to wait?" Once you've answered that question, you can decide on the maximum size of all files on a particular Web page. A common answer will be a file size that takes no more than one minute to download, thus limiting all content on a single Web page to under 60K. That means the HTML file and all the graphics. If you don't think that is important, keep in mind that surveys have shown that well over 50 percent of users will not wait even 30 seconds for a Web page to download before they go elsewhere. If you design a page that takes too long to download, you are going to scare away your visitors (that is, your customers).

Web File Formats

Several different file formats are widely used on the Internet, each with its pros and cons. This section discusses how to decide which format is best for you.

GIF and GIF Animation Formats

The GIF format is especially useful for line-art images rather than photographs. It is easy to create this type of graphic in CorelDRAW because of the geometric shapes that are usually involved. For example, suppose you have a simple image such as the file cd4web.cdr supplied with this book.

Now you need to decide how big you want the image to be on your Web page. This sizing information should be in pixels because that is the only way to truly measure an image on the Web. You want to use this image as a button, so we'll assume that a width of 150 pixels would be about right. The correct size for any graphic can be dependent on a number of factors, and there is no exact number. A good way to figure the size in CorelDRAW is to set your rulers to use pixels. Another way is to treat each inch as 100 pixels; thus, if you want the image to be

150 pixels, you can just make it 1.5 inches wide. Do the math yourself: the resolution is 100 dpi (dots per inch) and that is multiplied by 1.5 inches to give us 150 pixels. You can resize it easily by changing the width value on the Property Bar, making sure that the Maintain Proportional Sizing or Aspect Ratio button is depressed.

At some point, the image must be converted into a bitmap. This can be done either within CorelDRAW or during the export process. Here you will do both so you can see how both approaches work.

1. Choose <u>B</u>itmaps | Convert to Bitmap to display the dialog box shown in Figure 33-2.

2. In the Color textbox, you can choose either 24 Bit - 16 Million Colors or Paletted (8 bit). The GIF format can save only up to 256 colors, so you may as well choose Paletted now.

3. Set the Resolution value to 100 dpi. Remember that earlier we decided that 1 inch equals 100 pixels. You'll probably see other materials telling you to use 72 dpi or 96 dpi. If you do so, you just make the math more difficult. For Web graphics, resolution is a completely meaningless number.

4. Your choice on <u>A</u>nti-aliasing is dependent on several factors. If you anti-alias a file, the file will be larger because there will be more colors. And if you want to have transparency, you will run into problems with what is called the *halo effect*. In this example, there is a red outline on the object. To anti-alias, various shades of color between red and white will be

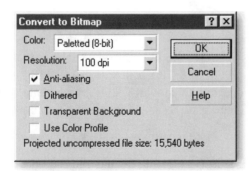

FIGURE 33-2   The Convert to Bitmap dialog box

added. If only white can be transparent, you'll have a number of light pink pixels that won't be transparent. So when the image is put onto a Web page with a nonwhite background, those light color pixels will create a "halo." Other than negatives, anti-aliasing is the best choice here. In this case, we'll assume our Web background is white and leave Anti-aliasing checked.

5. Although checking Dithered will give you an image that is closer to the original, it will also create a larger GIF file since dithering is difficult to compress. We suggest that you don't use dithering, especially on line art.

6. Checking Transparent Background will have no effect when you export the file. Check this option only if you want to use the file within CorelDRAW for other purposes. When it is checked, you won't have a white box around the graphic. In theory, you can use this transparent background if you were to use the bitmap in other programs that support alpha channels.

7. Make sure that Use Color Profile is not selected. Otherwise, you will see a terrible color shift in the image. Note that you also have to turn off Calibrate colors for display in the Tools | Options | Global | Color Management dialog box. If you do so, what you see onscreen will be what you get. Otherwise, you may get radically different colors. Color profiles are important only for images to be printed.

8. Click OK.

Now your image will be a bitmap stored in the CorelDRAW file. Just to make sure that you've done everything correctly, select the bitmap, and press ALT-ENTER to bring up the bitmap's properties. You should see a dialog box similar to the one shown in Figure 33-3.

If the pixel size of the bitmap does not seem correct, you should start the whole process over again. Carefully check each step to make sure that you followed all of the instructions. Unfortunately, one little mistake can throw off everything in this exercise.

You've now seen one way to convert vector artwork into a bitmap, but there is another way. There is no reason that you can't do both, but one of them is definitely required.

1. Choose File | Export (CTRL-H) to display the Export dialog box discussed in Chapter 24.

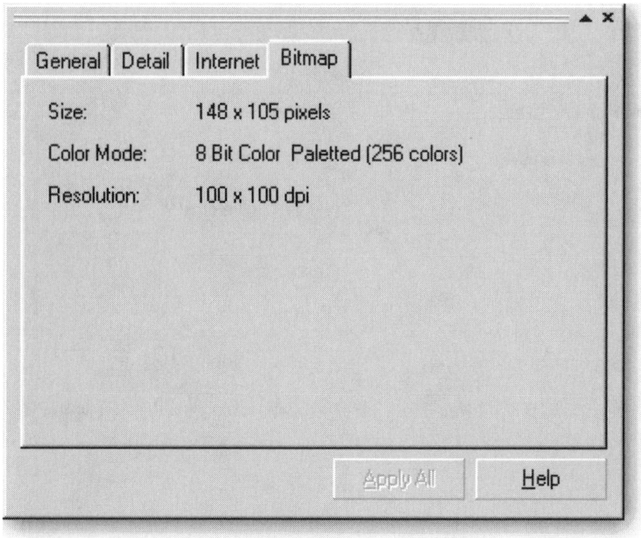

General | Detail | Internet | Bitmap |

Size: 148 x 105 pixels

Color Mode: 8 Bit Color Paletted (256 colors)

Resolution: 100 x 100 dpi

Apply All   Help

FIGURE 33-3   The Object Properties Docker

2. Give your file a name, such as cd4web.gif. Although it may seem unimportant at first, the case of the name is extremely important. Windows does not differentiate between uppercase and lowercase letters, but UNIX does. Since much of the Internet is based on UNIX computers, you must be careful to always spell a filename correctly, including the case of the letters. A good rule is to always name files in all lowercase to avoid any confusion.

3. In the Files of type drop-down list, choose GIF - CompuServe Bitmap.

4. Check the Selected only check box.

5. Click the Export button, and you'll be presented with the Bitmap Export dialog box shown in Figure 33-4.

6. In the Color section, select Paletted (8-bit), and make sure that Dithered is not checked. Dithering may produce a more attractive graphic, but at the expense of size. Again, make sure that Use color profile is not checked. And again, we'll use anti-aliasing. Remember the pros and cons of anti-aliasing we discussed earlier.

33

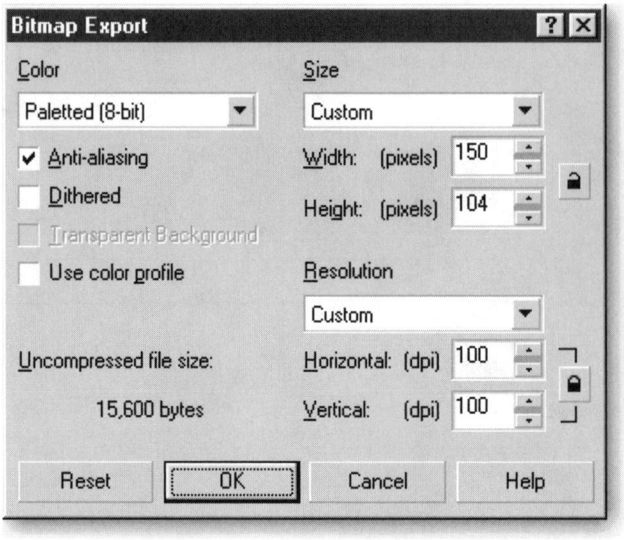

FIGURE 33-4 The Bitmap Export dialog box

7. In the Size section, choose 1 to 1 from the drop-down list. The Width and Height values will change automatically.

8. In the Resolution section, select Custom from the drop-down list, and type **100** into either the Horizontal or Vertical textboxes. The other value should automatically change.

9. Click OK.

One way or another, your graphic has now been converted to a bitmap. The GIF file format contains several special options that you may want to use. These options are presented in the GIF Export dialog box shown in Figure 33-5.

The GIF Export dialog box will automatically be displayed just after the Bitmap Export dialog box when you are exporting to GIF format. In the upper-left corner of the dialog box is the original image, and the upper-right corner contains a preview of your graphic.

One of the benefits of the GIF format is that it offers transparency. That means you can select a single color that will be hidden when placed on a Web page. Since

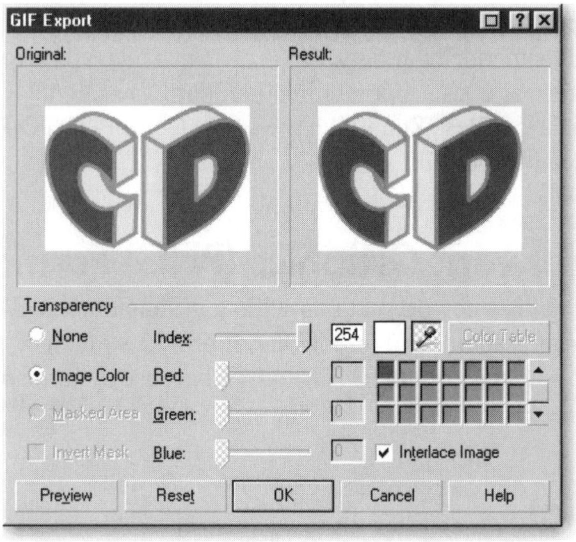

FIGURE 33-5   The GIF Export dialog box

most graphics aren't rectangular, this can be very useful. When exporting from CorelDRAW, the only options available are None and Image color. You'll notice that there are other options, but they are available only when exporting from Corel PHOTO-PAINT.

If you want transparency, select Image color. You can select the color you wish to be transparent from the palette, but it may be difficult to distinguish the exact color you want. A better way is to click the eyedropper in the preview window of the original image on the color you wish to be transparent. In our example, a white box appears around the image. Click with the eyedropper on the white box, and white will be selected in the palette and in the Transparency section of the dialog box. Now you just need to specify the GIF file in your Web page, and you'll be all set.

You now need to determine whether you want to interlace the file. If you choose Interlace Image, a crude version of the image will initially appear on the Web page, and then this image will gradually improve as more data is downloaded. The overall download time is not any quicker; it just appears to be quicker since the crude image appears first. If your image is very small, you probably should not use interlacing, but on larger images you should.

Here you have worked through the process of creating a GIF file completely within CorelDRAW. In reality, you should use CorelPHOTO-PAINT to do much

33

of the conversion work. It provides options to decrease the color depth to fewer than 256 colors and several options for choosing those colors. It can create smaller files that are vastly superior in quality.

The GIF file format does support animation, but CorelDRAW does not allow you to create animation files. You will have to use Corel PHOTO-PAINT if you want to create an animated GIF.

Portable Network Graphics (PNG) Format

The PNG file format is a new format that will soon supplant the GIF format. It can support 24-bit graphics and interlacing. It provides much better support for transparency, but you must use PHOTO-PAINT because the transparency requires that a mask be created.

JPEG Format

JPEG was developed to store 24-bit images in a small file. It accomplishes this by using lossy (note that this is not "lousy" misspelled) compression. Each time you open and then resave a JPEG image, it degrades in quality. The amount of degradation is directly related to the amount of compression, so the greater the amount of compression, the worse it will look. Nevertheless, this format provides a great way to put photographs on the Internet in full color. Be sure to keep a copy of the original file before JPEG compression, however, just in case the quality drops too much.

JPEG does not support transparency and works only on 24-bit images. A new variation on JPEG allows it to save a "progressive" image, which is basically the same as interlacing. However, these progressive JPEG files cannot be viewed in older Web browsers and other software (such as early versions of CorelDRAW).

To export to JPEG format, marquee-select the graphic, go to File | Export, and choose JPEG Bitmaps (JPG) from the Save as type drop-down list. Check Selected only. Give the file an appropriate name and location, and then click the Export button. Next you will see the Bitmap Export dialog box that we discussed in the GIF Export section. Make sure to select RGB Color (24-bit) in addition to setting the resolution and other options before clicking OK.

The JPEG Export dialog box, shown in Figure 33-6, provides several more options. This dialog has been significantly upgraded from earlier versions. As with the GIF Export filter, two previews show you a before and after view of the image.

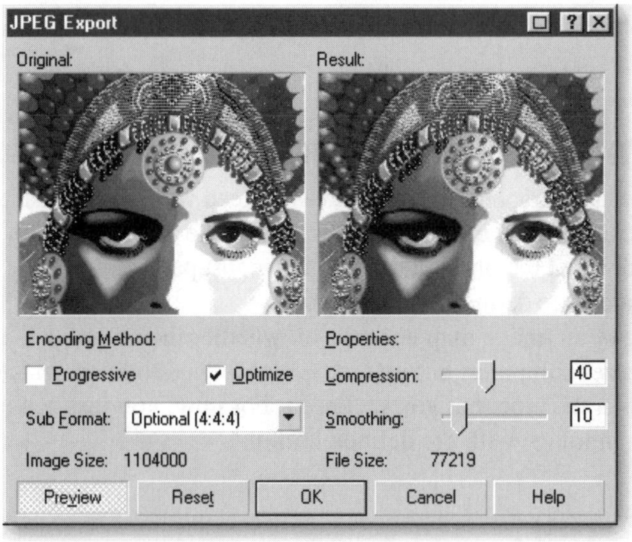

FIGURE 33-6   The JPEG Export dialog box

You have several options for the Encoding Method. The first option, Progressive, performs a function much like interlacing. It is supported by Netscape Navigator 3.*x* and later and Microsoft Internet Explorer 3.*x* and later. Selecting Optimize will generally decrease the file size. Under Sub Format, there are two choices: Standard (4:2:2) and Optional (4:4:4). Compression is the main control that will shrink the size of the file. Leaving the slider all the way to the left will produce a file that most resembles the original but with less compression. If you move the slider to the far right, the file will be very small but may be of very low quality. Remember that JPEG is a lossy format, and so when the file is reopened, it may lose some or all of its detail. At any time you can click the Preview button to see exactly how the compression is affecting the quality of the image. And at the very bottom of the dialog box are two numbers showing the size of the image in memory and of the resulting JPEG file.

Below Compression is the Smoothing slider. By using smoothing, you can sometimes squeeze the files a little bit more. It should always be used when you are working with a paletted image but is much less necessary when you are working with 24-bit images. It is helpful if there is a large area of plain background. Smoothing should be decreased when the file includes text because it will become difficult to read. Experiment with all these settings until you get the right amount of quality and compression. Once everything looks good, click the OK button.

Creating Image Maps and Web Pages

Image maps are large graphics that have areas defined within them that correspond to hyperlinks. The image map usually includes button-like images that can be clicked as if they were individual buttons, but they really are just parts of one large image in which various areas are defined in HTML code.

The coding of an image map depends on whether the mapping is done on the client or the server computer, but you really don't need to know much about the coding other than the type that you will need. For now, you just need to worry about creating an image with the defined hotlinks.

Assigning URLs

Any object you create in CorelDRAW can have a URL assigned to it. To do this, you'll need to activate the Internet Objects toolbar, shown here.

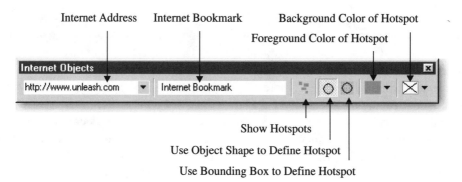

To activate this toolbar, right-click the gray area immediately surrounding the buttons on any of the toolbars currently on the screen. From the pop-up menu, select the Internet Objects toolbar. Another method for assigning URLs is to use the Object Properties Docker, which you can access by pressing the ALT-ENTER shortcut key with an object selected. It is shown here in an undocked state.

The following instructions are for the Internet Objects toolbar, but they should work equally well in the Object Properties Docker.

1. Select the object to which you wish to assign a URL.

2. On the Internet Objects toolbar, type the full URL in the Internet Address box, or choose an existing URL from the drop-down list.

3. If you wish to assign a bookmark to the object, type it in the Internet Bookmark box.

4. Click the Show Internet Objects button. (It is the button just to the right of the Internet Bookmark box.) Objects that have been assigned a URL can be clearly identified by a color and hatch pattern when this button is depressed.

5. The next two buttons specify whether the object's hotspot is defined by its shape or by its bounding box. Choose one of these buttons. If the shape is a complex shape, it is best to choose the bounding box button.

6. The next button lets you assign a foreground color to the object. This color will be displayed as crosshatching on the screen. It will not be used in the final rendering of the object when it is exported to a bitmap or when it is printed. Select a foreground color from the drop-down color palette.

7. Another drop-down color palette is found at the far right of the toolbar. This specifies the background color of the selected object. Select a background color from the palette.

33

Note that the foreground and background colors are used only to call your attention to any objects that have been tagged with a URL. If you change these colors with no objects selected, the colors you choose will apply to all objects that have a URL assigned. If you change the colors with an object selected, they will apply only to the selected object.

Creating Web Forms

CorelDRAW 8 added numerous new features for creating Web pages in addition to graphics. The biggest addition was in the area of elements for Web forms. Again, we'll caution you that these features are a quick way to create a sample page to show a client, but they are not a good choice for actual use on the Web. When you choose Edit | Insert Internet Object, you are presented with a child menu containing each of the various elements that you can create, as shown here:

Java applet
Embedded file

Simple Button
Submit Button
Reset Button
Radio Button
Check Box
Text Edit Field
Text Edit Box
Popup Menu
Options List

To fully understand how each of these elements work, you need to have some knowledge of HTML and its syntax. We'll show you how to edit the properties of one of the elements, and then you can explore the other types on your own, since they all work similarly.

With the child menu displayed, select Options List, and the object will be attached to your cursor. Click the page where you would like it displayed, and it will be inserted. Although it seems as though it can be resized, resizing won't have any effect. The Property Bar will allow you to assign a name to the element, which will be used when the form is processed by a CGI script.

For this particular element, you'll need to populate the list with data. Select the object, and press ALT-ENTER to bring up the Object Properties dialog box. We need to work with the List tab of the dialog, shown next:

In this case, several changes can be made. By default, you can select multiple items from the list when it is displayed in a Web browser, but you can disable this feature if you want. Visible Rows specifies how many items will initially be visible. If the items don't all fit, scrollbars would be provided automatically in the browser. The list can either drop down or not, based on whether you select Drop Down Menu or Options List.

The last, and most important, part is for the entry of the data. Anything you place in the Label column will be displayed in the browser. The value is what is sent to the CGI script. To the left of each label element is a check box. If it is checked, this item will be selected by default.

NOTE *If you are creating forms and don't understand these options, you should pick up a good reference book on HTML.*

33

For the form to work properly, you'll need to define the method in which it is to be processed. With nothing selected, right-click the page, and choose Properties from the pop-up menu. This will bring up the Object Properties window shown here:

The first item you must enter is the URL of the CGI script that will be used to process the script. This script will be different for each user as it is supplied by the company that hosts the Web page. The Method and Target entries will also be specified to you by the Web host, so you should discuss the appropriate values with them.

NOTE *If you do not enter values for how to process the form, you will receive error messages upon exporting the file.*

As you are designing a Web page, it is extremely important to try and line up each element in some sort of grid. When you export the page to HTML, the page layout will commonly be created by a table. The easier the elements fit within a grid, the less complex the table will be.

Preparing for Export

Before you export the file for the Web, you should check to see if there are any potential problems. Choose Window | Dockers | HTML Object Conflict to bring up the HTML Conflict Analyzer Docker window shown here. Note that we've undocked it.

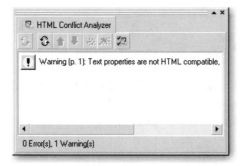

Click the far-left button to analyze the current document. As you can see in the image shown here, one warning has been brought to our attention. This particular error is warning us that some text is not HTML compatible. This just means that the text will be converted to a bitmap and not regular text. Fix this problem by selecting the text and choosing Text | Make Text HTML Compatible, and the warning will disappear from the HTML Conflict Analyzer. Note that only Paragraph Text can be converted to HTML Compatible. Note, however, that there are elements supported in regular text that will not be supported in HTML text.

To get a full list of the errors that are being checked, select Tools I Options I Document I Publish To Internet I HTML Conflicts, and you'll get the dialog box shown in Figure 33-7.

HTML conflicts are just another part of your workspace (see Chapter 34), so if there are particular warnings that you want checked on one type of project and not on another you can save them to a custom workspace. Each of the warnings is self-explanatory.

Exporting to HTML

When you have your page all finished, it is time to export it to HTML. Choose File I Publish To Internet to get the dialog box shown in Figure 33-8.

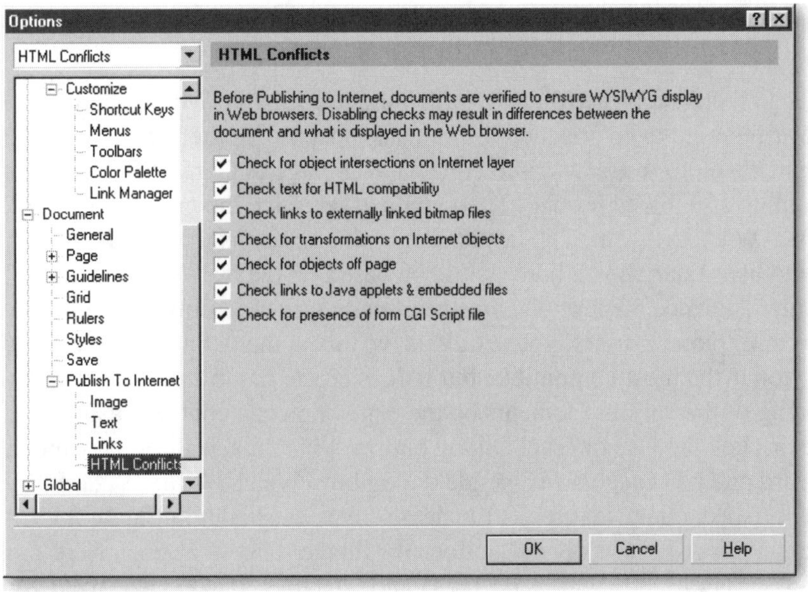

FIGURE 33-7   Options HTML Conflicts dialog box

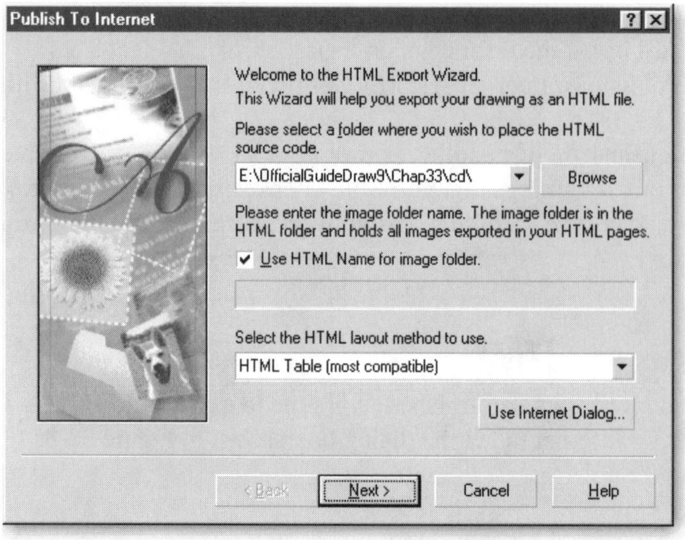

FIGURE 33-8 The initial Publish To Internet Wizard dialog box

Your first choice is the folder in which the resulting HTML file will be stored. If there are images to be created, you can also specify another subfolder where they will be stored. A great way to create a Web page in CorelDRAW is to import each graphic as a linked bitmap. Then you can optimize the graphics and not have CorelDRAW export them. The last choice in this screen is the HTML layout method to use. Your choice here should be based on the browser being used by your target audience. Unless you are specifically targeting only Netscape 4 users or Internet Explorer 4 users, you should leave this at the default of HTML Table. This option is the most compatible, but it does create complex tables to retain positioning of the various elements on the page. You can continue using the Wizard or click the Use Internet Dialog button, which takes all of the elements in the Wizard and places them in a single dialog box. We'll use the Wizard. Once you are finished, click Next to get the next screen, as shown in Figure 33-9.

This screen gives you several options for images. These options were described earlier in the sections on JPEG and GIF files. If you have sized your bitmaps correctly, make sure that you don't check Resample bitmaps to screen resolution, as the images will be incorrectly resized. Clicking Next again will bring you to Figure 33-10.

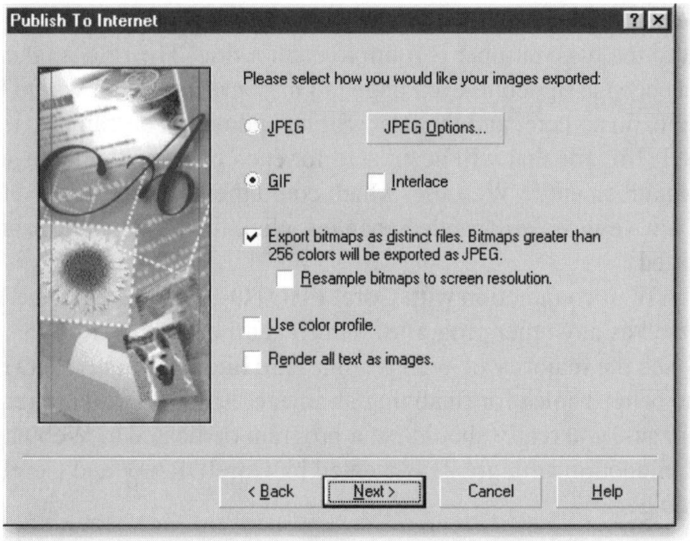

FIGURE 33-9   The Publish To Internet Wizard dialog box for selecting image options

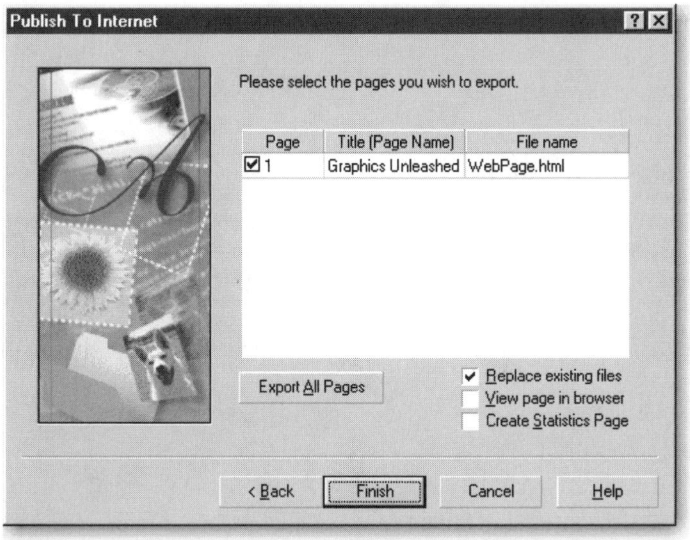

FIGURE 33-10   Last screen of the Publish To Internet Wizard for naming each page

Each of the pages in your CorelDRAW file will be listed. You can place a check mark next to each page that you wish to export or press the Export Δll Pages button. Next to the page number is room to enter a title. The title is taken from the name that has been assigned to each page tab in your file. If you would like to change a name, do so here, and the tabs will be updated. You can also specify the name of the HTML file that will be created for each page. In theory, a single CDR file could contain an entire Web site, which could then be exported to HTML all at once. Once you've made any needed changes, click the Finish button, and the file will be exported.

CorelDRAW in conjunction with Corel PHOTO-PAINT can create Web graphics as well as any other programs. You'll get the best results by using both programs. Since the majority of Web graphics are bitmaps, Corel PHOTO-PAINT is usually the better choice for finalizing an image. Lastly, if you are required to create Web pages, you really should get a program dedicated to Web page design to work in conjunction with graphics created by CorelDRAW and Corel PHOTO-PAINT.

CHAPTER 34

Setting Options and Customizing the User Interface

CorelDRAW 9

W e all work in different ways, and the options and interface of CorelDRAW are not optimal for everyone's style of working. Luckily, you can change almost everything in CorelDRAW to make it more to your liking. This chapter walks you through the many settings found in the Options dialog box and discusses the customization that you can do.

When you first install CorelDRAW, a number of options are already set for you. Corel tries to set default values that are appropriate for the majority of people. Nevertheless, you will want to change many of these settings to get the most benefit from the options. All of the options described here can be accessed with the Tools | Options (CTRL-J) command. The Options dialog box provides more than sixty dialog boxes full of information. This section describes each of these dialog boxes and their settings.

Along the left side of the Options dialog box is a tree structure of all the types of settings that you can adjust. If there is a plus (+) sign next to a category, subcategories are available. Just click the +, and they will be revealed. To hide them again, click the minus (−) sign that replaces the + sign to collapse the tree.

Workspace

The concept of workspaces was added in CorelDRAW 8. This makes it easy for several users to share the same installation of CorelDRAW, and for each one to work with a different customized environment. Or you may want different settings based upon the type of project you're working on. Workspaces allow you to save the user interface settings and defaults for each person or project so that you can easily return to those settings as needed. Figure 34-1 shows the Workspace section of the Options dialog box.

At the top of the dialog box, you can see which workspace is currently loaded. Unless you have changed it, it should read "_default." Just below that is a list of all the available workspaces. Initially there is the _default workspace and several other workspaces that mimic CorelDRAW 8 and Adobe Illustrator. You'll also note that the author has already created a workspace.

To create a new workspace, simply click the New button. This will bring up the dialog box shown in Figure 34-2.

First, you'll need to enter a name for the new workspace. Make sure to give it a descriptive name so that you can remember its purpose. Next, you need to choose the existing workspace to base it on. Choose the one that is most similar to what you want in the new workspace so you'll have fewer changes to make. Last, you need to enter a description of the new workspace. Make sure to expand on the name you gave it so

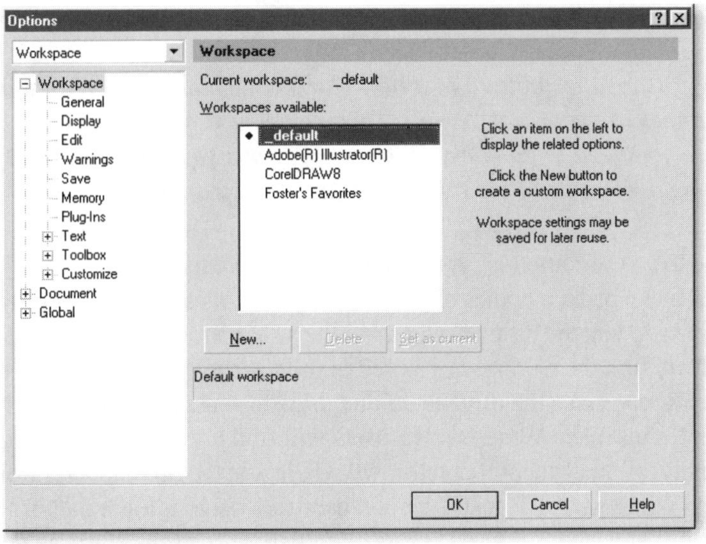

FIGURE 34-1 Options Workspace dialog box

that there is no question about how this workspace is best used. Once you're finished, click OK to get back to the main Workspace dialog box.

If you wish to delete a workspace, simply select it from the list on the left, and click the Delete button. The most important thing to do is to select a workspace that you want to use. Once selected, click the Set as current button, which will put

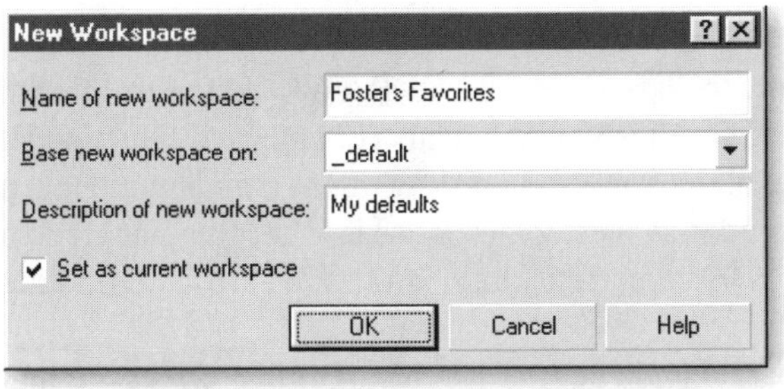

FIGURE 34-2 New Workspace dialog box

the workspace into use. As you'll see in the next few pages, a number of settings can be controlled by a workspace.

 TIP *Copy the _default to a new workspace name instead of making changes to the actual default. This way, you'll always have the default in case you need to go back. This also prevents your custom workspace from being overwritten by a reinstall or deleted by an uninstall.*

If you move to a new computer, you can move the workspace as well. It is also a good idea to make backup copies of your workspaces in case they get corrupt. Having backups will save you the time of recreating the workspaces. In Windows 9x, you will most likely find the workspaces stored in the x:\drawdir\workspace\coreldraw9 folder where x represents the drive letter and drawdir represents the folder in which CorelDRAW is installed. Windows NT users will find it located at x:\ntfolder\profiles\ username\application data\corel\coreldraw9 where x is the drive letter, ntfolder is the folder where Windows NT is installed, and username is your login name.

Inside this folder, you'll see a series of folders named the same as your workspaces. Once you have a workspace you really like, copy the whole folder someplace else, and you've got a backup.

General

Bring up the General dialog box shown in Figure 34-3 by clicking the General option under Workspace in the Options tree structure.

Undo Levels

It happens all the time. You do something such as deleting an object that you think you no longer need, and then you realize that it is needed after all. No problem— simply use the Edit | Undo (CTRL-Z) command. In the good old days of CorelDRAW, you could undo only the last action. CorelDRAW 5 increased this limit to 99. The limit is now 99,999, which is way too many for any user. Every action that can be undone will be stored in memory, so setting this at a high number can quickly drain your system's resources. A nice compromise is to set Regular Undo to 10. Note that the default setting is 99, which can drain your system resources rather quickly and cause instability.

There is a separate undo setting labeled "Bitmap effects" that relates to the effects that you apply using the Bitmap menu. Since these effects are usually even

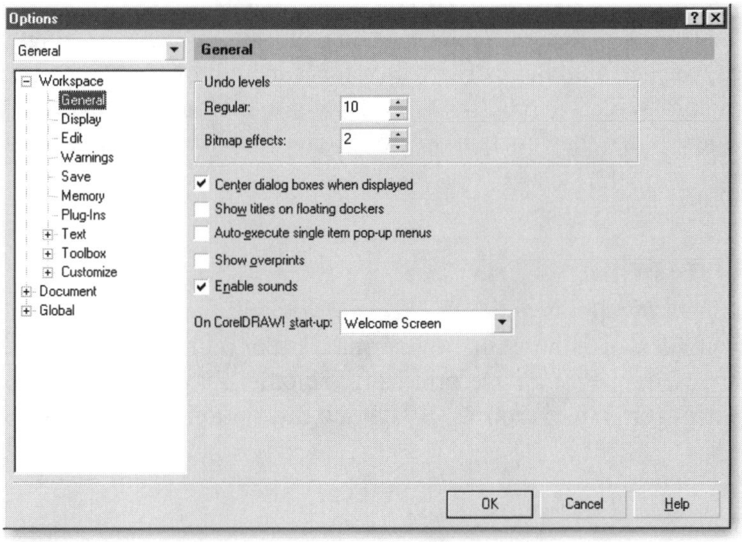

FIGURE 34-3   Options General dialog box

more memory intensive than regular operations, you'll want to keep this setting
much lower. The maximum value here is 99, and the default is 2. You may want to
change this value to 3 or 4 just so you can undo more than two effects, but keep in
mind that these operations are memory intensive.

Center Dialog Boxes

Do you ever find yourself moving a dialog box to a certain position on the screen
only to find that it doesn't appear there the next time it is used? By default, Center
dialog boxes when displayed is checked. This means that all dialog boxes will be
automatically centered. If you uncheck this option, the dialog boxes will remember
their last position and not automatically center themselves.

Floating Dockers

When you undock Dockers, you have the option of having a title bar on them or
having just a couple of gray lines. There is really no need to have a title bar unless
you find it more attractive. By default the title bar is turned off. Check Show titles
on floating dockers if you want them to appear.

34

Auto-Execute Single Item Pop-Up Menus

Some of the pop-up menus that appear when you right-click have a single item. In those cases, you can automatically execute that function by checking Auto-execute single item pop-up menus. You'll see later that you can customize the right-click pop-up menus so that they contain only one item. In this case, auto-execution is quite helpful.

Show Overprints

When the Show overprints option is checked, you will see a hatching pattern on any object for which there is an overprinted fill or outline. Three types of hatching are used: one for an overprinted fill, another for an overprinted outline, and yet another for both overprints. By default this option is turned off.

Sounds

New to CorelDRAW 9 is the ability to associate sounds with certain actions you perform. By default this ability is activated. You can turn it off by unchecking the Enable sounds checkbox. If you want to use the sounds, you'll need to visit the Sounds Control Panel in Windows to assign sounds to the various actions.

On CorelDRAW! Start-Up

When you started CorelDRAW for the first time, you were presented with a dialog box that asked you what task you wanted to perform. You may have just selected something to get rid of this box. If you want to change the setting to one of the other options, choose it from the On CorelDRAW! start-up drop-down list.

Display

The Display Options dialog box is discussed in Chapter 11.

Edit

Click the Edit option under Workspace in the tree structure of the Options dialog box to get the dialog box shown in Figure 34-4.

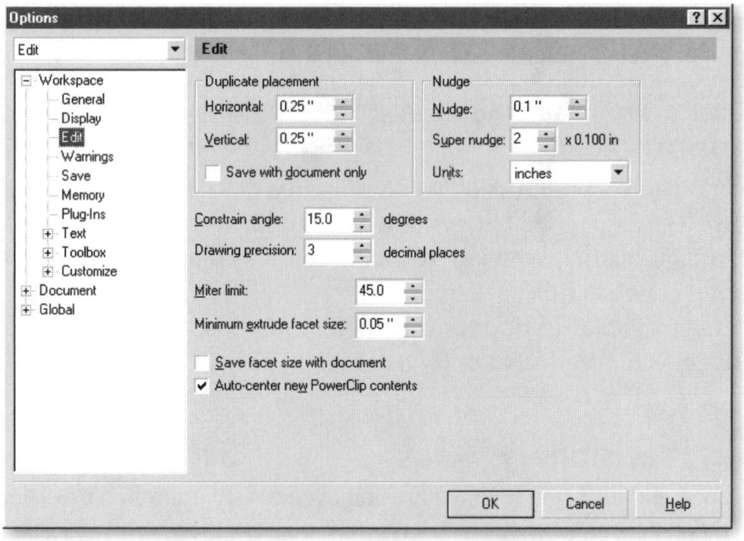

FIGURE 34-4   The Options Edit dialog box

Duplicate Placement

When you create a duplicate (CTRL-D) or a clone, it will be offset from the original object by the values you enter in the Horizontal and Vertical boxes. Many users like to change these values to 0 so duplicates are placed directly on top of the original object. Remember that you can also quickly create a duplicate on top of the original object by pressing the + key on the numeric keypad. The values set here will not have an effect when the + key is used. Checking the Save with document only box will restrict this change to the current document only; it won't change future documents.

Nudge

Nudging objects and nodes is a great way to get them exactly where you want them. The arrow keys on the keyboard will move an object by the amount specified here. Super nudge is the Nudge function on steroids. Hold down the SHIFT key when you click the arrow keys, and the nudge amount will be multiplied by the super nudge

34

value. This simple shortcut key provides an easy way to move objects. You can also select the type of Units you wish to use for your Nudge value. By default the unit is inches, but many users prefer to changing it to other systems.

Constrain Angle

As you work within CorelDRAW, you can use the CTRL key to constrain a number of functions. The angle used to constrain is a multiple of what is entered here. This value will affect rotating, skewing, adjusting control points, drawing straight lines, and adjusting Fountain fills.

The default value of 15 degrees is sufficient for most users, but you may find that a different value works better for a particular project.

Drawing Precision

CorelDRAW 6 and its 32-bit architecture achieved nearly unlimited precision. The level of precision also meant that every number was displayed with extra significant digits—which were usually zeros. The Drawing precision is the maximum number of digits that will appear after a decimal point. The default is 3 and will be more than sufficient for most artists. Those who create technical drawings may wish to increase this value slightly, but the days of flaunting precision are over!

Note that trailing zeros are no longer displayed at any time. Only significant digits are displayed to the precision you specify. The number displayed will be rounded if significant digits are not displayed.

Miter Limit

The Miter limit value determines the angle size below which miter joints will not be created at the corners of objects. If you draw an object with angles below the specified limit, the joints will be beveled. This feature eliminates the problem of corner joints extending far beyond the actual corners at small angles.

Minimum Extrude Facet Size

When you are extruding objects, sometimes a series of objects will be created to simulate the shading necessary to make the object look realistic. The number of objects created is controlled by the Minimum extrude facet size value. The higher the value, the fewer the number of objects. For most uses, the default is just fine.

Since this value will rarely need to be changed, you can select Save facet size with document to save the size with a particular document.

Auto-Center New PowerClip Contents

When you PowerClip an object inside of a container, you can check Auto-center new PowerClip contents to automatically center the object being PowerClipped within the container. This option is on by default. In most situations, you will find it easier to manually place the objects relative to one another, and therefore you'll want this option turned off.

Warnings

Select Warnings under Workspace in the tree structure of the Options dialog box to get the dialog box shown in Figure 34-5.

Various CorelDRAW functions may not perform as you originally expected. For example, Texture Fills will support only RGB colors even though you can

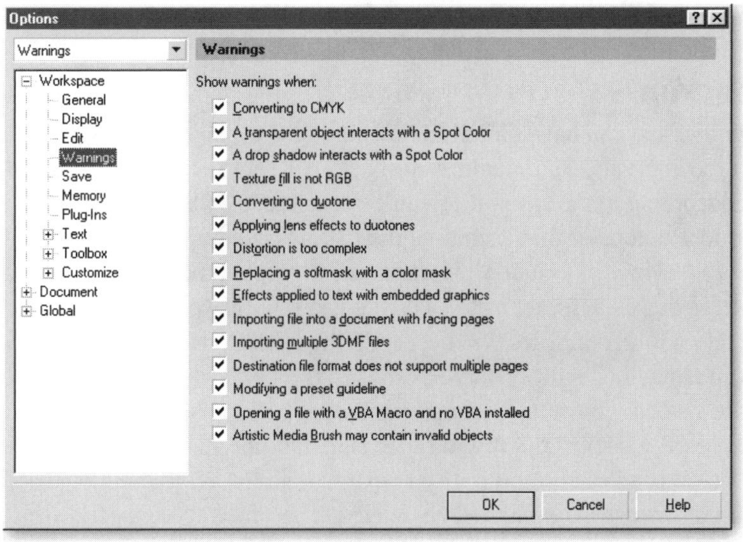

FIGURE 34-5   The Options Warnings dialog box

select colors in other models. These colors will then be converted back to RGB. A warning dialog box will tell you that your colors will be converted. Here is an example of this warning:

All of the other warnings are for problems that can affect you in a way that you might not expect. Unless there is a specific problem that does not concern you, you should leave them all checked until you understand them well enough to turn them off.

Save

Select Save under Workspace in the tree structure of the Options dialog box to get the dialog box shown in Figure 34-6.

Auto-Backup

As a safety net, you can have CorelDRAW automatically back up your work at specified time intervals. By default, Auto-backup is set to 10 minutes. You should set this value according to the amount of work that you are willing to recreate should you lose your file. Remember that each time the file is backed up, the computer will take some time for saving, so you don't want to be interrupted too often. By default, your file is saved in the same folder as the .cdr file itself, but if you select Always back-up to and specify a folder, all files will be sent to the folder you specify. To avoid auto-backup altogether, simply uncheck the Auto-backup check box.

Any file saved by the auto-backup feature will be clearly labeled as a file that has been automatically backed up. It will be labeled with the filename "Autobackup of *filename*" so you can easily find it. If you exit CorelDRAW gracefully (that is, if the program doesn't crash), the file will be deleted. Therefore, the only time this file remains is when you have run into a problem.

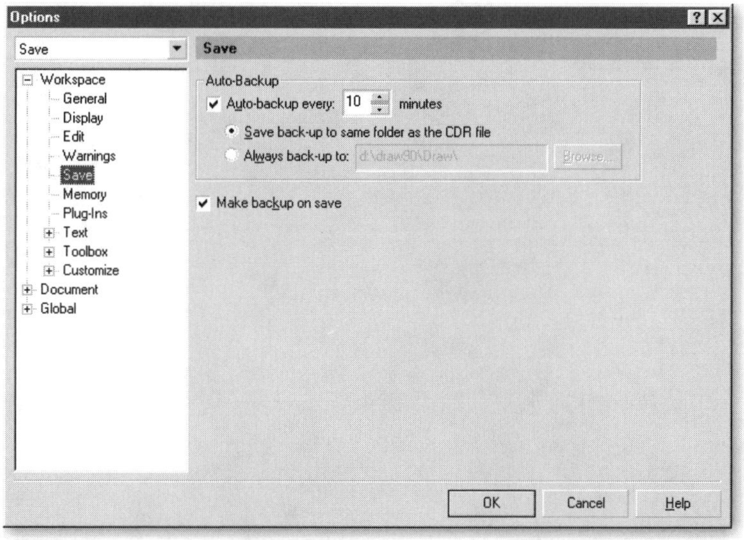

FIGURE 34-6 The Options Save dialog box

Make Backup on Save

As you save a file, you can have the previous version of the file saved as Backup_of_filename.cdr by checking the Make backup on save check box. This is yet another safety net to keep you from losing any important data. Since this feature will keep two copies of files on your hard drive, you may want to turn it off. If you leave this option activated, you may want to clean up your files on a regular basis so your hard drive does not fill up.

Memory

Select Memory under Workspace in the tree structure of the Options dialog box to get the dialog box shown in Figure 34-7.

Swap Disks

In the Swap Disks section, you can specify a Primary disk and Secondary disk. Should CorelDRAW need more memory than you have in your system, it can use

34

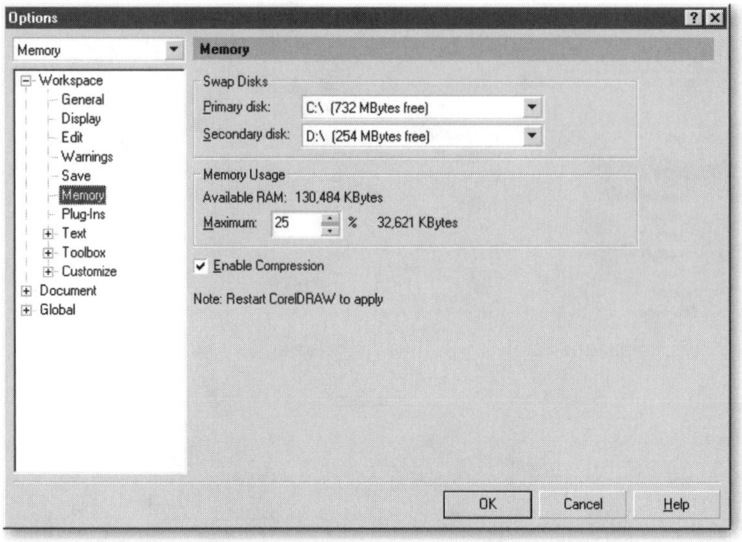

FIGURE 34-7 The Options Memory dialog box

hard disk space as temporary memory. Most programs use the Windows swap file, but CorelDRAW uses its own file so that it doesn't overload the Windows swap file. From either drop-down list, select the drive where you wish the swap file to be placed. The amount of space that is free on that drive is displayed. If there isn't at least 100MB free, it is probably not a good idea to use that drive.

Memory Usage

Memory usage will first report to you exactly how much RAM you have available to programs. You can specify a Maximum percentage of that memory that CorelDRAW can use. In Figure 34-7, we have specified 25 percent, which provides 32,621KB of memory on our system. If you have a high number of bitmap undos or plan to use a lot of bitmap effects, you should increase this to 50 percent. Raising it to a higher number could have adverse effects, especially if you plan on running other programs at the same time as CorelDRAW.

Compression

Selecting the Enable Compression check box will automatically compress the bitmap data in the swap file. There is no advantage to turning this option off.

 NOTE   *For the memory options to take effect, you have to restart CorelDRAW, as mentioned in the dialog box.*

Plug-Ins

The Options Plug-Ins dialog box lets you add third party Adobe PhotoShop compatible plug-in filters such as Alien Skins Eye Candy filter.

Text

Select Text under Workspace in the tree structure of the Options dialog box to get the dialog box shown in Figure 34-8.

Edit Text on Screen

You can enter text in two different ways when you click the text cursor in the drawing window. By default, you can type the text directly in the drawing window, but if you deselect Edit text on screen, you'll immediately go to the Edit Text dialog box.

Drag-and-Drop Text Editing

When text is selected, you can drag it and drop it into a new location when editing text on the screen. This feature is supported only when Drag and drop text editing is checked. This feature can be very sensitive and therefore somewhat difficult to use. This means that you may occasionally move text that you didn't intend to move, and at other times you won't move the text that you do want to move.

Show Selection Handles While Editing

When you are editing text, you can choose to have the object handles and the X in the middle of the object continue to display after a brief pause in editing. By

34

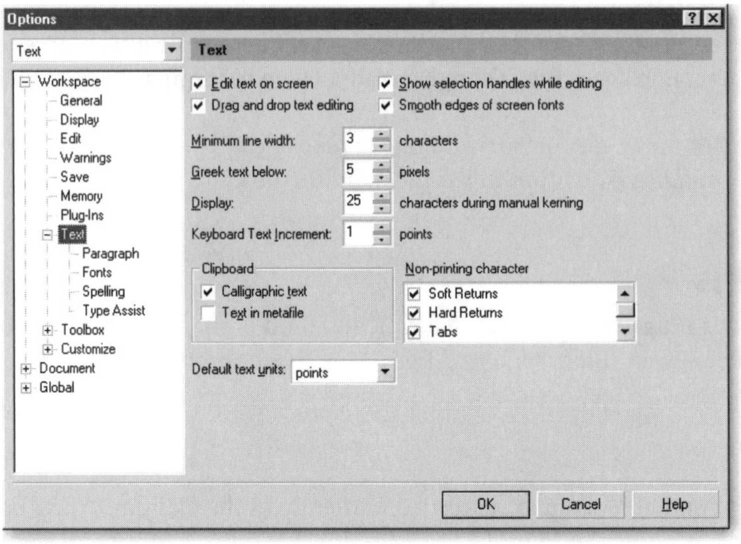

FIGURE 34-8   The Options Text dialog box

default the Show selection handles while editing check box is checked, but if you find the handles distracting or unnecessary, you can deselect this option.

Smooth Edges of Screen Fonts

The ability to antialias the edges of fonts was added in CorelDRAW 7. Checking the Smooth edges of screen fonts check box will activate this feature. By default, it is checked. If your display uses less than 65,000 colors, you will not able to use this feature.

Minimum Line Width

When working with small blocks of Paragraph Text, you may find it difficult to fit many text characters in the frame's width. The Minimum line width setting specifies the minimum number of characters allowed on a line.

Greek Text Below

When text becomes too small to accurately display on the screen, it is greeked. Greeked text appears as a gray line instead of as individual text characters. The Greek text below value specifies the minimum number of pixels high that a character must be; otherwise, it will be greeked. Text that is greeked will display much faster than the text itself.

Display During Kerning

As you manually kern text, the screen will display the number of characters specified in the Display parameter box.

Keyboard Text Increment

The Keyboard Text Increment box lets you specify the amount of change in text when you use the CTRL-8 or CTRL-2 shortcut keys. By default, this option is set to 1 point. Note that this does not affect the CTRL-4 and CTRL-6 shortcut keys, which select the next size in the font size drop-down list.

Clipboard

When you copy text to the clipboard, you can choose to have the text retain calligraphic effects. You can also specify whether the metafile format retains the text as text or converts it to a graphic. By default, text is converted to a graphic.

Default Text Units

When working with text in CorelDRAW, the units used are points. You can change these units by selecting another unit from the Default text units drop-down list.

Nonprinting Characters

If you choose Text I Show Non-Printing Characters, the types of nonprinting characters checked here will be displayed. By default, all types of characters are selected.

34

Paragraph

Select Paragraph under Text in the tree structure of the Options dialog box to get the dialog box shown in Figure 34-9.

Show Linking of Text Frame

CorelDRAW 9 lets you see which text frames are linked to others. When one frame is selected, a small line will be shown between the frames. You will also see the page number if the linked frame is on a different page. Check Show linking of text frame to activate this feature. By default, it is checked.

Show Text Frames

By default, paragraph text frames are displayed onscreen when you are editing the text within them. But if you deselect the Show text frames check box, you will see only the text.

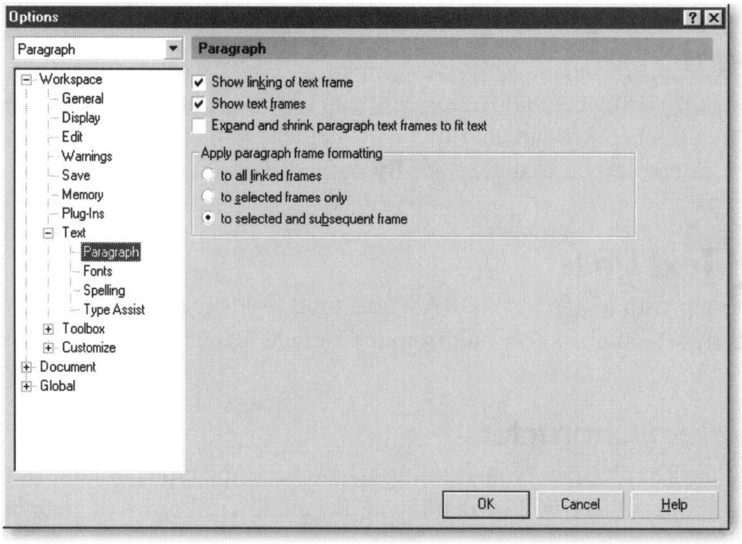

FIGURE 34-9   Options Paragraph dialog box

Expand and Shrink Paragraph Text Frames

As you are typing Paragraph Text onscreen, the paragraph text frame can be automatically resized to fit the amount of text if you check Expand and shrink paragraph text frames to fit text.

Paragraph Frame Formatting

When you make changes to the formatting of a paragraph frame, such as in the number of columns, you can have the changes apply to all linked frames, to selected frames only, or to selected and subsequent frames.

Fonts

Select Fonts under Text in the tree structure of the Options dialog box to get the dialog box shown in Figure 34-10.

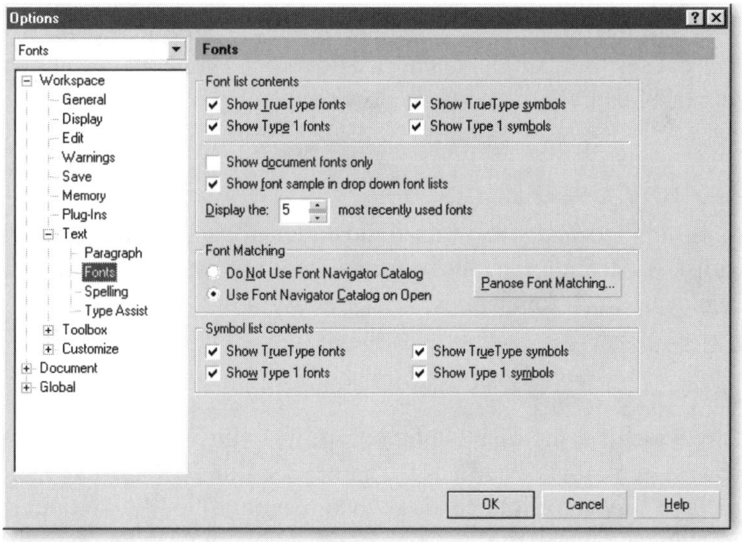

FIGURE 34-10   The Options Fonts dialog box

Font List Contents

Your font list may often include extra fonts that you don't wish to have in the list. You can obviously uninstall those fonts, but if they all come from the same type of font, you can turn them off within CorelDRAW. You have the option of displaying TrueType or Type 1 fonts and symbols, so if you don't want to see symbol fonts, simply uncheck those options. If you work in a PostScript-only environment, turn off the display of TrueType fonts.

 TIP   *A quick way to change the fonts displayed is to right-click the Font drop-down list on the Property Bar.*

Show Document Fonts Only

Another way to really shorten the font list is to display only the fonts used within the current document. To activate this option, simply check Show document fonts only. Note that with this option activated, you will not be able to choose any new fonts.

Show Font Samples

As you scroll through the font list, a sample of the font will be shown. If you would rather not see this sample, uncheck Show font sample in drop down font lists. Having this feature turned on can slow the display of the list.

Most Recently Used Fonts

The names of the fonts that you've used most recently appear at the top of the Font drop-down list. By default, the most recent 5 fonts are listed. You can change this value to display up to 20 font names.

Font Matching

CorelDRAW 9 includes the Font Navigator utility, which helps you to manage the fonts on your system. It is described in Chapter 32. CorelDRAW can include the fonts in the Font Navigator font catalog when opening files. Any required fonts will be automatically installed if the Use Font Navigator Catalog on Open option is selected. If you would prefer for this not to affect opening files, select Do Not Use Font Navigator Catalog. The Panose Font Matching information is discussed in Chapter 32.

Symbol List Contents

Just as you can control which fonts appear in the drop-down list, you can control which types of fonts appear in the Symbols roll-up. By default, only symbol fonts in both formats are shown.

 TIP *A quick way to change the symbol fonts that are displayed is to right-click the Symbols drop-down list.*

Spelling

The Spelling options are discussed in Chapter 28.

Type Assist

Type Assist is a fantastic tool for helping correct typographical errors. The Type Assist options are described in Chapter 28.

Toolbox

When you select the plus sign (+) next to the toolbox, CorelDRAW displays a list of the tools in the tree structure of the Options dialog box. Click the tool that you want to change, and the dialog box will show you all of the applicable options for that tool.

Pick Tool

Select Pick Tool from the tree structure of the Options dialog box to get the dialog box shown in Figure 34-11.

People used to using CAD programs may want to check the Cross hair cursor box to use this option. The small cursor will be replaced by a cursor with crosshairs that extend completely across the drawing window. By default, the crosshair cursor is turned off.

Selecting Treat all objects as filled allows you to select objects by clicking anywhere inside the object instead of just on the outline. This option is activated by default, unlike in some previous versions. If this option is checked, you may find it difficult to select an object behind the front object.

34

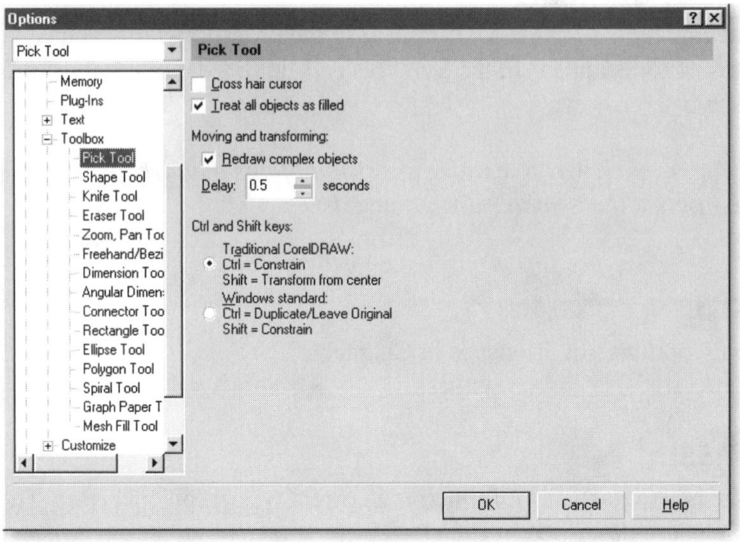

FIGURE 34-11   The Options Pick Tool dialog box

As you move or transform objects, you can display the changes by checking Redraw complex objects. The changes are displayed only when you stop moving your cursor for a period of time longer than that set in the Delay parameter box. By default, this option is turned on with a delay of 0.1 second.

Traditionally, the CTRL key has been used to constrain objects, and the SHIFT key to transform objects from the center. Now you have the option of using the Windows standard, where the CTRL key duplicates objects and the SHIFT key constrains objects. If you choose the Windows standard, the ALT key transforms objects from the center.

Note that if you are using CorelDRAW on a Macintosh, these keys work according the standard Macintosh conventions. The SHIFT key is used to constrain objects, and the COMMAND key will transform objects from the center.

Knife Tool

Select Knife Tool from the tree structure of the Options dialog box to get the dialog box shown in Figure 34-12.

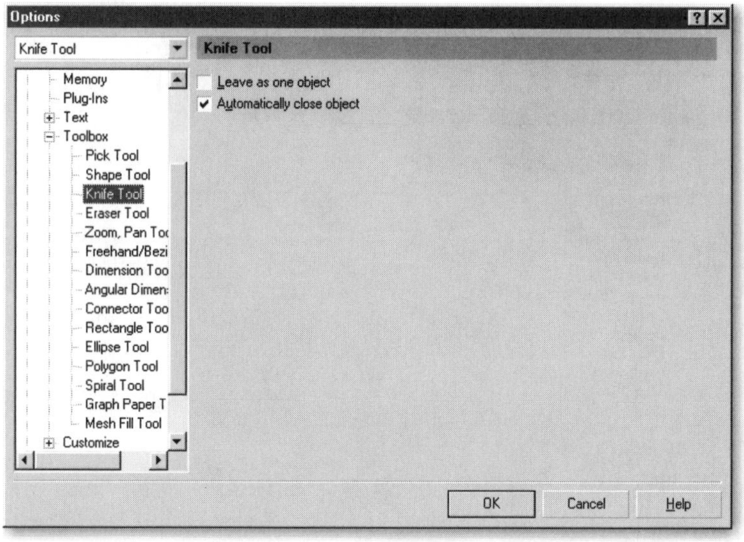

FIGURE 34-12   The Options Knife Tool dialog box

You can select two options to be applied when you use the Knife tool to cut an object. You can leave the pieces combined into a single object by checking the Leave as one object check box. By default, the objects will not remain combined. Checking Automatically close object will automatically create a closed path from objects that have been cut using the Knife tool, so they can be filled. By default, the objects will be closed.

Eraser Tool

Select Eraser Tool from the tree structure of the Options dialog box to get the dialog box shown in Figure 34-13.

The eraser thickness determines how much of an object is erased as you drag your cursor over it. By default, Thickness is set to 0.25 inch. You can choose to clean up the extra nodes when all erasing is finished by selecting Auto-reduce nodes of resulting objects. By default, this option is checked.

Zoom and Pan Tools

All of the options for the Zoom and Pan tools are described in Chapter 11.

34

The Options Eraser Tool dialog box

Freehand and Bézier Tools

Select Freehand/Bezier Tool from the tree structure of the Options dialog box to get the dialog box shown in Figure 34-14.

Freehand smoothing determines how closely CorelDRAW tracks your freehand drawing when it calculates the nodes used in the object you are drawing. The lower the number, the higher the number of nodes that will be created as CorelDRAW tries to recreate the line to match your drawing as closely as possible. This number can be any value between 0 and 100, with the default being 100.

The Autotrace tracking option works much like Freehand tracking except that it is used when you use the Autotrace tool to trace bitmaps.

The Corner threshold option determines whether smooth nodes or cusps are used when you draw a freehand or autotraced line. Lower numbers produce more cusp nodes, and higher numbers produce more smooth nodes. This number can be any value between 1 and 10, with the default being 5.

The Straight line threshold option works similarly to the Corner threshold option. A smaller number produces more curve segments when you are drawing a line, and a larger number produces more straight-line segments.

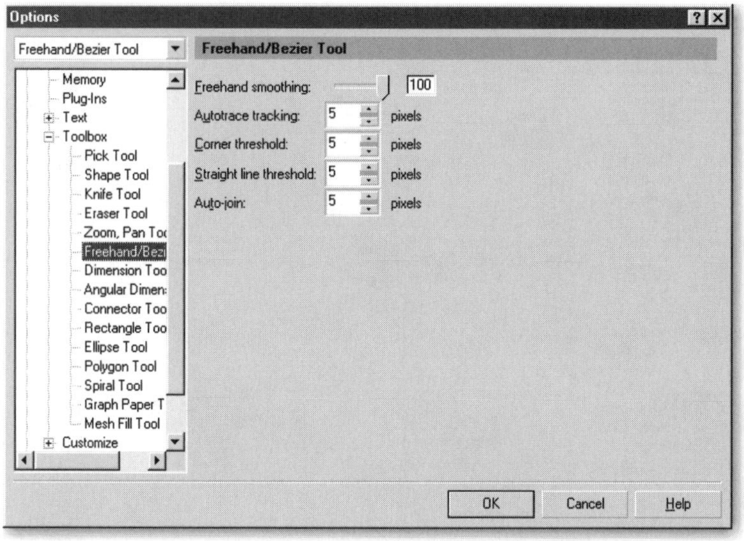

FIGURE 34-14

The Auto-join option determines how close, in pixels, the two end nodes of an object must be before they are joined. If you enter a low number, you will have to be more accurate in your drawing.

Dimension Tool

Select Dimension Tool from the tree structure of the Options dialog box to get the dialog box shown in Figure 34-15.

Again, the values entered for the Dimension tool are simply the default values that will appear on the Property Bar when drawing dimension lines. All of the options for dimension lines are discussed in Chapter 4.

Angular Dimension Tool

Select Angular Dimension Tool from the tree structure of the Options dialog box to get the dialog box shown in Figure 34-16.

Just as with the Dimension Tool, the values entered for the Angular Dimension tool are simply the default values that will appear on the Property Bar when drawing angular dimension lines. All of the options are discussed in Chapter 4.

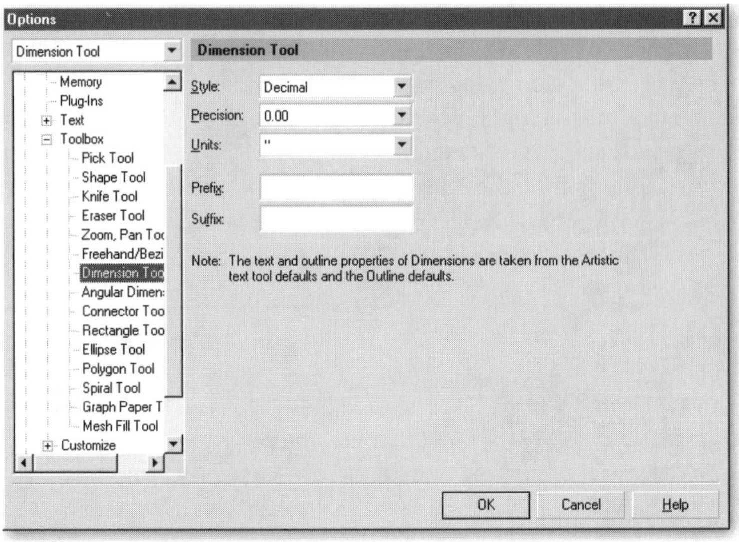

FIGURE 34-15 The Options Dimension Tool dialog box

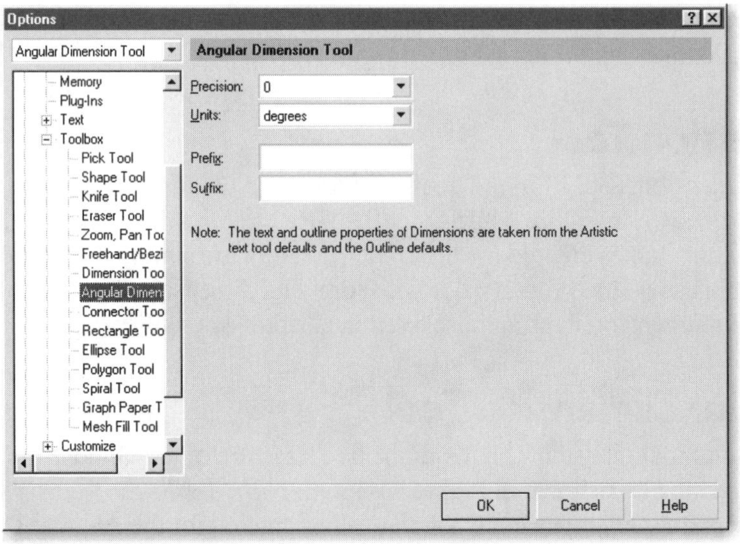

FIGURE 34-16 The Options Angular Dimension Tool dialog box

Connector Tools

Select Connector Tools from the tree structure of the Options dialog box to get the dialog box shown in Figure 34-17.

Connector lines can be set to either Snap to closest node or Lock to connector node. These defaults will be reflected in the Property Bar as you draw connector lines. All of the options for connector lines are discussed in Chapter 4. Straight line threshold determines at what point a line will be considered straight or if an elbow is inserted in the line. The default is 5 pixels.

Rectangle Tool

Select Rectangle Tool from the tree structure of the Options dialog box to get the dialog box shown in Figure 34-18.

Chapter 3 discusses the corner roundness for rectangles. The value set here will be the default roundness for any new rectangles. By default, the roundness is zero—that is, the corners of rectangles will not be rounded at all.

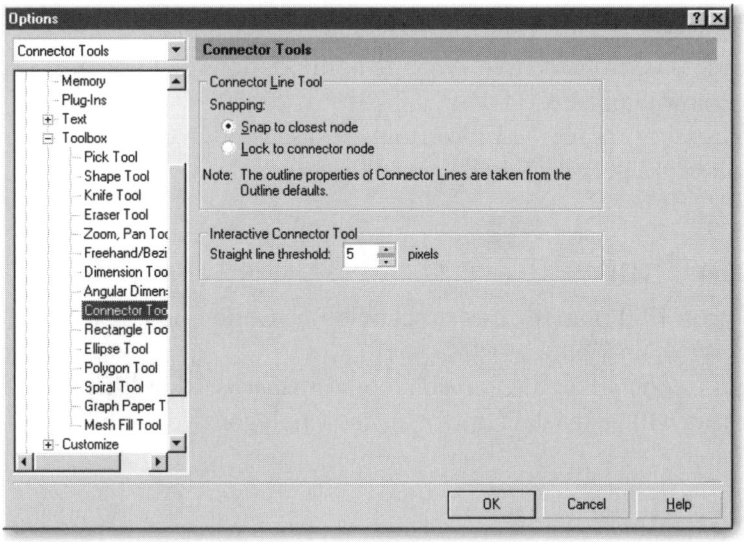

FIGURE 34-17   The Options Connector Tool dialog box

34

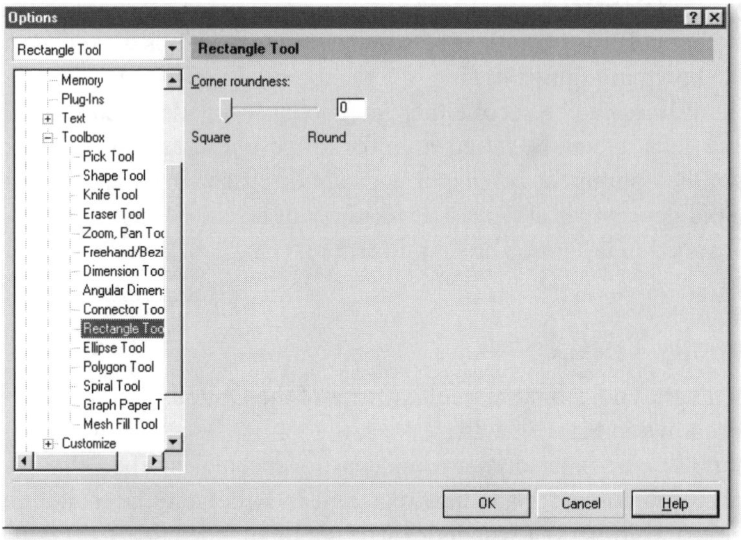

FIGURE 34-18   The Options Rectangle Tool dialog box

Ellipse Tool

Select Ellipse Tool from the tree structure of the Options dialog box to get the dialog box shown in Figure 34-19.

The options shown for the Ellipse tool are discussed in Chapter 3. The values set here will be the defaults for any new ellipses you draw.

Polygon Tool

Select Polygon Tool from the tree structure of the Options dialog box to get the dialog box shown in Figure 34-20.

The options shown for the Polygon tool were discussed in Chapter 3. The values set here will be the defaults for any new polygons you draw.

Spiral Tool

Select Spiral Tool from the tree structure of the Options dialog box to get the dialog box shown in Figure 34-21.

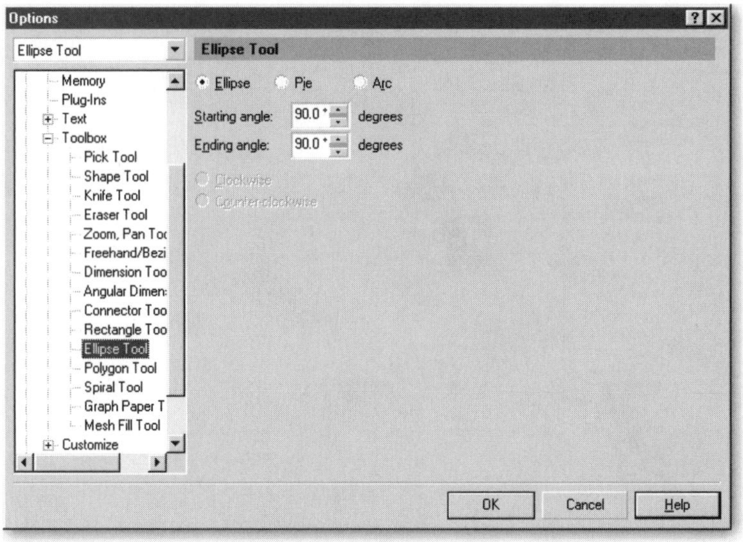

FIGURE 34-19   The Options Ellipse Tool dialog box

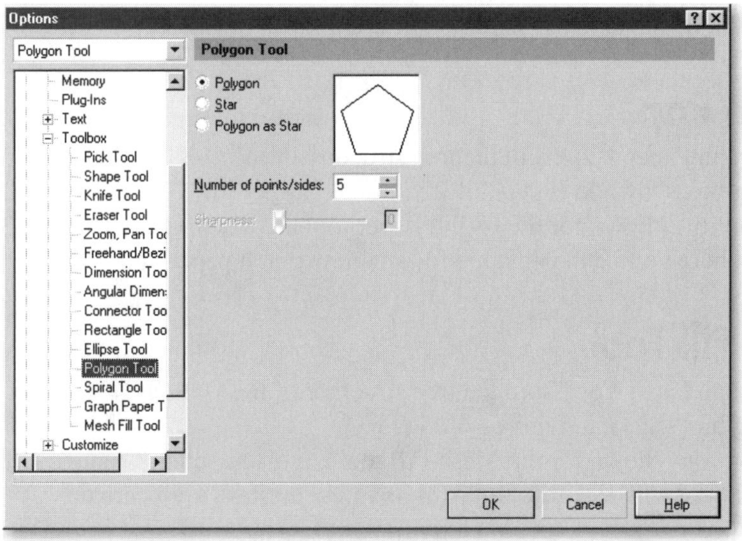

FIGURE 34-20   The Options Polygon Tool dialog box

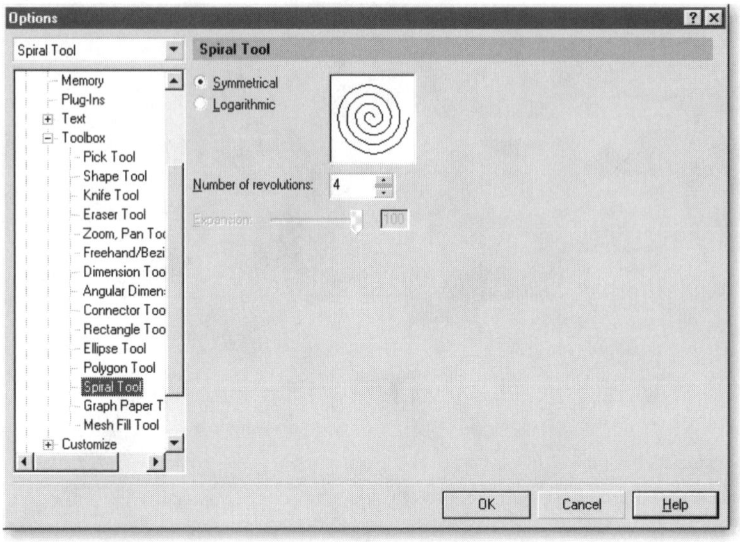

FIGURE 34-21   The Options Spiral Tool dialog box

The options shown for the Spiral tool are discussed in Chapter 3. The values set here will be the defaults for any new spirals you draw.

Graph Paper Tool

Select Graph Paper Tool from the tree structure of the Options dialog box to get the dialog box shown in Figure 34-22.

The options shown for the Graph Paper tool are discussed in Chapter 3. The values set here will be the defaults for any new graph paper you draw.

Mesh Fill Tool

Select Graph Paper Tool from the tree structure of the Options dialog box to get the dialog box shown in Figure 34-23.

The options shown for the Mesh Fill tool are discussed in Chapter 9. The values set here will be the defaults for any new mesh fills you create.

Customizing the User Interface

CorelDRAW 6 ushered in a new era of customization for Corel products. No longer are you forced to use only the tools in the format given to you. Now you can rearrange

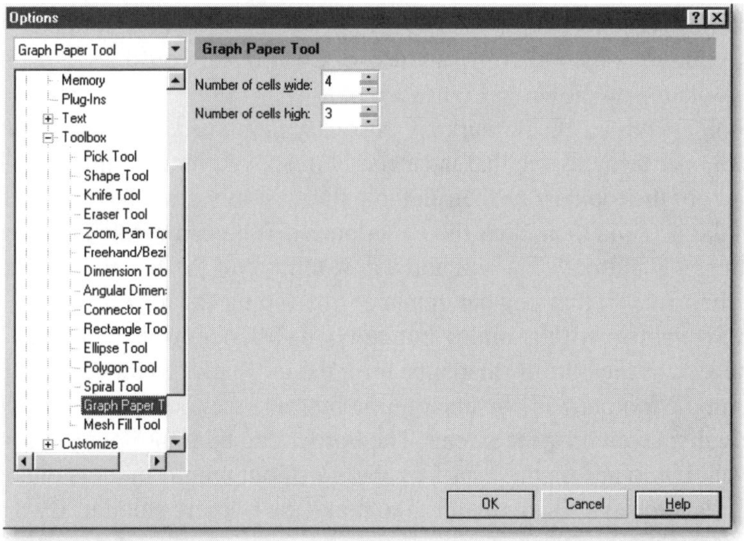

FIGURE 34-22   The Options Graph Paper Tool dialog box

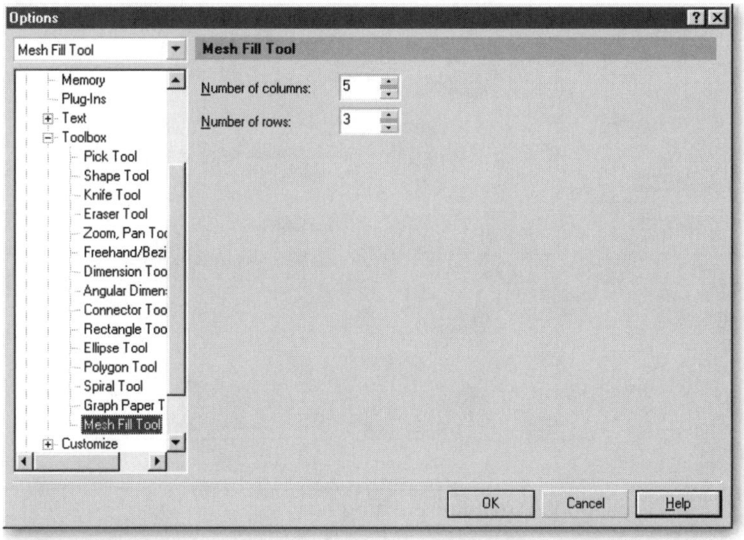

FIGURE 34-23   The Options Mesh Fill Tool dialog box

your toolbars, menus, and keystrokes and even write macros so you can work as productively as possible. CorelDRAW 9 takes customization even further.

When you select the plus sign (+) next to Customize, you'll see a list of the available toolbars, as shown in Figure 34-24.

The toolbars with a check mark are currently displayed. You can easily display other toolbars or turn off one that is currently displayed by clicking its check box. To reset any of the toolbars to their default state, simply click the name of the toolbar in the list, and then click the Reset button. You can create new toolbars by clicking the New button. This will add a new toolbar to the list and immediately highlight the name so that you can rename it by typing the new name.

In the Size portion of the dialog box are two slider controls that allow you to choose the size of the buttons that appear on the toolbars and the size of the border surrounding the toolbars. If you enlarge the buttons, the toolbar may not be completely displayed on your screen. The border can be important because you can right-click it to access the list of toolbars without reentering this dialog box, but if you want to save space, feel free to make the borders smaller. By default, both are set to Small.

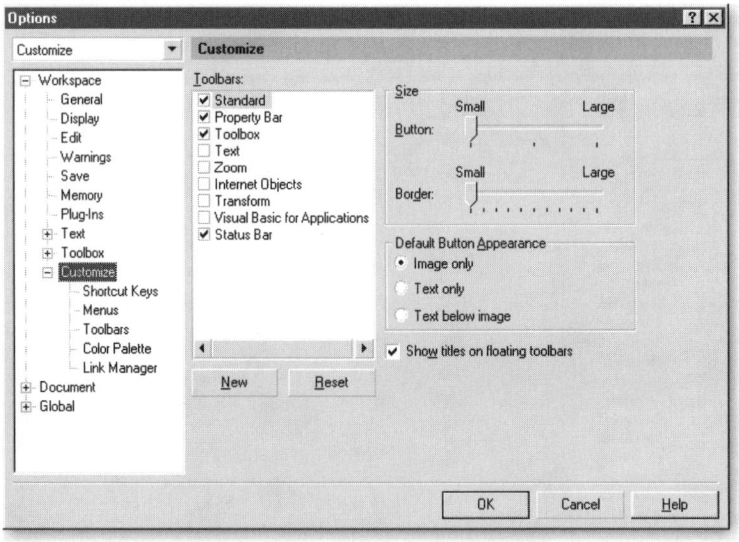

FIGURE 34-24   The Options Customize dialog box

Lastly, you can choose whether to use the <u>S</u>how titles on floating toolbars option. By default, any toolbar that is not docked will have a title bar just like a normal dialog box, but since this takes up more room, you can turn this option off. Another option allows the buttons on toolbars to be Image only, Text only, or Text below image. By default, they are set to Image only, but you can select the option that best meets your needs.

Shortcut Keys

It seems that each new version of CorelDRAW uses different keyboard shortcuts. Relearning new keystrokes with each new version can be frustrating. However, now you can customize the shortcut keys. Select Shortcut Keys from the tree structure of the Options dialog box to get the dialog box shown in Figure 34-25.

On the left side of the screen is a list of all of the available commands, grouped into folders based on their functionality. Work your way through the command tree until you find a command you wish to change. When the command is

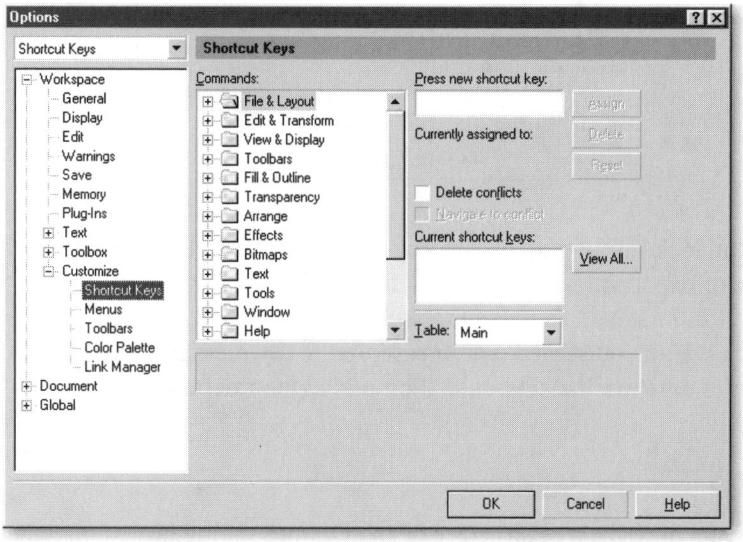

FIGURE 34-25   The Options Shortcut Keys dialog box

selected, the Current shortcut keys window will display the shortcut, if any, that is currently assigned to that command.

To enter a new shortcut, place your cursor in the Press new shortcut key box, and type the new keystrokes. When you've done this, the Assign button will become available. Click Assign to assign the new shortcut. If a conflicting shortcut exists, it will be listed. If you check the Navigate to conflict on assign check box, you'll automatically be sent to the conflicting command immediately after you click the Assign button. You can also select the Delete conflicts shortcut if you want it removed.

When you are editing text, the shortcut keys change to common shortcut keys used in other applications that edit text. The Table drop-down list lets you choose between the Main set of shortcut keys and those used for Text Editing.

To see a list of all of the keyboard shortcuts, click the View All button. The following dialog box will appear:

You can look through the list of keystrokes on the screen, print it for future reference, or export it to an ASCII text file.

Since it is quite easy to make these changes, CorelDRAW also provides a way to get back where you started just in case you really mess things up. Click the Reset button to return the keyboard shortcuts to their default settings.

Menus

Select Menus from the tree structure of the Options dialog box to get the dialog box shown in Figure 34-26.

The left window displays a list of all the commands that can be included on a menu, grouped by the category of command. The figure shows the commands in

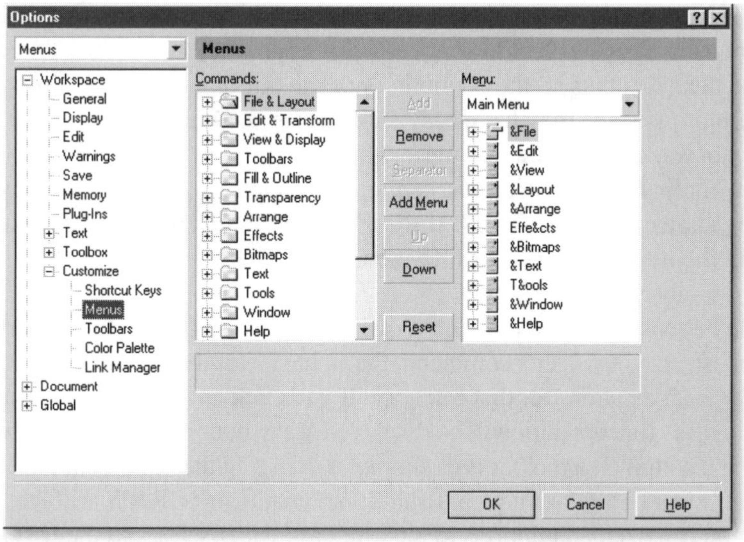

FIGURE 34-26   The Options Menus dialog box

the Arrange category. The right window shows the commands that are currently included in the drop-down menu. To add your own commands, simply click the command you want in the left window, and then click the Add button. To place the command where you want it, select the command you want it to appear below before clicking Add. If you happen to miss, the Move Up and Move Down buttons can help you to move the command into place.

You can add or remove separators as well. These are the little lines that appear in the drop-down menu to separate logically-grouped commands.

One of the neatest uses of customization is to create your own menu for storing your favorite commands. The only problem with this feature is that your menu is on only your own computer, so using someone else's computer can get confusing! Don't forget that the Reset button will set everything back to the defaults if things get too crazy.

TIP   *The drop-down list in the upper-right corner of the dialog box allows you to select the various pop-up menus within CorelDRAW. So you can customize them in the manner described previously.*

34

Toolbars

Earlier you saw how to select the toolbars that appear on the screen. You can also customize their contents so they contain only the buttons you want. You may not use many buttons since they have easy shortcut keys. Other commands are strangely absent, and a button for these would be great.

Select Toolbars from the tree structure of the Options dialog box to get the dialog box shown in Figure 34-27. If the toolbar contains buttons that you don't want, drag them from the toolbar into the Options dialog box. They'll no longer be part of the toolbar.

To add buttons, you need to first select the category that you want from the categories list. As you select a command, the right side of the dialog box will display all of the available buttons for that category. If you click any of the buttons, a description of its functionality will be displayed at the bottom of the dialog box.

Placing a button on a toolbar is as simple as dragging the button onto the toolbar you desire. If you don't drop it on a particular toolbar, CorelDRAW will create a new toolbar. You can even add buttons to a particular Property Bar. At the lower-left

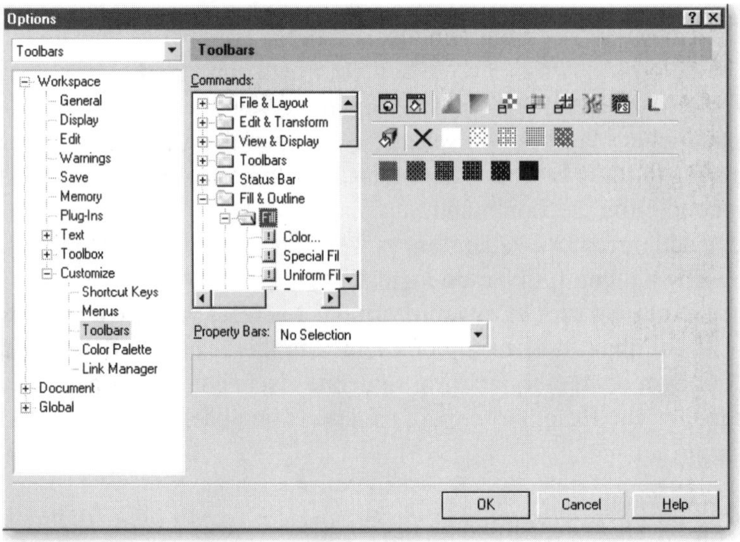

FIGURE 34-27   The Options Toolbars dialog box

corner of the dialog box is the Property Bars drop-down list. Select the Property Bar to which you want to add a button, and the Property Bar on the main screen will change accordingly. Now just drag the desired button onto the Property Bar.

If you really want to create your own graphic for a toolbar button, right-click directly on the toolbar button while you are customizing. Select Properties from the pop-up menu that appears to get the dialog box shown in Figure 34-28.

Here you have a simple bitmap editor for editing the button graphics. You can either directly edit the graphic here, or copy a graphic from another application (such as Corel PHOTO-PAINT) and paste it here using the CTRL-V shortcut key.

Color Palette

Select Color Palette from the tree structure of the Options dialog box to get the dialog box shown in Figure 34-29.

Selecting Wide Borders will leave a small amount of gray space between each color swatch on the palette. If you deselect this option, the colors are placed next to one another so that you can fit more colors in one row. The Large swatches check box controls the size of each color swatch in the palette. By default, it is not selected so

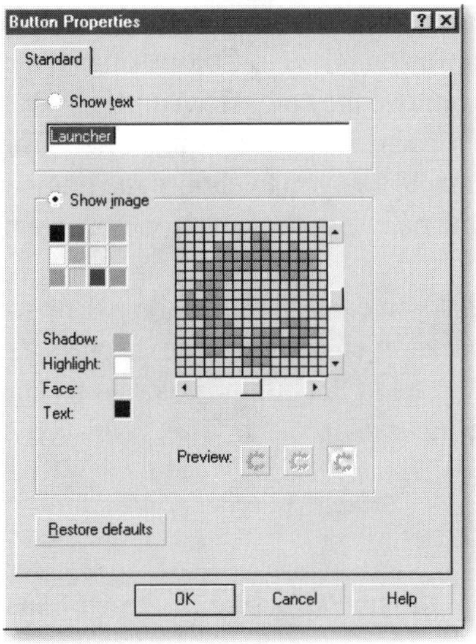

34

FIGURE 34-28   Button Properties dialog box

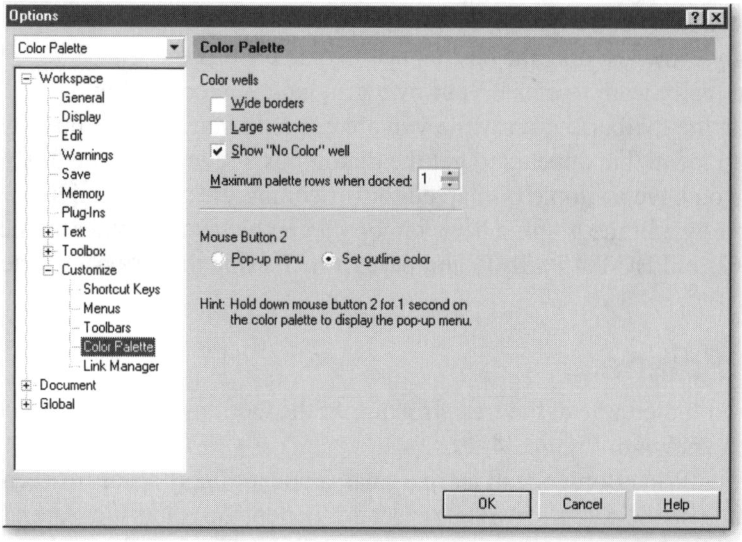

FIGURE 34-29   The Options Color Palette dialog box

that the color wells are considered "small." The Show "No Color" well option is one that creates a lot of confusion. The No Color well is the box with the X in it that signifies that you want to remove the color from a fill or outline. We sure couldn't imagine working without it because we use it quite often. The Maximum number of rows while docked num box allows you to choose the numbers of rows of swatches that will be shown when the palette is docked. You may want to increase this number to show more colors on the screen.

You probably know that you can right-click the palette to set the outline color. You can change this so that right-clicking instead displays a pop-up menu. If you leave the right mouse button set to Set outline color, you can hold the button down for a second or two to display the pop-up menu. This gives you the best of both options.

Link Manager

Select Link Manager from the tree structure of the Options dialog box to get the dialog box shown in Figure 34-30.

The Link Manager Docker gives you a way to check various links in your document. The Options Link Manager Docker allows you to control how they are

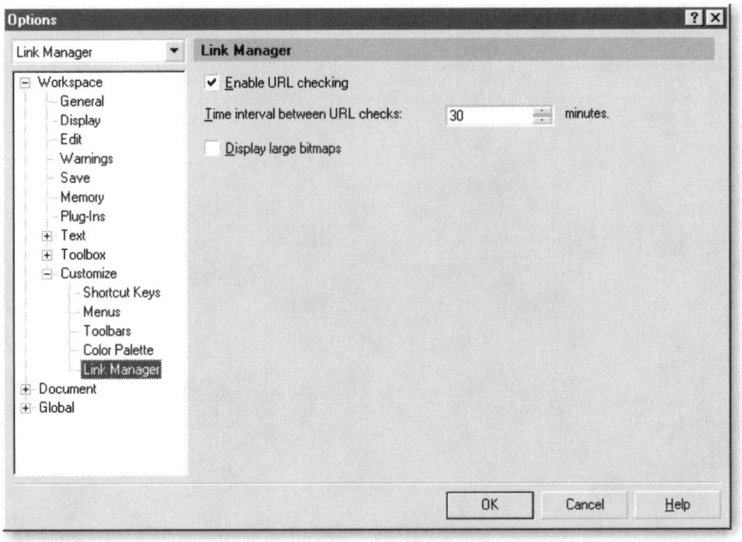

FIGURE 34-30   The Options Link Manager dialog box

checked. Enable URL checking will allow CorelDRAW to go onto the Web and check the validity of hyperlinks in your document. By default, these links are checked every 30 minutes, but you can control this by changing the value in Time interval between URL checks. You can also choose to Display large bitmaps instead of the default small ones.

Document

Select Document from the tree structure of the Options dialog box to get the dialog box shown in Figure 34-31.

The first check box asks if you want to Save options as defaults for new documents. When it is checked, the other options become available. Each of the options underneath Document in the tree structure within the dialog box are also repeated with check boxes. You are asked whether the changes you make in the other dialog boxes will apply to just the current document or to any new documents. Place a check mark in all categories that you wish to be defaults. Only those options set prior to entering the Options dialog box will be saved.

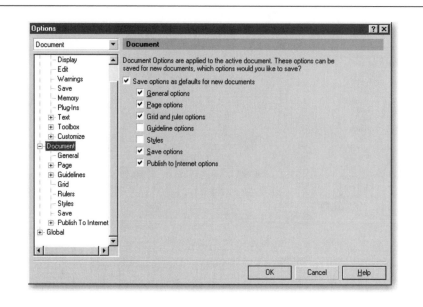

FIGURE 34-31   The Options Document dialog box

General

Select General from the tree structure of the Options dialog box to get the dialog box shown in Figure 34-32.

The Display drop-down list includes each of the five display modes that were described in Chapter 11. Select the view that you wish to be the default. It is initially set to Enhanced View. A new option added in CorelDRAW 8 is the ability to fill a curve that is not closed. By default, CorelDRAW 9 works just like previous versions, but by selecting Fill open curves, you can change this behavior. Another new feature is the ability to increase the size of a bitmap when an effect needs to have a few more pixels around the edge of the bitmap. If Auto inflate bitmap for bitmap effects is checked, CorelDRAW will increase the bitmaps in size as needed. Finally you can choose the Resolution that will be used when you create bitmap-based features such as Drop Shadows, Bitmap Extrusions, and Interactive Transparencies. By default Resolution is set to 200 dpi.

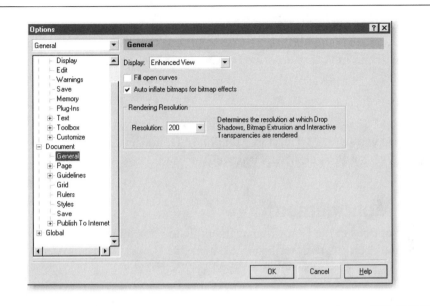

FIGURE 34-32   The Options General dialog box

Page

All of the options in the Page dialog box and the subsections of Size, Layout, and Background are described in Chapter 25.

Grids and Guidelines and Rulers

All of the options in the Grids and Guidelines dialog box as well as the Rulers dialog box are described in Chapter 13.

Styles

All of the options in the Styles dialog box are described in Chapter 29.

Save

All of the options in the Save dialog box are described in Chapter 24.

34

Publish To Internet

All of the options in the Publish To Internet dialog box and the subsections of Image, Text, and Links are described in Chapter 33.

Global

The options you select in the Global section of Options will affect not only CorelDRAW, but PHOTO-PAINT as well.

Color Management

All of the options in the Color Management dialog box and the subsections of General and Profiles are described in Chapter 22.

Printing

All of the options in the Printing and the subsections of Preflight are described in Chapter 26. Select Driver Compatibility from the tree structure of the Options dialog box to get the dialog box shown in Figure 34-33.

At times you want certain settings to apply only when you print to a specific printer. This dialog box allows you to select which overrides should apply to each of your printers.

Bitmap Effects

All of the options in the Bitmap Effects dialog box are described in Chapter 22.

Filters

When you first installed CorelDRAW, you were asked which filters you wanted to install. At the time, that list may have seemed mind boggling. You may have just moved on because it was too confusing, or you may have selected only a few filters to conserve hard drive space.

In earlier versions of CorelDRAW, you had to reinstall the program to change the filters installation, and if you didn't like their order in the Open/Import or Export dialog box, you were forced to carefully edit an .ini file. Now managing filters is quite easy.

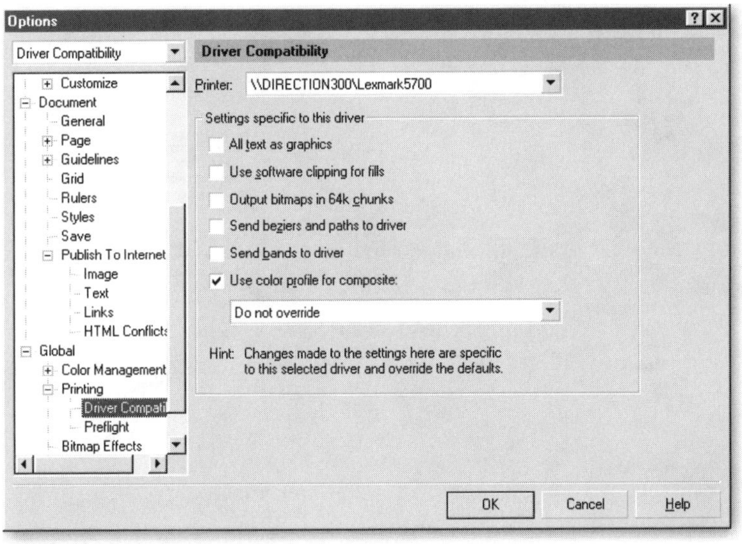

FIGURE 34-33   The Options Driver Compatibility dialog box

Select Filters from the tree structure of the Options dialog box to get the dialog box shown in Figure 34-34.

Adding and Deleting Filters

When Filters is selected, you're presented with two lists of filters. The left window shows all of the possible filters that can be installed. The right window shows the filters that are currently active, listed in the order in which they appear in the Open/Import dialog box. Available filters are divided into the categories Raster, Vector, Text, and Animation. Click the + sign next to any category to expand the list. If the list is already expanded, click the – sign to compress the list.

If you want to add a filter, find it in the list in the left window, and select it. Click the Add button in the middle of the dialog box, and the filter will now appear in the list of active filters. Deleting filters is just as easy. Select the filter in the left window, and click the Remove button.

To reorder the filters, select a particular filter, and use the Move Up and Move Down buttons to position it in the list. The order you see in the list of active filters is the order used in the Open/Import and Export dialog boxes. Most people use only five to ten filters on a regular basis, so moving those you commonly use to

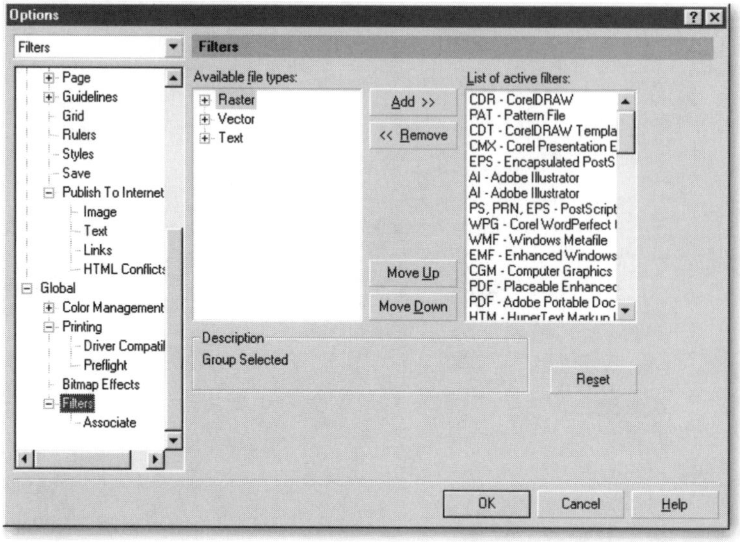

FIGURE 34-34   The Options Filters dialog box

the top of the list will save you the trouble of always scrolling through the list to find the filter you need.

With all of the customization features available, you can occasionally back yourself into a corner. Clicking the Reset button will put all of the filters back into the default configuration, so if you ever feel that you've messed up the filters beyond repair, just click Reset and start over.

Associate

Select Associate from the tree structure of the Options dialog box to get the dialog box shown in Figure 34-35.

When you view files in Explorer, each file is associated with a particular program. Sometimes you won't want that association in effect for a particular file format, and other times you'll want to associate a file format with CorelDRAW. Here you can specify which formats are associated with CorelDRAW.

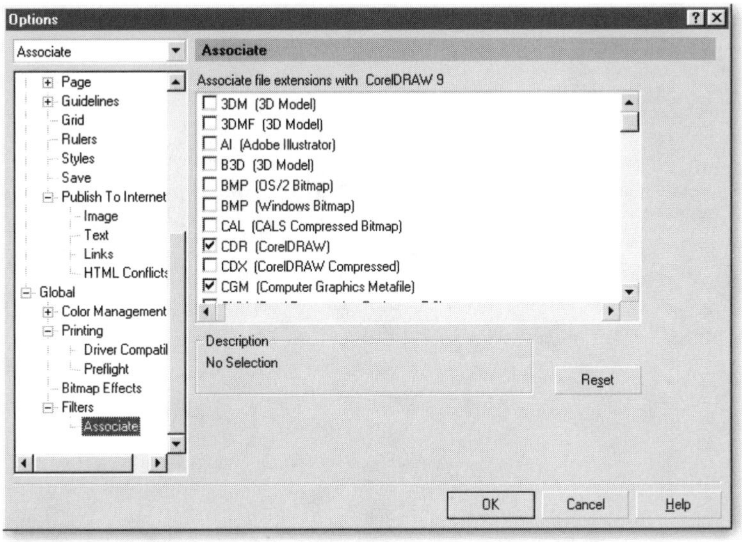

FIGURE 34-35 The Options Associate dialog box

The file formats are listed in alphabetical order. To the left of the file format is a check box. Any format that is checked will be associated with CorelDRAW 9. You may want to add the formats that you use most often, but remember that any formats that are associated with CorelDRAW can't be associated with anything else. For example, you may use .tif files quite a bit and want them associated with CorelDRAW, but wouldn't you rather have them associated with Corel PHOTO-PAINT? The nice thing is that if you make a mistake, you can easily change the associations, which wasn't true in past versions.

You may want to further customize CorelDRAW by adding more toolbars or buttons, changing the menu structure, and even adding some custom keystrokes. What about changing the shortcut keys so they are the same as in another of your favorite applications? You can do all of this by using the Customize options that have been described in this chapter.

34

CHAPTER 35

Automation of CorelDRAW

CorelDRAW 9

S everal releases back, Corel added presets to CorelDRAW. Then CorelDRAW 6
introduced scripts. Presets were easy, but limited. Scripts could do lots of things,
but you needed to be a programmer to write them. Now these features have been
rolled together to provide a lot of power, and creating a script is now easy for all users.
It's as simple as using your VCR, and certainly not as difficult as setting its clock!

Using Scripts

To work with scripts, you'll need to get the Script and Preset Manager Docker
onscreen. To do this, select Tools | Corel SCRIPT | Script and Preset Manager.
Initially, it will be displayed as a Docker. We've undocked it so that it takes up a
little less room. You'll see two folders in the window, as shown here. One of them
contains the presets that were included with CorelDRAW 6. The other contains
the scripts that have been included with CorelDRAW 9. Note that the presets are
scripts in this release; they are kept separate only for purposes of clarification.

Some of the scripts and presets require that an object be selected onscreen.
Others require nothing at all. If something is required, you will receive an error
message telling what you need to do to continue.

Just to get an idea of how scripts work, let's run one of the sample scripts.

1. Double-click the Scripts folder so you can see each of the scripts that are supplied with CorelDRAW 9.

2. Select the script called "Calendar" by clicking on it.

3. To run the script, double-click it or press the Play button (the right-pointing arrow).

This particular script is actually a wizard for creating a calendar, so once it starts, you'll see the dialog box shown in Figure 35-1.

The first screen doesn't really do anything. Click Next, and you'll see the dialog box shown in Figure 35-2.

The Calendar Wizard asks which paper size you wish to use for creating your new calendar. The list is limited when compared with the list that CorelDRAW provides, but you can always select another size later. So select a size, and click Next to get the dialog box for selecting page orientation. You can choose either Portrait or Landscape. Once you've made your selection, click Next to get to the dialog box shown in Figure 35-3.

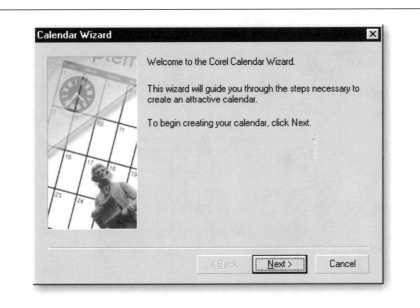

35

FIGURE 35-1   Opening screen of the Calendar Wizard

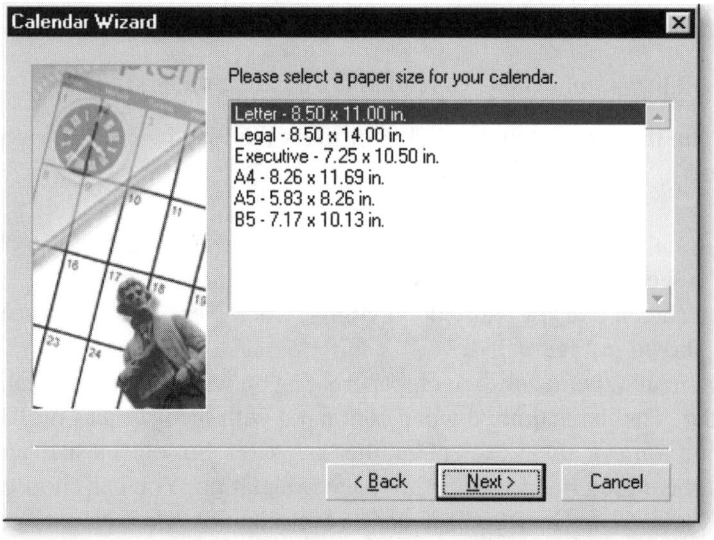

FIGURE 35-2 Calendar Wizard dialog box for selecting paper size

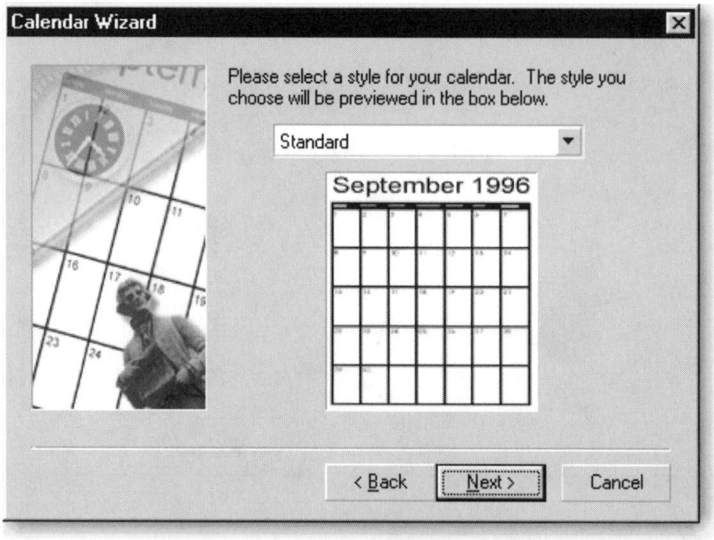

FIGURE 35-3 Calendar Wizard dialog box for selecting a style

You can select three calendar styles. The Standard calendar puts the month and year at the top. Other choices allow you to place that information on the left or right side instead. Once you've made your selection, click Next. You'll now be asked if you wish to choose a font. This will bring up a familiar dialog box for font selection. When you've chosen a font, click Next to get to the dialog box shown in Figure 35-4.

There are two check boxes here that will enable you to add either a picture or a border to the calendar. Click the check box for the option you want, if any, and then press the Select File button. This brings up a standard file selection dialog box. Find the image you want, and press OK. As the Wizard informs you, it is probably not a good idea to add both a picture and a border, because there will be little room left for the calendar. When you've finished, click Next to get to the dialog box shown in Figure 35-5.

The last choices you need to make are the starting month for the calendar you are creating and the total number of months you need. The default selection is the

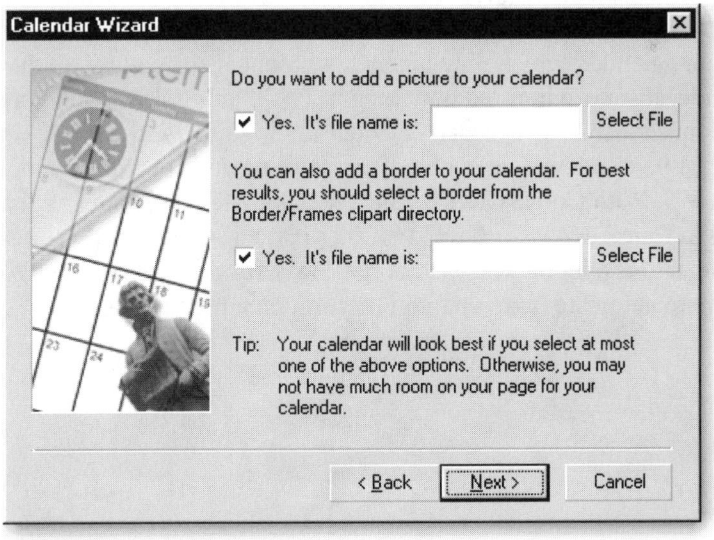

FIGURE 35-4   Calendar Wizard dialog box for adding pictures and borders

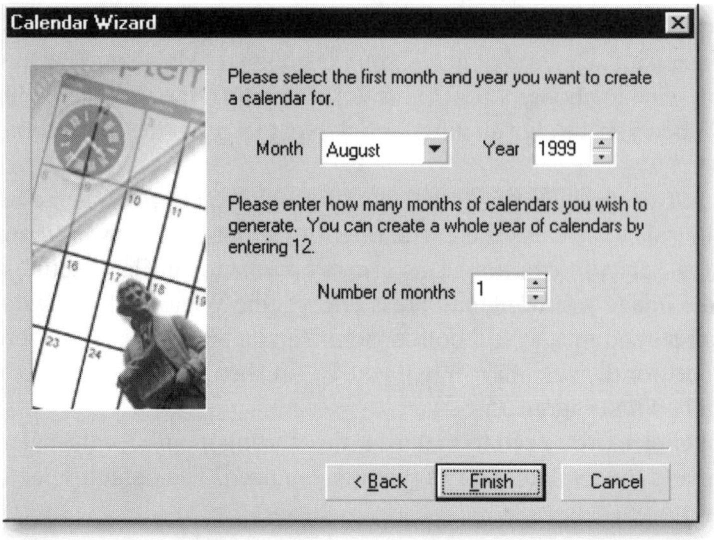

FIGURE 35-5   Calendar Wizard month selection dialog box

current month (it will print only that month). But if you need a whole year, just select 12 months. Then click Finish, and relax while the script goes to work creating your calendar, which may take a few minutes, depending on the speed of your machine. Just keep in mind how long it would have taken you to create the calendar from scratch. The finished calendar is shown in Figure 35-6.

The script you've just seen is one of the most powerful scripts included with CorelDRAW 9. With CorelSCRIPT, you can automate just about any feature that is included in CorelDRAW or Corel PHOTO-PAINT. Creating a script such as the Calendar Wizard is a lot of work and is not a task for the average user. However, it is quite easy to automate tasks that you perform on a regular basis.

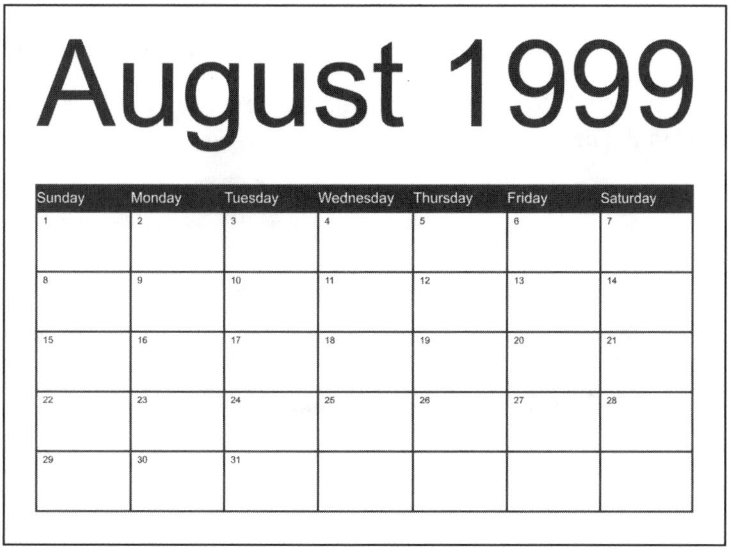

August 1999

Sunday	Monday	Tuesday	Wednesday	Thursday	Friday	Saturday
1	2	3	4	5	6	7
8	9	10	11	12	13	14
15	16	17	18	19	20	21
22	23	24	25	26	27	28
29	30	31				

FIGURE 35-6   The finished calendar

Recording Scripts

You've seen how to play back a script that has already been created. Now let's create a simple drop shadow script so you'll see how easy it can be to create your own scripts.

1. Start with a large piece of Artistic Text.

2. With the text selected, click the red Record button at the bottom of the Script and Preset Manager window. It's the one on the far right.

35

3. Make a duplicate of the text with the CTRL-D shortcut key combination.

4. Color the new text black or whatever color you want for the shadow.

5. Select Arrange | Order | To Back, and the new copy of the text will be placed in the back.

6. Use the Nudge arrows to move the shadow to exactly the place where you want it to be.

7. Click the Stop button (the square one in the middle).

You'll now be presented with the Save Recording dialog box shown here:

Save Recording	? ⨉
Save in: 📁 Scripts	▾ 🔼 📷 🔳 🔲

📄 Presets
📄 Scripts

File name:	DropShadow.csc	Save
Save as type:	Script Files (*.csc) ▾	Cancel
Description:	Simple Drop Shadow	

8. Give the new script a File name and a Description, and then click Save.

The script you've just created should now be shown in the Script and Preset Manager window. Note that you may need to click the yellow folder button at the top of the window to back up one level. Play it back on another object if you like. This script is certainly not as elaborate as the drop shadow effect that comes with CorelDRAW, but you can see how easy it is to automate a task you perform quite often. All you have to do is perform the task manually once, and it will then be recorded for future use.

 CAUTION   *Not all commands are supported by the scripting language, such as converting Artistic Text to Paragraph Text. CorelDRAW 9 has implemented many more commands in the scripting language than in past releases.*

Editing Scripts

So far, you've seen the kind of scripting that any user of CorelDRAW can work with, but those of you who wish to take scripting to another level can make some major modifications. Just be aware that these advanced scripting techniques may get your hands a little bit dirty!

Select Tools | Corel SCRIPT | Corel SCRIPT Editor, and you'll be presented with the Corel SCRIPT Editor program shown here:

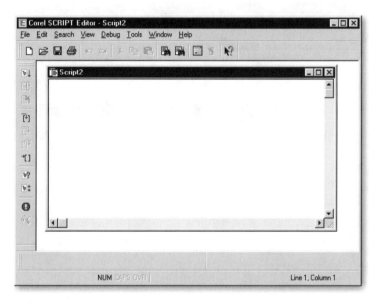

The Script Editor is used to work with the programming code directly and it isn't nearly as friendly as the recording functions built into CorelDRAW. It is to be used for modifying the scripts you've recorded or to write a new script from scratch using the scripting language. The syntax used is very similar to that of Microsoft's Visual Basic.

This is a full-blown programming language, and we can't give full coverage to the programming aspects in this book, but every command, along with its syntax. is described fully in the Help files. Another way to learn how the commands work is to record the activities you wish to script and look at what the recorder creates for you.

When you've finished with your script, you'll notice several options in the File menu for creating .exe, .dll, .cao, and .csb files. These features give you a way to compile your script so that the code can be protected. To learn more about writing scripts, we strongly suggest that you study the Help files.

35

Creating an Interface

If you really want to dress up your scripts, you can create dialog boxes to gather user input. To do this, we suggest you use the Dialog Editor. Select Tools | Dialog (F2) to get to the Dialog Editor. The toolbar will change to give you the tools you need to draw various elements of the dialog box. You'll also see that a new window has opened to show you the dialog box you are designing, as shown here:

When you close the dialog window, you'll see that the programming code that describes the dialog box has been entered into your script. To make further changes, select Tools | Dialog with your cursor somewhere in the code that creates the dialog box.

To learn more about creating dialog boxes, we again suggest that you consult the Help files that accompany the program. They explain each of the tools and how best to use them.

Creating a Sample Script

Now that you've learned the basics, we'll show you a simple script that will give you capabilities that CorelDRAW doesn't include. We'll write a script that will draw a rectangle of a precise size and a precise corner radius. Doing this without a script requires that you closely watch the Property Bar or several guidelines.

Simple scripts can be created by recording your actions within CorelDRAW, but in this case, we wish to create something that cannot be done using the tools in CorelDRAW and so we can't record it. Also, we want to design a dialog box to make our function look to users as if it is an integral part of CorelDRAW.

There can be two parts to creating a script. Some scripts don't need to gather user input, and therefore they include only one part. But when user input is required, a user interface must be designed. For this sample, we need to get the height, width, and corner radius from the user. While the user interface can be created in code, it is usually easier to design it with the dialog editing functions provided with Corel SCRIPT Editor. This allows you to design in a WYSIWYG environment.

When you first open the dialog editor, Tools | Dialog (F2), you will see a blank dialog box in the main window. As you begin creating your dialog box, the code for the dialog box will be generated in your script. The first thing we want to do is change the title bar of the dialog so that it says "Draw Rectangle of Exact Size." To do this, right-click on the dialog box itself, and choose Attributes from the pop-up menu. Changing the value of the "Text" field will change the title bar. If you wish to name the dialog box for reference within the script, change the text in the "Value" field. Let's go ahead and enter "DrawRectDialog" in that field. Also change the width to 204 and the height to 77. These numbers were determined by sizing the dialog box after adding the controls. We'll enter them now, but you can always adjust them to your liking later. After clicking OK, you should see the changes on the dialog box.

The next step is to put some controls on the dialog box. The first control will be a "group box," which draws a box around several different control items. It helps you visually group similar controls on the dialog. While it may not be necessary for this simple script, it could come in handy if this script is expanded later. The fifth item down in the toolbox is used to create a group box; it is the icon with the rectangle and the small "XYZ" on it. Click on that icon, and then drag out a rectangle on the dialog

35

box just like you were creating a rectangle in CorelDRAW. You'll now see the group box labeled "GroupBox1". We want to change the name as well as several other attributes of this box. Right-click on the group box, and choose Attributes from the pop-up menu. Change the text to "Desired Rectangle Size", the Position to 0,0, and the size to 140 wide by 25 high. Again click OK, and look at what you've got.

We now need to add two boxes for user input with labels above them. The second icon down is for adding text; it contains the letters *Aa* on it. Click on this icon, and then drag a rectangle inside of the group box. Once you've let go of the mouse, the rectangle will be drawn with "Text1" inside of it. Right-click on it, and choose Attributes just as with the other items. Change the text to "Height", the Position to 5, 10, and the Size to 25, 8. Click OK, and you'll see your changes. Also take a look at the script window to see the code that has been created. We now need a box for the user input of the Height. Choose the third icon down to create this "text box." Drag out a rectangle to the right of the word *Height*, and you'll now see a white rectangle. Again right-click, and choose Attributes. The Value field contains the name of the variable that the user's input will be stored in. Let's change this to DesiredHeight$. For those who haven't done any programming in the past, the dollar sign indicates that we will be receiving a string of text. We'll convert it to a number later. Let's change the Position to 30, 8 and the Size to 35, 13.

Creating the other label and textbox works exactly the same. The second box should have a text label of "Width" with a textbox to its right holding the DesiredWidth$ variable. Go ahead, and adjust the size and position so that these items will line up with the Height pair of controls.

We also want to add a section to enter the Radius values. Using what you've already learned, draw another group box containing four textboxes to contain the four radius values. We also added some explanatory text so that users will understand how it works. Assign the variable DesiredRadiusX$ to each textbox, replacing the *X* with a number. After adding these controls, you should see something similar to the example shown in Figure 35-7. The only thing missing at this point are the OK and Cancel buttons.

Buttons are created with the sixth tool down in the toolbox. It has a flyout just like in CorelDRAW, and the buttons we want are on the flyout. The second button across has a green checkmark and is the control for an OK button. Select that tool, and drag a rectangle on the right side of our dialog box. It should draw a button with "OK" on it. Now return to the flyout, and choose the third button across, which has the red *X* through it. This is the Cancel button. Again drag out a rectangle to get a button with the word *Cancel* on it. Size and position these buttons to your liking, either by stretching and dragging or by adjusting the attributes as we've done with the other

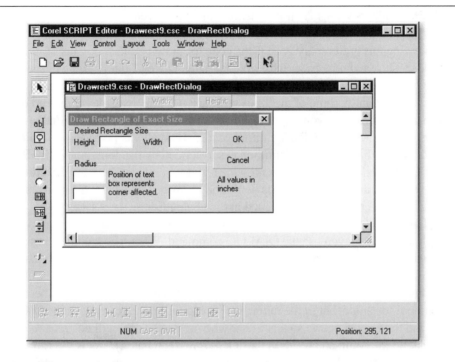

FIGURE 35-7   The dialog box as it looks in the Dialog Editor

controls. You should now have a complete dialog box. Close the Dialog Editor window, and you'll be returned to the Corel SCRIPT Editor.

You'll now see the code for the dialog box that we created. The programming language used in Corel SCRIPT is similar to that in Microsoft's Visual Basic. For those of you that have used this product, writing scripts will come fairly easily. For those who haven't programmed before, this language is not difficult to learn.

The first thing you should do in any program is put in some information about the program itself right at the top of the file. To add comments to a file, you use the REM command. We want to add a comment telling a little about the program so we'll add the line "REM Draw rectangle of specified size." It is also quite common to add a comment regarding the ownership of the program. Therefore, you'll see the next line is a copyright notice.

Now we want to give some of our variables a default value. This is so that when we bring up the dialog box, numbers will already be in each of the fields. So, we'll add a line "DesiredHeight$="1"" followed by a similar line for DesiredWidth$ and

35

the DesiredRadius$ values. You'll remember that those were the names we gave to the Value field in the textboxes created in the Dialog Editor.

Following this preliminary code is the code for drawing the dialog box. Look at the code closely, and remember what you did in the Dialog Editor. You will see the name of the control first, followed by four numbers indicating the position and size of the control. Finally, some of the items have text or variable names at the end of the line. At a future time, you might feel more comfortable creating your dialog boxes right here in Corel SCRIPT Editor because the syntax is fairly easy to follow. Also notice that the dialog box definition is surrounded by the commands BEGIN DIALOG and END DIALOG. This is so the script will know where the definition begins and ends, and it also gives the definition a name. In this case, the name is DrawRectDialog, the name we assigned in the Dialog Editor.

OK, now we're ready to do some programming. First we need to bring up our dialog box. To do so, you use the DIALOG command. When you call the command, you need to assign it to a variable so that you know what happened when the dialog was closed. If the user clicks OK, it will return one number, clicking Cancel will return another, and so on. For this exercise, we don't care about the number because we want our rectangle, but in the future, we should differentiate between the OK button and the Cancel button so that a user who presses Cancel will not get a rectangle. So the command is "ret=DIALOG(DrawRectDialog)." ret is the name of the variable that will tell us what the user pushed, and the name of the dialog box is in the parenthesis.

The numbers entered by the user are now stored in the variables. We need to create a routine that draws a rectangle. To begin a routine, you enter the command "WITHOBJECT "CorelDraw.Automation.9". "WITHOBJECT" tells it to use a particular object (that means a program), and "CorelDraw.Automation.9" is the name of the object. Basically that means to do whatever we tell you in CorelDRAW 9.

To draw a rectangle, we use the CreateRectangle command. That's pretty simple to remember, right? What gets difficult is remembering how each of the measurements get used by the command. So we added a REM showing how the command is used. It reads "REM .CreateRectangle height, width, bottom, right, radius1, radius2, radius3, radius4," which means that we need to add eight numbers after the CreateRectangle command. Also note that all commands are preceded by a period. Now we just need to calculate each of these numbers.

The numbers entered in the dialog box are entered as text, and not numbers, so we have to convert them. The VAL command will take the numbers as text and convert them into numbers. So we use the command "RectHeight=val(DesiredHeight$)" to do this conversion. This command is followed by a similar one to convert the Width and Radius values.

All of the drawing commands in the Corel SCRIPT language use the base measurement of one tenth of a micron. Most of us don't normally work in microns, so we will convert the measurement to inches as we draw the rectangle using the FROMINCHES command.

Now let's draw the rectangle. Remember that we need to use the FROMINCHES command with each value, or we will get tiny rectangles. Two of the numbers needed are for the bottom and right side of the rectangle. Deciding the placement of the rectangle will be left for a future exercise so we'll just use 0. Therefore, the entire command is:

```
.CreateRectangle FROMINCHES(RectHeight), FROMINCHES (RectWidth),
0, 0, FROMINCHES (RectRadius1), FROMINCHES (RectRadius2),
FROMINCHES (RectRadius3), FROMINCHES (RectRadius4)"
```

The last thing we need to add is the END WITHOBJECT command. This means that we're using whatever object we were using. In this case, we're done with Draw. When you're done, your screen should look similar to Figure 35-8. Note that the .CreateRectangle command does not fit completely in the window shown. If you remember, this script is included on the CD in this book, as described in Chapter 3.

Now we're ready to see if the script works. Make sure CorelDRAW 9 is running, and then minimize it so that you can see the Corel SCRIPT Editor. You'll find the Run command in the Debug menu, or you can just press F5 to start the program. It will bring up the dialog box we designed, as shown in Figure 35-9. Go ahead, and try it to see what you get.

The really interesting thing about using the script is that you can specify the radius for the rectangle's corners in inches. You can't do this in Draw itself! But there is something else that the script does that is actually a side effect. Run the script again, and type in 4 inches for each of the six measurements. You should get a shape similar to that shown in Figure 35-10. You can't create this without a script since CorelDRAW limits the amount of radius to one half of the shortest side of a rectangle when you do it manually. So not only can we be really accurate, but we can also do things that can't be done any other way.

 TIP *If you've created a script and want to give it a custom icon, there are just a couple of steps. First, create a graphic on the drawing page. Then right-click on the CSC file in the Script and Preset Manager Docker and choose Create Thumbnail.*

```
Drawrect9.csc *                                                    _ □ ✕
REM Draw rectangle of specified size
REM Copyright (c) 1999 by Unleashed Productions, Inc. All Rights Reserved.

DesiredHeight$="1"
DesiredWidth$="1"
DesiredRadius1$="0"
DesiredRadius2$="0"
DesiredRadius3$="0"
DesiredRadius4$="0"

BEGIN DIALOG DrawRectDialog 204, 77, "Draw Rectangle of Exact Size"
     TEXTBOX  30, 8, 35, 13, DesiredHeight$
     TEXTBOX  100, 8, 35, 13, DesiredWidth$
     TEXTBOX  3, 40, 35, 13, DesiredRadius1$
     TEXTBOX  100, 40, 35, 13, DesiredRadius4$
     TEXTBOX  3, 55, 35, 13, DesiredRadius2$
     TEXTBOX  100, 55, 35, 13, DesiredRadius3$
     OKBUTTON  145, 4, 50, 16
     CANCELBUTTON  145, 23, 50, 16
     GROUPBOX  0, 0, 140, 25, "Desired Rectangle Size"
     TEXT  5, 10, 25, 8, "Height"
     TEXT  75, 10, 25, 8, "Width"
     GROUPBOX  0, 30, 140, 45, "Radius"
     TEXT  150, 45, 45, 30, "All values in inches"
     TEXT  40, 40, 55, 30, "Position of text box represents corner affected."
END DIALOG

ret=DIALOG(DrawRectDialog)

WITHOBJECT "CorelDraw.Automation.9"

     REM .CreateRectangle height, width, bottom, right, radius1, radius2, radius3, radius4

     RectHeight=val(DesiredHeight$)
     RectWidth=val(DesiredWidth$)
     RectRadius1=val(DesiredRadius1$)
     RectRadius2=val(DesiredRadius2$)
     RectRadius3=val(DesiredRadius3$)
     RectRadius4=val(DesiredRadius4$)

     .CreateRectangle FROMINCHES(RectHeight), FROMINCHES (RectWidth), 0, 0, FROMINCHES (Rec

END WITHOBJECT
```

FIGURE 35-8   The script as seen in Corel SCRIPT Editor

FIGURE 35-9   Our script as it is being run

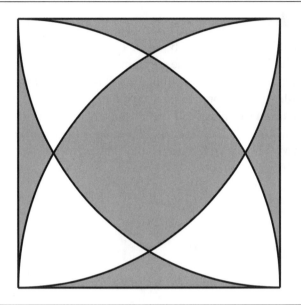

FIGURE 35-10   An interesting side effect of our script

Visual Basic for Applications

New to CorelDRAW 9 is the inclusion of Microsoft's Visual Basic for
Applications as a way to automate CorelDRAW. You can access it through Tools |
Visual Basic | Visual Basic Editor. Scripts that have already been written can be
run by choosing Tools | Visual Basic | Play. Because Visual Basic for Applications
is a complicated program in its own right, complete with third-party books on
how to use it, we will not cover it here. The actual commands used to control
CorelDRAW are the same commands used by Corel SCRIPT. The main difference
is the commands that are not specific to CorelDRAW.

In this chapter, you saw how you can automate your use of CorelDRAW. In
some cases, a feature is provided as a script rather than an extra menu command or
dialog box. You'll also find that third parties can provide scripts that can further
extend the capabilities of DRAW.

35

The End Is Near

If you've made it this far, you should be an expert at using CorelDRAW. We've covered most of the features within the program. While we feel that we've covered all of them, we don't assume that something hasn't been overlooked along the way. Check the Help files to get information on anything that we may have missed or that was added in a maintenance release. If you're still having trouble, let us know, and we'll see if we can help. We'll also regularly post updates on our Web page, so come, and visit http://www.unleash.com often. Happy drawing!

PART VI

Appendices

APPENDIX A

About the CD-ROM

COREL.COM

CorelDRAW 9

Enclosed in the back of this book is a CD-ROM loaded with sample files, useful software, and multimedia tutorials. To get the most out of the CD, you should load the readme.htm file in your browser. It includes complete details of what is included, where to find it, and lots of useful links to Web sites of interest to CorelDRAW users. Below is a list of exactly what is included on the CD:

- Sample Files described in the chapters of this book

- BrowserMaster v2.02 Evaluation

- EyeBrowse v2.2 Evaluation

- EZ Metrics v1.0 Evaluation

- HomeSite v4.0 Evaluation and Value Pack

- Netscape Communicator v4.5

- ROMCat v3.3 and Clip-Art Catalogs

- ThumbsPlus v4.0 Evaluation

- Vakcer Project Tracker v1.6 Evaluation

- Click 'N Learn Multimedia Tutorials

- Useful Links to Web sites

APPENDIX B

Production Notes

CoreIDRAW 9

This is the sixth CorelDRAW book we've authored, and we can happily say that this is the third book produced entirely on a PC.

We captured screens with Corel CAPTURE 8 & 9, as well as by simply copying screens to the clipboard. These images were often edited utilizing Corel PHOTO-PAINT 8. This editing mainly consisted of cropping out an item or highlighting it with a filter. The screens are real-world examples; they were not specially produced for the purposes of this book. If you do notice a difference between the screens in the book and those on your system, it may be that the dialog box has changed since the previous release. Scanning was done using a Hewlett-Packard 4c and 6100c.

All the text was written in Microsoft Word 97 using a custom style sheet that translates smoothly into Corel VENTURA. The layout of the book was created in Corel VENTURA 8. The color pages were all created directly in CorelDRAW, with the most fantastic artwork being taken from winners of Corel's World Design Contest. We've credited the artist on images that were not created by the authors.

The fonts used in this book are Times, Futura Condensed Extra Bold, Futura Condensed Light, and Futura Medium.

APPENDIX C

Author Biographies

CoreIDRAW 9

We are often asked how we got to this point in our lives, so we've spelled out all the important details for you.

Foster D. Coburn III

Foster began using Ventura Publisher 1.0 to produce a programming magazine while attending the University of Kansas back in the 1980s. He also started his own little company, Smart Typesetting, to produce various projects for clients.

As Smart Typesetting grew, a product called CorelDRAW 1.0 came along and did some incredible things that Ventura couldn't do. Soon Foster was doing a lot of work using this wonderful new package.

Along the way, he created some little shareware utilities and even helped create some fonts for inclusion in Microsoft's TrueType Font Pack 2. Then in 1993 the writing bug caught hold, and he created *CorelDRAW! 4 Unleashed.*

That first book led Smart Typesetting to morph into the current Unleashed Productions, Inc. Foster and Pete teamed up to put on CorelDRAW seminars throughout the United States and even at a few international destinations. Foster also co-authored three more books, *CorelDRAW 5 Unleashed, CorelDRAW 6 Unleashed* and *CorelDRAW 7: The Official Guide.*

The books and seminars led to a videotape series on CorelDRAW and Corel PHOTO-PAINT for versions 6, 7 and 8 and a version 9 series should be available by the time you read this. In addition to the one-day seminars, Unleashed Productions now conducts three-day Boot Camps for those who want to learn CorelDRAW inside and out.

Unleashed Productions continued to grow in 1999. A utility, EZ Metrics, was created to aid CorelDRAW users in making technical illustrations. You'll find a working demo version of the product on the CD in this book. They also began selling a series of multimedia CD-ROMs and doing Web design for a number of clients. The biggest growth has been at the companies Web site (http://www.unleash.com) which has grown to be a terrific resource for anyone creating graphics, especially with CorelDRAW and Corel PHOTO-PAINT.

Foster can be contacted by e-mail at foster@unleash.com; by mail at P.O. Box 7008, Cave Creek, AZ 85327; or by phone at (480) 595-0065. You may also want to visit the Unleashed Productions Web site at **http://www.unleash.com** for more information on Foster and Unleashed Productions, Inc.

Peter A. McCormick

Peter McCormick became involved with art and computers relatively late in life. At age 40 he discovered a latent talent for painting on canvas. This discovery eventually led him to the world of computer art. In 1992, at age 53, he discovered computers and CorelDRAW. It was love at first byte. He entered Corel's World Design contest that first year and was awarded Grand Prize in the Landmarks division for an image called Venice. That image appeared on the August 1992 cover of *PC Magazine* following the contest.

Peter then met and teamed up with Foster Coburn at a CorelDRAW users group and began creating ads for businesses in the Phoenix area. During this same period, Peter and Foster co-authored a series of books titled *CorelDRAW Unleashed* along with a third author, Carlos Gonzalez of Phoenix. The books were so popular that they have been translated into several languages. This success lead to the co-authoring of *CorelDRAW The Official Guide* books for versions 7,8, and 9. They too have been translated into several different languages as well.

Peter and Foster have trained more than 8,000 CorelDRAW users over a five-year period. In November 1996 they traveled to London, where they were presenters at Corel World UK. Besides writing *CorelDRAW 9: The Official Guide* Peter teaches CorelDRAW and Corel PHOTO-PAINT at Unleashed Production's boot camps throughout the year at Unleashed Production's training facility in Phoenix, Arizona. The boot camps are three days of intense training on the current version of CorelDRAW and Corel PHOTO-PAINT.

Besides writing books, Peter writes occasional articles for the *Corel User Magazine* in the UK and the German version of *Corel Magazine.*

Peter writes for the real-world user of CorelDRAW. Rather than showing how to create complicated drawings, he wants readers to learn and understand the complexities and functionality of the program. Once readers learn how to use CorelDRAW's tools and effects, they can apply their own unique talents and become the World Design Contest winners of the future.

Peter can be contacted by e-mail at pete@happyaccident.com; by mail at 13726 Aleppo Dr., Sun City West, AZ 85375; and by phone at (623) 584-8403. You may also want to visit his new web site Happy Accident.com at **http://www.happyaccident.com** for more information on Peter.

C

Index

C

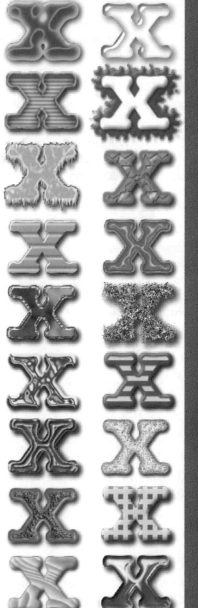

Get Technical with CorelDRAW!

E Z • M E T R I C S

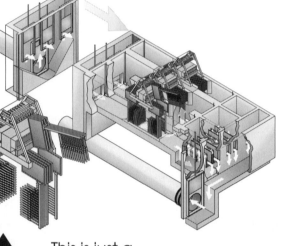

This is just a sample of what can easily be created with EZ Metrics!

With this interface you're just clicks away from great technical illustrations!

By itself, CorelDRAW is a very powerful program. But it is lacking some of the features required by technical illustrators. EZ Metrics was created to fill that void. Now it just takes a few clicks to convert an orthographic drawing into one of five different axonometric drawings such as Isometric, two forms of Dimetric, and two forms of Trimetric. EZ Metrics also makes it easy to move and extrude objects in the third dimension based on the type of drawing you are creating. We are simply automating features that already exist in CorelDRAW. Functions that require a number of steps and lots of math are reduced to a single click. What this all means is that you will be saving time while creating some fantastic technical illustrations.

EZ Metrics isn't the only program of its kind, but it is the best. It's flexible, it's accurate and best of all, it's easy to use. You get the ability to create all five types of axonometric drawings instead of just isometric. We've also added a bunch of features for tracking the transformations. The Extrude Depth and the orthographic size of an object are stored for later reference. Each of the transformations requires only a single click. And as you can see in the image at left, the interface is very streamlined so that you can concentrate on your drawing! Lastly, EZMetrics supports CorelDRAW 7, 8 and 9 all in one program. So no matter which version you use, we're ready for you!

We know that with a technical tool like this, you want to know if it will meet your needs. So we encourage you to install the demo version supplied with this book and give it a test drive. We haven't disabled anything because we want you to put it to work. After you've tested it for 14 days, we're sure that you'll be willing to

Order Now!
(800) 736-8973 or
www.unleash.com/ezmetrics

ThumbsPlus

This form is for single-user copies only. Please contact
Cerious Software for information on multi-user licensing!

Name: _____

Address: _____

City: _____ State: _____

Country: _____ Postal Code: _____

Phone: _____ Fax: _____

E-mail address: _____

Payment:

☐ Check enclosed
☐ Credit Card (Visa, MC, Amex, Discover)

⬚⬚⬚⬚ ⬚⬚⬚⬚ ⬚⬚⬚⬚ ⬚⬚⬚⬚

Expiration Date: ⬚⬚ / ⬚⬚

_____
Authorized Signature

You will receive the latest release of ThumbsPlus on CD-ROM with sample images and a copy of Mandelbrot
for Windows. Please send this form, with $59.95, to:

Cerious Software, Inc.
1515 Mockingbird Ln. Suite 1000
Charlotte, NC 28209 USA

You may also fax this form to 704-529-0497, or call us toll-free at 1-877-CERIOUS (1-877-237-
4687) to order.

Special Offer - $20 off!

Great Companion to CorelDRAW 9 Suite!

AVAILABLE AT:
http://www.vakcer.com

VAKCER Project Tracker is the perfect time-tracking utility if you run any business that provides a PC software service. Give your customers the benefit of precise hourly billing by generating reports on exactly how long it took to put their project together. Since VAKCER Project Tracker can be configured to run automatically, there's no need to keep an eye on your system clock. No more "approximating" when a project began and when it ended!

PRODUCT HIGHLIGHTS

⚙ Automatic application recognition and time and cost recording.

⚙ Automatically subtracts time when mouse or keyboard activity is not present. (Customizable unattended mode preset time.)

⚙ Over 300 Windows applications supported, and Application List Internet Live Update.

⚙ Individual cost rates for each application.

⚙ Manager module to update, move, split, backup, restore or export data.

⚙ Automatically launches on startup and opening the previous project.

⚙ One-click projects open/create (hundreds of projects could be activated).

⚙ Message board with non-intruding warning messages.

⚙ Backup/Restore project feature.

⚙ Complete project time/cost printed reports.

⚙ Job ticket with all necessary information about the project (Contact information, billing details, data transfer media, etc.).

VAKCER
Project Tracker
Time, Cost, Projects, and Files Manager

Put away the stopwatches and quit looking at that clock on the wall! Finally, a time tracking utility for easy and precise billing!

VAKCER Project Tracker Main Window.

The active application and document is tracked and time /cost constantly updated automatically in project records.

VAKCER Project Tracker Project Properties Window.

Fast access to project information, statistics, print, edit, tracking options, and preset manager. Full 32 bit application with latest programming advantages.

About the CD

The CD that comes with this book is full of images from the book's chapters so that you can follow along with the exercises in the book. These files are CorelDRAW files (with the .CDR extension) and you will need to have CorelDRAW installed to view these images.

The CD also contains a variety of software products and utilities for you to experience, a collection of multimedia tutorials to help you learn more about using CorelDRAW and links to a selection of premiere Web sites which you're sure to find useful.

How to Install the CD

1. Insert the CD into your computer CD-ROM drive

2. If the CD does not start itself, click on your Start menu, select Run, and type in the letter of your CD drive. Then click on OK and you'll be presented with a window that contains all of the folders on the CD.

3. The folders you see contain the tutorial images from the book's chapters, and the demo software that the authors have selected to include. Double-click on any of the folders to access their contents. Also, double-click on the ReadMe file in this window to read all about the products included on the CD, to link to a variety of great CorelDRAW and other graphics-related Web sites (including Web sites of Corel PHOTO-PAINT Add-Ons and Plug-Ins), and also links to the home pages of the software products on the CD so that you can get more info about these products.